Inventing Leadership

NEW HORIZONS IN LEADERSHIP STUDIES

Series Editor: Joanne B. Ciulla
Professor and Coston Family Chair in Leadership Ethics, Jepson School of Leadership Studies,
University of Richmond, USA

This important series is designed to make a significant contribution to the development of
leadership studies. This field has expanded dramatically in recent years and the series provides an
invaluable forum for the publication of high quality works of scholarship and shows the diversity
of leadership issues and practices around the world.

The main emphasis of the series is on the development and application of new and original
ideas in leadership studies. It pays particular attention to leadership in business, economics and
public policy and incorporates the wide range of disciplines which are now part of the field. Global
in its approach, it includes some of the best theoretical and empirical work with contributions to
fundamental principles, rigorous evaluations of existing concepts and competing theories, historical
surveys and future visions.

Titles in the series include:

Beyond Rules in Society and Business
Verner C. Petersen

The Moral Capital of Leaders
Why Virtue Matters
Alejo José G. Sison

The Leadership Dilemma in Modern Democracy
Kenneth P. Ruscio

The New Russian Business Leaders
Manfred F.R. Kets de Vries, Stanislav Shekshnia,
Konstantin Korotov and Elizabeth Florent-Treacy

Lessons on Leadership by Terror
Finding Shaka Zulu in the Attic
Manfred F.R. Kets de Vries

Leadership in Context
The Four Faces of Capitalism
Mark N. Wexler

The Quest for Moral Leaders
Essays on Leadership Ethics
Edited by Joanne B. Ciulla, Terry L. Price and Susan E. Murphy

The Quest for a General Theory of Leadership
Edited by George R. Goethals and Georgia L.J. Sorenson

Inventing Leadership
The Challenge of Democracy
J. Thomas Wren

Inventing Leadership

The Challenge of Democracy

J. Thomas Wren

University of Richmond, USA

NEW HORIZONS IN LEADERSHIP STUDIES

Edward Elgar

Cheltenham, UK • Northampton, MA, USA

Published by
Edward Elgar Publishing Limited
Glensanda House
Montpellier Parade
Cheltenham
Glos GL50 1UA
UK

Edward Elgar Publishing, Inc.
William Pratt House
9 Dewey Court
Northampton
Massachusetts 01060
USA

A catalogue record for this book
is available from the British Library

Library of Congress Cataloguing in Publication Data
Wren, J. Thomas, 1950–
    Inventing leadership : the challenge of democracy / J. Thomas Wren.
        p. cm. — (New horizons in leadership studies)
    Includes bibliographical references and index.
    1. Political leadership. 2. Political leadership—Philosophy.   I. Title.
    JC330.3.W74 2007
    303.3'4—dc22

2006028690

ISBN 978 1 84064 955 0 (cased)

Printed and bound in Great Britain by MPG Books Ltd, Bodmin, Cornwall

For Suzanne, and Jack

Contents

Foreword

The words *leader and leadership* carry quite a bit of historical baggage with them. In America, they not only describe people and activities, but they are often used to give a compliment: 'She is a leader!' or 'Now that's leadership!' This is not the case in Italy or Germany, where two twentieth century leaders behaved so badly, that the very words for leader, *duce* and *Führer*, were exiled from both languages. The idea of a leader is a social and historical construction and as such, it is also laden with moral values.

This book unpacks the historical baggage of leadership and in doing so, helps us better understand how we think and feel about leaders today. J. Thomas Wren traces the evolution of the idea of leadership in Western culture and in particular in America. The history of the idea of leadership is intimately tied up with the history of democracy. As Wren argues, both democracy and leadership require people to believe in certain fictions. According to Wren, the main fictions that people need to believe in are: leaders are wise and virtuous, the people are sovereign, and the fiction of leadership itself. He notes that the term *leadership* first shows up in Webster's dictionary in the 1818. The emergence of the concept marked an important change. It represented the decline of deference toward elites and a new model of social relations. The invention of the word leadership signaled a new way of thinking about who should lead.

Wren's account of the invention of leadership is far more than just an interesting story. His analysis has profound implications for the world that we live in today. It shows us why democracy is not simply a matter of setting up the right institutions, voting and picking out the right leaders. It requires a number of internalized beliefs about who we are as human beings, how we think about ourselves in relation to society, the values that we hold, and the way that we think about freedom equality and justice. Such ideas evolve and become embedded in cultures over time. They take on different shapes, depending on the history of a culture. People come to believe these fictions only when they correspond or make sense in the world in which they live. Since these fictions are matters of belief, not matters of knowledge, people internalize them and they become implicit in ideas about leaders and leadership. Wren's history isolates the variables that shape what people need to believe to have a democracy and to select competent and moral leaders, and to be good citizens. These variables help us better understand the difficulties of developing democracies in the Middle East, the chronic problems with leadership in many African nations, and the malaise of leadership and democracy in the U.S. and some other Western nations.

I am delighted to have this book in the New Horizons of Leadership series. It is a book that needed to be written. Without a comprehensive understanding of where our ideas about leadership come from, any analysis of leadership will always seem incomplete.

Joanne B. Ciulla, PhD
Series Editor, New Horizons in Leadership Studies
17 August 2006

Preface

As the new century dawned, the nonpartisan organization Freedom House supplemented its annual survey of the status of democracy and freedom in the world with a special report reflecting back upon the century just completed. The report concluded: 'The findings here are significant. They show a dramatic expansion of democratic governance over the course of the century.' Indeed, 'in a very real sense, the twentieth century has become the "Democratic Century"'.[1]

The momentum toward democracy appears to have continued into the twenty-first century, albeit not without some attendant controversy. This reality poses some of the most fundamental challenges for state making and the operation of the polity ever witnessed in human history. Longstanding democratic regimes such as the United States and Great Britain confront disconnection between their ideals and their realities, and must deal alike with sweeping egalitarianism, claims of social and economic inequities, increasing diversity and allegedly inefficient and unresponsive political structures. Emerging democracies face these and perhaps greater challenges. These were well articulated at the Jepson School of Leadership Studies at the University of Richmond (Virginia), which recently hosted a lecture series entitled 'Transitions to Democracy'. In its supporting materials, it was noted that 'the Cold War has ended, apartheid has crumbled, and once-entrenched dictators have departed. The old regimes, however, have not simply turned into democracies overnight. We see instead the hopeful beginnings of long and uncertain transitions to new political arrangements. These may one day call themselves democracies,' the Jepson program continued, 'but they are likely to be different in important ways from each other and from most Americans' fixed ideas of what "democracy" looks like.'[2]

We face, then, a period every bit as important and significant as that now-hallowed time in the late eighteenth century when the great minds of the day contemplated an appropriate response to the emergence of popular sovereignty. And, indeed, while certainly not 'the end of history', the present challenges can be seen as a part of, and perhaps the culmination of, centuries of grappling with the conception of rule by the people. The Jepson School lecture series posed the relevant questions: 'What possible outcomes lie ahead? What factors affect the reconstruction of institutions, the reallocation of resources, and the rethinking of social values and priorities that complicate transitions to democracy [and, I might add, reforms of existing democracies]?' And, perhaps most important, 'How might these considerations lead to a more useful understanding of democracy itself?'[3]

These are not superficial questions, and our responses must aspire to an intellectual rigor worthy of them. The ensuing analysis is not light reading nor is it intended to be. However, this book is intended to be an initial step toward an informed dialogue among those most concerned with the creation and reform of effective democratic polities (which means this book is for everyone). It does not claim to encompass all of the critical issues posed by the demands of democracy, but instead chooses to address perhaps the most important one: leadership in a democracy. Nor does this work pretend, even within this narrow sphere, to be the last word; rather, it hopes to become among the sources to which the people and their leaders can turn with profit when seeking a constructive dialogue about the means and ends of democracy.

While a more substantive discussion begins in the Prologue, below, it is useful here to sketch out the content and approach of this text. The focus of our ensuing discussions is not democracy *per se*, but rather the central dynamic within democratic polities, a dynamic we will label *leadership*. There will be little of the structural approach traditional to political science, other than to acknowledge with political scientists Philippe Schmitter and Terry Lynn Karl that 'democracy does not consist of a single set of institutions. There are many types of democracy, and their diverse practices produce a similarly varied set of effects.'[4] It is to be anticipated that the foundational principles discussed herein will be adapted as needed to the specific demands of various polities.

The focus herein will be upon leadership in democratic regimes. Although the construct will receive more intensive treatment in the text proper, it is important to indicate here the value of the concept as the organizing construct of our discussion of democracy. The reason is that *leadership*, as the term will be used in this text, is the essential dynamic of democratic functioning. Indeed, as historian Edmund S. Morgan has perceived, leadership only becomes important in the context of such democratic functioning. At the conclusion of a long analysis of the rise of popular sovereignty in the seventeenth and eighteenth centuries, Morgan wrote: 'The word "leader" is old, but "leader*ship*" was a term that no one seems to have felt a need for as long as the qualities it designates remained an adjunct of social superiority. The decline of deference and the emergence of leadership signaled the beginnings not only of a new rhetoric but of a new mode of social relations and a new way of determining who should stand among the few to govern the many.'[5]

Our study of leadership, then, is nothing less than an exploration of this 'new mode of social relations'; in particular, the relationship of rulers and ruled in regimes committed to ultimate power in the people. This consideration of leadership as the interrelationship of rulers and the people as they seek to achieve societal goals reveals the central dilemma of democracy. As Schmitter and Karl point out, regimes committed to popular sovereignty still require '*rulers*, persons who occupy specialized authority roles and can give legitimate commands to others. What distinguishes democratic rulers from nondemocratic ones are the norms that condition how the former come to power and the practices that hold them accountable for their actions.' This requires, in turn, a consideration of the place and role of '*citizens*', who are, according to Schmitter and Karl, 'the most distinctive elements in democracies'.[6]

Our examination of this new mode of social relations we are calling the leadership relation brings in its train unexpected complexities. Sociologist Matthew Trachman notes that although equality is generally considered to be the nodal point of modern democracies, 'yet paradoxically, leadership is an inherently unequal relationship.... Given the fact that democratic cultures are egalitarian and yet leadership relations are inegalitarian,' he continued, 'we should not be surprised to find that modern democrats are resolutely ambivalent about leadership.' In fact, wrote Trachman, 'it is this ambivalence ... that gives form to the relationship of leadership to democracy.'[7]

In sum, this focus upon leadership goes to the very heart of a democratic society's functioning. It can reveal insights that are otherwise overlooked or masked by attention to less vital aspects of democracy. Indeed, as Trachman suggests, 'those of us who are studying leadership are studying one of the most important discursive developments of the modern democratic age'.[8]

The first task of this book, and it is a task it attempts to take seriously, is an intellectual one. If we are to confront the challenges of modern democracy in a productive fashion, we need to be straight on our underlying principles. We need, in political scientist Michael Sandel's phrase, a 'public philosophy' of leadership in a democracy. Sandel elaborates: 'By public philosophy,' he wrote, 'I mean the political theory implicit in our practice, the assumptions about citizenship and freedom that inform our public life.' This will not be as simple as it might first appear. As Sandel explained, 'A public philosophy is an elusive thing, for it is constantly before our eyes. It forms the often unreflective background to our political discourse and pursuits.' In fact, 'in ordinary times, the public philosophy can easily escape the notice of those who live by it'.[9] Sociologist Matthew Trachman echoed this point in terms of modern conceptions of leadership in a democracy. He found that, much like the rest of the surrounding culture, notions of leadership go 'largely unnoticed'; they are 'simply taken for granted'. For Trachman, there is a need to 'awaken ourselves to culture's conventions', particularly when it comes to the leadership relation.[10]

More specifically, it can be argued that, for all of democracy's seeming ubiquity, those who partake in it, as well as those who study it, have not articulated a public philosophy that makes sense of the 'new mode of social relations' that accompanies it. Worse, it can be argued that there is no such coherent philosophy, articulated or not. Political scientist and leadership scholar James MacGregor Burns has made the point well. In pre-democratic times, he argued, a 'hierarchical world (the world of the father, the priest, the lord, the king, the Pope) ... was grounded in the doctrine of authority'. But, 'beginning in the seventeenth and eighteenth centuries,' he continued, 'the doctrine of authority began to be undermined by the bulwark of equality'. Surely, thought Burns, this was a salutary development, but it was unaccompanied by a parallel intellectual justification for the new relationships between rulers and ruled that came in its train. As Burns put it, 'while authority had been overthrown, nothing had come to replace it. ... No new, democratized and radicalized doctrine arose to salvage the authentic and relevant in authority and link these strengths to a doctrine of leadership ... with the power and sweep of the old doctrine of authority but now emphasizing followers and leaders.' In consequence, Burns explicitly put forth 'a call for the creation of a doctrine of leadership that could function in the democratic world in the way that the doctrine of authority functioned in the monarchic world'.[11]

This is a clarion call from one of the most astute observers of the modern scene. One of the objectives of this book is to initiate a response to Burns's invitation. It aspires to facilitate the creation of a philosophy of leadership in a democracy, and in so doing to raise the level and efficacy of modern debates concerning the challenges of democracy. Its first task will be to identify certain key fundamental premises and assumptions that underlie past and current interpretations of the leadership relation. Arguments about democracy and leadership are rooted in such foundational matters.

This brings us to the chosen title for this book, which is intended to reflect its approach. The title is *Inventing Leadership*, which quite consciously recalls Edmund S. Morgan's history of popular sovereignty cited above, whose title is *Inventing the People: The Rise of Popular Sovereignty in England and America* (a decade earlier Garry Wills had produced a volume entitled *Inventing America: Jefferson's Declaration of Independence*).[12] The use of the concept of 'inventing' constructs such as 'the people', a conception of 'America', or, in this case, 'leadership', is similar in each case. Morgan explains it in terms of the creation of a 'fiction', that is, of an idealized belief in some societal structure, construct or relationship. Such fictions are necessary if society is to function, because they generate support for the polity. In Morgan's telling of it (for example), there was first the fiction of the divine right of kings. No one could prove the veracity of this concept, but only through the acceptance of the fiction were the monarchs able to rule successfully. He also argued that the notion of 'the people' is a fiction, incapable of precise definition but nonetheless necessary in order to support regimes grounded in popular sovereignty. So too is 'leadership' a fiction, a socially constructed concept of the appropriate relations between rulers and the people. It is perhaps an even more amorphous construct than 'the people', but it is equally important that the members of the polity 'buy in' to its characteristics if democracy is to flourish.

And therein lies the rub. As Burns has pointed out, there is no agreement as to the essence of this relationship between the few (the rulers) and the many (the constituent population), the fiction we here label leadership. Because there has been no clarity in this essential fiction of a democracy, we are at sea, with no clear 'public philosophy'.

This book will seek to redress this failing by providing the reader with a historically-informed analysis of the construct of leadership. Its fundamental approach is captured by Kenneth Ruscio, author of another volume in this estimable Edward Elgar series. According to Ruscio, 'contemporary critiques of democracy, no matter how insightful, pay almost no attention to the political philosophical foundations of leadership'. Like Ruscio's, this work 'is an attempt to fill that void, but it does so by adopting the very different strategy of stepping back from today's events, not by immersing ourselves into them. If it sheds light on the current state of democracy, it will be because it has removed itself from the present to examine the complex and confusing legacy handed down from a number of influential, insightful, and imaginative thinkers.' In sum, Ruscio asserts, and I concur, that 'ideas do matter.... The intricacies of the arguments of our intellectual [forebears] has been lost along the way.' That is to say, 'the literature on political leadership in democracies rarely draws from political philosophy in any systematic or explicit manner'. What is needed, and what the following analysis seeks to provide, is the 'historical development of democratic thought, the analytical constructs it provides, and the competing perspectives it brings to ongoing debates' about leadership in a democracy.[13]

This volume will analyze the problems of leadership in a democracy in a substantive and textured way. It will draw together insights from classical philosophers, historical case studies, and the work of modern historians, political scientists, leadership scholars and practitioners. The analysis will unfold at several levels. First, the study will be grounded in history. It is impossible to understand properly a concept as complex as leadership in a modern democracy without a thorough examination of its historic roots. This work will trace the emergence of the construct of leadership, and the many tensions inherent in democratic functioning that have been present from its beginnings.

Second, this study will move beyond historical description and engage in the analysis of the principal responses to the challenges of leadership in a democracy. Indeed, there has been no simple, monolithic answer to the inherent tensions of democracy. Instead, a plethora of systems, ideas, proposals and ideologies have filled – and muddled – the field. One of the tasks of this study is to identify and explore some of the principal solutions that have been proposed. Moreover, because these various approaches to democracy stem from differing assumptions, values, and even ideologies, it is also necessary to isolate the contrasting 'first principles' that underlie past and current debates over leadership in a democracy. This will be linked to a frank evaluation of the strengths and weaknesses of each approach. Only with such background understanding can one hope to address profitably the challenges of leadership in our postmodern democracies.

Specifically, the organization of this volume has a logic to it that is important to understand. In Part One, 'Inventing the Leader', we will trace the emerging conception of the leader in the Western intellectual tradition. Drawing upon classical texts by Plato, Aristotle, Aquinas, Machiavelli and Harrington, we will construct the enduring image ('fiction') of the ideal leader in both unitary states and republics. Part Two, 'Inventing the People', traces the antithesis of the emerging dialectic, drawing heavily upon the work of historians Edmund S. Morgan and Gordon S. Wood, and political scientist James A. Morone. Part Three will address the attempts at synthesis, and is appropriately entitled 'Inventing Leadership'. Because there has been no consensus concerning this new relationship between rulers and ruled, we must instead trace out the most insightful and influential attempts at defining this new relation. We thus begin with a consideration of two early efforts to come to terms with the relationship between the few and the many, those by James Madison and Alexis de Tocqueville. The dominant approaches of the modern era are addressed in chapters on liberalism (with a focus on John Locke, John Stuart Mill, John Rawls and Robert Nozick), and communitarianism (Aristotle, Rousseau, Hegel and a host of modern commentators such as Benjamin Barber, Alasdair MacIntyre, Robert Nisbet, Michael Sandel and Michael Walzer).

It is important to note that the first three Parts of this volume noted above are not merely descriptive, but analytical. The Prologue (below) sets forth a protocol of questions labeled the 'template of leadership', which is designed to draw out the key assumptions about leaders, the people, and the relationship between them. When applied to the various writings parsed out in this volume, it both clarifies the complexities of what is a muddled intellectual tradition and facilitates comparisons and contrasts. The template also allows individuals to isolate and identify their own 'implicit theories of leadership' – that is, their own assumptions and premises about the leadership relation – and thereby to raise the level of debate from polemic to reasoned analysis.

All this sets the stage for Part Four of this book – 'Reinventing Leadership'. This concluding section is unabashedly normative, drawing upon the insights of the past as well as modern leadership scholars, game theorists, recent developments in the field of conflict resolution and the like, to fashion proposed reforms to our democratic polities. Indeed, this volume will culminate with a series of specific proposals for reform, based upon explicitly stated values and first principles. The reform package will include suggestions for changes in democratic theory, the rethinking of social values, the reallocation of resources and the reconstruction of institutions to create a just and workable democracy. Most important, it will suggest how the social relation that we call leadership can play a catalytic and determining role. What rescues it from the scrapheap of modern democratic polemics is that it consciously attempts to model how the approach of this volume can lead to a more productive discourse on democracy. That is to say, it expressly provides responses to the queries posed by the template of leadership, and thus lays bare for all to see the rationale underpinning the proposed reforms (my own 'implicit theory of leadership'). This does not, of course, guarantee agreement – indeed, the proposals contained herein will, at various points, enrage those on both the left and the right – but, because the assumptions are clear, the ensuing debate will likely be over substance.

There are, of course, no easy solutions, nor solutions that will be readily accepted by all. At the very least, however, the reader of this book should come away with a perception of the difficulties inherent in the implementation of a viable regime grounded in the power of the people. This should be coupled with an appreciation of the role that leadership plays in the functioning of a democracy. More importantly, this book aspires to bring debate over the operations of leadership and democracy from the realm of impassioned polemics to the substantive rationality of the discussion of first principles and their impact upon the operation of the polity. Once the intellectual underpinnings and premises of our respective views of democracy and leadership are out in the open, the diverging premises of many of our debates will be laid bare. Even those who disagree with the conclusions of this monograph will be the better for having confronted its arguments. Perhaps most important of all, this work may cause its audience – scholars, students, public intellectuals and others interested in a working democracy – to use its contents as a call to arms regarding the reform of leadership in a democracy.

The enduring value of this volume, then, will not be the specific policy proposals of Part Four, but its framing of democratic discourse in leadership terms, its attempts to raise the level of democratic debate by placing it within its historical context, and its creation of a framework through which we can engage one another in productive debate concerning the challenges of democracy.

We stand on the threshold of a critical era; let us hope our efforts to understand leadership will facilitate our efforts to make a better and more just world.

NOTES

1. Freedom House, 'Democracy's Century: A Survey of Global Political Changes in the 20th Century' (2001), http://www.freedomhouse.org/reports/century.html
2. Jepson School of Leadership Studies, 'Transitions to Democracy', text from promotional materials for lecture series, 1999.
3. Ibid.
4. Philippe C. Schmitter and Terry Lynn Karl, 'What Democracy Is ... and Is Not', *Journal of Democracy* 2 (1991): 76.
5. Edmund S. Morgan, *Inventing the People: The Rise of Popular Sovereignty in England and America* (New York: W.W. Norton & Company, 1988), p. 306.
6. Schmitter and Karl, 'What Democracy Is ... and Is Not', pp. 76–77 (see note 4).
7. Matthew Trachman, 'Historicizing Leadership / Democratizing Leadership Studies,' (unpub. ms; used with permission of the author), pp. 17–19.
8. Ibid., p. 24.
9. Michael J. Sandel, *Democracy's Discontent: America in Search of a Public Philosophy* (Cambridge: Harvard University Press, 1996), p. 4.
10. James MacGregor Burns, quoted in Trachman, 'Historicizing Leadership / Democratizing Leadership Studies', p. 1 (see note 7).

11. James MacGregor Burns, *Leadership* (New York: Harper & Row, 1978), p. 28, and Trachman, 'Historicizing Leadership / Democratizing Leadership Studies', pp. 5–6.

12. Morgan, *Inventing the People* (see note 5); Garry Wills, *Inventing America: Jefferson's Declaration of Independence* (New York: Houghton Mifflin Company, 1978).

13. Kenneth P. Ruscio, *The Leadership Dilemma in Modern Democracy,* New Horizons in Leadership Studies (Cheltenham, U.K.: Edward Elgar Publishing, Ltd., 2004), pp. 2, x.

Acknowledgments

I am grateful to Edward Elgar's series editor Joanne Ciulla, who came to me one day and asked if I would be willing to write up in book form the ideas about the intellectual heritage of leadership I have been contemplating, researching and teaching for a number of years. In addition to the obvious intended outcome of enlightening my readers, the process has done me the good service of requiring me to weave together a series of seemingly disparate threads in my research, each seemingly distinct yet all addressing similar fundamental issues.

This volume could not have been completed without the generous allocation of time and resources allotted to me for this purpose by Kenneth Ruscio, Dean of the Jepson School of Leadership Studies at the University of Richmond, Virginia. In addition, as usual, Cassie King, research assistant and editor extraordinaire, deserves enormous credit for her efforts to bring clarity to my language and accuracy to my citations.

The staff at Edward Elgar Publishing has been ever supportive. I thank in particular Alan Sturmer, who has patiently endured one missed promised deadline after another. Tara Gorvine has been ever supportive, and Kate Emmins has graciously shepherded the text to completion.

Finally, as is ever the case, I owe the greatest debt of gratitude to my family, Suzanne and Jack, whose love and support appear to have no bounds.

Prologue: of fictions, implicit theories, and leadership in a democracy

The role of leadership in a democracy is a perplexing one. Democracy is grounded in, and indeed is the ultimate manifestation of, a belief in popular sovereignty – power in the people. It presumes popular participation in government, yet there is evidence enough that the people do not always govern themselves well. Leaders have ever been called upon to rescue democratic societies from their foibles. Unfortunately, the very notion of leaders in a democracy is rife with tensions. Reality dictates that there must be 'leaders' of some sort; the few must govern the many in any social grouping of size. Moreover, a belief in wise and virtuous leaders acting for the common good has a long and honorable pedigree. But, in modern times, democratization and egalitarian values have undercut the deference necessary to follow such virtuous leaders – if any there be. Likewise, individualism and diversity have undermined the very notion of the common good. Many recent scholars and practitioners have sought to avoid the perceived evils of leaders by championing a participationist approach to the workings of democracy, but many thoughtful observers remain unconvinced that merely gathering stakeholders together yields wise policy. The difficulties of creating and maintaining an effective democracy remain patent.

If concentration shifts from 'leaders' to 'leadership', however, new possibilities begin to unfold. Leadership should be understood as an influence relation among leaders and followers that facilitates the accomplishment of group or societal objectives.[1] This shifts the focus from the leaders to all members of the polity, and suggests an ongoing process of mutual influence. The central tensions of a democracy remain, but the leadership process, if properly understood and implemented, holds the promise of mediating those tensions. For example, one of the central dilemmas of democracy arises when there is a belief in the power of the people, yet at the same time a distrust of the ability of the people to govern well. Leadership is a construct that seeks to mediate that dilemma through the actions of leaders, structural constraints and the utilization of appropriate processes. In a similar vein, leadership, rightly understood, mediates the tension in a democracy between the desire for strong and visionary leaders and the deeply held values of participation, egalitarianism and diversity. In short, leadership, both as a construct and a reality, promises to hold the key to a viable, functioning democracy in our postmodern world. It is the intent of this volume to explore the role of leadership in a democracy, and to put forward specific proposals to help implement an effective leadership process.

In addition to a definition of leadership, an accompanying definition of democracy must be proffered. As Raymond Williams has noted, 'Democracy is a very old word but its meanings have always been complex'.[2] For centuries – really until the nineteenth century – democracy was viewed by most as an evil – the equivalent of mob rule. Since then, the term has been held hostage to (that is, defined to accommodate) various ideologies.[3] This text will adopt a variation of the definition of political scientists Philippe C. Schmitter and Terry Lynn Karl. Those scholars begin by 'broadly defining democracy ... as a unique system for organizing relations between rulers and the ruled'. This book will somewhat modify their more precise definition by stating that 'democracy is a system of governance in which ultimate sovereignty resides in the people (however defined) and in which rulers are held accountable for their actions in the public realm by citizens, acting directly or indirectly'.[4]

Juxtaposing the two operative definitions helps to justify the many instances in this narrative in which democracy and leadership are treated as virtually inseparable. If democracy is 'a unique system for organizing relations between rulers and the ruled', and leadership is 'an influence relation among leaders and followers that facilitates the accomplishment of group or societal objectives', the leadership process in a democracy might be viewed as simply democracy at work.

The close connection between democracy and leadership does not lessen the complexities posed by their interrelationship. It simply means that the specific leadership challenges in a democracy will echo the challenges for democracy itself: the need to secure sound action and policy in a regime based upon a conception of power in the people.

To pursue this study, it is necessary to introduce two constructs that will serve as vehicles to carry this analysis forward. Specifically, it is important to understand the concepts of *fictions* and *implicit theories of democracy and leadership*.

FICTIONS

The intellectual frame that will guide the ensuing analysis is the notion of societal 'fictions', which requires some explanation. Historian Edmund S. Morgan pioneered the use of fictions as vehicles to explain historical developments.[5] His words may help to introduce the subject. Morgan argues that political society is built upon a series of fictions. In Morgan's words, '[A]ll government rests on the consent, however obtained, of the governed.... The success of government thus requires the acceptance of fictions, requires the willing suspension of disbelief....' He goes on to provide several examples of prominent fictions: 'Government requires make-believe. Make-believe that the king is divine, make believe that he can do no wrong or make believe that the voice of the people is the voice of God. Make believe that the people *have* a voice or make believe that the representatives of the people *are* the people. Make believe that governors are the servants of the people....'[6] None of these assertions are completely true in actual fact, yet people in certain societal situations have acted as if they were true.

Fictions, then, are idealized notions of what should be; they are societal beliefs in ideal values and organizing structures. Although the term 'fiction' carries a pejorative connotation, such idealized beliefs are necessary for any polity to function. Without such fictions, government could not stand, because it is such idealized conceptions that induce the governed to accept the regime. Equally important for our purposes, it is upon such fictions that leadership is based. As David Hume commented in 1758, 'Nothing is more surprising ... than to see the easiness with which the many are governed by the few.... When we enquire by what means this is brought about, we shall find ... 'tis on opinion only that government is founded.'[7] If we are to understand the complex interrelation between democracy and leadership, we will need to identify the ideals – the fictions – that constitute these constructs, and thereby maintain the people's allegiance.

This becomes all the more important when one realizes the dynamism of the relationship between fictions and reality. Fictions, by their very nature, are idealized notions of what should be; they are only imperfectly related to how things really operate in the real world. Nonetheless, fictions, in order to be maintained, must bear some relation to reality. When the fiction and reality get too far apart, tension builds, and one of two things must happen. Either the fiction must change (this is often a revolutionary event), or the reality must change to bring it more into conformity with the fiction (this is called reform).[8] Indeed it can be argued that it is the tensions between existing fictions and reality that drive historical change. Any aspirations to reform leadership in our present democracy, then, must begin with an assessment of the congruence of existing fictions and current reality.

This notion of the role of fictions helps to make sense of the ensuing analysis. This book will trace the rise and development of a series of related fictions that have been central to our issue of leadership in a democracy. The ideals contained in these fictions are, in essence, our 'first principles', and will serve as the touchstone for our analysis. An evaluation of the nexus between these fictions and contemporary reality will provide a means of assessing the propriety and success of various attempts to implement leadership in a democracy, and also serve as the catalyst for proposed reforms.

Specifically, this study will treat three fictions that are related in a dialectic of sorts. Part I will draw upon a range of classical philosophers and commentators to discern the emergence of a fiction of the ideal of a leader. As we shall see, despite considerable differences in time and context, the substance of this 'classical ideal' will remain remarkably stable, applying alike to regimes with and without popular participation. This classical ideal of the leader continues to have considerable influence even today. This 'thesis' will in time be joined by its antithesis, the fiction of the people. Part II will trace the emergence of a conception of the people and, gradually, the further (fictional) gloss of power in the people – popular sovereignty. With the emergence of this dialectic (at the end of the eighteenth century) there appears the important synthesis that will be the focus of our further consideration: leadership. As Edmund S. Morgan states in the conclusion to his study of the rise of popular sovereignty, 'The word "leader" is old, but "leader*ship*" was a term that no one seems to have felt a need for as long as the qualities it designates remained an adjunct of social superiority. The decline of deference and the emergence of leadership signaled the beginnings not only of a new rhetoric but of a new mode of social relations and a new way of determining who should stand among the few to govern the many.'[9]

The remainder of this volume will address 'this new mode of social relations and [its] new way of determining who should stand among the few to govern the many'. Part III, then, will explore this new fiction we call leadership and its various permutations over the past two centuries. Part IV will return to the dynamics of fictions and reality, and assess how well current conceptions and practices of this fiction leadership meet the realities of our postmodern world. It is in the context of this discussion that proposals for the remaking of leadership in a democracy will arise.

Fictions thus form the analytical framework for our study. However, there is yet another construct whose function it is to allow the sort of in-depth analysis necessary for a thorough treatment of our subject. It is to that construct we now turn.

IMPLICIT THEORIES

The analysis of leadership in a democracy in historical and contemporary context is complicated by the fact that the various approaches to democracy and leadership begin from quite different and often conflicting basic assumptions and premises. Unless these are articulated and understood, it is impossible to compare and analyze adequately the historical solutions for the dilemmas of democracy. Moreover, when one turns to contemporary discourse on democracy, these differing starting points stir much of the passion that fuels the disagreements. Only if these basic assumptions are brought out into the open can one hope for current debate over the workings of democracy to move beyond polemics and into a reasoned discussion of substantive differences. This book will make every attempt to isolate and identify the base assumptions of the approaches under study, and to suggest the implications for the workings of leadership in a democracy. When it comes time for promulgating proposed reforms, the underlying assumptions and premises will be laid bare. This will permit and encourage informed debate and disagreement.

Political scientist Benjamin Barber labels such beginning points as constituting an 'inertial frame', which he defines as 'a starting point or rest position from which a theorist launches his argument'. They represent, according to Barber, a 'pretheoretical substratum over which theory can be laid'.[10] To be sure, much of modern democratic theory is grounded in such assumptions.[11] However, in this analysis, such foundational assumptions will go by a different name. Adapting a term used by modern leadership theorists, they will here be called 'implicit theories' of leadership and democracy. According to the leadership scholars, implicit theories are filters through which individuals perceive the actions of others. These filters determine whether or not the individual attributes to the perceived actor or action the term 'leader' or 'leadership', respectively.[12] To be sure, the use of this construct in this volume differs from the role it plays as a psychological filter as portrayed in the leadership literature. At the same time, it goes beyond Barber's conception of inertial frame, which he views as merely the starting point for deductive theory building. As used here, an implicit theory has both the Barberian attribute of logical premise and the aspect of more active intellectual engagement with perceived reality drawn from the leadership studies. That is to say, in this volume, implicit theory operates both as the foundation for one's articulation of the proper functioning of democracy and leadership and as the lens through which he or she evaluates other solutions to democracy's challenges. This more dynamic conception best captures the multiple roles played by one's assumptions and premises in the discourse over leadership and democracy.

Although each contributor to the discourse brings a unique constellation of assumptions and premises to the debate, it is possible to identify several common issues that each has to confront. It is the resolution of these core issues that creates one's 'implicit theory' and largely determines one's perspective and course of action in approaching leadership in a democracy.

CREATING A TEMPLATE FOR LEADERSHIP ANALYSIS

In order to make analytical sense of the myriad sources upon which this volume draws, and to serve as a basis for proposals for reform, this study will apply a protocol of analytical questions that are designed to isolate and identify key premises and assumptions pertaining to leadership, thus creating a template for leadership analysis. This approach has several benefits. First, it is a way of pulling together quite disparate sources and focusing upon their leadership implications. The scope of the ensuing analysis will be quite extensive. It will explore with some care the works of political philosophers, political scientists, historians, sociologists and other commentators on democracy. Many of the sources utilized do not explicitly address leadership; often, it is necessary to distill from each the leadership implications. In creating a template that addresses identical issues for each source, it makes them comparable, thus facilitating analysis. Second, by drawing out the suppositions of each commentator or approach in this manner, it serves the purpose of clarifying points of disagreement among observers of leadership in a democracy. Finally, by categorizing the various responses of a long and rich history of individuals and societies to the challenges posed by leadership in popular regimes, we are afforded a catalogue of potential solutions for contemporary leadership challenges.

Before turning to the specifics of our 'leadership template', a word of clarification is in order. It is the argument of this volume that the actual fiction of 'leadership' – and the term itself – did not come into popular usage until the late eighteenth and early nineteenth centuries. However, we will be applying the analytical framework provided by the 'leadership template' to all aspects of the ensuing study, even those antedating the emergence of the construct itself. This is legitimate, in the sense that issues relating to leaders and the people and the relations between them have always been relevant. In sum, the template identifies some eternal 'leadership issues' that existed long before the term itself came into being as an adjunct of modern democracy. With this potential confusion resolved, we can turn to the protocol of queries which make up our analytical 'leadership template'.

What is the Leadership Challenge?

The initial task in the analysis of each approach to leadership in a democracy is identifying how the commentator or approach defined the central challenge to the implementation of a successful polity. While it is true that all governments face certain generic problems such as the keeping of good order and the accomplishment of societal objectives, each commentator whose thought is detailed in this volume uniquely defines a specific leadership challenge that must be addressed. The perceived challenge may be the result of specific historical conditions, the ideology of the commentator, or both, but it is this definition of the problem that goes a long way toward explaining the content and tenor of the response.

The identification of the perceived leadership challenge is also useful in terms of our continuing analysis of the role of fictions in understanding leadership in a democracy. That is to say, for any version of the fiction of leadership to achieve hegemony, that fiction must appropriately identify the essential challenges facing society, and adequately respond to them. By beginning our analysis with an identification of each commentator's basic starting point, we can begin to assess how well each approach to leadership serves its intended purpose, and thereby to evaluate its success as a societal fiction.

What is the Perception of Human Nature?

What appears at first blush to be a rather cosmic question more suited to a metaphysical analysis is in actuality one that is central to an ultimate understanding of the social relation we call leadership. For example, one's assumptions about whether humans are by nature social or independent, selfish or altruistic, rational or irrational, or incorrigible or capable of improvement, determines in great part one's view of leadership and democracy as well as one's proposed solutions to perceived challenges to both.

Unfortunately, few commentators take the care to identify explicitly their assumptions in this regard. Accordingly, our answers to this question must often be the result of logical implication, and thus remain somewhat suspect. Nevertheless, to the extent that such assumptions can be laid bare, the resulting insights into the nature of the leadership fiction that is created can be quite useful.

Are the People Capable of Governing?

This question is, perhaps, a subset of the previous query, but the issue is so central to the operation of a democracy that it deserves separate treatment. Whether or not the people are capable of governing themselves may be the most important foundational assumption related to leadership in a democracy. If the conclusion is that the people are not capable, it poses a fundamental problem that must be addressed – and opens the way for many leadership solutions. Even the opposite assumption – that is, that the people do have the capabilities to govern themselves – leaves many important issues unresolved. How, then, the various approaches to leadership resolve this issue is worthy of careful study.

What is the Proper End or Purpose of Leadership?

Every fiction relating to leadership has its own *raison d'etre*. Each articulates an image of what constitutes the desired outcomes of the relation among leaders and the people. One important task of any leadership analysis is to identify those desired ends.

Although it can take many forms, this question of the nature and purpose of government and leadership often involves consideration of the existence and nature of the common good. Commentators and approaches differ as to whether such a thing exists, how it is defined, and how it is to be achieved. In applying this leadership template to the sources addressed in the text, a consideration of each commentator's conception of the common good is both useful and unavoidable.

The answers to such questions, in turn, depend in part upon the commentator's values and value hierarchy. These, too, need to be identified. Even where multiple observers agree upon the same basic set of values – say, liberty, equality and justice – the definition of these terms can be quite divergent. Thus, for example, whether one stresses positive liberty or negative liberty, equality of opportunity or equality of condition, or distributive or procedural justice – and how one ranks them in priority – can lead to dramatically differing conclusions concerning the appropriate processes and structures to be implemented. Therefore care must be taken to attempt to discern these nuances in every approach under study.

What is the Epistemology of Leadership? (How Do We Know What to Do, or if What We are Doing is Correct?)

This question of the protocol refers to the issue of how one knows what is the proper action to take in any given situation. This can take many guises. Differing approaches to leadership, for example, posit various 'external' standards or 'independent grounds' by which to judge the propriety and success of actions. Examples of such external standards include truth, the actions of the market, the greatest good for the greatest number, natural rights, law and the like. On the other hand, in some versions of the leadership fiction, the issue is not so much what one looks to, but whom we rely upon to make the determination. Still others rely upon a given process to establish an acceptable course of action. By identifying, to the best of our ability, the epistemology of leadership for each approach to leadership, we reveal many assumptions about the leadership relation, and gain some insight into how it should operate. I will normally shorten this template question to 'What is the Epistemology of Leadership?'

What is the Role of the Leader?

This issue is often the first one that comes to mind when thinking about leadership, but in the logic of this protocol it is so interrelated with the responses to other queries in the protocol that it belongs well down the list. It is an important issue nonetheless, and we need to cull from our various sources the specific expectations of the leader.

This question embraces several possible subtopics. They include the threshold issue of who should lead, as well as role expectations. In addition, in this study of regimes grounded in the sovereignty of the people, any consideration of leader behavior will also include issues related to representation.

Moreover, although this topic will be addressed in more detail later, we must make the connection between a commentator's view of proper leader behavior and the commentator's underlying ideological orientation. For example, one of the great divides in the contemplation of leadership is between those who favor an *elitist* approach and those who champion a *participationist* approach. Expectations of leader selection and leader behavior (as well as of follower behavior, below) are part and parcel of such foundational assumptions. Thus, someone who adheres to an elitist conception of leadership will probably call for a leader who has the ability to perceive the interests of society and act upon them – a philosopher king, or at the very least someone drawn from an aristocracy of merit. That leader will then have considerable latitude in his or her actions. In contrast, those who reject elite theories and embrace a participationist model will undoubtedly call for a much different leader role, one geared to the needs of the followers, or perhaps facilitating the debates among follower interests.

What is the Role of the People?

This question is in many ways the obverse of the preceding one. In the study of leadership in a democracy, this issue is both unavoidable and surpassingly important. What may come as a surprise to some may be the variation in responses the respective commentators and approaches provide, which is often a function of the elitist/participationist divide mentioned above.

For each commentator or approach to leadership in a democracy depicted below, there must be an explication of this issue. The varying responses will go a long way toward helping us to understand the core philosophy and approach of the commentator under study.

How Should Leaders and the People Interact?

A derivative issue that deserves separate attention is the dynamics of the interaction between leaders and the people. Another way to frame this issue in a democratic context is: 'What is the appropriate relationship between the few and the many?' This query forces us to look at the leadership process itself.

This question is in many ways the culmination of the responses to the other questions of the protocol. Many of the same issues are raised again, but in a manner more directly related to the functioning of the polity. Representation, for example, must be revisited, but this time in a more holistic manner that suggests the dynamics of the relationship between the representative and his or her constituents. Again, implicit theories will drive the debate. A participationist who believes that there is no independent ground for determining the rightness of actions will view the process itself as all-important, and strive to structure interactions in such a way as to maximize the contributions of followers. One who adopts the classical liberal emphasis upon representative democracy will call for quite a different dynamic. One whose core value is justice may advocate a leadership structure and process that is different still. Again, the purpose of identifying and analyzing this issue across time is to gain thereby a further understanding of the operations of leadership in a democracy.

How is the Matter of Diversity and Minority Interests Addressed?

This is another of those questions that is in reality a subset of the previous query, but which is important enough for separate consideration. As is the case with many of our template questions, not all commentators address this basic issue. For example, the issue of diversity was ignored or assumed away until relatively recently. Concern for minority interests has a longer track record, but this, too, has received uneven attention. For a well-working democracy, of course, such matters must be addressed successfully. The ensuing analysis will attempt to suggest at least the implications of each approach for this fundamental issue.

What Institutions and Processes Must be Designed to Accommodate the Premises and Assumptions about Leadership Articulated in the Responses to the Leadership Template?

This is the all-important issue of application. The previous questions of the protocol are designed to elucidate the core assumptions relevant to leadership in a democracy. If these premises are to become workable, structures, institutions and processes must be devised to realize them in practice. An attempt will be made in each instance to identify what these structures, institutions and processes might be. It is here that various fictions of leadership get transformed into some form of functioning reality. This will also provide an opportunity to evaluate the closeness of the match between the fiction and the reality. This, in turn, will provide grist for the mill of proposed future reform of leadership in a democracy.

In applying this 'leadership template' to the contents of this volume, an attempt will be made to do so in a consistent manner, in order to derive the greatest analytical benefit from its use. However, given the great disparity in sources utilized herein, some flexibility is required. Not all sources address each of the questions of the protocol. In many cases, the leadership template will be applied at the conclusion of an often lengthy explication of the commentator's argument. To avoid unnecessary repetition, the discussion of the template will draw upon the previous analysis in a summary manner. In other cases, the template itself will drive the analysis. Whatever the format, the intent is to highlight the leadership implications in an organized manner suitable for comparison and analysis.

This Prologue has introduced the principal analytical tools that will shape this analysis. The point is that we can gain no clear understanding of the role and purpose of leadership in a democracy unless we can unravel the tangled threads of underlying values, intended purpose and modes of implementation of leadership in a democracy. The use of fictions and implicit theories help us to accomplish this level of understanding. Only after these have been made clear – in both historical and contemporary context – can we hope to address the central challenges of leadership in a democracy.

NOTES

1. This definition is akin to, but not completely congruent with, that found in Joseph C. Rost, *Leadership for the Twenty-First Century* (Westport, Conn.: Praeger Publishers, 1991). It is sufficiently broad to carry our analysis for the moment. A more detailed explication of the term leadership must await the final sections of this text.
2. Raymond Williams, *Keywords* rev. ed. (New York: Oxford University Press, 1983), 93.
3. Ibid., 93–98.
4. Philippe C. Schmitter and Terry Lynn Karl, 'What Democracy Is … and is Not', *Journal of Democracy* 2 (1991): 75–88.
5. Edmund S. Morgan, *Inventing the People: The Rise of Popular Sovereignty in England and America* (New York: W.W. Norton & Company, 1988). This book will serve as the principal resource for Part II of this volume. Note that political scientist James A. Morone also asserts that the notion of 'the people' is a fiction: Morone, *The Democratic Wish: Popular Participation and the Limits of American Government* (New York: Basic Books, 1990), 7.
6. Morgan, *Inventing the People*, 13.
7. Morgan begins his book with an epigraph from David Hume's 'Of the First Principles of Government':

   Nothing is more surprising in those, who consider affairs with a philosophical eye, than to see the easiness with which the many are governed by the few; and to observe the implicit submission with which men resign their own sentiments and passions to those of their rulers. When we enquire by what means this wonder is brought about, we shall find, that as Force is always on the side of the governed, the governors have nothing to support them but opinion. 'Tis therefore, on opinion only that government is founded; and this maxim extends to the most despotic and most military governments, as well as to the most free and most popular.

   David Hume, *Essays and Treatises on Several Subjects*, 1758 edition, quoted in Morgan, *Inventing the People*, 13.
8. Morgan, *Inventing the People*, 14.
9. Ibid., 306.
10. Benjamin R. Barber, *Strong Democracy: Participatory Politics for a New Age* (Berkeley: University of California Press, 1984), 26–28.
11. Several of these democratic theories will be addressed in Parts III and IV of this volume.
12. *See*, for example, Billy J. Calder, 'An Attribution Theory of Leadership', in Barry M. Staw and Gerald R. Slancik, eds, *New Directions in Organizational Behavior* (Chicago: St. Clair Press, 1977), 179–204; Dov Eden and Uri Leviaton, 'Implicit Leadership Theory as a Determinant of the Factor Structure Underlying Supervisory Behavior Scales', *Journal of Applied Psychology* 60 (1975): 736–741; H. Kirk Downey, et al., 'Attribution of "Causes" of Performance: A Constructive, Quasi-Longitudinal Replication of the Staw (1975) Study', *Organizational Behavior and Human Performance* 24 (1979): 287–9. More recently, Robert J. House and associates apply implicit leadership theory to explain differences in perceptions of leadership across cultures: Robert J. House, et al., *Culture, Leadership, and Organizations: The GLOBE Study of 62 Societies* (Thousand Oaks, Calif.: Sage Publications, 2004).

PART I

Inventing the Leader

1. The classical ideal of the leader

The initial fiction that was created or 'invented' in response to the challenges of societal governance was the conception of the appropriate leader. This fiction arose quite logically as societies confronted challenges of organization and the accomplishment of mutual goals in a variety of settings. Despite the variety of contexts and a diversity of challenges often unique to each society, the societal construct that emerged as the appropriate response to such needs was remarkably similar in varied locales and across time.[1] This conception we will label 'the classical ideal of the leader'. The first two chapters of this volume explore the nuances of this invented notion of the paragon of a ruler. The content of this fiction will prove to be extraordinarily enduring and continues to influence our perceptions of leadership to the present day.

It is possible to introduce and to convey the essential substance of the classical ideal through the careful study of the thought of two of the Western tradition's great commentators, Plato and Thomas Aquinas. Although widely separated in time and context, their writings were central to the creation of the fiction and provide insights into its most notable characteristics. In this chapter, these two exemplars of the fiction serve to portray the views of the leader that were to have such staying power.

PLATO

The writings of Plato have been the subject of considerable controversy over the years. Two academic debates in particular are relevant to the present analysis. One interpretive disagreement is over whether Plato intended his *Republic* as a political tract, or whether his extensive treatment of political structure and operations was merely intended as an illustration of his larger concern with the nature of justice. The second debate concerns Plato's seeming shifts of emphasis in his later works, in particular his *Epistles*, the *Statesman* and the *Laws*. While relevant, the resolution of neither question detracts overmuch from the current analysis. The debate over the *Republic* is academic in both the literal and figurative sense of the term. It is of course literally a debate among academicians, but more important, Plato's actual intent becomes less crucial when one views his writings as the genesis of an enduring fiction. Whatever Plato intended, his works from an early date have been accepted as a political statement, and it is that impact that has shaped the emerging fiction of the leader.[2] Similarly, Plato's consideration of the rule of law as opposed to that of men in his later work could be viewed either as the impact of experience or as merely the realistic application of his earlier ideas. While there is evidence to support the former interpretation, either explication fits well with an approach that embraces the impact of reality upon the operation of a fiction.[3]

More important is the context within which Plato wrote these treatises. The *Republic* was written in the aftermath of the Peloponnesian War, when chaos, instability and frequent swings to tyranny (and the judicial killing of his mentor Socrates) made it appear to Plato that democracy was insufficient to the task of creating and maintaining a just state. His *Letters*, *Statesman* and *Laws* emerged after long observation of the difficulties of ruling and the formative experience of two attempts to reform government in Sicily.[4] In all cases, Plato's writings on the nature of leaders and leading stem from his observation of specific societal occurrences, but his conclusions have assumed far larger significance. It is to the specifics of his arguments that we now turn.

Plato began his dialogue in the *Republic* by posing the question of the nature of justice. The discussion quickly turned, however, to how one might structure a just state. Before turning to Plato's proposed solutions to this conundrum, it is useful to consider the problems that he perceived in existing states. There can be little doubt that Plato reserved his harshest criticism for the workings of democracy.

Plato acknowledged the need for a state of some kind, yet voiced skepticism about how most states operate. He began by noting that 'a state comes into existence because no individual is self-sufficing; we all have many needs'. As a consequence, 'we call in another's help to satisfy our various requirements; and when we have collected a number of helpers and associates to live together in one place, we call that settlement a state'.[5] Unfortunately, all states quickly become subservient to the interests of the predominant party. Although a state might be ruled by one, the few or the many, 'in every case the laws are made by the ruling party in its own interest'.[6]

In particular, argued Plato, a democratic state is dangerous because its intrinsic values lead to abuse and tyranny. Democracies are based upon the values of liberty and equality. These seem innocuous enough – even desirable – but in democracies people always take them to excess. 'In such a state the spirit of liberty is bound to go to all lengths.' As a result, 'the citizens become so sensitive that they resent the slightest application of control as intolerable tyranny, and in their resolve to have no master they end by disregarding even the law, written or unwritten'. So too the value of equality leads to ruin. In a democracy, each citizen 'gives himself up entirely to the passions'. Moreover, 'he will set all his pleasures on a footing of equality … declaring that one appetite is as good as another and all must have their equal rights'. Here, too, the outcome is the same: 'His life is subject to no order or restraint'. The consequence of democracy, then, is anarchy, which can be redeemed only by a tyrant. 'So,' Plato concluded, 'the only outcome of too much freedom is likely to be excessive subjection, … which means that the culmination of democracy is … the cruelest extreme of servitude under a despot.'[7]

Plato was especially tuned in to the implications for leaders in a democracy. In a democracy the people do not recognize what is best for them, particularly with respect to who should lead them. He spun an allegory involving sailors to make his point. Plato asked his auditors to imagine a ship on the high seas. 'The sailors are quarreling over the control of the helm', he began. 'Each thinks he ought to be steering the vessel, though he has never learnt navigation and cannot point to any teacher under whom he has served his apprenticeship. What is more,' Plato added, 'they assert that navigation is a thing that cannot be taught at all, and are ready to tear to pieces anyone who says it can.' The sailors 'take control of the ship, make free with its stores, and turn the voyage, as might be expected of such a crew, into a drunken carousal'. Such constituents clearly have no conception of the appropriate person required to lead them. Instead, 'they cry up as a skilled navigator and master of seamanship anyone clever enough ... in persuading the master to set them in command. Every other kind of man they condemn as useless. They cannot understand that the genuine navigator can only make himself fit to command a ship by studying the seasons of the year, sky, stars, and winds, and all that belongs to his craft.' Moreover, 'they have no idea that, along with the science of navigation, it is possible for [the navigator] to gain, by instruction or practice, the skill to keep control of the helm whether some like it or not'.[8]

Nor did Plato leave the problem of leading a democracy at the level of allegory. He made it quite clear that in such a state a wise leader has almost no hope of success. Instead, only those who cater to the whims of the masses will be successful. In a democracy, the people 'honour as a good and profoundly wise person any obsequious flatterer who ... can minister agreeably to their humours, which he is clever enough to anticipate'.[9] In such a state, the better sort will never succeed in the role of a leader. Because 'the multitude can never be philosophical', Plato concluded that 'it is bound to disapprove of all who pursue wisdom'.[10]

Despite his seeming pessimism regarding the operation of states and particularly leaders in a democracy, Plato harbored a hope that there is a solution to rampant self-interest and injustice in a polity. The solution returns to the matter of the proper leader. Given the fact that this solution appears to buck the reality he perceived all around him, Plato acknowledged that his proposal presents a paradox. Nevertheless, he says, 'I must state my paradox'. He then presents one of his most famous passages: 'Unless either philosophers become kings in their countries or those who are now called kings and rulers come to be sufficiently inspired with a genuine desire for wisdom; unless, that is to say, political power and philosophy meet together ... there can be no rest from troubles ... for states ... .' A bit later he added, 'There will never be a perfect state or constitution ... until some happy circumstance compels these few philosophers who have escaped corruption but are now called useless, to take charge, whether they like it or not, of a state which will submit to their authority; or else until kings and rulers or their sons are divinely inspired with a genuine passion for true philosophy.'[11]

This, then, was the answer to society's troubles, if only it could be instituted. The evils of political society could be resolved if only the right kind of leader could be found, trained, and placed into power over a rightly constructed state. Plato devoted a great deal of the remainder of the *Republic* to elaborating upon this basic insight.

Given the fact that his conceptualization of the ideal leader has proven to be seminal, it behooves us to explore Plato's construct in some detail. He took considerable care to address the required traits and characteristics of the desired leader. He acknowledged that 'it is our business to define, if we can, the natural gifts that fit men to be guardians of a commonwealth, and to select them accordingly'.[12] They must, first and foremost, be 'lovers of wisdom'. This 'philosopher, with his passion for wisdom, will be one who desires all wisdom, not only some part of it'. Another necessary trait is that he evince 'a love of truth and a hatred of falsehood that will not tolerate untruth in any form'. Such a leader will be 'free from the love of money, meanness, pretentiousness, and cowardice, ... quick to learn and remember, magnanimous, gracious, the friend and kinsman of truth, justice, courage, and temperance'. He will, 'above all, possess within himself all that is necessary for a good life'. Assuming such men can be found, Plato asked his auditors in rhetorical fashion, 'would you entrust the care of your commonwealth to anyone else?'[13]

Such leaders did not just grow on trees. A society that wished such men (or women – Plato held out this possibility) at the helm could develop such leaders only through a long and rigorous process of selection and education. As usual, Plato went directly to the point: 'How are these Guardians to be brought up and educated?' he asked.[14] In response to his own query, Plato sketched out his plan. It began with the selection of candidates with the potential to be philosophical leaders. 'We must', said Plato, 'find out who are the best guardians of this inward conviction that they must always do what they believe to be best for the commonwealth.' To do so, 'We shall have to watch them from earliest childhood and set them tasks in which they would be most likely to forget or to be beguiled out of this duty'. Such tests served to winnow out undeserving candidates. 'Whenever we find one who has come unscathed through every test of childhood, youth, and manhood, we shall set him as a ruler to watch over the commonwealth.' This, added Plato, 'may be taken as an outline of the way in which we shall select Guardians to be set in authority as Rulers.'[15]

Selection, however, was only the first step. Once selected, leader candidates were to pursue an elaborate training process that spanned decades. Plato set forth a detailed educational plan designed to prepare society's leaders. In its general outlines, this training program progressed according to the following guidelines: 'Boys and youth should be given a liberal education suitable to their age, and, while growing up to manhood, they should take care to make their bodies into good instruments for the service of philosophy. As the years go on in which the mind begins to reach maturity, intellectual training should be intensified. Finally, when strength fails and they are past civil and military duties, let them range at will, free from all serious business but philosophy.'[16] The specifics of the education included higher education in mathematics and moral philosophy. Part of this education must involve the fine arts. Plato championed 'the decisive importance of education in poetry and music; … a proper training of this kind makes a man quick to perceive any defect or ugliness' and 'he will … grow into a man of noble spirit'.[17] Even participating in the theater, on a limited scale, could prove helpful. 'If they act,' Plato insisted 'they should, from childhood upward, impersonate only the appropriate types of character, men who are brave, religious, self-controlled and generous.' Such 'reproduction of another person's gestures … or states of mind, if persisted in from youth up, grows into a habit which becomes second nature'.[18]

This educational process could not be abbreviated or hastened. As Plato envisioned it, it would take literally decades before a leader would achieve sufficient wisdom to step into his or her assigned role. Partly this was because wisdom requires considerable life experience. As Plato put it, 'these Guardians we are to bring up will never be fully cultivated until [they] can recognize the essential Forms of temperance, courage, liberality, high-mindedness, and all other kindred qualities'.[19] This takes a considerable amount of training and experience. The outcome of this elaborate educational process, however, was a cadre of ideal leaders, trained equally in philosophy and the practicalities of governing.

One challenge that accompanied the training of a cadre of philosophers to lead the state was then getting these good men to consent to rule. Philosophers, by Plato's own definition, concerned themselves with such eternal 'Forms' as Goodness and Beauty. As a consequence, 'the life of true philosophy is the only one that looks down upon offices of state, and access to power must be confined to men who are not in love with it'. Nevertheless, rule they must. 'Whom else', asks Plato, 'can you compel to undertake the guardianship of the commonwealth, if not those who, besides understanding the best principles of government, enjoy a nobler life than the politician's and look for rewards of a different kind? ... Is it not ... certain after what has been said,' he continued, 'that a state can never be properly governed either by the uneducated who know nothing of the truth or by men who are allowed to spend all their days in pursuit of culture?'[20] Accordingly, for the good of the state, these philosophers must be forced to be also kings. As Plato put it, 'It is for ... [the] founders of the commonwealth ... to bring compulsion to bear on the noblest natures'. Referring back to his 'allegory of the cave', Plato noted that these philosophers 'must be made to climb the ascent to the vision of Goodness, which we have called the highest object of knowledge; and, when they have looked upon it long enough, they must not be allowed ... to remain on the heights, refusing to come down again to the [people] or to take any part in their labors and rewards'.[21] With leaders trained as philosophers who were then forced to be kings, Plato had invented the institutional solution to the ills of society.

However, the installation of wise leaders was only a part of the answer. Equally important were the desired ends or purposes of these ideal leaders. Above all else, the overarching objective of the philosopher king should be to create a state that models the ideals of philosophy. The ultimate goal of philosophy is knowledge of the Good. The concomitant end of statesmanship ('politics') is human well-being or happiness; that is, the 'Good' for man.[22] The philosopher king must assure this translation from the ideal to the practical. As Plato portrayed it, the leader 'will sketch in the outline of the constitution. Then, as the work goes on, he will frequently refer to his model, the ideals of justice, goodness, temperance, and the rest, and compare with them the copy of the qualities he is trying to create in human society.'[23] If he does his work aright, the result will be a perfect society.

Harbored within this effort on the part of the ideal leader to create a perfect society are several issues relating to the appropriate relationship between the leader and the people. At all times, the leader must act in the interests of the people and the common good. Thus, Plato makes clear that the object of a leader's actions must be the true interest of his followers. 'No leader, insofar as he is acting as a ruler,' said Plato, 'will study or enjoin what is for his own interest. All that he says and does will be said and done with a view to what is good and proper for whom he practices his art ... . The genuine ruler's nature is to seek only the advantage of the subject.'[24] This means that the ideal leader must act in the interests of the common good. As Plato phrased it, 'our aim in founding the commonwealth was not to make any class specially happy, but to secure the greatest possible happiness for the community as a whole'. Leaders, then, must 'be full of zeal to do whatever they believe is for the good of the commonwealth and never willing to act against its interest'.[25]

The fact that Plato championed the interests of the people and the commonwealth did not mean that he similarly championed their active participation in governing. This should come as no surprise, recalling his earlier searing indictment of democracy. Although acting for the interests of all the people, the leader in Plato's schema had full responsibility for the direction of the state. Others contributed to the functioning of society as their gifts allowed, but Plato stressed that their roles were strictly delimited. Nonetheless, this strictly ordered and hierarchical society was in the interests of all. Indeed, this polity manifested the culmination of all of Plato's efforts: a just society. How Plato reached this conclusion requires, perhaps, some elaboration.

The foundational principle that governed leader–follower relations in Plato's *Republic* was that everyone should know their place in society. Plato built his commonwealth on the assumption that each individual would bring different talents to society as a whole. 'No two people are born exactly alike', he said. 'There are innate differences which fit them for different occupations.' Those with the most courage, for example, were best suited to become soldiers. Ultimately, Plato divided society into three major groupings: rulers, soldiers and the producing classes.[26] These he ranked in a hierarchy of importance. 'All of you in this land are brothers,' he said, 'but the god who fashioned you mixed gold in the composition of those among you who are fit to rule, so that they are the most precious quality; and he put silver in the Auxiliaries, and iron and brass in the farmers and craftsmen.' It was of the utmost importance that individuals be assigned to the proper group. 'There is none that needs to be so carefully watched as the mixture of the metals in the souls of the children. If a child … is born with an alloy of iron or brass, [the leaders] must, without the smallest pity, assign him the status proper to his nature and thrust him out among the craftsmen or farmers. If, on the contrary, these classes produce a child with gold or silver in his composition, they will promote him, according to his value.'[27]

Plato's stress upon the importance of maintaining one's proper place in society is key to his ultimate argument, and deserves further analysis. First, the relationship between the leaders and the people is absolutely clear: the governors should govern, and the people should be content to follow the guidance of their philosopher kings. This made perfect sense, following the logic of Plato's polity. 'We have come to see who are the philosophers and who are not', Plato argued. 'Since the philosophers are those who can apprehend the eternal and unchanging, while those who cannot do so, but are lost in the mazes of multiplicity and change, are not philosophers, which of them ought to be in control of a state?'[28] His famous allegory of the cave explains how only the philosopher, who has emerged from the cave and had the opportunity to understand the true Forms of Goodness and Beauty should rule over those others [the people] who remain behind and perceive only shadows of what is real and true.[29] Thus, 'good government and well-being depend entirely upon such [leaders]'. These are, in fact, 'genuine [leaders] who will be the last to bring harm upon the commonwealth'.[30] For the people's part, on the other hand, 'men will need self-control; and for the mass of mankind that chiefly means obeying their governors. … Anyone who cannot obey shall not practice his art in our commonwealth.'[31] Although seemingly harsh, it was for Plato a self-evident reality.

The rigid specification of roles among the members of the polity was likewise absolutely essential to the achievement of the ideal state. Part of this was for efficiency's sake. As Plato put it, 'our intention … was to set the … citizens to work one man at one task for which his nature fitted him'. But it went much deeper than that. To allow a departure from the assigned roles was to invite the kind of anarchy that had led democracies to tyranny. Plato spun out for his listeners the probable progression of events if such a deviation were permitted. 'It would be harmless', he acknowledged, '… were it not that, little by little, this lawless spirit gains a lodgement and spreads imperceptibly to manners and pursuits, and thence with gathering force invades men's dealings with one another, and next goes on to attack the laws and constitution with wanton recklessness, until it ends by overthrowing the whole structure of public and private life.'[32]

Although his narration of the consequences of members of the polity stepping out of their assigned roles appears at first blush overdrawn, Plato's intensity on this issue stems from his final and most important reason for championing rigid societal roles: they exemplified the answer to the question that began the dialogue, that is, the nature of justice. Having devoted considerable effort to depicting the ideal state, Plato returned to this original question. Turning to his auditors, he said: 'Your commonwealth is established. The next thing is to bear upon it all the light you can … in the hope that we may see where justice is to be found in it.'[33] He elaborated by first restating the 'universal principle, that everyone ought to perform one function in the community for which his nature best suited him. … I believe,' he then asserted, 'that that principle, or some form of it, is justice.'[34] Justice, then, is realized by keeping the parts distinct; and having each individual perform only that role which is suited to him. In so doing, each individual will be assured of his due rights, and the state will be in harmony.[35] Thus, 'any shifting from one order to another is not only utterly harmful to the community, but one might fairly call it the extreme of wrongdoing. And you will agree,' Plato concluded, 'that to do the greatest of wrongs to one's own community is injustice.'[36] Plato's state, then, served as the guarantor of justice in the community.

All this also helps to explain why both leaders and followers would accept the proposed state, and it can be said to have the consent of the governed, even though they do not participate in its rule. Plato likened it to the virtue of temperance in an individual. Applied to an individual, temperance 'means that within himself, in his soul, there is a better part and a worse; and that he is his own master when the part which is better by nature has the worse under control'. So too with the state: 'This state of things will [likewise] exist in your commonwealth, where the desires of the inferior multitude will be controlled by the desires and wisdom of the superior few'. Therefore, 'in our state, if anywhere, the governors and the governed will share the same conviction on the question who ought to rule. … Temperance … extends throughout the whole gamut of the state, producing a consonance of all its elements from the weakest to the strongest.' As a result, 'we are entirely justified in identifying with temperance the unanimity or harmonious agreement between the naturally superior and inferior elements on the question which of the two should govern'.[37] Indeed, 'the people will look upon their rulers as preservers and protectors'.[38]

It was unthinkable that a polity that guaranteed leaders who would assure justice should meet with objection. Indeed, Plato intimated that the proposed state would approach a utopia. 'It will unite the citizens in harmony, making them share whatever benefits each class can contribute to the common good, and its purpose in forming men of that spirit was not that each should be left to go his own way, but that they should be instrumental in bonding the community into one.'[39] 'Our state,' he continued, 'having been founded and built up on the right lines, is good in the complete sense of the word. … Obviously, then, it is wise, brave, temperate, and just.'[40] The very nobility of this vision promised to resolve the paradox Plato identified at the outset. It will be recalled that Plato's paradox was his championing of philosopher kings in the very teeth of his observation that the people had no use for the wisdom of philosophers, but preferred instead leaders who catered to their whims. Plato was now more optimistic about the possibility of public acceptance. 'You must not condemn the public so sweepingly', he informed his listeners. 'They will change their opinion, if you avoid controversy and try gently to remove their prejudice against the love of learning. Repeat our description of the philosophic nature and of his pursuits,' he continued, 'and they will see that you do not mean the sort of person that they imagine. ... For what is the ground left to dispute? It would be absurd to deny that a philosopher is a lover of truth ... no other [leader] will be so completely good and enlightened.' As a consequence, the people 'will hardly give preference to those imposters whom we have ruled out. ... The public, when they see that we have described him truly,' Plato concluded, 'will be reconciled to the philosopher and no longer disbelieve our assertion that happiness can only come to a state when its lineaments are traced by an artist working after the divine pattern.'[41]

Plato in his *Republic*, then, invents a leader as the appropriate response to the societal challenges he perceived. His conceptualization of that leader we might call the 'classical ideal' of the leader, and it was to prove to be extraordinarily influential and enduring. The essential characteristics of Plato's invention can be briefly summarized. First, the ideal leader is *wise*. Wisdom is the essence of philosophy, and the appropriate leader is the only one in society that attains this essence. Such a leader really does know what is best for society, and will be by nature compelled to act upon that knowledge. All others in society necessarily defer to his (or her) judgment and direction. Second, the ideal leader is *virtuous* in the classic sense of 'civic virtue'. That is to say, the leader will subsume his or her own interests to those of the community as a whole. Finally, this wise and virtuous leader *acts for the common good*. The result of having such a leader in place (in a society properly structured as Plato decrees) is the ideal state, in which the interests of all are served, and the good life is possible.

Plato's invention of the classical ideal of a leader is a fiction, and he acknowledged as much. In a conversation with his brother Glaucon in the dialogue, Plato turns to his brother. 'We have been constructing in discourse the pattern of an ideal state. Is our theory any the worse, if we cannot prove it possible that a state so organized should actually be founded?' 'Surely not', replied Glaucon. 'That, then, is the truth of the matter', continued Plato. 'Can theory ever be fully realized in practice? Is it not in the nature of things that action should come less close to truth than thought? ... Then you must not insist', he told Glaucon, 'upon my showing that this construction that we have traced in thought could be reproduced in fact down to the last detail. ... If we can discover how a state might be constituted in the closest accordance with our description[,] ... will not that content you? It would be enough for me.'[42] The fact that the classical ideal is a fiction makes it no less powerful. As an ideal, as a proposed solution to society's ills, it still has great potency, and continues to figure into our calculus when confronting the challenges of our contemporary society.

Before leaving Plato behind, it is worth our while to trace a related theme that he took up in his later writings. Although we digress somewhat from our focus upon the leader, the ensuing analysis is not unrelated, and Plato's use of another fiction – 'the rule of law' – became a precedent for many later attempts to grapple with the challenges of leadership. Let us turn, then – albeit briefly – to this other Platonic invention that would prove to be so influential.

Plato's discussion of the role of law in the leading of a commonwealth has been subject to various interpretations. Some have held that his seeming shift in emphasis was the result of hard experience in seeking to implement the rule of a philosopher king. Others argue that the rule of law was simply his way of achieving his goal in practice, 'the closest accordance with our description', as he explained it to Glaucon.[43] The ensuing analysis adopts the learn-as-you-go interpretation, but in reality, this academic debate has little relevance for the purposes of this study. Regardless of Plato's motivation, his ultimate conclusions regarding the uses of the law created a model that many have emulated over the years. Moreover, both interpretations exemplify the dynamic tension between fiction and reality that has driven many reforms in leadership. Let us turn, then, to Plato's consideration of the role of law in leading a state.

Our starting point can be Plato's experience in attempting to apply his theories. There can be little doubt that a formative moment in Plato's life was his experience in Sicily. In 367–366 B.C.E., Plato was invited by his friend Dion to visit Sicily and advise Dion's uncle, Dionysius, who had become the tyrant of Syracuse, on the art of ruling. Dionysius, as it turned out, was more comfortable acting despotically than adhering to Plato's advice, and the entire experiment ended disastrously. Plato, on a subsequent visit, was imprisoned, and Dion was assassinated.[44] Somewhat later, in a letter to the friends of Dion (commonly referred to as *Epistle VII*), Plato appeared chastened, and volunteered a new and interesting possibility regarding the leading of the state. In that letter, he did not express regret at the attempt to institute his ideals. He noted that when Dion had called him to Syracuse, 'Above all I was ashamed lest I appear to myself as a pure theorist, unwilling to touch any practical task'. The experience with Dionysius, however had been sobering. Having viewed it up close and firsthand, Plato could say with confidence that 'the despotic power benefits neither ruler nor subjects … and no one grasps at the prizes it offers except petty and illiberal souls who know nothing of the divine and human goods that are now and for all time good and just'. Having failed utterly to reform the state he found in Syracuse under such an unjust leader, Plato now offered an alternative approach to such rule. 'Do not subject Sicily nor any other state to the despotism of men,' he concluded, 'but to the rule of law; that at least is my doctrine.'[45] This seeming shift to a role for law became a topic to which Plato devoted considerable attention in his later years. In particular, he developed his thinking in the *Statesman* and the *Laws*.

In the *Statesman*, Plato explored both the rule of men and the rule of law. Specifically, he began to come to grips with the dilemma he confronted in Sicily and reflected upon in *Epistle VII*. Simply stated, the issue with which Plato grappled was the problem of how to reconcile the fiction of the philosopher king with reality. It was – and remains – a challenge to any supporter of the classical ideal. Plato's somewhat stumbling attempt to address this difficult issue is an object lesson for anyone who strives to base the rule of the state upon meritorious leaders akin to Plato's model. As we shall see, in the *Statesman* Plato never fully resolved the contradictions created when reality (in the form of less-than-ideal leaders) conflicts with the fiction of rule by philosopher kings. Nevertheless, he appears to be feeling his way along the path toward a possible solution in the form of the rule of law. As will become clear, however, Plato in the *Statesman* never became fully comfortable with the substitution of the rule of law over the rule of men. He returned to this challenge in his last great work, the *Laws*.

In the *Statesman*, Plato reasserted his commitment to the need for wisdom in ruling the state, but took a somewhat more analytical approach than had been the case in the *Republic*. He began by recognizing the common typology of states, that is, kingly monarchy, tyranny, aristocracy, oligarchy and democracy. Those categorizations, however, were based, according to Plato, upon mistaken criteria. Classification was normally 'defined by these criteria – one, few, and many, wealth and poverty, force and consent, [or] whether … [the state] be accompanied by written laws or without laws'. Plato disagreed.

'The criterion in the things in question must not be few, nor many, nor consent nor lack of it, nor poverty nor wealth', he argued, but instead 'some sort of knowledge.'[46] Changing the criterion to knowledgeable rulers led to a different approach to the evaluation of constitutional forms.

Plato considered the implications. He turned to the question of how this would impact one's evaluation of a democracy. In his typical dialogic fashion, Plato posed the question to his audience: 'Does it seem that a mass of people in the city are capable of acquiring the expertise?' He rejected the very idea. In a city of a thousand men, neither one hundred men nor fifty men could be expected to acquire the requisite knowledge. 'Among a thousand men there would never be so many top [checker] players ... let alone kings. ... As a consequence of this, I think we must look for correct rule in relation to some one person, or two, or altogether few.' It is this measure of knowledgeable rulers that must determine one's evaluation of a state's constitution. 'It must then be the case', he asserted, that the proper constitution 'is the one in which rulers would be found truly possessing expert knowledge ... whether they rule according to laws or without laws, over willing or unwilling subjects and whether the rulers are poor or wealthy.' The conventional criteria offer 'no principle of correctness', and thereby need not 'be taken into any account at all'. Instead, the good state is one in which the rulers 'act to preserve it on the basis of expert knowledge and what is just making it better than what it was so far as they can. This is the constitution which alone we must say is correct.'[47]

Thus Plato sets out as a model of governance his earlier invention of the classical ideal. Indeed, he perhaps never captured its essence so succinctly as when he said, 'The truest criterion of correct government ... is the one according to which the wise and good man will govern the interests of the ruled'.[48] This, then, is 'the Statesman' to whom the dialogue is dedicated. Plato devoted considerable attention to how such a statesman might utilize his expertise, including the useful metaphor of the 'leader as weaver'.[49] More important for our purposes in exploring the rule of law, however, is Plato's recognition that his fiction might not comport with reality.

While Plato began his analysis in the *Statesman* with a reassertion of his belief in the philosopher king, he also recognized that current leaders fell short of the ideal. It almost went without saying that large aggregations of people could not have the requisite expertise to rule. 'If some sort of kingly expertise exists,' Plato observed, 'neither the collection of the people that consists of the rich, nor all the people together, could ever acquire this expert knowledge of statesmanship.'[50] Worse still, neither did contemporary leaders have the necessary skills. He noted that 'the statesmen who belong to our present era are much more like their subjects in their natures and have shared in an education and nurture closer to theirs'.[51] Plato's scan of the contemporary political landscape, then, offered little solace for one who was committed to the classical ideal of the leader.

This, in turn, led him to contemplate other options for securing a good and just state. In the *Statesman,* for the first time, Plato considered seriously the pros and cons of the rule of law as a substitute when the reality of poor leaders seemed to make a mockery of his commitment to the fiction of the classical ideal. Plato began by evaluating the potential role of law in states that had philosopher kings in place. At one level, having such a leader obviated entirely the need for systematic rules of law. By definition, the leader was far wiser than any law. Such leaders would 'be carrying out whatever sort of rule they do on the basis of expertise ... Rulers ... truly possessing expert knowledge' should operate as they deem necessary, 'whether they rule according to laws or without laws.'[52] Thus, an enlightened ruler had the right to ignore law and custom in ruling, so long as he ruled justly. Whether the leader 'does what is not to the benefit of the citizens, or what is to their benefit, must ... be the truest criterion of correct government'.[53]

At another level, however, Plato recognized that even though the concept of general laws was flawed in theory, such laws might be a practical necessity, even in a state ruled by an ideal ruler. Plato found himself weighing the pros and cons of laws. On the one hand, a general law cannot serve the interests of all men. 'Law could never accurately embrace what is best and more just for all at the same time, and so prescribe what is best.' There are too many 'dissimilarities between human beings and their actions'; moreover, 'practically nothing in human affairs remains stable'. Such realities prevent any attempt to set forth 'any simple decision in any sphere that covers all cases and will last for all time'.[54] Given this fundamental theoretical flaw in general laws, Plato posed the question: 'Why then is it ever necessary to make laws, given that law is not something completely correct? We must find out the cause of this.'[55] The answer stemmed from the demands of necessity. 'The [leader], ... the person who will direct [the people] in relation to justice and their contacts with one another ... will never be capable, in prescribing for everyone together, of assigning accurately to each individual what is appropriate for him. Instead he will, I think, set down the law for each and every one according to the principle of "for the majority of the people, for the majority of cases, and roughly, somehow, like this," whether expressing it in writing or in unwritten forms, legislating by means of ancestral customs.'[56] Recall, however, that in a state ruled by a philosopher king, such general laws were a mere convenience. The leader could ignore such laws, if as a consequence the result was 'more just, better and finer'.[57]

Plato now turned to the matter of states ruled by lesser men, men who did not measure up to the standards of the classical ideal. This posed a problem. He had already made more than clear that 'a mass of any people whatsoever would never be able to acquire this sort of expert knowledge and so govern a city with intelligence'.[58] Plato mulled over a possible solution. Perhaps, 'when ... a king ... is [not] ... immediately superior in body and mind, it is necessary – so it seems – for people to come together and write things down, choosing after the traces of the truest constitution'.[59] That is, 'we must look for that one constitution, the correct one, in relation to a small element in the population, few in number, or even a single individual, putting down the other constitutions as imitations'. Then, the people 'ought to employ the written documents that belong to this [ideal state], and save themselves in that way'. Such a state that is modeled upon wisdom rather than possessing it itself will of course have different rules. As Plato explained, 'The principle that no one in the city should dare do anything contrary to the laws ... is very correct and fine as a second choice, when we change the [assumption regarding the availability of a statesman-leader]'. Viewing it from this perspective, the rule of law appeared to hold promise as a viable substitute for the ideal leader, if one were careful to ensure that no departures were permitted from the substituted code of laws. Plato saw some benefit to laws in such situations, provided they 'have been established on the basis of much experiment, with some advisors or other having given advice on the subject'. This indeed might be the 'second-best method of proceeding', so long as 'neither individual nor mass ever [is permitted] to do anything contrary to these – anything whatsoever'.[60]

At first blush, then, Plato appears to be reconciled to the utility of the rule of law in certain circumstances. It can serve as a useful adjunct to the philosopher king, although he is in no ways bound by it. More important for our later analysis, Plato suggests that the need for a rule of law is particularly important when there is widespread participation in government by the people (and consequently an absence of philosopher kings). In such cases, carefully constructed rules of law, explicitly modeled after ideal states, can act as a proxy for wisdom.

At the same time, Plato in the *Statesman* is never fully reconciled with this line of reasoning. The sticking point is his belief in eternal Forms of Goodness, Justice and Beauty that only true philosophers can grasp.[61] Anything less, any 'imitation', is flawed at best, and potentially dangerous to the well being of the state. If there be not leaders who can perceive and act upon what is Real, then who we have as leaders are really nothing better than those who had been left behind in the cave, seeing only shadows. Citing Socrates, Plato asks: 'Do we wonder, then, at all the evils that turn out to occur in such constitutions ... when a foundation of this sort underlies them, one of carrying out their functions according to written rules and customs without knowledge?'[62] Such constitutions 'are not genuine, and not really constitutions at all, but imitations'.[63] This has enormous – and dangerous – consequences for both leaders and the state. Plato finally concluded that 'we must ... remove those who participate in all these constitutions, except for the one based upon knowledge, as being, not statesmen, but experts in faction; we must say that, as presiding over insubstantial images, on the largest scale, they are themselves of the same sort, and that as the greatest imitators and magicians they turn out to be the greatest sophists among sophists.'[64] And again: 'Although removing [such a sophist] from among those who really are in possession of the art of statesmanship and kingship is a very difficult thing to do, remove him we must if we are going to see plainly what we are looking for.'[65]

The conclusion of the *Statesman* found Plato deeply ambiguous about both the role of men and the rule of law in achieving a good and just state. He never wavered with respect to his core belief in his invented fiction of the classical ideal of the leader. What troubled him was the tension between that fiction and reality. After his experience in Sicily and in the *Statesman*, Plato expressed concern that rule by philosopher kings may not be possible. In the *Statesman*, he contemplated the solution he introduced in *Epistle VII*, the rule of law. However, after flirting with this as both a practical and satisficing solution, Plato ultimately could not bring himself to endorse it wholeheartedly. For him, in the *Statesman*, the rule of law remained too pale an imitation of the ideal.

The issues thus framed by Plato in the *Statesman* continue to be of relevance to the respective roles of the leader and the law in society. The tension between the idealist and the realist positions continues to be a fault line among students of the law. Plato himself was not done with the topic. In his last, great work, the *Laws*, he again took up the gauntlet of the rule of law in society.

The setting of the *Laws* is that of a group of fellow travelers who undertake a discussion of the desired attributes of a proposed new city in Crete. The content of the *Laws* appears to embody a distinct shift of emphasis toward the practical application of Plato's previous theories. It is perhaps not overly surprising that this, the last of his great works, has such a pragmatic aspect. Certainly his experience in Syracuse had caused him to rethink the practical application of his ideals, and we have seen his initial grapplings with this dilemma in the *Statesman*. Still, the shift in perspective is substantial, and like much else in his oeuvre, this has been the subject of considerable debate among scholars. Again, the academic fisticuffs need not overly detain us here, other than to identify the essential issues. The seeming tension between the *Republic* and the *Laws* has been subject to two interpretations. One explanation – the one adopted in this volume – is that Plato was engaged in an intellectual odyssey that led him to a more realistic application of his initial formulation. The other is that the *Laws* was simply the most specific application of a consistent body of ideas that he had sustained essentially unchanged throughout his works. Regardless of the respective merits of the two schools of thought, the important point for our current analysis is that in the *Laws*, more than in any other dialogue, Plato embraced the rule of law as the proper mode of achieving the just state. It is this outcome that was to figure so importantly in subsequent discussions of leadership.[66]

Let us turn, then, to the insights of Plato's *Laws*. Whatever else might be said about the *Laws*, it is clear that Plato's ultimate goal of a virtuous state remained consistent with his earlier works. 'The proper object of true political skill', he said, 'is not the interests of private individuals but the common good. That is what knits a state together … If the public interest is well served, rather than the private, then the individual and community alike are benefited.'[67] The objective of both individual and state is to 'become as virtuous as possible'.[68] Given this overarching vision for the state, Plato began to consider how that vision could be realized in an admittedly imperfect world.

One of Plato's strategies for achieving this virtuous state lay in its constitutional structure. In the *Laws*, he sought a middle ground between the perceived evils of a dictatorship and a democracy. 'There are two mother-constitutions, so to speak, which you could fairly say have given birth to all the others. Monarchy is the proper name for the first, and democracy for the second. The former has been taken to extreme lengths by the Persians, the latter by [Athens]; virtually all others are varieties of these two. It is absolutely vital for a political system to combine them, if … it is to enjoy freedom and friendship applied with good judgment.'[69] Looking more specifically at his two examples, he noted: 'One state was over-eager in embracing the principles of monarchy, the other in embracing only the ideal of liberty; neither has achieved a balance between the two.'[70]

The Persians, for their part, 'were too strict in depriving the people of liberty and too energetic in introducing authoritarian government, so that they destroyed all friendship and community of spirit in the state. And with that gone,' Plato continued, 'the policy of rulers is not framed in the interests of their subjects and the people, but to support their own authority.' This was unacceptable. 'So let's have done with the Persians. Our conclusion is that the empire is badly run … because the people are kept in undue subjection and the rulers excessively authoritarian.'[71]

'Next,' Plato went on, 'we come to the political system of Attica [Athens]. We have to demonstrate, on the same lines as before, that complete freedom from all authority is infinitely worse than submitting to a moderate degree of control.' In the old days, 'we Athenians had the same experience as the Persians. They [the leaders], of course, reduced the people to a state of complete subjection, and we encouraged the masses to the opposite system of unfettered liberty.' Unfortunately, this movement away from rigid laws 'gave the ordinary man not only a taste for breaking the laws … but the general arrogance to set himself up as a capable judge … [This] proved to be the starting point of everyone's conviction that he was an authority on every thing, and of a general disregard for the law. Complete license', concluded Plato, 'was not far behind.'[72]

Plato's conclusion was to advocate a governmental structure that involved elements of both states. The goal of government, he reiterated, was 'the freedom, unity, and wisdom of the city'. Having looked at the two chief strands of government, he posed the question: 'Which of these two constitutes correct government?' His answer was that a state needed both 'a moderate authoritarianism and a moderate freedom.'[73] The further question was how to achieve such a balance of competing ends. It is not coincidental that the conversation of those fellow travelers in Plato's dialogue turned to a consideration of the rule of law.

In the *Laws*, Plato seems to have moved beyond his reservations about the rule of law that he had articulated in the *Statesman,* although he began his argument from a familiar starting point. He repeated his mantra about the desirability of having a philosopher king. Moreover, he repeated also his belief that the rule of law held no sway over such a leader. 'If ever by the grace of God some natural genius were born, and had the chance to assume such power, he would have no need of laws to control him. Knowledge', he explained, 'is unsurpassed by any law or regulation; reason, if it is genuine and really enjoys its natural freedom, should have universal power.'[74] But, elaborating upon his observations in the *Statesman* and *Epistle VII*, Plato acknowledged that reality did not match his treasured fiction. Referring to the philosopher king, Plato made his point succinctly. 'But as it is such a character is nowhere to be found, except a hint of it here and there.' This reality led him rather seamlessly to embrace the solution that had troubled him in the *Statesman*. 'That is why', he said, 'we need to choose the second alternative, law and regulations which embody general principles, but cannot provide for every individual case.'[75]

Unlike in his earlier work, Plato here expressed no ambivalence about the rule of law. To the contrary, he took pains to explain why it was necessary in such an imperfect world. 'It is vital that men should lay down laws for themselves and live in obedience to them', he said. 'Otherwise, they will be indistinguishable from wild animals of the utmost savagery.' It is, indeed, the very absence of virtuous leaders that calls forth the need for law. 'The reason is this', Plato explained. 'No man has sufficient natural gifts *both* to discern what benefits men in their social relationships *and* to be constantly ready and able to put knowledge to the best practical use.'[76] Thus, Plato ultimately came to terms with the need for the rule of law as the best way to achieve his desired ends in a flawed world. 'Where the ruler of a state is not a god but a mortal,' he observed, 'people have no respite from toil and misfortune.' The rule of law provided the closest approximation to the ideal state Plato had been seeking all along. Although one could no longer be secure in relying upon a virtuous leader to achieve the ends of society, that did not mean that one should not make the attempt to secure such objectives by some other means. 'The lesson is that we should make every effort to imitate [the good life]; we should run our public and private life, our homes and cities, in obedience to what little spark of immortality lies in us.' The way to do this, Plato concluded, was to 'dignify these edicts of reason with the name of "law"'.[77]

Once he had established the need for law, Plato took pains to elaborate further upon the purposes that law could serve. One function that law performed was to advance and preserve the common good. The object of the state was 'not the interests of individuals but the common good',[78] and the rule of law could help to assure this. Indeed, 'laws which are not established for the good of the whole state are bogus laws'.[79] Another function of the law was that it could rein in wicked rulers. Here, Plato came close to suggesting that *all* rulers were ultimately bad, a far cry from his earlier stance. 'Even if a man did get an adequate theoretical grasp of the truth … ', Plato explained, 'he might attain a position of absolute control over a state, with no one to call him to account.' While this seemed to be precisely Plato's point in the *Republic*, here he was less sanguine. 'In these circumstances,' Plato now believed, 'he would never have the courage of his convictions, he would never devote his life to promoting the welfare of the community as his first concern, making his private interests take second place to the public good. His human nature will always drive him to look to his own advantage and the lining of his own pocket. ...'[80] Only by the restraints of law could such leaders be controlled.

If one pauses for a moment and reflects, it is clear that Plato was advocating a surrogate for the classical ideal. That ideal, it will be recalled, called for a wise and virtuous leader acting for the common good. Plato's articulation of the purposes of a rule of law paralleled that closely. He called for laws to further 'the good of the whole state' and to ensure that leaders acted in the interests of all. Furthermore, he said, all regimes 'rightly start ... with *virtue* ... [as] the aim of laws'.[81] In the *Laws*, then, Plato appears to have been willing to consider a much more pragmatic route to his desired end of the good state, and used the rule of law to secure it.

A state based upon the rule of law rather than that of men has different and important implications for leaders. Plato appears to distinguish two phases in the establishment of a state under the rule of law. The initial phase has the challenge of establishing the rule of law itself. Here, Plato appears more comfortable with his previous view of the role of the leader. If there is a virtuous lawgiver, 'nothing could be quicker or easier' than acquiring 'a good set of laws'. If such a wise leader can be found in the early stages, 'you usually get a rapid and trouble-free transition' to the new regime. Without such a wise leader, 'it is difficult for a state to acquire a good set of laws'.[82] There remains, then a significant chicken-and-egg challenge at the founding of a state. Plato still relies upon wise leaders to initiate a regime designed to ensure good leaders. However, the difficulty is mitigated somewhat by the fact that statebuilders can look to already-established regimes as models.

Once the rule of law is in place, however, the role of the leader changes. Here, Plato makes a statement in the *Laws* that is stunning when compared to the role that leaders played in his earlier works. Turning to his companion on the journey who was seeking advice as to how to structure the proposed new Cretan state, Plato said, 'In your new state we aren't going to appoint a man to office because of his wealth or some other claim like that, say strength or stature or both'. Instead, said Plato, 'We insist that the highest office ... must be allocated to the man who is best at obeying the established laws'. This rather breathtaking (for Plato) assertion suggests how far his ground had shifted. He then rammed the point home. 'Such men are usually referred to as "rulers", and if I have called them "servants of the laws" it's not because I want to mint a new expression but because I believe that the success or failure of a state hinges on this point more than on anything else.'[83] The role of leader, then, had evolved. When Plato aspired to create a perfect state based upon philosophers ruling as kings, it made perfect sense for such leaders to be above the law. Once Plato turned his attention to designing a state peopled by more mortal rulers, wisdom and virtue became embodied in the rule of law rather than in individual leaders. This being the case, it was equally logical that in this case the rule of law must reign supreme over the ruler.

It is not that Plato had totally abandoned his previous ground. For one thing, there was still a definitive need for a leader, because such a man continued to have a better understanding of how the state should operate. 'Each and every assembly and gathering for any purpose whatsoever should invariably have a leader', Plato stated.[84] 'The cool-headed and sober', he went on, 'should guide and cooperate with these laws by taking command of those who are not sober.'[85] Indeed, '[it] is a case of mismanagement ... if [an assembly or gathering] is carried on without a sober leader to control it'. Taking the metaphor one step further, he added: 'Surely you appreciate that a drunken statesman, or commander of anything, will always make a total wreck of his ship ... or whatever else he may be directing'.[86]

Furthermore, the leader, after a fashion, still maintained a level of understanding that most of the populace did not. It was not that the leader was without knowledge; only that now, rather than using his knowledge to place himself above the law, he used it to educate the populace about the virtues of law. 'The lawgiver will ... lift the fog that clouds our judgment', said Plato. His task was to help people to see that the law embodied justice and was thus worthy of support. 'He will persuade us that our ideas of justice and injustice are like pictures drawn in perspective. Injustice looks pleasant to the enemy of justice, because he regards it from his own personal standpoint, which is unjust and evil; justice, on the other hand, looks *un*pleasant to him.'[87] But the wise leader would help the people to understand that the law operates in the interests of justice for all, and as such was the cornerstone of the state.

The leader needed knowledge of another fashion as well, and in addressing it Plato necessarily revisited the concept of the role and training of the good leader. His reflections also went to the heart of the dilemma of securing good leaders in a world peopled by fallible humans. Plato addressed the dilemma of the leader directly. In his dialogic fashion, he posed this question to his fellow travelers: 'And if the ruler of a *state* were obviously ignorant of the target at which a statesman should aim, would he really deserve the title "ruler"? Would he be capable of ensuring the safety of an institution whose purpose he entirely failed to appreciate?' 'Certainly not', replied his auditors. This led Plato to consider the qualifications for leaders in the state. 'Well, then, ... if our settlement of this territory is to be finished off properly, it looks as if we shall have to provide it with some constituent that understands (a) this target we have mentioned – the target of the statesman, (b) how to hit it, and (c) which laws (above all) and which persons have helpful advice to give and which not ... .' Regardless of what person or entity that stepped into the role, 'that body must possess virtue in all its completeness'.[88] This meant a special education for such leaders. 'So it looks as if we have to compel the guardians ... to get an exact idea of the common element in all four virtues – that factor which, though single, is to be found in courage, restraint, justice, and wisdom, and thus in our view deserves the general title "virtue"'. Thus, 'if our guardians are going to be *genuine* guardians of the laws they must have *genuine* knowledge of their real nature, and they must be articulate enough to explain the real difference between good actions and bad, capable of sticking to the distinctions in practice'.[89]

'So,' he asked at last, 'is there any institution, or constituent part of our state qualified and prepared to function as an organ of protection?'[90] In keeping with the pragmatic character of the *Laws*, Plato actually goes so far as to envision a political entity that would embody the type of leaders needed in the proposed state. In addition to a group of Guardians of the Laws, there should be a Council carefully selected to ensure that the best men were included. 'We ought to have in the state a council with the following range of membership. The ten Guardians of the Laws who are currently the eldest were to convene together with all persons who have won awards of distinction and the travelers who had gone abroad to see if they could discover any special method of keeping a legal code intact ... In addition, each member had to bring a young man of at least thirty years of age, but only after selecting him as particularly well qualified by natural abilities and education.'[91] This group of leaders would need special training, in order to be 'duly primed by the course of studies we've described'. Once educated, this 'Council of Authorities ... shall be constituted the legal protector of the safety of the state ... and if ... this wonderful council of ours can be formed, then the state must be entrusted to it'.[92] With such a body of leaders in place, '[Our] idealistic dreaming ... will all come true, provided the council members are vigorously selected, properly educated, and made into guardians whose powers of protection we have never seen excelled in our lives before'.[93]

Plato's peroration on the type of leaders needed in the new Cretan city marks a fascinating turn in this dialogue he wrote so late in life. In a sense, he has returned to his fiction of the classical ideal, but a classical ideal adapted to life under the rule of law. He retains the requirements of a wise leader who understands the nature of virtue and justice, one who acts for the good of the entire community rather than that of the individual. Such a leader under the rule of law, however, has to operate within the parameters set forth by that law. This is Plato's compromise with reality. When his actual experiences demonstrated that the philosopher king was a will-o'-the-wisp, he turned – rather grudgingly – to a more realistic formulation. Even though a philosopher king could not be counted upon, leaders carefully selected and carefully trained could still provide service to the state. Their task was to protect and enforce the law, and to educate the citizenry regarding the efficacy of the rule of law. All this was a corollary to the proposition that the rule of law embodied a fair approximation of the ideals of justice that Plato had always pursued. Since the rule of law – rather than the wisdom of the philosopher – held the key, it was right and proper that leaders operate within its purview.[94]

Our study of Plato's works, then, has uncovered two core fictions that have been seminal in our understanding of the leader and his or her role. The first, the 'classical ideal' of the leader, articulates an image of the proper leader that still dominates much of our thinking. The notion of a wise and virtuous leader who operates for the common good is one with considerable currency today. Plato's second 'invention', the rule of law, similarly imbues our current notions of a proper polity. It is important to understand, however, that Plato concocted the rule of law as a mechanism to fulfill the original purposes of the good leader, and to the extent possible, he continued to rely upon leaders who fulfilled the classical ideal, even under a rule of law. Both fictions were to have considerable longevity and influence.

While Plato provided the archetypal model of the classical ideal of the leader, it is useful to take a brief look at the insights of one other commentator who applied this fiction to monarchies. That writer is Thomas Aquinas. The contribution of Aquinas does not reinvent the fiction, but provides us with an example of how differing contexts and challenges can yield differing emphases or 'glosses' on the core conception of the ideal leader.

THOMAS AQUINAS

The writings of Thomas Aquinas were, predictably enough, a function of his political and intellectual context, although the latter predominated. Politically, Aquinas wrote during a period when monarchies were struggling to free themselves of the demands of both powerful vassals and the Church. Aquinas was, first and foremost, a man of the church, and a product of the France of Louis IX (1226–1270), whose power was hemmed in to a certain extent by the nobility. As a result, in his most famous work, *Summa Theologica*, he defended a form of mixed monarchy as the proper constitutional form.[95] The ensuing analysis, however, is dedicated to exploring Aquinas's conception of the role and purposes of the leader. To understand that, it is much more important to grasp his intellectual concerns. The text that is most illuminating regarding his view of the leader is not *Summa Theologica*, but a more obscure text called, variously, *On the Government of Rulers*, or *On the Kingdom, to the King of Cyprus*.[96] In that work, Aquinas addresses directly his version of the classical ideal.

It was the intellectual sphere that provided both the genesis of Thomas Aquinas's writing and the specific challenge that caused him to consider the proper role of the leader. As a general statement, it is safe to say that his Christian religious beliefs were the most significant influence upon his writing. More specifically, Aquinas was, in the words of Timothy Fuller, 'suffused with awareness of the spiritual destiny of mankind'. His goal was to create institutions and practices that would comport with this destiny. Although teleological, Aquinas's approach did not embrace absolute predetermination; there was an important role to play for human reason and free will. This, in turn, led to an important role for a leader. Although a society was ultimately 'in God's hands', a person in authority could 'be a help or a hindrance in setting the conditions under which we each must seek our path to the common, final destination'. The leader, then, was to play a pivotal role in facilitating efforts to achieve a godly community. 'The ordering of earthly life', to quote Fuller again, 'must be made as compatible as possible with the higher task of seeking the fulfillment of the spiritual life and the supernatural or heavenly end of our existence.'[97] For Aquinas, then, the challenge was different from that which Plato conceived. Plato had sought a good leader to achieve a just society in the face of the perceived disarray of his times. Aquinas looked instead to a leader who could help create conditions where the members of society could achieve divine salvation. Intriguingly, their conclusions were not all that different, although Aquinas stressed differing aspects of the classical ideal and thereby made an important contribution to the received fiction of the ideal leader.

Aquinas, of course, also had more secular influences upon his thinking. Chief among these was Aristotle. We will treat Aristotle in the next chapter; here we need mention only his rational approach to the study of the proper working of society. This meshed well with the quest of Aquinas in his efforts to unify faith and reason in seeking answers to society's problems. It was Aquinas himself who perhaps best stated his topic and his approach in the Prologue to *On the Government of Rulers*. There, he stated, 'It occurred to me that what I could best offer a king was to compose a book about the kingdom. In it, to the best of my ability, I would diligently bring to light the origin of the kingdom and what pertains to the office of king, according to the authority of divine scripture, and teaching of philosophers, and the examples given by those who praise rulers.'[98] Let us turn now to the insights that Thomas Aquinas brings to the classical ideal of the leader.

As he stated in his Prologue, his first task was 'to bring to light the origin of government'. Aquinas thus began his argument with an Aristotelian explanation of the need for government. 'If it were suitable for humans, like many other animals, to live alone,' he said, 'they would need nothing to direct them to their end ... But,' he continued, 'more than in any other animal, it is natural for human beings to be social and political animals.' Since 'one person acting alone is not enough to obtain a sufficient life, so it is natural for human beings to live in a society of many'.[99] That being the case, 'it is necessary that among human beings there be that through which the multitude may be governed'. To reverse the logic, 'only those who are directed in living well by the same laws and the same government are reckoned to belong to one multitude'.[100]

This gathering together into a society, and the forming of governments, was for more than the sake of convenience. According to Aquinas, there was an overarching purpose to societal efforts. Indeed, it was his focus upon this purpose that constituted Aquinas's chief contribution to the fiction of the classical ideal of the leader. For Aquinas did not focus so much, as Plato had done, upon the personal qualities of the leader. His stress was upon the outcomes he valued so much. Therefore, it is useful to consider the proper ends of governments and leaders.

According to Aquinas, the common good was the desideratum of all government. This notion, then, deserves further attention. The common good was something different, and superior to, the interests of individuals: 'That which is individual,' said Aquinas, 'is not the same as that which is common'. Although men 'differ by their individual characteristics', they 'are united by what they have in common'. The bottom line for Aquinas was that 'the good of the multitude is greater and more divine than the good of one'.[101] This gave rise to a peculiar definition and application of the term 'virtue'. 'The end of a multitude gathered together', he said, 'is to live according to virtue.' This was, however, not so much a conception of individual virtue as it was 'civic' virtue, where virtue consists of subsuming one's own interests to the good of the whole.[102] Aquinas perhaps elucidated this notion of virtue best when he noted that 'when the public has contempt for the good, everyone is devoted to their own profit and enthusiasm for virtue ceases, and everyone prefers reward for the honor that comes from virtue'.[103] This focus upon shared purpose led Aquinas often to equate the common good to unity and peace. 'The good and wellbeing of a multitude joined in society is that its unity should be preserved, and this can be called peace',[104] he said.

This need for unity, in turn, led to a natural demand for governments and leaders. 'The multitude would be broken up and dispersed unless there were something to take care of what pertained to the good of the multitude.' Thus, there must be 'some general governing strength ... to attend to the common good of all members'.[105] This desideratum also became for Aquinas the measure of a proper government. 'There is,' he wrote, ' both a right approach and one that is not right in the government of a multitude ... If, therefore, the one governing ordains ... the common good of the multitude, the government will be right and just ... But if the government is ordained to the private good of the one governing, the government will be unjust and perverse.' As a consequence, 'the more effective a government is in preserving the unity and peace [that is, the common good], the more useful it will be'.[106] Indeed, 'a government becomes unjust when it spurns the common good of the multitude and seeks the private good of the governing element. The more it recedes from the common good, the more it is an unjust government.'[107] Having determined that the common good is the measure of successful states, Aquinas turned to the traditional typology of constitutions and evaluated them according to his central criterion.

Again drawing upon his Aristotelian heritage, Aquinas defined three forms of bad states. The first had but a single ruler acting against the common good. 'One alone who brings about an unjust government by seeking individual profit from the government, and not the good of the multitude ... is called a tyrant ... But if more than one, although still a few, bring about an unjust government,' he continued, 'it is called "oligarchy", that is, the rule of the few.' Finally, 'if the many exercise an unjust government it is named "democracy", that is, the hegemony of the people'. Thus the term 'democracy' continued to have the bad connotations that had attended the term since the days of Plato and Aristotle. As Aquinas depicted it, the evil of democracy 'occurs when the plebeian people oppress the rich through the might of the multitude. Then, the whole people will act as if it were a single tyrant.'[108] The danger of a tyranny of the majority overriding some externally determined standard of worthiness such as the 'common good' (we will discover other such standards in the course of this work) remains a central challenge of modern democracy.

Aquinas also noted that 'just governments' could be 'distinguish[ed] in a similar way', and proceeded to outline a typology of good governments. Again drawing upon Aristotle, he observed: 'if some multitude administers the government, it is called by the common name "polity" ... But if a few virtuous ones administer a government of this kind, it is called "aristocracy", that is the best hegemony or hegemony of the best ... But if one alone is involved with just government,' he concluded, 'that one is properly called "king."'[109]

Having delineated the six possible types of government, and more specifically, the three types of 'good' government that strive for the common good, Aquinas turned to a ranking of the forms of good government. 'I must ask', he began, 'whether it is more expedient for a province or city to be governed by many or one.' The way to answer such a query was simply to apply his criterion. 'This can be considered with respect to the end of government ... . The more effective a government is in preserving the unity of peace,' he continued, 'the more useful it will be.' This articulation of the criterion made his task of ranking governments easy. 'It is evident,' he said, 'that what is one itself can better bring about unity than can many ... . Therefore,' he was able to conclude, 'the government of one is more useful than that of many.'[110] This preference for the single ruler (the 'king') as the preferred route to the common good had partly to do with the greater efficiency of a single ruler. If the 'many are said to be united to the degree they approach to one', it stands to reason 'it is better for one to govern the many, who only approach to one', Aquinas explained. The primacy of the single ruler was confirmed by looking to the Oneness of God; to nature, where 'there is ... one king among the bees'; and to the experience of actual states, where 'provinces and cities that are governed by one king rejoice in peace, flourish in justice, and are gladdened by their affluence. ... It follows nicely,' he concluded, 'that a human multitude is best governed by one.'[111] Thus, 'if the government is just, a kingdom is better than an aristocracy and aristocracy better than polity, since the more the governing element is one, the more the government will be useful'.[112]

By the same token, the criterion of the common good created quite a different ranking of unjust governments. 'Just as it is more useful for a force working for good to be more one, so it is more harmful if a force working for evil is one, than if it is divided.' When a single ruler operates unjustly, 'such a one twists the common good of the multitude to that one's own good alone'. Consequently, 'if the government is unjust, the more the ruling element is one, the more harm it will do'.[113] 'Consider the evils that arise from tyrants', Aquinas went on. 'The consequence of tyrants having contempt for the common good and seeking their private good is that they burden their subjects in various ways'. 'Therefore,' Aquinas concluded, 'we must flee this government.'[114]

The fact that he found that 'tyranny is more harmful than oligarchy, and oligarchy is more harmful than democracy'[115] was no endorsement of democracy. Aquinas merely preferred the most inefficient of states when the ruling element was seeking its own ends rather than the good of the community. All things being equal, the government of the many was to be avoided if possible. Aquinas identified two essential evils in government by the people. First, by its very nature, democracy is more prone to disunity, the bane of the common good. 'Dissension,' he said, 'which usually follows from the government of the many, is contrary to the good of peace, which is the chief good of the social multitude.' Worse, government by the people is actually more likely to lead to tyranny than any other form of government. Taking a leaf from Plato's book, Aquinas noted that 'the government of the many turns into tyranny not less, but perhaps more frequently, than that of one. After the government has been led to dissension, it often happens that one of them gets the upper hand over the others and alone usurps lordship over the multitude.' Thus, while 'it might seem that government of kings ... should be especially avoided on account of tyranny, in fact, a tyrant is not less, but more likely to arise under the government of the many. So,' Aquinas finally ended, 'it remains simply that it is more expedient to live under one king than under the government of many.'[116]

If Thomas Aquinas's first objective in *On the Government of Rulers* was to explore the origins of government and its optimal mode of rule by a king, the remainder of his contribution to that work was dedicated to an exploration of the powers and responsibilities of such a just ruler. As he put it in his Prologue, he now concerned himself with 'what pertains to the office of king'.[117] Thus, having devoted such efforts to justifying the rule of a single individual, he turned to a further consideration of the need for a leader and his role. In so doing, Aquinas provided an important variant of Plato's version of the classical ideal.

Aquinas began his book by announcing his 'intention ... to explain how we understand the title king'. Having established the propriety of one-man rule, he turned to the task at hand: 'We must now consider what the office of king is and what sort of person a king ought to be'.[118] There needed to be such a leader, if for no other reason than 'there needs to be something that directs all things ordained to one end, which might be achieved in various ways, so that they might achieve the due end by a direct path'. He observed that 'humans proceed in various ways toward their intended end, which the diversity of human endeavors and actions demonstrates, and so they need something directing them to their end'.[119] That having been said, Aquinas devoted considerable attention to the topic of what constituted an ideal leader in the society he envisioned.

In the Thomistic view, the first and foremost requirement of a leader was that he be a good man (little consideration was given to women as leaders). 'First,' said Aquinas, 'it is necessary for those whom it pertains to promote a king to choose someone of such a condition that makes it unlikely that he will decline into tyranny.' More to the point, the good leader should be a godly man. Citing the biblical book of 1st Kings, Aquinas recalled that 'the Lord ... sought [as a king] a man according to his own heart'.[120] Therefore, he continued, 'let the king know that this is the office that he has taken up, that he in his kingdom is as the spirit in the body and God in the world'.[121]

Such a vision of kingly nature made for some rather lofty expectations of kingly behavior. It certainly limited the pool of potential kings. 'Human beings are not suited to perform the same offices equally', Aquinas acknowledged, and the demands placed upon kings were such that only the best of men need apply.[122] Turning to the behavior expected of leaders, Aquinas stressed how high the standards really were. 'If he diligently reflects upon this [that is, his role as God's surrogate],' observed Aquinas, 'two things will happen. On the one hand, zealousness for justice will be kindled in him when he considers that he was put in this position so that he might exercise judgment in his kingdom in the place of God. On the other hand,' continued Aquinas, 'he will acquire the gentle qualities of mildness and clemency, when he reckons individuals under his government as his own members.'[123] Such a leader would also keep constantly in mind the ultimate purpose of human life and society. 'Since heavenly beatitude is the end of the life that we live well at present, it pertains to the office of king to procure the good life of the multitude to make it suitable for heavenly beatitude.' This meant, in simple terms, that a leader should 'order those things which lead to heavenly beatitude and forbid their contraries, as far as possible'.[124]

This, in turn, led to a rather straightforward articulation of a leader's obligations. The overarching guideline was to rule virtuously. 'If it is characteristic of virtue to render the work of a person good', Aquinas noted, 'it seems as if working a greater good would be characteristic of a greater virtue'. This 'greater good' was the work of a king. If God acknowledges the good works of individuals, 'How much more, therefore, must those who make a whole province rejoice in peace, who hinder violence, who serve justice, who with their laws and precepts determine what persons should do, receive human praise and be rewarded by God?'[125] Aquinas went on to give leaders a more specific charge.

As we have seen, the primary obligation of the ruler was to rule for the common good. 'When the office of king establishes the good life among the multitude,' said Aquinas, 'he should attend to its preservation.'[126] Recalling Aquinas's conflation of peace, unity and the common good, it is not surprising to find him saying, 'The unity of the multitude, which is called peace, must be procured through the industry of that which governs'. Referring to 'the multitude united by the chain of peace,' Aquinas asserted that 'the multitude must be constituted in the unity of peace'.[127] Unfortunately, there was sometimes 'an impediment to the public good'. This occurred when individuals acted unvirtuously; that is, against the public interest. There is a 'perversity of human will, so that persons either are indolent when it comes to doing those things that the republic requires, or they harm the peace of the multitude when they disturb the peace of others by transgressing justice'.[128] Thus, another expectation of the leader was to ensure justice. Citing Augustine, Aquinas said 'We do not call Christian rulers happy because they have commanded for a long time, … or because they have tamed the enemies of the Republic, … rather, we call them happy if they command justly'.[129] The good leader, then, 'should compel those subject to him to avoid iniquity and lead them to virtuous works by laws and precepts, handing out a reward to those who observe it and punishments to those who transgress it'.[130] Lastly, the ruler also had the more mundane responsibility of ensuring a productive state. There must be, concluded Aquinas, 'a sufficient abundance of necessities for living well … through the industry of that which governs'.[131]

The responsibilities of the leader to secure justice and the common good had important implications for the relationship among leaders and followers. Clearly, Aquinas viewed the role of the leader as paramount. 'What I have said makes it apparent', he wrote, 'that the king ought to have precedence over all human affairs and order them by the command of his government … .'[132] This was true not only because it was more efficient to grant the leader such power over followers, but also because, simply put, a leader was more valuable to society than any individual follower. As Aquinas phrased it, 'in every art and potency, those are more laudable who govern others well than those who conduct themselves well according to another's direction … . The king is, therefore, worthy of a greater reward, if he guides his subjects well, than any of his subjects, if they conduct themselves well under the king.'[133] Such power and reward were only justified, however, if the king ruled rightly. And to rule rightly was to return to the leader's duties toward his subjects. 'Good kings' must 'zealously intend the common profit', and 'demonstrate that they love their subjects.'[134]

This obligation to serve the interests of subjects brought Aquinas to a conclusion unknown to Plato. For Aquinas, there was at least some sense that followers had the right to expect good governance from their leaders, and had certain (limited) options available to them if these expectations were not met. As we have seen, the *raison d'etre* of society and government was to foster the ability of the community at large to enjoy the peace, security and unity necessary to achieve the ends of divine salvation. Anything that threatened to get in the way of this primary obligation must be thwarted. This applied to leaders as well. Although the leader in Aquinas's perfect state should be superior, that does not imply that he should be unrestrained. The first objective was prevention. As Aquinas put it, 'the government of the kingdom must be so deposed as to remove the occasion of tyranny from the king who has been instituted. At the same time, his power should be tempered, so that he can not easily decline into tyranny.'[135]

If prevention should fail, Aquinas was willing to consider other options. Indeed, Aquinas provided a veritable dissertation on the possible responses of followers who found themselves in such an unhappy situation. Aquinas listed several levels of response. 'If it [that is, tyranny] is not excessive, it is more profitable to tolerate a slack tyranny for a time than to go against the tyranny and become involved in many dangers, which are more serious than the tyranny itself.'[136] Certainly in such a case resistance should not reach the level of regicide; 'it would be dangerous to the multitude … to bring about the death of those who preside, even if they are tyrants'.[137] Nevertheless, to the extent that the authority of the king derived from the people, 'the same multitude can, not unjustly, depose a king that they instituted or bridle his power, if he should abuse the royal authority tyrannically. Nor should such a multitude be thought to be acting unfaithfully when it abandons the tyrant, even if it had previously subjected itself to him in perpetuity.' This was because the leader had broken his compact with the people. In this case, 'he deserves to have his subjects not preserve their pact with him by not behaving faithfully to the government of the multitude, as the office of king demands'.[138] On the other hand, if the king had been put into place by someone other than the multitude, 'they must wait for a remedy for the worthlessness of the tyrant from that superior'.[139] Ultimately, 'if human aid against a tyrant is not to be had, recourse must be made to God'. However – Aquinas gives one last caution – 'for the people to deserve this benefit from God, it ought to cease from its sins'.[140]

The moral note that Aquinas sounded as he reflected upon possible remedies for the evil leader is consonant with his entire work. In *On the Government of Rulers*, he sought to respond to the principal challenge of society as he saw it. That challenge was the daunting one of creating a society that maximized the potential for its inhabitants to achieve divine grace. In the secular sphere, at least, the responsibility for this, according to Aquinas, lay in large part upon the leader. In devoting a work to kingdoms and kings, Aquinas 'invented' a leader that appeared most likely to secure the desired end.

The leader he invented shared many characteristics with the one Plato invented to meet a different societal challenge. Both versions of the ideal demanded a wise and virtuous leader committed to the common good, which became the essence of what we have here labeled the classical ideal of the leader. But while Plato devoted considerable time to securing a leader (or his surrogate) who had the abilities to achieve the desired goal, Aquinas's approach to the classical ideal emphasized less individual leader traits and more the accomplishment of desired ends. This is in one sense no more than a gloss on Plato's original invention. The shift, however, had important implications, not least the rather dramatic departure Aquinas took regarding the role and status of followers.

For Plato, the superiority of the leader foreclosed any sense of active followers. For Aquinas, although he too championed the superiority of the good leader, his focus upon the results (the common good), led to a shift in viewing the relationship among leaders and followers. If the goal was not being attained, the overwhelming need to remedy the situation permitted more follower activism than Plato would ever contemplate.

In terms of the long-term contribution to our notions of the leader, Aquinas thus gives us a richer palette with which to paint our ideal. While his approach shared the same primary colors with Plato (that is, the notion of a wise and virtuous leader dedicated to the common good), Aquinas's brush did not apply these colors in the same proportions. That is to say, his focus upon the common good was sufficient to highlight that good for future generations. And, like Plato's grappling with the role of the leader versus the rule of law, Aquinas's championing of the common good continues to both hearten and haunt those seeking good government in our world today.

Plato and Thomas Aquinas, then, are giants in the intellectual history of our understanding of the term 'leader'. Before we turn to a further investigation of this fiction in a context closer to our chief concern of democracy, it is helpful to pause briefly to consider the similarities and contrasts between the two, drawing our inspiration from the two interpretive vehicles that drive this study: fictions and implicit theories.

CONCLUSION: FICTIONS AND IMPLICIT THEORIES

In the Prologue to this study, we identified fictions and implicit theories as important interpretive frameworks of our study of leadership in democracy. Although we have thus far discussed only two commentators, and those commentators have addressed only one aspect of the construct we will eventually label leadership – that is, the leader – these frameworks already prove helpful. They help to clarify the significance of the work of Plato and Aquinas for our larger study and suggest how and why their work has continuing relevance for those of us who seek to make sense of leadership in a democracy. Let us turn then, to each construct in turn.

One interpretive vehicle that we identified in the Prologue was that of implicit theories. This construct, which we carefully defined for the purpose of this study, embodies both fundamental assumptions and lenses through which one interprets phenomena. One's implicit theories are, more often than not, left unarticulated. Nonetheless, their impact upon one's proposed solutions to societal problems – and one's judgment of the proposed solutions of others – is formidable. Implicit theories become ever more important as we move into the higher complexity of the full leadership relation, but they are not unimportant, even here. It is certainly worth our while to identify some examples of how they affected the thinking of both Plato and Aquinas.

What is the Leadership Challenge?

As perhaps befits two individuals living 1500 years apart, Plato and Aquinas perceived two differing leadership challenges. Plato lived in disordered times; his leadership solutions were prompted by a perception that democracy was not working: it devolved into license and anarchy, which ultimately created a tyrannical society characterized by injustice. While Plato was looking to the perceived problems of his present, Aquinas had a slightly different focus. Plato saw a society careering out of control; Aquinas's concern was not so much to remedy a current crisis, but to create a society that would ultimately be worthy of godly approval.

Plato and Aquinas are but two examples of the central role which the diagnosis of the challenge plays in one's proposed solutions. Plato's presentist concern with the people and their leaders demanded immediate and substantial reform of current realities. Aquinas, living in more stable times and maintaining a more teleological approach, exhibited more flexibility in the means to his desired ends. Nonetheless, it is informative that, even given the differences in the leadership challenges they faced, both concocted solutions that we have identified as consonant with what we have deemed as the classical ideal of the leader.

What is the Perception of Human Nature?

In the face of their respective challenges to the creation of a good society, each commentator inevitably was led to consider the nature of the human condition. Both agreed that humankind needed to band together to survive; hence the need for government. Moreover, both detected severe weaknesses in the abilities of human beings to respond productively to the demands such society imposed. Plato in particular believed that individuals had little control over their passions. This was, indeed, one of the principal sources of the crisis he detected. Aquinas took a more judicious view. He acknowledged that individuals could be selfish, and indeed there was a seeming 'perversity of the human will' that tended to lead them to bad behavior. At the same time, he also maintained that humans were capable of overcoming such deficiencies, with the proper guidance. This was another of the distinctions between the two commentators that led to subtly differing glosses on the respective roles of leaders and followers.

Are the People Capable of Governing?

On this important question, Plato and Aquinas again differed in some respects, although both shared the same essential conclusion that the people were not to be relied upon as the engine of government. Plato, as usual, was unequivocal on the matter. In his view, the people were totally incapable of governing themselves, and, perhaps worse, had a natural inclination to choose inappropriate leaders to lead them (although he held out hope that they could be convinced to acquiesce in the rule of Plato's philosopher kings). Aquinas appeared somewhat more neutral on the issue, since he considered all forms of government possible, and even favored democracy in certain situations. Yet this is somewhat deceiving. It is clear that Aquinas ultimately thought the people could not govern themselves well. His ideal state, after all, was that of a single ruler acting for the common good, and he advocated rule by the people only in bad situations – precisely *because* they cannot rule well: they are so inefficient as to be the least harmful.

Again, however, there was a subtle distinction between the two that would have important implications for the potential operation of the leadership relation. Plato held that, except for the few philosophers who could be trained also to become kings, there was no reason to expect individuals to have the ability to do more than the limited scope of activity of which they were by nature capable. Indeed, to attempt otherwise was for Plato the definition of injustice. Aquinas also recognized that persons varied in their personal capabilities, but he believed in the ultimate perfectibility of man. In any event, his focus upon desired ends shifted attention away from the extended castigations of the people that characterized Plato. It is, perhaps, no coincidence that Thomas Aquinas ultimately was willing to contemplate people taking an active role in remedying the abuses of tyranny. Again, these differences in fundamental assumptions – implicit theories – had an enormous impact upon each commentator's conclusions.

What is the Proper End or Purpose of Leadership?

In the logic of implicit theories of leadership, once a commentator has diagnosed the situation and considered the ability of the people to respond to it, attention turns to what to do about the perceived problem, who should bear the responsibility for crafting and implementing the response, and a consideration of the processes and structures needed to do so. This process begins with the question of the ultimate purpose, or end result, of the leadership process.

For Plato, the proper end of leadership was identical to the purposes of society in general: human well-being or happiness. This was not to be achieved, however, through democratic conceptions of liberty and equality. Indeed, commitment to these principles was at the root of the leadership crisis Plato perceived. Instead, leadership should help the society achieve justice, which in turn required a focus upon good order. Only in a well-ordered society could the larger ends of leadership – a commitment to justice, truth, beauty and wisdom – be secured.

Thomas Aquinas viewed the proper end of leadership somewhat differently. Rather than being remedial, Aquinas looked forward. His goal was to create a state that allowed and encouraged men to become godly, and fit for eternal salvation – a sort of linking together of Augustine's City of Man and City of God. To achieve this, believed Aquinas, it was the responsibility of leadership to create a society committed to the common good. This, in turn, required a society characterized by unity and peace.

Although their visions for society differed – as befitted two men who faced vastly differing challenges – both were to come up with solutions involving leaders with similar characteristics. This suggests the reason for much of the staying power of the classical ideal: it seemed to serve so many different leadership challenges equally well. Before turning to that key facet, however, there is another question of the protocol that requires attention.

What is the Epistemology of Leadership?

Another example of differences in the implicit theories of the two had to do with their differing definition of what we sometimes call their *independent grounds*. That is to say, each looked to distinct (but related) standards by which to measure a successful leader and society. Plato's independent ground, or standard by which to judge the good leader, was knowledge of the Good – known only by the true philosopher (this was modified in his later works to allow for the surrogate of the law). Although not wholly different, Aquinas's independent ground was the common good. It had more to do with the facilitating conditions for the pursuit of divine grace – peace, unity and justice.

Again, subtle differences in the underlying measure of success yielded distinct outcomes, in this instance, how one went about achieving the desired results. Plato was committed to the substantive outcome of the good society, but his focus was upon *who* was capable of implementing this – that is, the enlightened leader. Later, as we have seen, he appeared to substitute the rule of law for the role of the leader. Aquinas, for his part, looked less to the implementing individual or institution, and more to the end itself (the common good). While Plato was content to leave the determination of this to an unfettered leader (or the law), Aquinas was less concerned with the vehicle of the desired end (although he concluded that a leader molded in the style of the classical ideal was best), and judged success solely by the outcome of a society committed to a common good of peace and unity. This would lead to slightly differing expectations of the leader–follower relationship.

What is the Role of the Leader?

The leader occupied the primary place in the schemes of both Plato and Aquinas, albeit in somewhat differing ways. One of the threshold issues related to the role of the leader is that of who should lead. As we have seen, Plato had a definitive response. It was the 'philosopher king', that individual possessed of wisdom, courage, temperance, and the many other virtues that allowed him (or her) to perceive the Good, and thereby lead a just society. Later in life, when he became convinced that such a leader was unlikely, we have seen how he turned to the rule of law as an alternative. Although he then advocated the rule of law, not of men, even under the rule of law Plato expected 'the better sort' to play an important role. Aquinas, for his part, also looked to a leader with exceptional qualifications. He went so far as to say that the leader should be a good man who approached godliness. Both, it becomes clear, sought a leader who fit the expectations of the classical ideal: an individual who manifested wisdom, virtue and a commitment to the common good.

Once an appropriate leader was in place, attention could turn to what type of action or activity could be expected of him (or, in Plato's case, potentially, her). In his ideal state, Plato granted the philosopher king *carte blanche* in ruling that state; by definition, he or she would never act otherwise than in the interests of the whole. Accordingly, no detailed blueprint of expected actions was necessary. This changed somewhat when the infallibility of the leader came into question, and as a consequence the rule of law was imposed. Now Plato felt an obligation to spell out the duties of the leader. A wise leader, for example, was necessary to help the populace frame the governing documents. Likewise, a leader of superior intelligence and virtue (although necessarily somewhat short of a philosopher king) should be involved in the correct interpretation and implementation of the law, and to educate the people regarding the value of following the law.

Thomas Aquinas also granted a great deal of latitude to the leader, but perhaps because Aquinas held more realistic expectations about the nature of who would serve, he was more forthcoming about his obligations. Aquinas, as we have seen, sought efficiency in a leader. He was to be a directing and unifying force, utilizing the strength of his position as the single ruler to reach most effectively the goal of the common good. In so doing, the Thomistic leader was asked to exhibit a zealousness for justice while at the same time demonstrating his love for his subjects. He was expected, in other words, to emulate on earth the rule of God in heaven.

In sum, both Plato and Aquinas represent well the approach that looks to strong and virtuous leaders to play the principal role in resolving the ills of society. This, in turn, had consequences for the role of followers.

What is the Role of the People?

In the ideal fiction of both Plato and Aquinas, the people played virtually no active role in the governing of the state. For Plato, this was because they simply lacked the competence to do so. This was not to say that the constituents of the state had no competence; indeed, they were often superior at certain things such as farming, the military and the like. It was the duty of the people, according to Plato, to perform such functions to the best of their abilities. Thomas Aquinas, on the other hand, in his essay on leadership directed to the King of Cyprus which is the subject of study here, paid very little attention to the role of the people in day-to-day affairs. He, like Plato, called for a strong leader to direct affairs, and an active role for the people was not contemplated. The one important exception to this statement will be discussed in the next section.

That these commentators envisioned little role for the people should come as no surprise. Plato and Aquinas were chosen for analysis in this chapter, after all, as exemplars of the classic view of the leader in states with little popular participation. As we shall see, however, many of their views would be adapted to polities grounded in the people.

How Should Leaders and the People Interact?

Given the premise that the people were not expected to play an active part in governance, the interactions between the two are predictable: the relationship was expected to be hierarchical, with little mutual interchange of views. However, even this straightforward expectation was not without its importance for other versions of the polity. It introduced the conception of *deference*. It was expected that those who were in the inferior position – that is, the people – would willingly accept that status because they recognized the superior capabilities of their leaders. This was to become an aspect of leader–follower relations that was to be extraordinarily long lived and consequential.

Although both commentators had similar expectations for the role of the people in normal times, Thomas Aquinas added an important exception. Drawing upon a long tradition that harked back to Cicero and others in classical times, as well as a robust theme of political philosophy in the Middle Ages, Aquinas allowed for a remedy in cases of tyranny. Although carefully delimited and hedged by restrictions, in such instances he held out the possibility of the propriety of popular action to end the abuse. While this did not quite reach the status of the later 'contract' approach to government, it nonetheless set forth some expectation for good governance that emanated from the people themselves. This, too, would not be unimportant in later times.

How is the Matter of Diversity and Minority Interests Addressed?

In brief, it can be said that neither Plato nor Aquinas concerned themselves with either diversity or minority rights. Diversity was not even recognized as an issue, particularly by the ancient Greeks, who specifically excluded from their political councils all who were not adult male 'citizens'. Nor was Thomas Aquinas concerned with such differences. His worldview tended to think of all men as children of God, and a concern for difference was simply not a part of his mindset. So, too, was the case with the interests of minorities. However, it is worth noting how the emphasis upon the common good in the classical ideal tended to militate against such concerns for minority interests. First, almost by definition, there should be no interests apart from those of the whole. Moreover, the idea of minority interests was, if anything, seen as an evil. When Aquinas, for example, defined the common good in terms of 'unity', the idea of claims by an aggrieved group against the majority (represented by the leader) took on the color of disloyalty, at best. Again, a stance on one of our protocol of leadership questions by these early commentators presaged an issue of enormous importance in later times.

What Institutions and Processes Must be Designed to Accommodate the Premises and Assumptions about Leadership Articulated in the Responses to the Leadership Template?

As befits an implicit theory, the answer to this question of synthesis is imbedded in the earlier analysis. It is useful, however, to summarize the leadership applications here. Plato's principal objective was to create a structure that would ensure a society committed to justice and the good life. This amounted to placing each individual in the position where he (or she) could make use of his or her virtues and abilities. In terms of the leadership relation, this meant the creation of a sophisticated program for leader recruitment and education, at the end of which the reins of the state were handed over to the resulting philosopher king.

It was in his later writings, when his desired fiction did not appear to comport with reality, that Plato spelled out another and promising institutional solution to the problem of bad leadership. It was, as we have seen, the rule of law. Together with leaders who fit the image of the classical ideal, this notion of the rule of law was another important contribution to the ongoing challenge of creating appropriate fictions to meet the realities of ruling the people wisely and well.

Thomas Aquinas likewise made his contributions to the ongoing tradition. As a student of Aristotle, and as a keen observer of some of the abuses of his own age, he was not so opposed to any checks upon the leader as had been Plato. Nevertheless, his ideal remained that of a single, strong leader characterized by wisdom and committed to the common good – that is, the classical ideal of the leader. Aquinas did, however, also acknowledge the possibility of evil leaders, and began to think through what possibilities might be available to an oppressed polity.

This summary catalogue of responses to the protocol of the leadership template reveals something about the implicit theories of leadership that each commentator brought to their respective task. It also suggests how the contents of one's implicit theory has significant consequences for one's ultimate policy proposals. This will become more clear as this type of analysis is extended to other commentators in other contexts. As the results of various applications of the leadership template accrue, we will be in a position to compare, contrast, criticize, and ultimately to create our own solutions to the challenges of leadership in a democracy.

Having now analyzed the implicit theories of our initial two commentators, we can turn to the larger issue of the fictions that resulted. These initial examples of thoughtful commentators reflecting upon the idea of the leader are perfect examples of the genesis of what we have deemed a 'fiction'. This, it will be recalled, is a construct normally created in response to perceived problems and challenges in society. It is, in effect, an idealized solution to these problems. Fictions are designed both to exemplify core values and to serve as templates designed to gauge and evaluate the extent to which reality matches the ideal. Although often (but not always) acknowledged as fictions, these constructs have enormous staying power and influence. They are also quite dynamic. To the extent that reality and fiction diverge, some outlet for the resulting tension usually surfaces. This might be in the guise of reform (attempts to change reality to meet the fiction), or, in extreme cases, revolution (usually, the replacing of an existing fiction with another).

Plato provides us with an early example of each of these dimensions. In response to the perceived challenge of democracy-cum-tyranny, Plato invented the fiction of the ideal leader, the philosopher king, who was wise and virtuous and intent upon securing the common good. This fiction, even during the course of Plato's intellectual life journey, came face to face with a divergent reality. As a consequence, Plato restated his fiction in the more institutionalized form of the rule of law.

So, too, did Thomas Aquinas respond to a perceived societal challenge by constructing a fiction. Aquinas did not invent his out of whole cloth (he relied in particular upon Aristotle), but his fiction made an important contribution to the construct we have labeled the classical ideal of the leader. Thomas Aquinas's societal challenge was the problem of creating a society and government best designed to allow the inhabitants to achieve divine salvation. His invention of the ideal leader paralleled Plato's in many ways, but, as we have seen, it had a focus upon securing the common good, which in turn led to a slightly differing approach toward achieving the desired societal consequences.

These early articulations of the fiction of the leader were to have a lasting impact. We will continue to see their consequences to the present day.

Plato and Thomas Aquinas are giants in the intellectual development of our notion of the term 'leader'. However, both envisioned their ideal leader in a political context virtually unfettered by the influence of the people. In a book dedicated to studying the role of leaders in a democracy, it is important to see how the classical ideal of the leader played out in contexts that involved the participation of the people. It is to that topic that the next chapter turns.

NOTES

1. This study will focus solely upon the Western tradition. Since modern democracy is ultimately a product of the Western cultural tradition, this otherwise narrow focus appears justified.
2. By way of example, both Aristotle and Cicero address Plato's conclusions as political pronouncements. *See* Aristotle, *The Politics*, trans. Carnes Lord (Chicago: University of Chicago Press, 1984); Cicero, *De Officiis*,

trans. Walter Miller, vol. 21 of *Cicero in Twenty-eight Volumes* (Cambridge, Mass.: Harvard University Press, 1968), 87–91.

3. For an accessible discussion of such matters, *see* Francis MacDonald Cornford, Introduction to *The Republic*, by Plato (New York: Oxford University Press, 1962); John M. Cooper, Introduction to *The Statesman* and *The Laws*, by Plato, in *Plato: Complete Works* (Indianapolis: Hackett Publishing Company, 1997); R.F. Stalley, *An Introduction to Plato's Laws* (Indianapolis: Hackett Publishing Company, 1983), 13–22.

4. Ibid.

5. Plato, *The Republic of Plato*, trans. Francis MacDonald Cornford (New York: Oxford University Press, 1962), 369b, c. Cornford's edition of the *Republic* has been rather heavily edited, chiefly through Cornford's rearrangement of the original text into a more logical narrative. Nevertheless, his translation and presentation provide the clearest explication of the ideas traced herein. Here, and in all subsequent texts of Plato referenced, citations will be in the universal 'Stephanus' numbers to facilitate ease of reference.

6. Ibid., 338d, e; 339a.

7. Ibid., 561–566.

8. Ibid., 488a–d.

9. Ibid., 426b–e.

10. Ibid., 494a.

11. Ibid., 473c, d, e; 499a, b.

12. Ibid., 374e.

13. Ibid., 387d, e; 474b, c; 475b, c, e; 486b; 487a, e.

14. Ibid., 376b, d.

15. Ibid., 413c–e; 414a.

16. Ibid., 408b, c.

17. Ibid., 401d, e.

18. Ibid., 395c, d.

19. Ibid., 402c.

20. Ibid., 520d, e; 521a; 519b, c, d.

21. Ibid., 519b, c, d.

22. Cornford, Introduction to *The Republic*, 211 (see note 3).

23. Plato, *Republic*, 501a, b.

24. Ibid., 342e; 347d.

25. Ibid., 420b; 412c, d, e.

26. Ibid., 370ff.

27. Ibid., 415a–f.

28. Ibid., 484a, b.

29. Ibid., 514a–517a.

30. Ibid., 421a.

31. Ibid., 389d, e; 401b, c.

32. Ibid., 423a, d; 424b, d.

33. Ibid., 427d.

34. Ibid., 432b.

35. Cornford, Introduction to *The Republic*, 120 (see note 3).

36. Plato, *Republic*, 435b.

37. Ibid., 430c, d; 431a, c, d, e; 432a.

38. Ibid., 463a, b.

39. Ibid., 519d, e; 520a.

40. Ibid., 427e.

41. Ibid., 499d, e; 501c, d; 500d, c.

42. Ibid., 472e–473b.

43. *See* Stalley, *An Introduction to Plato's Laws*, 13–17 (see note 3).

44. Ibid.

45. Plato, *Epistle VII*, in *Plato: Complete Works*, ed. John M. Cooper, 328c, 334c, d.

46. Plato, *Statesman*, in *Plato: Complete Works*, ed. John M. Cooper, 291d, e; 292a, c.

47. Ibid., 292e; 293a, d, e.

48. Ibid., 296d, e.

49. *See*, e.g., ibid., 279a, b; 305c–e; 306a; 310a.

50. Ibid., 300e.

51. Ibid., 275c.

52. Ibid., 293a–e.

53. Ibid., 296d, e.

54. Ibid., 294a, b.
55. Ibid., 294d, e.
56. Ibid., 294d, e.
57. Ibid., 296c, d.
58. Ibid., 297b, c.
59. Ibid., 301d, e.
60. Ibid., 297b–e; 300b, c.
61. There is a relatively convincing argument that Plato drifted away from his focus upon Forms and the tension between universals and particulars in his later dialogues. However, this mode of framing the issue is the neatest way to capture his continuing concern with achieving an ideal state in light of a divergent reality. *See* Stalley, *An Introduction to Plato's Laws*, 21–22 (see note 3).
62. Plato, *Statesman.*, 301e; 302a.
63. Ibid., 293d, e.
64. Ibid., 303c.
65. Ibid., 291c.
66. *See* the discussions in Cooper, Introduction to *The Laws*, 1319; Stalley, *An Introduction to Plato's Laws*, 14, 20–22 (see note 3).
67. Plato, *Laws*, in *Plato: Complete Works*, ed. John M. Cooper, 875a, b.
68. Ibid., 707d.
69. Ibid., 693d, e.
70. Ibid., 693e.
71. Ibid., 697c, d; 698a.
72. Ibid., 701b, c.
73. Ibid., 701e.
74. Ibid., 875c, d.
75. Ibid.
76. Ibid., 874e; 875a.
77. Ibid., 713e; 714a.
78. Ibid., 874e; 875a.
79. Ibid., 715b.
80. Ibid., 875a–d.
81. Ibid., 631a.
82. Ibid., 711a, e; 712a.
83. Ibid., 715b, c, d.
84. Ibid., 640a.
85. Ibid., 671d.
86. Ibid., 640e; 641a.
87. Ibid., 663b, c.
88. Ibid., 962a–d.
89. Ibid., 964b, c; 965c, d; 966b.
90. Ibid., 962a–d.
91. Ibid., 960d, e; 961a, b.
92. Ibid., 968a, d; 969b, c.
93. Ibid., 969b, c.
94. Because our focus is on the role of the leader, the preceding analysis does not address the role of the people in Plato's proposed state. It can be argued that while Plato contemplated a greater concern for popular acceptance of the laws, his essential thrust of deference to the wisdom of one's ruler remained intact. *See* Plato, *Statesman*, 297b–e; 300b, c; Plato, *Laws*, 656c; 657a–b; 659a–c; 669a–c; 689e; 690b; Cooper, Introduction to *The Laws*, 1318; Stalley, *Introduction to Plato's Laws*, 13, 15 (see note 3 for details).
95. James M. Blythe, Introduction to *On the Government of Rulers*, by Thomas Aquinas (Ptolemy of Lucca) (Philadelphia: University of Pennsylvania Press, 1997), 13.
96. Thomas Aquinas, *On the Government of Rulers*, trans. James M. Blythe (Philadelphia: University of Pennsylvania Press, 1997). The first part of this work is sometimes called *On the Kingdom, to the King of Cyprus*. There is also complexity as to its authorship. Aquinas probably wrote that first part, from the beginning to Book 2, chapter 4. Ptolemy of Lucca probably wrote the remainder. It was probably composed in the 1260s or 1270s.
97. Timothy Fuller, ed., *Leading and Leadership* (Notre Dame, Ind.: University of Notre Dame Press, 2000), 72–73.
98. Aquinas, *On the Government of Rulers,* I.1.3. Note that the citation format will again be that of a universal notation that facilitates ease of reference to multiple editions of the text. The passage cited here translates into Book I, Chapter 1, Section 3.

99. Ibid., I.1.3.
100. Ibid., I.1.6; I.15.6.
101. Ibid., I.10.3.
102. Ibid., I.15.6.
103. Ibid., II.3.5.
104. Ibid., I.3.1.
105. Ibid., I.1.6.
106. Ibid., I.2.1; I.3.2.
107. Ibid., I.4.3.
108. Ibid., I.2.2.
109. Ibid., I.2.3.
110. Ibid., I.3.1–2.
111. Ibid., I.3.3–5.
112. Ibid., I.4.2.
113. Ibid.
114. Ibid., I.4.5–6.
115. Ibid.
116. Ibid., I.6.1–4.
117. Ibid., I.1.3.
118. Ibid., I.13.1.
119. Ibid., I.1.1–2.
120. Ibid., I.7.2.
121. Ibid., I.13.3.
122. Ibid., I.16.5.
123. Ibid., I.13.3.
124. Ibid., I.16.2.
125. Ibid., I.10.3–4.
126. Ibid., I.16.5.
127. Ibid., I.16.4.
128. Ibid., I.16.5.
129. Ibid., I.9.6.
130. Ibid., I.16.6.
131. Ibid., I.16.4.
132. Ibid., I.16.1
133. Ibid., I.10.2.
134. Ibid., I.11.4.
135. Ibid., I.7.1. Aquinas pursues methods of accomplishing this in *Summa Theologica*. See, for example his discussion of mixed government and limiting the powers of kings at 1.2.105.1–2.
136. Aquinas, *On the Government of Rulers*, I.7.3 (see note 98).
137. Ibid., I.7.6.
138. Ibid., I.7.7.
139. Ibid., I.7.9.
140. Ibid., I.7.10,12.

2.   The classical ideal in republics

Thus far we have traced the classical ideal of the leader in the context where one might expect it to take its purest form, that is, in regimes ruled exclusively or primarily by a single individual. Plato and Thomas Aquinas, then, could spin out their fiction of a wise and virtuous leader serving the common good without the messy detail of popular participation in governing. This, of course, was not the case in many regimes in ancient and later times. Some form of participation by the people existed in most city-states in ancient Greece, and the Roman republic, a polity that lasted for some six hundred years, embraced a role for the people. Somewhat later there arose the republics of the Renaissance, and the early modern age saw the emergence of a new and important conceptualization of the role of the people (a development we will trace in Part II). Certainly, a volume dedicated to exploring leadership in a democracy must account for the nuances placed upon the classical ideal of the leader by some level of popular participation in government.

Fortunately, there exist some sophisticated and influential treatises that address the issue of ruling a republic. In particular, three stand above the rest as veritable titans in conceptualizing the role of the leader in such regimes. Those three – Aristotle, Niccolo Machiavelli and James Harrington – are the subject of this chapter's investigation. Each considered deeply the respective roles of the people and their rulers, and each 'invented' in response a conception of the leader that was fully in line with what we have labeled the classical ideal. These commentators take on especial significance when it becomes clear that theirs is the intellectual heritage that informed the first modern attempts to establish regimes grounded in the people. Let us turn, then, to a consideration of these contributors to the classical ideal.

ARISTOTLE

With the possible exception of Plato, Aristotle ranks as the most influential philosopher of all time. He occupies a place that straddles the intellectual developments traced in the preceding chapter and this current one. Aristotle was a contemporary and student of Plato, and addressed many of the same issues, although his responses to similar questions were often markedly different from those of his mentor. His influence during the Middle Ages, and particularly upon Thomas Aquinas, was so dominant that Aquinas referred to him simply as *philosophus*, the 'philosopher'. Moreover, Aristotle's work, the *Politics,* in the words of scholar Carnes Lord, 'would play a significant role in the revival of republican political thought in Italy throughout the early Renaissance'. Indeed, as Machiavelli scholars Harry C. Mansfield and Nathan Tarcov suggest, 'Aristotle was the dominant figure – in either the foreground or background – of the political science of Machiavelli's time'. When we turn to the key contributions of the seventeenth-century English political philosopher

James Harrington, we will find Harrington's chief interpreter, scholar J. G. A. Pocock, citing Machiavelli as Harrington's primary intellectual inspiration and arguing that Harrington's proposed polity was essentially Aristotelian. Thereby does Aristotle serve not only as the lynchpin of our analysis here, but in the words of Lord, as 'an invaluable perspective on the intellectual underpinnings of modern political philosophy'.[1]

It is useful to begin our analysis of Aristotle by briefly suggesting the latter's departures from his mentor Plato in the realm of political philosophy. Aristotle, being a contemporary of Plato, confronted the same challenge of seeking a political system that would allow his fellow Greeks to achieve the good life. However, Aristotle took a different approach and came up with different answers. For openers, Aristotle did not believe that universals or Forms existed apart from particulars. This differentiation in initial premise led to a dramatically different approach. For Aristotle, rather than beginning with a notion of an ideal Form of Good or Beauty or Justice as did Plato, instead began his philosophy with observations of particular objects – in this instance, specific political systems. His focus was not so much on beginnings, but on desired ends, a teleological approach we have already seen mimicked in the Thomistic focus upon the common good. Thus we will begin our analysis presently with Aristotle's conception of the nature and purpose of the state, for from this all else flowed.[2]

More specifically, Aristotle rejected Plato's basic assumption about the availability of philosopher kings. For Plato, such leaders existed because the 'gold from god' was allocated to only a few, while all others had some more base metal. Aristotle agreed in principle that such should 'always rule, where this is possible'. Unfortunately, this 'was not possible, because all are equal in their nature', or at least the 'gold' of wisdom 'is ... mixed in the souls of some at one time and others at another'. As a result, such philosopher kings 'no longer arise today. ... [Today] there are many persons who are similar, with none of them so outstanding as to match the extent and claim to merit the office.'[3] Aristotle's observations thus led him to another route, traced in his *Politics*.

That classic work has been called 'the earliest attempt to elaborate a systematic science of politics'. Scholar James M. Blythe provides perhaps the most cogent summary of Aristotle's opus. In it, said Blythe, Aristotle introduced 'the notion that politics could be analyzed objectively, broken down into the various kinds of governments and purposes for which governments were instituted, using historical examples to demonstrate how each worked and how each could fail. He raised the question of what form of government was best absolutely, best in practice, best for most people, and best in certain circumstances.'[4] Because most of the *Politics* is devoted to a republican political order, it is an ideal starting point for our current analysis.

Aristotle began by tracing the genesis of the state and defining its nature. 'Man is by nature a political animal', he said. This created the need for cities, for 'just as man is the best of animals when completed [that is, when joined with other humans], when separated ... he is worst of all'. A city, or state, then, is simply 'a certain multitude of citizens'. It was his definition of 'citizen', however, that demonstrated Aristotle's republican leanings. 'A citizen' was 'whoever is entitled to participate in an office involving deliberation or decision.' Thus, by definition, 'the city is the multitude of such persons'. Accordingly, Aristotle began his study by carefully delineating the type of leader–follower relationship that was the subject of his inquiry. He specifically excluded rule over dependent and subservient individuals such as was characteristic of household government. Instead, Aristotle was interested in 'political rule', which was 'rule ... over free and equal persons'.[5] Although this could take many forms, this primary focus of Aristotle already had set his study apart from that of Plato.

Given Aristotle's teleological bent, the proper ends of the city or state became all important. Aristotle was quite clear as to the purposes the state was to serve. 'We see that every city is some sort of partnership,' he noted, 'and that every partnership is constituted for the sake of some good .... The partnership that is most authoritative of all ... aims at the most authoritative good of all. That', he continued, 'is what is called the city or political partnership.'[6] Thus, the state existed 'not only for the sake of living but rather primarily for the sake of living well. ... The political partnership must be regarded, therefore, as being for the sake of noble actions, not for the sake of living together.'[7] Aristotle went on to define more specifically what he meant by this good life in a political community. It meant living virtuously. 'It is evident that virtue must be the care of every city.' And civic virtue, it will be recalled, had everything to do with subsuming one's individual interests to the good of the whole. 'The political good is justice,' he explained, 'and this is the common advantage.'[8] Ultimately, then, the way to achieve the good life in this community of citizens, according to Aristotle, was to secure the common good. 'It is evident, then', he noted, 'that those regimes which look to the common advantage are correct regimes according to what is unqualifiedly just, while those which look only to the advantage of rulers are errant.' Thus, 'whether the one or the few or the many rule with a view to the common advantage, these regimes are necessarily correct, while those with a view to the private advantage of the one or the few or the multitude are deviations'.[9]

In setting forth the common good as the essential criterion for the good state, Aristotle thereby introduced his classic analysis of the various forms the state can take. These he actually divided according to two criteria: whether one, few or many rule, and whether the ruling group governed for the common good or for its own good. In summary, Aristotle distinguished 'three correct regimes – kingship, aristocracy and polity – and three deviations from these – tyranny from kingship, oligarchy from aristocracy, and democracy from polity'. Aristotle went on to elaborate, beginning with a discussion of the good types of government. 'Now of monarchies, that which looks toward the common advantage we are accustomed to call kingship; [rule by] the few ... we ... call aristocracy – either because the best persons are ruling, or because they are ruling with a view to what is best for the city and for those who participate in it; and when the multitude governs with a view to the common advantage, it is called by the term common to all regimes, a polity.' Each of these constitutional forms had a dark side, when the common good no longer was the end of government. 'Tyranny', Aristotle went on, 'is monarchy with a view to the advantage of the monarch, oligarchy with a view to the advantage of the well off, democracy with a view to the advantage of those who are poor; none of them', he emphasized in conclusion, 'is with a view to the common gain.'[10]

Aristotle was not content to create a typology of constitutions. Because each of the good types of government easily disintegrated into its evil twin,[11] Aristotle was faced with the challenge of advocating a form of constitution that seemed best fitted to sustaining a stable regime committed to the common good. As befitted his practical orientation, he noted: 'For one should study not only the best regime, but also that regime that is the best possible and similarly also the regime that is easier and more attainable for all'.[12]

Aristotle proceeded analytically. He began with reality as he perceived it. He acknowledged that most states were constituted primarily of the rich few and the poor majority. Moreover, Aristotle knew that each group tended to pursue its own self-interest. 'Those of the popular sort assert that justice is resolved by the majority, while those of the oligarchic sort assert that it is whatever is resolved by [those with] the greater property.' Unfortunately, said Aristotle, 'Both involve inequality and injustice. For if [justice is] whatever the few [decide] it is [indistinguishable from] tyranny ... . But if it is what the majority [decide] on the basis of number, they will act unjustly by confiscating the property of the rich few.'[13] This brought Aristotle to the issue of 'what the authoritative element of the city should be'.[14] His solution was to involve somehow all the interests in a balanced state. 'Since it happens that there are two parts of which the city [is constituted], rich and poor, whatever is resolved by both or a majority [of both] should stand as authoritative.' In sum, he recognized that 'if a regime is going to be preserved, all the parts of the city must wish it to exist and continue on the same basis'.[15]

Aristotle set out to invent just such a polity. For inspiration he turned to his earlier work in ethics, for, in the end, he believed that 'the good of the individual cannot be separated from the good of the community'.[16] Accordingly, he considered 'what regime is best and what way of life is best for most cities and most human beings'. Referring to his *Nichomachean Ethics*, he noted that 'If it was correctly said in the [discourses on] ethics that the happy life is one in accordance with virtue, and that virtue is a mean, then the middling sort of life is best – the mean that is capable of being attained by each sort of individual'.[17] Turning to the state, Aristotle applied this insight by relying upon what he called the 'middling element' to bridge the gap between factions. The importance of these individuals who were neither rich nor poor was that they exhibited the key attribute necessary for successful participation in a republic: independence. On the one hand, the poor 'do not know how to rule but only how to be ruled, and then only in the fashion of a master'. On the other, the wealthy 'do not know how to be ruled ... but only to rule in the fashion of rule of a master ... . It is clear, then,' concluded Aristotle, 'that the political partnership that depends on the middling sort is best ... for it is readiest to obey reason.'[18]

This led to his proposal for a constitutional form that has become known as 'mixed' government. The objective was to have a polity that contained elements of all groups, but which relied primarily upon the wisdom and independence of those of middling means. 'It is clear, therefore,' Aristotle explained, 'that the political partnership that depends on the middling sort is best ... and those cities are capable of being well governed in which the middling element is numerous, most particularly if it is superior to both [of the other classes].' This was because 'it will tip the scale and prevent opposing excesses from arising ... For tyranny arises from the most headstrong sort of democracy, and from oligarchy, but much less from the middling sorts of regime.' Thus, 'where the multitude of middling persons predominates ... there a lasting polity is capable of existing'.[19]

What Aristotle had in mind, in its essence, was a government that would partake of an aristocratic regime in the sense of the definition provided above: where 'the best persons rule' and that rule was 'with a view to what is best for the city and those who participate in it'. Thus, rule should be by the virtuous and for the common good. The leaders should be selected 'in accordance with virtue', and virtuous men, it will be recalled, are 'those who are respectable by nature ... [and] ... have no wish to aggrandize themselves', but instead have a view to the interests of all.[20] This sort of language should be familiar by now, because it echoes what we have come to call the classical ideal of the leader.

Aristotle's invention of an idealized ruler to head his state thus appears to be firmly within the tradition initiated by Plato and, as we have seen, picked up and carried forward by Aquinas. However, establishing such a ruler in a state that also embraced an important role for the people necessitated a more sophisticated consideration of the relationship between the people and their rulers. Aristotle was up to the challenge, and it befits our ultimate study of leadership in a democracy to elucidate how he viewed the people, their leaders, and the relationship between them.

Almost by definition, given the fact that his chief focus was on republics, Aristotle held the people and their role in higher esteem than had Plato. However, his was a cautious endorsement of their role. Aristotle challenged those who held 'that the multitude should be the authoritative element rather than those who are best but few'. He did, however, acknowledge that this assertion, 'while questionable, ... perhaps also involves some truth'. Here Aristotle appeared willing to grant the possibility that 'the many, of whom none is individually an excellent man, nevertheless can when joined together be better – not as individuals but all together – than those [few who are considered the best]'. This collective phenomenon, where the people as a whole might supersede in virtue any individual member of the populace, was possible 'because they are many, each can have a part of virtue and prudence', and, presumably the total could conceivably exceed the sum of the parts. This was not necessarily the case, however. As we will see in more detail below, Aristotle thought that such virtuousness was probably only 'true of a certain kind of multitude'.[21]

Although Aristotle gave an endorsement of the people in limited situations, he was certainly no friend of democracy. For one thing, democratic regimes were often no more than a reaction to previous oligarchic rule. In such democracies, 'since oligarchy is defined by family, wealth, and education, the opposite of these things are held to be characteristically popular – lack of birth, poverty, and vulgarity'.[22]

Worse, democracies mistook the proper end of government, favoring freedom and equality over justice. There could be little question that freedom was the core value of democracies. As Aristotle put it, 'the presupposition of the democratic sort of regime is freedom, ... and it is regarded by those of the popular sort as the defining principle of the regime'. The problem was that 'they define freedom badly'. The term was interpreted to mean, among other things, the right 'to live as one wants' and 'not being ruled by anyone, or failing this, ... being ruled and ruling in turn'. In democracies, then, freedom meant 'doing whatever one wants. ... But this is a poor thing,' he said, 'and is the opposite of what is advantageous.'[23]

One of the problems with freedom as it was practiced in democracies was that it encompassed a commitment to equality that led to a perversion of justice. 'The justice that is characteristically popular', Aristotle noted, 'is to have equality on the basis of number and not on the basis of merit. Where justice is of this sort,' he continued, 'the multitude must necessarily have authority, and what is resolved by the majority must be final and must be justice, for, they assert, each of the citizens must have an equal share [in determining the outcome].' When 'justice is held to be something equal,' he concluded, 'equality requires whatever the multitude resolves as authoritative'. This, too, 'is a poor thing'.[24] Thus did Aristotle become the first to identify the evils of a tyranny of the majority, a dilemma that will occupy a goodly portion of our later analysis.

Moreover, democracy tended to promote evil leaders, with disastrous results. The democratic tendency toward class factionalism was a recipe for unrest. 'Democracies undergo revolution,' he said, 'particularly on account of the wanton behavior of the popular leaders', who 'egg on the multitude' against men of property.[25] Worse, leaders of democracies preyed on the foibles of the people to create tyrannies. As Aristotle explained it, in democracies 'the popular leader is a flatterer of the people'. This 'flatterer is held in honor by ... the base, for they delight in being flattered'. Once deceived, it was only a short step to tyranny. Only a debased populace would be so misled, Aristotle reasoned. It all went back to the necessity for independence among politically active participants in the state. 'Tyranny is friendly to the base', Aristotle concluded. 'No one would do this who had free thoughts.'[26]

Aristotle thus confronted something of a dilemma. He had accepted the reality and even the desirability of popular participation in states. However, those states with unalloyed popular power led to unacceptable ends: injustice and tyranny. His resolution of this dilemma was two-pronged. First, he carefully defined who exactly it was that he meant when he spoke of the people who were to participate in government. Second, and more important for the purposes of our discussion, he relied upon a carefully thought out hierarchy of leaders.

Because of their importance to the regime, Aristotle was at great pains to define precisely who among the people should participate in his invented republic. It will be recalled that, when Aristotle had acknowledged the potential for virtue in the people, he had done so quite carefully. 'Whether this [virtue] ... can exist in the case of every people and every multitude is not clear', he had said. 'But nothing prevents what was said from being true of a certain kind of multitude.'[27] That 'certain kind of multitude' consisted of citizens who were individually virtuous in the republican sense of the term. Aristotle acknowledged that in order to understand his argument 'the virtue of the citizen must be grasped in some sort of outline'. He went on to explain that 'though citizens are dissimilar, preservation of the partnership is their task, and the regime is [this] partnership'. This meant, according to Aristotle's logic, 'the virtue of the citizen must necessarily be with a view to the regime'.[28]

This commitment to the common good was linked to the capacity to exercise independent judgment, thus qualifying the individual to participate in the governing of the republic. 'The capacity to rule and be ruled is [to be] praised', he said. 'The virtue of a citizen of reputation is held to be the capacity to rule and be ruled finely.'[29] And, it should be recalled, Aristotle had clearly delineated between those who had such capacity to rule and be ruled freely and those who did not. He had begun his discourse by specifically excluding dependent and subservient persons, such as were commonly found in households, from a role in republican government. This independence, in turn, would manifest itself in virtue, because it was only those who were sufficiently independent to resist the siren call of self-interest who could remain focused upon the common good. Translated into pragmatic terms, this meant that the participants in a republic had to have sufficient property to avoid dependence upon others. This excluded, for Aristotle, the participation of those who were poor and dependent. 'One of the questions concerning citizens still remains', he noted. 'Is he truly a citizen to whom it is open to participate in office, or are vulgar persons also to be regarded as citizens?' Aristotle did not hesitate. 'The best city', he said, 'will not make a vulgar person a citizen.'[30] One answer, then, to the dilemma of popular government was to limit the sort of people who were permitted to participate. Historian J.G.A. Pocock, in discussing later disciples of Aristotle such as James Harrington, would depict this as 'the ... ideal of propertied independence and the Aristotelian ideal of citizenship founded upon it'.[31]

Aristotle next turned to his other solution to the dilemma posed by popular participation in government. It involved the invention of a system of virtuous leaders and citizen followers acting together to ensure the attainment of the common good. Despite his efforts to ensure an independent and virtuous citizenry, Aristotle did not fully trust such citizens to rule the state. It was, again, a function of the dose of pragmatism that Aristotle characteristically brought to his analysis. Despite best efforts, he acknowledged the reality that while 'it is possible for one or a few to be outstanding in virtue, ... where more are concerned it is difficult for them to be proficient with a view to virtue as a whole'.[32] Something else was needed, and that something Aristotle tried to supply by creating a polity that took advantage of the virtues of the constituent parts of society.

Aristotle's mixed republic, with its inclusion of the citizens as active participants in governance, made this endeavor more complex than that which had confronted Plato. In Aristotle's republic, 'the good and wealthy and well born, as well as a political multitude apart from this ... all ... exist in a single city'. This in itself was enough to create 'a dispute as to which should rule' that was unknown to Plato.[33] Even without the increased complexity of Aristotle's reality, Aristotle did not accept Plato's assumptions about the availability of a philosopher king. 'If there [were] one person so outstanding by his excess of virtue', noted Aristotle, '... such a person would likely be a god among human beings.' As attractive as such a vision might seem, Aristotle discounted the likelihood of such a leader appearing. He therefore accepted the more daunting task of creating a governing structure among 'those who are equal in stock and capacity'.[34]

Having pretty much eliminated the single or kingly ruler as a realistic element in his polity, Aristotle devoted his attention to how a polity composed of the few and the many should be ruled. He suggested that rulers in his republic should have special attributes. As he put it, 'Those who are going to rule in authoritative [that is, important] offices ought to have three things: first, affection for the established regime, next a very good capacity for the work involved in rule, third, virtue and justice'.[35] Translated into the terms of our ongoing discussion, Aristotle was looking for wise and virtuous leaders committed to the common good – that is, the classical ideal.

The next task was to identify who among the populace had the requisite characteristics to serve as a leader. Aristotle had no doubt that such individuals existed. 'There must', he thought, 'of necessity be certain persons who are capable of ruling and who perform public service for the city ... either continuously or in turn.' There must, in other words 'be certain persons who share the virtues of political [rulers]'.[36] Once found, concluded Aristotle, 'those capable of ruling best should rule'.[37]

The challenge remained of identifying these men. A logical place to look was among men of property. This was not due to their wealth *per se*. Indeed, said Aristotle, 'election on the basis of wealth is oligarchic', which was one of the evil forms of government. What Aristotle was looking for was not wealth but virtue, for 'election in accordance with virtue [was] aristocratic' in the best sense of that term.[38] The connection between having a moderate amount of property and civic virtue was twofold. First, sufficient property made an individual independent, a necessary condition for virtue. Second – and this was particularly relevant when it came to the duties of ruling – having sufficient property allowed an individual to have the leisure to contemplate the common good. On the other hand, 'the menial element ... having little property, so as to be incapable of being at leisure ... [cannot serve as rulers]'.[39] Aristotle appeared to look with favor upon the example of the Greek reformer Solon. Although Solon permitted the people some role in the polity (more on this presently), when it came to selecting leaders, 'all the offices established by him were to be chosen from among notable and well-off persons ... the Labourers, had no part in any office'.[40]

In sum, Aristotle advocated looking to the better sort for his leaders, but it was understood that these men would rule virtuously on behalf of all. Those who rule would be 'those who are respectable by nature'; they 'will be the sort who have no wish to aggrandize themselves'.[41] The result would be a society where the common good was secured and justice done to all.

Aristotle was astute enough to recognize, however, that a regime grounded in popular participation could not simply rely upon a Platonic deference to a cadre of select leaders with no provision for contributions from a broader segment of society. He devoted considerable reflection to the challenges posed by participation by the people. Despite the theoretical possibility that the multitude, as a group, might have virtue, Aristotle was unwilling to rely upon this slim reed. He struggled to find a role for the people that would serve their legitimate interests without jeopardizing the good of the state. He contemplated 'the question ... over what [matters] free persons or the multitude of citizens (those being whoever is neither wealthy nor has any claim at all deriving from virtue) should have authority'. Considering the matter carefully, he concluded that 'having them share in the greatest offices is not safe: through injustice or imprudence they would act unjustly in some respects and err in others. On the other hand,' he continued, 'to give them no part and for them not to share [in the offices] is a matter for alarm, for when there exist many who are deprived of prerogatives and poor, that city is necessarily filled with enemies.'[42]

Aristotle negotiated the dilemma by turning to a consideration of what the possibilities were for political participation in a republic. 'There are', he decided, 'three parts in all regimes with respect to which the excellent lawgiver must attempt to discern what is advantageous for each. ... One is the part that is to deliberate about common matters; the second, the part connected with offices – that is, which offices there should be, over what matters they should have authority, and in what fashion the choice [of persons to fill them] should occur; and third, the adjudicative part.'[43] These differing functions provide the solution to the dilemma: participation can be allocated according to the abilities of the populace.

Again he looked for his inspiration to Solon. The Greek reformer had acknowledged the necessity of involving the people in governing, but feared the evils of overmuch influence. Solon's solution was 'to have granted only the most necessary power to the people, that of electing to office and auditing'.[44] Aristotle noted that Solon 'arranges to have them both choose officials and audit them, but do[es] not allow them to rule alone'. Aristotle agreed with such an approach. Common citizens, he thought, were incapable of ruling the state. In Aristotle's view, 'what is left, then, is for them to share in deliberating and judging'.[45]

In application, this meant for Aristotle a two-tiered system of governance. 'It is ... advantageous', he noted, ' ... to have all elect to the offices to audit and adjudicate, but for persons elected on the basis of assessments [property holding] to hold the offices.' He was willing to grant to the people the role of the 'deliberative element' in the state, with power to discuss policy. However, 'the few have authority to veto measures' suggested by the many. Leaders were to come from the better sort. Such leaders of the republic should be 'elected on the basis of assessments', with those who were to hold the more important offices drawn from those with 'the greater assessments'. Only through such a bifurcated system could a state wed the participation of the many and the wisdom of the few. 'Those who govern themselves in this way', he concluded, 'must necessarily be finely governed.'[46] The lower elements of society, admittedly, 'are kept inferior but are done no injustice'.[47] Thus were justice and the common good served.

Aristotle's conceptualization of the relationship between leaders and the people is significant for our subsequent study of democracy, and thus deserves more thorough analysis. Throughout his work, Aristotle was careful to make a distinction between leaders and followers. This distinction, however, varied somewhat, depending upon the make-up of the state under consideration. It is clear that in states where one could discern a different level of virtue among the members of the respective classes, those with the most virtue (which amounted to those having sufficient property to be independent and enough leisure to be able to contemplate the common good) should rule.

Where all members of the polity were essentially equal in wealth, status and condition, however, Aristotle's evaluation became more complex. 'There is', he noted, '... a sort of rule in accordance with which one rules those who are similar in stock and free.'[48] Here, although all citizens had essentially the same attributes, Aristotle still maintained that a distinction existed between ruler and ruled. 'The virtue of ruler and citizen is not the same', he said. 'We assert that the excellent ruler is good and prudent, while the [excellent] citizen is not necessarily prudent.'[49] The distinction had to do with the requirements placed upon rulers. As Aristotle explained it, 'Prudence is the only virtue peculiar to the ruler. The others, it would seem, must necessarily be common to both rulers and ruled, but prudence is not a virtue of the ruled, but rather true opinion.' He used a metaphor to illustrate the point. 'For the one ruled is like a flute maker, while the ruler is like a flute player, the user [of what the other makes].'[50] At another point in the discourse, somewhat shifting the metaphor, Aristotle argued that 'the ruler must have complete virtue of character (for a work belongs in an absolute sense to the master craftsman, and reason is a master craftsman), while each of the others [that is, the ruled] must have as much as falls to him'.[51]

In such regimes of equality, Aristotle faced the further challenge of reconciling the leveling aspect of equal inherent virtue in the citizens with the demands of greater virtue required of the rulers. He resolved the conundrum through the concept of rotation in office. 'When [the regime] is established in accordance with equality and similarity among the citizens,' he explained, 'they claim to merit ruling in turn.'[52] In this way the roles of ruler and ruled were linked symbiotically. 'The ruler learns [his role] by being ruled ... it is not possible to rule well without having been ruled. Virtue in [each of] these cases is different, but the good citizen should know and have the capacity both to be ruled and to rule, and this very thing is the virtue of a citizen – knowledge of rule over free persons from both [points of view].'[53] One way to implement this is to look to age and experience. 'That governors should excel their subjects is undeniable', Aristotle pointed out. 'How all this is to be effected, and in what way they will respectively share in this government, the legislator has to consider.' Fortunately, 'Nature herself has provided the distinction when she made a difference between old and young of the same species, of whom she fitted the one to govern and the other to be governed'.[54] This experience as both ruler and ruled in societies characterized by equality served the interests of both. 'For unless the ruler is moderate and just,' Aristotle asked, 'how will he rule finely? And unless the ruled is, how will he be ruled finely?'[55]

Aristotle, then, provides us with important new insights into our notions of the appropriate leader. In responding to a similar political context as his mentor Plato, he took a different approach, addressed differing problems, and came to somewhat distinctive conclusions, all of which have added to our understanding of the classical ideal of the leader.

Aristotle's approach clearly differed from that of Plato. Aristotle preferred to operate within the constraints of the reality that he perceived in his surrounding political context, rather than erect his system upon a pre-existing and universal Form of the Good as had Plato. Instead, Aristotle carefully articulated the desired ends of justice and the common good, and devoted all his efforts to their achievement. This teleological approach permitted considerable flexibility as to the means used to secure these ends.

This difference in approach was matched by a subtle shift in the definition of the problem addressed. Plato, as we have seen, distrusted democracy and the notion of rule by the people, and devoted his efforts toward restraining their actions. Aristotle was no friend of democracy, but he recognized that popularly based republics were a dominant political reality of his time. So instead of wishing such regimes away, Aristotle set out to discover how states grounded in popular participation could be structured to reach the desired ends of justice and the common good.

Similar to Plato, the pursuit of answers to this challenge led Aristotle to a comprehensive consideration of the nature of the state, its purposes and the respective roles of leaders and followers. The shift in attention to and acceptance of republican forms, however, led to a subtle redefinition of the idea of the leader and his (still his) role. It was here that Aristotle added his glosses to the fiction of the classical ideal of the leader.

Aristotle, like Plato (and Aquinas who was to come later), concluded that the leader must be wise and virtuous and committed to the common good. The fact that Aristotle was contemplating rule in a state with popular participation, then, did not alter the need for a leader with the characteristics we have come to identify as the classical ideal. Thus, it becomes clear from our study of Aristotle that this sort of leader is not restricted to regimes without popular sovereignty. At the same time, the popular premise of Aristotle's state required some adjustments to the notion of the classical ideal.

In those republics (perhaps the majority) that consisted of groups of differing virtue, it was imperative that those possessing the most virtue somehow be assured of capturing the primary ruling roles. This Aristotle sought to secure by inventing a political system most likely to assure 'aristocratic' rule by the best men by means of a two-tiered polity. In doing so, Aristotle confronted and resolved a challenge that never really troubled Plato, that is, how to provide for a role for the less virtuous who were nevertheless participants in the polity. Thus Aristotle modified the pure classical ideal of Plato to embrace the contributions of those who did not fully meet the ideal. Though it involved some machinations of the polity, Aristotle was able to create a model that preserved, for the most part, wise and virtuous leaders acting for the common good.

Aristotle contributed another gloss to the classical ideal of the leader when he turned his attention to states where all citizens were of essentially equal virtue. In this rather special case, he was able to demonstrate that the very position of the leader demanded differing qualities and virtues. A leader needed a quantum of prudence as the custodian of the common good that others in the state could safely do without.

Thus did Aristotle delineate a version of the fiction of the leader fitted for government grounded in the people. His insights would be carried forward and elaborated by others, most notably Niccolo Machiavelli and James Harrington. Before we turn to the contributions of these commentators, however, we must pause briefly to consider one other theme of Aristotle's work, the now-familiar issue of the role of the rule of law in the leading of a society.

We have seen how Plato rather belatedly and reluctantly came around to advocating a rule of law when he saw that the reality of the Greek city-state did not conform to the rule of philosopher kings. Aristotle came to a similar conclusion concerning the need for law, but for different reasons. Aristotle was never so confident in the godly nature of his rulers, nor was he as suspicious of the virtue of the people. Still, he came to view the rule of law as a safeguard for the accomplishment of the desired ends of justice and the common good, especially in regimes where the many were dominant.

For Aristotle, the rule of law obviated many of the risks inherent in rule by man. 'One who asks law to rule', he wrote, '... is held to be asking god and intellect alone to rule, while one who asks man adds the beast.' Law, he continued, 'is intellect without appetite'. When men seek to rule virtuously, 'it is clear that in seeking justice they are seeking impartiality'. This lends itself well to a rule of law, for 'law is impartiality'.[56] Hence, 'it is better if [leaders] judged not at discretion but in accordance with written [rules] and the laws'. In sum, 'it is better if all these things are done in accordance with law rather than in accordance with human wish, as the latter is not a safe standard'.[57] This did not obviate human rule, of course. 'With respect to political arrangements,' he acknowledged, 'it is impossible for everything to be written down precisely, for it is necessary to write them in universal fashion, while actions concern particulars.'[58] Thus, 'The law should rule in all matters, while the offices and the regime should judge in particular cases'.[59] Still and all, the principle remained: the rule of (presumably objective) law could go a long way toward ensuring that Aristotle's ends of justice and the common good were achieved.

This was especially true for states that did not have the benefit of leaders conforming to the classical ideal. We have already noted Aristotle's concerns with democracy, one of the perverted constitutional forms. In such regimes, precisely the wrong sort of leaders achieve power. 'The popular leader and the flatterer are the same or comparable ... they become great through the people having authority in all matters.' In such democracies, 'the multitude has authority and not the law. ... On account of their not being ruled by law, ... flatterers are held in honor, and this sort of [rule of] the people bears comparison to tyranny.' On the other hand, 'in cities under a democracy that is based on law a popular leader does not arise, but the best of citizens preside'.[60] Aristotle came to a similar conclusion with respect to regimes ruled by the few. 'When ... not law but officials rule [in oligarchies],' he noted, 'this is the counterpart among oligarchies to tyranny among monarchies.'[61]

Thus Aristotle, in addition to echoing Plato's use of the rule of law to supersede leaders who fell short of the classical ideal, also introduced the concept that the rule of law can moderate the excesses of regimes of the people. This would prove useful in later formulations of the relationship between leaders, the law and the people.

Aristotle was the first of an interconnected trilogy of writers who did the most to articulate the classical ideal of the leader in popular regimes. The others were Niccolo Machiavelli and James Harrington. It is to their writings that we now turn.

NICCOLO MACHIAVELLI

If Aristotle was the first Western commentator to address the issue of leading in a regime based upon popular participation, Niccolo Machiavelli was the most important. Although Machiavelli drew inspiration from Aristotle (it has been said that 'Aristotle was the dominant figure – in either the foreground or background – of the political science of Machiavelli's time'),[62] it was Machiavelli that had the greatest influence in his own time and later. While one can trace Aristotle's influence upon later thinking in an indirect way, there is a discernible lineage from Machiavelli to such early modern theorists as James Harrington, and from both to men such as James Madison, who sought to implement the classical ideal in an era of emerging democracy.[63] Moreover, Machiavelli explored the nature of leaders and their role in republics in considerably more depth and sophistication than had his predecessor Aristotle. These two factors make Machiavelli a central figure in the emergence of the fiction of the classical ideal of the leader in popular regimes.

The Machiavelli who has become known in popular circles in modern times is the Machiavelli of *The Prince*, that highly readable and somewhat shocking booklet of advice designed to maintain princely rulers in power. It is not *The Prince*, however, that stands as Machiavelli's enduring monument to the western tradition of leading. That appellation belongs to his *Discourses on Livy*.[64] In the words of the translators of this work, 'the *Discourses* ... by contrast [to *The Prince*] is a long, forbidding, apparently nostalgic, obviously difficult, but decent and useful book that advises citizens, leaders, reformers, and founders of republics on how to order them to preserve their liberty and avoid corruption'.[65] There has been much scholarly debate over the issue of the relationship of *The Prince* and the *Discourses*. A close student of both will certainly see some elements of *The Prince* in the *Discourses*, but two aspects of the latter cause it to stand independently, and give to it its importance. The first has to do with the topic addressed. While *The Prince* is avowedly about rule in one-man states ('principalities'), the *Discourse* is just as assuredly about rule in republics. That in itself is sufficient to treat the two works as distinct. Second, and not unrelated to the first, is the fact that Machiavelli's objective in the *Discourses* is to create a state devoted to the common good. *The Prince* can be interpreted to do the same in the sense that Machiavelli was seeking an orderly existence through the peace and order of the state, but his methods certainly appeared to twist traditional conceptions of the common good unreasonably. It is this focus upon the common good in popular regimes that has made the *Discourses* such an influential work.

As has been the case with each of our previous commentators, Machiavelli wrote in response to a perceived challenge. Italian politics was in a state of considerable flux in the early sixteenth century, and he set out to discover how regimes of various types could achieve stability and success. In doing so, he became a paragon of the Renaissance and its complicated interaction with reality. The literal meaning of 'renaissance' is the rebirth of something that has passed away, in this instance the lessons and learning of classical antiquity. Machiavelli certainly purported to tread this path, as he looked to the insights that could be gleaned from the history of the Roman republic as reported by Livy. As Machiavelli himself put it, 'He who considers present affairs and ancient ones readily understands that all cities and all peoples have the same desires and the same traits and that they have always had them'. Therefore, 'He who diligently examines past events easily foresees future ones ... and can apply to them the remedies used by the ancients'. Unfortunately, 'because these considerations are neglected or are not understood by those who read ... or are not known to rulers, the same dissensions appear in every age'. According to Machiavelli, 'not a single prince or republic now resorts to the examples of the ancients'.[66] In seeking to resurrect the wisdom of the ancients, however – and in keeping with the Renaissance in general – Machiavelli achieved far more than restoring the insights of the past. Rather, he advanced and improved upon the conclusions of those who had gone before, and in the process created a modern outlook on the state and its leaders. His insights and recommendations, then, became seminal to our current fiction of the leader.

Let us turn, then, to our analysis of Machiavelli. Much like Aristotle (and Aquinas), Machiavelli framed his analysis of republics and their operation in terms of the desired ends of government. Indeed, a parsing of the *Discourses* reveals considerable overlap with its progenitors. Throughout the text Machiavelli continually makes reference to that desideratum of Plato, Aristotle and Aquinas, the common good. 'Not individual good but common good is what makes cities great', he said. Moreover, 'without doubt the common good is thought important only in republics, because everything that advances it they act upon'. On the other hand, 'the opposite happens when there is a prince; then what benefits him usually injures the city, and what benefits the city injures him'.[67] The obverse of the common good, of course, is the classical notion of civic virtue, wherein the individual subsumes his private interest to the interest of the community. Such virtue also characterized Machiavelli's ideal state. According to him, excellent leaders 'subordinat[e] all of their own advantage to the common good'.[68] So, too, with citizens: 'A republic without citizens of reputation cannot last and cannot in any way be governed well', he noted. 'A person advising well and acting better, for the common good, gains reputation.' In sum, 'A well-ordered republic ... opens the ways ... to those who seek support by public ways, and closes them to those who seek it by private ways'.[69] Machiavelli also echoed those earlier works in his emphasis upon justice. Leaders, he said, should be chosen according to 'who was the most prudent and most just'.[70]

In addition to the classical commitment to virtue, justice and the common good, Machiavelli added a stress upon the values of liberty. 'Experience has shown', he commented, 'that cities never have increased in dominion or riches except while they have been at liberty.' Indeed, in language that at times almost eerily anticipated the later arguments of Friedrich Nietzsche, Machiavelli took Christianity to task for undermining the vigor of mankind and its love for freedom. As a consequence, modern times, to Machiavelli, fared worse than had the classical age. 'There are in the world fewer republics than in ancient times, and as a result, the people do not have such great love for freedom as then.'[71] Part of his task, as he saw it, was to regenerate republics and their love of liberty.

Machiavelli began his analysis with the traditional survey of the forms of government, ending – as Aristotle had – with a recommendation of a mixed regime that had the characteristics of a republic. His typology of governments and their cycle of declension were familiar – it echoed both Aristotle and the Roman commentator Polybius. He held that 'there are six kinds of government, of which three [tyranny, oligarchy and democracy] are very bad; the three others [princedom, aristocracy and popular government] are good in themselves, but so easily corrupted that even they come to be pernicious'. Thus a princedom slid into tyranny, aristocracy into oligarchy, and popular government into democracy. Unfortunately, 'this is the circle in which all states revolve as they are governed and govern themselves'. This meant that a 'founder of a state' could establish one of the preferred types 'for a short time only, because no precaution can be used to make certain that it will not slip into its contrary'.[72]

This pessimism was relieved by the same mechanism that had occurred to Aristotle, the institution of a mixed form of government. 'I say, then, that all the said types are pestiferous, by reason of the three good and the viciousness of the three bad.' Fortunately, 'those who have been prudent in establishing [governments] ... have avoided each of these kinds by itself alone and chosen one that partakes of them all'. Such a mixed regime is 'more solid and more stable, because each one keeps watch over the other'. Looking to history for support for this proposition, Machiavelli noted that Lycurgus of Sparta had managed this balance well, and 'made a state that lasted more than 800 years, with the highest reputation for himself and the peace for the city'. Solon in Athens, on the other hand, erred by granting too much power to the people. 'Organizing a state there governed only by the people', Machiavelli noted, '... made it of ... a short life.' Previewing his infatuation with the Roman republic, Machiavelli turned to it for the best example of mixed government. That system of Consuls, Senate and Tribunes (representing the people) proved ideal. 'Never,' he explained, 'in order to give authority to the aristocrats, did she take all authority away from the kingly element, nor did she entirely remove the authority of the aristocracy to give it to the people, but continuing her mixed government, she was', he concluded, 'a perfect state.'[73]

It is important to square Machiavelli's advocacy of mixed government with his championing of republics. In actuality, there is less of a contradiction than might at first appear. Having made the case for a mixed government consisting of the one, the few and the many, Machiavelli nevertheless insisted that the best manifestation of this balance occurred in republics. Republics, by definition, embrace some form of popular participation, and as a consequence it is relatively easy to conceive of the few and the many as central elements of the polity. The 'kingly' contribution is more problematic. Aristotle had faced the same challenge when he, too, had simultaneously championed republics and mixed government. He had negotiated the tension by asserting that individuals akin to Plato's philosopher kings did not exist, and consequently focused his attention almost exclusively upon the interactions of the few and the many. Machiavelli, on the other hand, did not define away the kingly leader, but instead created (as we will see) a deep reservoir of possibilities for individual leaders in a republic. It is important to realize, however, that such leaders were not any sort of hereditary monarch, but instead fit more closely the Platonic ideal.[74]

Having begun his analysis by echoing the work of earlier authors, Machiavelli now departed from his classical roots and made important new statements about the nature and role of the people and their leaders in a republic. It was to be these innovations that would shape ensuing efforts to define the role of the leader in popular regimes.

One of Machiavelli's innovations was a much more sophisticated and nuanced view of the people and their role. He was willing to accept that the people could be mistaken, and at times even evil.[75] However, he also went far beyond Aristotle and all other previous writers in perceiving the potentialities of the people. Indeed, Machiavelli specifically rejected the traditional wisdom concerning the people. Livy, for example, had held that 'Nothing can be more unreliable and more inconstant than the multitude', and 'all other historians' had maintained similar views. Machiavelli disagreed.[76]

The people, thought Machiavelli, were really no different in their essence from a prince. 'The nature of the multitude is no more to be blamed than is that of princes,' he argued,' because all err equally when all are free to err without considering right and wrong. ... I say, then, about that fault of which writers accuse the multitude, that all men individually can be accused of it and chiefly princes, for he who is not regulated by laws will commit the same errors as the ungoverned multitude.' Thus the prince 'who is not regulated by the laws will commit the same errors as the ungoverned multitude'. Moreover, 'it is easy to make sure of this, because there are and have been many princes, and the good and wise ones have been few'. Moreover, the same holds true when one compares princes and peoples under a rule of law. 'I conclude, then, against the common opinion, which says that the people, when they are rulers, are variable, changeable, and ungrateful, for I affirm that in those sins they do not differ from individual princes. And anybody who accuses both the people and the princes surely tells the truth.' The fallacy lay chiefly in thinking that princes were somehow better than the people. One might condemn the people, Machiavelli acknowledged, 'but in excepting princes he deceives himself'.[77]

His analysis led Machiavelli to a conclusion about the nature of the multitude that far surpassed Aristotle's tepid contemplation of the possibility of virtue in the people if considered as a whole. Although recognizing the foibles of the people, Machiavelli also saw a positive side. Indeed, 'a people that commands and is well organized will be just as stable, prudent, and grateful as a prince, ... even though he be thought wise'. He went further still, and argued that the people, whether operating under a rule of law or not, could be trusted more than a prince. As we have seen, both people and princes had flaws, 'and the variation in their actions comes not from a different nature – because that is the same in all men'. Nevertheless, 'If we are to discuss either people or prince when unrestrained,' Machiavelli argued, 'fewer defects will be seen in the people than in the prince, and they will be smaller and easier to remedy'. That was because 'when a people is wholly unrestrained, the foolish things it does are not to be dreaded; no existing evil is to be feared, but rather what such evil can produce, for amid confusion it can produce a tyrant. ... On the other hand, a prince set loose from the laws will be more ungrateful, variable, and imprudent than a people.' A similar conclusion ensues under a rule of law. 'If then,' Machiavelli continued, 'we are discussing a prince obliged to keep the laws and a people chained by laws, we shall see more worth in the people than in the prince.' This was because the people had more respect for 'the laws under which both of them live'.[78]

All this led Machiavelli to his most strident conclusion. The more he compared people and princes, the more of a champion of the people he became. Ultimately he can be found making statements such as these: 'I say that a people is more prudent, more stable, and of better judgment than a prince. Nor is it without reason that the voice of the people is likened to that of God. ... Governments by the people are better than those by princes. ... If we consider all the people's faults, all the faults of princes, all the people's glories and all those of princes, the people will appear in goodness and in glory far superior.'[79]

Machiavelli, then, has brought our conceptualizations of the importance of the people to new heights. Part II of this volume is dedicated to tracing the triumph of this important development. Yet Machiavelli's contribution to the notion of leading the people remains untapped. As we have seen in the above analysis, Machiavelli did not view the people as completely virtuous. Two other circumstances were necessary before they could contribute to the achievement of the ends of the state. One was the rule of law. The other was the role that must be played by appropriate leaders. We will turn our attention to each in turn. Once we have elaborated Machiavelli's scheme in its entirety, his contributions to our understanding of the role a leader can play in a popular regime should be evident.

Machiavelli's discussion of the people had stressed the importance of the rule of law for both leaders and the people in a republic. At several points in his analysis, he had advocated a regime 'regulated by laws'. Throughout his *Discourses*, Machiavelli reiterated the positive role for the rule of law. One key function of law was to force men to live according to their better natures. 'Men never do anything good except by necessity', he said, 'hence it is said that … the laws make them good.'[80] By 'establishing rewards for good deeds and penalties for evil ones', the law can serve 'to bridle human appetites and to take from them every hope of erring without punishment'. The same principle applied to leaders. 'When establishing magistrates,' Machiavelli advised, 'the people ought to put a guard over magistrates to keep them good.'[81] At a more macro level, laws keep order in society. 'Where there is plenty of choice and excessive freedom is possible, everything is at once filled with confusion and disorder.'[82] Law can in this case exercise both a positive and negative function. In its negative role, laws can punish those who 'under cover of good do evil, and so … harm liberty'.[83] But law can also provide a positive outlet for societal tensions. In this guise it can provide for institutions that have 'the power to bring before the people, or before some magistrate or council, charges against citizens who in any way sin against free government'. Law thus 'provides an outlet for the discharge of those partisan hatreds that develop in cities in various ways … . When these hatreds do not have an outlet for discharging themselves lawfully, they take unlawful ways that make the whole republic fall.'[84]

All this presumes that the laws are framed and executed appropriately. In the first instance, the laws must conform to the values of the community. As Machiavelli put it, 'Because just as good morals, if they are to be observed, have need of the laws, so the laws, if they are to be observed, have need of good morals.'[85] Once in place, such laws must be obeyed by all – to include both the leaders and followers. 'To violate law [is] not in accord with good government', Machiavelli argued. 'For I do not think there is a thing that sets a worse example in a republic than to make a law and not keep it, and so much the more when it is not kept by him who has made it.'[86]

A regime under the rule of law, then, has the best chance of securing the desired ends of government. As Machiavelli summed it up: 'In short, to conclude this subject, I say that governments by princes have lasted long, republican governments have lasted long, and both of them have needed to be regulated by the laws; because a prince who can do what he wants to is crazy; a people that can do what it wants to is not wise'.[87] So, under a rule of law, citizens 'feel secure and comforted', and 'a city lives in freedom for a long time'.[88]

If the rule of law was one strategy for assuring that states with popular participation achieved stability and the common good, another was the actions of appropriate leaders. Indeed, Machiavelli provides a more thorough and sophisticated investigation of the nature and role of leaders in a popular regime than does any other commentator. Moreover, there is an original character to Machiavelli's treatment of the leader that brings new understanding to the fiction of the ideal leader. He manages to unite the insights of the past with a decidedly modern conceptualization of the leader. That is to say, while we find the essential characteristics of Machiavelli's leader to be consonant with the classical ideal of the leader, he adds a detailed study of how leaders are instrumental in founding republics and remedying their defects. In the process, Machiavelli's work introduces us to some of the dilemmas of leading in a popular regime. In the *Discourses*, leaders sometimes act independently and even ruthlessly for the common good and with the ultimate objective of making the republic perfect. The dilemmas thus posed continue to occupy us to this day.

Machiavelli began by recognizing the need for a leader. He pointed out 'the helplessness of a multitude without a head', and noted that 'weak and bad advised republics do not know enough to make [tough decisions] and do not know how to gain themselves honor from … necessities'.[89] As was his wont, he provided many examples from ancient times where the people had enough wisdom to turn to leaders. 'The Capuans', for example, '… being at variance with one another, … judged it necessary to have in their city a Roman citizen who could reorganize and reunite them.' Similarly, 'moved by this example and forced by the same need, the people of Antuin also asked for a prefect'.[90]

Having established the need for a leader, Machiavelli turned to a consideration of the source and nature of his ideal leader. In this, he again drew from the past for inspiration while at the same time striking out in new directions. Aristotle had looked to those with property as the most likely source for his leaders, and Machiavelli concurred in part. 'I believe it to be very true', he said, 'that rarely if ever do men of humble fortune come to high rank without force and without fraud.'[91] Nevertheless, Machiavelli was open to leaders of ability, no matter what their social standing. He praised the polity that conveyed 'the knowledge that poverty did not close [the] road to whatever rank and honor, and that men went to seek Ability whatever house she lived in'.[92] Similarly, Machiavelli appeared to agree with Plato that the education of leaders was important. 'When your education has been quite different,' he observed, 'it renders you too of another kind, and … it makes you know the world better.'[93] Yet Machiavelli came nowhere near advocating the type of rigorous training for leaders that Plato had done. Here, Machiavelli was closer to Aristotle and Aquinas in his focus upon the manifested characteristics and abilities of the leader.

When Machiavelli turned his attention to the desired traits of a leader, he recapitulated the classical ideal. That ideal, it will be recalled, called for a wise and virtuous leader acting for the common good. Machiavelli used precisely this language in depicting his ideal leader. He stressed 'what can be done by a good and wise man, and how much good he can bring about, and how much he can benefit his country when, by means of his goodness and ability', he addresses the needs of his state. Such a leader of a republic must exhibit civic virtue and a commitment to the common good. 'His way is wholly for the benefit of the state and does not in any respect regard private ambition … he … loves solely the common good.'[94] In sum, concluded Machiavelli, 'Nothing makes [a leader] so much esteemed as to display extraordinary ability … in keeping with the common good, that shows the [leader] as high-minded or liberal or just, and [he] gets to be a sort of proverb among [the people]'.[95]

Not only does this portrayal of the desired leader evoke the classical ideal, it also suggests a Platonic leader in the sense that Machiavelli appears to call for leaders of extraordinary abilities to lead the state. Aristotle had downplayed reliance upon extraordinary men, but Machiavelli resurrects this notion to a certain degree. Once we have examined the roles

Machiavelli holds out for leaders of a republic, his emphasis becomes more understandable. Along with the increased expectations and demands upon a leader, however, come hard questions about leading in a regime grounded in popular participation. Machiavelli does little in the way of resolving these tensions, but they will be central to many later grapplings with leadership in a democracy.

In his examination of the role of leaders in a republic, Machiavelli's analysis was both thorough and unvarnished. Of course wise and virtuous leaders were necessary to the everyday operation of a popular regime, but Machiavelli focused upon those critical moments where the success and very existence of the republic were at risk. In these situations, Machiavelli unabashedly advocated the obligations of individual leaders, often operating, akin to Plato's philosopher kings, above and beyond popular participation and control. It was in such circumstances that Machiavelli set out for us some of the central dilemmas of leading in regimes based upon the people.

One of these critical moments occurred at the founding of the republic. 'This we must take as a general rule:' he declared, 'seldom or never is any republic or kingdom organized well from the beginning ... except when organized by one man. Still more, it is necessary that one man alone give the method and that from his mind proceed all such organization.' Thus individual activity on the part of the leader was necessary, but it must be directed toward appropriate ends. 'Therefore,' continued Machiavelli, 'a prudent organizer of a republic and one whose intention is to advance not his own interests but the general good, not his own posterity but the common fatherland, ought to strive to have authority all to himself.' Machiavelli went on to provide numerous examples from history, citing leaders 'who, because they appropriated to themselves sole power, could form laws adapted to the common good'.[96]

In his efforts to create this end of a republic dedicated to the common good of all, Machiavelli acknowledged that at times unseemly means might be necessary. 'A prudent intellect will [never] censure anyone for any unlawful action used in ... setting up a republic', Machiavelli maintained. Looking to the Roman republic as an example, he cited with approval the actions of Romulus in killing his brother, because 'what he did was done for the common good and not for his own ambition'. Thus, when it came to the evaluation of such actions on the part of the founders of republics, it was by their fruits that one knew them. Romulus was justified, in retrospect, because he immediately followed his fratricide with the creation of the Roman republic. 'This', concluded Machiavelli, 'testifies that all the first arrangements for that city were more in conformity with a constitution free and according to law than one that was absolute and tyrannical.'[97]

Romulus had demonstrated his virtue as a leader by handing over the reins of the regime to its inhabitants. This served as an important model, for Machiavelli believed that the single leader should continue to rule only for so long as was necessary to create the republic. As he phrased it, 'though one alone is suited for organizing, the government organized is not going to last long if resting on the shoulders of only one'. A republic 'is indeed lasting when it is left to the care of many, and its maintenance rests upon many'. There was a logic to this. 'The reason is that just as a large number are not suited to organize a government, because they do not understand what is good for it on account of their diverse opinions, so after they become familiar with it they do not agree to abandon it.'[98] There is implicit within this logic an important insight about the respective roles of leaders and followers in a republic. At base, such a polity must rely upon the people for its continued existence. Yet at certain crucial moments, the multitude 'do[es] not understand what is good for it', and a leader must step in. At the same time, a virtuous leader must recognize when authority must be shifted back to the people.

Machiavelli's founding leader recalls the philosopher king of Plato who, by his very nature of understanding the Good, could legitimately operate without restriction, so long as he did so in the interests of the common good. Machiavelli, however, acknowledged (at least implicitly) an external standard of morality that made actions such as those by Romulus suspect. This moral dimension raised a barrier, and posed a dilemma for anyone who aspired to lead a republic. Machiavelli posed the issue with his usual clarity: 'To reorganize a [republic] for living under good government assumes a good man, and to become prince of a state by violence assumes an evil man; therefore a good man will seldom attempt to become a prince by evil methods, even though his purpose be good; on the other hand a wicked man, when he has become prince, will seldom try to do what is right, for it never will come into his mind to use rightly the authority he has gained wickedly.'[99] So, although Machiavelli justified harsh means for the good end of state building, he also acknowledged that it would be difficult to secure a leader who would adopt such otherwise evil means for the virtuous purpose of achieving the common good. And those who did not succeed in achieving this balance could justifiably be castigated. Such leaders, 'though able, to their perpetual honor, to set up a republic … , turn to tyranny. Nor do they realize how much fame, how much glory, how much honor, security, quiet, along with satisfaction of mind, they abandon by this decision, and into what infamy, censure, blame, peril, and disquiet they run.' Thus, concludes Machiavelli, 'the founders of a tyranny are as deserving of censure as those of a republic … are deserving of fame'.[100] Machiavelli leaves us with a nice puzzle: how to secure the kind of strong and even ruthless leader required to create a republic, yet who retains the moral sensibilities to serve only the common good.

If the founding of republics was one occasion when a strong leader was necessary, so too was there a need for this sort of leader when the republic was in peril. Looking back at the examples of the ancients, Machiavelli noted the frequent use of 'dictators' when republics were in danger. Drawing upon his favorite example, he pointed out how 'the Romans determined to use their chief remedy against urgent perils: they set up a Dictator, that is, they gave power to one man to make decisions without any consultation, and without any appeal to … whatever he decided'. This device, said Machiavelli, 'was always very useful in all the emergencies that … endangered the Republic'.[101]

Although even by Machiavelli's time the term 'dictator' had come to signify tyranny, he was quick to put such misconceptions to rest. 'Some writers have condemned those Romans who devised for that city the scheme of setting up a Dictator, believing that it was in time the cause of tyranny in Rome. …' Machiavelli disagreed, and went on to provide a tutorial regarding the dictatorship. 'Anyone who holds this belief', he maintained, 'has not examined the matter well, but accepts it contrary to all reason.' It was 'not the name or rank of Dictator [that] made Rome a slave, but the power … gained through prolonged military command. … The Dictator, in fact, as long as he was set up according to general laws and not by his own authority', Machiavelli explained, 'always did good to the city.' This was his key point. 'To republics, indeed, harm is done by magistrates that set themselves up and by power obtained in unlawful ways, not by power that comes in lawful ways.' Thus these strong leaders were not the problem. 'It is apparent', he pointed out, 'that never in Rome during so long a course of time did any Dictator do the Republic anything but good.'[102] Nor was the problem with dictatorship as a concept. Tyranny arose only when such a device was used imperfectly. Machiavelli thus took care to set out the conditions necessary to ensure that this sort of strong leadership served the republic well. When the Roman dictatorship worked well, 'three things ... worked together: the dictatorship lasted but a short time; the Dictator's power was limited; the Roman people was not corrupt. These conditions', Machiavelli concluded, 'made it impossible for the Dictator to go beyond bounds and injure the city.' To the contrary, again, 'experience shows that he always benefited her'.[103]

The fact that these emergencies that called forth a dictator arose after the founding of the republic led Machiavelli to a subtle but important departure from the previous example of a strong leader operating prior to the founding of the republic. Since the republic was now in existence, it was subject to the rule of law. Therefore, it was imperative that the rule of law be maintained. As Machiavelli explained it, 'It is not good that in a republic anything should ever happen that has to be dealt with extralegally. The extralegal action may turn out well at the moment, yet the example has a bad effect, because it establishes a custom of breaking laws for good purposes; later, with this example, they are broken for bad purposes.' The problem could be remedied easily enough, however. It was only a matter of providing a mechanism for such dictatorship in the laws of the republic. Machiavelli put it thus: 'A republic will never be perfect if with her laws she has not provided for every thing, and furnished a means for dealing with every unexpected event and laid down a method for using it'.[104]

Machiavelli's discussion of the use of the law to provide for these emergency situations also made a contribution to the understanding of the respective roles of the people and their leaders in a republic. On the one hand, the need for such a dictatorship stemmed from a weakness of the people also found at the time of the creation of the republic. The people were simply not up to the task of either creating a republic or maintaining it during a crisis. In the latter event, Machiavelli was quite specific in his assessment of popular capabilities in an emergency. 'The normal legal procedures of republics are very slow,' he noted, 'since no council or official can do anything independently, but each one must for many things have approval of another; in reconciling these various opinions time is lost. Because of this delay,' he concluded, 'their provisions are very dangerous when they must provide against some thing that does not permit loss of time.'[105] Given this weakness in the people at critical times, Machiavelli's solution of the legal provision for a dictatorship with appropriate restraints as to its grant of power and longevity was rather creative. By approaching the issue in this manner, the ultimate authority of the people was not compromised. Machiavelli knew well the dangers that lurked if such restrictions were not in place. 'When I say that authority [that is, the dictatorship] given by free vote never injures any republic,' he explained, 'I presuppose a people never bringing itself to give it, except with proper limitations and at proper times ... because an absolute authority in a very short time corrupts the matter [that is, the people/republic], and makes itself friends and partisans.'[106] If done correctly, however, all would be well. Indeed, Machiavelli posited that 'those republics that cannot against impending danger take refuge under a dictator or some such authority will in serious emergencies always be ruined'.[107]

Emergencies were one thing, and could be dealt with through such means as a dictator. Far more dangerous, because much more insidious, was what Machiavelli called 'corruption' in a republic. The term 'corruption' did not connote the common meaning of today

– dishonesty in public affairs. In Machiavellian terms, corruption had a precise meaning and important implications for a republic. It had both private and public aspects. In the private sphere, corruption was the opposite of virtue; that is, it meant the falling away from the commitment to the public good and the turn to the pursuit of private interests. His example, predictably enough, came from the late Roman republic, where the citizens had become 'wicked', and 'no longer had regard for virtue', creating a state where 'the powerful proposed laws, not for the common liberty but for their own power, and for fear of such men no one dared speak against these laws'. The result was that 'the people were ... forced into decreeing their own ruin'.[108] In the public sphere – and not unrelated to this failure among individuals – corruption meant the degeneration of the balance of mixed government caused by the encroachment of one of the constituent groups upon the others, in consequence of which the polity was undone and tyranny resulted.

The effect of corruption in a republic was catastrophic. 'Where ... goodness does not exist,' Machiavelli wrote, 'nothing good can be expected.' In a republic that was corrupt, the people were 'always the servants of the few and of the more powerful'. The rule of law disappeared, and 'in a corrupt city men have to seek glory in other ways than they do in a city still living in accordance with law'.[109] A corrupt republic, then, represented the antithesis of everything that the virtuous republic aspired to be. Serious problems required dramatic solutions, and Machiavelli was fearless as a theorist. His solution struck to the heart of the challenge, and again he relied upon the leader to play the principal role in serving the polity's greater interests.

The only remedy for corruption in a republic was a return to first principles. 'The way to renew them,' Machiavelli explained, 'is to carry them back to their beginnings, because all the beginnings of ... republics ... must possess some goodness by which they gain their first reputation and first growth.' In the wise republic, this could be achieved proactively by provision in its constitution and laws for the occasional revisiting of its original purposes or even by 'good examples' by 'good men' (presumably leaders).[110] Once a republic had become corrupt, however, such approaches were insufficient, and more drastic measures were required. Again drawing upon the Roman example, he recounted how 'the Roman people no longer had regard for virtue. To have maintained Rome free it would have been necessary to change not only its laws but its orders – that is, its fundamental institutions or constitutions.'[111] This was akin to founding a new republic, and, perhaps not surprisingly, Machiavelli's solution echoed his earlier call for a virtuous leader, acting independently.

Thus, for Machiavelli, a corrupt republic called for the emergence of a leader akin to that needed at the founding of a republic. The regeneration of the republic meant 'restoring esteem for virtue ... through the simple virtue of one man' although this man would in all probability have to 'act outside the law'.[112] Because the people were corrupt, 'necessity demands' that government in such a state 'be inclined more toward kingly rule [that is, rule by one virtuous man] than towards popular rule'.[113] Indeed, as Machiavelli put it, 'where the [republic] is so corrupt that the laws are not restraint enough, along with them some greater force must of necessity be established, namely, a kingly hand that with absolute and surpassing power puts a check on the over-great ambition and corruption of the powerful'.[114] Only by the efforts of such a strong leader can the republic 'become good'.[115]

Here, as in the founding of republics, the moral issue of such leadership occupied Machiavelli's attention. In both cases, even as the leader was acting to secure the good of the republic, his actions at times contravened traditional conventions of morality. He acknowledged that a leader who sought to bring the republic back to virtue 'must use entirely extralegal means'. Being a consequentialist, Machiavelli was less concerned with the means–ends issue than he was with the more practical difficulty of finding a leader willing to do bad for good. A leader in such a situation needed to use such means 'as few can or will use'. Moreover, in language similar to that used in the earlier discussion, Machiavelli bemoaned the fact that 'a good man will seldom attempt ... evil methods, even though his purpose be good', while a 'wicked man ... will seldom do right'.[116] Thus the problem for a corrupt republic was finding a truly virtuous man. Once found, Machiavelli, much like Plato and his philosopher king, was quite comfortable with his harsh methods on behalf of the public good.

It was not always in times of crisis that strong leaders were needed. Machiavelli perceived that the people, for all their ostensible virtue, could be misguided, and take the republic down wrong and dangerous paths. Here, too, it was necessary for a leader to step in and save the multitude from the error of its ways. We have already seen that Machiavelli had a nuanced view of the people. We have seen him claim that the people, when regulated by laws, were as wise and virtuous as any prince. At the same time, the people were not infallible. As Machiavelli put it with his typical bluntness, 'sometimes good decisions are not made in republics'. At times, the multitude does not perceive the subtle or hidden aspects of a proposed policy. 'When in a plan put before the people the gain is apparent, even though the loss be hidden beneath ... always the multitude can be easily persuaded to approve. Likewise the multitude is always with difficulty persuaded to accept proposals in which ... loss appears, even if beneath ... is hidden ... gain.'[117] Machiavelli concluded by observing 'how far wrong the opinions of men often are, ... for often their decisions ... are contrary to all truth'.[118]

Nevertheless, Machiavelli also believed that governments of the people were not doomed to a purgatory of mistaken choices and missed opportunities. There existed a solution to the dangers of a misguided multitude. It was the role and duty of enlightened leaders – leaders akin to the classical ideal – to enlighten the people and show them what was in their real interest. Machiavelli pointed out that 'whenever [the people's] beliefs are mistaken, there is the remedy of assemblies, in which some man of influence gets up and makes a speech showing them how they are deceiving themselves'.[119] In a similar fashion, 'an uncontrolled and rebellious people can be spoken to by a good man and easily led back unto a good way. ... I conclude, then, that there is no more reliable or more necessary means for checking an incensed multitude than the presence of a man whose aspect makes him appear worthy of veneration and who is worthy of it.'[120] Thus, again, Machiavelli turned to an enlightened leader to ensure the success of a regime ostensibly grounded in the people.

Machiavelli's discussion of the role of leaders in a republic raises important issues relating to the capability of the people to govern and the role of leaders in a regime grounded in the people. All of Machiavelli's examples of the need for a strong leader role – that is, the founding of a republic, times of emergency, corruption and unwise popular decisions – stemmed from a similar cause: the inability of the people to govern well. This appears to contrast sharply with his earlier championing of the abilities of the people. Elsewhere in the *Discourses*, it will be recalled, Machiavelli boldly stated that 'the voice of the people is likened to that of God', and he contended that 'a people is more prudent, more stable, and of better judgment than a prince'.[121] It is important to seek to resolve this seeming contradiction in Machiavelli's thinking, for within it lies a nuanced and sophisticated understanding of the respective roles of leaders and the people in a popular regime.

The most obvious apparent contradiction in Machiavelli's argument is actually the easiest to resolve. His favorable comparison of the people to a 'prince' is just that: he was comparing the wisdom and judgment of the people to the run-of-the-mill prince, and not to a virtuous leader who met the requirements of the classical ideal. While there was no reason for the people to take a back seat to a prince, it is evident that Machiavelli thought that leaders after the fashion of the classical ideal should be deferred to.

Yet there is subtlety to Machiavelli's understanding of the people and their capabilities. Although he cited instances when wise leaders were needed, he never fully retreated from his contentions about the wisdom and virtue of the people. While the people, if left unguided, could err, they also had wisdom enough to recognize their failings and to defer to their betters in important matters. Citing Cicero and Virgil, Machiavelli noted that 'the people, though they are ignorant, can grasp the truth, and yield easily when by a man worthy of trust they are told what is true … . If they see some man weighty in his piety and his high qualities, they stand silent and with open eyes.'[122] Machiavelli thus offered the comforting opinion that a misguided 'people can be spoken to by a good man and led easily back into a good way'.[123]

Equally comforting was Machiavelli's belief that, when left to their own devices, the people knew enough to select wise and virtuous leaders. It was true, Machiavelli admitted, that in normal times the people sometimes erred in their choice of leaders. 'It always has been and always will be true', he said, 'that in republics great and exceptional men are neglected in times of peace'.[124] Fortunately, in times of need, the people could be trusted to select well. In such situations, never 'will a people ever be persuaded that it is wise to put into high places a man of bad repute and of corrupt habits'.[125] Thus, the republic 'need not avoid the popular judgment in particular … about the distribution of offices and dignities, because in this alone the people do not deceive themselves'.[126] When he turned to examples, it was clear that the types of leaders Machiavelli had in mind were the better sort, the aristocracy of virtue. Looking again to Rome, he recounted how the populace had demanded a voice in government and had been rewarded with the office of Tribune. 'This desire of theirs [for participation in government] was reasonable', Machiavelli opined. But an interesting development occurred when it came time to choose who should fill this office. Despite the reasonableness of popular participation in theory, 'When they had to judge men of their own class individually, they recognized their weakness, and decided that no one of them deserved what they believed all of them together deserved. Hence, ashamed of them, they turned to those who did deserve high office'. Accordingly, 'when in the choice of these Tribunes the Roman people were permitted to choose plebeians entirely, they chose only nobles'.[127]

In sum, then, Machiavelli makes several important contributions to the developing fiction we have come to call the classical ideal of the leader. First, he elaborated in much greater detail the nature and role of the people. To a much greater degree than anyone previously, Machiavelli championed the wisdom and virtue of the people. True, they could err, but they were prudent enough to know when they needed guidance, and wise enough to select appropriate leaders to help them. Second, Machiavelli detailed the role of leaders in popular regimes. Far more than had Aristotle, Machiavelli invented a neo-modern conceptualization of the strong leader. Equally important, he demonstrated that such leaders were consistent with a regime premised upon the participation of the people. Implicit within that complex dynamic is a moral paradox concerning the (necessary?) use of extralegal power to achieve ends necessary to the continuance of the state. Finally, Machiavelli served as the transmitter and mediator of the classical ideal as it descended from the ancient ages to modern times. If Aristotle was the wellspring of thinking about the leader in popular regimes, it was Machiavelli who took that tradition, modified it and transmitted it to a modern audience. It was Machiavelli, not Aristotle, who served as the reference and the inspiration for those thinking about the role of the leader and the people in the early modern world.

This leads us to the third of our triumvirate of intellectuals who shaped our notions of the leader in popular regimes. If Aristotle was the original source of this tradition, and Machiavelli its chief reviser and transmitter, it was James Harrington who addressed some of the unresolved issues pertaining to the classical ideal of the leader. And it was Harrington who most directly impacted the thinking of eighteenth-century statesmen such as James Madison, who actually sought to implement the classical ideal of the leader in modern polities characterized by the dominant role played by the people.

JAMES HARRINGTON

James Harrrington has been called 'the central figure' in the transmission of Machiavelli's ideas and 'the chief translator of Machiavelli into English political, legal, and historical terms'. Indeed, it has been said that Harrington was 'the first to achieve a paradigmatic restatement of English political understanding in the language and world-view inherited through Machiavelli'. This section, then, will trace a 'current of ideas' that derived from Aristotelian and Machiavellian roots, but which was transformed by Harrington and came to be a central intellectual heritage for those who later confronted the challenges of leading in a democracy.[128]

As has been the case with each of our other commentators, Harrington wrote in response to perceived societal challenges that appeared to call for a thoughtful political response. In Harrington's case, however, the challenge was perhaps more palpable and more immediate. Harrington drafted his most important works in the England of the 1650s, when the monarchy had been swept away and the king executed, to be replaced by a series of polities that ranged from a republic to the unitary military rule of Oliver Cromwell. So, although we will find Harrington's chief work to be quite fanciful in format, it was nevertheless intended as a serious and considered solution to the specific needs of Interregnum England.

The chief vehicle for Harrington's argument was a long and 'tiresome Utopian fantasy' entitled *The Commonwealth of Oceana*. It was, in the words of one historian, 'a model of government so bewildering in its detail that it could scarcely have had a wide reading, … but the fact that *Oceana* is virtually unreadable did not prevent the ideas in it from finding their way into popular tracts and gaining wide acceptance in both England and America in the seventeenth and eighteenth centuries'. In its substance, Harrington drew upon the tradition we have traced in this chapter to depict 'England as a classical republic and the Englishman as a classical citizen'. It was, in response to the challenges of the time, a 'blueprint for … a government without a monarchy or House of Lords'. Yet it became much more, for in the words of one Harrington scholar, 'the consequences of [this work] were felt to the American Revolution and beyond'.[129]

Indeed, it is worth mentioning briefly at this point the role Harringtonian thought played in the development of the American colonies and, more importantly, in American political thought. In the first instance, Harrington was to have a significant impact when several of the American proprietary colonies were founded later in the seventeenth century. When John Locke, acting as secretary to the Earl of Shaftesbury (one of the proprietors of the Carolina colony), was asked to create a constitution for that colony, he modeled it after Harrington's *Oceana*. As befitted any document patterned after Harrington's often bizarre model, this attempt did not meet the demands of reality. Nevertheless, it suggested the power of Harrington's ideas. Later, William Penn also emulated Harrington in an initial plan for Pennsylvania that met a similar fate.[130] More important was Harrington's intellectual impact. In the late seventeenth and early eighteenth centuries in England, a group of intellectuals and polemicists now called 'neo-Harringtonians' adapted his thought to the exigencies of their time. Although this group remained on the fringes of British political thought, historian Bernard Bailyn has demonstrated convincingly that it was this intellectual heritage that had the greatest impact upon American revolutionaries.[131] Most important for purposes of this study, Harrington, in the words of one careful historian, 'was to have a long-continuing influence on the subsequent history of popular sovereignty'.[132] For example, when it came time for James Madison to concoct a plan of government for the new American nation, he relied heavily upon David Hume's *Idea for a Perfect Commonwealth*. Hume's work, in turn, 'was an attempt to improve on Harrington's *Oceana*'.[133] This continuing influence makes James Harrington a central figure in our current study. In the following analysis, we will seek to identify his major contributions to our notions of the role of the leader in a popular regime.

Being a student of Machiavelli and firmly within the tradition of the classical ideal, it is no surprise that Harrington's work echoed many of the same themes that are by now familiar. For example, he agreed with earlier writers that the ultimate purpose of government was the common good. 'Government', he said, '… is an art whereby a civil society of men is instituted and preserved upon the foundation of common right or common interest.' This necessitated for Harrington, as it had his predecessors, a commitment to the classical notion of civic virtue, with its emphasis of public good over private interest. 'Wherefore,' Harrington continued, 'if we have anything of piety or of prudence, let us raise ourselves out of the mire of private interest unto the contemplation of virtue.'[134]

Harrington also restated the ancient typology of constitutional forms, with its three forms of good government by the one, few and many, respectively, which degenerated into a similar number of perversions, where the dominant group sought its own advantage rather than the good of the whole.[135] However, it was Harrington's discussion of this classical commonplace that led him to identify and address two central problems he felt were inadequately handled by earlier writers. In his resolution of these problems, he contributed materially to later conceptions of the roles of the leaders and followers in a popular state.

The first of the problems Harrington confronted grew out of the traditional view of the declension from good forms of the state (monarchy, aristocracy and polity) into the corrupted forms of tyranny, oligarchy and democracy ('anarchy' in Harrington's typology). He was, in the first instance, concerned with interweaving the aristocratic element with that of the people without incurring unacceptable rule by a corrupt elite. In a larger sense, Harrington was tackling the proper relations between leaders and the people. He noted that 'there is not a more noble or useful question in the politics than that which is stated by Machiavel whether means were to be found whereby the enmity that was between the senate and people [in Rome] might have been removed'.[136]

The second problem that occupied Harrington involved the traditional solution of the rule of law. Make no mistake: Harrington favored the rule of law as the salvation of a republic. He took pains to contrast governments under a rule of law with others. 'Government (to define it *de jure* ...) is an art whereby a civil society of men is instituted and preserved upon the foundation of common right or common interest, or (to follow Aristotle and Livy) it is the empire of laws and not of men.' In contrast, 'government (to define it *de facto* ...) is an art whereby some man, or few men, subject a city or nation, and rule according unto his or their private interest, which, because the laws in such cases are made according to the interest of a man or of some few families, may be said to be the empire of men and not of laws'. Harrington made no bones about which was preferable. 'The liberty of the commonwealth', he asserted, 'consisteth in the empire of her laws, the absence of which would betray her unto the lusts of tyrants; and those I conceive to be the principles upon which Aristotle and Livy ... have grounded their assertion that a commonwealth is an empire of laws and not of men.'[137]

At the same time, however, Harrington was among the first to examine the fiction of the rule of law in the harsh light of reality. He cast aside the façade of neutrality that had masked the realities of the rule of law. He posed the question starkly: 'But seeing they that make the laws in commonwealths are but men, the main question seems to be how a commonwealth comes to be an empire of laws and not of men? or', to put it another way, 'how the debate and result of a commonwealth is so sure to be according to reason, seeing they who debate and they who resolve be but men?'[138] This was, indeed, the proverbial 'elephant in the room', which previous writers had chosen to ignore.

Harrington, then, faced these two independent but related challenges. The first was to invent a polity that would have the proper balance of aristocracy and democracy (Harrington's – at that time – idiosyncratic term for the virtuous form of government by the many). A related challenge was to ensure that the rule of law that resulted truly reflected the common good and not the particular interest of one group. He addressed both challenges via a brace of solutions that creatively reconfigured the basis for participation in a republic and which established an innovative political mechanism that ensured leaders who emulated the classical ideal while at the same time capturing the benefits of popular participation.

In the first part of his package, Harrington invented a new foundation for republican government. His insight emerged from his study of the classical cycle of constitutional forms. Harrington put forward one observation that he thought explained all. His basic principle he articulated as follows: 'Lands, or the parts and parcels of a territory, are held by the proprietor or proprietors ... in some proportion, and such ... as is the proportion or balance of dominion or property in land, such is the nature of the empire'. With this insight, Harrington returned to the classical cycle, this time adding his twist to the proceedings. 'If one man be the sole landlord of a territory', he argued, ' ... his empire is absolute monarchy. If the nobility ... be landlords ... it makes [for an oligarchy] ... and if the whole people be landlords, or holding the lands so divided among them, that no man, or [few] … men, overbalance them; the empire is a commonwealth.'[139] Power, then, was for Harrington linked to the possession of property, and this gloss helped make intelligible the classical cycle.

More important in terms of his immediate challenge presented by the Interregnum in England, Harrington used the same principle to create his own version of English history. In sum, he argued that the evolving distribution of land ownership both explained English political history and provided the key to resolving the challenges of the present. According to Harrington's history, both lands and power had been in the hands of the king and the nobility prior to the accession of Henry VII in 1485. Thereafter, Henry, for his own purposes, had 'reduced the property both of the crown and of the nobility while increasing that of the yeoman and gentry'. Power had consequently shifted in a parallel direction, evidenced by the rise in influence of the House of Commons in the sixteenth and seventeenth centuries. Particularly in recent years, Harrington thought that he could perceive a movement toward a commonwealth of freeholders. This underlying historical and economic development, more than any specific political acts, had brought England to its current juncture.[140]

Harrington, however, intended his insight to be much more than a mere descriptor of English history. He went on to posit a normative aspect to the widespread possession of property and its impact upon the English polity. Property, argued Harrington, conferred certain benefits that were essential to wise and virtuous policy making in a republic. 'Equality of estates causeth equality of power,' he argued, 'and equality of power is the liberty not only of the commonwealth, but of every man.' Conversely, 'where there is inequality of estates, there must be inequality of power, and where there is inequality of power, there can be no commonwealth'.[141]

Moreover, Harrington, in a somewhat convoluted argument, suggested that this widespread distribution of property resolved the problem of 'interest' that he had first broached when deconstructing the rule of law. According to Harrington's logic, 'interest' occurred in several different forms, and each form of interest generated in turn its own particular form of 'reason'. As Harrington described it, 'At first there is private reason, which is the interest of a private man. Secondly, there is reason of state, which is the interest of the ruler or rulers…. Thirdly, there is that reason which is the interest of mankind of the whole.' It was this last that was key to Harrington's argument. It represented 'a common right, law of nature, or interest of the whole, which is more excellent, and so acknowledged by the agents themselves, than the right or interest of the parts only'. If, as Harrington argued, 'the interest of mankind be the right interest, then the reason of mankind must be right reason'. If so, then the task was to assure that government came as close as possible to achieving the interest of mankind, and thus 'right reason'. How to do so? Harrington put forward a proposition. 'Now compute well,' he began, 'for if the interest of popular government come nearest unto the interest of mankind, then the reason of popular government must come nearest unto right reason.'[142] Looking back once more at his version of English history down to the present day, Harrington believed that contemporary England, with its widely distributed ownership of land, stood at the cusp of an era when public interest and law would be one, and 'right reason' would rule the land. 'For the balance, swinging from the monarchical into popular, abateth the luxury of nobility and, enriching the people, bringeth the government from a more private into a more public interest, which ... [by all portents was] coming nearer ... unto justice and right reason.'[143]

If England was approaching a system of land distribution that permitted such laudable results, Harrington was taking no chances. He called for the institutionalization of a widespread distribution of land among the citizens of the commonwealth. In *Oceana*, his fanciful model for English government, he introduced a concept first seen in Aristotle: 'A kind of law for fixing the balance in lands is called agrarian', he said. More specifically, 'An equal agrarian is a perpetual law establishing and preserving the balance of dominion, by such distribution that no man or number of men within the compass of the few or aristocracy can come to overpower the whole people by their possession in lands'. And, as we already know, 'if the whole people be landlords, or hold the lands so divided among them, that no one man ... or few ... overbalance them' what results is a commonwealth, and, more importantly, a regime where the real public good is likely to be attained.[144]

Harrington was not, however, content to rely merely upon a mechanistic distribution of land to secure his ends, and indeed he recognized that his equal agrarian was insufficient to accomplish them fully. In particular, he acknowledged that widely distributed ownership of land was inadequate, standing alone, to ensure that the common good would be properly served. Being a realist, he knew that self-interest would not suddenly disappear. 'But it may be said that the difficulty remains yet,' he allowed, 'for be the interest of popular government right reason, a man doth not look upon reason as it is right or wrong in itself, but as it makes for him or against him.' Any viable system of government, he knew, must 'be able to constrain this or that creature to shake off that inclination which is more peculiar to it, and take up the common good or interest. ... [A]ll this', he continued, 'is to no more end than to persuade every man in a popular government not to carve himself of that which he desires most, but be mannerly at the public table, and give the best from himself unto decency and the common interest.'[145] Other critics, he knew, could weigh in with another objection. 'But there be [some] that say (and think it a strong objection): let a commonwealth be as equal as you can imagine, two or three men when all is done will govern it; and there is that in it, which notwithstanding the pretended sufficiency of a popular state, amounteth unto a plain confession of the imbecility of that policy.'[146] This objection, in effect, addressed Harrington's second problem, that of creating a polity in which the aristocratic classes behaved virtuously and where both the aristocracy and the people could draw upon their respective strengths to assure the good of the commonwealth.

Harrington moved to resolve both challenges with a creative model for leading in a popular regime. He introduced his invention by means of two parables. The first may be called 'the parable of the girls', and addressed the matter of ensuring that private interests did not predominate over the general interest. Harrington began by pointing out 'that such [a system] may be established as may, nay must, give the upper hand in all cases unto common right or interest, notwithstanding the nearness of that which sticks unto every man in private, and this in a way of equal certainty and facility, is known even to girls'. He elaborated: 'For example, two of them have a cake yet undivided, which was given between them. That each of them therefore may have that which is due, "Divide", says one to the other, "and I will choose; or let me divide, and you shall choose." If this be but once agreed upon, it is enough; for ... she divides equally, and both have right.' Albeit simple, this process is also profound. 'That which great philosophers are disputing on in vain', observed Harrington, 'is brought unto light by two silly girls: even the whole mystery of a commonwealth, which lies only in dividing and choosing.'[147] In this case, the general interest was served by a simple structural expedient.

Of course, Harrington's solution of 'dividing and choosing' faced some difficulties when applied to a commonwealth. Chief among these was the question of who was to divide, and who to choose. This led him to a consideration of the differing capacities of the participants in a commonwealth, and ultimately to the matter of leading. Harrington introduced the topic with another parable, one that we can call 'the parable of the six and the fourteen'. Fortunately, he argued, the matter of who divides and who chooses was not all that difficult. 'Nor hath God ... left so much unto mankind to dispute upon as who shall divide and who choose,' he explained, 'but established them for ever into two orders, whereof the one hath the natural right of dividing, and the other of choosing.' He turned to his next parable. 'A commonwealth is but a civil society of men', he said. 'Let us take any number of men, as twenty, and forthwith make a commonwealth. Twenty men,' he continued, 'if they be not all idiots – perhaps if they be – can never come together but there will be such difference in them that about a third will be wiser, or at least less foolish, than all the rest. These upon acquaintance, though it be but small, will be discovered and (as sheep that have the largest heads) lead the herd. ... ' The process by which this occurred could not be more natural, 'for while the six, discussing and arguing with one another, show the eminence of their parts, the fourteen discover things that they never thought on, or are cleared in divers truths which had formerly perplexed them'. This, in turn, created a natural and beneficial relationship. 'In matters of common concernment, difficulty, or danger, they hang upon [the] lips [of the six] as children upon their fathers, and the influence thus acquired by the six, the eminence of whose parts is found to be a stay and comfort to the fourteen, is ... the authority of the fathers.' Harrington acknowledged what his parable had established: 'Wherefore this can be no other than a natural aristocracy diffused by God throughout the whole body of mankind to this end and purpose, and therefore such [leaders] as the people have not only a natural but a positive obligation to make use of as their guides'.[148]

Harrington thus identified who were to be the 'dividers': those members of a natural aristocracy who had the wisdom and virtue (recall the classical ideal) to debate and discuss matters of public policy, a function that the people – the 'fourteen' – should leave in their hands. But this was not to be a one-way street. The people also had an important role as the 'choosers', based upon the capacities that they brought to the commonwealth. The people, it will be recalled, although they had not the wisdom of the few, nevertheless best represented the common interest. As Harrington put it, 'whereas the people, taken apart, are but so many private interests, but if you take them together they are the public interest', which led to a familiar litany: 'the public interest of a commonwealth ... is nearest that of mankind, and that of mankind is right reason'.[149] Thus, Harrington concluded, 'as the wisdom of the commonwealth is in the aristocracy, so the interest of the commonwealth is in the whole body of the people'.[150] In this way Harrington merged the parable of the girls with the parable of the six and the fourteen; creatively, he advocated a system whereby the capacities of the few and those of the many could be harnessed, as with the girls, for the good of the whole.

Having set forth the underlying principles of his polity, Harrington turned to their implementation. His essential challenge was to institutionalize 'dividing and choosing', or, in the language of the commonwealth, 'debating and resolving'. It was necessary, in other words, 'to distinguish the two actions and the two groups' who were to perform them.[151] Harrington proceeded to do this by inventing the fantastical Commonwealth of Oceana.

The initial task was to distinguish who among the population at large were to be the few, and who the many. This Harrington accomplished by separating the people into two classes according to annual income. All freemen (servants were excluded) who had an annual income exceeding one hundred pounds were members of 'the horse', while those with less were of the 'foot'.[152] Such a property qualification to demark the elite appeared at first blush to contradict Harrington's advocacy of a natural aristocracy of merit, but he put forward a justification for his distinction. In identifying the few, he was searching for a 'nobility', defined not according to riches or title, but by 'virtue', in the classical sense of civic virtue. Such virtue, argued Harrington, was inextricably linked to a certain degree of wealth. This provided them not only with an Aristotelian independence, but also the leisure to contemplate and pursue the common good. Such a 'nobility', identifiable as those 'who live upon their own revenues in plenty, without engagement either unto the tilling of their lands or other work for their livelihood ... are ... necessary unto the natural mixture of a well-ordered commonwealth'. Unless one has personages of some wealth, he asked, 'how else can you have a commonwealth that is not altogether mechanic?' The problem with 'mechanics' was that they 'are so busied with their private concernments that they have neither leisure to study the public, nor are safely to be trusted with it'. But if one had wealth, '... his share be such as gives him leisure by his private advantage to reflect upon that of the public'.[153]

Having differentiated the people into the few and the many, Harrington assigned to each group its institutional embodiment. The few, that is, the natural aristocracy, were the basis of the senate, which was to be relatively small (a membership of three hundred), and indirectly elected. Members were to be drawn entirely out of the 'horse'. This yielded, according to Harrington, the necessary wise leaders. 'The six then approved of', he said, referring back to his parable, '... are the senate, not by hereditary right, nor in regard to their hereditary estates only, ... but by election for their excellent parts, which tendeth unto the advancement of the influence of their virtue or authority that leads the people.'[154] There was also to be a popular assembly, which was made up of both the 'foot' and the 'horse' in a ratio of four to three, thus giving the people a slight predominance in that body. This assembly of approximately one thousand members was to be elected by direct popular vote from geographic districts.[155]

Once the few and the many had achieved institutional manifestation in Harrington's model, it remained to assign them their respective roles. These roles amounted to, in the language of the girls, 'dividing' and 'choosing'. The role of the senate was to 'divide', or in the language of the commonwealth, to 'debate and propose'. As Harrington put it, 'Wherefore the office of the senate is not to be commanders but counselors of the people, and that which is proper unto counselors is first to debate the business whereupon they are to give advice'. Once debated, 'the decrees of the senate are never laws, nor so called'. Rather, 'it is their duty ... to propose in the case unto the people'. Harking back to his model and his parables, Harrington pointed out that 'the senate is no more than the debate of the commonwealth. But to debate is to discern', he continued, 'or put a difference between things that being alike are not the same, or it is separating and weighing this reason against that reason against this, which is [akin to the] dividing [of the cake]'.[156]

The role of the popular assembly was to 'choose', or in the language of the commonwealth, to 'resolve'. Given the logic of his model, this was an inescapable conclusion. As Harrington framed it, 'The senate then having divided, who shall choose? Ask the girls,' he responded to his own question, 'for if she that divided must have chosen also, it had been little worse for the other, in case she had not divided at all, but kept the whole cake unto herself. … Wherefore,' he concluded, 'if the senate have any further power than to divide, the commonwealth can never be equal.' Thus there was no 'remedy but to have another council to choose'. This certainly should not be a council of the few. 'The wisdom of the few may be the light of mankind,' he acknowledged, 'but the interest of the few is not the profit of mankind, nor of a commonwealth.' Given Harrington's previous discussion of the venue of true interest in a commonwealth, the proper roles were obvious. 'Wherefore, seeing we have granted interest to be reason, they [the few] must not choose, lest it put out their light; but as the council dividing consisteth of the wisdom of the commonwealth, so the assembly … choosing should consist of the interest of the commonwealth.'[157] The interest of the commonwealth, that is, the sense of the common good, Harrington had already posited, lay in the people. Thus, the popular assembly should choose (or decide, or resolve).

In Harrington's model, the respective roles of the few and the many were strictly delimited. Just as 'that right of debate, as also of proposing to the people, be wholly and only in the senate, without any power at all of result,' so too 'the power of result be wholly and only in the [representative body of the] people, without any right at all of debate'.[158] The process worked like this: 'The senate having passed a decree which they would propose to the people, cause it to be … published, … [then] they choose their proposers … The [popular assembly] being assembled at the day appointed and the decrees proposed, that which is proposed by authority of the senate and commanded by the people is the law of Oceana.'[159]

Harrington's model was extremely complex, and included an executive branch whose duty it was merely to execute the laws. It also embraced other innovations such as rotation in office and the secret ballot, in his attempt to assure the continued influence of the people and prevent the emergence of factions and improper influence peddling.[160] In its essence, however, it was an attempt to secure the common good over private interest, and to create a polity in which both the few and the many could achieve a political capacity that furthered the ends of the commonwealth. How well he achieved his goals, and the implications for leading in a regime based upon the people, deserve further attention.

One way to assess Harrington's efforts is to consider how well he accomplished the goals he set out for himself. We identified earlier two central concerns that appeared to occupy Harrington. The first was the matter of how to integrate properly the many and the few in a commonwealth, particularly with respect to the functions of leading. The second issue, on its surface, addressed the age-old topic of the rule of law, but in reality plumbed the deeper point of how one achieves the general interest or the common good in a polity filled with individual interests. For both issues, Harrington devised a brace of solutions. First, he posited a new basis for relationships and the role of power in society, and second, he put forward a novel system of relating and leading. Let us assess the implications.

When Harrington broached the problems concerning the rule of law, he was in essence acknowledging the existence of private interests in society, even among lawmakers, that could result in laws that did not serve the common good. Believing, however, that society came closest to the common interest and 'right reason' when the whole of mankind was involved in the process, Harrington sought ways by which popular participation in the commonwealth could be assured. He found this in a new theory of power in a polity. According to Harrington, power followed resources, in particular land ownership. Given this premise, it was a relatively small step to advocate a system of land distribution that assured widespread participation and influence. However, Harrington was not so naïve that he could comfortably assume that the public interest would magically appear. He thought that achieving the common good required the twofold strategy of balancing interests and tapping into the capacities of the few and the many. The wisdom of the few would be enhanced by the sense of the general interest in the many, in a system carefully structured to assure that both contributions were protected.

It may be useful here to pause and consider the implications and significance of Harrington's treatment of 'interest' in a society. His contributions are many, but three in particular stand out. The first is his reliance upon landed property (in the main) as the basis for influence in a state. This was not totally new, and in some senses echoed Aristotle, but Harrington took it further, and his successors took it further yet. One of the central tenets of the 'neo-Harringtonians' who, in turn, influenced American state makers so profoundly, was their assumption about the wisdom and necessity of widespread property ownership in a balanced republic. This was to create a legacy and spawn an ideological divide in American history that remains visible to this day. We will be discussing the impact of this ideological divide upon leadership in a democracy in Part III of this volume.

Another important contribution by Harrington related to his conceptualization of the common good. Harrington, as have all the other commentators in this tradition of the classical ideal that we have been tracing, strongly believed in the notion of common interest or common good. Moreover, he joined such predecessors as Aristotle and Machiavelli in believing that, somehow, the people as a whole were more virtuous – more likely to pursue the common good – when they acted as a group, rather than when acting individually. However, Harrington was also more realistic in his acknowledgment and acceptance of the continued existence of 'interest'. His parable of the girls and the structural processes of the ensuing polity were directed at minimizing the influence of interest. In this sense, Harrington, although fully within the classical republican tradition and its commitment to civic virtue, nonetheless was in some senses a precursor to later, more sophisticated attempts at dealing with interests in a democracy. These, too, will be a topic of discussion later in this volume.

Related to this is a third Harringtonian contribution. With his discussion of the role of interests in the rule of law, he provided the good office of bringing out into the open for public consideration the strengths and weaknesses of this solution for human foibles that had been a favorite for millennia. This insight, too, spawned an ideological split of sorts within legal circles, but more important is the fact that, after Harrington, no one can with any pretense of intellectual honesty rely smugly upon the 'rule of law' without confronting these Harringtonian realities. Harrington's creative attempts to resolve this challenge may not pass muster, but they can serve as a useful starting point for others.

Let us now turn to Harrington's issue of how to integrate properly the many and the few in a commonwealth. This issue can be recast in terms of the respective roles of leaders and followers in a republic, and as such places James Harrington squarely within the compass of our current study.

In addressing this issue, Harrington drew upon the same solutions that he had tapped in resolving the matter of interest in a republic, although his analysis in this context was, perhaps, somewhat more sophisticated. Harrington had come to this issue of leaders and followers through his study of Machiavelli. As much of a fan of Machiavelli as Harrington was, he nevertheless did not agree with all of Machiavelli's analyses and conclusions. One of these departures had to do with Machiavelli's conclusions concerning the tensions between patricians and plebeians in Rome. The cause of the problems in Rome was not, as Machiavelli would have it, the actions of corrupt leaders or unvirtuous followers, so much as it was a flaw in the underlying allocation of property, and the resulting power relations. As Harrington put it, 'Machiavel, in this as in other places, having his eye upon the division of patrician and plebeian families as they were in Rome, hath quite mistaken the [issues] of this commonwealth'. Rather than focus upon the conflicts, Machiavelli should have looked to the underlying social and political structures. For 'a commonwealth that is internally equal hath no internal cause of commotion', and 'a commonwealth internally unequal hath no cause of quiet'.[161] It was in the context of this discussion that Harrington advocated an 'agrarian' law of wide property distribution, for if the members of the commonwealth could be thus equalized in power, abuses between the leaders and the people could be essentially eliminated. Such a commonwealth need not fear either convulsions or unfairness as had characterized Rome. 'For, as no man shall show me a commonwealth born straight that ever became crooked, so no man shall show me a commonwealth born crooked that ever became straight. Rome', Harrington continued, 'was crooked in her birth ... her twins the patrician and plebeian orders came ... into the world one body but two heads, or rather two bellies. ...' On the contrary, Harrington was confident that his Oceana (England) had avoided this problem. 'My lords', he concluded, in one of the many meandering speeches that characterize his tome, 'if I have argued well, I have given you the comfort and assurance that, notwithstanding the judgment of Machiavel, your commonwealth is safe and sound.'[162] And, although few have adopted Harrington's prescriptions in any specificity, we will find that as we contemplate the solutions for effective leadership in modern democracy, his argument for equalizing power among stakeholders will retain its currency.

Of course, Harrington's analysis went much deeper than the mere redistribution of property. He also considered carefully the proper relations between the many and the few, and created an innovative system designed to tap the best capacities of each. Harrington's model, in effect, amounted to a new system of leading, with new expectations of both leaders and the people. Our further discussion of leadership in a democracy requires a closer look at the roles of leaders and the people in Harrington's commonwealth.

Let us explore, then, in more detail, Harrington's conceptions of the leader and his role, as well as that of the people, and the relationship between them. We have seen that Harrington did not in all cases agree with the arguments of Machiavelli. So, too, it was when it came to the topic of the role of leaders. Although Machiavelli and Harrington joined in adopting the classical ideal – both believed that whoever it was that was leading must be wise and virtuous and committed to the common good – there was substantial disagreement over who should lead in specific circumstances. There was, however, one situation in which both agreed entirely.

Both Machiavelli and Harrington believed that the founding of a republic or commonwealth, regardless of what happened after, was the work of one man who embodied the classical ideal. Harrington asserted 'first, that the legislator [that is, the founder of a republic] should be one man, and secondly that the government should be made altogether, at once'. Here he cited his predecessor. 'It is certain, saith Machiavel, that a commonwealth is seldom or never well turned or constituted, except it have been the work of one man.' More important, this individual leader must be 'a wise legislator, and one whose mind is firmly set not upon private but the public interest'. And, again like Machiavelli, the leader's ends justified his means. 'Nor shall any man that is master of reason blame such extraordinary means as in that case shall be necessary, the end proving no other than the constitution of a well-ordered commonwealth.' Thus Harrington agreed with Machiavelli about the need for a conquering hero such as Cromwell (Harrington called him 'Olphaus Megalator' in his fanciful Oceana), or at least a wise legislator ('Lord Archon' in the text).[163]

Once the founding of the commonwealth was complete, however, Harrington no longer felt the need to return to the single leader-as-savior that Machiavelli had called for when the republic became corrupted. This in large part was due to the underlying structure of the commonwealth discussed previously. If the initial 'legislator' had done his job aright and established an equal agrarian, the commonwealth was 'born straight', and unlikely to need rescuing by a single leader. This being the case, Harrington turned his attention to what sort of leader(s) were needed in the normal course of events.

In such a normal course of events, Harrington relied not upon a single leader, but upon a cadre of leaders who represented 'the six', that is, a 'nobility' of wisdom and virtue which could be relied upon to provide proper policy direction. If 'you would have popular government', Harrington asserted, '...the superstructures of such government ... require a good aristocracy'.[164] Indeed, 'a nobility or gentry in a popular government ... is the very life and soul of it'.[165] This nobility, it will be recalled, was a natural aristocracy that had sufficient wealth and leisure to attend to the public interest. From this it is clear that the leaders of the commonwealth constituted an entire class of individuals who fit the classical ideal. Such a group, then, was 'a true aristocracy and provides the people with their natural leaders'.[166]

While Harrington continued in the tradition of the classical ideal of the leader(s) in republics, what distinguished him from his predecessors was the extent to which he relied upon the people as principal participants in the polity. Aristotle had grounded his approach upon the assumption that the people (at least those with a certain level of independence and wealth) would be active members of the state, and Machiavelli had penned some dramatic rhetoric about the abilities of the people, but it was left for Harrington to expand upon this notion and give it institutional viability.

Harrington's faith in popular participation was grounded in two foundational principles, both of which he extrapolated forward from his classical republican roots. First, Harrington picked up on a long tradition of respect for the potential capabilities of the people, when taken as a whole, and if not overmuch is asked of them. As he pointed out, 'It is noted out of Cicero by Machiavel that the people, albeit they are not so prone to find out the truth of themselves, as to follow custom or run into error, yet, if they be shown the truth, they not only acknowledge it and embrace it very suddenly, but are the most constant and faithful guardians and conservators of it'.[167] Thus, if one recalls the parable of the six and the fourteen, one realizes that this wisdom is somewhat truncated. Not all the people could be counted on to have the wisdom and virtue necessary to make policy; Harrington thought perhaps one in three had this capacity, and it was this subset who constituted 'the six', the natural aristocracy of the polity. Nonetheless, the 'fourteen' could be counted on to have sufficient wisdom, when acting as a whole, to recognize the general interest. Equally important, they had sufficient insight to recognize and select appropriate leaders from their numbers.[168] The second foundational principle undergirding popular participation was the Aristotelian notion of independence. As one historian of Harrington summed it up, 'The freedom characteristic of popular governments depends on the independence of the voting population and their representatives, and that their independence in turn rests on the secure possession of sufficient property in land to support them and render them free of coercion'.[169]

One of Harrington's innovations, however, was his willingness to extend these principles to the great majority of the people. While Harrington was Aristotelian in his belief that the possession of property was a gauge of the necessary independence of a citizen, his liberal agrarian made sure that this advantage was widely distributed. In the words of his closest student, Harrington was positively 'democratic ... in his willingness to extend citizenship to the poorest that was not a servant'.[170] Harrington's fictional Oceana, of course, was to presage future reality, and the implications are the topic of much of the remainder of this volume.

One implication that became immediately apparent was the need for some sort of representation. Given the widespread basis of political participation, the people needed to select their own 'leaders', or representatives to Harrington's popular assembly. To him, representation was simply a matter of necessity. 'As the wisdom of the commonwealth is in the aristocracy, so the interest of the commonwealth is in the whole body of the people,' he said, 'and whereas this, in case the commonwealth consist of a whole nation, is too unwieldy a body to be assembled.' Therefore, 'it should seem that, without a representative of the people, your commonwealth consisting of a whole nation can never avoid falling either into oligarchy or confusion'. Of critical importance, however, was the requirement that the representatives of the people must not depart in form or function from those they represented. 'This council', Harrington insisted, 'is to consist of such a representative as may be equal, and so constituted as can never contract any other interest than that of the whole people.'[171] Therefore he insisted that the popular assembly, as nearly as practicable, must replicate the people at large. Although Harrington appeared to view the emergence of representation as a mere convenience, the idea of some of the people representing the interests of others (more specifically, some representing the interests of the whole) was to have significant implications for leading in a regime grounded in the people. Harrington either did not perceive these implications, or left them for others. So we, too, will reserve our discussion of representation in a democratic republic for our later consideration of the fiction of leadership.

Along with the new focus on the people came the opportunity to explore in more depth the relations between leaders and the people in a popular republic. There were, indeed, important implications attending Harrington's system of the people and the natural aristocracy who were to be their leaders working together as they sought to achieve the common good. As we have seen, he believed in elite leaders proposing policy, but he opposed Machiavelli's notion that such leaders could do so without the people's overt consent. In articulating this relationship, Harrington negotiated a delicate balance between equality and inequality in the state. In the words of Harrington scholar J.G.A. Pocock, Harrington 'presupposes ... that some personalities possessed the capacity to engage in what he called "debate," others only that necessary to do what he called "resolve," and that differentiation was (a) natural, and (b) that between higher and lower intelligences. With that,' continues Pocock, 'the principle of inequality was introduced; ... however, ... there was a presumption of equality as well.' As Pocock explains it, 'Harrington's republic ... rested upon a relation of equality between persons who were unequal in their capacities'. Thus arose a quintessentially political relationship between the leaders and the people that captured and tapped the possibilities of this equality-within-inequality. Pocock concludes that 'Harrington was designing a system of proportionate rather than numerical equality, in which the respective weights assigned to aristocracy and democracy mattered less than the functional and ethical relationships between them, and there was nothing contrary to his notion of equality in weighting the balance against the numerical principle'.[172] In the process, Harrington accorded new status and legitimacy to the people. In Harrington's work, 'the body of the people [must have] the opportunity of virtue, which means partaking in decisions directed at the common good and according authority where it is due to the goods of mind displayed by others'.[173]

Along with Harrington's nuanced view of equality within the state, there arose an equally sophisticated characterization of the relationship between leaders and the people. It was an association marked by an intriguing mix of deference and mutual respect. On the one hand, the parable of the six and the fourteen, and the institutional articulation Harrington derived from that parable, demanded that the many yield to the wisdom of the superior few in policy formation. In this manner, the principle of deference made its appearance. As Harrington put it when discussing the people, 'You shall find them to have ... a bashfulness in the presence of the better sort or wiser man, acknowledging their abilities by attention, and according it no mean honor to receive respect from them'.[174] Yet the notion of deference is inadequate to depict fully the relationship between leaders and the people. Harrington believed that 'as the wisdom of the commonwealth is in the aristocracy, so the interest of the commonwealth is in the whole body of the people'.[175] Indeed, 'in truth an army may as well consist of soldiers without officers, or of officers without soldiers, as a commonwealth (especially such an one as is capable of greatness) of a people without a gentry, or of a gentry without a people'.[176] Thus, in Pocock's analysis, 'If the Many choose the Few by showing them deference, there is a real sense in which the Few must defer to the Many. Only on these principles will equality, authority, and virtue be simultaneously guaranteed.'[177] Only the two, working together in mutual respect, could achieve wise policy for the common good in a popular regime.

THE IMPLICIT THEORIES OF THE CLASSICAL REPUBLICANS

Having explored in some detail the thought of three classical republican writers, we can now apply the template of leadership in order to discern their 'implicit theories of leadership'; that is, their premises and assumptions concerning the central elements that comprise the phenomenon of leadership. The purpose is to uncover the essence of the leadership implications of classical republicanism, without undo repetition of the preceding analysis. Again, the purpose is analytical; this will serve our ongoing study of the challenges of leadership in a democracy. We turn, then, to the now-familiar protocol of questions that make up our leadership template.

What is the Leadership Challenge?

Predictably enough, our classical republican commentators were responding to differing problems grounded in their peculiar contemporary contexts. What is intriguing is the fact that, although each addressed unique contemporary political challenges, at the heart of each writer's argument was the essential challenge of maintaining leaders characterized by the classical ideal in regimes characterized by popular participation.

In terms of the immediate political problem faced, Aristotle perceived a wide variation in the governance of republics in ancient Greece, and sought, in the manner of a detached scholar, to identify the best structures and practices. Machiavelli similarly noted a lack of stability in the republics of Renaissance Italy, and, as an admirer of the ancients, set out to provide guidance for the regeneration of strong republics. Harrington faced a more immediate challenge: he wrote during the turbulent period after the regicide of Charles I, and sought to create a republican polity that could bring prosperity and tranquility to England.

Despite their differing contemporary challenges, at base each confronted a similar foundational problem: each sought to reconcile the stability and favorable societal outcomes associated with strong leaders adhering to the classical ideal with a polity that was grounded in popular participation. This in itself makes our consideration of the classical republican writers essential to our larger task of contemplating leadership in a democracy.

What is the Perception of Human Nature?

The classical republican commentators all agreed that the human condition required individuals to come together to form states in order to survive. Plato had begun from a similar premise, but these writers went far beyond his functional analysis and claimed, with Aristotle, that men were by nature 'social and political animals', and actually *needed* others in order to realize fully their complete nature.

Another assumption of the classical republicans was that, within the sometimes exceedingly narrow confines of the individuals defined as citizens, all were essentially free and equal. In this, too, we find a notable departure from Plato and even Aquinas.

Finally, regarding an issue that goes directly to the next issue of the ability of the people to govern, the republicans took a rather nuanced view of the essential competence of the people. Given the previous recriminations of Plato, those who contemplated regimes involving popular participation held a much more positive perspective. On the other hand, in many respects they agreed with Plato that the people were often likely to be mistaken, and at times even evil. This tension, applied to our focus upon political life, can best be detailed in response to the next query.

Are the People Capable of Governing?

To a much greater degree than anyone previously, the classical republicans championed the wisdom and virtue of the people, when considered in general. Moreover, they considered the people capable of participating in government, when one allows for the caveat that this extended only, to take Aristotle as an example, to 'citizens' carefully defined (in a circular manner) as those capable of governing. James Harrington was to take an enlarged view of the scope of citizen participation, but only after carefully structuring the situation to achieve the same result.

For all their encomiums of the people, this did not translate into unlimited confidence in government by the people. The republicans were every bit as skeptical of unadulterated democracy as had been Plato. They acknowledged that the populace often engaged in selfish (that is, nonvirtuous) behavior, frequently failed to see beyond their own immediate gratification, and in other respects simply acted unwisely. In addition to the now familiar threat of a descent into tyranny was now added the specter of the tyranny of the majority.

All this necessitated that the people receive the proper guidance, which brought our classical republicans back to the need for leaders patterned after the classical ideal. This raised a further problem, in that the people could not be consistently counted upon to choose wise leaders, although the republican commentators were not wholly pessimistic about the people's wisdom in this area.

Taken all in all, the classical republican commentators faced a challenge of rather formidable proportions, as they labored to create a government linked to the people, even though the constituency was flawed.

What is the Proper End or Purpose of Leadership?

One of the things that exacerbated this new challenge of involving the people was the fact that the classical republicans had not changed what had become the traditional conception of the ends of government, nor the values that accompanied it. Although there was much more of an acceptance of the notion of political equality and some discussion of the value of liberty, the focus of these classical republicans remained the traditional one of achieving the good life. Each of the commentators confirmed that the good life was captured in the concept of the common good, and moreover that this good could be best achieved through leaders and the people practicing civic virtue. As we have seen, what made this more problematic in republics was the fact that this expectation extended to the people, who often failed to meet the required standard.

What is the Epistemology of Leadership?

Given the commitment to the common good, the classical republicans – just like Plato and Aquinas – had to conceive of some method by which society could determine whether or not this good had been achieved. In this the republicans again modeled the traditional approach: they still relied upon leaders patterned after the classical ideal to determine the common good and how to achieve it, supplemented by the rule of law.

It is worthy of noting, however, that in republican theory the rule of law took on a subtly different role as an independent standard to assure actions in pursuance of the common good. In Plato's writings, it will be recalled, the rule of law was called upon as a substitute in situations when the desired type of leader could not be secured. It retained this aspect for the republicans, but now it was also a method of keeping in check the people, who now had some role in government. There thus came to be championed the notion of 'the rule of law, and not of men'. It will also be recalled that only with the writings of James Harrington did we see an acknowledgment of the fact that this, too, remained problematic, since the law was made by men and thus was not intrinsically neutral. We will review Harrington's solution in our response to the final question of this protocol.

What is the Role of the Leader?

While, as we have seen, the classical republicans took a more positive view of the people than had the other traditional political theorists, all agreed that a sufficiently virtuous citizenry was unlikely. Moreover, even with the best of citizens, good leaders would still be needed; as Machiavelli put it, 'a multitude needs a head'. Given the need for leaders, the classical republicans called for those that met precisely the same criteria that we have seen articulated by other theorists: wisdom, civic virtue, a sense of justice and a willingness to work for the good of the people. It was, in sum, the classical ideal of the leader.

One contribution the republican commentators did make was to develop a way of identifying appropriate leaders. Plato, it will be recalled, devised an elaborate educational system that culminated in philosopher kings. The republicans also held open the possibility that anyone could become a member of the necessary 'aristocracy of merit', but each believed that property ownership served as an appropriate indicator of the necessary skills. This was not because wealth was valued *per se*, but because men of property had the necessary independence from want to exhibit civic virtue, and also the leisure necessary to rule.

Once the matter of who should become leaders was determined, the classical republican depiction of the leaders' duties tracked quite closely the discussion of other traditional theorists. Such leaders were expected to use their superior wisdom and virtue to act in the interests of the people. The extent of the reliance upon leader expertise is made evident by those situations in which these theorists (particularly Machiavelli and Harrington) were willing to leave leaders unfettered in times of crisis and at the creation of republics.

What is the Role of the People?

Given the continued reliance upon leaders, one of the republicans' more intriguing challenges was delineating the role of followers. After all, by definition republics involved some participation by the people, but the fact remained that none of the commentators were friends of democracy. Faced with this dilemma, each of the theorists under study took a slightly differing tack.

Given his concern about the potential evils of rule by the people, in which he often parroted Plato, Aristotle's initial solution was to limit popular participation to a narrowly defined group of individuals who were likely to display the necessary civic virtues. Accordingly, all 'citizens' needed to have a certain amount of property, with all the civic advantages that accompanied such ownership. 'The best city', he intoned, 'will not make a vulgar person a citizen'. Even with the meticulous screening of popular participation, Aristotle carefully delimited the role of popular involvement to 'deliberating and adjudicating'. Those aspects of ruling that required more foresight and skill were reserved for leaders.

Machiavelli, for his part, also allocated a limited role for the people, even though he held their wisdom (taken as a whole) in rather high esteem. One of the great elements of that wisdom, after all, was their willingness to choose and follow men of higher wisdom and virtue. In times when the polity was under stress, Machiavelli allocated an even smaller role to the people, and instead vested virtually unlimited authority in leaders. Even in more normal times, he sought to limit them through the rule of law. Thus Machiavelli tried to walk the thin line between permitting popular participation and restricting its dangerous tendencies. In this, he confronted the dilemma that has ever after haunted proponents of popular government.

James Harrington moved the farthest toward popular participation, and in doing so he can be viewed as a transitional figure in our narration of the development of popular sovereignty. Harrington expanded the electorate and required the people's overt consent to policies of state. Still, he carefully delimited the role of the people (the 'fourteen' in his parable of the fourteen and the six) to the Aristotelian role of deliberation (in Harringtonian terms, 'deciding'). He also did Aristotle one better by setting up a mechanism – the equal 'agrarian', or redistribution of property – that ensured citizens of appropriate virtue.

Taken together, we see in these republican commentators a sincere effort to reconcile some of the tensions posed by the continued adherence to leaders of the classical ideal in regimes characterized by the participation of the people. A part of that apparent tension was dissipated by the expected relations between leaders and the people.

How Should Leaders and the People Interact?

The most important element of the relations between leaders and the people in classical republican theory was the continued expectation that general citizens would defer to their betters, that is, their leaders. This assumption was so pervasive as to go almost unspoken, although each of the commentators made the point clearly. This expectation of deference to one's betters (leaders) is perhaps the single defining distinction between classical republics and modern democracy. It continued more or less unabated in the works of each of our commentators.

The one partial exception – and it is an exception that would take on considerable significance – could be found in the writings of Harrington. There, it will be recalled, *all* members of the polity played an equal, if distinct, role: the aristocracy of merit hammered out policy, and the common people had to approve it. In this ingenious system, the many still deferred to the few in traditional ways, but, perforce, the few also had to defer to the many. The system was set up to take advantage of the respective advantages of each group – the wisdom of the few, and the sense of the common interest that was the province of the many. This division of labor continues to hold promise for the challenges of modern democracy.

Although little remarked at the time, one other element of Harrington's writings held considerable portent for the future. It had to do with his concept of representation. To the extent that the leaders of the classical republics of Aristotle and Machiavelli could be deemed to be 'representatives' of the people, they were representatives of the *trustee* type. That is, these representatives were acknowledged to be somehow better and wiser than the constituents they represented, and were expected to utilize that superiority on behalf of the whole. This view of representation survived intact in Harrington's conception of the elite senate, but quite a different view emerged in his assembly of the people. This was a representative body created purely out of necessity: the entire populace could not meet to transact business. But because it was intended to act as a proxy for the whole people, its members were not expected to be or act differently from their constituents. These representatives were *delegates*. This distinction would figure in many future attempts to create governments grounded in the sovereignty of the people.

How is the Matter of Diversity and Minority Interests Addressed?

In our analysis of the emergence of the classical ideal in monarchical states, we noted that the issues of diversity and the interests of minorities were rarely a consideration. They were either defined away, or simply transformed, as in Plato's case, into rigidly construed hierarchies (those with courage were soldiers and so on). Moreover, the very notion of a 'common good' militated against any sense of divergent interests. Many of the same dynamics operated in the thinking of the classical republicans. The membership of the polity was often rigidly controlled (Aristotle), or homogeneity was assumed (Machiavelli), or forcibly created (Harrington's redistribution schemes). Moreover, the conception of a good that was truly common still held sway.

However, it is also worthy of note that these classical republicans also perceived the possibility of a tyranny of the majority, and in this sense, by implication, recognized the existence of opposing interests. Plato had acknowledged similar concerns in decrying democracy, but the matter was much more immediate for those contemplating states with popular participation. The resolution, however, was fairly simple: the classical republicans simply distinguished the will of the majority from the common good, and relied upon leaders of the classical ideal to ensure that the latter triumphed over the former. It was not until more modern times that such issues occupied theorists' serious attention.

What Institutions and Processes Must be Developed to Accommodate the Premises and Assumptions about Leadership Articulated in the Responses to the Leadership Template?

Again, this is a summary question, and it is not necessary to do more than highlight the strategies proposed by our commentators, already discussed in some detail. In response to the challenge of creating a polity dedicated to rule by leaders of the classical ideal in regimes that also had popular participation, each of our theorists devised creative solutions.

Structurally, Aristotle sought to resolve the age-old cycle of declension among the various constitutional forms by creating a mixed polity, although his 'mix' involved chiefly economic classes. A polity, he argued, must have participation from the two classes of rich and the poor, to offset the evils of each. The real key, however, was the predominance of the 'middling sort', those possessed of just enough property to have independence and virtue. (Although he did not go so far as to ensure this through any kind of redistributional mechanism, we will see that Harrington would). In Aristotle's efforts to assure the proper influence of the appropriate leaders, he established a two-tiered mechanism wherein all (citizens) would vote for leaders, but only those with the requisite property qualifications could actually serve. Thereafter, the leaders handled policy making, while the people were restricted to deliberating upon elite initiatives and adjudicating. Like most in the early tradition of political theorizing in the West, he also held out a role for the rule of law as a structural constraint upon all participants.

Machiavelli advocated a similar mixed regime, although it was more influenced by the Roman example of Consuls, Senate and Tribunes. In truth, Machiavelli did not devote a great deal of attention to the specifics of structuring the polity, although he, too, placed considerable reliance upon the benefits conferred by the rule of law.

Harrington, as we have seen, erected the most elaborate political structure to assure the achievement of his leadership goals, creating an innovative political mechanism that both ensured leaders patterned after the classical ideal and the benefits of popular participation. To achieve his objective of a virtuous citizenry, his state required widespread land ownership. He was, however, no enemy of elite leadership. His elaborate utopia named Oceana depended upon the wisdom and the initiative of such leaders in its senate. That body, it will be recalled, was made up only of the elite (the 'horse'), and was indirectly elected. Even the popular assembly had only a plurality of four common property holders (the 'foot') to every three of the elite.

While Aristotle and Machiavelli well represent the ideas of the powerful republican tradition, it was Harrington who was the most ingenious in a structural sense. His willingness to redistribute wealth (and therefore power) to achieve desired ends, his specific inclusion of all the people in every major policy decision, his innovative attempt to tap the wisdom of the better sort (an elitist approach) as well as the good sense of the people (a participationist approach), and his marriage of differing conceptions of representation, mark James Harrington as one of our most important sources of inspiration as we continue to confront the challenges of leadership in a democracy.

TOWARD A NEW IMPLICIT THEORY AND A NEW FICTION

During the course of this chapter, we have continued to trace the evolution of the classical ideal of the leader – the fiction that the leader of society must be wise, virtuous and serve for the common good. Having traced the emergence of the fiction in essentially monarchical states, this chapter looked to its manifestation in republics. The trilogy of writers treated in this chapter remained firmly within the tradition of the classical ideal. Each believed that the state must be led by men of wisdom and virtue, who always keep the general good in mind. However, these commentators faced the additional burden of applying the classical ideal to states characterized by popular participation.

These writers succeeded in inventing regimes that permitted popular participation, but the implications of their work went far beyond this. In justifying their states, these classical republican writers lifted the conception and the role of the people to new levels. Aristotle and Machiavelli had composed rhetoric about the virtues of the people, a rhetoric that amounted to a new implicit theory about their capabilities. Gone were the contempt and derision of Plato, to be replaced by a new, if qualified, respect for the people. Harrington built upon this new assumption about the nature of the people to create a new role for them, a state that truly relied upon the people, working with their natural leaders to secure the common good.

This new implicit theory regarding the people eventually gave rise to a new fiction – the fiction of the people. The invention of this fiction of the people served as the antithesis to our thesis of the leader, and eventually would lead to a synthesis we call leadership. It is to the development of this new fiction that we now turn.

NOTES

1. Forrest E. Baird and Walter Kaufmann, 'Aristotle', in Baird and Kaufmann, eds., *Ancient Philosophy* 3rd edn. (Upper Saddle River, N.J.: Prentice Hall, 2000), 305; Carnes Lord, Introduction to Aristotle, *The Politics*,

trans. Carnes Lord (Chicago: University of Chicago Press, 1984), 23–24; Harry C. Mansfield and Nathan Tarcov, Introduction to Machiavelli, *Discourses on Livy,* trans. Mansfield and Tarcov (Chicago: University of Chicago Press, 1996), xxvii; J.G.A. Pocock, 'Machiavelli, Harrington, and English Political Ideologies of the Eighteenth Century', *William and Mary Quarterly,* 3rd ser., 22 (1965): 551, 555–556, 567, 569; *see* Pocock, *The Machiavellian Moment: Florentine Political Thought and the Atlantic Republican Tradition* (Princeton: Princeton University Press, 1975).

2. Baird and Kaufmann, 'Aristotle', 305.
3. Aristotle, *Politics,* trans. Carnes Lord (Chicago: University of Chicago Press, 1989), 1264b, 10–13; 1261a, 8–10, 35–40; 1261b, 1; 1313a, 2–8. Note that citations to Aristotle's work follow the universal notation first used by Immanuel Bekker in 1831, and refer to pages, columns and lines, respectively.
4. Lord, Introduction to Aristotle, *The Politics,* 1; James M. Blythe, Introduction to Thomas Aquinas, *On the Government of Rulers,* trans. James M. Blythe (Philadelphia: University of Pennsylvania Press, 1997), 19.
5. Aristotle, *Politics,* 1253a, 1–3, 30–40; 1255b, 17–20; 1274b, 30–42; 1275b, 16–18.
6. Ibid., 1252a, 1–6.
7. Ibid., 1280a, 31–32; 1280b, 40; 1281a, 1–3; 1252b, 28–30.
8. Ibid., 1280b, 6–7; 1282b, 14–17.
9. Ibid., 1279a, 16–19, 27–31.
10. Ibid., 1279a, 33–38; 1279b, 4–10; 1289a, 25–30.
11. *See,* for example, ibid., 1295a, 15–25; 1307a, 6–9.
12. Ibid., 1288b, 35–40.
13. Ibid., 1318a, 18–33.
14. Ibid., 1281a, 10–38.
15. Ibid., 1318a, 18–33; 1270b, 20–23.
16. Lord, Introduction to Aristotle, *Politics,* 19 (see note 3).
17. Aristotle, *Politics,* 1295a, 25–38. His reference is to Aristotle, *The Nichomachean Ethics,* 1101a, 14–16.
18. Aristotle, *Politics,* 1295a, 33–40; 1295b, 1–40.
19. Ibid., 1295b, 35–42; 1296a, 1–20; 1296b, 15–40; 1297a, 5–10.
20. Ibid., 1273a, 25–26, 38–43; 1273b, 1; 1267a, 1–2, 7–13, 36–45; 1267b, 1–8.
21. Ibid., 1281a, 40–45; 1281b, 15–17, 20–21.
22. Ibid., 1317b, 37–40.
23. Ibid., 1317a, 37–42; 1317b, 1–17; 1310a, 25–39.
24. Ibid.
25. Ibid., 1304b, 20–25.
26. Ibid., 1313b, 38–42; 1314a, 1–2.
27. Ibid., 1281b, 15–17, 20–21.
28. Ibid., 1276b, 18–20, 27–30.
29. Ibid., 1277a, 25–31.
30. Ibid., 1277b, 33–35; 1278a, 7–8.
31. Pocock, 'Machiavelli, Harrington, and English Political Ideologies of the Eighteenth Century', 581 (see note 1).
32. Aristotle, *Politics,* 1279a, 38–41.
33. Ibid., 1283b, 1–10.
34. Ibid., 1284a, 1–15.
35. Ibid., 1309a, 32–35.
36. Ibid., 1291a, 35–40; 1291b, 1–5.
37. Ibid., 1273b, 3.
38. Ibid., 1273a, 25–26.
39. Ibid., 1291b, 23–28.
40. Ibid., 1274a, 15–22.
41. Ibid., 1267b, 1–8.
42. Ibid., 1281b, 22–34.
43. Ibid., 1297b, 35–41; 1298a, 1–3.
44. Ibid., 1273b, 28–43; 1274a, 1–22.
45. Ibid., 1281b, 22–34.
46. Ibid., 1298a, 3–8; 1298b, 37–40; 1318b, 27–35.
47. Ibid., 1267b, 1–8.
48. Ibid., 1277b, 7–17.
49. Ibid., 1277a, 13–16, 23–24.
50. Ibid., 1277b, 25–29.
51. Ibid., 1260a, 15–19.

52. Ibid., 1279a, 7–13.
53. Ibid., 1277b, 7–17.
54. Aristotle, *A Treatise on Government*, trans. William Ellis (London: J.M. Dent & Sons, 1900), 226–27.
55. Aristotle, *Politics*, 1259b, 30–40; 1260a, 1–8.
56. Ibid., 1287a, 25–35; 1287b, 1–10.
57. Ibid., 1270b, 27–30; 1272a, 36–39; 1272b, 5–8.
58. Ibid., 1269a, 8–18.
59. Ibid., 1292a, 30–40.
60. Ibid., 1292a, 1–40.
61. Ibid., 1292b, 5–10.
62. Harry C. Mansfield and Nathan Tarcov, Introduction to Machiavelli, *Discourses on Livy*, xix (see note 1).
63. *See generally* Pocock, *The Machiavellian Moment: Florentine Political Thought and the Atlantic Republican Tradition* (see note 1).
64. The official title is *Discourses on the First Ten Books of Titus Livy,* or sometimes *Discourses on the First Decade of Titus Livius*, although all versions of the title are commonly abbreviated to *Discourses on Livy*, or simply *Discourses.*
65. Mansfield and Tarcov, Introduction to Machiavelli, *Discourses on Livy*, xx (see note 1).
66. Niccolo Machiavelli, *Discourses on the First Decade of Titus Livius*, in Machiavelli, *The Chief Works and Others*, trans. Allan Gilbert (Durham, NC: Duke University Press, 1965), I, Preface; I, 39. Note the citation will be in the universal format of citing by book and chapter.
67. Ibid., II. 2.
68. Ibid., I. 2.
69. Ibid., III. 28.
70. Ibid., I. 2.
71. Ibid., II. 2. *See,* for example, Friedrich Nietzsche, *On the Genealogy of Morality*, ed. Keith Ansell-Pearson, trans. Carol Diethe (Cambridge: Cambridge University Press, 1994). Machiavelli was not opposed to conflict in the pursuit of liberty, but it must be understood that the freedom that he espoused was not the liberty of anarchy, but the ordered liberty to be found in a mixed regime under the rule of law. *See* Machiavelli, *Discourses*, I. 4; II. 24.
72. Machiavelli, *Discourses,* I. 2.
73. Ibid.
74. For a discussion of the superiority of republics, *see* ibid., II. 2; III. 9.
75. *See* ibid., I. 3; I. 57; II. 22; III. 16. One of the remedies was the actions of the leader. *See* the discussion below.
76. Machiavelli, *Discourses*, I. 58.
77. Ibid.
78. Ibid.
79. Ibid.
80. Ibid., I. 3.
81. Ibid., I. 24; I. 40; I. 42.
82. Ibid., I. 3.
83. Ibid., I. 46.
84. Ibid., I. 7.
85. Ibid., I. 18.
86. Ibid., I. 45.
87. Ibid., I. 58.
88. Ibid., I. 16; I. 24.
89. Ibid., I. 38; I. 44.
90. Ibid., II. 21.
91. Ibid., II. 13.
92. Ibid., III. 25.
93. Ibid., III. 31.
94. Ibid., III. 30; III. 22.
95. Ibid., III. 34.
96. Ibid., I. 9.
97. Ibid.
98. Ibid.
99. Ibid., I. 18.
100. Ibid., I. 10.
101. Ibid., I. 33.

102. Ibid., I. 34.
103. Ibid.
104. Ibid.
105. Ibid.
106. Ibid., I. 35.
107. Ibid., I. 34.
108. Ibid., I. 18.
109. Ibid., I. 49; III. 8.
110. Ibid., III. 1; III. 8.
111. Mansfield and Tarcov, Introduction to Machiavelli, *Discourses on Livy*, xxiv (see note 1).
112. Ibid., xxv.
113. Machiavelli, *Discourses*, I. 18.
114. Ibid., I. 55.
115. Ibid., I. 17.
116. Ibid., I. 17–18.
117. Ibid., I. 53.
118. Ibid., II. 22.
119. Ibid., I. 4.
120. Ibid., I. 54, 58.
121. Ibid., I. 58.
122. Ibid., I. 4, 54.
123. Ibid., I. 58.
124. Ibid., III. 16.
125. Ibid., I. 58.
126. Ibid., I. 47.
127. Ibid.
128. J.G.A. Pocock, 'Machiavelli, Harrington, and English Political Ideologies of the Eighteenth Century', *William and Mary Quarterly* 22 (4): 551–552, 569; Pocock, Introduction to James Harrington, *The Political Works of James Harrington* (Cambridge: Cambridge University Press, 1977), 15.
129. Pocock, Introduction, 15, 42; Edmund S. Morgan, *Inventing the People: The Rise of Popular Sovereignty in England and America* (New York: W.W. Norton & Company, 1988), 85, 157.
130. Morgan, *Inventing the People*, 129–130.
131. Bernard Bailyn, *The Ideological Origins of the American Revolution* (Cambridge: Belknap Press of Harvard University Press, 1967), 34–35, and *passim. See also* Pocock, 'Machiavelli, Harrington, and English Political Ideologies of the Eighteenth Century', 573, and *passim* (see note 128).
132. Morgan, *Inventing the People*, 86 (see note 129).
133. Ibid., 286; *See* Douglass Adair, '"That Politics May be Reduced to a Science": David Hume, James Madison, and the Tenth Federalist', *Huntington Library Quarterly* 20 (1957): 343–360.
134. James Harrington, *The Commonwealth of Oceana*, in Harrington, *The Political Works of James Harrington*, ed. J.G.A. Pocock (Cambridge: Cambridge University Press, 1977), 161, 169.
135. Ibid., 162.
136. Ibid., 272.
137. Ibid., 161, 170.
138. Ibid., 171.
139. Ibid., 163–164.
140. Ibid., 194–198. *See also* Morgan, *Inventing the People*, 155–156 (see note 129).
141. Harrington, *Oceana*, 170, 199.
142. Ibid., 171–172.
143. Ibid., 202.
144. Ibid., 164, 181.
145. Ibid., 172.
146. Ibid., 182.
147. Ibid., 172.
148. Ibid., 172–173.
149. Ibid., 280–281.
150. Ibid., 173.
151. *See* discussion in Pocock, Introduction to James Harrington, especially at 66–67 (see note 128).
152. Harrington, *Oceana*, 213.
153. Ibid., 258–259.
154. Ibid., 173.

155. For a brief summation of the institutional essence of Harrington's complex model, *see* his 'Epitome of the Whole Commonwealth', found in Harrington, *Oceana*, 333–337. *See also* Harrington, *Brief Directions Showing How a Fit and Perfect Model of Popular Government May Be Made, or Understood*, in Harrington, *The Political Work of James Harrington*, ed. J.G.A. Pocock (Cambridge: Cambridge University Press, 1977), 583–598.
156. Harrington, *Oceana*, 173.
157. Ibid.
158. Harrington, *Brief Directions*, 596.
159. Harrington, *Oceana*, 335–336.
160. Ibid., 174, 181.
161. Ibid., 274–275.
162. Ibid., 276, 278.
163. Ibid., 206–207.
164. Ibid., 257.
165. Ibid., 167.
166. Pocock, Introduction to James Harrington, 68 (see note 128).
167. Harrington, *Oceana*, 284.
168. Ibid., 182.
169. Morgan, *Inventing the People*, 156 (see note 129).
170. Pocock,, 'Machiavelli, Harrington, and the English Political Ideologies of the Eighteenth Century', 556 (see note 128).
171. Harrington, *Oceana*, 173, 279–280.
172. Pocock, Introduction to James Harrington, 65–67 (see note 128).
173. Ibid., 67.
174. Harrington, *Oceana*, 268.
175. Ibid., 173.
176. Ibid., 183.
177. Pocock, Introduction to James Harrington, 107 (see note 128).

PART II

Inventing the People

3. A new conception of the people

With his careful attention to the role of the people in an ideal state, James Harrington was an important contributor to the emergence of a second fiction that has come to dominate Western conceptions of societal governance. This fiction – 'the people' – is now the fundamental and unquestioned desideratum of democracies. In their seminal document establishing a regime grounded in a conception of the people, the American Founding Fathers appended a preface indicating that the new system actually stemmed from this wellspring of governmental legitimacy. '*We the People* of the United States, in Order to form a more perfect Union', they wrote, '… do ordain and establish this Constitution for the United States of America.'[1] A few generations later, in the midst of one of the great challenges to the viability of such an undertaking, President Abraham Lincoln felt compelled in his Gettysburg Address to articulate the fundamental organizing principle of American government and the underlying objective of the American Civil War: 'that government of the people, by the people, for the people, shall not perish from the earth'.[2]

This 'fiction' of 'the people' is such a commonplace today that few recognize its fictional status (much like Kuhnian paradigms, fictions firmly entrenched appear as simple reality). It may come as a surprise to some that the construct of 'the people' is of relatively recent origin. Clearly such observers as Aristotle and Machiavelli had some sense of an entity that could be labeled 'the people', but the notion of the people as the constitutive element of government came much later. Indeed it can be said that the fiction of the people arose from the political vortex that was seventeenth- and eighteenth-century England and America. Moreover, the ideal of 'the people' has been anything but static. It has indeed proven to be a protean concept that continues to evolve down to the present day.

This segment of our study will trace the emergence and permutations of this notion of 'the people'. It is, we will find, a story of some complexity, and a fiction containing many nuances with implications for democratic leadership. While the consideration of our initial fiction, the classical ideal of the leader, necessitated a careful parsing of the seminal works that embodied that fiction, we are fortunate to be graced with excellent studies of the phenomenon of the people. Two award-winning studies in particular will serve as our guide. The first is the monograph that, more than any other, inspired this study as a whole. Historian Edmund S. Morgan, in his *Inventing the People: The Rise of Popular Sovereignty in England and America*,[3] not only introduces the interpretive vehicle of the fiction, but also provides a superb narrative of the rise of one particular fiction: the people. Morgan's study ends at the founding of the American republic. Another study, this one by a contemporary political scientist, rounds out our analysis. James A. Morone's *The Democratic Wish: Popular Participation and the Limits of American Government*[4] serves as the inspiration for our tracing of the subsequent dynamics of the fiction of the people.

These two works, together with the interpretive gloss provided by the author of this volume, will place the emerging fiction of the people within the framework of this study and should lead, ultimately, to a more sophisticated understanding of leadership in a democracy.

THE EMERGENCE OF 'THE PEOPLE'

Edmund Morgan, as indicated above, is one of the few authors relied upon in this volume who specifically frames his analysis in terms of 'fictions' (interestingly, James Morone, the other inspiration for this chapter on the people, is the other). Morgan's work thus fits nicely within our ongoing analysis. Let us trace his argument.

Morgan begins his exploration of the emergence of the fiction of the people by looking to the fiction that preceded it.[5] That fiction, which might be called 'the divine right of kings', dominated England until well into the seventeenth century. Like all successful fictions, there were sound reasons for its emergence and longevity. For one thing, it was a way of making sense of reality: England (and most of the rest of Europe) had been ruled by hereditary monarchies for centuries, and the divine right explanation served the interests of both leaders and followers in maintaining stability. England, argues Morgan, had a more specific reason for embracing divine monarchy. It stemmed from the Englishman's unreasoning hatred of Catholicism. A king with the imprimatur of God, so the reasoning went, could stand on a plane of equality with the pope.[6]

This divine monarch, however powerful, had certain expectations placed upon him. Part of being 'divine' entailed acting toward subjects in a manner entirely recognizable as akin to the classical ideal of the leader. It was a fiction embraced by all parties. 'The king, 'says Morgan, 'proclaimed himself as the source of all law and the giver of all good things.' His subjects were eager to believe that 'the king is wise and good'. As Morgan summarized it, 'the king in his body politic always wanted what was best for his subjects'. And, because 'God's lieutenant could do no wrong', England had a more than fair facsimile of the classical ideal.[7]

In the event, it was this expectation of flawless leading that contributed to the emergence of a new fiction. This new fiction emerged, as most do, in response to a disparity between the ideal of the previous fiction and the reality that confronted it. In England in the seventeenth century, there arose a group of men who, for their own personal interests, were more than willing to utilize this disparity to challenge existing power relations.

The fiction of the divine right of kings contained two components. 'The first', as we have seen, 'was that God's lieutenant could do no wrong; the second was that every one else ... was a mere subject.'[8] The problem was that in seventeenth-century England neither leaders nor followers fit the ideal. Even the most rudimentary knowledge of English history makes it clear that the early Stuart kings, James I and Charles I, were a far cry from the perfection expected of a leader. James I headed a corrupt and, most thought, immoral court, and created a contentious relationship with a series of Parliaments as he consistently sought to free himself from fiscal dependence upon that body through novel approaches to taxation and revenue. Charles I was much more threatening. He fostered innovations in finance, administration and religion. His imposition of new taxes and novel ways of collecting traditional ones without the consent of Parliament were seen as unconstitutional. His appointed administrators were perceived as corrupt and evil, his royal judges biased against the rights of the people. Charles sought, through the hated Archbishop Laud, to introduce Arminianism into the Church of England, which many interpreted as a move toward even more hated Catholicism. When Charles I tired of his dealings with a recalcitrant Parliament, he simply dissolved it, and ruled without Parliament for eleven years. As a result of all this, few subjects concluded that either monarch was acting in the best interests of the whole, as the classical ideal required.

If the fiction did not match the reality with respect to the leaders, neither did the followers act like the submissive and obedient subjects the fiction demanded. Members of Parliament in particular posed a challenge for the traditional way of thinking. The institution of Parliament itself was problematic. It was an institution in which a group of elite men represented the remainder of the population in important governmental functions. Parliament thus held some sort of intermediary standing in the leader–follower constellation that was itself difficult to assimilate into a fiction calling for all subjects to be subservient to the king.[9] This was exacerbated by the actions of the members of Parliament during the first half of the seventeenth century. As the early Stuart kings sought to implement their policies, members of Parliament took a series of decidedly non-subservient actions in their attempts to rein in the kings and their ministers. These included the passage of a Petition of Right asserting legal and political guarantees to the followers, limitations on the king's right to rule without Parliament, impeachments and bills of attainder (in effect the legislative conviction and execution) of the king's ministers, rising in arms against the king, and ultimately beheading Charles I.

With a reality such as this confronting the ideal of an all-knowing and benevolent monarch ruling over happily subservient subjects, it is small surprise that the divine right of kings had a difficult time maintaining itself as the dominant fiction of England in the mid-seventeenth century. As Morgan puts it, by the 1640s 'the charade could no longer be sustained. The fictions of divine right and the subjection of subjects had been strained too far, not only by the king but by the Commons themselves.' Indeed, in the challenges that the House of Commons eventually raised against the king, 'the Commons had elevated themselves to the point where they were contending with the king less as subjects than as rivals. And that kind of contest', asserts Morgan, 'could not be conducted under the old ground rules.' From this derived the logical conclusion that was to serve as the basis for a new fiction. The reality of the conflict between king and Commons in the 1640s 'required a transfer of divine sanction from the king to his people and their representatives'. As Morgan sums it up, 'The divine right of kings had never been more than a fiction, and … it led to the fiction that replaced it, the sovereignty of the people'. And, although it was to take considerably more time amid considerable complexity, this new ideal 'made way, indeed, for the new fictions of a world where all men are created equal and governments derive their powers from those who govern'.[10]

Morgan suggests that the key formative period of the notion of the people in governing was during the time of the English Civil War and the Interregnum, that period when England was ruled without a king.[11] This era, stretching from 1640 to 1660, was a time of considerable intellectual ferment that accompanied the roiling political and social scene. Not only did the major players like members of Parliament seek to find a new justification for government, but this period was also a fertile time for extremely radical ideas in the social and religious spheres. Some of the ideas that will become a part of this story came from the radical fringe of English intellectual life. Intriguingly, some ideas that were too radical for England in the seventeenth century took root in America in the eighteenth and nineteenth centuries.

As the resistance to the king unfolded in the 1640s, an intellectual challenge presented itself to those seeking to rein in Charles I. As Morgan phrases it, 'the fictions that centered in the divine right of kings were not adequate to support the challenge that Parliament was now mounting to the king's authority. A new ideology, a new rationale, a new set of fictions was necessary to justify a government in which the authority of kings stood below that of the people or their representatives.'[12] As is often the case, new fictions grow out of – or are made to *seem* to grow out of – something that had been believed in the past. So it was with the emerging fiction that power resides in the people. 'Revolutions in thought', says Morgan, 'frequently take the forms of shifts of emphasis, with old ideas not repudiated, but put to new uses.' In the case of England, 'the old ideology of divine right had not generally excluded the people from a nominal role in the creation of kings. Some vague sort of popular consent or choice in the distant past, renewed from time to time in the coronation ceremony, was at least implied…. The origin of English government could thus be placed in the actions of Englishmen themselves in a comfortably distant and nebulous past.' As a result, 'it was not necessary … for the supporters of Parliament against Charles I to invent a popular basis for government, but simply to expand and make more explicit the supposed role of the people in originating and defining government'.[13] In the hurly-burly of a very real contest for control of England, then, the Parliamentary leaders made a quite logical – to them – extension of a previous fiction.

Perhaps the clearest articulation of the new wrinkle on an old fiction came from Parliamentarian Henry Parker. Parker 'envisioned a nation that existed before it had a king or any other governing officer'. In this state of nature, 'the people of the nation, exercising their God-given powers, chose to be governed by kings in hereditary succession (they might have chosen any other form of government)'.[14] When the early Stuart kings had abused the power thus conferred upon them by the people, 'the people through their representatives could rightly resist him and in the last resort depose him'.[15] The new polity that was to be established – what this would be was unclear and the subject of much debate – would thus derive from the authority of the people.

Of course all of this was a fiction – the putative state of nature and the popular determination to overthrow the king. Morgan acknowledges that 'the new Parliamentary fictions strained credulity as much as the old. The divine right of kings had emphasized the divine character of the king's authority without giving much attention to the act in which God was supposed to have commissioned him.' In the same vein, 'the sovereignty of the people, emphasizing the popular character of governmental authority, rested on supposed acts of the people, both past and present, that were almost as difficult to examine as acts of God'. Indeed, Morgan argues, 'The very existence of such a thing as *the* people, capable of acting to empower, define, and limit a previously nonexistent government required a suspension of disbelief. History recorded no such action.' But this was beside the point. 'The impossibility of empirical demonstration is a necessary characteristic of political fictions', explains Morgan. 'In the absence of historical record Parker and his friends could reconstruct the original donation of the people in terms that gave to Parliament a determining power in its dispute with the king.'[16]

This analysis raises the question of why such an obvious invention out of whole cloth could have prevailed. The answer is complex. In point of fact, there was a wide array of responses to the Parliamentary initiative, and each of them, in its own way, contributed to the ultimate understanding of the fiction of the people. Some individuals, of course, opposed the whole notion of government stemming from the people. The Royalists in particular sought to discredit the idea of Parliament sitting as leaders of a sovereign people. Their strategy was to undercut Parliament's argument by taking the notion of popular sovereignty to its logical extreme, and thereby to make the fiction so unattractive that no self-respecting elite leader could agree to it. The Royalists first attacked the very notion of 'the people'. How could such an entity be defined? Taking Parliamentary rhetoric to its logical conclusion, the 'people' should include both women and children! And even if one could define who constituted this body called the people, it would nonetheless remain impossible ever to decipher the 'will' of the people. To ground a government upon such ephemera was ludicrous. And if even this difficulty were negotiated, if, that is, some way was found to distill the will of the people, this still did not ensure the Parliamentary conclusions. If, argued the Royalists, the people *did* have the power to place Parliament at the head of government, those same people could also opt to *remove* Parliament, and even return to kingly rule![17]

The Royalist objections to popular rule haunt it still, and a goodly portion of our later discussion will be devoted to addressing such issues. This attack exposed the 'soft underbelly' of the Parliamentary position on two counts. First, for all their rhetoric about government being grounded in the people, the Parliamentarians meant nothing of the sort. Their intent in inventing the new fiction was to use it as a weapon against the king. 'The immediate objective of the change in fictions', explains Morgan, 'was to magnify the power not of the people themselves, but of the people's representatives', that is, Parliament. This was entirely a debate among elites; 'it did not originate in popular demonstrations against the king, but in the contest between king and Parliament'.[18] 'In endowing the people with supreme authority', Morgan concludes, '... Parliament intended only to endow itself.'[19] In other words, Parliament was quite happy to use the fiction of the people to justify its own rule, but it had no intention of using the logic of its own argument actually to grant real power away from itself and to the people. As Morgan put it, 'Although the new ideology might safely encourage a greater degree of popular participation in government than the old, its purpose was the same, to persuade the many to submit to the government of the few. It would not do to encourage the unruly to shelter under an illusion that they were the people.'[20] This disparity between rhetoric and reality eventually would create a dynamic that carried notions of 'the people' to new heights, but that result still lay in the future.

Even more threatening to the Parliamentarians at the time, however, was the Royalist charge asserting the ability of the people to overthrow even Parliament as their leaders. This charge hit home, because by the late 1640s, in all probability, most common Englishmen probably *did* want the king to remain in power. Indeed, just as the Parliamentary leaders were espousing their place as representing the will of the people most vociferously, precisely the opposite was the case. This requires, perhaps, some explanation. When Charles I had abused many of the perceived rights of Englishmen in the 1620s and 1630s, and when he seemed to be moving the Church toward Catholicism, it is probably safe to say that most of the English people sided with Parliamentary efforts to rein him in. But over the course of the 1640s Parliament became more and more radical – placing unheard of restraints on the king, killing his chief ministers, waging war on the king, trying to impose their brand of religion upon England, and ultimately, killing the king. At each more radical turn, more Englishmen could not stomach the Parliamentary action, and dropped their support. By 1649, popular support for Parliament had largely dissipated.

Confronted on the theoretical front by Royalists and with perceived dissension from below, Parliamentary proponents responded with an argument that contained ideological assumptions destined to have some significance. Polemicists rejected the very notion that Parliament could be acting against the interests of the people. 'Parliament', they said, 'was not simply the representative of the people, it *was* the people.' As a consequence, Parliament 'can do no wrong' and, while 'Kings seduced may injure the commonwealth … Parliament cannot'.[21] This perceived identity between representatives and the people would also loom large in the evolution of the character of popular sovereignty.

With its rhetoric of omniscience and concern with the good of the whole, Parliament seemed to be espousing yet one more version of the classical ideal. Unfortunately, the frame of reference of many Englishmen was not that of an ideal leader, but of Charles I at his worst. To many, Parliament with its articulation of government grounded in the people sounded suspiciously like the fiction it had replaced – the divine right of kings, where an unchecked cadre of leaders acted in ways seemingly contrary to the common good. In those years of intellectual ferment prior to 1660, it is not surprising that some radical writers attempted to shape the emerging fiction of popular sovereignty to move it closer to actual rule by the people, as well as to address the dilemma of how to control a government that claimed its imprimatur from the people.

Radical ideas were commonplace in those decades. There were social utopians, anarchists, religious extremists and many others giving vent to all manner of schemes and theories. Among them was one group of political activists and theorists who were to have a profound impact upon future conceptualizations of rule by the people. Although relegated to the footnotes of English history, the ideas of this group – the Levellers – were to take root in America.

The Levellers were a group of men closely connected to certain factions in the Parliamentary army during the latter stages of the Civil War. These men 'were committed to the supremacy of Parliament over the king', but, like many others, 'became increasingly discontented with the existing Parliament'.[22] They sought to 'set limits, in the name of the people, on what [Parliament] could do. They wanted not only to give more people a hand in electing Parliament but also to give *the* people a way of exercising their sovereignty outside Parliament and with a necessary superiority to Parliament.'[23] The most cogent and articulate expression of their ideas was expressed in the form of a proposed 'Agreement of the People'. That document contained many specific proposals, such as the elimination of the king and House of Lords, nearly universal suffrage, annual elections and proportional representation. 'To such a reformed House of Commons they would have given all the powers of the central government.'[24]

More important than any specific provision, however, was the concept embodied in the Agreement that the people stood apart from and superior to their representatives in Parliament. As the Agreement stated, the 'power of this and all future representatives of this nation is inferior only to theirs who choose them'.[25] In thus separating the people from the government – even though the government stemmed from the people – 'the Levellers indeed had identified the central problem of popular sovereignty, the problem of setting limits to a government that derived its authority from a people for whom it claimed the sole right to speak'.[26] The Levellers, then, agreed with the new idea expressed by the supporters of Parliament that ultimate power lay in the people; they had no argument with the premise of the new fiction. Nevertheless, they had seen this power abused by Parliament, and sought some manner of applying the fiction in a way that resolved the problem posed by the unlimited exercise of the people's power. Their solution of having 'the people' separate from, and superior to Parliament was then, their chief contribution to the evolving conception of government of the people.

The Levellers never really worked out just how the people might exercise some constraint upon the people's government. And, indeed, the solution was not really fully articulated until the Americans faced a similar problem in the 1770s and 1780s. Nevertheless, a few of the English radicals in the 1640s and 1650s took up the gauntlet, and suggested various ways in which government of the people could be held close to its source of authority. Although England never fully adopted any of these proposed solutions, they would become central to the American struggles with the same issue, and indeed, they have continued relevance in the ongoing effort to reconcile leadership and democracy.

The problem with government of the people as practiced by Parliament in the 1640s and 1650s is captured nicely by Morgan. 'By the 1650s,' Morgan writes, 'it was apparent that the new fiction, in the absence of a clear distinction between sovereign and subject, and in the absence of any higher expression of popular will, could endow an existing government with absolute and arbitrary powers beyond anything that England's kings had ever exercised.' This was because 'the new fictions, by placing authority and subjection, superiority and inferiority in the same hands, could deprive people, who were actually subjects, of effective control over a government that pretended to speak for them – a form of tyranny that popular sovereignty continues to bring to peoples all over the world.'[27] Morgan continues: 'What popular sovereignty did require, in the eyes at least of those who thought seriously about it, was a means by which some body or bodies capable of doing so could speak decisively and authentically for the people, so as to contain government … within the framework and the limits which that speaking body prescribed for it. It was widely acknowledged that the people could not speak for themselves – there were too many of them.'[28]

In searching for some mechanism for reining in arbitrary government allegedly based upon the people, various ideas were thrown about. Each of them, at one point or another, have factored into the American political experiment with popular government. Indeed, it was in this context that our friend James Harrington composed his chief works. Harrington tried to keep government close to the people by basing it upon widely-held land ownership, and ensuring that there would be an assembly that as nearly as possible reflected the people at large. This assembly, it will be recalled, was to approve all proposals put forward by an elite senate. Another approach was suggested by clergyman George Lawson. He sought to keep the government nearer to the people by emphasizing local institutions.[29]

It was Henry Vane, however, who hit upon the most significant tactic. Vane advocated what Morgan calls 'The People's Two Bodies'.[30] According to Vane's plan, the people would come together in one representative body as a 'constituent assembly' – we would call it a constitutional convention – to create the overarching framework of the government to be established. Subsequently, the people would elect a separate body – a legislature – to implement and execute that government. In other words, the people were to set the rules through their first 'body', and then rule through their second body. Vane's plan sounds almost like a gimmick, and perhaps it was; certainly when the Americans implemented it the same men were often elected to each body. At the same time, however, having a constituent body that met to set constraints upon the potential actions of the subsequent legislature and then dispersed did serve the purpose of placing restraints upon the popular assembly. As Morgan puts it, 'the idea of having an elected convention that would express enduring popular will in fundamental constitutions superior to government was a viable way of making popular creation and limitation of government believable. It was fictional,' he acknowledges, 'for it ascribed to one set of elected representatives meeting in convention a more popular character, and consequently a greater authority, than every subsequent set of representatives meeting as a legislature.' Nevertheless, this fiction that stemmed from the early grappling with problems associated by rule in a popular regime was to have enormous influence. 'It never came into use in England,' Morgan admits, 'but it was reinvented in the American Revolution.'[31]

As indicated, the ideas of Vane, the Levellers and others would become enormously important to the development of conceptions of rule by the people, but not in England, and not even in America until the Revolution and after. Before we turn to the American variety of popular sovereignty, however, we need to complete the story of popular sovereignty in England. It took a different form than would rule by the people in America, but it, too, became an important part of the American heritage, and continues to inform our discussions of leadership in popular regimes.

The distinctive aspect of the English version of popular sovereignty was its limited nature. The climax of the English saga (at least, that is, until the nineteenth century) lay in the events of the English Civil War and Interregnum and the subsequent reaction (some would say counter-revolution) to them. The culminating event was the Glorious Revolution of 1688–1689. This 'revolution' could be justified, and was, by such luminaries as John Locke, in terms of popular sovereignty. However, in so justifying this revolution, the revolutionaries were very careful not to take notions of popular sovereignty too far.[32]

To clarify, it is necessary to pick up again the thread of English history. We have already depicted in part the chaotic twenty years stretching from 1640 to 1660, with their civil wars, regicide, the experiment with Parliamentary dominance in the English Republic, and ultimately the dictatorship of Oliver Cromwell. In 1660, the people of England, vastly tired of strife, dissension and uncertain government, took the occasion of Cromwell's death to invite the son of Charles I to regain the throne of England. With the 'Restoration', as it came to be called, Charles II assumed the throne and a new page in English history turned.

It is safe to say that the English people were heartily sick of the dislocations of the preceding twenty years, many of which they blamed on their experiment with popular sovereignty. It *seemed*, at any rate, a time when the idea of government by the people should have been squelched. However, such was not to be the case. Although the concept of popular sovereignty continued to be tainted to a certain degree, circumstances remained that kept the notion alive. When a new crisis of governing arose as a result of the actions of the later Stuart kings, the idea of government stemming from the people became useful again. At that point, the notion of popular sovereignty emerged from its quiet eclipse. However, the radical possibilities bandied about in the 1640s and 1650s were shunned, and a much more 'cautious' approach ensued.[33]

Let us first turn our attention to the conditions that kept alive the idea of government stemming from the people. First was the continued presence of Parliament. Even in the years immediately after 1660, when the 'Cavalier Parliament' was exceedingly deferential to Charles II, the very existence of Parliament demanded some acknowledgment of the role of the people in governing. Parliament by now had an enormous institutional history, and it was clearly linked – somehow – with the people. Since it was equally clearly a part of the governing structure of the kingdom, the conclusion was inescapable that the people were a part of the governing calculus. England, then, remained a unique monarchy, and events would shortly awaken those sleeping notions of popular sovereignty.

Those events constituted the second enabling condition that allowed notions of government grounded in the people to resurface. In brief, the next two Stuart monarchs – Charles II and James II – were no more politically astute than their predecessors had been, and they eventually squandered the good will that attended the Restoration. Charles II was a spendthrift whose profligate spending kept him dependent upon Parliament. His relations with that body were characterized by dissembling and distrust, and when subsequent Parliaments grew restive, he orchestrated a campaign to dominate Parliament by manipulating elections to that body. Perhaps worse, Charles II appeared to be moving toward Catholicism, that most hated and feared of religions. His Declarations of Indulgence, which granted Catholics freedom of religion, created a firestorm of protest. And there was good reason to suspect Charles's motives: he went so far as to enter into a secret treaty with the Catholic king of France in which he promised to convert in return for financial subsidies. Things went from bad to worse when his brother James II ascended the throne. James II was openly Catholic and, ignoring the unhappy experience of his predecessor, announced another Declaration of Indulgence. James undercut Parliament by unilaterally suspending laws and ruling arbitrarily. Like his brother, he sought to control Parliament by 'packing' it with his supporters. Within a scant three years, James II had by 1688 managed to unite virtually all factions in England against him. The result was what is called the Glorious Revolution, when the elite of England invited William and Mary of Holland to take over the throne of England. When William landed with his army, James II vacated the throne and the country, and England gained new sovereigns in what has been called a 'bloodless revolution'.

It was in the context of these remarkable and unprecedented events that the fiction of popular sovereignty was resurrected in England. Something of the sort was needed to explain and legitimate what had occurred. In casting about to justify this breach in the normal succession, some commentators turned once again to popular sovereignty, going back to the myth that the people, not God, really chose the king.[34] What was distinctive about this return to the people as the wellspring of government was its limited nature. No one pursued any of the more radical implications of the fiction as had the Levellers or Henry Vane during the 1640s and 1650s. Although lip service was paid to the people's theoretical role, there was no thought of actually returning to a 'state of nature' where the people might have real power to reconstitute the polity. Instead, the revolutionaries' 'brand of popular sovereignty stressed adherence to the ancient constitution of king, Lords, and Commons'. Although the monarch had changed, 'their actual efforts … all assumed the unaltered continuance of the existing government'.[35]

That is not to suggest, however, that things remained the same. Although the tripartite division of government remained intact, Parliament took the occasion of the accession of William and Mary to restate and restructure the relationship between the monarchs and Parliament. The Declaration of Rights, and later the Bill of Rights, assured that Parliament would henceforth be the predominant partner in the governance of the nation. It is important to note, however, that this accretion of power went to Parliament as the representatives of the people, and not to the people themselves. Morgan notes that 'England did not achieve – and never would – a formulation and establishment of its constitution by a popular sanction or authority separate from its government. Popular sovereignty in England was to be exercised, as from its inception, by Parliament, or more particularly by the House of Commons.'[36]

Before turning to the American experience, which was to have a more radical outcome, it is useful to explore the reasons the English revolutionaries were so cautious in their handling of popular rule. Their concerns with the fiction form the basis for some continuing contemporary debates over rule by the people. There were two principal perceived threats associated with acknowledging any real power in the people. The first was a concern with social stability. No one wanted to open the door to the near anarchy of the 1640s and 1650s. After the Civil War and Interregnum, popular sovereignty still had a rather bad name.

Perhaps more important to the Parliamentary elites was a concern related to societal stability: maintaining their own hegemony. There was, in other words, a concern about the political implications of popular sovereignty. As had been the case during the Civil War, the Parliamentary elites who 'invented' the people and their sovereignty did so for selfish reasons. In a sense, in both instances these elites were using this fiction to advance their own power. What no one wanted in the 1680s was to imply that popular sovereignty was what it said it was: power in the people. As Morgan puts it, 'The sovereignty of the people was a convenient, perhaps a necessary, fiction for a convention bent on disinheriting and displacing a monarch whose beliefs and conduct offended ... the vast majority of his subjects. But the sovereignty of the people', Morgan reminds us, 'would lose its usefulness if taken literally.'[37]

We have, then, in England in the seventeenth century, the emergence of a conception of the people as the constitutive part of government. This new fiction had dramatic implications, but somewhat ironically, it was in England utilized merely as a justification to legitimize the hegemony of a certain elite. This desire for social, political and economic hegemony also characterized the desires of elites in the American colonies, who also sought to manipulate the fiction of popular sovereignty to their own ends. Unfortunately for the future of elite hegemony, conditions and events in America conspired to carry the notion of power in the people to its logical conclusions. This evolution in the fiction of popular sovereignty took a very long time to complete, and indeed continues to the present day. Our eventual consideration of leadership in a democracy requires that we understand the American version of the people and their role.[38]

It is difficult to exaggerate the importance that the English experience with popular sovereignty in the seventeenth century had for the American colonists. They embraced that English experience as their own, and constantly drew upon it (not always accurately), usually in, ironically, their spats with the mother country. Yet at the same time, the American experience was different from that of England, and the outcomes different. Again, it is Edmund S. Morgan who provides the best depiction of these important developments.

From the outset of English colonization on the American continent, there were two striking differences between the Americans' experience with popular sovereignty in the seventeenth century and their English counterparts. First and foremost, the English colonists in America embraced the notion of popular sovereignty far more readily than had their brethren in England. This was a simple function of the reality of the New World. 'The facts of life in North America', writes Morgan, 'dictated ... a degree of popular participation in government that would make the sovereignty of the people – the people of the colonies – a more plausible fiction, a fiction closer to fact, than in England itself.'[39] The groundwork was laid early in the seventeenth century. Several of the American colonies, especially in New England, had begun with a 'compact' theory of government, thereby confirming patently and explicitly the participation of the people in the formation of government, an event English commentators had had to conjure up out of whole cloth. Take, for example, the Mayflower Compact and the Fundamental Orders of Connecticut, where groups of individuals explicitly bound themselves together in a body politic.[40] Added to this was the reality that, contrary to England, the vast majority of (adult white male) Americans either owned property, or had the reasonable expectation of doing so. It was property ownership that in England guaranteed active political participation, and the widespread availability of this perk automatically made popular participation in government more likely in the colonies. Then, too, everywhere in the colonies it made sense to have local assemblies to aid the royal governors. Because local conditions were so unique, policy decisions had to be decided on the ground. Moreover, the quick rise of the economy and society of the colonies led to the emergence of local elites, who demanded a say in their governance. Taken together, these factors virtually required a colonial governance structure that remained close to its popular roots.[41]

Ironically, this more universal commitment to the people as a constituent part of government in the American colonies was joined by another attribute that made the colonies distinct from the mother country. 'While colonial governments from the beginning depended more visibly on popular consent than the government of England,' observes Morgan, 'there was less occasion in the colonies than in England for the development or articulation of ideas about popular sovereignty.'[42] Thus in the very decades when the English intellectual world was in an uproar over the notion of popular sovereignty, the American colonists, who knew it most firsthand, were strangely quiet. The reason is not far to seek. Because they were more-or-less happy with the status quo, there was no incentive, as there had been in England under the abusive Stuarts, to articulate justifications for reconstituting the regime. This quietude had other benefits. For one, it kept the colonists and their emerging brand of popular government out of the limelight. Second, the lack of discussion allowed widely differing interpretations of appropriate popular participation to coexist peaceably. 'The result', says Morgan, 'was a situation in which the sovereignty of the people could be accepted as the basis of government in the colonies without anyone having to decide what people endowed whom with what powers. There might be a variety of opinions on the question, but they could be left unexpressed.'[43]

Even though the American colonists did not push the issue of popular sovereignty, important groundwork was being laid for the time when, during the Revolutionary crisis, the American variant of rule by the people would come to the fore. As the seventeenth century progressed, many of the constitutions of the 'Restoration colonies' (that spate of proprietary colonies created after 1660 such as Pennsylvania and Carolina) had provisions for extensive popular involvement, and it became assumed that all colonial government would have some form of popular participation through assemblies.[44] Meanwhile, as the political cultures of the colonies became more mature in the eighteenth century, the political reality of the colonies gave even more credence to notions of popular sovereignty in America. Not only did the assemblies assert more and more authority during a series of battles with colonial governors, but also elite factions in the assemblies more and more looked to the people for support of their various causes.[45]

On the eve of the Revolutionary crisis, several generalizations about the status of the fiction of the people as the wellspring of government can be asserted. First, popular sovereignty was a bedrock belief among American colonists. Morgan notes that 'by the eighteenth century, the sovereignty of the people was taken for granted'.[46] Second, it can be said that the theoretical implications of popular sovereignty had not caused nearly as much trouble in America as they had in England. 'The sovereignty of the people in the colonies, insofar as it was embodied in representation,' says Morgan, 'had not departed so far from fact as to induce the kind of protest evoked in England.'[47] Finally and importantly – and this conclusion is not quite so obvious – the rhetoric of popular sovereignty in the colonies had not threatened any major upheaval of the existing social order.

This last point may require some elaboration. Although the colonial elite were much less well defined than their counterparts in England, by the late seventeenth century colonial society had stabilized to the point where an identifiable and somewhat stable elite had emerged. These societal leaders, like those in England, had neither desire nor intention of giving up status and power to those below them. 'Such men,' Morgan points out, 'while identifying themselves with the people, had no more desire to subvert the social order than did the governors with whom they contended. Appeals to the people, in the colonies as in England,' Morgan continues, 'came from the top down.' As Morgan sums it up, for all the differences between England and the American colonies in terms of the embracing of popular sovereignty, on the eve of the Revolution the reality of American politics remained surprisingly similar to England: the elites maintained hegemony in a social and political system supposedly grounded in the people. 'In other words', writes Morgan, 'popular sovereignty, in the colonies, as in England, became the prevailing fiction in a society where government was traditionally the province of a relatively small elite. Although the new fiction slowly widened popular participation in the governing process, those who made use of it generally belonged to that elite and employed it in contests with other members.'[48]

In sum, the new fiction about the sovereignty of the people, which caused such lamentation and gnashing of teeth in England, had been accepted unconditionally in the American colonies. This acceptance was an entirely pragmatic one, and had not been accompanied by a lot of philosophical treatises exploring the implications of the concept. Moreover, down to the eve of the Revolutionary crisis, Americans of all strata had been more-or-less content with retaining the existing power structure. However, as we have seen, America was not England, and the conservative English interpretation of popular sovereignty was destined to be transmuted into a more radical American version that would eventually fuel a democratic revolution throughout the Western world.

The American experience had always held more possibilities for a more substantive role for the people in governing. The early political compacts among the first settlers had suggested as much, and the subsequent reality of widespread political participation and powerful local assemblies had confirmed this early promise. However, with a few minor exceptions in the seventeenth century, the American colonists had never felt the need to challenge the existing social hierarchy, and as a result the elite colonial leaders, like those in England, had been able to imbibe safely the benefits of popular sovereignty without risk. Partly this was a function of the fact that the colonials never felt the need to articulate their interpretation of popular sovereignty or its implications. To the extent that they thought about it at all, most rather superficially accepted the English interpretation as equally applicable to the colonial experience.[49] But such was not the case, and in the crucible of the American Revolutionary crisis and after, Americans had to think through what they really meant by 'the people', and their wielding of power. As a consequence, the doctrine of popular sovereignty took on new forms, with new implications.

The issue which served as the catalyst for this intellectual transformation was that of representation. This has ever been the most complex of concepts in a regime grounded in the people.[50] The very concept of representation contains within it an inherent 'enigma', which goes to the heart of leader–follower relations. As Morgan puts it, 'The people are the governed; they are also, at least fictionally, the governors, at once subjects and rulers'.[51] The contradiction occurs when the people select representatives to voice their will, while at the same time the representatives are expected to 'rule' the people.[52] There are, of course, various ways that the contradiction can be worked out, and the time-honored method that the elite had adopted was to embrace a version of the classical ideal. Perhaps the best-known articulation of this was Edmund Burke's response to instructions from his constituents. His argument, in its essence, was that the representative (leader) should be wise and virtuous enough to think for himself. Indeed, the elite leader might well be better able to perceive the real interests of followers than the followers themselves. Moreover, the elected leader, continued Burke, had to look beyond the narrow interests of his local constituency, and instead be cognizant of the wider, general good.

When the crisis in British–American relations boiled over in the 1760s and 1770s, one of the flash points was just this concept of representation. Although the American elites had embraced the Burkean approach on the domestic front, the debates over 'no taxation without representation' pushed them toward a differing version of this relation.[53] The British had responded to American protests by articulating the traditional notion of representation in the guise of Thomas Whately's famous notion of 'virtual representation'.[54] This, in turn, forced American intellectuals into framing an alternative version of representation. 'It pushed', in Morgan's words, 'the colonists into a strenuous affirmation of the local, subject character of representation, in which they ... repudiated Whately's view....' Indeed, 'it became a cardinal principle of Americans in the revolutionary period that the only legitimate representation of any people, the only persons who could consent to acts of government for them, were persons whom they had personally chosen for the purpose'.[55] The colonists went further yet. They held that 'a representative ought not only to be directly chosen by his constituents, but ought to be one of them, ought to live among them and share their local circumstances'.[56] In a famous passage from John Adams, the representative body should be 'a portrait in miniature of the people at large.... It should think, feel, reason, and act like them.'[57]

All this made perfectly logical sense in the context of the imperial debate. However, almost unbeknownst to the colonists, this localistic stance had profound implications for the notion of popular sovereignty. By refusing, in effect, to have the elite represent them in Britain, they had opened the doors for a similar application in their own world. As Morgan points out, 'they could scarcely turn their backs on the view of representation that had impelled them to the separation. But that view, so crucial for crushing the pretensions of representatives from a distant nation, posed problems' when Americans turned to creating new governments for themselves.[58] Make no mistake: the men who drafted the first state constitutions were, for the most part, the same elite who had held power prior to the Revolution. And – again make no mistake – they had no intention of relinquishing their hold on power. When they erected governments via these state constitutions, they took care to place power where they traditionally had held sway: in the assemblies. But the Revolution had unleashed social, economic and political forces that had been gathering force for decades,[59] and as a result there was a burst of activity on all fronts by men who had traditionally been quiescent and willing to defer to their 'betters'. On the political front, the Revolutionary rhetoric provided them with an intellectual legitimation of their new activism. Now common men stood for election, quite openly representing the interests of their compatriots (often debtors). To the elite steeped in the traditions of the classical ideal and notions of a unitary common good, this constituted a crisis. To the elite, 'it was the people's representatives who now threatened to destroy the union and to disgrace the whole idea of popular sovereignty'.[60]

The American elite countered with their famous attempt to put things aright – the Constitution. The details of that attempt will be the subject of a later chapter;[61] here the important matter is to distill from this whirl of events the key developments regarding the emerging fiction of the people in government. There were essentially three. The first was a function of pragmatic reality. The outcome of the early American experience was the emerging reality that the common people actually had a role to play in government. This was implicit from the founding of the colonies, became much more patent as a result of the American Revolution, and would culminate in the nineteenth century and beyond.[62]

The second outcome was intellectual; specifically, a new conceptualization of the relations between leaders and the people. In working through the debate with Britain over representation, American revolutionaries articulated an alternative mode of relation between representative and represented. The notion of creating a representative body closely tied to localities and serving as nothing more than a mirror of constituent wishes was quite a departure from the traditional norm. Although many American elites came to regret this shift and sought to recant, others (Anti-Federalists and their intellectual descendants) embraced the new version, and this divide became one of the fault lines of the ongoing American polity.[63]

The third outcome is not as obvious, but again Edmund Morgan gives good service in identifying it and suggesting its significance. It was no less than the creation or invention of an 'American' people, separate from and superior to the government that represents them. This was just what the Levellers had advocated, but, it will be recalled, their radicalism had been buried in the conservative reaction of the Restoration. When popular sovereignty resurfaced at the time of the Glorious Revolution, it was the milder kind that equated the people with the representative body of Parliament. In England, then, Parliament *was* the people, and the British have never moved beyond such a conception. In America, the Framers devised a different conception of the people. Morgan describes this development: 'Even before the convention met, Madison recognized that it could achieve the objectives he had in mind for it only by appealing to a popular sovereignty not hitherto fully recognized, to the people of the United States as a whole'. Madison, then, 'envisioned a genuine national government, resting for its authority, not on the state governments and not even on the peoples of the several states considered separately, but an American people, a people who constituted a separate and superior entity'.[64]

This invention of a people separate from and superior to government could be viewed as the greatest legacy of the American founding. Certainly it was among the most profound. The remainder of this volume will be dedicated to addressing the consequences, in terms of how the people and their leaders negotiated the new relationship demanded when a sovereign people and their leaders must act together to achieve societal objectives. Before turning to this analysis, however, it is necessary to pursue this construct of 'the people' as it has evolved to the present day.

'THE PEOPLE' AS A PROTEAN FICTION

If historian Edmund S. Morgan provides us with insight into the emergence of the people as a viable fiction in the polity, political scientist James A. Morone demonstrates how that fiction can evolve, take on new forms, and indeed serve as an engine of reform. Morone's innovative work is entitled *The Democratic Wish: Popular Participation and the Limits of American Government*. In it, he portrays a model of how the American political system has repeatedly drawn upon the concept of 'the people' to fuel reform movements that have, as one consequence, consistently (although not uninterruptedly) enlarged the understanding of what constitutes the people. Morone is, at bottom, a scholar of governmental administration and bureaucracy. His study stresses the rather mixed administrative results stemming from these periodic evocations of the people in the call for reform. His treatment of the conception of 'the people' is merely an explanatory vehicle for the continuing growth of government and bureaucracy. As Morone himself says, however, 'I suspect that variations of the pattern I describe – the democratic wish – could also illuminate political issues which I did not pursue here'.[65] In this segment, we are going to take advantage of Morone's implied invitation and draw from his analysis a narrative of the evolving fiction of the people in the American experience.

For Morone, perhaps better than any modern scholar, does understand the power of the fiction of the people and its consequences. There can be no doubt that he understands the fictional quality of the construct. 'Ultimately,' he says, '"the people" is ... a powerful political fiction ... it is a myth.'[66] Moreover, 'the democratic ideals that inspire reformers are, like any myth, unattainable'. Nevertheless, in the course of American political history 'a consensus over the mirage of the people cut through the political factions and enabled the creation of new political institutions [and] ... new images of the people.'[67] It is upon those 'new images of the people' that this study will focus, rather than the institutional consequences.

It is perhaps best to begin our discussion with the interpretive vehicle that drives Morone's analysis: 'the democratic wish'. This 'wish' is the engine that propels all reform movements, and does so in the name of the people. According to Morone's innovative approach, the 'democratic wish' is really a 'yearning'. When things appear to be mishandled in government, this latent yearning comes to the surface. This yearning, he argues, 'is an alternative faith in direct, communal democracy ... the people would, somehow, put aside their government and rule themselves directly'.[68] 'The key to the ideology', Morone elaborates, 'is an image of the people – a single, united, public entity with the capacity … to … solve the troubles that plague the nation. [This] populist ideal is not simply the rhetorical flourish that strikes the modern ear. Nor is it merely a call for more responsive government.' In the democratic wish, 'the people would be governors as well as constituents, political agents as well as principals. They would act by and for themselves.' This, Morone asserts, 'is nothing less than an alternative locus of political authority. Somehow, power will be seized from the government and vested in the people themselves.'[69] He concludes: 'the democratic wish imagines a single, united people, bound together by a consensus over the public good which is discerned through direct citizen participation in community settings'.[70]

In Morone's interpretation, this call for returning 'power to the people' is anything but haphazard. According to Morone, such calls follow a predictable pattern, and yield similar results: 'a more open political system, marked by newly legitimated groups'.[71] It is useful to expound his model. 'The American democratic ideology,' Morone posits, 'sets a recurrent pattern into motion. Each successful call to the people progresses, roughly speaking, through four stages. First, the process begins (as it ends) in … political stalemate…. Ideology, interests, and institutions all block change … With time, pressures for reform mount. The stalemate is broken when proponents of change transform the debate by invoking the democratic wish. We reach the second stage,' Morone continues, 'when the call for the people provokes a popular response.' Then 'broad political movements take up the populist call; Americans attack the status quo and demand changes that will empower the people'. It is here that the fictional quality of the construct proves invaluable. This call for '"the people" covers a multitude of factions. This helps explain why the democratic wish introduces change … easily…. Even when social tensions are sharp, contending factions can converge on a set of symbols that appear to promote the interests of each.'[72] 'The third stage begins', according to Morone, 'with the implementation of new political institutions.' Unfortunately, 'once reforms are in place, the image of a united republican *Volk* evaporates into the reality of classes and interests scrapping for partisan advantage.' This brings on 'the fourth stage', which 'is a return to the first – the reassertion of … political equilibrium (around a new status quo).'[73]

As indicated, this analysis will be less concerned with the institutional ins and outs of this model than it will the light it sheds upon developing conceptions of the people. Although this is not Morone's primary focus, he acknowledges the implications his work has for the fiction of the people. 'Precisely because they were designed to empower the people,' he says, 'the new organizations [created during the stages of the model] facilitate the participation of new groups' in the polity, who then 'contend for political legitimacy.' The result is indeed 'newly legitimated groups'.[74] It is to this aspect of Morone's work that we now turn our attention.

Morone begins his study of America's populist journey by looking to the events of the American founding. In an analysis similar to Morgan's narrative, Morone finds that Americans of the Revolutionary generation formulated a new definition of the people. Morone's emphasis, however, differs somewhat from that of Morgan, in a way that allows us to trace a continued dynamism in the fiction of the people.

Morgan and Morone begin from the same premise, that in the Revolutionary era a new vision of the people based upon 'actual' representation as opposed to the former 'virtual' representation came to the fore. This shift, argues Morone, had important implications for notions of 'the people'. Virtual representation carried with it certain assumptions about society, the people and their leaders. As Morone puts it, 'the implicit vision of society is one of stability, aristocracy, deference, and only a small number of political interests'.[75] Ideas of actual representation had quite different assumptions. The belief that representatives of the people should be merely a microcosm of the people at large, and should 'think, feel, reason, and act' like them, contained within it the assumption that the people are wise and an implication of popular activism. From this, as Morgan also points out, came the first manifestation of a conception of the people as the driving force in governing.

For all the seeming attractiveness of this 'democratic wish',[76] problems with this new conception of the people immediately presented themselves. Chief among these was 'its murky definition of the constituency itself. What (or whom) should the assemblies mirror? … "The people" [was] not a concrete entity. The colonists were seeking an assembly that would "think, feel, and reason" like a fiction....'[77] Moreover, this new 'people', however defined, was not acting in ways that traditionally had been expected or acceptable. Indeed, in place of the old deference to their betters, there was the 'spread of political contagion' during which '"new men" entered American politics'.[78] The result was, as Morgan also notes, the emergence of individuals representing narrow interests on the American political scene, a development that appeared to fly in the face of all traditional conceptions of virtue and commitment to the common good.

Clearly, as the American experiment in government based upon the people progressed, some began to have second thoughts about defining the people in such a way that challenged the established political order and cherished notions of how government should operate. Those who were most troubled by these developments were the elite, who set about the task of inventing a new, more palatable, definition of the people, one that was more consistent with older notions of virtue and the common good. This movement culminated in the Constitutional Convention. Morone and Morgan agree that the Founders were, in Morone's words, 'debating a new constitution rooted in a radically different vision of the people' than was the current norm.[79]

The interesting point is that Morgan and Morone come up with differing, yet not totally incompatible, ways of portraying this new conception of the people. Morgan, as we have seen, depicts the invention of a new 'American' people, separate from and superior to government, a portrayal that enabled the Framers to erect a new, national government designed to remedy the evils of the recent past. Morone, on the other hand, champions the famous Madisonian tactic of creating such a large republic that various factions of the people could not easily unite to do evil. As Morone puts it, 'The Framers reconstructed the collective people seeking a shared interest into a pluralistic population pursuing its multitude of private concerns'.[80]

The difference between these two interpretations is worth remarking upon. In one sense, it reflects a divide in the historiography of the Founding period, and indeed one of the major fault lines of all subsequent political discourse in America. Morgan focuses more upon a communal definition of the people, while Morone takes a more liberal, interest-group approach. This tension between communitarian and private, between republican and liberal, has become the very warp and woof of American politics (as Morone clearly acknowledges in his model of political development). It is an ideological divide of sufficient import to occupy several later chapters in this volume.[81] Yet there is no right or wrong in the debate, because both strains of American thought coexisted side by side, often, as was the case of Madison, in the same individual.[82]

Nonetheless, if Morgan's interpretation helped us to understand better the emergence of the people as a separate fiction, it is Morone's approach that lends itself to our task of pursuing the implications of that fiction. Morone's analysis yields two important insights. First, he identifies the first of many calls to 'the people' in times of crisis, a response that would characterize the American political process down to the present day. Second, Morone argues that the view of the people emerging out of the Founding period was nothing less than 'a new conception of popular sovereignty'.[83] This new conception was one that embraced private interests in the polity. Although Morone may overstate this move to interest group liberalism, there can be no question that private interests began to play a role in American politics as never before. In terms of our continuing study of the evolution of notions of 'the people', it is a quite useful vehicle. Once 'the people' become a collection of interests, it becomes possible for individual interest groups to claim the right of participation, a dynamic that fuels the story of the expanding fiction of the people we are about to relate.

Before turning to the later developments, however, it is important to get a 'baseline' sense of who constituted 'the people' during this early period. As Morone makes clear, the early vision of the people, even at its most all-encompassing, had its limitations. In the early Republic, the construct of the people embraced only those individuals who in the classical republican tradition were deemed worthy of participation in government – adult white males who owned sufficient (usually real) property to render them independent and virtuous. Obviously, this definition of the people was rather narrow: 'women, black people, native Americans, and men without property' were excluded.[84] But American history is characterized by nothing if not dynamism, and things were about to change, albeit gradually and haltingly. That is the tale Morone helps to delineate.

One of the most dramatic instances of a shift in the conception of who constituted 'the people' occurred during the Jacksonian period. Changes in the definition of the people were often, although not exclusively, a response to economic, social and demographic changes. Such was certainly the case during the Jacksonian period. In the first decades of the nineteenth century, a sea change took place in American society.[85] Those decades were characterized by 'emerging capitalism, the evolving frontier, the arrival of immigrants, ... [the rise of notions of] manifest destiny, [and] slavery'.[86] The results were twofold. First, as we will detail in more depth in a later chapter,[87] many of these social and economic changes opened up new opportunities for the common man, and Americans rushed to take advantage of such opportunities, in the process completely overturning the traditional elite-dominated culture. Second, and more relevant to our study of the fiction of the people, these were 'disorienting changes that challenged [America's] political discourse and ... conceptions of American self'.[88]

The resulting tensions inevitably found their way into the political sphere. There they encountered Andrew Jackson, one of the most astute politicians in American history. Jackson became one of the first to muscle his way to the front of the charging popular herd by embracing the new prominence of the common man. Indeed, although his actions often belied his words, Jackson 'invok[ed] the rhetoric so persuasively he was often said to embody it'. In doing so, he 'updated "the people" for a new era'.[89] Tapping the popular energy and disorientation, Jackson 'fashioned vivid imagery to fix blame and offer corrections. Using the language of the people to explain and justify, Jackson reconstructed' the very image of the people.[90]

The result was nothing less than a revolution in the conception and role of the people. In Morone's terms, 'Americans have rarely pursued their democratic wishes with the fervor they showed in the second quarter of the nineteenth century'.[91] This was reflected most obviously in the suffrage, which achieved 'universal' (that is, white male) status by mid century. This wide franchise was accompanied by 'booming political participation, and an era named after "the common man"'.[92] Thus Jackson, in embracing the people, 'broadened the conception of the people for the new era of bourgeois capital and burgeoning cities'. Those deemed fit for membership in 'the people' now extended beyond the Jeffersonian 'planters and farmers'. Jackson 'broadened "the people" to embrace artisans and mechanics in the cities, ... laborers, [and immigrants]'.[93]

However, although the definition of the 'political people' – those entitled to be active in the polity – was broadened considerably during the Jacksonian era, the fiction of the people remained far from all-encompassing. Women were generally not included, and 'the Jacksonian Democrats ... willingly accepted slavery' and 'Native Americans were brutally driven from their lands'.[94]

In sum, however, it can be said that circumstances in the first half of the nineteenth century were conducive to a significant new understanding of the fiction of 'the people'. While the events of the Revolutionary era created the first sense of the people as an entity separate from and superior to their government, the Jacksonian period gave the fiction a new scope and dynamism that it has never lost. It was to be a 'Jacksonian' people that would ultimately create the most perplexing problems for leadership.

If we ignore the racial politics of the post-Civil War period – a theme we will take up in the context of the modern civil rights movement presently – the next important shift in the fiction of the people, according to Morone, occurred during the Progressive era. Morone characterizes the Progressive movement as the culmination of a series of reform movements that had been active in the decades after the Civil War. That period, he notes, 'was cluttered with causes and reformers – Populists, Prohibitionists, Suffragettes ... Knights of Labor', and others.[95] Drawing upon their respective themes and others, the Progressives proposed an ambitious agenda of reform. Partly as a consequence of its multiple constituency, the Progressive agenda was broad, and indeed not always consistent. 'The Progressives won changes', points out Morone, 'ranging from railroad regulation ... to women's suffrage....'[96]

Among several other achievements, the Progressive movement, like the American Founders and the Jacksonians, were able to re-cast the fiction of the people in ways that conformed to a new social reality. Again, a similar dynamic was in evidence. Like their predecessors, the Progressives grounded their call for reform in terms of returning power to the people.[97] And, again, 'the ambiguous image of "the people" served to meld an uneasy coalition of interests and philosophies'.[98] Indeed, 'the Progressives resolved the contradictions within their reform agenda by invoking an idealized people, united by a yearning for the public interest'.[99] More specifically, 'by the turn of the century, reformist rhetoric and image had reconstructed the people into victims of oppression'.[100] In this manner, concludes Morone, did the Progressive movement 'fashion ... [reform] around their version of the fictitious people'.[101]

The Progressive impact upon the fiction of the people was manifested in two ways. First, it encouraged a modernized version of the people more in tune with the emerging modern, industrialized state America had become. This development was not always clear cut or unambiguous. As Morone points out, the Progressive movement contained its own contradictions, which were reflected in contrasting views of the people. Morone elaborates: 'There were competing definitions of the Progressive people. One variant – articulated by Herbert Croly, Walter Lippmann, and the Bull Moose-era Theodore Roosevelt – embraced the great scale of twentieth-century America. Their constituency was a single national people, mobilized in opposition to the concentration of power. In the alternate, more populist version of William Jennings Bryan, Robert LaFollette, and Woodrow Wilson, democracy resided in the 'collective will' of small communities across America.'[102] Thus, admits Morone, 'Progressives ... were not able to root their unitary people in a concrete constituency'. Nonetheless, 'Croly and the national Progressives moved the people off the land entirely and found a new republican promise in the industrialization of the twentieth century.'[103] The second and more obvious alteration in the fiction of the people brought about by the Progressives was the inclusion of women in the polity. 'Like the revolution-aries and the Jacksonians, Progressives expanded the franchise, this time with voting rights for women.'[104]

As has ever been the case in our evolving fiction of the people, the advances in terms of inclusion were not unalloyed. Although women secured the suffrage during the Progressive era, the Progressives were far from totally admirable in their conceptualization of the people. They were 'suspicious of the immigrants who gathered in the eastern cities, nervous of the farmers who flocked to the Populist party in the Midwest, unsympathetic to the poor whites in the South'.[105] Indeed, many Progressive reforms 'served to disenfranchise illiterate voters, most conspicuously the black voters in the South. Ironically, even the Progressives' central democratic achievement, women's suffrage, helped subvert the political influence of urban immigrants.'[106]

Nevertheless, the contributions of the Progressives to the definition of the political people should not be minimized. As Morone sums up, 'The Progressives, for all their democratic shortcomings, won political rights for a still larger class when they finally secured the Nineteenth Amendment'.[107] Moreover, their willingness to contemplate a 'people' suitable to a modern industrialized state paved the way for an important, if slightly novel, shift in the dynamics of the fiction of the people.

Indeed, the Progressive movement laid the groundwork for a development that occurred during the New Deal that has considerable significance for the continuing dynamism of the fiction of the people in America. The development in question was the emergence of organized labor as a contributing part of the democratic polity during the New Deal. This is important for our understanding of the modern dynamics of the fiction of the people because it suggests that the fiction is viable at varying levels of scale. That is to say, our understanding of who might be included as legitimate members of the political community operates not only at the most visible level of the franchise. It is also a function at the more subtle level of various groups and interests in society who may develop political clout by demonstrating to hegemonic groups that their voices deserve to be heard as legitimate members of 'the people' in a democracy.

The New Deal was the perfect environment for the development of such permutations in our understanding of who can be substantive participants in the political community. This was due to the New Deal's peculiar openness to the contributions of various organized groups, a development often referred to as 'interest group liberalism'.[108] As Morone describes the phenomenon, New Deal agencies 'differed from the old largely in the eagerness with which they accommodated private interests…. Progressives,' he explained, 'had tried to render government neutral by ending special favors; if the New Dealers were neutral, it was because they seemed to endow favors on every organized group. The … widely acknowledged reality was constituency service: defining, even organizing private interests that could be accommodated within the governing coalition.'[109] Indeed, 'the [New Deal] effort to empower independent experts over narrowly delineated arenas systematically turned politics away from a universalistic people; it advantaged narrow organized interests by organizing narrow functional political arenas'.[110] This approach 'inverted the Progressive idea [of government by neutral specialists and experts]…. The failure of [Progressive] scientific administration was not merely inevitable but good.' Instead, administrators should be 'instructed by the people through a sort of political market. A group or interest that felt strongly about a matter would mobilize for political action.' This approach, argues Morone, 'subordinated the administrative state to democratic politics. A sprawling bureaucracy pursuing its self interests in consort with private groups (pursuing theirs) was conjured into a vast democratic market responding to citizen wishes as they were articulated by organized groups.'[111] The New Deal, then, reinvented how the people were to be conceptualized, and how they would relate to their government. This fiction of interest group democracy was to dominate much of the remainder of the twentieth century. The consequences for the fiction of the people were profound. 'Previously suppressed interests mobilized, [and] they were given new political ground on which to challenge dominant elites.'[112]

A classic example of one subset of 'the people' gaining political clout and thus becoming a part of the political people was the case of labor in the 1930s. Prior to that decade, 'the bias of American labor policy tilted, often violently, against working-class organizations'.[113] As had been the case of the other shifts in the definition of the people addressed in this chapter, the transformation, when it came, arose out of shifting economic and social circumstances. By the early twentieth century, America was confronted with 'a flood of new, unskilled workers', and by the 1930s, the Great Depression had rendered their situation almost untenable.[114] The opportunity for labor's emergence was provided by a series of legislative and administrative initiatives instigated by the federal government. In its vast, semi-chaotic response to innumerable societal needs, Roosevelt's administration spawned a cornucopia of attempted solutions. Among these was a series of measures that would ultimately permit organized labor to take its place among those with clout in the political process – and thereby become members of the 'political people'.

One of the earliest and most enigmatic measures was the National Industrial Recovery Act of 1933. Although intended to aid existing hegemonic groups in the industrial sector, in typical early New Deal fashion, the Act was a sprawling and somewhat disorganized legislative attempt to revive the economy. One somewhat incongruous provision was Section 7(a), which asserted that employees 'should have the right to organize and bargain collectively through representatives of their own choosing and shall be free from the interference, restraint, or coercion of employers of labor'.[115] Although this language sounded promising for labor in their attempts to gain more clout in the workplace, in reality only a few unions – most notably John L. Lewis and the mineworkers – sought to take advantage of this provision, and they were fiercely resisted.[116]

It was in some of the myriad New Deal agencies that were created at the same time, however, where labor really began to make progress in its efforts to become a recognized political force. The National Recovery Administration (NRA), for example, 'established a political arena in which New Deal labor policy could be fought out'. As 'workers, unions, and industry fought for control of the NRA',[117] the agency provided a 'political arena in which New Deal labor policy could be [debated]', and, in the process, it 'legitimated ... labor's demands'.[118] The increasingly vociferous calls on the part of labor for fair treatment amounted to far more than just leverage at the bargaining table; labor wanted nothing less than to be accepted as participants in the emerging New Deal democracy. As Morone puts it, 'The American workers were not emphasizing substantive benefits such as wages, hours, or improved working conditions; instead they struck over representation, over voice'.[119] This 'political' activity on the part of labor led to the creation of the National Labor Board, and later, the National Labor Relations Board. It was these bodies, Morone asserts, that 'altered public sector politics by institutionalizing the workers' view of representation within the government'.[120]

As the politically sensitive Roosevelt tacked leftward in 1935, he embraced the Wagner Act, which amounted to, in Morone's words, a 'Magna Charta' for labor, institutionalizing into law the principal components of labor's agenda. Although obviously a victory for workers in their negotiations with employers, the Wagner Act also confirmed a new place for labor in the political firmament. As a direct result of this act, 'the labor movement began to reconstitute itself.... The Committee (later Congress) of Industrial Organizations ... rejected the restrictive craft union philosophy and started organizing industrial workers.' The ultimate result was momentous for the definition of the American political people. 'By the end of the decade,' Morone concludes, 'the independent unions had become legitimate players in a political economy that repressed them for more than a century.'[121]

In sum, after the 1930s, 'working class organization entered American politics', and the political people came to be 'defined ... broadly enough to include labor'.[122] This was a different sort of revision of the fiction of the people. Here, no expansion of the franchise was contemplated or occurred. Yet the fiction of the people was expanded just as surely as if a new class had been granted the suffrage. The subtleties of enhanced political influence can, indeed, trump in impact the mere legalistic access to the ballot box. If the definition of the American 'people' continues to demonstrate vitality and dynamism, it will largely be a function of such more subtle shifts in real power as achieved by organized labor during the New Deal and after.

Our final example from Morone's text partakes of both variants of the shifting conceptions of the people in the twentieth century. That is to say, when we look to the civil rights movement, we see the larger development of yet another group acquiring the franchise and thus becoming in law a part of the political people. At the same time, Morone's analysis also demonstrates how black Americans have taken a page from the labor movement in the sense that they have sought to move beyond being merely *de jure* members of the people, and have, with varying degrees of success, become in fact successful participants in the American democracy.

The story of the civil rights movement and its impact upon American definitions of the political people arguably has its roots as far back as 1619, when the first slaves were imported into colonial Virginia, but a more direct antecedent were the developments in the years immediately following the Civil War. Those years of seeming acceptance of black Americans into the political people by means of the Civil War Amendments and various measures of the Radical Republicans were never as thoroughgoing as might first appear. Moreover, most of the few gains accomplished, especially in the South, were swept away in a white counter-revolution during the later decades of the nineteenth century and the early years of the twentieth. In those years, in both the South and the North, 'the white establishment maintained supremacy by rigidly excluding blacks from politics'. The hegemonic whites 'relied upon political tactics elaborated in the three decades following the Civil War: violence, race hatred, and legal machination'.[123] As America moved toward the middle decades of the twentieth century, 'black Americans faced legal segregation in the South; [and] political and economic inequity throughout the nation'.[124]

The legal standing of blacks as an equal part of the American people began to shift noticeably at mid-century. There can be little doubt that the Supreme Court decision of *Brown v. Board of Education* was a watershed moment in the struggle by American blacks to take their place among the people. Although a close reading of the American civil rights movement will show that this decision was but part of a large and continuing movement for equal treatment, *Brown* changed everything. As Morone explains, 'The Court's decision did not end segregation; by altering the political rules, however, it prompted a citizen's movement which ultimately transformed racial politics'.[125] After *Brown*, 'black Southerners took advantage of the shifting legal bias and began to mobilize a mass movement'.[126] And, 'with each wave of protest, the government conceded some of the citizenship rights that had been formally promised by the courts'.[127] The culmination of black American legal entry into the ranks of the political people was undoubtedly the Civil Rights Act of 1964.

However, as suggested above, while the court decisions and civil rights legislation gave blacks *de jure* political status, it was another, less obvious, development that marked the arrival of *de facto* participation in the political affairs of the nation. According to Morone, it was not until the War on Poverty in the 1960s that black Americans began to enjoy real power at the local level. As usual for such developments, this did not occur in a social vacuum. The black gains were a part of a larger social movement that characterized that decade in American history. 'In the 1960s,' he says, 'another mass movement invoked democracy.... It demanded participation, celebrated grass roots community, proclaimed the consensus of the people, mobilized previously oppressed Americans, and won new political rules and institutions.'[128]

In particular, argues Morone, 'the War on Poverty launched the next stage of the democratic political pattern. Black Americans were mobilized and aroused.' Moreover, 'the new program gave them a focus within the state itself'.[129] Within the War on Poverty, the catalytic event was the creation of Community Action Agencies to direct the 'War' at the local level. Because these local agencies had to have minorities compose at least one-third of their governing boards, they 'took the excluded minority populations and thrust them into local politics'. In so doing, these organizations 'opened one agency of the state to black Americans, redefining them as a legitimate group within the constellation of American interests'.[130] The hegemonic groups holding sway at the local levels did not, of course, surrender their prerogatives to the newly empowered group either willingly or gracefully. In almost all localities bitter battles over power, turf and participation raged. This was, according to Morone, beneficial in its effect. 'The sheer fact of the conflict ... signaled a more profound development – an incipient black mobilization for power in local American politics.'[131] The result was then, significant. 'Thousands of black Americans (along with members of other minority groups) got an opportunity to participate in local politics.... In this fashion, a new generation of American leaders entered a political process that had violently shunned them.'[132]

Again, as has been the case in each of our other examples of the expansion of the definition of the people, the result was not an unmitigated success. Certainly 'Black Americans won a significant place within the political system. They dismantled the most egregious forms of racial oppression and became active participants [in politics]. Still,' Morone notes, 'in the United States it is not easy to mobilize political power for righting economic wrongs.' Viewed from the perspective of today, 'economic indicators continue to tell a dismal story about race in America'. Therein lies an important lesson about continuing efforts to reformulate the people in a democracy. Looking again to the experience of black Americans, Morone asserts that 'the legacy of the struggle for black rights is, at best, mixed'. The movement's 'accomplishments should not be minimized. Black Americans have won a significant and growing role in a political system that violently excluded them.... But the nation's disheartening racial schism remains. African-Americans are still worse off than other groups....'[133] The lesson appears to be this: efforts to expand notions of 'the people', whether *de jure* or *de facto*, are neither easy nor, in reality, ever fully complete. Such efforts remain among the most problematic challenges to a functioning democracy.

Looking back at the argument we have constructed from the raw materials of Morone's analysis, we can see how the fiction of the people continues to be a vibrant and protean construct. Ever since the moment the concept of 'the people' arose as an identifiable element of the American experiment, the definition of the people has grown and evolved. Although one is tempted to depict this evolution as a kind of inevitable process powered by some sort of 'flywheel of democracy', the reality is much more complicated. Each turn of the 'wheel' was spurred by idiosyncratic facilitating social and economic conditions, and each turn took on its own peculiar attributes. Moreover, this evolution of 'the people' has not been some whiggish march toward a full democracy. There have always been winners and losers, and this continues to be the case. Also of importance is the subtlety introduced in our consideration of twentieth century developments. We have seen that the dynamism of the fiction of the people is much more than the mere extension of the suffrage to new groups. It is also the securing of power and equality by individuals and groups that already formally have the vote. It is in this last manifestation that 'the people' retains its vitality today. And, as Morone points out to us, in this invention of 'the people' lies our future. 'The image of the people is fanciful', he acknowledges. 'It conjures up that universal interest – beyond the friction of class or race or gender or economic interest.... What the legacy of "the people" offers us is not imaginary unity but an affirmation of our shared needs and aspirations, of who we are and what we aspire to be.'[134]

THE IMPLICIT LEADERSHIP THEORIES OF POPULAR SOVEREIGNTY

In this chapter we have not parsed the writings of particular commentators, but rather have traced, with the help in particular, of the works of modern scholars like the historian Edmund S. Morgan and political scientist James A. Morone, the emergence of a conception of 'the people' in whom the sovereignty of the polity resided. This dramatic development held within it some important shifts in the underlying premises and assumptions that we have been tracing as fundamental to the leadership relation. It is worthwhile, then, to look once more at the protocol of questions that comprise our template of leadership, in order to discern the 'implicit theories' undergirding the new fiction of the people.

What is the Leadership Challenge?

As might be expected in an intellectual transformation that evolved over nearly four hundred years, the perceived challenges that evoked claims of a separate and identifiable 'people' were quite varied. Nonetheless, the responses to these disparate challenges all tended in the same direction: toward a sense of the people as the wellspring of government.

At the beginning of our narrative, that is, in seventeenth-century England, the perceived challenge was the abuses of the Stuart kings, and the call to the people was no more than a stratagem to buttress the claims of the Parliamentary elite. The rhetoric of seventeenth-century English politics became transformed when eighteenth-century American colonists faced the problem of perceived British oppression. In response to British arguments about the nature of representation (among other things), the Americans fashioned a more thoroughgoing idea of the role of the people, which was subsequently refined (and debated) in the critical years of the early republic. Thereafter, if Morone is to be believed, evolutions of the construct of the people were engendered by recurring perceived crises, each, in turn, sparked by changing economic and social developments. Taken together, it can be said that the move toward modern conceptions of the people and their role has been a product of a succession of responses to quite pragmatic challenges in the political world, as a new fiction was needed to justify desired ends.

As we shall see in the remainder of this text, this new fiction took on a life of its own. It was then that the most important leadership challenge presented itself: how to secure competent leaders (presumably patterned after the classical ideal) in a regime devoted to the new fiction of the sovereignty of the people. That challenge will occupy succeeding chapters.

What is the Perception of Human Nature?

The developments we have traced in this chapter were not, for the most part, the work of political philosophers, but instead the consequence of quite pragmatic political struggles. As such, we find little overt attention paid to such esoteric matters as the nature of man. However, implicit in the developing debate was a distinction of some consequence. It is best deciphered by looking to the emerging tension between conceptions of representation. Under the classical ideal (with the partial exception of James Harrington), the proper form of representation was taken to be the 'trustee' type, in which representatives acted upon their own superior insights to further the good of the whole. With the rise of the concept of the people as constituent power, there arose the contrary conception of the representative as mere 'delegate' of the people. This distinction had many important implications, several of which will be explored in more detail below. In terms of the view of human nature (our topic here), these contrasting conceptualizations of representation marked a divide between those who believed that all mankind had similar interests (which could be captured and advanced by a 'trustee' type of representative), and those who held that humans were more individualistic, with distinct interests best represented by a 'delegate'.

For a very long time, this dichotomy remained unstated and its implications unexplored. It would become, however, one of the fault lines of leadership in modern democracies.

Are the People Capable of Governing?

Given the fact that this chapter traces the emergence of a concept of the people and popular sovereignty, the answer to this question would appear obvious. To the contrary, however, this issue continued to be one of controversy, and indeed remains so today. That being said, there is no gainsaying the fact that, with the emergence of the construct of the people as a distinct and constituent part of the polity, the notion of the capability of the people to govern became a commonplace – as a fiction. The debates came when attempts were made to make the fiction a reality. Again, this is a topic that receives considerable attention in the remainder of this volume.

A brief summation of how this issue played out in the historical narration just completed may clarify the matter. Under the pure doctrine of the divine right of kings, it was a truism that the people could not – and should not – rule. In England, even at the very beginning of our narration, this assumption was compromised by the existence of Parliament. Parliament was an unusual, even unique, institutional development, but its existence suggested a notion that the people had some role in governing. At most however, it was of the sort consistent with that of classical republicanism, characterized by elite dominance, with little real commitment to an idea of popular competence.

During the seventeenth century, we saw the Parliamentary elite utilize the rhetoric of the sovereignty of the people, but they did not intend by that to mean either that the people were actually sovereign, or that they had the capability of governing. Both those attributes remained the province of the elite. The problem (for the elite) was that the rhetoric suggested otherwise. This was exacerbated in the American colonies, where actual conditions were such that logic led to an enhanced sense of the power and capability of the people to govern. During the Revolutionary crisis, the logic of the debate over representation with Britain led even the American elite to affirm the essential logic of popular sovereignty.

By the nineteenth century, this assumption became a truism, and today in American democracy one would be hard pressed to find anyone challenging the capability of the people to govern. The fiction has become that dominant. But another of the challenges of democracy is the fact that the reality of popular behavior often gives the lie to the fiction. As we will see when we turn to our consideration of James Madison, Alexis de Tocqueville and numerous modern commentators, this premise of the capability of the people has sometimes posed severe difficulties for friends of good government. This, too, becomes a topic of our continuing attention.

What is the Proper End or Purpose of Leadership?

Heretofore, the proper end of leadership could be summed up in the term 'the common good'. That notion retains its currency, and continues to influence thinking about leadership to this day. However, with the emergence of the construct of the people as a sovereign entity, there came to be important shifts in the rationale and purpose for leadership.

The first transition involved the idea of the common good itself. For most of the period under study – up until the period of the American Revolution – the construction of the common good continued along traditional lines. The Parliamentary elite in England, and the elites of the American colonies, continued to argue for a unitary common good that they were best equipped to identify and pursue. At about the time of the American Revolution, however, a competing formulation arose, and again, it was most detectable in the innovations in conceptualization of representation. In the more extreme forms of representation as localistic delegation, one could say that the end of leadership became less some esoteric and unitary common good, but rather, simply, the interests of the respective constituencies, whatever those interests might be. Again, at the time, this important innovation went largely unremarked. Moreover, it never fully replaced the more traditional version. For example, James Morone's characterization of the 'Democratic Wish' that he argues drove American reform was largely a harking back to the ideals of the traditional notions of the common good. Nonetheless, the newer and more individualistic approach coexisted with the old, and has become another of those 'fault lines' of American politics. Our subsequent investigation of the liberal and communitarian fictions will explore this in some depth.

Another important implication of this new fiction of the people and their role was even more fundamental. Although, again, it took some time for the issue to become patent, the developments of the period under study suggested a wholly new purpose for the leadership relation: freedom and equality. Some assumptions about the freedom and equality of citizens had been inherent in republican political theory, but in republican thought these attributes had been considered as a baseline necessity in order for the polity to achieve the common good. Now, rather than merely a means to an end, the new fiction of the people created the possibility that freedom and equality were ends unto themselves. A premise ('implicit theory') along these lines held large implications for how the leadership relation should be structured. Again, this will be the subject of close scrutiny as we turn to the fiction of leadership itself.

What is the Epistemology of Leadership?

In the tradition of the classical ideal, this was, again, a relatively simple matter. In regimes in which such leaders held sway, it was assumed that the wise and virtuous leader – by definition – knew the common good, and the means to achieve it. In general, it was safe to answer the question by indicating *who* should make the determination. With the emergence of the people as the constituent power, significant new complexities arose, complexities that have not yet been fully resolved.

In the traditional approach, which continues to have potency today, it was within the province of the leader to ferret out what was best for the people, and the followers could safely rely upon his or her conclusions. With the emergence of the people as the focus and constituting power of the polity, another possibility arose. Now (at least in one version of the fiction), the success of public policy was not reliant upon the wisdom of elite and farseeing leaders, but a function of the people themselves, who determined whether or not the policy achieved its intended consequences. With this, the simplicity of the epistemology of leadership disappeared. What remained was a fiercely contested battle over by whom, how and by what standard this determination could be made. Some ways of organizing our thinking about this debate will be a part of our introduction to leadership in the next chapter. It is safe to conclude that no definitive resolution has been made, and is perhaps not possible. One of the purposes of the remainder of this study, however, is to identify the various approaches suggested, and to conclude with specific recommendations for our contemporary world.

What is the Role of the Leader?

The rise of popular sovereignty posed two new possible interpretations regarding the leader in the polity. The first involved the threshold issue of who might be qualified to become a leader. Under the classical ideal, which characterized divine right and the English version of Parliamentary sovereignty, as well as many more contemporary views, the leader was someone special, possessing superior virtue and wisdom. However, another possibility arose once the sovereignty of the people became a reality, particularly that version which called for representatives who were mere delegates. Once the representative assembly was 'a portrait in miniature' of the people, a new expectation arose. Representatives, at any rate, were expected to be no different from their constituents. This leveling of leaders and followers quite clearly held important implications for the relationship between them (we will turn to this presently).

The second novel conceptualization regarding the leader went more directly to the role he or she might play. For those who continued to advocate some version of the classical ideal – and they were many – the answer was familiar: the leader had the responsibility to discern and direct the populace along paths that led to the securing of the common good. Now, there arose beside this more traditional interpretation a less leader-centric version. At one extreme, the leader became the mere servant – even the minion – of the people. Even among those who did not take things quite this far, the newly enhanced role for the people shifted the expectations of leader behavior. This could vary from being an articulator of popular opinion to a facilitator of a process that leads to popular consensus.

As might be expected, there has been no definitive resolution of the appropriate role of the leader in a democracy. One service that this volume provides (in the next Part) is to gather together several of the more important responses to this question for review and evaluation.

What is the Role of the People?

In an era when the sovereignty of the people came to prominence, it should come as no surprise that there was a transformation in the expectations of the role the people should play in the polity. At the same time, these expectations were more complex than might at first appear.

At the beginning of this period of transition, under the fiction of the divine right of kings, the people were expected to be purely passive, not unlike those in a Platonic regime. In England, even in the early days, these expectations were thwarted. The very existence of Parliament suggested some role for the people, but it must be remembered that Parliament was very much an elite institution. Even after it gained ascendancy after the Glorious Revolution, England at most resembled the republics of the classical ideal. In such republics, it will be recalled, the role of the people remained quite limited. Although there had been some early arguments for an expanded role for the people among the Levellers and some of the French Huguenots, it was in the American colonial experience that a sense grew that the common people really did have a role in government. With the events of the American Revolution and after came the first assertions of an all-encompassing sovereignty of the people. As we have seen, much of the rest of American history has involved refining exactly what this fiction entails.

Thus, although there was a gradual widening of the conception of the role of the people, what that meant in reality has been the subject of considerable controversy. This can best be addressed under the rubric of the next query of our leadership protocol.

How Should Leaders and the People Interact?

This question, it will be recalled, ferrets out the dynamics of the expected relationships between leaders and followers. As such, it reveals much about complexities raised by the seemingly simple assertion of popular sovereignty.

Again, a brief tracing of developments will help to elucidate the issue. Although the rhetoric used would come to have great importance, the narration of the rise of Parliament in England was, in some respects, less one of popular sovereignty than a move from a Platonic fiction (the divine right of kings) to one more in line with the classical republican fiction, where there was some participation by propertied citizens, but the burdens of leading remained with a virtuous elite. In other respects, however, this seemingly traditional outcome was accompanied by important new ideas about the relations between leaders and followers. In devising a rationale to resist the Stuarts, English political commentators drew upon a tradition that reached back to Cicero and Aquinas to articulate a contract theory of government that placed limitations upon leaders. This development will be explored in greater detail in a later chapter; here, we can note merely that, with the emergence of such contract conceptualizations, the people became, in theory at least, the equal of their leaders.

This still begged the question of how the two should relate. This issue brings us back to the competing versions of representation that have played such a key role in our analysis. In seventeenth-century England, the members of Parliament most certainly saw themselves as trustees – indeed, they went so far as to proclaim that they *were* the embodiment of the people, and thus their deliberations, by definition, represented the common good. But this rhetoric about being one with the people was quite dangerous to their position. This language could – and did, under American circumstances – morph into the 'delegate' version of representation. If representatives and represented were identical, the former had no claim to superiority over the latter. If anything, since sovereignty was acknowledged to be in the people, a new possibility arose: the people could actually be *superior* to their leaders.

What this meant in terms of leader–follower relations was a total reversal of traditional assumptions and practices. Under the traditional, trustee-type of relation, the relationship was characterized by deference on the part of the people toward their superior leaders. But when representatives (leaders) became mere delegates of their constituents, a quite different relationship ensued. Now it became logical for the people to issue 'instructions' to their leaders, and expect them to be obeyed.

What complicated things was that neither approach gained unchallenged ascendancy, and democratic political thought ever since has been a mishmash of one version or the other or, often uncomfortably, some mixture of the two. The remainder of this volume will attempt to decipher this dynamic in more recent attempts at conceptualizing leadership in democracy, and ultimately, making some recommendations as to how to proceed in the future.

How is the Matter of Diversity and Minority Interests Addressed?

With the advent of the new fiction of the people as sovereign, issues of diversity and minority interests inevitably arose. Intriguingly, so long as the turn to the people still partook of the assumptions inherent in the classical ideal, such concerns could be pushed aside. To the extent that one still remained dedicated to a monolithic common good that fairly represented the needs of a homogeneous society, such issues as diversity and minority interests were moot. But such an idyllic conceptualization never really took hold, if for no other reason than the fact that the Stuart kings seemed to be pursuing strategies at odds with the interests of the people. That being the case, some stratagem was needed to protect interests that diverged from those championed by the leader.

The idea that members of society might not be homogeneous, but rather characterized by diversity and difference, was a surprisingly late addition to the political consciousness of democratic polities. Certainly, as we shall see in the next Part, it had begun to dawn on such commentators as James Madison, although Madison expended as much effort to allay the effects of 'faction' as to embrace it. But in more modern times, it became such a commonplace that a political philosophy labeled 'interest group liberalism' could be embraced by many.

Acknowledging differences and distinct interests is not the same as effectively protecting them, however. One of the tactics for the protection of interests that emerged was a stress upon *rights*. From the Petition of Right through the Declaration of Rights to the American Bill of Rights and after, this became a bulwark against oppression. Moreover, the primacy of rights was easily adapted to the needs of minorities, once the 'oppressor' became not a king but the majority. This particular strategy came to be a central tenet of what we will later style the 'liberal fiction', and will be the subject of closer scrutiny later in this volume.

Others have sought (with varying degrees of success) other strategies for the protection of minorities in a democracy and the championing of diverse interests. Again, we will be looking closely at some of these approaches, from the insights of Alexis de Tocqueville to the protections suggested by the 'liberal fiction'. Most would agree, however, that this challenge to leadership in a democracy has been only imperfectly resolved. It is to be hoped that the remaining segments of this text offer some hope for a better future.

What Institutions and Processes Must be Designed to Accommodate the Premises and Assumptions about Leadership Articulated in the Responses to the Leadership Template?

One of the purposes of applying our leadership template to the emerging fiction of the people has been to demonstrate how the easy answers of the past are no longer so pat. In responding to each question of the protocol, an effort has been made to suggest the conflicting, tentative and complex nature of the responses, once the sovereignty of the people is assumed. This state of affairs is not to be bemoaned, but welcomed. When the sovereignty of the people is accepted as appropriate and right, as democracy most certainly does, the very complexity of the challenges posed allows for more flexibility in responding.

Thus we have laid out before us an entire smorgasbord of possible strategies and remedies. Some, we have already previewed. For example, some version of Plato's virtuous leader still holds its attractiveness to many. The creative institutional solutions of Harrington's 'dividing and choosing' approach, or Vane's 'constituent convention', still hold possibility. So, too, do such redistributional policies of Harrington and the role of the rule of law that has exercised such a hold on so many of our commentators. In the next Part of this volume, as we turn more specifically to the issues of leadership itself, such potential remedies for the challenges of democracy will proliferate. It is only at the end of this volume that some organized attempt will be made to draw from that smorgasbord to create specific institutional and policy recommendations. Even then, the proposals will only be those of the author; there will be an explicit invitation to each reader to assemble his or her own responses to the perceived challenges – but only after he or she has articulated his or her idiosyncratic answers to the protocol of questions in the leadership template. Only then will the inevitable ensuing debate become informed.

It should be clear by this point that the rise of the fiction of the people marked a transitional point in the history of human affairs. Before turning more specifically to the institutional and policy consequences, we need to look more closely at a new underlying construct that emerged and energized all who came to contemplate life in a democracy.

TWO FICTIONS IN NEED OF A THIRD FICTION

In the first two Parts of this volume, we have been introduced to two dominant fictions in the Western tradition. The first to arise was what we have deemed the classical ideal of the leader. This fiction was based upon an implicit theory that the responsibility for ruling lay with the 'better sort'. As we have seen, this fiction addressed the perceived needs of all, evidenced by the obligation to serve disinterestedly and for the common good. Over the course of centuries, this fiction of the ideal leader took on many guises in response to differing societal challenges. The underlying principles remained the same in both monarchical and republican states. Moreover, careful observers took pains to puzzle out how this well-intended ideal could be made to work in practice. From an early date such innovations as the rule of law have been proposed as mechanisms to ensure that the underlying principles of the classical ideal would be realized. This classical ideal of the leader has had enormous staying power. It continues to inspire and inform societal expectations of the leader.

In more recent times, a second fiction has emerged: the fiction of the people. From an early date, commentators and philosophers in the republican tradition have acknowledged and addressed the existence of the people in such regimes. However, it was not until the seventeenth century that a conception of the people as a separate, constitutive part of the polity began to emerge. This newer fiction has come to dominate the Western tradition and indeed, appears to be on its way to becoming the dominant fiction worldwide. Just as the fiction of the leader has changed and evolved in response to changing societal conditions, so too has the fiction of the people exhibited a continuing dynamism. It is today the most central construct of modern Western regimes.

The difficulty is that these two dominant fictions are not necessarily compatible with one another. The implicit theories that undergird the two fictions are quite different. While the one assumes that the source of governing is an enlightened elite, the other, implicitly at least, views the wellspring of government in the people. Equally problematic may be the classical ideal's implicit theory about an identifiable and prevailing common good. These and other tensions between the two dominant fictions of the Western tradition pose what is perhaps the most pressing and most important challenge faced by Western democracies. What this thesis and antithesis require is a synthesis. What is needed is some way to ensure good leaders in regimes based upon the people, government that secures the good of the people when that good is at best difficult to ascertain, and at worst may be multiple and inconsistent 'goods'. Such a challenge requires something new in our experience, the invention of a new fiction that holds the possibility of addressing these most complex of problems.

It should come as no surprise that these issues have not gone unrecognized. Some of the world's great minds have pondered such matters, and, indeed, whole ideologies have grown up around this fundamental challenge of creating a polity that can successfully negotiate the tensions posed by these conflicting fictions. The new fiction that has resulted is the most complex – and most important – yet studied. It is to this new fiction – a fiction we call *leadership* – that we now turn.

NOTES

1. From the engrossed copy in the National Archives. Original spelling, capitalization and punctuation have been retained.
2. Abraham Lincoln, 'Gettysburg Address', in *The Writings of Abraham Lincoln*, ed. Arthur Brooks Lapsley (New York: P.F. Collier & Son, 1906), 7: 20.
3. Edmund S. Morgan, *Inventing the People: The Rise of Popular Sovereignty in England and America* (New York: W.W. Norton & Company, 1988).
4. James A. Morone, *The Democratic Wish: Popular Participation and the Limits of American Government*, rev. ed. (New Haven: Yale University Press, 1998).
5. The ensuing analysis of divine right is taken from Morgan, *Inventing the People*, 17–37.
6. Ibid., 18.
7. Ibid., 21–22, 30.
8. Ibid., 21.
9. Ibid., 22–23.
10. Ibid., 35–37.
11. The following discussion is taken from Morgan, *Inventing the People*, 55–77.
12. Ibid., 56.
13. Ibid., 57.
14. Ibid., 58.
15. Ibid.
16. Ibid., 58–59.
17. Ibid., 61–63.
18. Ibid., 58.
19. Ibid., 65.
20. Ibid., 60.
21. Ibid., 64.
22. Ibid., 67.
23. Ibid., 68.
24. Ibid., 69.
25. 'An Agreement of the People for a Firm and Present Peace upon Grounds of Common Right and Freedom, 28 October 1647', in Andrew Sharp, ed. *The English Levellers* (Cambridge: Cambridge University Press, 1998), 94.
26. Morgan, *Inventing the People*, 70 (see note 3).
27. Ibid., 83.

28. Ibid., 82.
29. Ibid., 85–89.
30. Ibid., 89–91.
31. Ibid., 91.
32. Ibid., 94–121, *passim*.
33. Ibid.
34. Ibid., 102–106.
35. Ibid., 102–103.
36. Ibid., 120.
37. Ibid., 118.
38. The remainder of this chapter will trace the emergence of the people as the constitutive element in the American polity in broad brush strokes. The focus will be upon the development of an operable construct called the 'people'. A more detailed narration of the emergence of actual democracy will be found in Chapter 5.
39. Morgan, *Inventing the People*, 122 (see note 3).
40. Ibid., 123.
41. Ibid., 123–125.
42. Ibid., 125.
43. Ibid., 134.
44. Ibid., 128–130.
45. Ibid., 135–141.
46. Ibid., 143.
47. Ibid., 147.
48. Ibid., 148.
49. This is an oversimplification. The complexities of late colonial society, economics and politics will be treated in more depth in Chapter 5.
50. *See* for example, J.R. Pole, *Political Representation in England and the Origins of the American Republic* (London: Macmillan, 1966); Morgan, *Inventing the People*, 38–54 (see note 3).
51. Morgan, *Inventing the People*, 38.
52. Ibid., 237.
53. Ibid., 240–245.
54. Ibid., 240.
55. Ibid.
56. Ibid., 241.
57. Quoted in ibid., 241.
58. Ibid., 244–245.
59. The details of these developments will be the subject of Chapter 5.
60. Morgan, *Inventing the People*, 254 (see note 3).
61. *See* Chapter 6, below.
62. This story of democratization is addressed in part in the second section of this chapter. It is addressed more thoroughly in Chapter 5.
63. Chapters 8 and 9 detail the two principal ideological currents in American democracy.
64. Morgan, *Inventing the People*, 267 (see note 3).
65. Morone, *The Democratic Wish*, xii (see note 4).
66. Ibid., 7, 22.
67. Ibid., 23, 11.
68. Ibid., 1.
69. Ibid., 5.
70. Ibid., 7.
71. Ibid., 4, 12.
72. Ibid., 9–11.
73. Ibid., 11–13.
74. Ibid., 12, 28.
75. Ibid., 40.
76. Ibid., 33.
77. Ibid., 41.
78. Ibid., 36, 12.
79. Ibid., 62.
80. Ibid., 63.
81. *See* Chapters 8 and 9, and *passim*.
82. Madison will be the topic of Chapter 6.

83. Morone, *The Democratic Wish*, 127 (see note 4).
84. Ibid., 41.
85. These developments will be treated in more detail in Chapter 5.
86. Morone, *The Democratic Wish*, 76, 79.
87. *See* Chapter 5.
88. Morone, *The Democratic Wish*, 76, 79.
89. Ibid., 75.
90. Ibid., 80.
91. Ibid., 74.
92. Ibid.
93. Ibid., 78, 82, 114.
94. Ibid., 75, 324.
95. Ibid., 97.
96. Ibid., 106.
97. Ibid., 96.
98. Ibid., 98.
99. Ibid., 123.
100. Ibid., 109.
101. Ibid., 99.
102. Ibid., 113.
103. Ibid., 114–115.
104. Ibid., 110.
105. Ibid., 114.
106. Ibid., 124.
107. Ibid., 127. The Nineteenth Amendment granted suffrage to women.
108. Ibid., 133.
109. Ibid., 132.
110. Ibid., 133.
111. Ibid., 136.
112. Ibid., 162.
113. Ibid., 145.
114. Ibid., 151.
115. Ibid., 157.
116. Ibid., 163.
117. Ibid., 168.
118. Ibid., 162.
119. Ibid., 166.
120. Ibid., 184.
121. Ibid., 174–175, 178.
122. Ibid., 146, 159,
123. Ibid., 188–189.
124. Ibid., 188.
125. Ibid., 186.
126. Ibid., 206.
127. Ibid., 187.
128. Ibid., 141.
129. Ibid., 226.
130. Ibid., 239, 244.
131. Ibid., 233.
132. Ibid., 246–247.
133. Ibid., 251–252.
134. Ibid., 337.

PART III

Inventing Leadership

4. A new social relation

With the emergence of the people as a central construct of the polity, the familiar landscape of leading in the traditional sense became the unknown territory of attempting to achieve societal goals in a world where many of the previous guideposts for proper relating between the many and the few had been swept away. It was this foundational challenge to the old order – a shift in underlying reality, if you will – that demanded a new fiction that could encompass both leaders and the people. It is to the emergence of this fiction that we now turn. This chapter identifies the genesis of this new fiction and revisits our theoretical framework of implicit theories as they will be applied to the new fiction of leadership. This should prove beneficial as we attempt to identify and dissect the variety of proposed solutions to the challenges posed by the emergence of the people. In this way we can better critique the various historical attempts at inventing a successful leadership relation and ultimately, to suggest new ones better suited to today's leadership context.

THE EMERGENCE OF THE FICTION OF LEADERSHIP

The need for a new fiction to accommodate the new reality of a sovereign people is one of the consequences of the narrative of the preceding chapter. The rise of the fiction of the people created a sort of vacuum that demanded a new fiction to replace it. Modern sociologist Matthew Trachman cited the French political philosopher Claude Lefort when he argued that 'with the rise of modern democracy, the place of power, which had been occupied by the monarch's body, has become what Lefort terms an empty place. While, for instance, in a democracy we say the people rule, the people are not a real substantial entity.'[1] Hence the need was for something to fill that vacuum, and that something was a new conceptualization of leaders and the people working together to achieve societal objectives. This new conceptualization we call *leadership*.[2] The new conceptualization was (is) a fiction, just as the leader and the people are fictions. Nevertheless it serves the central societal purpose of making understandable a new reality, and of creating a normative ideal of the type of social relation among leaders and followers to which we can aspire.

This requires a tracing of the emergence of the new fiction. Perhaps it is not surprising that it was historian Edmund S. Morgan who first adumbrated the new construct that emerged as a result of the developments detailed in his study of the fiction of the people. Although Morgan's analysis only hinted at the new fiction that was to prove so important to a modern democratic world, his was the first to link the emergence of the people to a new demand for leadership. Morgan's insights are thus worthy of our attention.

As we saw in the previous chapter, the emergence of the fiction of the people was not planned, or even intended. Throughout his detailing of the rise of popular sovereignty, Morgan continually acknowledged that the construct of the people was one that was invented by elites for their own purposes. By the eve of the American Revolution, he wrote, 'Popular sovereignty had been successfully directed for more than a century to support the beneficiaries of England's social hierarchy and of America's attenuated version of it'. The problem, as we shall explore in more detail in the next chapter, was that 'there was nothing in the doctrine itself … to require the assignment of popular powers to one set of men or women than another. While making it possible for the few to govern the many, popular sovereignty offered, in itself, no prescription for restricting membership in the few to the sort of people who had traditionally expected it'.[3]

This, in turn, posed significant problems for those who wished to preserve the *status quo ante*. Morgan looks no farther than to American Founding Father James Madison. 'He had invented a sovereign people,' acknowledges Morgan, 'but he had assumed an existing social structure in which the people would know and recognize and defer to their natural leaders.'[4] This, as Morgan points out and we explore in more depth in the next chapter, was a false assumption. Indeed, as Morgan points out, 'From the beginning the egalitarian implications of the doctrine had rested uneasily beneath the deference that the better sort expected from the rest of the population, a deference that was supposed to place the better sort "naturally" in positions of authority in the church and the armed forces as well as in the state'. Such deference 'died a slow death, but every contest in which the few appealed to the many dealt it a blow. By the end of the eighteenth century in America and somewhat later in England', the traditional relationship between governors and governed had withered away.[5]

The need for a new relationship, a new fiction, to sustain the new reality became evident. As Morgan indicated in his peroration, 'The word "leader" is old, but "leadership" was a term that no one seems to have felt a need for as long as the qualities it designates remained an adjunct of social superiority. The decline of deference and the emergence of leadership signaled not only a new rhetoric but of *a new mode of social relations and a new way of determining who should stand among the few to govern the many* [emphasis supplied].'[6] This need was addressed by the new fiction, and 'by the end of the eighteenth century… something that we call "leadership" was taking its place in the ordering of society'.[7]

While the historian Morgan posits the emergence of a new social construct in the concluding passages of his study of popular sovereignty, it is sociologist Matthew Trachman who offers the best analysis of its emergence. In so doing, he provides an important point of departure for our own analysis of leadership in a democracy. Trachman's academic training is a key to many of his insights. As a sociologist, he takes a different perspective from that of the historian or political scientist, the disciplines usually linked to the study of political developments. As Trachman freely admits, 'My disciplinary training is as a sociologist. It is important to point this out,' he continues, 'because in many ways my approach to studying leadership has been influenced by a sociological perspective.' Trachman goes on to explicate what this means. 'Sociologists claim that members of a culture exist in a social context that is largely unnoticed – it is simply taken for granted. Members of a culture assume that their culture is simply natural or inevitable.' Here is where the sociologist makes a contribution. 'In order to awaken ourselves to culture's conventions,' explains Trachman, 'sociologists try to make the familiar seem strange – we aim to disrupt common sense, so that we can begin to understand and analyze common sense.'[8]

Trachman's approach is directly relevant to our ongoing study of fictions. In effect, what he is attempting to accomplish is to help us to see our own fiction more clearly. Fictions have ever been a difficult concept to embrace. Somehow, *other* people's fictions are easier to detect than our own. For example, most in the modern world would have little difficulty in perceiving the divine right of kings as a fiction. Perceiving popular sovereignty as a fiction is a bit more problematic for us, since it is our own definition of reality. Perhaps most difficult yet is the fiction of leadership, because it is a social relation that we take for granted. This is where Trachman can contribute to our understanding. By taking a step back and viewing leadership from the perspective of a sociologist, he helps to bring an otherwise amorphous political and social fiction into focus. Trachman's commitment to elucidating an otherwise unrefined societal construct meshes nicely with the strategy of this volume.

So too does his framing of his analysis of leadership in historical perspective. As Trachman suggests, 'We need to historicize the discourse – that is, to treat it as emerging at a particular historical moment and in response to a particular historical problem'.[9] His approach, so congruent with the premises of this study, makes Trachman's work particularly useful to our current study. Let us turn first to his historical analysis.

Borrowing a leaf from Morgan, Trachman endeavors to date the initial appearance of the term 'leadership'. In doing so, he builds upon the insights of Hannah Arendt. As Trachman puts it, 'Arendt would tell us that one way to date the actual birth of a general historical phenomenon like leadership is to find out when the word leadership appears for the first time. To find out when the word was first used is crucial in Arendt's approach', Trachman explains, 'because she argues that concepts are introduced into our political vocabulary because new ways of appearing among our fellow humans need to be named.'[10] As Arendt herself puts it, 'Each new appearance among men stands in need of a new word, whether a new word is coined to cover the new experience or an old word is used and given an entirely new meaning'.[11] Trachman applies this to leadership. 'I will focus on when the word leadership was first used,' he says, 'because I am convinced that the development of the concept was part of an historic elaboration of a new way of appearing.'[12] Looking then to the concept of leadership, Trachman finds that the historical moment in which the term emerged can be rather precisely dated. The contemporary sources suggest that the word leadership first appeared in print in the first half of the nineteenth century. This is reinforced by the work of scholar Joseph Rost, whose 'extensive search of dictionaries of the English language ... showed that the first appearance of leadership in a dictionary of the English language was in Noah Webster's *American Dictionary of the English Language* (1818)'.[13]

If Arendt is to be believed, this emergence of a new term in the lexicon was anything but accidental, and deserves careful analysis. 'In a sense,' acknowledges Trachman, 'the question Arendt might suggest for us is what exactly was it that was new about the world of nineteenth-century America, the world which seems to have first articulated the concept of leadership.'[14] The answer had everything to do with the developments we have been tracing. 'The claim that I would like to stake out here', asserts Trachman, 'is that the emergence of the discourse of leadership is connected to the emergence of the modern democratic world and to modern democratic ways of appearing. I will argue that the discourse of leadership needs to be thought of as a socio-conceptual product of what Tocqueville called the democratic revolution.'[15]

Trachman finds considerable support for his contention in the leadership literature. 'Alvin Gouldner [in the 1960s] claimed that an explicit concern with leadership was a product of the democratic world.' According to Gouldner, 'an extensive and articulate concern with leadership is a phenomena conditioned by modern democratic values'.[16] A decade later, one of the foundational figures in the field of leadership studies, James MacGregor Burns, agreed, but was not sanguine about the outcome. As Trachman summarizes it, 'Burns linked the creation of the discourse of leadership to the decline of the hierarchical world.... Yet, beginning in the seventeenth and eighteenth centuries, the doctrine of authority began to be undermined by bulwark of equality.' Although Burns links 'the discourse of leadership' to 'democratic ways of appearing', to use Trachman's terms, he does not believe that discourse has achieved a successful outcome. Burns 'points ... to the "absence of a doctrine of leadership with the power and sweep of the old doctrine of authority, but now emphasizing followers and leaders'. Burns thus calls 'for the creation of a doctrine of leadership that could function in the democratic ... world in the way that the doctrine of authority functioned in the monarchic ... world'.[17] The fact that one of the giants of current leadership scholarship can both link leadership to democracy and suggest that we have yet to get the fiction right affirms the timeliness of our continuing discussion.

Trachman, then, provides an important service in helping us to recognize that the construct of leadership was indeed something new in the world. 'Rather than defining leadership as an omnipresent feature of the human condition,' he concludes, 'the usage of the concept [must be] placed in its proper historical context. The discourse of leadership [should be] treated as emerging at a particular historical moment, in order to name a new way of appearing among others.'[18] 'Leadership, then, needs to be thought of as a socio-conceptual product of the modern democratic revolution. From its inception, and to this day, the discourse of leadership has remained attached, at least in some degree, to a democratic way of appearing.'[19] It was (and is), in its essence, a new fiction created to make sense of (and, in some instances, to manipulate) a new reality, a reality where the people had new predominance.

The remainder of this volume explores various historical and contemporary configurations of the new fiction, and proposes a new variant of the fiction of leadership. Before turning to that task, however, we need to turn again to our analytical framework of implicit theories, in order that we can evaluate the respective approaches to leadership.

THE IMPLICIT THEORIES OF THE LEADERSHIP RELATION

Throughout this volume we have been using what we call the leadership template to elucidate the 'implicit theories' of leadership. Here we draw upon our prior analysis, but now, with our attention at last upon the fiction of leadership itself, it is necessary to lay the groundwork for our subsequent analysis. Accordingly, prior to our study of a variety of models of the leadership relation, it is useful to elaborate upon our template of leadership.

It should come as no surprise from the above discussions of the implicit theories underpinning the fictions of the leader and the people that various approaches to leadership in a democracy can begin from quite different and often conflicting basic assumptions and premises. Unless these are articulated and understood, it is impossible to compare and analyze adequately the historical and contemporary solutions for the dilemmas of leadership in a democracy. When one turns to the current discourse on leadership in a democracy, these differing starting points – often unacknowledged by the disputants – stir much of the passion – and not a little of the confusion – that characterizes these disagreements. Only if these basic assumptions are brought out into the open can one hope for current debate over the workings of democracy to move beyond polemics and into a reasoned discussion of substantive differences. When it comes time for promulgating proposed reforms in the last section of this volume, we will hold our own proposals up to the harsh light of their implicit premises and assumptions. This will allow reasoned debate over these proposals, and hopefully elevate the debate to a level of rational discourse.

Although each contributor to the discourse on leadership in a democracy brings a unique constellation of assumptions and premises to the debate, it is possible to identify several common issues that each has to confront. Indeed, there are certain issues that are so central to the fiction of leadership in a democracy that every attempt to construct a working model of the relation between leaders and followers must confront and resolve them. It is the resolution of these core issues that creates one's 'implicit theory' and largely determines one's perspective and course of action in approaching leadership in a democracy. These issues comprise the protocol of our leadership template; it is to these core issues that we now again turn.

What is the Leadership Challenge?

For any version of the fiction of leadership to achieve hegemony, of course, the fiction needs to address successfully the chief dilemmas and challenges posed by the emergence of the people as the constitutive power in the regime. Such challenges are legion, yet at its most fundamental level, the essential challenge of leadership in a democracy is to achieve a synthesis between the 'thesis' of the classical ideal of the leader and the 'antithesis' of the sovereignty of the people. All other matters are merely derivative. Our focus, then, will be upon how this challenge might be framed and resolved.

One way to characterize the dilemma inherent in this challenge is to depict it in terms of *elitist* versus *participationist* approaches to leadership. This tension in democratic polities has been summarized best by Matthew Trachman. 'Either we get an "elitist" view which understands democracy to be a "threat" to leadership,' he says, 'or a participation-ist view which understands leadership to be a "threat" to democracy.'[20] Or, as political scientist Bruce Miroff phrases it, 'American devotees of leadership have trusted the nation's political salvation to the hands of a leadership elite, while treating followers as a secondary and inferior lot. Radical democrats have feared leadership as inherently destructive of democracy and have counted instead on the enthusiastic and capable efforts of leaderless equals.'[21] Note that each scholar uses the term 'leadership' interchangeably with 'elite rule'; neither applies the term in the manner it will be used in this text – as connoting leaders and followers working together to achieve societal objectives. Nevertheless, they each point out a very real tension between 'elitists' and 'participationists'. This tension, a tension that has infused democratic workings since their inception, is worthy of some elaboration.

One horn of democracy's dilemma is posed by elitism. At its most basic, according to Thomas Dye and Harmon Zeigler, 'the central proposition of elitism is that all societies are divided into two classes: the few who govern and the many who are governed'. In such a scenario, '*elites* are the few who have power; the *masses* are the many who do not'.[22] The elitist approach, however, has come to mean more than the simple recognition that the few always rule the many. In its more normative form, elitism calls for the deference to leaders with supposedly higher levels of knowledge and ability to govern society. Thus, there are two branches of the elitist argument, which we can call the realist and the normative. Let us look into each in more detail.

The realist branch of elitist theory simply holds that elite rule in a democracy is inevitable. According to this view, 'elites, not masses, govern *all* societies. Elites are not a product of capitalism, or socialism, or industrialism or technological development. All societies – socialist and capitalist, agricultural and industrial, traditional and advanced – are governed by elites.' Indeed, 'individuals in all societies, including democracies, confront the iron law of oligarchy. As organizations and institutions develop in society, power is concentrated in the hands of [the few].'[23]

Whether or not the *realpolitik* of the realists is correct, another branch of the elitist school nonetheless asserts that elites *should* rule, even in a democracy. This interpretation holds that there are those with higher levels of 'education, ... knowledge, ... [and] ability', who should take their place at the head of the polity.[24] According to Trachman, 'Elitists argue that democracy needs [such elite leaders] if it is to fulfill its promise'. Without wise and virtuous elite leaders, one ends up with a '"standardized mediocrity" ... at the price of standards and distinctiveness'.[25]

The other horn of democracy's elitist–participationist dilemma is the participationist viewpoint. Participationism, despite existing in several different forms, is simply a stance in favor of giving decision-making power to the people. From this perspective, the vitality of democracy and the quality of decisions that are made depend upon mass political participation. 'Participationists', explains Trachman, 'contend that democratic peoples are self-regulating, and the notion that they need to subordinate themselves to an individual who represents some higher moral standard that they themselves have not attained, is elitist claptrap.'[26]

The opposing conclusions of these two approaches to ruling in a democracy identify a fault line among theories of democratic leadership. The dilemma for those seeking to construct a workable conception of leadership is that both approaches have their virtues and their flaws. The elitist view has ever had its attractions. It is difficult not to be lured by the siren call of great and virtuous leaders looking out for our good. Moreover, an argument can be made for the claim that some individuals *are* more capable than others, and so have some claim to positions of influence. On the other hand, it takes no imagination for anyone living in the twenty-first century to realize the down side of relying upon individual leaders purportedly acting on our behalf. Similarly, the belief in widespread citizen participation is so much a commonplace as to appear almost trite. The potential weakness in the participationist approach lies in the question of whether the people are willing and able – or can be fully trusted – to have sovereign authority in a democratic state. Part of the problem is the lack of popular commitment to the endeavor. Bruce Miroff has noted that 'put into practice, however, a pure participatory democracy has often appeared too demanding for most people [with its] ... endless meetings, [and] intrusions on personal life and privacy'.[27] It is also a matter of expertise. Miroff states, 'Committed democrats must confront not only the difficulties in citizen participation but also the limitations of citizens' understanding.... When the scale of public action grew beyond the world hymned by Jefferson and the township celebrated by Tocqueville, citizens were called to make judgments on matters of which they could have little experience or expertise.'[28] Dye and Zeigler point out the more nefarious side of popular rule. 'Despite a superficial commitment to the symbols of democracy,' they argue, 'the masses have surprisingly weak commitments to the principles of individual liberty, toleration of diversity, and freedom of expression when required to apply these principles to despised or obnoxious groups or individuals.' Recent examples have included 'racial hatred, anti-intellectualism, class antagonisms, [and] anti-Semitism'.[29]

Clearly, a successful fiction of leadership will have to negotiate this tension. Pure, unalloyed democracy appears neither feasible nor even desirable. Yet the reality of popular sovereignty forbids swinging too far in the direction of elite rule. The reality is that there must be both leaders and the people operating in tandem in our democracy. The dilemma for leadership is that we need to balance the power and abilities of the elite with the will of the people.

What is the Perception of Human Nature?

One foundational issue that inevitably affects one's perceptions and conclusions about both leadership and democracy is the perception of the nature of man, and of the human condition. Whether one believes mankind is at base good or evil is at the heart of one's commitment to a polity grounded in the people. Related to this is one's assumptions about whether man is unregenerate or perfectible. One has to go no further than the contrasting approaches of Thomas Hobbes and John Locke to perceive the dramatically differing leadership theories that can spring from such disparate starting assumptions. So too, do assumptions concerning man's sociability impact one's conclusions about how man's interactions should be structured and regulated. Somewhat later in this volume we will turn our attention to one of the great ideological divides in the history of leadership in a democracy, that of the liberal/individualistic approach, which begins with the assumption that men are at base solitary beings seeking out their own interests, and the republican/ communitarian approach, which assumes that man by nature is 'political' in the sense that he exists and reaches his fullest potential only in concert with his fellow man. Related to this divide are differing assumptions concerning whether man is at base competitive or collaborative. Such diverse implicit theories clearly make for widely divergent conclusions about how the relations among men, and among leaders and the people, should be structured. It should be equally obvious that some of these differences are unlikely to be bridged fully. Nevertheless, the open articulation of such foundational premises provides the best hope for a constructive dialogue.

Are the People Capable of Governing?

This issue arose most dramatically as a consequence of the emergence of the fiction of the people, and was discussed in the previous chapter. Once we turn to the fiction of leadership – that is, to the invented conceptions of the ideal influence relation among leaders and followers that facilitates the accomplishment of group or societal objectives, the question takes on added significance. The very nature of that 'influence relation', after all, is fundamentally shaped by the assumptions about the capability of the people to govern.

As we have seen in our earlier discussion, the emergence of democracy brought with it essentially two stances on the matter. The first, implicit in the centuries-old tradition of the classical ideal of the leader, holds that the people as a whole cannot be trusted – not fully, at any rate – to govern themselves wisely, and therefore need the guidance of wiser and more virtuous leaders. This, of course, tracks closely the elitist school of leadership, as well as the trustee form of representation. The opposite stance is the implicit theory underlying the participationist approach to leadership and the delegate form of representation. This argument maintains that the people themselves are capable of governing, and indeed, are the best positioned to know the common good.

Much of the friction between opposing sides in both theoretical discourses regarding leadership in a democracy and in ongoing policy debates stems from differing assumptions concerning this very issue. It is important, in our subsequent analysis, to bring these differing implicit theories to light.

What is the Proper End or Purpose of Leadership?

Readers of the earlier chapters of this text will recognize that, prior to the modern era, the answer to the question of the proper end of leadership could be succinctly answered by reference to the 'common good'. Moreover, prior to the emergence of the notion of the sovereignty of the people, there was little concern over what that term entailed or how it was to be discerned and implemented. Both the discerning and the implementing were the tasks of the wise and virtuous leader, who, by definition, was responsible for securing the common good of all.

With the momentous events of the seventeenth and eighteenth centuries, however, the issue rather suddenly became much more complicated. We have already traced the impact of the rise of the fiction of the people, and how it challenged traditional notions of who was to determine the common good. But these years also generated an even more fundamental challenge. As we will detail in a subsequent chapter, those years also were the breeding ground for a political philosophy (we will call it 'liberalism') that questioned the very conception of a common good. As we embark upon our study of various approaches to leadership, it may be useful to sketch out in more detail the debates surrounding the common good in a democracy.

The notion of the desired end of leadership as the common good is somewhat problematic, given the fact that some factions deny the existence of such an entity. The discussion here, however, is intended to be sufficiently broad so as to encompass all points on the spectrum. Certainly the concept has been deeply troubling for modern democracies, and the differing perspectives that have been taken concerning the existence and attainment of such a construct explain much of the conflict among leadership models. Some of the principal formulations are briefly summarized below.

The conceptualization of the common good with the longest pedigree in the Western tradition is that stemming from the civic republican tradition. In that tradition, there was a deep commitment to the idea of a common – truly common – good. There was a belief in 'a powerful, shared common interest' which was 'a distinct public interest with an objective existence of its own'. In short, this powerful tradition maintained that there was such a thing as the common good, that it could be ascertained by astute leaders, and that there would be a citizen 'consensus about the common good'.[30]

In striking contrast is the view of the common good often associated with the liberal tradition.[31] 'Rejecting classical notions of public good', those in the liberal tradition disdained the idea that there might be a unitary and ascertainable common good.

Instead, they 'left individuals to define and pursue their own self interest'. According to the dominant strain of liberalism, the free interplay of private interests would, as in Adam Smith's *Wealth of Nations*, culminate in something akin to the public interest.[32] A modernized variant of this approach is embodied in the world view sometimes called interest-group liberalism. In this approach, society's interests are represented in 'countervailing centers of power'. These competing centers 'can check one another and keep each interest from abusing its power'. Public policy results from 'an equilibrium of interest interaction', in which 'the resulting policy is therefore a reasonable approximation of society's preferences'.[33]

In our contemporary world, with its stress on participation by all and its diversity, another, more cautious, conceptualization of the common good has come into play. With the liberals, this school rejects the notion of a unitary common good. For these individuals, the focus has moved away from the content of the outcome of societal debates and instead focuses in on the process of the debate itself. That is to say, in this process-oriented approach, the stress is upon making sure that all the 'stakeholders' have the opportunity to participate on something near an equal basis, and that the debate itself allows all views to get a fair hearing. If these procedural safeguards operate correctly, the outcome, almost by definition, is acceptable, and, because all have participated in its formulation, it could even be considered as a 'common' good.[34]

The above brief summary does not exhaust the litany of responses to the challenge of the common good in a democracy, but it sets forth the chief parameters of the debate. There is, as we have seen, debate over whether the common good is a unitary entity to which all can accede, or a composite of individual interests, or perhaps even a nonentity that can only be approximated in the give and take of democracy. There is disagreement over whether the common good is an end to be achieved or is merely a process of interaction. How one conceives the common good, then, goes a long way toward determining how one will approach the operations of democracy and leadership.

Closely related to conceptions of the common good are the hierarchies of values that guide various constructions of the leadership fiction. The distinctions here are often subtle and rarely clearly articulated, yet they exert a substantial impact upon one's perceptions of the obligations of the leadership relation. Modern democracies were founded upon such iconic declarations of values as 'life, liberty, and the pursuit of happiness', or 'liberty, equality and fraternity', but such widely accepted enunciations mask substantive differences in interpretation and priority. Some, for example, stress the negative liberty of the absence of governmental interference in one's private affairs, while others champion the positive liberty that comes from having sufficient economic and political resources. Equality can mean the equality of opportunity or the equality of condition. Another widely accepted value, justice, can take on quite different meanings. Other values are overtly antagonistic. Equality and fraternity, for instance, can be at odds with conceptions of liberty. Such distinctions can be elaborated almost without end. For our purposes, the important thing is that the relevant values that inform each approach to leadership, and their interpretation, must be identified and articulated. This is not only conducive to a more informed evaluation of the proposed leadership solution, but it also tends to bring clarity to heated disputes among rival claimants whose arguments are – often unknowingly – grounded in contrasting definitions of a common term.

What is the Epistemology of Leadership?

The various conceptualizations of the proper end of leadership – discussed above in terms of the common good – imply differing standards by which participants in a democracy can discern appropriate policy and gauge success. For example, those adhering to an elitist approach – which includes the classical ideal – are more concerned with who is placed into a position to discern and implement the common good than with its content. Participationists, on the other hand, look to processes that incorporate widespread citizen activity in the policy-making process. Classical liberals take yet a different approach: they seek to establish institutional structures that ensure protection of individual initiative.

In addition to differences concerning how appropriate policies are determined, the epistemology of leadership in a democracy holds varying answers to the question of how one knows whether or not any chosen action is successful. Put another way, it is the question of the standard by which one judges the propriety and success of actions. Numerous 'external standards' or 'independent grounds' have been posited over the years, to include absolute truth, the action of the market, the protection of property, the greatest good for the greatest number, natural rights, law and the like. Some reject independent grounds entirely, and embrace a relativistic approach to all actions. Regardless of the standard chosen, the very choosing of such a measure of success or failure represents an important implicit theory of leadership.

What is the Role of the Leader?

As was discussed in our previous chapter concerning the fiction of the people, the role of the leader in modern democracies is also a topic of considerable controversy. One can easily imagine the contrasting role for the leader in an elitist as compared to a participationist approach to leadership. And, obviously, a 'trustee' type of representative will experience different expectations from a 'delegate' type. Moreover, some of the more modern conceptualizations of the operations of a democratic state evince considerable ambiguity about the role of leaders. Some proponents of classical liberalism are much more concerned with the protection of rights than with the leader, while many modern communitarians seemingly reject the very idea of a leader as elitist.

What is the Role of the People?

This, too, inevitably came up in our discussion of the emergence of the fiction of the people, and we need not be overly repetitive here. The expected role for the people is in many ways the obverse of that of the leader. That is to say, to the extent that one harbors elitist assumptions, the role for the people is by that much reduced. The opposite is the case for participationists. In a similar manner, the expected role of the people is quite distinct in a regime with trustee-type representation as compared to that of the delegate type. And again, the potential roles of both leaders and followers are also captured in a more dynamic way in answering the next question of the protocol.

How Should Leaders and the People Interact?

This query regarding the interactions among leaders and the people really embraces two related issues. Both involve leadership, which, in Edmund Morgan's words, is 'a new mode of social relations and a new way of determining who should stand up among the few to govern the many'.[35] The first issue is that of representation, and the second is the dynamics of the process that occurs between leaders and the people. Although such topics inevitably came up in discussing our two previous fictions, with our consideration of the fiction of leadership they come front-and-center. It is therefore worth our while to introduce them in more detail as preliminary to our continuing analysis.

Let us first turn our attention to the concept of representation. Somewhat ironically, adherents of both the elitist and participationist approaches to leadership in a democracy confront a similar challenge in the issue of representation. All but the most rabid of participationists acknowledge that, at some level, the many must choose representatives to transact the business of governing. As Thomas Dye and Harmon Zeigler acknowledge, '... even if it were desirable, mass government is not really feasible in a large society'. This reality brings us again to the notion of fictions. Dye and Zeigler continue: 'Lincoln's rhetorical flourish – "a government of the people, by the people, for the people" – has no real world meaning'. Instead, 'the democratic solution to the practical problem of popular government is the development of institutions of representation ... as bridges between individuals and their government'.[36] This aspect of popular government must be understood if we are to assess intelligently the workings of government by the people. The construct of representation, however, is not so simple as it might first appear. There are differing versions, with differing expectations placed upon both representative and constituents, that reflect the ideological divide that we have been tracing. It is to those that we now turn.

One classic approach to representation is commonly known as 'virtual' representation. This approach actually encompasses a constellation of assumptions about the appropriate relationship and behavior of both representative and constituent that it is important to identify. Virtual representation has a long history, but the term itself springs from Thomas Whately, a British official who responded to American colonial cries of 'no taxation without representation' with this famous passage: 'None are actually, all are virtually represented, for every member of Parliament sits in the House, not as a Representative of his own constituents, but as one of the August Assembly by which all the Commons of Great Britain are represented'.[37]

Embodied within Whately's notion of virtual representation are important assumptions about the polity and those who represent it. His assertion that 'all the Commons of Great Britain are represented' suggests that, as James Morone explains it, 'the constituency was a single entity bound together by a single interest – the general good. Representatives stood not for individual citizens or cities or causes, but for the country.'[38] Or, as Edmund Burke would have it, 'Parliament is not a congress of ambassadors from different and hostile interests which interests each must maintain, as an agent and advocate, against other agents and advocates, but Parliament is a deliberative assembly of one nation, with one interest, that of the whole – where not local ... prejudices ought to guide, but the general good.... You choose a member, indeed, but when you have chosen him he is not a member of Bristol, but he is a member of Parliament.'[39]

Implicit in this mode of representation is the conception of the representative as trustee for his or her constituents. Trachman notes that 'representation took a ... form in which followers deferred to [representatives] on the basis of their demonstrated virtue, not on the basis of public persuasion on substantive matters'.[40] Again, it was Edmund Burke who said it best. 'Certainly,' he said, '...it ought to be the happiness and glory of a representative to live in the strictest union, the closest correspondence, and the most unreserved communication with his constituents. Their wishes ought to have great weight with him; their opinions high respect; their business unremitted attention.... But his unbiased opinion, his mature judgment, his enlightened conscience, he ought not to sacrifice to you, to any man, or to any set of men living.... Your representative owes you, not his industry only, but his judgment; and betrays, instead of serving you, if he sacrifices it to your opinion.'[41] As Morone capsulizes it, 'Burke would loosen the linkages between citizenry and state. He would limit [representation] to natural leaders....'[42] Such a view of the polity, say Dye and Zeigler, 'envisioned decision making by representatives of the people, rather than direct decision making by the people themselves'.[43]

Quite different was the alternative view of representation. In response to British championing of virtual representation, explains Morone, the American colonists articulated 'what is sometimes called the microcosm view of representation. As John Adams put it, the legislature "should be an exact portrait, in miniature, of the people at large ... it should think, feel, reason, and act like them" ... Here', comments Morone, 'was the reverse of the Burkean view: not the wisest doing what is best for the people, but the typical doing what the people themselves would have done.'[44]

Just as virtual representation contained certain assumptions about the polity, constituents and representatives, so too did the microcosm view of representation. If virtual representation assumed that the relevant constituency was the British people as a whole, the assumptions of the microcosm view that arose in America were more localistic. Part of this distinction, Edmund Morgan points out, had simply to do with the logic of the Revolutionary debate. In their need to respond to Whately's claim of virtual representation, the Americans claimed the opposite. 'In the course of a dozen years of resisting those [British] measures the colonists insisted, again and again, that a representative derived his only legitimacy, his only authenticity, his only being from his attachment to and identification with his particular constituents.'[45] However, the intellectual logic of the Revolutionary debate was also reinforced by the reality of the American colonists. Morone again provides the relevant analysis. 'England and her colonies moved toward their break articulating sharply different theories of political representation, each imbedded in the styles and mores of their respective social orders', he explains. 'Colonial representation contrasted with English practice at almost every point. ... Constituencies were small, ... [and] assembly seats generally reflected the flux in the populace [and] ... the breadth of the franchise.' These realities 'led legislators to take a distinctly local view of their roles'.[46]

Another contrasting assumption that was inherent in the microcosm view was that the people themselves were capable – had it been logistically possible – to concoct wise public policy. This approach assumed that 'the people participating in civic affairs is how the public good is discerned ... if [representatives] could be like the people – if [the people] could somehow be reproduced in the assembly chamber – they were more likely to think, feel, and reason their way to the common good'.[47] This conception also changed the expectations of the role of the representative. If virtual representatives were expected to act as trustees, the microcosm approach expected them to act as delegates. 'Many colonies ... imposed residency requirements, elections were held annually, instructions on specific matters common', all with the intention of ensuring that representatives did not stray from the will of the people.[48]

Virtual representation and the microcosm view constitute opposite ends of a spectrum of possible conceptualizations of the relationship between governors and governed in a polity based upon the people. The possible variants are limitless, but one other approach to representation has become central to modern democracy, and deserves some discussion here. This form of representation has come to be associated with liberalism. In this variation, the people elect representatives who appear most likely to serve their perceived interests. These representatives then interact in the legislative body based upon these perceived interests to craft policy.

It should come as no surprise that this approach to representation, too, comes encumbered with pivotal assumptions about the nature of the polity, representatives and constituents. This approach is grounded in the liberal assumption that society is made up of distinct interests, and that the appropriate polity is one where, in the words of Dye and Zeigler, 'public policy ... is an equilibrium of interest interaction – that is, competing interest-group influences are more or less balanced, and the resulting policy is therefore a reasonable approximation of society's preferences'.[49] This type of representative relation partakes of elements of both types depicted above. The people in this construction are neither policy makers themselves nor completely passive. 'Individuals can influence public policy by choosing between competing elites in elections.' Moreover, 'elections and parties allow individuals to hold leaders accountable for their actions.' Representatives in such a system are expected to reflect the specific interests of their constituency, which harks back to the localism of the microcosm view. On the other hand, in this approach the representatives have superior 'skills in leadership, information about issues, knowledge of democratic processes, and skill in organization and public relations'.[50] Thus representatives also fit the elite categorization of the virtual approach.

These variations in conceptions of representation suggest, then, another dilemma for leadership in a democracy. If representation is indeed the point of nexus between leaders and followers, it is thus a critical issue that must be resolved well. The results are matters of consequence. The dialectical debate between elitism and participationism has the potential to be mediated by the mode of representation adopted as a part of the leadership fiction. Representation, then, links together elite leaders with the will of the people, and thus may be one method of bridging two disparate ideological streams.

We have discussed thus far the challenges posed by the respective elements of our definition of leadership: the roles of leaders and followers, and the ends toward which they direct their actions. There is yet another aspect of this new social relation called leadership to which we must attend. It is the nature of the interaction itself, the dynamic interchange between leaders and followers as they interact in the face of contextual challenges in pursuit of desired ends. This we can call the *leadership process*, and it embodies all of the issues and dilemmas outlined above.

As we proceed through the attempts of various commentators, scholars and practitioners to fashion a fitting leadership relation for a democracy, we must pay attention to the dynamics of the resulting process. When we ultimately turn to a consideration of the process of leadership, then, it will be our attempt at integrating the many criss-crossing currents of our discussions, with an emphasis upon the dynamic aspects of the interactions among the participants. The dilemmas confronted by those who contemplate an appropriate leadership process are those inherent in all the dilemmas outlined above; the challenge of creating the process is essentially the challenge of inventing the new fiction of leadership. Again, there will be many times when this dynamic will not be fully articulated by the chosen commentator, and it will be necessary to indulge in educated speculation. Regardless, it should be a visible part of our analysis, in order that it might be understood, critiqued, and, ultimately, improved upon.

How is the Matter of Diversity and Minority Interests Addressed?

Although this issue arose only tangentially in the historical periods covered thus far (when there was a belief in a common good and an assumption that society was homogeneous), with the rise of democracy and liberalism, concerns about minority rights and diverse interests have come to the fore. With the coming of democracy, the very definition of majority rule posed difficulties for minorities, and commentators and practitioners were quick to acknowledge the problem. And with the gradually increasing inclusiveness of democracy, the issue of dealing with diversity arose. In our upcoming analyses of variations of the leadership fiction, we will see varying attempts to address these fundamental challenges. Some will seek institutional protections for those not in the majority; others will look to procedural safeguards; while still others will focus on attitudinal adjustments. In the end, a successful democracy will require a leadership solution that addresses the matter of minority rights and diversity.

What Institutions and Processes Must be Designed to Accommodate the Premises and Assumptions about Leadership Articulated in the Responses to the Leadership Template?

Much of the remainder of this volume will be devoted to providing the answer to this question. We will engage, in other words, in inventing the fiction of leadership.

INVENTING THE FICTION OF LEADERSHIP

Having depicted the need for this new social relation we call leadership as a result of the emergence of the fiction of a sovereign people, and having set out in some detail the analytical template we will use in our further engagement with this phenomenon, the remainder of this volume will be devoted to a careful exploration of the principal attempts at inventing a fiction designed to fit the new reality of popular sovereignty. In the remainder of Part III, several of the most consequential attempts at creating a workable fiction of leadership will be put forward. Each, in turn, we will subject to analysis and critique. For each approach to leadership, it will be necessary for us to evaluate both the consistency between the approach's implicit theories and its proposed institutions and processes, and how well it resolves the challenges of leadership in a democracy. With the wisdom born of that analysis, and with a renewed look at present realities, Part IV will propose reforms for the future success of leadership in a democracy.

Before turning to the historical attempts at creating a useable fiction, however, it is important to explore in more depth the historical context within which leadership became a salient notion. It is only with a more thorough understanding of the challenges posed by the emergence of the people as a political force that we can appreciate the proposed solutions.

NOTES

1. Matthew Trachman, 'Historicizing Leadership / Democratizing Leadership Studies', (paper delivered at the annual meeting of the International Leadership Association, Toronto, Canada, November 2000), 7. This discussion will draw upon two distinct works by Trachman with identical titles. The first, cited here, is a conference paper. It will hereafter be cited as Trachman, 'Historicizing Leadership / Democratizing Leadership Studies [A]'. The second source with this identical title is a more formal article, still in manuscript form. It will be cited as Trachman, 'Historicizing Leadership / Democratizing Leadership Studies [B]'. All citations are with the permission of the author.
2. Note that this depiction of leadership parallels closely the definition provided at the beginning of the Prologue to this book.
3. Edmund S. Morgan, *Inventing the People: The Rise of Popular Sovereignty in England and America* (New York: W.W. Norton & Company, 1988), 292.
4. Ibid., 286.
5. Ibid., 305.
6. Ibid., 306.
7. Ibid., 305.
8. Trachman, 'Historicizing Leadership / Democratizing Leadership Studies [A]', 1.
9. Trachman, 'Historicizing Leadership / Democratizing Leadership Studies [A]', 2.
10. Ibid., 3.
11. Hannah Arendt, *On Revolution* (New York: Penguin Books, 1963), 35, quoted in Matthew Trachman, 'Historicizing Leadership / Democratizing Leadership [B]', 1.
12. Trachman, 'Historicizing Leadership / Democratizing Leadership Studies [A]', 3.
13. Trachman, 'Historicizing Leadership / Democratizing Leadership Studies [B]', 3, citing Joseph C. Rost, *Leadership for the Twenty-First Century* (New York: Praeger, 1991), 40.
14. Trachman, 'Historicizing Leadership / Democratizing Leadership Studies [A]', 3.
15. Ibid., 4.
16. Trachman, 'Historicizing Leadership / Democratizing Leadership Studies [B]', 5, citing Alvin Gouldner, *Studies in Leadership: Leadership and Democratic Action* (New York: Russell & Russell, 1965), 4.
17. Trachman, 'Historicizing Leadership / Democratizing Leadership Studies [B]', 5–6. The reference is to James MacGregor Burns, *Leadership* (New York: Harper & Row, 1978), 25.
18. Trachman, 'Historicizing Leadership / Democratizing Leadership Studies [B]', 2–3.
19. Ibid., 5.
20. Trachman, 'Historicizing Leadership / Democratizing Leadership Studies [B]', 8.
21. Bruce Miroff, *Icons of Democracy: American Leaders as Heroes, Aristocrats, Dissenters, and Democrats* (New York: Basic Books, 1993), 347.
22. Thomas R. Dye and Harmon Zeigler, *The Irony of Democracy: An Uncommon Introduction to American Politics*, 9th edn. (Belmont, CA: Wadsworth Publishing Company, 1993), 2.
23. Ibid., 2, 8.
24. Ibid., 3.
25. Trachman, 'Historicizing Leadership / Democratizing Leadership Studies [B]', 8, 10.
26. Ibid., 12.
27. Miroff, *Icons of Democracy*, 348 (see note 21).
28. Ibid.
29. Dye and Ziegler, *The Irony of Democracy*, 18 (see note 22).
30. James A. Morone, *The Democratic Wish: Popular Participation and the Limits of American Government*, rev. edn. (New Haven: Yale University Press, 1998), 41–43.
31. The republican and liberal traditions constitute the poles of American political discourse. Each will be treated in more depth in subsequent chapters.
32. Morone, *The Democratic Wish*, 15.
33. Dye and Zeigler, *The Irony of Democracy*, 10–11 (see note 22).
34. Perhaps the best example of this approach is Ronald A. Heifetz, *Leadership Without Easy Answers* (Cambridge: Belknap Press of Harvard University Press, 1994).
35. Morgan, *Inventing the People*, 306 (see note 3).
36. Dye and Zeigler, *The Irony of Democracy*, 8 (see note 22).
37. Thomas Whately, quoted in Morone, *The Democratic Wish*, 39 (see note 30).
38. Morone, *The Democratic Wish*, 39.
39. Quoted in ibid., 39.
40. Trachman, 'Historicizing Leadership / Democratizing Leadership Studies [A]', 5.
41. Edmund Burke, quoted in Morgan, *Inventing the People*, 218 (see note 3).

42. Morone, *The Democratic Wish*, 40 (see note 30).
43. Dye and Zeigler, *The Irony of Democracy*, 7 (see note 22).
44. Morone, *The Democratic Wish*, 40.
45. Morgan, *Inventing the People*, 244 (see note 3).
46. Morone, *The Democratic Wish*, 36–38.
47. Ibid., 44.
48. Ibid., 37.
49. Dye and Zeigler, *The Irony of Democracy*, 11 (see note 22).
50. Ibid., 10–11.

5.   The challenge of democracy

The appearance of the new social relation that we now call leadership was a product of the intersection of a complex constellation of historical circumstances, the most momentous of which was the growth of democracy. Although we have already traced the rise of a conception of popular sovereignty, that conception, as we have seen, was consistent with any number of political forms. In seventeenth-century England, for example, popular sovereignty was seen as entirely consistent with the continuation of elite rule. And, as we will see in some detail in the next chapter, such Founding Fathers as James Madison were quite comfortable with a regime that was grounded in the people, yet which fell far short of a democracy. But it was democracy that ultimately emerged as the dominant reality, and it is the peculiar circumstances of democracy that pose the greatest challenges for modern leadership. This chapter is devoted to a more detailed exploration of the rise of democracy, and the specific implications which that would have for those attempting to craft a new fiction – leadership – to meet its demands.

To pay attention thus to the historical roots of democracy is justified by the symbiotic relationship that has characterized democracy and leadership. As sociologist Matthew Trachman states, 'On the one hand the discourse of leadership has been shaped by the emergence of modern democracy. On the other hand modern democracy itself has been shaped by the emergence of the discourse of leadership. In a sense,' Trachman continues, 'leadership needs to be examined as both influenced by its origins in the modern democratic world and yet also influencing the shape modern democracy has come to take. What I am arguing for,' he concludes, 'is a narrative of simultaneous development; that is, that the discourse of leadership and modern democracy develop concurrently.' In order to begin that narrative, Trachman harks back to the insights of Hannah Arendt. 'Arendt's fundamental suggestion', he notes, 'is that we ask about the new way of appearing that leadership was intended to name by looking into the historical context in which the word leadership was first used.'[1] This chapter provides the narration of historical origins that Trachman and Arendt find so important.

Fortunately, such a narration currently exists in the award-winning work of historian Gordon S. Wood. His *The Radicalism of the American Revolution*[2] traces the emergence of democracy rather than leadership *per se*, but his thoroughgoing analysis makes it rather easy to extrapolate the leadership implications of the economic, social, political and intellectual developments of the late eighteenth and early nineteenth centuries. This chapter, then, will trace Wood's argument and add an analytical gloss intended to highlight the leadership implications of his conclusions.

Wood asserts that his book represents 'an inquiry into the democratization of early America'. More specifically, Wood provides a reinterpretation of the impact and consequences of the American Revolution. 'We have tended to think of the American Revolution as having no social character, as having virtually nothing to do with society, as having no social cause and no social consequences.... If we measure the radicalism of revolution by the degree of social misery or economic deprivation suffered, or by the number of people killed or manor houses burned,' he admits, 'then the conventional emphasis on the conservatism of the American Revolution becomes true enough.' Wood, however, means to stake out a larger claim. 'But if we measure the radicalism by the amount of social change that actually took place – by transformations in the relationships that bound people to each other – then the American Revolution was not conservative at all. On the contrary, it was as radical and revolutionary as any in history.... In fact, it was one of the greatest revolutions the world has known, a momentous upheaval that not only fundamentally altered the character of American society but decisively affected the course of history.... By the time the Revolution had run its course in the early nineteenth century,' Wood concludes, 'American society had been radically and thoroughly transformed. One class did not overthrow another; the poor did not supplant the rich. But social relationships – the way people connected to one another – were changed, and decisively so. By the early years of the nineteenth century the Revolution had created a society fundamentally different from the colonial society of the eighteenth century. It was in fact a new society unlike any that had ever existed anywhere in the world.' America had become 'the most liberal, democratic, and modern nation in the world'.[3]

Although Wood does not label those changed social relationships as leadership, leadership was among the most important manifestations of this shift. Equally significant, the move toward modernism posed – often for the first time – many of the central challenges relating to leadership in a democracy that we continue to confront. It behooves us, then, to trace Wood's argument with some care.

A REPUBLICAN PRELUDE

The move toward modernism and democracy did not occur suddenly. It had its roots in developments prior to the American Revolution. Accordingly, an understanding of the developments that gave rise to the 'discourse of leadership' requires that we must begin our narrative several decades prior to the Revolutionary crisis itself. For it was in those decades that changing social conditions and catalytic events caused the Americans to move beyond their original 'monarchic' social relations toward something new. This shift was not a full-blown transition to democracy, but rather, initially, to republicanism.

The implications of this early attachment to classical republicanism are profound. Republicanism itself proved to be a fiction inadequate to the dynamics of the early American nation, and it was eventually supplanted by social relations that were, in Wood's phrase, 'unlike any that had ever existed in the world before'. Nevertheless, this early exposure to classical republican ideas has left an indelible legacy. We will find that the social relations (and implicit theories) of classical republicanism closely resembled many of those previously articulated in our earlier analysis of the classical ideal of the leader in republics, which links this early American experiment with the past. Moreover, many of the assumptions about leadership in a modern democracy can be traced to these republican roots, and much of the conflict and confusion generated by current debates over leadership in democracy stem from the fact that one side of the debate argues from implicit theories that derive from the presumptions of classical republicanism.[4] It is of more than mere historical interest, then, that motivates our analysis of this early stage in the American response to the developments of the Revolutionary era.

In order to understand the American version of republicanism, it is necessary to first understand what preceded it. As Wood puts it, 'To appreciate the extent of the change that took place in the Revolution, we have to re-create something of the old colonial society that was subsequently transformed'. This 'old colonial society' exhibited a social relation Wood characterizes as 'monarchism'. 'Despite all the momentous transformations that had taken place since the seventeenth-century settlements,' Wood says, 'mid-eighteenth-century colonial society was in many ways still traditional – traditional in its basic social relationships and in its cultural consciousness…. The theoretical underpinnings of their social thought still remained largely monarchical.'[5]

More than anything else, monarchism was characterized by hierarchy and inequality. The American colonists 'may not have known much of real kings and courts, but they knew very well the social hierarchy that the subjection and subordination of monarchy necessarily implied'. Indeed, 'in the eighteenth century … it was nearly impossible to imagine a civilized society being anything but a hierarchy of some kind'.[6] Such hierarchy imposed certain expectations of participant relationships. Monarchical relationships were 'personal relationships of dependence, usually taking the form of those between patrons and clients, [which] constituted the ligaments that held this society together and made it work'. Those lower in the hierarchy were expected to acknowledge the superiority of those higher. 'The popular "deference" that historians have made so much of', observes Wood, 'was not a mere habit of mind; it had real economic and social force behind it.'[7] Such relationships stretched beyond the social and economic to include the political. 'Translating the personal, social, and economic power of the gentry into political authority was essentially what eighteenth-century politics was all about. Everywhere it was the same: those who had the property and power to exert influence … created obligations and dependencies that could be turned into political authority.'[8]

Inevitably coupled with such notions of hierarchy was an assumption of inequality among members of the polity. 'Living in a monarchical society meant, first of all', argues Wood, 'being subjects of the king. This was no simple political status, but had all sorts of social, cultural, and even psychological implications…. Since the king … was the "*pater familias* of the nation," to be a subject was to be a kind of child, subordinated to a political dominion. In its starkest theoretical form, it implied a society of dependent beings, weak and inferior, without autonomy and independence.'[9] It worked at all levels of society. Although the American colonists were known for their independent streak, 'Many colonists who were quick to scorn all forms of legal or contractual dependence, many who owned their own land and prided themselves on their independence, were nevertheless enmeshed in diffuse and sometimes delicate webs of paternalistic obligation inherent in a hierarchical society'. Even the 'most radical whigs', such as John Trenchard and Thomas Gordon in England, from whom the colonists imbibed their most revolutionary ideas, 'did not expect equality between men'.[10] There was, in sum, writes Wood, 'one great horizontal division that cut through [colonial society] with a significance we can today scarcely comprehend – that between extraordinary and ordinary people, gentlemen and commoners. Although the eighteenth century was becoming increasingly confused over who precisely ought to make up these basic groups, there was little question that in all societies some were patricians and most plebeians…. More than any other distinction, this difference between aristocrats and commoners, between gentlemen and ordinary people, made manifest the unequal and hierarchical nature of the society.'[11]

Note that this hierarchy and inequality were not necessarily evil; indeed, in its best usages, this social relation embodied the classical ideal of the leader. Just as we were able to trace the classic ideal in early monarchic forms of government, so too here was the classical ideal manifest. Modeling the classical ideal, the leader in the eighteenth century monarchic world was seen to be truly superior to those he led. Rulers were drawn from the aristocracy, and 'compared with [ordinary people] ... the members of the aristocracy were very different. They were those "whose Minds seem to be of a greater Make than the Minds of others and who are replenished with Heroic Virtues and a Majesty of Soul above the ordinary Part of our Species."'[12] 'Important offices were supposed to be held only by those who were already worthy and had achieved economic and social superiority.'[13] Such 'officeholders relied on their own respectability and private influence to compel the obedience of ordinary people. Common people could become hog reeves or occupy other lowly offices, but they had no business exercising high political office, since, in addition to being caught up in petty workaday interests, they had no power, no connections, no social capacity for commanding public allegiance and deference.'[14]

The fact that eighteenth-century expectations of monarchical leaders drew upon the fiction of the classical ideal can be seen in other justifications for such elite rulers. One characteristic of the ideal leader continued to be independence from self-interest and worldly obligations. Only 'independent gentlemen of leisure and education [were] expected to supply leadership for government'.[15] Beneath 'all these strenuous efforts to ... [assure] gentility [in leaders] lay the fundamental classical characteristic of being free and independent. The liberality for which gentlemen were known connoted freedom – freedom from material want, freedom from the caprice of others, freedom from ignorance, and freedom from having to work with one's hands.'[16]

This independence was to be utilized for the benefit of all. The ideal leader in a monarchic social relation was expected to look out for the welfare of those below him, indeed to act for the common good of the whole. Ordinary people 'were presumably unimaginative and unreflective and rarely saw beyond their own backyards and their own bellies'.[17] Leaders, on the other hand, had the wisdom and independence, and an obligation to think and act in the interests of the entire society.

In such ways did the classical ideal of the leader become manifest in American colonial society. It is a worthwhile endeavor to consider the implications of these monarchic relationships. According to Wood, 'A society organized like this accentuated the differences between the few and the many, gentlefolk and commoners, and gave meaning to the age-old distinction between rulers and ruled. "In all hierarchical Societies whatsoever," it was said, "there are, and must be, people that lead, and people that are led."'[18] The implications are enormous. As Wood puts it, 'we will never appreciate the radicalism of the eighteenth-century revolutionary idea that all men were created equal unless we see it within this age-old tradition of difference'.[19] Moreover, 'the stability of this political system thus depended on the social authority of political leaders being visible and uncontestable'.[20] 'In this face-to-face society,' argues Wood, 'particular individuals – specific gentlemen or great men – loomed large, and people naturally explained human events as caused by the motives and wills of those who seemed to be in charge.'[21] 'No presumption about politics',

Wood stresses again, 'was in fact more basic to society and separated it more from the emerging world of the nineteenth century.'[22]

Despite all the legitimately monarchical aspects of American colonial society, by the eighteenth century conditions were ripe for a shift to a new form of social relation, one that may be labeled republican. Part of the explanation lay in the unique institutional and political configuration of the British monarchy itself. We have previously traced the English political history of the seventeenth century, culminating in the Glorious Revolution and the ascendancy of Parliament.[23] This history – peculiar to England and not replicated elsewhere – gave the British monarchy republican overtones that were unique.

The political heritage of the seventeenth-century English experience ran deep. As a result of that century-long struggle against tyranny, argues Wood, 'Englishmen everywhere [to include the American colonists] simply made poor subjects for monarchy, and they were proud of it. The king had his birthright to the crown, but the people had theirs too. They were "free-born Englishmen" and they had rights and liberties that no other people in the world enjoyed. They had in fact,' Wood goes on to suggest, 'more rights and liberties than any traditional hereditary monarchy could accommodate, and consequently the British monarchy was very different not only from any other but also from what it had been in the days of James I.' Indeed, 'In the years following the Glorious Revolution of 1688 [the British] had become increasingly aware of the marvelous peculiarity of their limited monarchy'.[24] In particular, contrary to the premises of traditional monarchy, 'Representation in the House of Commons even allowed for the participation of His Majesty's subjects in the affairs of government.... Although few Englishmen could vote for representatives, they always had a sense of participating in political affairs.'[25] In sum, concludes Wood, 'By continental standards the English monarchy was scarcely a real monarchy.... Their famous "limited" or "mixed" monarchy was in fact a republicanized one.'[26]

The republican tendencies of the British monarchy were reinforced by the social conditions prevalent in the American colonies. Chief among these was the reality of relative equality among members of the colonial societies. 'Equality did not mean that everyone was in fact the same, but only that ordinary people were close in wealth and property to those above them and felt freer from aristocratic patronage and control than did common people elsewhere in the Western world.'[27] Wood depicts the realities of colonial life: 'In some places people moved around so rapidly and in such numbers that society as people had known it was not easily re-created. Hierarchies that gradually emerged out of raw frontier areas were necessarily jerry-built and precarious.... In such a raw society distinctions were hard to come by, and those who sought to rule had difficulty sustaining their authority.' Throughout the colonies, argues Wood, 'social distinctions remained tenuous, ... politics turbulent, and [the] structure of authority continually subject to challenge'.[28] 'This description of the truncated nature of American society is familiar', claims Wood. 'Both eighteenth-century observers and historians ever since have repeatedly commented on the egalitarian character of colonial society. America, it seemed, was primed for republicanism. It had no oppressive established church, no titled nobility, no great distinctions of wealth, and no generality of people sunk in indolence and poverty. A society that boasted that 'almost every man is a freeholder' was presumably a society ideally suited for republicanism.'[29]

Alongside the reality of colonial life was a readily available fiction that seemed to encompass the needs of the moment. We have previously traced the long heritage of classical republican thought in the Anglo-American experience. In Wood's version of this intellectual heritage, 'republicanism was the ideology of the Enlightenment. In the eighteenth century to be enlightened was to be interested in antiquity, and to be interested in antiquity was to be interested in republicanism.' The classical writers depicted in previous chapters were well known to thinking individuals of the eighteenth century. Indeed, 'all the ancient republics – Athens, Sparta, Thebes – were familiar to educated people in the eighteenth century ... but none was more familiar than Rome.... Those Roman writers ... set forth republican ideals and political and social values that had a powerful and lasting effect on Western culture.'[30] As we have seen, these Roman conceptualizations were transmitted through Machiavelli and ultimately culminated in the writings of James Harrington in the seventeenth century and the 'neo-Harringtonians' in the eighteenth.[31] By the eve of the American Revolution, 'Classical republican values existed everywhere among educated people in the English-speaking world, but nowhere did they have deeper resonance than in the North American colonies'.[32]

The nexus of egalitarian social realities and an ideology or fiction that appeared well-matched to it set the stage for significant changes. Gradually, the old ways of relating eroded away. 'Republicanism did not replace monarchy all at once', argues Wood, 'it ate away at it, corroded it, slowly, gradually, steadily, for much of the eighteenth century. Republicanism seeped everywhere in the eighteenth-century Atlantic world, eroding monarchical society from within, wearing away all the traditional supports of kingship, ultimately desacralizing monarchy.'[33] Thus, 'the Americans did not have to invent republicanism in 1776; they only had to bring it to the surface. It was there all along.'[34]

When the Americans were forced by the Revolutionary crisis to invent their own forms of government, it was quite natural that these governments would take on a republican cast. Indeed, as early as 'the middle of the eighteenth century these social changes were being expressed in politics'. And, says Wood, 'popular principles and popular participation in politics, once aroused, could not be easily put down, and by the eve of the Revolution, without anyone's intending, or even being clearly aware of what was happening, traditional monarchical ways of governing through kin and patronage were transformed under the impact of the imperial crisis'.[35] When the conflict with Great Britain reached the point at which the American revolutionaries began to contemplate the creation of new governments, a new view of appropriate social relations in the polity guided them. 'To eliminate those clusters of personal and familial influence and transform the society became the idealistic goal of the revolutionaries,' argues Wood. 'Any position that came from any source but talent and the will of the people now seemed undeserved and dependent.... A republic presumed, as the Virginia declaration of rights put it, that men in the new republic would be "equally free and independent."'[36]

If the Americans turned to republicanism in the Revolutionary era, it behooves us to explore in more detail the nature of their beliefs, and the implications for the relations between leaders and the people. Predictably, the form of Revolutionary republicanism was a product of the perceived specific historical challenges that gave rise to the Revolutionary crisis itself. In both England and America, but particularly in England, a group of critics attacked the emerging political reality of England after 1690. 'This social criticism was steeped in classical republican values'; they claimed that the monarchy was succumbing to 'luxury, selfishness, and corruption'.[37] This last charge – corruption – was the most dangerous. By that term the critics did not mean simply dishonest dealings; they meant that there was corruption in the classical republican sense of the term – that individuals were placing self-interest above the good of the whole. This, as we have seen in our discussions of classical republican thought, was lethal to a well-functioning polity. The remedy was a return to classical republican virtue. According to Wood, 'Virtue ... lay at the heart of all prescriptions for political leadership in the eighteenth-century English-speaking world'. Specifically, 'the virtue that classical republicanism encouraged was public virtue.... Public virtue was the sacrifice of private desires and interests for the public interest. It was devotion to the commonweal.'[38]

The stress upon public virtue held important implications for leaders of the new regime. It seemed to require, for instance, leaders who emulated the classical ideal. As Wood puts it, 'These appeals to antiquity made anything other than a classical conception of leadership difficult to justify. It was,' Wood explains, 'almost always classical standards ... that British opposition writers invoked to judge the ragged world of eighteenth-century politics. They placed the character of republicanism – integrity, virtue, and disinterestedness – at the center of public life.... Political leaders were held to ancient republican standards ... the civic humanist ideal of disinterested public leadership.'[39]

The focus upon disinterested leaders led in turn to the conception of rule by an elite. Theoretically, this was an aristocracy of merit, and, in the words of one revolutionary, 'all offices lie open to men of merit, of whatever rank or condition'.[40] In reality, however, the old republican stress upon independence and wisdom in a society's leaders kept the pool of potential leaders relatively small. 'Of course, the revolutionary leaders did not expect poor humble men – farmers, artisans, or tradesmen – themselves to gain high political office.'[41] This was because 'common people and others involved in the marketplace were usually overwhelmed by their interests and were incapable of disinterestedness.... Of course they were not to be the leaders of society. Although republicanism compared to monarchy rested on a magnanimous view of common people,' argues Wood, 'it retained a patrician bias in regard to office holding.' Even good republicans 'believed that important public office ... ought to be filled only with "the better sort".' Furthermore, at the time of the Revolution, 'for many this disinterested leadership could only be located among the landed gentry'.[42] These would most likely be the 'liberally educated, enlightened men of character' demanded by the classical ideal.[43]

The American experiment with republicanism, however, had a significance far beyond its attempt actually to apply the classical ideal of the leader to a reformulated polity. It also encompassed the recognition of the people as a constitutive element of the state. The American Revolution marked the first time that the notion of popular sovereignty, which, as historian Edmund S. Morgan has shown us, had its roots in the seventeenth century,[44] gained official legitimation as the core ideology of the state. As Gordon Wood puts it, 'Overnight modern conceptions of public power replaced older archaic ideas of personal monarchical government.... Popular consent now became the exclusive justification for the exercise of authority.'[45]

Along with this came new expectations of the people as well. In a polity grounded in public virtue, 'it followed that only autonomous individuals free from any ties and paid by no master were qualified to be citizens'.[46] Such citizens likewise had to grapple with new sorts of relations with their fellows. They needed to 'create once and for all new, enlightened republican relationships among people', relationships that demanded new responsibilities and new attitudes.[47]

The republican approach to the polity contained within it several key assumptions or 'implicit theories' about the nature of man, the proper relationships among citizens and between citizens and leaders, the reason for government, and the ultimate end that guides all action. It is essential to articulate each of these premises. Republicanism carried with it a rather beneficent view of man's nature and capabilities. 'Man was by nature a political being', which meant that he 'achieved his greatest moral fulfillment by participating in a self-governing republic'. Such republican citizens had to be 'virtuous – that is, willing to sacrifice their private interests for the sake of the community'. Moreover, 'this virtue could only be found in a republic of equal, active, independent citizens'.[48] Not all citizens were capable of ruling the polity, of course. Yet, if not fully capable of being leaders themselves, the fact that republicans had faith in 'the ability of the common people to elect those who had integrity and merit presumed a certain moral capacity of the people'.[49] The role of those leaders, once selected, was central. As Wood puts it, 'the people [were] allowed a share of participation in government, but ultimately [republicans] ... believed that the secret of good government ... lay in ensuring that good men – men of character and disinterestedness – wielded power'.[50] Once those leaders were selected, the people in the ideal republican state should defer to them as they steered the ship of state toward the only acceptable end – the achievement of a single, unitary common good.

The novel requirements of a republican polity created the impetus for a new way of relating that would have profound implications. Wood is extravagant in his claims about republicanism. He claims that the republicanism that emerged in the eighteenth century was 'revolutionary'. In fact, argues Wood, 'it was in every way a radical ideology – as radical for the eighteenth century as Marxism was to be for the nineteenth century. It challenged the primary assumptions and practices of monarchy – its hierarchy, its inequality, its devotion to kinship, its patriarchy, its patronage, and its dependency. It offered new conceptions of the individual, the family, [and] the state....' Wood goes on to depict republicanism in a way consistent with the argument being developed in this volume. Says Wood, 'Indeed republicanism offered nothing less than new ways of organizing society. It defied and dissolved the older monarchical connections and presented people with alternative kinds of attachments, new sorts of social relationships.'[51] Although Wood does not label it as such, the new social relation that was emerging during the Revolutionary crisis was one that we call leadership.

Yet, in many ways, the republicanism of the American Revolutionary era was only a prelude. As Wood puts it, 'the disintegration of the traditional monarchical society of paternal and dependent relationships prepared the way for the emergence of the liberal, democratic, capitalistic world of the early nineteenth century'.[52] It is to the rest of the story, to the story of the emergence of a society arguable modern, and its implications for leadership, that we now turn.

THE TRANSITION TO DEMOCRACY

Republicanism was revolutionary in its explicit grounding of government in the people and its disdain for traditional paternalistic relations grounded in in-born inequality. However, as we have seen, the utopian republicanism of the American revolutionaries was entirely consistent with longstanding expectations of the proper relationships between leaders and the people. The American state makers of the 1770s consciously embraced what we have deemed the classical ideal of the leader. Although we have seen that such a view of leaders stretched back to antiquity, the actual and overt adoption of this ideal by American revolutionaries was, in Woods' term, 'breathtaking'. This was because 'as hard-headed and practical as they were, they knew that by becoming republican they were expressing nothing less than a utopian hope for a new moral and social order led by enlightened and virtuous men'. Indeed, Wood suggests, 'It would be difficult to exaggerate the importance of these new enlightened republican ideals of gentility for the American revolutionary leaders.... We shall never understand the unique character of the revolutionary leaders until we appreciate the seriousness with which they took these new republican ideals.... No generation in American history has ever been so self-conscious about the moral and social values necessary for public leadership.'[53] Indeed, for Wood, 'their soaring dreams and eventual disappointments make them the most extraordinary generation of political leaders in American history'.[54]

The fact that these utopian republican expectations about societal leadership were to be disappointed had everything to do with the stunning developments that reached full flower in the decades after the American Revolution. Wood points out that 'the Revolution had set loose forces in American society that few realized existed, and before long republicanism itself was struggling to survive'.[55] What was to replace it was something entirely new in the history of the world: a vast, individualistic, egalitarian, commercial democracy that required the invention of a new leadership relation, a task that to this day has been imperfectly consummated.

The social, economic, political and intellectual dynamics 'set loose' by the American Revolution had been latent in American society during the decades prior to the Revolution. Wood suggests that 'the history of America in the decades between the 1740s and the 1820s is the story of these various revolutions. The imperial crisis with Great Britain and the American Revolution were simply clarifying incidents in this larger story of America's democratic revolution.'[56] In order to understand fully the dramatic outcomes of these societal movements, then, it is necessary to look briefly at their beginnings in the years prior to the Revolution.

In those years, argues Wood, 'powerful forces were accelerating and changing everything'. Indeed, 'these forces were the most important sources of the late-eighteenth-century democratic revolution'. Wood acknowledges that 'they were not unique to America, they were Western-wide.... All Europe experienced democratic revolution in the late eighteenth century, but in America this democratic revolution was carried further than elsewhere.'[57] How these forces played out in America, then, is a matter of some importance.

In the years prior to the Revolution, 'extraordinary demographic and economic developments, moving as never before, reshaped the contours of the society'.[58] The primary demographic reality was an extraordinary 'growth and movement of people.... This demographic explosion, this gigantic movement of people, was the most basic and most liberating force working on American society during the latter half of the eighteenth century, and it would remain so for at least another century after that.'[59] The implications for relations between leaders and the people were profound. In this fluid society, 'the social hierarchy seemed less natural ... and more man-made, more arbitrary'. As a result, subordinates and inferiors felt more independent, more free, than they had in the past.... Everywhere ordinary people were no longer willing to play their accustomed roles in the hierarchy…. [They were] less deferential, less passive, less respectful of those above them.'[60]

If this were not enough, 'coupled with this demographic expansion – and nearly equal a force in unsettling the society – were the spectacular changes taking place in the American economy'. The most significant development was the emergence of a vibrant internal economy within the colonies. According to Wood, 'almost everywhere in the colonies … growing numbers of small farmers, many for the first time in their lives, were drawn into producing "surpluses" for the market'.[61] In addition, a growing number of farm families were 'becoming part-time manufacturers and entrepreneurs'. These developments represented a 'momentous shift of the basis of American prosperity from external to internal commerce'. There developed, in short, 'an inland trade in the colonies' which amounted to 'a new kind of business world … involving the extensive exchange of goods and services'.[62]

For our purposes, the significance of this new economy lay in the new social relations that resulted. Prosperity was more widespread, leading to a diminution of social hierarchy. 'Common people now had the financial ability to purchase "luxury" goods that previously had been the preserve of the gentry.' This 'social emulation' reduced the obvious differences between the 'better sort' and ordinary people.[63] But it was more than merely a change of appearances that emerged from the new economy. Very real and substantive shifts in the way individuals related to one another also resulted. The inland trade, and in particular the rise of paper money that facilitated it, 'opened up possibilities for increasing numbers of people to participate more independently and more impersonally in the economy'.[64] Moreover, the rapid increase in borrowing and indebtedness caused many personal relationships to be replaced by impersonal, legalistic ones. Wood depicts how 'the new commercial borrowing involved formal, signed, interest-bearing instruments of credit, often between people who did not know each other well…. These written contracts represented very different obligations from [before].' They were, among other things, 'exclusively economic rather than being part of some ongoing social relationship based on personal familiarity'.[65] An unintended consequence of the new economic reality, then, were social relationships that were 'more independent and more free' than anything that had been known before.[66]

Even religious developments in the colonies in the years preceding the Revolution worked to undercut traditional deferential relationships within society. Although certainly at least in part a response to the unsettling demographic and economic changes detailed above, the religious upheaval of the mid-eighteenth century also contributed to the rapid breakdown of traditional societal relationships. Labeled by historians the 'Great Awakening', this religious movement was emotional, evangelical, and resulted in a great upsurge in religious participation. Resistance to the movement by conservatives often meant traditional church communities were split into 'Old Side' and 'New Side' congregations. Again, the important implications were social. 'By challenging clerical unity, shattering the communal churches, and cutting people loose from ancient religious bonds, the religious revivals became in one way or another a massive defiance of traditional authority.'[67]

Given all the social forces operating to undercut traditional deferential relationships between leaders and the people, it should come as no surprise that these trends should also manifest themselves in the political arena. Even before the Revolution, 'the growing independence of smaller and middling … farmers from traditional patronage connections manifested itself … [in a] number of contested elections.' In these elections, '"worthy gentlemen" were being pressed by "abject competitors"',[68] in ways quite contrary to the implicit assumptions that buttressed the classical ideal of the leader.

If the social and economic conditions of the pre-Revolutionary period operated to undercut traditional notions of deference to elite leaders, the problem was exacerbated by the fact that the leaders themselves somehow did not seem to fit the classical ideal. In the first place, American elites did not fit the classical model of a superior class of individuals. The problem, as Wood articulates it, was 'the weakness and incompleteness of American social hierarchy.... By English standards, the colonial aristocracy was a minor thing – at best composed of middling and lesser gentry only.... Although real and substantial distinctions existed in colonial America, the colonial aristocracy was never as well established, never as wealthy, never as dominant as it would have liked.' To complicate matters, 'the American aristocracy, such as it was, was not only weaker than its English counterparts; it also had a great deal of trouble maintaining the desired classical independence and its freedom from the marketplace'.[69] As Wood sums it up, 'there were numbers of educated well-connected professional men or gentlemen of independent fortune who were capable of living up to the classical ideals of political leadership that dominated eighteenth-century culture. But there were, it seemed, never enough of these to go around. As a result, more than one established gentleman complained of the extent to which colonial assemblies contained too many members who were not gentlemen in any sense, much less gentlemen educated in a classical ... mode.'[70] And, because 'elites also had trouble living up to the classical republican model of leadership, ... challenges to their authority were common'.[71]

The very fact that there were 'challenges to authority' suggests that it was not only the truncated elite who were at the heart of the problem. The other half of the equation was the reality that the people in American colonial society were not so properly deferential as the classical model expected. There were several reasons for this. There was, of course, a rich political and intellectual tradition inherited from the seventeenth-century English battle against tyranny. The American colonists lived in 'a liberty-loving whig-dominated world'.[72] In addition to this intellectual heritage, part of the explanation lay in the colonists' material well-being. In contrast to the English example, 'most American farmers owned their own land.... Freehold tenure in America was especially widespread, and freehold tenure ... "excluded all ideas of subordination and dependence".' The 'radical importance of this land ownership', argues Wood, 'cannot be exaggerated; even before the Revolution it gave Americans a sense of egalitarian separateness'.[73]

Moreover, the emergence of the new commercial society depicted above also helps to explain the new forms of social relations that were emerging. For example, we have seen 'the new conception of contract as a consensual bargain between equal parties'. This had important implications when applied to social relations. Once members of society 'came to think of ... superior-subordinate relationships as only deliberate and positive bargains between two parties', a whole new relation evolved. 'The contractual relationship now often presumed an equality....' In such contractual relationships 'authority ... commanded little natural respect. Allegiance was becoming a mere business arrangement, a coincidence of interests. This contractual imagery,' concludes Wood, 'mingled with and colored all paternal and superior-subordinate relationships.' As a result of the contractual nature of the relationship between superiors and subordinates, 'allegiance, which had once denoted the loyalty of an inferior to a superior, now became virtually indistinguishable from consent'.[74]

Once relations became based upon 'consent', the consequences were 'momentous'. Applied to the political sphere, the idea of leaders ruling only with the consent of the people, Wood suggests, 'touched on awesome questions'. For example, 'Did this mean that rulers were not to be "great men," perhaps not even gentlemen? Were rulers really "of the same species … and by nature equal" with those who ruled?' Would people respect rulers who were not buttressed by the traditional societal supports?[75] Although such questions were nascent at the time, the catalytic event that was the American Revolution would bring such queries into ever-higher relief.

The long-term economic, social and political developments that served to undercut classical republicanism were inchoate and barely recognized prior to the Revolution. Nothing deterred the American revolutionaries in their sincere, if utopian, effort to create a polity based upon civic virtue, a perception of a unitary common good, and a reliance upon leaders who fit the classic ideal. However, these pre-Revolutionary developments might be likened to hot embers, which were fanned into flame by the events of the Revolution and the years immediately thereafter. Eventually, those flames became a conflagration that swept all before it. To understand the democratic revolution which was about to take place, it is necessary to explore the impact of the Revolution and the events of the early American republic.

The American Revolution was, in Wood's words, 'the greatest utopian movement in American history. The revolutionaries aimed at nothing less than a reconstitution of American society…. They sought to construct a society and government based on virtue and disinterested public leadership and to set in motion a moral movement that would eventually be felt around the globe.' Unfortunately for these republican state builders, 'the ink on the Declaration of Independence was scarcely dry before many of the revolutionary leaders began expressing doubt about the possibility of realizing their high hopes'.[76] Much of the difficulty can be attributed to the visible emergence of those trends that we have traced prior to the Revolution.

As we have seen, one problem was the people themselves. Prior to the Revolution, the common people of America had not been as deferential as elite leaders would have liked, due partly to the fact of their economic independence. Now the other side of the commercial coin became apparent: those who were becoming so deeply engaged in the new commercial markets were not likely to practice civic virtue, to subsume their individual interests to the advancement of the common good. After the Revolution, argues Wood, 'expectations of raising one's standard of living … seeped deeper and deeper into society and had profound effects on the consciousness of ordinary people. Instead of creating a new order of benevolence and selflessness, enlightened republicanism was breeding social competitiveness and individualism.' In sum, by the 1780s, 'the American people seemed incapable of the degree of virtue needed for republicanism. Too many were unwilling to respect the authority of their new elected leaders and were too deeply involved in trade and moneymaking to think beyond their narrow interests or their neighborhoods and to concern themselves with the welfare of their state or their country.'[77]

So, too, there was the continuing problem of leaders whose traits and behaviors seemed inconsistent with the classical ideal. Here, too, the seeds of the problem antedated the Revolution, but the Revolution itself greatly exacerbated its impact. As Wood depicts the scene, 'in many of the greatly enlarged and annually elected state legislatures, a new breed of popular leader was emerging who was far less educated, less liberal, and less cosmopolitan than the revolutionary gentry had expected. These new popular leaders were exploiting the revolutionary rhetoric of liberty and equality to vault into political power and to promote the partial and local interests of their constituents at the expense of what the revolutionary gentry saw as the public good.'[78]

It is a familiar interpretation that 'the federal Constitution of 1787 was in part a response to these popular social developments, an attempt to mitigate their effects by new institutional arrangements. The Constitution, the new federal government, and the development of independent judiciaries and judicial review were certainly meant to temper popular majoritarianism.' We will turn to the details of this story in the next chapter. But to the extent that the federal Constitution was designed as a counter-revolutionary system designed to preserve prior social relations and the political hegemony of a 'virtuous' elite, it ultimately failed. As Wood puts it, 'no constitution, no institutional arrangements, no judicial prohibitions could have restrained the popular social forces unleashed by the Revolution'.[79]

The changes in American society in the years after the Revolution were obvious and momentous. The societal trends that had their seeds in the middle decades of the eighteenth century reached full flower in the decades after the Revolution. Wood again tells the story best: 'In the decades following the Revolution,' he says, 'American society was transformed. By every measure there was a bursting forth – not only of geographical movement but of entrepreneurial energy, of religious passion, and of pecuniary desires. Perhaps no country in the Western world has ever undergone such massive changes in such a short period of time.'[80]

In part, these developments were a continuation of longstanding social movements. But they were also spurred by the Revolution itself. In the economic sphere, 'no event in the eighteenth century accelerated the capitalistic development of America more than did the Revolutionary War. It brought new producers and consumers into the market economy, it aroused latent acquisitive instincts everywhere, and it stimulated inland trade as never before.' As a result, 'America was soon to become ... a scrambling business society dominated by the pecuniary interests of ordinary working people'.[81] The implications were of tremendous consequence. As Wood sums it up, the 'popular social forces unleashed by the Revolution ... swept over even the extended and elevated structure of the new federal government and transformed the society and culture in ways no one in 1776 could have predicted. By the early nineteenth century, America had already emerged as the most egalitarian, most materialistic, most individualistic ... society in Western history. In many respects this new democratic society was the very opposite of the one the revolutionary leaders had envisaged.'[82]

If the demographic and economic changes in American society were dramatic, undoubtedly the development with the most significant implications for the leadership relation was the emergence of the socio-intellectual conception of equality. We have already depicted American society, even before the Revolution, as the most egalitarian in the world. Prior to the Revolution, however, this equality was more of a social reality than an announced societal value. It was the American Revolution, with its Enlightenment roots, that first promulgated equality as a central societal value. This was captured most lastingly in Jefferson's phrase in the Declaration of Independence that 'all men are created equal'. Yet even this statement had its limits. The Founding Fathers, 'in embracing the idea of civic equality ... had not intended to level their society'. They saw equality as quite consistent with their ideal of a deferential society. 'By equality they meant most obviously equality of opportunity, inciting genius to action and opening up careers to men of talent and virtue.'[83]

How this limited notion of equality came to be transmuted into something much more radical is the real story of the American Revolution. It did not take long for the version of equality championed by the gentlemanly elite to come under attack. The most profound debate over the meaning and significance of this term – and its implications for leadership – came during the debate over the Constitution in the 1780s.

The acknowledged craftsman of the Constitution, James Madison, had constructed a sophisticated system designed to acknowledge the new realities while at the same time preserving the classic ideal of leadership. Madison will be the subject of intensive analysis in the next chapter; here, we can be content with Wood's synopsis of Madison's approach. Madison was among the first to acknowledge 'the reality of interests in America', and had departed sufficiently from classical republican notions to 'acknowledge the degree to which private interests of various sorts had come to dominate American politics'. His new federal system was designed 'to allow these diverse competing interests free play in the continent-sized national republic created by the Constitution'. However, Madison and his fellow founders 'were not modern-day pluralists. They still clung to the republican ideal of an autonomous public authority that was different from the many private interests of society.' Such an authority would still pursue the classical goal of the unitary common good, and would be manned by 'disinterested gentry who were supported by proprietary wealth and not involved in the interest-mongering of the market-place'.[84] Such men were, in Madison's words, 'men who possess most wisdom to discern and most virtue to pursue the common good of the society'.[85] It was in the context of this institutional arrangement that the Founding Fathers espoused equality. They wished an equality of opportunity that was most likely to recruit the kinds of virtuous leaders that the polity needed. Madison had no notion that all people were equal in any absolute sense. Although he believed in government by the people, most were unequal to the task of governing themselves. At best, they possessed sufficient 'virtue and intelligence to select men of virtue and wisdom' to lead them.[86]

But, importantly for the future of the debate over the proper functioning of leadership, Madison and the Federalists (the name chosen by supporters of the Constitution) were not the only voices to weigh in regarding the proper relations between leaders and the people. Opponents of the Constitution, called Anti-Federalists, articulated quite a different view, a view that was to have profound implications. Again, it is Wood who brilliantly distills their argument.

'Because the Constitution seemed to be perpetuating the classical tradition of virtuous patrician leadership in government,' he writes, 'the Anti-Federalists felt compelled to challenge that tradition. There was, the Anti-Federalists said repeatedly, no disinterested gentlemanly elite that could feel "sympathetically the wants of the people."' In reality, such an elite 'had its own particular interests to promote. However educated and elevated such gentry might be, they were no more free of the lures and interests of the marketplace than anyone else.' The consequences of such thinking, argues Wood, 'were immense and indeed devastating for republican government. If gentlemen were involved in the marketplace and had interests just like everyone else, they were really no different from all those common people – artisans, shopkeepers, traders, and others – who had traditionally been denied a role in political leadership because of their overriding absorption in their private occupational interests. In short,' continues Wood, 'the Anti-Federalists were saying that liberally-educated gentlemen were no more capable than ordinary people of classical republican disinterestedness and virtue and that consequently there was no one in society equipped to promote an exclusive public interest that was distinguishable from the private interests of people.'[87]

In addition to undercutting republican implicit theories concerning the existence of a unitary, discernible common good and the availability of a wise and virtuous elite to lead the society toward such a good, the Anti-Federalists challenged the Founding Fathers' limited understanding of equality, and indeed, their entire vision of proper social order. If the Anti-Federalists were to be believed, 'American society could no longer be thought of either as a hierarchy of ranks or a homogeneous republican whole'. Instead, they 'saw a society more pluralistic, more diverse, and more fragmented with interests.... Society, they said, was not a unitary entity with a single common interest but a heterogeneous mixture of 'many different classes or orders of people, ... *all equal to one another* [emphasis supplied].'[88]

In this way the Anti-Federalists came to be among the first to espouse a new, radical type of social relation that was destined to inform (and trouble) notions of leadership from that day to this. 'The Anti-Federalists lost the battle over the Constitution,' writes Wood, 'but they did not lose the war.... Their popular understanding of American society and politics was too accurate and too powerful to be put down.'[89] In particular, their conception of equality has become 'the single most powerful and radical ideological force in all of American history. Equality became so potent for Americans because it came to mean that everyone was really the same as everyone else, not just at birth, not in talent or property or wealth, and not just in some transcendental religious sense of the equality of all souls. Ordinary Americans came to believe that no one in a basic down-to-earth and day-in-day-out manner was really better than anyone else. That,' concludes Wood, 'was equality as no other nation has ever quite had it.'[90]

In terms of the emerging leadership relation, the triumph of such radical notions of equality appeared to sound the death knell for ideas of a polity composed of virtuous and superior leaders and deferential citizens. Indeed, 'equality became the rallying cry for those seeking to challenge every form of authority and superiority, including the rank of gentleman'. The result was 'Americans ... became the first society in the modern world to bring ordinary people into the affairs of government – not just as voters but as actual rulers. This participation of common people in government', suggests Wood, 'became the essence of American democracy.'[91]

Such a shift had obvious and dramatic implications for how leaders and the people relate; it was indeed this shift to democracy that we have suggested necessitated the invention of a new fiction that we have labeled leadership. Before turning to an analysis of the principal leadership responses to this challenge, it is helpful to follow Hannah Arendt's advice, and to take a more analytical look at this key moment in history when the term 'leadership' was invented to meet a new reality.

THE IMPLICIT LEADERSHIP THEORIES OF DEMOCRACY

In the previous two chapters, we have applied our template of leadership to, respectively, the fiction of the people and the emerging fiction of leadership itself. Doing the same now for democracy is less redundant than might at first appear. Although we have made clear the symbiotic relationship among the constructs of popular sovereignty, democracy and leadership, each is distinct, and each deserves separate treatment. Popular sovereignty, as we argued at the beginning of the chapter, embraces many political forms that do not achieve the broad sweep of democracy. Our treatment of leadership in the last chapter was intended only to frame the critical issues that must be addressed in any leadership analysis, and was therefore not specifically focused upon the challenges that democracy brings in its train. The depiction of democracy just completed should suggest the stunning new problems for leadership that appeared as a result of the rise of democratic ways of relating. In order to understand the challenges this new order posed for any purported leadership relation, it is necessary first to clarify how the assumptions – the implicit theories – of that society had shifted as a result of the sea change that was the emergence of democracy.

What is the Leadership Challenge?

We have seen a rather stunning shift in the nature of social relations as a result of the changes Gordon Wood has traced. The implications of all this, taken as a whole, were breathtaking. As Wood summarizes it, 'Democracy became for Americans more than the broader suffrage and the competitive politics of their political system.... Democracy actually represented a new social order with new kinds of linkages holding people together....' Continues Wood: 'There is no doubt that the new Republic saw the development and celebration of democratic social bonds and attachments different from those of either monarchy or republicanism and the emergence of democratic political leaders different from any that had ever existed anywhere in the history of the world'.[92]

But along with this modern polity came overwhelming challenges for leadership. Wood writes, 'The problems of governing this kind of society were overwhelming. If everyone in the society was interested and no one was disinterested, who was to assume the role of neutral umpire? Who was to reconcile and harmonize all these different clashing interests and promote the good of the whole?'[93] Indeed, one of the great dilemmas facing this new democratic world was the matter of how to secure appropriate leaders. For millennia, it had been understood that good leaders – whether in monarchies or republics – were those who could perceive the real interests of the people and act in their behalf. Suddenly, in nineteenth-century America, this no longer seemed to hold. What sort of leader, and what form of leadership relation he or she maintains with the newly-empowered people, remains the central challenge of leadership in a democracy.

As various commentators and practitioners were to confront this challenge, they inevitably faced the remaining questions of our leadership protocol. All would have to create their fictions in the face of the realities of democracy, which contained its own implicit responses to the issues contained in the leadership template, and thereby can be deemed the implicit theories of democracy. It is necessary, then, to attempt to identify the new premises and assumptions contained in the democratic world Wood described.

What is the Perception of Human Nature?

The new realities of nineteenth-century democracy appeared to demand a revision of the assumptions about the nature of man. First, any Aristotelean presumptions about the communal nature of the human condition seemed out of place. As Wood has depicted it, nineteenth-century Americans were wildly individualistic. Perhaps more damning for traditional ways of thinking was the apparent fact that men could no longer be considered virtuous in the classical sense. That is to say, no longer could it be assumed that individuals would be willing to subsume their own individual interests to those of the community as a whole. These two shifts in the underlying premises concerning the constituting body of the polity – that is, the people – alone were sufficient to require a modified approach to leadership.

Are the People Capable of Governing?

The response to this question demonstrates the distance ideas about governing had traveled. According to traditional ways of thinking, this new view of the people posed grave difficulties for their ability to govern. In classical republican thought, the people must have a modicum of civic virtue, and at least enough wisdom to choose their betters to lead them. Without such virtue, rule by the people was doomed to fail.

With the new realities, however, not only were the people capable of governing, but they could do so successfully without the kind of civic virtue previously thought necessary. The rationale for this rather shocking reversal was linked to the responses to other questions of the leadership protocol. For example, once the idea of a unitary common good went by the by, and once assumptions about the inherent superiority of leaders over followers were swept away, there was little to hinder the emergence of a belief that all could take an equal share in governing society. Moreover, since all had 'interests', and thus could not be seen as altruistic and above the fray, the argument became even stronger for the maximum participation of the people. The result was an almost unthinking belief in the capability of the people to rule themselves. This assumption was to cause all manner of grief for those later commentators who chose to question this reigning premise.

What is the Proper End or Purpose of Leadership?

We have seen that the traditional end of leadership has always been characterized as the common good. However, the new focus upon private interests turned the notion of the common good completely upside down. While both monarchic and republican approaches to the polity had viewed the common good as something wholly distinct from – and in most cases antagonistic to – private interests, now 'the pursuit of private interests was the real source of the public good'. In such a world, man's civic responsibilities were completely reversed from those required under republicanism. Now 'it was foolish to expect men to devote their time and energy to public responsibilities without compensation.... It became increasingly clear that society could no longer expect men to sacrifice their time and money – their private interests – for the sake of the public.'[94]

Given these radically different priorities, the purpose of government shifted as well. Where before it had been to secure the unitary common good, now the ideal polity would be characterized by 'the prevalence of private interests in government.... The object of government was the pursuit of private interests instead of the public good.'[95] Wood notes that 'this marked the beginning of what would eventually become the very staple and stuff of American politics – a consciously pluralistic, ethnic, interest-group politics'.[96]

What is the Epistemology of Leadership?

The epistemology of leadership also changed dramatically. In the republican worldview, one could judge the correctness of one's actions by measuring them against the yardstick of the common good. In the individualistic, egalitarian society of the nineteenth century, this comforting guidepost seemed no longer available. As Wood describes the situation, 'the result of all these assaults on elite opinion and celebrations of common ordinary judgment was a dispersion of authority and ultimately a diffusion of truth itself to a degree the world had never before seen. With every ordinary person being told that his ideas and tastes ... were as good, if not better, than those [of the elite] ..., it is not surprising that truth and knowledge became elusive and difficult to pin down. Knowledge and truth,' Wood argues, '... now indeed had to become more fluid and changeable, more timely and current....' As a result of this new frame, says Wood, 'Americans ... experienced an epistemological crisis as severe as any in their history'. Gradually, however, Americans did devise 'a criterion for determining who was right and who was wrong, and it was the opinion of the whole people.... Truth was actually the creation of many voices and many minds, no one of which was more important than the other. By the early nineteenth century,' concludes Wood, 'this newly enlarged and democratized public opinion had become the "vital principle" underlying American government, society, and culture.'[97]

What is the Role of the Leader?

Given the new assumptions, the traditional expectations of the leader – the classical ideal – appeared to have no place. The classical justifications for elite rule simply no longer seemed to hold. We have already seen that the notion of elite leaders as disinterested servants to society had been punctured. 'So much did private interests come to pervade [American politics] ... that many Americans found it harder and harder to conceive of disinterested leadership anywhere in society.... The idea that [elite leaders] were simply disinterested gentlemen, squire worthies called by duty to shoulder the burden of public service, became archaic.' To the contrary, the new commitment to interests 'meant that politically ambitious men, even those with interests and causes to advocate, could now run and compete for electoral office'.[98] This, in turn, led to a new view of the leader's role. 'Many Americans ... came to believe that what they once thought was true was no longer true. Government officials were no longer to play the role of umpire, and they were no longer to stand above the competing interests of the marketplace and make disinterested, impartial judgments about what was good for the whole society.'[99] In place of the traditional expectations came the acknowledgment that leaders were interested; the challenge became how to harness that interest in ways conducive to the needs of society. That challenge itself was mitigated, however, by the decreased role expected of leaders. In this new egalitarian democracy, the expectations regarding the people rose apace.

What is the Role of the People?

Perhaps the most momentous change in the leadership relation came about as a natural outgrowth of the developments previously described. It had to do with the role of the ordinary citizen in government. Wood points out that 'with these new ideas and practices came the greater participation of more ordinary people in politics. If men were alike, equal in their rights and in their interestedness,' it was reasoned, 'then there were no specially qualified gentlemen who stood apart from the whole society with a superior and disinterested perspective. All people were the same: all were ordinary and all were best represented by ordinary people.'[100] This had important implications. According to this logic, 'every man in society had interests, not just noblemen and gentlemen, and therefore every man in the society had the right to hold office in government'.[101]

The consequences were not only that ordinary men took part in ruling society – an outcome radical enough in its own right – but also that ordinary men held the key to wise social policy. Recalling our earlier discussion of the new epistemology of leadership, this meant that society really was in better hands now that its leadership had been taken over by the people. Wood summarizes it well: 'In a society of many scrambling, ordinary, and insignificant people, the power of genius and great-souled men no longer seemed to matter.... Greatness in America's colonial period may have been due almost entirely to the exertions of prominent individuals. But the American Revolution had created "something like a general will," in which the course of society was shaped "less by the activity of particular individuals" and more by "the mass of intellectual, moral, and physical powers."' In sum, 'plain ordinary people as individuals may no longer have been important, but together they now added up to a powerful force.... The individual was weak and blind ... but the mass of people was strong and wise.'[102]

Although this assumption came to be a commonplace in the early nineteenth century, we will find that it did not go unchallenged. Shortly we will turn, for example, to an analysis of the works of Alexis de Tocqueville, who strove mightily to moderate the impact of this democratic premise. It will continue to be a salient issue as we turn to modern considerations of leadership in a democracy.

How Should Leaders and the People Interact?

This new ideology of the common man and the stress upon private interests in government generated a new set of expectations regarding the proper linkages between leaders and the people. It seemed that all of the governing assumptions that had guided society – and the relations between leaders and the people – had suddenly been turned upside down. Merely a century before, men 'still took for granted that society was and ought to be ... [characterized] ... by degrees of dependency and that most people were still bound together by personal ties of one sort or another'.[103] By the early nineteenth century this presumption of social connection had disappeared in large part, as had the traditional deference paid to leaders. This was an extraordinary development. Gordon Wood again explains it well.

As Wood puts it, 'America had experienced an unprecedented democratic revolution that had created a huge sprawling society that was more egalitarian, more middling, and more dominated by the interests of ordinary people than any that had ever existed before'.[104] In such a culture, elite leaders were not only unnecessary; to some they were undesirable. The new commitment to the common man had left a lingering resentment of elite leadership. Ordinary men 'were sick and tired of being dismissed as factions, narrow, parochial and illiberal, and were unwilling to defer any longer to anyone's political leadership but their own'.[105] Indeed, 'so absurd was this designation "the better sort" in a republic "that the very terms become contemptible and odious in the estimation of the people"'.[106]

The question remained, of course, how leaders in this brave new world were to relate to the people. It is a problem never fully resolved, but a decent beginning can be had by once again returning to the issue of representation. It will be recalled that during the Revolutionary crisis American leaders, in responding to the British claims of 'virtual representation', had formulated a much more localistic version of representation, articulated most famously by John Adams when he called for representative assemblies to be a 'portrait in miniature' of the people at large. While this localistic approach served the revolutionary leaders well in their debates with Great Britain, it came back to haunt them when they attempted to ensure the continuation of the classical ideal (and their own hegemony) in the years following the Revolution.

Again, it was the debate over the Constitution that brought the matter to a head. The Founding Fathers – the Federalists – had crafted their Constitution in such a way as to remedy the self-interested localism they saw emerging all around them. Wood points out how 'the state legislatures were greatly democratized by the Revolution – by both the increase in the number of members in each assembly and broadening of the electorates'. As a consequence, 'men of even more humble and rural origins and less education than had sat in the colonial assemblies were now elected as representatives'. The substantive results were even more troubling. Rather than fulfill 'their republican responsibility to promote a unitary interest distinguishable from the private and parochial interests of people.... Each representative ... was concerned only with the particular interests of his electors.'[107] In response, the large electoral districts and the indirect elections of the Constitution were specifically designed to promote the election of the 'better sort' who would look beyond particular interests and keep the larger public good in view. Make no mistake: however ironic it was, the Federalists were advocating a form of virtual representation.

It was the Anti-Federalists who articulated a new version of representation designed to meet the new realities. They reversed the Federalist argument. The Anti-Federalists maintained that 'in such a pluralistic egalitarian society there was no possibility of a liberal enlightened elite speaking for the whole; men from one class or interest could never be acquainted with the "Situations and Wants" of those from another'. They concluded that 'the occupations and interests of the society were so diverse and discrete that only individuals sharing a particular occupation or interest could speak for that occupation or interest'.[108] In other words, 'the grass-roots Anti-Federalists concluded that, given the variety of competing interests and the fact that all people had interests, the only way for a person to be fairly and accurately represented in government was to have someone like himself with his same interests speak for him; no one else could be trusted to do so'. Wood suggests that 'momentous consequences eventually flowed from these Anti-Federalist arguments'. It was 'in these populist Anti-Federalist calls for the most explicit form of representation possible, and not in Madison's *Federalist No. 10*', that 'lay the real origins of American pluralism and American interest-group politics'.[109]

The emergence of democracy, and the notion of pluralism and interest group politics that Wood argues stems from the localistic, delegate style of representation that accompanied it, required commentators and practitioners alike to confront – really for the first time – the twin issues of minority interests and diversity.

How is the Matter of Diversity and Minority Interests Addressed?

Prior to the rise of democracy, these issues were more-or-less moot. The assumption of a unitary common interest well served by virtuous leaders negated any concerns along these lines. To the extent that we have seen any substantive developments, it was in response to leaders who abused their positions and tyrannized their constituents. It was in this context that a strong tradition of individual rights grew up in the English tradition, emulated and even expanded in the American experience. This was no small thing: the protection of individual rights would become a frontline defense for minorities in a democracy.

But the rise of democracy raised even more fundamental questions. Now, the threat to minorities was seen not just as an example of the abuse of the leadership role, but a part of the polity itself, endemic to democracy. Moreover, the vast social and economic changes depicted by Wood also undercut the assumption that society was by nature homogeneous, with a unitary interest. These changed realities demanded new and innovative institutional and procedural responses. The shift in conceptualizations of representation was only one manifestation. To be sure, these issues were not – and have not been fully resolved, but with the coming of democracy, they now take their place among the principal challenges that must be resolved in order to achieve a successful democratic polity.

What Institutions and Processes Must be Designed to Accommodate the Premises and Assumptions about Leadership Articulated in the Responses to the Leadership Template?

The task of designing new institutions and processes to accommodate the new assumptions of a democratic world has occupied the attention of theorists and practitioners to the present day. The remainder of Part III is devoted to a careful exploration of a number of influential attempts to create institutions and processes suited to the new realities. These attempts were nothing less than efforts at creating a new fiction: the new social and political relation we call leadership. We have defined that construct as 'an influence relation among leaders and followers that facilitates the accomplishment of group or societal objectives'. As we shall see, the creation of such an 'influence relation' embraces more than the mere interactions of the leaders and the people. Those interactions are grounded in the values and assumptions uncovered by the leadership template, and demand facilitating institutions to ensure their success. It is such a constellation of values, institutions and processes that make up the fiction we call leadership.

INTRODUCING THE FICTIONS OF LEADERSHIP

With the emergence of individualistic, egalitarian democracy as the dominant reality, the essential challenge of the modern political era was upon us. This challenge was to create a new fiction of leadership that successfully accommodated the novel assumptions, beliefs and social relations that accompanied the rise of modern democracy. This was – and continues to be – no easy task. Fortunately – and predictably, given the magnitude and importance of the challenge – many of the greatest minds in modern history have undertaken the endeavor.

As will become clear, these efforts at creating a political framework responsive to the demands of democracy were not monolithic. However, it is possible, if one will allow for a moment the latitude permitted by rough approximation, to categorize each of the approaches set forth below into one of three essential strategies. The first strategy was to attempt to merge the benefits of the traditional fictions of classical republicanism and the classical ideal with the new realities of democracy. In our forthcoming analysis, this approach will be represented by the works of James Madison, who operated before democracy had reached full flower, and Alexis de Tocqueville, who did not. Tocqueville was thus faced with the more formidable challenge of striving to keep alive the benefits provided by the classical ideal in the inhospitable environment of democracy. A second strategy was to embrace the individualism, commercialism and egalitarianism of the modern democratic world, and attempt to erect a polity that reflected it. This approach we will label 'the liberal fiction'. Although it would prove remarkably successful and durable, this strategy would also contain some inherent difficulties for the concept of leadership. A third strategy has been to attempt to turn back the clock and posit assumptions about humans and their relationships reminiscent of an earlier era (and/or of a society less individualistic than found in modern America). These proposals for ordering society and its institutions we discuss under the rubric of 'the communitarian fiction'. This approach, too, has its problems from a leadership perspective.

Taken together, these prototypes of the leadership relation allow us to perceive how the fiction of leadership has been 'invented' from differing perspectives over the past two centuries. Through analysis and critique, they can also serve as the foundation for a new fiction of leadership better suited to today's realities.

NOTES

1. Matthew Trachman, 'Historicizing Leadership / Democratizing Leadership Studies' (paper delivered at the annual meeting of the International Leadership Association, Toronto, Canada, November 2000), 1, 3, 7.
2. Gordon S. Wood, *The Radicalism of the American Revolution* (New York: Alfred A. Knopf, 1992).
3. Ibid., 3–7.
4. For a more thoroughgoing discussion of this *see* Chapter 9.
5. Wood, *The Radicalism of the American Revolution*, 11, 18.
6. Ibid., 18–20.
7. Ibid., 63.
8. Ibid., 89.
9. Ibid., 11–12.
10. Ibid., 57.
11. Ibid., 24–25.
12. Ibid., 28.
13. Ibid., 83.
14. Ibid., 85.
15. Ibid., 83.
16. Ibid., 33.

17. Ibid., 27.
18. Ibid., 73.
19. Ibid., 27.
20. Ibid., 86.
21. Ibid., 60.
22. Ibid., 86.
23. *See* Chapter 3.
24. Wood, *The Radicalism of the American Revolution.*, 13.
25. Ibid.
26. Ibid., 15, 98.
27. Ibid., 171.
28. Ibid., 123, 130–131.
29. Ibid., 123.
30. Ibid., 100.
31. *See* Chapter 2.
32. Wood, *The Radicalism of the American Revolution*, 109.
33. Ibid., 95.
34. Ibid., 109.
35. Ibid., 173–174.
36. Ibid., 177–178.
37. Ibid., 101. *See generally* Bernard Bailyn, *The Ideological Origins of the American Revolution* (Cambridge: Belknap Press of Harvard University Press, 1967).
38. Wood, *The Radicalism of the American Revolution*, 104.
39. Ibid., 103–104.
40. Ibid., 180.
41. Ibid.
42. Ibid., 106.
43. Ibid., 180.
44. *See* Chapter 3.
45. Wood, *The Radicalism of the American Revolution*, 187.
46. Ibid., 106.
47. Ibid., 169.
48. Ibid., 104.
49. Ibid., 234.
50. Ibid., 109.
51. Ibid., 96.
52. Ibid., 95.
53. Ibid., 196–197.
54. Ibid., 190.
55. Ibid., 225.
56. Ibid., 125.
57. Ibid., 124–125.
58. Ibid., 124.
59. Ibid., 125, 133–134.
60. Ibid., 145–146.
61. Ibid., 134–135.
62. Ibid., 138–139.
63. Ibid., 135.
64. Ibid., 140–141.
65. Ibid., 139–140.
66. Ibid., 142.
67. Ibid., 144–145.
68. Ibid., 143.
69. Ibid., 112–113.
70. Ibid., 121.
71. Ibid., 118.
72. Ibid., 156.
73. Ibid., 122–123.
74. Ibid., 162–166.
75. Ibid., 167–168.
76. Ibid., 229.

77. Ibid., 229–230.
78. Ibid., 229.
79. Ibid., 230.
80. Ibid., 232.
81. Ibid., 248, 250.
82. Ibid., 230.
83. Ibid., 233–234.
84. Ibid., 253.
85. Ibid., 254.
86. James Madison, quoted in *ibid.*, 234.
87. Wood, *The Radicalism of the American Revolution*, 255–256.
88. Ibid., 258.
89. Ibid., 259.
90. Ibid., 234.
91. Ibid., 243.
92. Ibid., 232.
93. Ibid., 296.
94. Ibid., 293–294.
95. Ibid., 247, 252.
96. Ibid., 245. This tendency in American politics will be explored in greater depth in our later treatment of liberalism. *See* Chapter 8.
97. Wood, *The Radicalism of the American Revolution*, 361–364.
98. Ibid., 257, 267.
99. Ibid., 294.
100. Ibid., 294–295.
101. Ibid., 246.
102. Ibid., 359–360.
103. Ibid., 6.
104. Ibid., 347.
105. Ibid., 275–276.
106. Ibid., 241.
107. Ibid., 250–251.
108. Ibid., 258.
109. Ibid., 259.

6. James Madison and the classical ideal

The new social relation we call leadership came about when the emergence of the people as the constitutive element of the polity required a rethinking of the relationship between leaders and their new sovereigns. Predictably, a tension arose between traditional ways of viewing the leader – the classical ideal – and the new fiction that held the people sovereign. In particular, as we saw in the previous chapter, the classical vision of the leader as more wise and more virtuous than the ordinary run of mankind came into conflict with the emerging democratic and egalitarian ethos of the early American republic. Even the classical ideal's commitment to an independent and unitary common good came into question. One of the great challenges facing those who attempted to frame a new leadership relation in those turbulent times consisted of the attempt to honor the commitment to the sovereignty of the people while still securing the advantages of the classical ideal, in which the pursuit of the public interest is carefully guided by wise and disinterested leaders.

No one took this challenge more seriously than did James Madison, one of the greatest political theorists and practical politicians of his (or any) age. Throughout a long career, Madison continually sought to secure what he believed to be the proper end of any polity, the common good. The challenge, as he saw it, was to do so in a popular regime. His tactics to achieve this goal were many and ingenious, but at base, all connected to the leadership relation. That is to say, Madison devised his remedies by carefully reflecting upon the proper roles of leaders, the people and the institutional ligaments that bound them together.

As a consequence of his lifetime of effort, James Madison became one of the most enigmatic, interesting and important figures in American political history. Historians and political scientists alike have long struggled with his apparent inconsistencies, spanning a long career, which seemingly have left an ambiguous legacy.[1] This chapter suggests a perspective on Madison's career that yields a sense of coherency, if not complete continuity, to his actions. Throughout his career, Madison faced a series of challenges to his core belief in popular sovereignty and his equally firm commitment to the common good. When these priorities came into conflict, Madison devised creative adaptations of the form and workings of the polity. In the process, he plumbed the possibilities inherent in his perception of the appropriate roles of the people and their leaders in a regime of popular sovereignty. The result was a series of brilliant improvisations that have become the cornerstone of our contemporary polity, and which continue to provide instruction to those who struggle with the challenges of leadership in a democracy.

MADISON'S CORE VALUES

In the beginning of his career, as at the end, Madison was committed to the creation of a polity that fit the 'genius' of the American people. In the early years he clearly articulated the two pole stars that would guide his efforts throughout a long career. Madison embraced wholeheartedly the new fiction of the people. He had an unquenchable faith in government by the people – popular sovereignty. 'The ultimate authority,' he argued, 'wherever the derivative may be found, resides in the people alone.' All governments are 'but agents and trustee of the people', he added; they must be 'dependent on the great body of citizens' and 'derive all … powers directly or indirectly from the great body of the people'.[2]

It was not enough, however, to create governments based on the people. Madison was also deeply committed to the creation of a polity consistent with the classical ideal. His focus was the purpose of such government – the common good. Madison's conception of the public good was unmistakable, and had substantive implications. Madison was heir to the republican tradition, in which, according to historian Gordon Wood, 'no phrase except "liberty" was invoked more often … than "the public good"'. Indeed, 'the peculiar excellence of republican government was that … by definition it had no other end than the welfare of the people: *res publica*, the public affairs, or the public good'.[3] As Madison put it, 'the public good, the real welfare of the great body of the people, is the supreme object to be pursued, and … no form of government whatever has any other value, than as it may be fitted for the attainment of this object'.[4]

Moreover, that public good was distinct, identifiable and enduring. Madison referred to 'the permanent and aggregate interests of the community',[5] and proceeded to outline what this encompassed. First and foremost, it involved 'the necessity of sacrificing private opinions and partial interests to the public good',[6] the classic definition of civic virtue. In addition, a regime committed to the common good must embody liberty and justice. This, in turn, required the substantive protection of both personal and property rights. It is his emphasis upon property rights that will most concern us here. The protection of property rights led to a just and stable society. Madison, drawing from David Hume, argued that 'justice is the end of government',[7] and that this justice consisted, as historian Drew McCoy phrased it, 'largely of a respect for the property rights of others'. 'Madison believed, above all', McCoy went on, 'in a permanent public good and immutable standards of justice, both of which were linked to the rules of property that stabilized social relationships and that together defined the proper ends of republican government.'[8] 'No government', Madison concluded, 'will long be respected, without being truly respectable; nor be truly respectable, without possessing a certain portion of order and stability.'[9]

In sum, in addition to a sincere commitment to popular sovereignty, Madison held to a conception of the common good characterized by a priority of the general interest over local or individual interests, and a polity devoted to liberty and justice in the form of the protection of individual liberty and rights of property. This, in turn, would lead to an orderly and stable regime.

The difficulty was that these core values proved to be often in conflict and were perhaps inherently so. As circumstances were to create challenges to one or the other of Madison's core values, he concocted a series of brilliant adaptations as he labored to devise solutions that addressed the perceived threat. The result, while surely not a dialectical process in the Hegelian sense, was nevertheless a succession of challenges created in part by his solution to each previous challenge. James Madison was thus a constant innovator, but one who always had the achievement of his higher goals in mind. In the process, Madison explored differing ways in which popular sovereignty might play out in practice, and in particular he tested various formulations of the proper relationship of the people to their leaders.

CHALLENGE #1: THE THREAT TO THE COMMON GOOD FROM THE PEOPLE

The first challenge to Madison's basic tenets emerged in the 1780s, when the new nation's commitment to popular sovereignty threatened Madison's conception of the public good. The developments of the 1780s are generally well known,[10] but Madison's 'take' on these matters is important. The 'symptoms ... are truly alarming', he wrote Jefferson.[11] Although Madison was fully aware of the weaknesses of the Confederation government,[12] his real concern was at the state level: 'No small share of the embarassments of America is to be charged on the blunders of our [state] governments', he wrote.[13] In particular he was aghast at the instability caused by new men in government, the threat to creditors inherent in paper money and debtor relief legislation, and a general slide toward chaos.[14] Perhaps his concern is best captured by his report to Jefferson of conditions in Virginia on the eve of ratification: 'Our information from Virginia is far from being agreeable. ... The people ... are said to be generally discontented. A paper emission is again a topic among them. So is an instalment of all debts in some places and making property a tender in others. ... In several Counties the prisons & Court Houses & Clerks offices have been willfully burnt. In Green Briar the course of Justice has been mutinously stopped.'[15]

The fact of these developments was bad enough; much worse were the implications. The activities at the state level challenged standards of property and justice, and led to a lack of 'wisdom and steadiness' in government.[16] As Madison put it, 'complaints are everywhere heard from our most considerate and virtuous citizens, equally the friends of public and private faith, and of public and personal liberty, that our governments are too unstable; that the public good is disregarded in the conflict of rival parties; and that measures are too often decided, not according to the rules of justice, and the rights of the minority party, but by the superior force of an interested and overbearing majority.'[17] That placed the issue in its starkest form: popular sovereignty appeared to be undermining the public good.

This realization led Madison to reflect upon the American experiment in popular sovereignty, and in particular upon the proper roles of the people and their leaders in securing the public good in such a regime. While applauding the Revolutionary Founders' commitment to rule by the people, Madison acknowledged that their perspective had been blinkered in the 1770s by their obsession with 'the overgrown and all-grasping prerogative of an hereditary magistrate'.[18] Viewing the disruptions of the 1780s, Madison perceived unanticipated difficulties with the existing form of rule by the people, which he detailed in a remarkable document written in early 1787 he titled *Vices of the Political System of the U. States*.[19] Having again detailed several of the abuses of this era of majoritarian rule, Madison contemplated the possible causes. He found two. The first lay in the leaders of such a regime, who often place 'ambition [and] personal interest [above the] public good'. While this was indeed relevant to the 1780s, it became more salient to Madison in the 1790s. In the decade of the '80s, he devoted more attention to the second source of concern, 'the people themselves'.[20]

As early as 1785, Madison had perceived the problem. 'True it is,' he had said, 'that no other rule exists, by which any question which may divide a Society, can be ultimately determined, but the will of the majority, but it is also true that the majority may trespass on the rights of the minority.'[21] This, Madison acknowledged, 'brings more into question the fundamental principle of republican Government, that the majority who rule in such Governments, are the safest Guardians both of public Good and of private rights'.[22] The essential problem was that the public good and the will of the majority might not be the same, and, as Madison wrote to Jefferson in 1787, one cannot assume that 'a majority with the public authority in their hands' will opt for 'the general and permanent good of the whole'.[23] Nor is this to be unexpected. Here, Madison, in his *Vices*, anticipated his famous discussion of factions and individual interest which would later appear in *Federalist No. 10*.[24] The bottom line, as Madison wrote in another context, is that 'interest leads to injustice', and as he concluded in *Vices*, 'whenever therefore an apparent interest or common passion unites a majority', this threatens the common good.[25]

The key issue of the age was how to reconcile popular sovereignty and the common good. As Madison was to put it in the *Federalist*, 'to secure the public good, and private rights against the danger of such a faction, … is then the great object to which our inquiries are directed'. In his famous phrase, Americans must find 'a republican remedy for the diseases most incident to republican government'.[26]

This issue forced Madison to do some deep thinking about the roles and capabilities of the people and their leaders in a regime of popular sovereignty. He developed a sophisticated and nuanced conceptualization of the abilities of the people, one capable of legitimizing a multiplicity of adaptive responses to a series of challenges to the common good under the rule of the people.

Madison began by acknowledging the premise of popular sovereignty, but with a caveat. In responding to Jefferson's call for frequent conventions, Madison had agreed that 'as the people are the only legitimate fountain of power, and it is from them that the constitutional charter … is derived; it seems strictly consonant to the republican theory, to recur to the same original authority' for any revisions. Quickly, however, he hastened to add: 'but there appear to be insuperable objections against the proposed recurrence to the people'.[27] The problem was that the people, as a whole, were not capable of such an undertaking. As he expressed in correspondence with Edmund Randolph, 'Whatever respect may be due to the rights of private judgment, and no man feels more of it than I do, there can be no doubt that there are subjects to which the capacities of the bulk of mankind are unequal',[28] and the making of a Constitution was one of them. It 'certainly surpasses the judgment of the greater part of them', he added to Jefferson.[29]

The matter went back to the issue of the public good. To expect the people as a whole to keep in mind the overarching interests of the general population, and to respect the property rights of the minority, was too much to ask, particularly in the passions of the moment. 'At present,' Madison commented, 'the public mind is neither sufficiently cool nor sufficiently informed for so delicate an operation'.[30] 'The *passions* therefore not the *reason*, of the public, would sit in judgment. But it is the reason of the public alone that ought to controul and regulate the government.'[31] 'Under all these circumstances,' he wrote to George Turberville, 'it seems scarcely to be presumable that the deliberations of the body could be conducted in harmony, or terminate in the general good.'[32]

In one respect, then, Madison had doubts about the people as the source of the common good. 'In a nation of philosophers', Madison wrote in *Federalist No. 49*, there need be no concern for achieving the common good. 'But a nation of philosophers', he went on to say, 'is as little to be expected as the philosophical race of kings wished for by Plato.'[33] As he put it to Jefferson, while 'enlightened Statesmen, or the benevolent philosopher' might be able to rise above faction and interest and majority passion, 'the bulk of mankind … are neither Statesmen nor Philosophers'.[34]

Nevertheless, those doubts were but one part of Madison's formulation. He joined his concerns about the people with a paradoxical yet ultimately complementary underlying faith that the people had sufficient virtue to support the public good. Madison was quite candid in this regard. 'As there is a degree of depravity in mankind which requires a certain degree of circumspection and distrust', he acknowledged, '… so there are other qualities in human nature, which justify a certain portion of esteem and confidence. Republican government', he asserted, 'presupposes the existence of these qualities in a higher degree than any other form.'[35] Indeed, 'to suppose that any form of government will secure liberty or happiness without any virtue in the people is a chimerical idea'.[36] Madison took solace from his own state of Virginia. 'The case of Virga. seems to prove', he wrote to Jefferson, 'that the body of sober & steady people, even of the lower order, are tired of the vicicitudes, injustice, and follies which have so much characterised public measures, and are impatient for some change which promises stability.'[37]

While these views of the people appear at first blush to be contradictory, in reality they were not, and it was Madison's vision of the role of popular leaders which bridged the gap. Madison recognized the need for leaders, even (perhaps especially) in a regime grounded in the people. 'There can be no doubt that there are subjects to which the capacities of … mankind are unequal', he had said. In such cases, 'they must and will be governed by those with whom they happen to have acquaintance and confidence'.[38] It had ever been so. Looking back through the ages, Madison noted that 'in every case reported by ancient history, in which government has been established with deliberation and consent, the task … has been performed by some individual citizen of pre-eminent wisdom and approved integrity'.[39] More recently, the example of Virginia added further proof. 'In Virginia,' he observed, 'the mass of people have been … much accustomed to be guided by their rulers on all new and intricate questions.'[40]

In a regime of popular sovereignty, the nature of these leaders and their relationship to the people became all-important. Madison stated the general principle to Edmund Randolph: there must be 'a fortunate coincidence of leading opinions, and a general confidence of the people in those who may recommend' such opinions.[41] But the specifics were critical. Appropriate leaders must be selected. Only 'the purest and noblest characters' were appropriate; those who 'feel most strongly the proper motives to pursue the end of their appointment'.[42] And those 'proper motives' went to the heart of the matter. 'The aim of every political constitution', noted Madison, 'is, or ought to be, first, to obtain for rulers men who possess most wisdom to discern and most virtue to pursue, the common good of society.'[43] Moreover, his view of what constituted that common good remained consistent. Such leaders should be 'individuals of extended views', who 'will give wisdom and steadiness' to government, and who are 'interested in preserving the rights of property'.[44]

Having carefully established the sort of leader he had in mind, Madison went on to articulate the nexus between such leaders and the people. Madison acknowledged his ambiguity concerning the capabilities of the people. Rejecting those in the Virginia ratifying convention who had no faith in the people, Madison stated 'I consider it reasonable to conclude, that they will as readily do their duty, as deviate from it'. However, he was not naïve. He could not 'place unlimited confidence in them, and expect nothing but the most exalted integrity and sublime virtue'. The saving grace lay in their relationship with their leaders. 'I go on this great republican principle, that the people will have virtue and intelligence to select men of virtue and wisdom. ... If there be sufficient virtue and intelligence in the community, it will be exercised in the selection of these men.'[45] This was the nub of it. Popular sovereignty and the common good were indeed compatible, if only leaders and followers united their particular virtues in pursuit of the common good. Much of the remainder of Madison's career was devoted to just this endeavor.

In confronting the essential challenge of the 1780s – the threat to the common good posed by majoritarian excess[46] – Madison was up for the task. His adaptive response to the dangers of majority passion at the state level – much of which found its way into the federal Constitution – is justly famous. While it is unnecessary to explore all the details of this familiar document, it is important to explore the extent to which Madison conformed to his articulated priorities of popular sovereignty and the common good.

There can be little doubt that Madison continued to view the common good, as he defined it, as the ultimate objective. Madison was well aware that by 1787 conditions were such that the public was looking for relief from the existing conditions. As he wrote to Jefferson, 'my own idea is that the public mind will now or in a very little time receive any thing that promises stability to the public Councils and security to private rights'.[47] This concern with what Madison would label the public good would be his guiding light throughout the Convention. On May 31, in one of his first addresses before the delegates, Madison assessed his charge: 'He [Madison] should shrink from nothing which should be found essential to such a form of Government as would provide for the safety, liberty, and happiness of the Community. This being the end of all our deliberations, all the necessary means for attaining it must, however reluctantly, be submitted to.'[48] This included, he added in remarks several weeks later, 'the necessity of providing more effectually for the security of private rights, and the steady dispensation of Justice. Interferences with these', he added, 'were evils which had more perhaps than any thing else, produced the convention.'[49]

Madison's efforts to preserve the common good were chiefly structural, and he kept his eyes on his ultimate objective at all times.[50] When he realized that a 'pure democracy' was 'no cure from the mischief of faction', and that 'the public good is disregarded in the conflicts of rival parties', he recommended a representative republic, which would 'refine and enlarge the public views ... and be more consonant with the public good'.[51] The same thinking led to his championing of a republic over a large area. Recognizing that 'in all cases where a majority are united by a common interest or passion, the rights of the minority are in danger, ... [t]he only remedy is to enlarge the sphere, & thereby divide the community into so great a number of interests & parties, that ... a majority will not be likely at the same moment to have a common interest separate from that of the whole or of the minority'.[52] Thus 'a coalition of a majority of the whole society could seldom take place upon any other principles than those of justice and the general good'.[53]

Madison also sought to create a polity which shackled the chief perpetrators of the indignities to the common good, the state governments. Besides the specific prohibitions of some of the more egregious state practices in Article I, section 10, Madison sought a strong national government. 'The necessity of a general Govt.', he explained, 'proceeds from the propensity of the States to pursue their particular interests in opposition to the general interest. This propensity', he continued, 'will continue to disturb the system unless effectually controuled.' Madison had a remedy: 'Nothing short of a negative [a national veto] on their laws will controul it'.[54] Again, the goal was the common good. 'The effects of this provision,' he wrote, 'would be not only to guard the national rights and interests against invasion, but also to restrain the States ... from oppressing the minority within themselves by paper money and other unrighteous measures which favor the interests of the majority.'[55]

While the examples could be multiplied, the point is clear: Madison continued to be guided by his perception of what constituted the common good as he advocated political structures which he believed would obviate current threats to that good, while at the same time establishing a polity which would provide lasting protection to the public interest. Perhaps less obvious is the extent to which Madison counted upon the 'right' sort of leaders to guide the new polity. Historian Gordon Wood has demonstrated the elite nature of Federalist constitutionalism, but Madison's own commitment to ensuring that the proper sort of leaders would be in place has been under-appreciated.[56]

His chief vehicle for securing proper leadership was the republican form itself. By creating a representative republic, it became possible actually to improve upon popular rule. Under a republic, it was possible to 'refine and enlarge the public views, by passing them through the medium of a chosen body of citizens [that is, leaders], whose wisdom may best discern the true interest of their country, and whose patriotism and love of justice, will be least likely to sacrifice it to temporary or partial considerations'. Under such a system, Madison concluded, 'it may well happen that the public voice pronounced by the representatives of the people, will be more consonant to the public good, than if pronounced by the people themselves'.[57] Madison explained this startling conclusion by demonstrating that the leaders of a republic, particularly a large republic, would be 'men who possess the most attractive merit, and the most diffusive and established characters',[58] and thereby would keep the public good in view.

A closer look at Madison's explanation of the specific departments of the new national government reinforces his emphasis on securing proper leadership for the new government. The House of Representatives demonstrates nicely his nexus between the people and their leaders. The House, he said, 'should rest on the solid foundation of the people themselves', and direct election of Representatives reinforced 'a clear principle of free Government'.[59] Despite its 'dependence on ... the people', the goal remained of 'obtain[ing] for rulers men who possess most wisdom to discern, and most virtue to pursue the common good of the society'.[60] This was to be achieved by the large electoral districts of thirty thousand people. 'In so great a number,' Madison noted, 'a fit representative would be most likely to be found.'[61]

The Senate, through its structure and the individuals who would make it up, was even more likely to uphold the common good. Indeed, that was its essential *raison d'etre*. In speaking of the Senate, Madison suggested 'that such an institution may sometimes be necessary, as a defence to the people against their own temporary errors and delusions. ... In these critical moments, how salutary will be the interference of some temperate and respectable body of citizens, in order to check the misguided career, and to suspend the blow meditated by the people against themselves, until reason, justice and truth can regain their authority over the public mind?'[62] Such a body required appropriate leaders, so Madison called for more stringent qualifications for eligibility, to ensure 'greater ... stability of character'.[63] This would also be ensured by the indirect election of that body.[64]

Given these precautions, Madison was relatively sure that the actions of its members would correlate to the 'prosperity of the community'.[65]

The executive and judiciary could also be expected to be inhabited by appropriate individuals, with a similar positive impact on the common good. Both the executive and judicial branches could be 'useful to the Community at large as an additional check agst. a pursuit of … unwise & unjust measures'.[66] Undoubtedly the President would be an individual 'of distinguished character' and 'an object of general attention and esteem',[67] also elected indirectly. The executive could be expected to use his rather formidable powers in pursuit of the public good. 'The independent condition of the Ex[ecutive] … will render him a just Judge', and help ensure 'the safety of a minority in Danger of oppression from an unjust and interested majority'.[68] The judiciary, to be nominated by that executive, who is 'likely to select fit characters', will be 'independent tribunals of justice [who] will consider themselves in a peculiar manner the guardians' of the public interest.[69]

In sum, throughout the new polity one could expect to find just the sort of leaders Madison had said were necessary for the accomplishment of the public good in a regime of popular sovereignty: men of broad views who would respect the property rights of the minority and seek the good of the whole, irrespective of factional politics. In other words, Madison sought to put in place the classical ideal of the leader.

Reviewing, then, the decade of the 1780s, Madison had confronted the first of his challenges to his twin beliefs in popular sovereignty and the common good, and had apparently succeeded marvelously in creating an adaptive response. Forced to articulate the fundamental premises of his political philosophy, he had used these premises to create an entirely new polity, grounded firmly in his core belief in popular sovereignty, which at the same time promised to quell the abuses of the people that threatened the common good. Overseeing it all – and fundamental to his system – was a network of leaders responsible to the popular will yet committed to the permanent, aggregate good of the community.

This adaptive response was brilliant in its own way, but Madison almost immediately (in the 1790s) faced another challenge to his core beliefs, which demanded a quite different adaptation of the polity.

CHALLENGE #2: THE THREAT TO THE COMMON GOOD FROM THE LEADERS

In the decade of the 1790s, Madison's commitment to his core values of popular sovereignty and the common good continued unabated,[70] but he was confronted with a somewhat unexpected development: the rise of Alexander Hamilton and his policies. The Hamiltonian program of a funded federal debt, a national bank, federal taxation and support for internal improvements and manufactures is well known. At first Madison rather moderately quibbled with his erstwhile collaborator over the wisdom of his initial proposals,[71] but before long he began to perceive a more sinister development. Soon he viewed the Hamiltonian policies as inimical to the common good.

In a sense, Madison should not have been surprised by the developments of the early 1790s: he had predicted them. Many times in the 1780s (most famously in *Federalist No. 10*), he had predicted the rise of various factions, to include 'those who are creditors … a manufacturing interest, a mercantile interest, a monied interest' as well as several others.[72]

Indeed, one of Madison's chief concerns during the 1780s had been 'the unreasonable advantage [existing conditions] give ... to the sagacious, the enterprising and the moneyed few, over the industrious and uninformed mass of the people. ... This', he continued, 'is a state of things in which it may be said with some truth that laws are made for the *few* and not for the *many*.'[73] Under Hamilton, such a situation appeared to be repeating itself.[74]

Madison had even predicted this problem with the apparent leaders of the society. While, as we have seen, Madison placed a great deal of faith in the efficacy of leaders with a larger view of the common good to forestall the evils of faction, he had foreseen that leaders could not always be trusted in a regime of popular sovereignty. In his 1787 *Vices of the Political System of the U. States*, Madison had acknowledged that popular leaders (at the state level) often placed 'ambition' and 'personal interest' above the 'public good'. These men, 'with interested views, contrary to the interest, and views, of their Constituents, join in a perfidious sacrifice of the latter to the former'. 'How frequently, too,' Madison warned, 'will the honest but unenlightened representative be the dupe of a favorite leader, veiling his selfish views under the professions of public good ... ?'[75] This, as time went by, was exactly what Madison thought Hamilton and his allies were about.

What troubled Madison the most was the threat to individual property rights, and the apparent championing of private interest over the public good. While the Hamiltonians were taking great care to protect and enhance their own property, it was at the expense of the property interests of the majority. 'Government is instituted', he said, 'to protect property of every sort. ... This being the end of government, that alone is a *just* government which *impartially* secures to every man whatever is his *own*. ... That is not a just government, nor is property secure under it, where' there are 'arbitrary seizures of one class of citizens for the service of the rest.'[76] This seemed to be the case in the early 1790s, when 'stockjobbers', who had become 'the pretorian band of the Government', were scouring 'the interior & distant parts of the Union in order to take advantage of the ignorance of holders' of old paper. Thus, 'the many ... [are] victims ... to the few'.[77] All this struck at the essence of government – the public good. Madison saw instead a government 'substituting the motive of private interest in place of public duty ... accommodating its measures to ... part of the nation instead of the benefit of the whole,' which threatened 'a real domination of the few, under an apparent liberty of the many'.[78]

In sum, the challenge of the 1790s was wholly different from the challenge of the 1780s. Rather than a democracy working against the interests of the common good, it was a small covey of leaders, operating under the auspices of the new polity Madison himself had done so much to create. Different challenges called for different reactions, and Madison's adaptive response in this circumstance was as creative and innovative as his earlier efforts. Madison's great contribution at this juncture was that he did not jettison the polity which he had so laboriously created; instead, he returned to his own original principles of popular sovereignty and the common good and, focusing upon his understanding of the proper role of leaders and followers in a regime of popular sovereignty, fashioned new 'tactical' methods of implementing that relationship to secure the ultimate triumph of the common good.

Because the source of the threat to the common good was now reversed – rather than from unruly state democracies, it now came from a 'financial aristocracy, led and encouraged by an officer of the executive department, who had acquired a dominant influence'[79] – Madison was led to rethink the proper role of leaders and the people. He recognized that the great bulk of the people agreed with his position. 'On the republican [Madisonian] side,' he wrote, 'the superiority of numbers is so great, their sentiments are so decided, and ... there is a common sentiment and common interest' in favor of reversing the Hamiltonian trend.[80] This led him logically to turn to the people for assistance in redressing the problem. Having established a government based on the people, Madison now argued that 'to secure all the advantages of such a system, every good citizen will be at once a centinel over the rights of the people; over the authorities of the confederal government; and over both the rights and the authorities of the intermediate governments'.[81]

This stance involved a seeming departure from his position in the 1780s, when he had fully trusted the people only to have virtue enough to select proper leaders. And, indeed, Madison did rethink the nexus between leaders and followers that he had posited in the 1780s, yet his final conclusions were less contradictory than might at first appear. In confronting the challenge of the 1790s, Madison returned to the issue of leaders and followers in an essay entitled *Who Are the Best Keepers of the People's Liberties?* Here, he did not suddenly abandon his concerns about the capabilities of the people; 'the people *may* betray themselves', he wrote, and the lessons of history – recent history – bore this out. Yet, as in the 1780s, his was not a totally negative view of the capability of the people. Then, he had acknowledged that the people had some 'virtue', certainly enough to choose enlightened leaders. Now, facing a small group of leaders who were not pursuing the common good, Madison expanded his view of the obligations of the people. Rather than followers who 'think of nothing but obedience, leaving the care of their liberties to their wiser rulers', Madison held that the new regime placed a larger responsibility upon the people. His answer, then, to the query 'who are the best keepers of the people's liberty?' was 'the people themselves. The sacred trust', he said, 'can nowhere be so safe as in the hands most interested in preserving it.' But Madison attached an important addendum to his seeming reliance upon the people and their wisdom. 'The people', he observed, 'ought to be enlightened, to be awakened', and 'to be united' in their efforts at oversight.[82] And the logical candidates to guide this process remained leaders who retained a sense of the common good. Madison, then, in responding to the unexpected development of misguided leaders in control of the new polity, adapted his view of the role of the people in a regime of popular sovereignty, but did not abandon his core belief that the people needed to be directed by those who knew better. Much of Madison's activity in the 1790s reflected this belief.

In devising a response to the perceived threat of the Hamiltonians, Madison had no fixed plan, but, as he wrote to Jefferson, he hoped to engage in 'the free pursuit of measures which may be dictated by Repubn. principles and required by the public good'.[83] As it turned out, the chief vehicles for mobilizing the people came through the shaping of public opinion through personal influence, newspapers and other print media, and ultimately, the resourceful creation of the first American political party. Ultimately, Madison was as creative and successful in facing his second challenge to his dual beliefs in popular sovereignty and the common good as he had been in addressing the first.

Given his views of the respective roles of leaders and the people, the concept of public opinion became key. Public opinion, which Madison defined as 'that of the majority', 'sets bounds to every government, and is the real sovereign in every free one'.[84] Madison recognized that 'all power has been traced up to opinion', and that 'the most arbitrary government is controuled where the public opinion is fixed'.[85] The problem was that 'the Country is too much uninformed, and too inert to speak for itself'.[86] 'How devoutly is it to be wished, then, that the public opinion of the United States should be enlightened', Madison wrote. The solution was to turn to appropriate leaders. 'In proportion as Government is influenced by opinion,' Madison observed, 'it must be so, by whatever influences opinion.'[87] Leaders were just such an influence.

Madison's tactics can best be demonstrated by way of an example. In 1793, as the policies of the Hamiltonians seemed to have reached dangerous proportions, Madison wrote to Jefferson with a plan. 'If an early & well digested effort for calling out the real sense of the people be not made,' he wrote, 'there is room to apprehend they may in many places be misled.' Having consulted with a fellow Virginia leader (probably Monroe), Madison outlined their strategy. 'We shall endeavor at some means of repelling the danger; particularly by setting on foot expressions of the public mind in important Counties, and under the auspices of respectable names.' He gave an example. 'I have written with this view to Caroline [county], and have suggested a proper train of ideas, and a wish that Mr. P[endleton] would patronise the measure. Such an example', he predicted, 'would have great effect.' Although drafted, proposed and marshaled through by leaders, the result 'would be considered as an authentic specimen of the *Country* temper'. The only real problem with the plan was a lack of acceptable leaders. 'The want of opportunities, and our ignorance of trust worthy characters', Madison concluded, 'will circumscribe our efforts in this way to a very narrow compass.'[88]

If personal appeals had their limitations, the use of the press had no such restriction. The 'circulation of newspapers through the entire body of the people', said Madison, would positively affect public opinion, and 'is favorable to liberty'.[89] In particular, Madison 'entertain'd hopes that a free paper meant for general circulation and edited by a Man of genius, of republican principles ... would be an acceptable vehicle of public information in many places not sufficiently supplied with it'.[90] He was thereupon instrumental in setting up his old schoolmate Philip Freneau as editor of the new *National Gazette*, and himself contributed more than a dozen essays to the initial editions. Madison and other republican leaders continued throughout the 1790s a steady drumbeat of articles and pamphlets designed to 'enlighten, awaken, and unite' the people to secure the common good.

The ultimate impact of this enlightened public opinion, Madison knew, must be felt at the ballot box. Here he teamed with Jefferson in one of his truly creative adaptations of the polity: the development of the first American political party. The process was a gradual, almost unplanned affair. In the early 1790s, anti-Hamiltonian political clubs known as 'Democratic Societies' had emerged to discuss current issues and to support appropriate candidates for political office. When the Federalist Washington denounced these societies in an annual message in 1794, Madison had responded sharply, labeling this an 'attack on the most sacred principle of our Constitution and of Republicanism'.[91] However, prior to 1796, as historian Robert Rutland reports, 'The Republicans as a party had been a somewhat sociable group of like-minded politicians without any fixed commitment to a philosophy or a leader'. However, subsequent events – such as the controversies over the Jay Treaty, widely seen by many as a sell-out of American interests to the British – had energized the group. Led in large part by Madison, Rutland notes that 'within twelve months this group gave way to a corps of politicians who knew that the cardinal sin in public life was to lose an election. They set themselves on a course to steer them to victory in local contests, statewide balloting, and finally to the presidential election [of 1800].'[92] This new party represented the first effort at such organized opposition in the new polity.

Madison was well aware of the link between this stratagem and his commitment to popular sovereignty and the common good. As early as 1792, he had detected the essential distinctions between his followers and those of Hamilton. Hamilton's 'party', he said, 'consists of those, who from particular interest ... are more partial to the opulent than to the other classes of society; and [have] debauched themselves into a persuasion that mankind are incapable of governing themselves'. This in turn, had implications for the common good. 'Men of these sentiments', wrote Madison, 'must naturally wish to point the measures of government less to the interest of the many than of a few.' Madison's followers, representing 'the mass of people in every part of the union' (who Madison labelled for the first time the 'Republican party'), were the opposite. They believed in 'the doctrine that mankind are capable of governing themselves', and are 'naturally offended at every public measure that does not appeal to the understanding and to the general interest of the community'.[93] Thus, somewhat ironically, Madison perceived that the emergence of the Republican party would eventually lead to the securing of the general good, even if it seemed to reinforce divisions in doing so. In a sense, then, Madison's party 'represented' the public good on the American political scene, and its ultimate triumph would re-establish the nexus between popular sovereignty and the public good.[94]

The creation of a disciplined party operation was Madison's consummate stratagem in his quest to preserve the common good through the mechanisms of the existing polity. Ultimately, he was successful in what came to be known as the 'Revolution of 1800', as he secured, in the words of historian Drew McCoy, 'relief from the impositions of a power-hungry minority faction ... through the republican principle of mobilizing popular opinion through the electoral system'.[95] It is, however, always darkest before the dawn. In the waning years of the 1790s, Madison faced a crisis of unprecedented proportions, which called for the application of all of the adaptations he had devised during the decade, and more.

The crisis, of course, was the passage of the Alien and Sedition Acts, the latter of which in particular seemed to strike at the heart of all of Madison's efforts of the preceding decade. Passed by the Federalists during the heat of partisan wrangling, the Alien Act allowed the president to arrest or expel any noncitizen. Even more troubling, the Sedition Act made it a crime to criticize the national government. Where Madison had come to champion the role of the people in overseeing the polity (with proper guidance from far-sighted leaders), the Sedition Act threatened to 'shut ... the eyes of the people ... on the conduct of those entrusted with power ... [and] tie ... their tongues ... from a just wholesome censure' of them.[96] Moreover it menaced the very survival of the elective process Madison relied upon so much by a strangulation of opposition parties. All in all, these acts represented the 'grossest contradictions' to 'the real principles & interests' of the public.[97] Indeed, this was, perhaps, the most serious threat to popular sovereignty and the common good yet. If the leaders in Congress could go along with the executive on this one, Madison worried, 'a majority in the H[ouse] of R[epresentatives] & 2/3 of the Senate seem to be ripe for everything'.[98] Worse, if the people will accept such tyranny, they are liable to 'an infatuation which does not admit of human remedy'.[99]

Rather than despair, however, Madison remained creatively adaptive. Part of his response simply echoed the tactics of the preceding years. Again it was to his ultimate faith in the people that he turned, again carefully guided by appropriate leaders. Newspapers played an important role. 'I am glad to find in general', he wrote Jefferson, 'that every thing that good sense & accurate information can supply is abundantly exhibited by the [Republican]

Newspapers to the view of the public.' The problem was, that even this was not enough. 'It is to be regretted', he went on, 'that these papers are so limited in their circulation ... .'[100] Something more was needed to bolster public opinion in the right direction. Historian Ralph Ketcham captures the essence of the ensuing strategy: 'The people and the Republican press needed some rallying point, some statement of principles and policy that could crystallize antiadministration sentiment. ... The two men agreed that the state legislatures might be the most effective and legally invulnerable organs of protest.'[101]

This was the genesis of Madison's famous Virginia Resolutions, and ultimately of his subsequent Virginia Report. Much has been made of Madison's seeming shift to a states' rights position in these documents, and there is something to the charge. But what is often overlooked is the fact that Madison was simply pursuing the objectives he had always pursued: the securing of the common good through the creative adaptation of the regime. True enough, he now gave much more latitude to the states than he had a decade earlier, when he had confronted a vastly different challenge to the common good. But this was not a sudden switch. As early as 1791, when he had begun to perceive that the new threat to the common good resided in the national government, Madison had begun to suggest that both state and national governments could guard the 'public liberty and the public welfare'.[102] This was the essential purpose of his language in the Virginia Resolutions, if one is to believe Madison's explication in the following year's Virginia Report. In the Resolutions, he argued, 'the appeal was emphatically made to the intermediate existence of the state governments, between the people and that [national] government, to the vigilance with which they would descry the first symptoms of usurpation, and to the promptitude with which they would sound the alarm to the public'.[103] Much later, when Madison's rhetoric was being used by the hated nullifiers, he would retreat from even this interpretation. As he would write to Edward Everett and Edward Livingston in 1830, the goal had simply been to supplement the other efforts to mobilize public opinion.[104]

In the face of the final crisis of the 1790s, then, Madison continued his strategy of the earlier years of the decade, and was ultimately successful in overturning the hated Alien and Sedition laws and, more importantly, in turning out the Federalists with their policies inimical to the common good. With the election of 1800, Madison largely achieved his objective of placing into power at the national level a cadre of leaders devoted to the common good.

Looking back at Madison's stances and activities of the 1790s, one sees a different Madison from that of the 1780s. Madison had confronted a new challenge in the '90s. Rather than the earlier threat to the common good posed by local majorities at the state level, this time he confronted a minority faction which had gained ascendancy in the national government and which pursued ends that Madison believed contravened the good of the people. In response, he rethought his earlier views of the nexus between leaders and followers in a regime of popular sovereignty. In the 1780s, he had articulated a commitment to rule by the people, but, in the face of seeming popular misbehavior, Madison had sought to mediate the rule of the people by ensuring a cadre of leaders who looked beyond interest and faction to the permanent and general interest of the people. Faced with unruly majorities, Madison trusted the people only to have sufficient wisdom and virtue to choose their betters to lead them. In the 1790s, the challenge was altogether different. Now faced with a group of leaders behaving improperly, Madison turned to the natural constituency for restraining the usurpers: the people. In so doing he had to revisit his earlier assumptions about the people and their role. Now he suggested that not only could the people be trusted to select appropriate leaders, but they also had the obligation to monitor closely those leaders' activities. This seeming shift, however, was not as dramatic as might at first appear. Madison did not suddenly become a believer in the enhanced capabilities of the people; only in their increased responsibility. It remained the duty of far-sighted leaders, with the general good in view, to 'awaken, enlighten, and unite' the people in opposition to designing leaders. This was the underlying purpose of the bulk of Madison's activities in the 1790s.

In the end, then, the Madison of the 1790s was really not all that much different from the Madison of the 1780s. He continued in his quest to secure what he conceived as the public good, and to do so without abandoning his faith in rule by the people. He achieved this through a series of creative adaptations of the polity. In the 1780s, this had required the wholesale restructuring of the polity itself. In the 1790s, it was more a matter of devising equally creative means to assure that the people were properly led in their role as 'keepers' of the general good.

CHALLENGE #3: THE THREAT TO THE COMMON GOOD FROM THE PEOPLE AND THEIR LEADERS

With the Republicans safely in power after 1800, the perceived tension between the operations of the polity and the common good receded. There were difficulties and dangers enough, as Jefferson's second term and most of Madison's presidency amply attest. Yet because the polity was led by the 'right' sort of leaders, and supported for the most part by the people, Madison was not overly troubled by the kinds of fundamental concerns about the polity that motivated much of his activity in the 1780s and 1790s. Of course the rump of the Federalist party was the source of a considerable amount of dissension, but they fell safely under the category of 'minority faction' that Madison had identified in *Federalist No. 10*, and could be dealt with through 'the republican principle, which enables the majority to defeat its sinister views by regular vote'.[105] Likewise the fundamentalists in Madison's own party, the 'Tertium Quids', were as yet but a minor annoyance.

The triumph of leaders and followers committed to the common good goes a long way to explain some of the otherwise puzzling policies pursued by Madison in the first fifteen years of the new century. As historian Robert Rutland explains it, 'now that both Virginians [Jefferson and Madison] were in the executive branch, their responsibility to the nation demanded that they examine every policy and make decisions on one criterion only: what course of action was dictated by the self-interest of the United States?'[106] This 'would turn Republican policy in new directions', adds historian Marvin Meyers. 'Madison as war president had felt the alarming weakness of the nation under stress.' The nation had lacked 'effective military forces, and the financial, industrial, and transportation facilities and resources needed to sustain' it. Moreover, the glow of postwar nationalism – as the *Richmond Enquirer* put it, 'the sun never shone upon a people whose destinies promised to be grander' – 'pointed to a program that could realize the possibilities'.[107] This makes sensible Madison's rather remarkable annual message of 1815. In it, in distinct contrast to his positions in the 1790s, he called for a national bank, a beefed-up military establishment, a protective tariff and, if the 'defect of constitutional authority' could be got over, a federally-funded program of internal improvements.[108]

It was this last issue, however – internal improvements – that was to foreshadow Madison's final trial. On his penultimate day in office, he was to veto the 'Bonus Bill', an act to fund such improvements. His ostensible reason was that this bill was not congruent with the Constitution.[109] Given, however, his constitutional 'flip-flop' regarding the national bank,[110] there was something more subtle at issue here. It was no less than Madison's final, and most difficult, challenge to his dual commitment to popular sovereignty and the common good.

If Madison's perception of the sorts of policies which could advance the public interest had advanced significantly since his days in opposition in the 1790s, his core beliefs had not. Certainly he never abandoned his commitment to popular sovereignty. In 1821 he wrote to John G. Jackson describing himself as 'having from the first moment of maturing a political opinion down to the present one, never ceased to be a votary of the principle of self-government'.[111] Nor did he alter his commitment to, or his definition of, the common good. In his last annual message to Congress, he closed with his wish and vision for the future: 'a Government pursuing the public good as its sole object'.[112] Madison continued to label 'the rights of property as well as of persons the two-fold object of political Institutions',[113] and remained concerned with 'the claims of justice',[114] and 'the purposes of order, justice, and the general good'.[115]

Now, however, Madison faced a new challenge to his lifelong pursuit of the common good in a regime of popular sovereignty. The new challenge was related to, but distinct from, the challenges of the past. In the 1780s, Madison sought to respond to a tyranny of the mass of the people through the creation of a governmental structure which would ensure that those who had wisdom and virtue to perceive the common good would have the power to pursue it. In the 1790s, when the common good was under attack by a minority of misguided leaders, Madison orchestrated a tactical campaign to restore to the helm leaders who could perceive and implement the common good. Now Madison faced the ultimate challenge: ostensibly good leaders and their followers swept along in a majoritarian tide which threatened the common good.

The sources of this ultimate challenge were twofold, stemming from contemporary societal changes and an ominous future. As we have seen, historian Gordon Wood has traced a sea change which took place in American values in the early decades of the nineteenth century. Previous commitments to communalism and public virtue were overwhelmed by social, economic and intellectual movements which made America by 1820 'the most egalitarian, most materialistic, most individualistic … society in Western history'.[116] This new individualism undercut Madison's assumptions about an enduring, unitary common good which could be elucidated and implemented by a virtuous elite. Instead, in the words of a contemporary, 'the public good is best promoted by the exertion of each individual seeking his own good in his own way'.[117] The political manifestation of this phenomenon was a sweeping democratization of the country at all levels which made the political leaders at all levels acutely sensitive to the will of majorities.[118] The future held its own concerns for Madison. As early as the Constitutional Convention Madison had predicted that 'in future times a great majority of the people will not only be without landed, but any other sort of property'. When that came to pass, 'the rights of property & the public liberty, will not be secure in their hands'.[119] That time now appeared nigh. In 1821, he noted that in the future the time would come when 'the Majority shall be without landed or other equivalent property', there will be a 'danger from an equality and universality of suffrage, vesting compleat power over property in hands without a share in it'.[120]

The problem facing Madison in one sense remained the one familiar from the 1780s. 'Where the people govern themselves,' he wrote in 1825, 'and where, of course, the majority govern, a danger to the minority arises from opportunities tempting a sacrifice of their rights to the interests, real or supposed, of the majority.'[121] Only now there was an exacerbating circumstance. While in the 1780s Madison could turn to enlightened leaders to rectify the abuses, now the leaders were part of the problem. The 1790s concern with renegade leaders was past; there was now 'sufficient control in the popular will over the Executive and Legislative departments'. Contrariwise, 'the great complaint now', Madison wrote in 1830, 'is, not against the want of this sympathy and responsibility, but against the results of them'.[122] In other words, now leaders – even of Madison's carefully-constructed national polity – were puppets of the people. Now 'if ... the powers of the General Government be carried to unconstitutional lengths, it will be the result of a majority of the States and of the people, actuated by some impetuous feeling, or some real or supposed interest'.[123] 'What is to controul Congress,' Madison asked plaintively, 'when backed & even pushed on by a majority of their Constituents, as was the case in the late contest relative to Missouri, and as may again happen in the constructive power relating to Roads & Canals?'[124]

Much of Madison's retirement was devoted to grappling with just this issue. Although many no longer shared his premise of a permanent, unitary common good, Madison continued to seek creative ways to adapt the new manifestation of popular sovereignty to his traditional notions of the common good. His initial impulse was to resurrect remedies of the past; when those did not prove efficacious, Madison explored new roles for the people and their leaders in his continuing quest.

Madison's initial impulse was to return to structural solutions such as he had implemented in the 1780s. He remained committed to the efficacy of a large republic and long terms of service. 'The security for the holders of property when the minority', he wrote, 'can ... be derived ... from the difficulty of combining & effectuating unjust purposes throughout an extensive country.' Again, this should secure the selection of appropriate leaders. 'Large districts are manifestly favorable to the election of persons of general respectability', he argued.[125] In addition, such districts provided 'the better for internal justice and order'. Likewise, long terms of service 'render the Body more stable in its policy, and more capable of stemming popular currents taking a wrong direction, till reason & justice ... regain their ascendancy'.[126] Unfortunately, given the new relationship between leaders and the people, these safeguards were no longer enough.

Nor was the kind of structural re-engineering Madison contemplated in his private writings in 1821, although these reflections provide an important insight into his adaptability to new conditions. In those private musings, Madison sought to devise a new legislative structure which would respond to the demands of the times. His initial concern remained the same as it had always been – the protection of property rights, and hence justice in society. Property holders, who in addition to a concern for property 'have at stake all the other rights common to those without property', remained essential guarantors of the common good. Thus 'some barrier against the invasion of their rights would not be out of place in a just & provident System of Government'. Nevertheless, Madison recognized, and sought to respond to, the new reality of recently-enfranchised masses. 'Under every view of the subject', he admitted, 'it seems indispensable that the Mass of Citizens should not be without a voice in making laws which they are to obey, & in chusing the Magistrates who are to administer them.' This posed a dilemma: on the one hand, to 'allow the right [of suffrage] exclusively to property' could mean 'the rights of persons may be oppressed'. On the other hand, to 'extend it equally to all' could mean that 'the rights of property or claims of justice may be overruled by a majority ... interested in measures of injustice'. Madison's solution was to weigh carefully a variety of possible legislative configurations which might protect both the new manifestation of popular sovereignty and his concern for the common good. This effort suggests that Madison was astute enough, and creative enough, to seek to devise a polity that could accommodate his dual interests.[127]

About a decade later, Madison had an opportunity actually to apply such musings in a policy-making setting. He was a delegate to the Virginia constitutional convention of 1829–1830, which had to grapple with these self-same issues. Virginia's constitution had not been revised since its promulgation in 1776, and its provisions favored the political hegemony of an eastern, slaveholding elite. In the ensuing decades, Virginia's population had increased enormously and expanded to the west, where slavery was much less of a factor. After decades of agitation on the part of those denied access to political power, the ruling elite had been forced to call a constitutional convention to redress the imbalance through a broader suffrage and the reapportionment of the legislature.[128]

Although Madison was quite elderly at this point, he consented to be a part of the deliberations. In his only speech during the proceedings, Madison began where he had left off in his writings in 1821: he acknowledged that both factions had legitimate concerns. 'It is sufficiently obvious', he said, 'that persons and property are the two great subjects on which Governments are to act; and that the rights of persons, and the rights of property, are the objects, for protection of which Government was instituted.' Moreover, 'These rights cannot well be separated'. On the one hand, a key concern was the need for 'a guaranty of the rights of the minority against a majority disposed to take unjust advantage of its power'.[129] On the other hand, the majority could not be ignored. 'It must be recollected ... that it cannot be expedient to rest a Republican Gov[ernment] on a portion of society having a numerical [minority]'. Indeed, it would be ideal if 'a State of Society could be ... framed in which an equal voice in making laws might be allowed to every individual bound to obey them'. Unfortunately, long experience had shown that it was 'unsafe to admit [all individuals] to a full share of political power'. The task of the convention, then, was to determine what 'limitations & modifications' would be required.[130]

Madison's proposed solution was twofold. First, he sought to broaden the definition of those who might be permitted to participate in the polity, but within carefully-defined parameters. The polity should now embrace 'every description of citizens having sufficient stake in the public order, and the stable administration of the laws'. Specifically, this meant that the previous freehold suffrage could now be extended to include 'House keepers & Heads of families'.[131] Second, the structure of the polity should be altered. On the one hand, the new men deserved representation in the government. On the other hand, in view of emerging majoritarianism, 'the only effectual safeguard to the rights of the minority must be laid in such a basis and structure of Government itself as may afford, in a certain degree, directly or indirectly, a defensive authority in behalf of a minority having right on its side'.[132] Therefore Madison advocated a lower house based upon the white male population, and an upper chamber based upon white males plus three-fifths of the slaves.

The actual document ultimately approved by the convention favored greatly the traditional interests (an outcome foreordained by the ruling elite's clever manipulation of the convention's membership). Although Madison professed himself pleased with the results, he well knew that no permanent solution had been found to this new democratic threat to the common good. (Indeed, a mere twenty years later, in 1850, Virginia would join the phalanx of states adopting universal white male suffrage). Nevertheless, Madison had operated in this convention, as he had in previous decades, according to consistent principles. As he phrased it a few years later in his autobiography, his concerns were 'the tranquillity of the State, and the capacity of man for self-government'.[133]

Madison, however, was always a pragmatist. He realized that, in the long term, all his structural inventiveness would go nowhere, given existing democratic attitudes. He recognized that despite his efforts 'Experience or public opinion require an equal & universal suffrage for each branch of the [national] Gov[ernment] such as prevails generally in the U.S.', and that solutions which might have been practical in the 1780s had been made more or less obsolete by the tides of change. He was forced to consider other possible responses to the challenge to popular sovereignty and the public good, and he did so by turning again to the roles and responsibilities of the people and their leaders.[134]

Reliance upon proper leaders had been the cornerstone of Madison's strategy for decades. Now that avenue had been truncated. It was not that Madison had entirely abandoned his faith in their utility. In the face of growing evidence that popular leaders were becoming the mere spokespersons for the majority, Madison noted that there remained a leadership role for property holders in the minority. Indeed, a 'security for the holders of property when [in] the minority, can ... be derived from the ordinary influence possessed by property, & the superior information incident to its holders'.[135] Moreover, the duty of such leaders was to serve as a beacon of good sense and good judgment. 'What is to controul Congress when backed & even pushed by a majority of their Constituents ...?' Madison answered his own question. 'Nothing within the pale of the Constitution but sound arguments and conciliatory expostulations addressed both to Congress & to their Constituents [supposedly by wise and virtuous leaders].'[136]

Unfortunately, the continued reliance upon exemplary leaders who had the larger common good in view was to prove a rather slim reed. The problem was that Madison's assumption about the proper relationship between leaders and followers had been turned on its head. While Madison had always expected followers to look for and accept guidance from their appropriate leaders, now the governing assumption seemed to be the opposite. As Richmond newspaper editor Thomas Ritchie put it, 'the day of prophets and oracles has passed; ... we are free citizens of a free country, and must think for ourselves'.[137] Madison had painful enough evidence of this in his own experience. In response to Edward Coles's call for Madison to act as a responsible leader for yet another generation of Americans, Madison replied: 'May I not appeal, also, to facts which will satisfy yourself of the error which supposes that a respect for my opinion ... would control the adverse opinions of others?' The fact was that Madison's opinions had been ignored on each of the principal issues then agitating the public conversations. 'On the subject of the bank, on that of the tariff, and on that of nullification, three great constitutional questions of the day,' he went on, 'my opinions, with the grounds of them, are well known.... Yet the bank was, perhaps, never more warmly opposed than at present; the tariff seems to have lost none of its unpopularity; whilst nullification ... is ... notoriously advancing with some of my best personal, and heretofore political, friends among its advocates.' Again, however, Madison displayed his willingness to adapt to the new reality. 'It must not be thought', he concluded, 'that I am displeased or disappointed at this result. On the contrary, I honor the independent judgment that decides for itself.'[138]

If leaders with a higher vision of the common good were no longer the avenue for the protection of those interests that Madison held dear, he perforce had to turn to creative adaptations of the role of the people. Specifically, in light of the new realities, Madison now had to rethink the role of the people in a regime of popular sovereignty. In a sense, this reconceptualization was merely the culmination of an ongoing process for Madison; in another sense, it required a significant departure from his previous thinking. We have seen that in the 1780s, when many of the threats to the common good appeared to stem from the people, Madison had trusted the people only to have sufficient virtue to elect appropriate leaders. In the 1790s, when the threat came from misguided leaders above, Madison had expanded this conception, and had championed the people as the watchdogs of the polity, although he still reserved to enlightened leaders the task of awakening and shaping this guardianship of the common good. By the 1820s, the inescapable demands of democratic individualism required that virtually all responsibility for the operation of the polity lay in the hands of the people themselves. In response, Madison was no less creative than before, albeit less successful, in his last attempt to reconcile popular sovereignty with his conception of the common good.

A threshold issue involved enhancing the capability of the people who now shouldered the enormous responsibility of a popular regime. Protection of the common good could now come only 'from the popular sense of justice enlightened and enlarged by a diffusive education'.[139] This was the heart of it. 'A popular Government, without popular information, or the means of acquiring it', Madison argued, 'is but a prologue to a farce or a tragedy; or, perhaps, both. Knowledge will forever govern ignorance; and a people who mean to be their own governors must arm themselves with the power which knowledge gives.' The benefits of a successful system of education coincided exactly with the needs of a democratic polity. Madison suggested that 'Learned institutions ought to be the favorite objects with every free people. They throw that light over the public mind which is the best security against crafty and dangerous encroachments on the public liberty'. Moreover, such schools could help respond to the needs of leadership. 'They are the nurseries of skilful teachers for the schools distributed throughout the community. They are themselves schools for the particular talents required for some of the public trusts, on the able execution of which the welfare of the people depends. They multiply the educated individuals, from among whom the people may elect a due portion of their public agents of every description; more especially of those who are to frame the laws....' The result would be the end Madison had long sought: a government characterized by 'the perspicuity, the consistency, and the stability, as well as by the just and equal spirit of which the great social purposes are to be answered'.[140]

Unfortunately, education was at best a long-term solution, dependent as well upon uncertain public appropriations. Madison well knew that the abuses he was currently witnessing required a more substantive, and more immediate, response. Here, Madison offered his last great creative contribution to the polity. It was a new form of Constitutional interpretation which sought to acknowledge the new locus of power in the people, while at the same time assuring the stability, concern for justice and the rights of property that had guided his efforts for so long.[141]

The new approach was not one that Madison came to easily; nor was it one that he would have desired had conditions permitted a different option. Madison had long viewed the Constitution as a salutary brake on popular passion, and he continued to argue that it was 'the duty of all to support it in its true meaning, as understood *by the nation* at the time of its ratification'.[142] Moreover, if that original interpretation was to be altered, it should be done according to the 'constitutional remedies' already in place, particularly 'amendment of [the] Constitution, as provided by itself'.[143] To the extent that matters of day-to-day interpretation arose, Madison preferred to rely on 'the Judiciary branch of the Government [as the] expositor' of the Constitution.[144] These procedures, if adhered to carefully, would yield the desired result: 'the substitution of law and order for uncertainty, confusion, and violence'.[145]

Regrettably, the practices of the time did not conform to Madison's ideal. In such legislation as the 'Bonus Bill', which condoned federally-funded internal improvements – as well as several other recent initiatives – Americans appeared to determine the constitutionality of a proposal according to its 'usefulness and popularity',[146] rather than upon traditional constitutional principles. The popular will, in other words, was running unchecked. In response to this popular challenge to proper constitutional interpretation, Madison had to rethink his traditionalist approach, and seek instead to devise a theory of constitutional interpretation which was more consonant with the existing reality.

The goal was the same as it had always been: to 'bring [these] measures to the test of justice & of the general good'.[147] At present, 'every new legislative opinion might make a new Constitution'. This promised 'an end to that stability in government and in laws which is essential to good government and good laws'.[148] Instead, there was a need for a new standard. 'The Constitution of the United States may doubtless disclose, from time to time,' Madison admitted, 'faults which call for the pruning or the ingrafting hand'. It was critical, however, that 'remedies ought to be applied, not in the paroxysms of party and popular excitements, but with the more leisure and reflection'. Only then could one be assured of 'the symmetry and the stability aimed at in our political system'.[149] Such a model for constitutional interpretation was what Madison now proceeded to devise.

What Madison now proposed, in the words of historian Drew McCoy, was 'a voluntary deference to the authority of ancestral intent'.[150] It was, in a sense, a reliance upon popular opinion, yet not upon the passions of the moment; it was that popular opinion which had withstood decades of testing and which had become the source of stability and expected rules of behavior. If a measure could pass the test of this sort of popular sanction, it was likely also to meet the objectives Madison maintained for the polity.

The most obvious case was that of the tariff. Madison had always thought the tariff constitutional, but in the face of intense opposition to it among his fellow Virginians and others, Madison now embraced far more evidence of its constitutionality than his traditional focus upon specific constitutional language and original intent. As he wrote to Joseph Cabell in 1828, he believed that the Constitution itself had always legitimated tariffs. If constitutional language were not enough, however, 'a further evidence … an evidence that ought of itself to settle the question, is the uniform and practical sanction given to the power by the General Government for nearly forty years, with a concurrence or acquiescence of every State Government throughout the same period, and, it may be added, through all the vicissitudes of party which marked the period'. Madison thus set forth an innovative method of constitutional interpretation designed to moderate majority passion. 'No novel construction, however ingeniously devised, or however respectable and patriotic its patrons', he wrote, 'can withstand the weight of such authorities, or the unbroken current of so prolonged and universal a practice.'[151] Moreover, this mode of constitutional interpretation moderated the tension between Madison's fundamental commitment to popular sovereignty and his coexisting concern for the public good. As he wrote to Cabell in other correspondence, 'a construction of the Constitution practised upon or acknowledged for a period of nearly forty years, has received a national sanction not to be reversed but by an evidence at least equivalent to the national will'. Such a demonstrated commitment to the legitimate will of the people would also yield the 'stability in that fundamental law ... required for the public good'.[152]

The issue of the national bank was even more revealing, because, as Madison himself admitted, it was an institution 'I had originally opposed as unauthorized by the Constitution' yet 'to which I at length gave my official assent [as president in 1816]'.[153] What was most intriguing was his justification, because he drew upon his new theory of defining the Constitution in terms of the popular will as manifested by longstanding practice. Madison was quite candid about this. 'My abstract opinion of the text of the Constitution is not changed', he acknowledged in 1831, yet 'in the case of a Constitution as of a law, a course of authoritative expositions sufficiently deliberate, uniform, and settled, was an evidence of the public will necessarily overruling individual opinions'.[154] By 1816, a national bank 'had been carried into execution throughout a period of twenty years with annual legislative recognitions ... with the entire acquiescence of all the local authorities, as well as the nation at large'. Thus the bank – through the longstanding demonstration of the popular will – was constitutional. Indeed, Madison would go so far as to say that 'under these circumstances, with an admission of the expediency and almost necessity of the measure', a veto 'would have been a defiance of all the obligations derived from a course of precedents amounting to the requisite evidence of the national judgment and intention'. Not only did this constitutional stance acknowledge the will of the people, it also prevented instability and injustice.[155]

On the other hand, many current issues, such as federally-funded internal improvements, did not have this sort of long-term popular sanction, and thus were constitutionally suspect. As Madison looked back upon the history of this issue, he noted that federal activity in the realm of internal improvements had been rejected in the Constitutional Convention as well as in the state ratifying conventions, and that not even Hamilton himself had been so bold as to believe that the Constitution permitted such a power.[156] Neither had constant practice and public acceptance sanctioned such a change in policy. As Madison noted, 'As a precedent, the case is evidently without the weight allowed to that of the National Bank, which ... had received reiterated and elaborate sanctions'.[157] That being the case, the only way to make such legislation constitutional was through the formal amending process. As Madison had put it in his penultimate annual message, 'any defect of constitutional authority which may be encountered can be supplied in a mode which the Constitution itself has providently pointed out'.[158]

The importance of Madison's stances on these issues lies in his underlying purpose. The essential problem that Madison saw in the emerging American polity was the lack of an effective check on majority passion, which potentially threatened private property rights, and hence justice and stability. As Madison put it, the concern was that 'the usefulness and popularity of measures' was 'the most dangerous snare' for prospects for the common good.[159] His solution was as creatively adaptive as any he had concocted in the past. Realizing that the structural solutions of the 1780s were unavailable to him, and that the current social and political realities had diluted the role of leaders in guiding the polity in the right path, Madison turned instead to a rule of constitutional construction. This rule honored his commitment to popular rule, yet constrained popular abuses by defining the polity's fundamental law in terms of longstanding practice. If space, in the form of the large republic, had helped to guarantee proper leadership and the common good in an earlier era, now time – in the sense of longstanding practice – was to serve a similar function, at least in terms of protecting Madison's notion of the common good from democratic majoritarianism.

Despite Madison's creative attempts to ensure stability, the protection of property rights, and justice in a majoritarian democracy, he gradually recognized that none of his proposed solutions were finding favor with the populace. Worse, the popular demand for internal improvements and, later, the nullification movement suggested that misguided popular passion was to be an ongoing reality. At the end of a long career devoted to seeking the congruence of rule by the people and the pursuit of the common good, Madison realized that a choice between these sometimes competing objectives needed to be made. When finally faced with this stark reality, Madison did not hesitate. As early as the 1820s, he had indicated his priority. In a letter to Jefferson, he had bemoaned the push for federally-funded internal improvements, and noted that 'the will of the nation being omnipotent for right, is so for wrong also'. Nevertheless, 'the will of the nation being in the majority, the minority must submit to that danger of oppression as an evil infinitely less than the danger to the whole nation from a will independent of [the majority]'.[160] Even earlier (in 1821), as he had been seeking to balance the interests of the majority and the minority, he had acknowledged that 'if no exact & safe equilibrium can be introduced, it is more reasonable that a preponderating weight sh[ould] be allowed to the greater interest than to the lesser'.[161] Thus, although the newly-emergent majoritarian democracy held profound concerns for Madison, he chose to cast his lot with this form of the polity as superior to any other yet devised.[162]

THE IMPLICIT LEADERSHIP THEORIES OF JAMES MADISON

James Madison has long enjoyed a deserved reputation as perhaps the greatest political theorist in the American experience. As he struggled with the successive challenges to his core beliefs, he, perhaps more than any other modern theorist, articulated his underlying assumptions about the human condition and the requirements of governing. In particular, in his responses to the fundamental issues we have identified as the 'template of leadership', he evinced quite a complex and sophisticated understanding of the challenge of leading the people. Because his reflections were among the first and most cogent of those confronting leadership in a regime of popular sovereignty, and because his solutions continue to shape the structure and workings of the American polity, Madison's responses to the protocol of questions of the leadership template are worthy of our consideration.

What is the Leadership Challenge?

The leadership challenge facing Madison, in various guises throughout a long career, can be summarized as the perceived need to devise appropriate institutions, mechanisms and processes to secure justice and the common good in a polity that – quite rightly, in Madison's view – looked to the people as the source of its justification and to their interests as the measure of its success. In most instances, this challenge, for Madison, transmuted into the more specific problem of the need to secure good leaders consistent with the classical ideal in ways consistent with the new reality of popular sovereignty. As we have seen, the formulation of this challenge varied as the political realities shifted over time. In the 1780s, the perceived problem lay in the people; a decade later it resided in the leaders, and at the end of his career, when democracy had reached full flower, the danger stemmed from both leaders and the people. Through it all, Madison consistently, and with considerable creativity, sought to establish a new social relation between the many and the few that could be labeled the first attempt at creating a fiction of leadership. It was in such efforts to reconfigure the traditional relations between leaders and the people that Madison came face to face with many of the issues posed by the template of leadership.

What is the Perception of Human Nature?

It was in confronting this threshold issue that Madison first gave evidence of the sophistication of his thinking concerning the challenges of rule in regimes grounded in the sovereignty of the people. He was, above all, a realist and pragmatist. He thought men capable of high aspirations and had the ability to look beyond themselves (civic virtue), but he also acknowledged that they often evinced a self-interested narrowness of purpose. Such contradictions did not make for simple solutions when it came time for creating political structures to serve the people's interests, but they made James Madison well suited as the creator of a fiction relevant to the emerging complexities of modernity. This question regarding human nature is, of course, inextricably linked to its political manifestation, which is the next topic of the leadership protocol.

Are the People Capable of Governing?

In this political manifestation of the human condition, Madison refused to give a definitive answer, instead contenting himself with addressing the subtleties in practice. Of one fact there was no doubt: Madison believed deeply that the people were the *basis* of government; that is, he was firmly committed to the principle of popular sovereignty. However, this did not mean that he was equally confident that the people could govern; his doubts about this spurred many of his innovations. Indeed, Madison's first leadership challenge in the 1780s was precisely the apparent reality that the people, given their head, would not govern wisely. Nevertheless, even though men were not 'angels', Madison acknowledged that a certain amount of popular wisdom and virtue inhered in the very concept of popular sovereignty. In the 1780s, he contented himself with the idea that the people had sufficient wisdom to choose their betters to lead them. Again in the 1790s, Madison expressed faith in the people to have the common sense to perceive the general good (à la Harrington), and to join efforts (by virtuous elite leaders) to roust out unvirtuous mentors. And, in the early nineteenth century, Madison, although still despairing of popular virtue regarding issues inspiring sudden popular passion, again was willing to defer to the long-term wisdom of the people. His call for education also suggested that he thought the people perfectible.

In summarizing Madison's positions on this matter, it becomes clear that he had some faith in the people's fundamental, underlying good sense, but that this was a slim reed to rely upon in the heat of political controversy, especially that which related to the individual interests of the populace. For this reason, Madison made various attempts to shape and steer popular opinion through institutional devices designed to emulate the good offices of the classical ideal. Madison remains an inspiration to those in the modern world who remain uncomfortable with the idea of democracy unrestrained.

What is the Proper End or Purpose of Leadership?

In this, Madison remained quite traditional, although he was more precise than many of his predecessors in defining his terms. Just as was the case with the classical ideal, Madison was firmly committed to the idea of the common good as the appropriate end of all political action. By defining it as the protection of individual and, in particular, property rights, his conceptions worked to the benefit of the dominant class. This, too, was entirely consistent with the classical ideal, which equated property ownership with leisure and independence, the two prerequisites for good leaders.

Madison, however, was among the first to contemplate what the common good might mean in a regime of popular sovereignty. As Madison thought it through, he became convinced that the common good was not the same as the will of the majority. This recognition lay at the base of his many efforts to secure his vision of the public interest even in the face of democratic passions and the reality of individual interests.

What is the Epistemology of Leadership?

One of the purposes of Madison's many institutional creations was to make it possible for there to be leaders of the type demanded by the classical ideal. To the extent that this was successful, such leaders could be relied upon to know what was in the interests of the people. To the extent, then, that Madison was able to apply the classical ideal to a regime of the people, the answer to this query could be the comfortable one offered by the classical ideal: simply rely upon the leader. Unfortunately, much of Madison's effort was occasioned by the reality that his ideal did not operate effectively. In the 1790s, for example, the leaders did not match the ideal, and in the nineteenth century, full-fledged democracy produced further problems.

Madison recognized, as had Harrington, that the common alternative of adherence to the rule of law was an inadequate substitute, because the laws were only as good as the men who made them. This was in part ameliorated when the 'rule of law' involved was a constitution, because Madison believed like Henry Vane that this form of law was likely to be wiser than mere legislative enactment. Thus, like Harrington again, it was Madison's desire to invent institutions that admitted of both the wisdom of virtuous leaders and the fundamental common sense of the people (this, for example, was an apt depiction of Madison's image of his party system).

Ultimately, as we have shown here, Madison had no effective answer to the challenge of the epistemology of leadership in a democratizing state. He eventually threw in his lot with the power of the people to decide policy, knowing full well that this would often lead to unwise policy. It is a challenge that remains with us still.

What is the Role of the Leader?

In Madison's fiction of leadership, the appropriate leader played an enormous role. When he stated that he was looking for a 'republican remedy', he meant the term literally. The schemes he devised to resolve the problems of popular government were very much in keeping with the expectations of the leader role in classical republicanism. The leader, ideally at any rate, was to provide the wisdom and disinterested virtue expected of the classical ideal.

As we have seen, Madison's initial solutions did not guarantee that appropriate leaders would rise to power, and his elitist remedies began to seem increasingly anachronistic as democracy began to reach high tide. Gradually Madison came to recognize that his desired role for the leader was doomed. In his later years, he never abandoned this as his preferred solution to the problems of democracy, but he came increasingly to understand that it was not a fiction destined to prevail in the egalitarian democracy of his later years. He was forced to turn to other devices (popular education, constitutional adjudication) that were neither successful nor entirely satisfactory to his conservative inclinations.

What is the Role of the People?

It is clear that the role of the people in Madison's line of thought shifted as conditions continued to evolve. As he progressed through the series of challenges to leadership narrated in this chapter, Madison gradually came to an expanded role for the people (although at the end of his career this was not a recommendation so much as a somewhat tired acknowledgment of reality). In the 1780s, the preferred role for the people was in the selection of appropriate leaders. The Constitution, with its huge electoral districts and indirect elections was designed to achieve this. A decade later, when faced with a small cadre of unvirtuous leaders, Madison called for more responsibility on the part of the populace. With the help of a virtuous elite, they were now to act as a 'sentinel' over their leaders. The mechanism for holding leaders accountable to the demands of the classical ideal was the political party. By the 1820s and 1830s, the reality was that the rising tide that was the passions of the people seemed to sweep all before it. This was something Madison abhorred, and had struggled against all of his life. It was, apparently, the role the people would play in this unprecedented democracy, and Madison simply had no effective solutions for it.

How Should Leaders and the People Interact?

The interaction of leaders and the people is the essence of this new social and political relation we call leadership. As such, it partakes of the responses to each of the preceding queries of the protocol. As the above narration makes evident, Madison was constantly innovating as he attempted to invent a relation that would solve the perceived challenges of government grounded in the people. At the core, though, his belief system was consistent:

the people needed some sort of wise and stabilizing influence, most desirably in the person of a leader. This did not mean, however, that the people were to be mere ciphers. Again, much like James Harrington, Madison believed that leaders and the people each had their respective virtues. Harrington, it will be recalled, looked to elite leaders in his senate to provide the wise discussion of policy alternatives, and to an assembly made up of a majority of commoners to provide their sense of the public interest when voting on proposals made by the elite. Madison was not quite so precise in his expectations, yet he never conceived of a polity in which the people had no opportunity to add their particular expertise, be it in choosing leaders or in holding them accountable. Madison's genius was to create institutions and processes that tapped the strengths of each.

By the 1820s, Madison's Harringtonian assumptions that leaders should make policy had been reversed in the popular consciousness, and it was left to someone like Alexis de Tocqueville to confront the new implicit theory of democracy. Tocqueville's version of the leadership relation is the subject of the next chapter.

How is the Matter of Diversity and Minority Interests Addressed?

Because James Madison was one of the first to perceive the dangers of the majority, he was also one of the early innovators in devising protections against majority abuse. Two of his solutions are justly famous. One had to do with the protection of individual rights. Drawing upon English and colonial traditions of enumerated rights he (somewhat reluctantly, for reasons unrelated to the rights themselves) authored the federal Bill of Rights. His real passion for the legal protection of individual liberty was more fully demonstrated in his championing of religious freedom at the state level. With such efforts, Madison became one of the early stalwarts of this strategy of devising legal bulwarks against majority oppression.

Madison's second strategy is equally famous. In his *Federalist Number 10* he explicated his strategy of protecting minority (read: elite) interests by establishing a large republic that made it unlikely that a 'majority faction' (defined as a grouping inimical to the public interest) could coalesce and oppress the minority. Although many have (wrongly) argued that Madison was thereby advocating interest-group politics – he was in fact attempting to avoid them – his acknowledgment of separate interests in society did indeed help to lay the groundwork for this modern approach to the interests of various minorities.

In sum, James Madison appears as one of the earliest, and one of the most influential, proponents of solutions to the newly-recognized danger of popular majorities. The impact of his ideas continues to the present day.

What Institutions and Processes Must be Designed to Accommodate the Premises and Assumptions about Leadership Articulated in the Responses to the Leadership Template?

In this, the implementation of the things needed for the desired leadership relation to operate successfully, Madison proved to be without equal. Particularly in the realm of institution building was he nonpareil. His Constitutional system, in all its intricacy and power, continues to structure American democracy. His invention of the party system, although, like his Constitution, now nearly unrecognizable when compared to its early formulation, has come to define the American political process. Madison's other initiatives, such as his suggested mode of Constitutional interpretation – in effect, a new form of the rule of law – have not had as much impact, but nevertheless may hold promise for future reforms.

James Madison built upon a long legacy that had engendered the classical ideal, but, when facing the new challenge of the sovereignty of the people, he proved remarkably innovative and far-sighted. In effect, he created one of the first versions of a new political relationship in which, in Edmund Morgan's words, the few had to stand up for the many. It was the first fiction of leadership.

THE MADISONIAN FICTION OF LEADERSHIP

James Madison was among the first, and certainly among the most important, of the individuals who turned their attention to the problems of leadership in that era when the emergence of popular sovereignty demanded such a new social relation. Madison was a veritable giant of his day, both an astute political theorist and a hard-nosed politician. He dedicated himself to finding some way to resolve what he felt to be the ultimate leadership challenge of his day, the challenge posed to achieving the common good of society when that society was based upon the power of the people.

In responding to this challenge, Madison proved himself to be virtually endlessly creative. He invented new institutions of governing designed to ensure the securing of the common good by assuring wise and virtuous leaders. When such leaders and the common good faced challenges from an unexpected quarter, Madison created the first political party as a vehicle for virtuous elite leaders to mobilize the people in the public interest. Later, when his commitment to leaders who emulated the classical ideal crumbled before the reality of rampant democracy, Madison, like Plato before him, turned to the law as the last bastion against popular unwisdom.

In each of these proposals, Madison was engaged in inventing a leadership relation that aimed at conquering the perceived challenge of his day. The fact that Madison ultimately failed to secure a polity that adhered to the classical commitment to elite and virtuous leaders directing the people toward an identifiable common good suggests that the reality of American society had outraced the traditional fiction that had served to guide polities for millennia.

Looking back upon Madison's experience, it seems safe to say that the challenges of democracy demanded something more than the stock leadership responses of classical republicanism. Here, perhaps, we find Madison's greatest contribution. He was astute enough to realize that reality had departed from the republican fiction of society as a communal body. He acknowledged the dominant role of private and conflicting interests in society. Yet Madison did not embrace this new reality so much as attempt to neutralize and overcome it. He maintained a belief in and a commitment to the essence of the republican fiction: that there was a common good that was both concrete and identifiable. Moreover, he agreed with the longstanding tradition that the best way to achieve this good was by putting in place wise and virtuous leaders dedicated to its accomplishment. One of Madison's great achievements, then, was his noble attempt to graft classical republican ideals on to the new democratic reality. His creative proposals moved beyond anything heretofore put forward, and he explored with profit the possibilities inherent in the relationship between the people and their leaders in a regime of popular sovereignty. If his solutions were not wholly successful, Madison's unique and varied response to the challenges he faced provide a rich source of inspiration for those who continue to confront the challenges of leadership in a democracy.

If Madison ultimately failed in his quest to link classical aspirations to the new democratic reality, there were others who followed him who met America's sprawling, commercial, individualistic and egalitarian democracy on its own terms, and sought, like Madison, to concoct solutions to the problems of leadership in such a modern society. Certainly the most insightful and influential of these was Alexis de Tocqueville. It is to his remarkable work that we now turn.

NOTES

1. Two recent major works on Madison address this topic in differing ways. See Jack Rakove, *Original Meanings: Politics and Ideas in the Making of the Constitution* (New York: A.A. Knopf, 1996) and Lance Banning, *The Sacred Fire of Liberty: James Madison and the Founding of the Federal Republic* (Ithaca, NY: Cornell University Press, 1995). *See also* Matthew Trachman, 'Historicizing Leadership / Democratizing Leadership Studies' (paper delivered at the annual meeting of the International Leadership Association, Toronto, Canada, November 2000), 1, 3, 7.
2. James Madison, 'Federalist No. 46', in William T. Hutchinson et al., eds, *The Papers of James Madison, Congressional Series*, 17 vols. (Chicago: University of Chicago Press, 1962–77; Charlottesville: University Press of Virginia, 1977–), 10:438–39. James Madison, 'Federalist No. 39', ibid., 10:379–80. *See* Marvin Meyers, *The Mind of the Founder: Sources of the Political Thought of James Madison*, rev. edn. (Hanover: University Press of New England, 1981), 408; Robert A. Rutland, *James Madison: The Founding Father* (New York: Macmillan Publishing Company, 1987), 33.
3. Gordon S. Wood, *Creation of the American Republic, 1776–1787* (New York: W.W. Norton & Company, 1969), 55.
4. James Madison, 'Federalist No. 45', in *Papers*, 10:429.
5. James Madison, 'Federalist No. 10', ibid., 10:264.
6. James Madison, 'Federalist No. 37', ibid., 10:364. See also Wood, *Creation*, 53–54.
7. James Madison, 'Federalist No. 51', ibid., 10:479.
8. Drew R. McCoy, *The Last of the Fathers: James Madison and the Republican Legacy* (Cambridge: Cambridge University Press, 1989), 41–42.
9. James Madison, 'Federalist No. 62', in *Papers*, 10:540. Note that this argument concerning Madison's commitment to the common good rather than the sum of individual goods is not without controversy. *See*, for example, Richard K. Matthews, *If Men Were Angels: James Madison and the Heartless Empire of Reason* (Lawrence, KS: University Press of Kansas, 1995) and Jennifer Nedelsky, *Private Property and the Limits of American Constitutionalism: The Madisonian Framework and Its Legacy*, (Chicago: Chicago University Press, 1990). Support for the author's position can be found in Banning, *The Sacred Fire of Liberty*; Rakove, *Original Meanings* (see note 1 for details); and McCoy, *The Last of the Fathers*. The sheer volume of Madison's mentions of conceptions of the 'public good' or similar references requires some attention to this notion.
10. *See generally* Wood, *Creation*, 391–425 (see note 3).
11. Madison to Thomas Jefferson, 19 March 1787, in *Papers*, 9:318.
12. Madison to Edmund Randolph, 25 February 1787, ibid., 9:299.
13. James Madison, 'Federalist No. 62', ibid., 10:538.
14. Ibid., 538–39. James Madison, 'Federalist No. 44', ibid., 421. 'Notes for Speech Opposing Paper Money', [c. 1 Nov. 1786], ibid., 9:158–59.
15. Madison to Jefferson, 6 September 1787, ibid., 10:164.
16. Madison to Caleb Wallace, 23 August 1785, ibid., 8:350.
17. James Madison, 'Federalist No. 10', ibid., 10:264.
18. James Madison, 'Federalist No. 48', ibid., 10:456.
19. James Madison, 'Vices of the Political System of the United States', ibid., 9:348–57.
20. Ibid., 9:354.
21. James Madison, 'Memorial and Remonstrance Against Religious Assessments, 1785', ibid., 8:299.

22. James Madison, 'Vices', ibid., 9:354.
23. Madison to Jefferson, 24 October 1787, ibid., 10:213.
24. James Madison, 'Vices', ibid., 9:355.
25. James Madison, 'Observations on Jefferson's Draught of a Constitution for Virginia', (sent to John Brown, 15 October 1788), ibid., 11:287. 'Vices', ibid., 9:355.
26. James Madison, 'Federalist No. 10', ibid., 10:267.
27. James Madison, 'Federalist No. 49', ibid., 10:461.
28. Madison to Edmund Randolph, 10 January 1788, ibid., 355.
29. Madison to Jefferson, 9 December 1787, ibid., 313.
30. Madison to Jefferson, 10 August 1788, ibid., 11:226.
31. James Madison, 'Federalist No. 49', ibid., 10:463. *See also* James Madison, 'Federalist No. 50', ibid., 10:471–72.
32. Madison to George Turberville, 2 November 1788, ibid., 11:331–32. *See also* Madison to Edmund Pendleton, 20 October 1788, ibid., 307.
33. James Madison, 'Federalist No. 49', ibid., 10:462.
34. Madison to Jefferson, 24 October 1787, ibid., 10:213.
35. James Madison, 'Federalist No. 55', ibid., 10:507–508.
36. Speech in Virginia Ratifying Convention, 20 June 1788, ibid., 11:163.
37. Madison to Jefferson, 9 December 1787, ibid., 10:313.
38. Madison to Edmund Randolph, 10 January 1788, ibid., 10:355.
39. James Madison, 'Federalist No. 38', ibid., 10:365.
40. Madison to Jefferson, 9 December 1787, ibid., 10:313.
41. Madison to Edmund Randolph, 10 January 1788, ibid., 10:355–56.
42. James Madison, 'Vices', ibid., 9:357. *See also* Speech in Constitutional Convention, 23 June 1787, ibid., 10:74.
43. James Madison, 'Federalist No. 57', ibid., 10:521. *See* Ralph Ketcham, 'Party and Leadership in Madison's Conception of the Presidency', *Quarterly Journal of the Library of Congress* 37 (1980): 249.
44. James Madison, 'Vices', in *Papers*, 9:355. Madison to Caleb Wallace, 23 August 1785, ibid., 8:350. James Madison, 'Observations', ibid., 11:287.
45. James Madison, Speech in Virginia Ratifying Convention, 20 June 1788, ibid., 11:163.
46. *See* James Madison, 'Observations', ibid., 11:287–288.
47. Madison to Jefferson, 6 September 1787, ibid., 10:164.
48. James Madison, Speech in Constitutional Convention, 31 May 1787, ibid., 10:21.
49. James Madison, Speech in Constitutional Convention, 6 June 1787, ibid., 10:32.
50. James Madison, 'Federalist No. 37', ibid., 10:360.
51. James Madison, 'Federalist No. 10', ibid., 10:264, 268.
52. James Madison, Speech in Constitutional Convention, 6 June 1787, ibid., 10:33.
53. James Madison, 'Federalist No. 51', ibid., 10:479.
54. James Madison, Speech in Constitutional Convention, 17 July 1787, ibid., 10:102.
55. Madison to Jefferson, 19 March 1787, ibid., 9:318.
56. Wood, *Creation*, 471–518 (see note 3).
57. James Madison, 'Federalist No. 10', in *Papers*, 10:268.
58. Ibid.
59. James Madison, Speech in Constitutional Convention, 31 May 1787, ibid., 10:19. James Madison, Speech in Constitutional Convention, 6 June 1787, ibid., 10:32.
60. James Madison, 'Federalist No. 52', ibid., 10:484. James Madison, 'Federalist No. 57', ibid., 10:521.
61. James Madison, 'Federalist No. 57', ibid., 10:524.
62. James Madison, 'Federalist No. 63', ibid., 10:546.
63. James Madison, 'Federalist No. 62', ibid., 10:535.
64. James Madison, 'Federalist No. 39', ibid., 10:378.
65. James Madison, 'Federalist No. 63', ibid., 10:545.
66. James Madison, Speech in Constitutional Convention, 21 July 1787, ibid., 10:109.
67. James Madison, Speech in Constitutional Convention, 19 July 1787, ibid., 10:108.
68. James Madison, Speech in Constitutional Convention, 4 June 1787, ibid., 10:25.
69. James Madison, Speech in Constitutional Convention, 21 July 1787, ibid., 10:110. James Madison, Speech in Constitutional Convention, 8 June 1787, in Gaillard Hunt, ed., *The Writings of James Madison*, 9 vols. (New York: G.P. Putnam and Sons, 1910), 5:385.
70. See James Madison, 'Spirit of Governments', in *National Gazette*, 18 February 1792, in *Papers*, 14:234; James Madison, 'Charters', in *National Gazette*, 18 June 1792, ibid., 14:191; Madison to Jefferson, 4 February 1790, ibid., 13:19–20; James Madison, Speech in 2nd Congress, 19 December 1791, ibid., 14:172.
71. See Madison to Hamilton, 19 November 1789, ibid., 12:449–51.

72. James Madison, 'Federalist No. 10', ibid., 10:265.
73. James Madison, 'Federalist No. 62', ibid., 10:539–40.
74. Madison to Hamilton, 19 November 1789, ibid., 12:450.
75. James Madison, 'Vices', ibid., 9:354.
76. James Madison, 'Property', in *National Gazette*, 27 March 1792, ibid., 14:266–67.
77. Madison to Jefferson, 24 January 1790, ibid., 13:4. Madison to Jefferson, 8 August 1791, ibid., 14:69.
78. James Madison, 'Spirit of Governments', ibid., 14:233.
79. Madison to Jefferson, 8 August 1791, ibid., 14:69.
80. James Madison, 'A Candid State of the Parties', in *National Gazette*, 26 September 1792, ibid., 14:372.
81. James Madison, 'Government', in *National Gazette*, 31 December 1791, ibid., 14:179. *See also* James Madison, 'Charters', ibid., 14:191.
82. James Madison, 'Who Are the Best Keepers of the People's Liberties?' in *National Gazette*, 20 December 1792, ibid., 14:426.
83. Madison to Jefferson, 2 September 1793, ibid., 15:93. *See* Rutland, *James Madison*, 107 (see note 2).
84. Madison to Jefferson, 24 October 1787, in *Papers*, 10:213. James Madison, 'Public Opinion', in *National Gazette*, 19 December 1791, ibid., 14:170.
85. James Madison, 'Charters', ibid., 14:192.
86. Madison to Jefferson, 2 September 1793, ibid., 15:93.
87. James Madison, 'Public Opinion', ibid., 14:170.
88. Madison to Jefferson, 27 August 1793, ibid., 15:75. For similar examples, *see* Madison to Archibald Stuart, 1 September 1793, ibid., 15:87–88; Madison to Jefferson, 2 September 1793, ibid., 15:92–93.
89. James Madison, 'Public Opinion', ibid., 14:170.
90. Madison to Edmund Randolph, 13 September 1792, ibid., 14:365.
91. Madison to Jefferson, 30 November 1794, ibid., 15:396.
92. Rutland, *James Madison*, 143 (see note 2).
93. James Madison, 'A Candid State of the Parties', in *Papers*, 14:371–72.
94. *See* Edward J. Erler, 'The Problem of the Public Good in the Federalist', *Polity* 13 (1981): 665–66.
95. McCoy, *The Last of the Fathers*, 91 (see note 8).
96. James Madison, 'Political Reflections', in *Papers*, 17:239.
97. Madison to Jefferson, 10 June 1798, ibid., 17:150.
98. Ibid., 17:151.
99. Madison to Jefferson, 3 June 1798, ibid., 17:142.
100. Madison to Jefferson, 5 May 1798, ibid., 17:126.
101. Ralph Ketcham, *James Madison: A Biography* (New York: The Macmillan Company, 1971), 394.
102. Ibid., 329. *See* for example, James Madison, 'Consolidation', in *National Gazette*, 3 December 1791, in *Papers*, 14:137–39.
103. James Madison, 'Report of 1800', ibid., 17:350.
104. Madison to Edward Everett, 28 August 1830, in *Writings*, 9:383–403. Madison to Edward Livingston, 8 May 1830, in *Letters and Other Writings of James Madison*, Philip R. Fendall, ed. (Philadelphia: Lippincott, 1865). 4:80. *See* McCoy, *The Last of the Fathers*, 142 (details in note 8); Rutland, *James Madison*, 248 (details in note 2).
105. James Madison, 'Federalist No. 10,' in *Papers*, 10:266.
106. Rutland, *James Madison*, 172 (see note 2).
107. Meyer, *The Mind of the Founder*, 208 (see note 2). *Richmond Enquirer*, 18 February 1815, in Rutland, *James Madison*, 231.
108. James Madison, 'Seventh Annual Message to Congress', 5 December 1815, in James D. Richardson, ed., *A Compilation of Messages and Papers of the Presidents, 1789–1897* 10 vols. (Washington: Government Printing Office, 1896–1899), 1:568.
109. Madison, 'Veto message', 3 March 1817, ibid., 1:576.
110. *See* discussion below.
111. Madison to John G. Jackson, 27 December 1821, in *Letters*, 3:245 (see note 104). See also 'Note on Constitutional Convention speech of 7 August 1787', 1821, in *Documentary History of the Constitution* (Washington: Government Printing Office, 1894–1905), 5:446–49; 'Majority Governments', 1833, in *Writings*, 9:520–24, 527–28 (details in note 69); 'Notes on Nullification', 1835–1836, ibid., 9:573–607; Madison to Edward Everett, August 1830, in *Letters*, 4:102; McCoy, *The Last of the Fathers*, 137 (details in note 8).
112. James Madison, 'Eighth Annual Message to Congress', in Richardson, *Compilation*, 1:579–80 (see note 108).
113. James Madison, 'Note on Constitutional Convention speech of 7 August 1787', in *Documentary History*, 5:446 (see note 111). James Madison, Speech in Virginia Constitutional Convention, 2 December 1829, in *Writings*, 9:360–61 (see note 69).

114. James Madison, 'Note on Constitutional Convention speech, 1821', in *Documentary History*, 5:441. Madison to Joseph C. Cabell, 18 September 1828, in *Writings*, 9:33.
115. Madison to John Adams, 22 May 1817, in *Letters*, 3:42 (see note 104). Madison to Joseph C. Cabell, 22 March 1827, ibid., 3:573. See Ketcham, 'Party and Leadership', 257 (see note 43).
116. Gordon S. Wood, *The Radicalism of the American Revolution* (New York: Alfred A Knopf, Inc., 1991), 230.
117. Statement attributed to Jefferson, ibid., 296.
118. McCoy, *The Last of the Fathers*, 91 (see note 8).
119. James Madison, Speech in Constitutional Convention, 7 August 1787, in *Papers*, 10:139.
120. James Madison, 'Note on Constitutional Convention speech of 7 August 1781', 1821, in *Documentary History*, 5:443 (see note 110).
121. Madison to Thomas Ritchie, 18 December 1825, in *Letters*, 3:507 (see note 104).
122. Madison to Edward Everett, August 1830, ibid., 4:99–100.
123. Madison to John G. Jackson, 27 December 1821, ibid., 3:246.
124. Madison to Spencer Roane, 6 May 1821, in *Writings*, 9:58.
125. James Madison, 'Note on Constitutional Convention speech', in *Documentary History*, 5:447–48 (see note 111).
126. James Madison, 'Majority Governments,' in *Writings*, 9:520–21.
127. James Madison, 'Note on Constitutional Convention speech,' 1821, in *Documentary History*, 5:441, 444–45, 448–49 (see note 111). McCoy, *The Last of the Fathers*, 194–95 (see note 8).
128. *See* Robert P. Sutton, *Revolution to Secession: Constitution Making in the Old Dominion* (Charlottesville, VA: University Press of Virginia, 1989); Alison Goodyear Freehling, *Drift Toward Dissolution: The Virginia Slavery Debate of 1831–1832* (Baton Rouge: Louisiana State University Press, 1982).
129. James Madison, Speech to Virginia Constitutional Convention, 2 December 1829, in *Letters*, 4:51–52 (see note 104).
130. James Madison, 'Memorandum on Suffrage', (distributed at the Virginia Convention of 1829–1830), in *Writings*, 9:359n.
131. Ibid.
132. James Madison, Speech in Virginia Constitutional Convention, 2 December 1829, in *Letters*, 4:52.
133. James Madison, 'Autobiography,' in Adair, ed., *William & Mary Quarterly* 2 (1945): 208.
134. James Madison, 'Note on Constitutional Convention speech', 1821, in *Documentary History*, 5:447 (see note 111). McCoy, *The Last of the Fathers*, 196 (see note 8).
135. James Madison, 'Note on Constitutional Convention speech', 1821, in *Documentary History*, 5:448. *See also* Madison to Edward Everett, August 1830, in *Letters*, 4:99 (see note 104).
136. Madison to Spencer Roane, 6 May 1821, in *Writings*, 9:58–59 (see note 69).
137. *Richmond Enquirer*, 3 January 1829, in McCoy, *The Last of the Fathers*, 121 (see note 8).
138. Madison to Edward Coles, 15 October 1834, in *Letters*, 4:367.
139. James Madison, 'Note on Constitutional Convention speech', 1821, in *Documentary History*, 5:448 (see note 111).
140. Madison to William T. Barry, 4 August 1822, in *Letters*, 3:276–77. *See also* Madison to Jefferson, 8 February 1825, in *Writings*, 9:219–20 (see note 69).
141. I am indebted here to the insights on Madison's constitutional interpretation put forward by Drew McCoy, in his *The Last of the Fathers*, especially chapters 2–4 (see note 8).
142. Madison to John G. Jackson, 27 December 1821, in *Letters*, 3:245. *See also* Madison to M.L. Hurlbert, May 1830, ibid., 4:74; James Madison, 'Outline', ibid., 20; Madison to George Thomson, 30 June 1825, ibid., 3:491; McCoy, *The Last of the Fathers*, 63–64.
143. James Madison, 'Outline', in *Letters*, 4:19. *See also* Madison to John M. Patton, 24 March 1834, ibid., 343. Madison to Joseph C. Cabell, 18 March 1827, ibid., 3:573. See McCoy, *The Last of the Fathers*, 71–72, 102–103, 126–28 (see note 8).
144. Madison to Jefferson, 17 February 1825, in *Letters*, 3:483 (see note 104). *See* Madison to Charles Jared Ingersoll, 25 June 1831, ibid., 4:183–87; Madison to Jefferson, 27 June 1823, ibid., 3:325; Madison to Roane, 2 September 1819, ibid., 3:143–44; Madison to Roane, 29 June 1821, ibid., 3:223; McCoy, *The Last of the Fathers*, 99–100.
145. Madison to Edward Everett, August 1830, in *Letters*, 4:97.
146. Madison to Monroe, 27 December 1817, ibid., 3:56. McCoy, *The Last of the Fathers*, 97–103 (see note 8).
147. Madison to Joseph C. Cabell, 18 September 1828, in *Letters*, 3:647.
148. Ibid., 3:642–43.
149. Madison to John M. Patton, 24 March 1834, ibid., 4:343.
150. McCoy, *The Last of the Fathers*, 83 (see note 8).
151. Madison to Joseph C. Cabell, 18 September 1828, in *Letters*, 3:642.

152. Madison to Joseph C. Cabell, 22 March 1827, ibid., 3:573.
153. Madison to C.E. Haynes, 25 February 1831, ibid., 4:165.
154. Ibid.
155. Madison to Charles Jared Ingersoll, 25 June 1831, ibid., 4:186.
156. Madison to Edward Livingston, 17 April 1824, ibid., 3:435–36.
157. Madison to Monroe, 27 December 1817, ibid., 3:55–56.
158. James Madison, 'Seventh Annual Message', 5 December 1815, in Richardson, *Compilation*, 1:568 (see note 108).
159. Madison to Monroe, 27 December 1817, in *Letters*, 3:56 (see note 104). Madison to Jefferson, 17 February 1825, ibid., 3:483.
160. Madison to Jefferson, 17 February 1825, ibid.
161. James Madison, 'Note on Constitutional Convention speech', in *Documentary History*, 5:446 (see note 111).
162. Madison to Thomas Ritchie, 18 December 1825, in *Letters*, 3:507.

7.   Tocqueville and the challenges of democracy

If James Madison was among the first individuals to contemplate the leadership challenges posed by the emerging fiction of a sovereign people, it was Alexis de Tocqueville who first confronted the problem in its starkest form: the egalitarian democracy which came to dominate the scene in the nineteenth century. His treatment of these issues, in his magisterial two-volume *Democracy in America*, is justly famous. A recent scholar has argued that 'there have been only two classics of American political theory', the *Federalist Papers* of Madison, Hamilton and Jay, and *Democracy in America*.[1] Moreover, Tocqueville's work has continuing relevance to the challenges of today's democracy. In the words of Sheldon Wolin, 'To reflect on present-day American politics invites reflection on *Democracy in America* and vice versa'.[2] In terms of our current study, Tocqueville's insights respecting the operation of leadership in a democracy merit careful study.

Tocqueville was well aware that in investigating the workings of American democracy he was encountering an entirely new phenomenon. While Madison had been only dimly – and reluctantly – aware of the emergence of egalitarian democracy, Tocqueville both acknowledged its reality and welcomed the opportunity to contemplate its implications. According to Tocqueville, 'To attempt to check democracy would be … to resist the will of God'.[3] Accepting the new reality, he proposed to study it analytically. 'I confess', he wrote, 'that in America I saw more than America; I sought there the image of democracy itself, with its inclinations, its character, its prejudices, and its passions, in order to learn what we have to fear and hope from its progress.'[4]

In doing so, Tocqueville affirmed that earlier commentators such as Madison had failed to confront in an adequate manner the new challenges to the proper governing of society that true democracy posed. 'The most powerful, the most intelligent, and the most moral classes of the nation have never attempted to control it in order to guide it', he said. 'Democracy has consequently been abandoned to its wild instincts, and it has grown up like those children who have no parental guidance….' To fill the void, 'I have sought to discover the evils and advantages which [democracy] brings. I have examined the safeguards used by the Americans to direct it, as well as those that they have not adopted, and have undertaken to point out the factors which enable it to govern society.' In short, 'a new science of politics is needed for a new world', and Tocqueville set out to produce it.[5]

THE NATURE OF DEMOCRACY

In the course of his extended observation of American society, Tocqueville came face-to-face with its dominant social characteristic: equality. It was, he said, 'an extraordinary phenomenon. Men are there seen on a greater equality in point of fortune and intellect, or, in other words, more equal in their strength, than in any country of the world, in any age of which history has the remembrance.'⁶ In America, 'the principle of equality is, therefore, a providential fact. It has all the characteristics of such a fact: it is universal, it is lasting, it constantly eludes all human interference, and all events as well as all men contribute to its progress.'⁷ 'The more I advanced in the study of American society,' Tocqueville continued, 'the more I perceived that this equality of condition is the fundamental fact from which all others seem to be derived and the central point at which all my observations constantly terminated.'⁸

Having identified the predominant social reality of the United States, Tocqueville quickly noted the political implications. 'It is impossible to believe', he asserted, 'that equality will not eventually find its way into the political world, as it does everywhere else.'⁹ Indeed, the manifestations were everywhere. 'I readily discovered the prodigious influence that this primary fact exercises on the whole course of society; it gives a peculiar direction to public opinion, a peculiar tenor to the laws; it imparts new maxims to the governing authorities and peculiar habits to the governed.'¹⁰

In particular, the American society of the early nineteenth century was committed, in a way unlike any other in the world, to the sovereignty of the people and democratic principles. 'The Anglo-Americans', Tocqueville observed, 'are the first nation who ... have been allowed by their circumstances, their origin, their intelligence, and especially by their morals to establish and maintain the sovereignty of the people.... In America, the principle of the sovereignty of the people ... is recognized by the customs and proclaimed by the laws; it spreads freely, and arrives without impediment at its most remote consequences.'¹¹ Indeed, 'The democratic principle ... has gained so much strength ... as to have become not only predominant, but all-powerful.... The people reign in the American political world as the Deity does in the universe. They are the cause and the aim of all things; everything comes from them, and everything is absorbed in them.'¹²

As a consequence, he concluded, 'If there is a country in the world where the doctrine of the sovereignty of the people can be fairly appreciated, where it can be studied in its application to affairs of society, and where its dangers and its advantages may be judged, that country is assuredly America'.¹³ Tocqueville used such observations as a launching pad for an analysis of democracy – and, for our purposes, its leadership implications – that continues to have resonance for us today.

THE PROBLEMS OF DEMOCRACY

Democracy in America is a sprawling, two-volume tapestry of American culture and politics in the 1830s. Despite its scope, it is possible to draw from its pages an identifiable set of problems posed by the emergence of egalitarian democracy. With the eye of a scientist, Tocqueville was able to discern the primary challenges posed by a regime in which actual sovereignty resided in the many. Moreover, it is also possible to distill from Tocqueville's narration a series of potential remedies for the ills of democracy, each with implications for leadership. This section will detail Tocqueville's recognition of the problems posed, and the next will work through his proposed remedies. The chapter will conclude with a consideration of the implications for leadership.

The most fundamental problem posed by America's turn to democracy was one seemingly inherent in the entity itself: the challenges posed by majority rule. Such a decision rule, acknowledged Tocqueville, was both desirable and inevitable. 'In the United States,' he said, 'the majority governs in the name of the people, as is the case in all countries in which the people are supreme.'[14] The difficulty lay in the unrestrained exercise of that power. He perceived that 'the very essence of democratic government consists in the absolute sovereignty of the majority; for there is nothing in democratic states that is capable of resisting it'.[15] In politics, the problem manifested itself in the legislature, since 'to concentrate the whole social force in the hands of the legislative body is the natural tendency of democracies; for this is the power that emanates most directly from the people'. This, in turn, led to the central problem of majoritarian democracy: 'This concentration of power is at once very prejudicial to a well-directed administration and favorable to the despotism of the majority'.[16]

For Tocqueville, then, the potential 'tyranny of the majority' loomed as the most worrisome product of democratic functioning. He found this to be a bit of a conundrum: on the one hand, majority rule appeared right and logical, yet it also proved too limiting. 'The advantage of democracy is not,' he wrote, 'as has been sometimes asserted, that it protects the interests of all, but simply that it protects those of the majority.' Tocqueville was confidant enough in the competence of the majority to discern and act in its own interests. 'Democratic laws', he said, 'generally tend to promote the welfare of the greatest possible number; for they emanate from the majority of the citizens, who are subject to error, but who cannot have an interest opposed to their own advantage.'[17] This left minorities, however, at a woeful disadvantage. 'A majority taken collectively is only an individual, whose opinions, and frequently whose interests, are opposed to those of another individual, who is styled a minority', he reasoned. 'If it be admitted that a man possessing absolute power may misuse that power by wronging his adversaries, why should not a majority be liable to the same reproach?'[18]

This led Tocqueville to the gist of the problem. 'Unlimited power,' he concluded, 'is in itself a bad and dangerous thing. Human beings are not competent to exercise it with discretion. In my opinion, the main evil of the present democratic institutions of the United States does not arise, as is often asserted in Europe, from their weakness, but from their irresistible strength. I am not so much alarmed at the excessive liberty which reigns in that country, as at the inadequate securities which one finds against tyranny.'[19]

It was the lack of a coherent program to withstand the tyranny of the majority that Tocqueville hoped to address. In his view, 'The Americans hold that in every state the supreme power ought to emanate from the people; but when once that power is instituted, they can conceive, as it were, no limits to it, and they are ready to admit that it has the right to do whatever it pleases'. Indeed, 'The omnipotence of the majority appears to me to be so full of peril to the American republics that the dangerous means used to bridle it seem to be more advantageous than prejudicial'.[20] Tocqueville would ultimately posit his own solutions, but first he continued his litany of other problems with American democracy.

A second problem stemmed from the same egalitarian social conditions that spawned American democratic institutions, but its impact was even more far-reaching and subtly damaging. It was the overweening power of public opinion. 'It is in the examination of the exercise of thought in the United States that we clearly perceive how the power of the majority surpasses all the powers with which we are acquainted in Europe', Tocqueville noted. In America, 'the majority possesses a power that is physical and moral at the same time, which acts upon the will as much as upon the actions and represses not only all contest, but all controversy. I know of no country in which there is so little independence of mind and real freedom of discussion as in America.'[21]

This evil was due, somewhat ironically, to the pervasive sense of equality found in the United States. 'The nearer the people are drawn to the common level of an equal and similar condition,' Tocqueville reasoned, 'the less prone does each man become to place implicit faith in a certain man or class of men. But his readiness to believe the multitude increases, and opinion is more than ever the mistress of the world.'[22] Thus, 'The same equality that renders him independent of his fellow citizens, taken severally, exposes him alone and unprotected to the influence of the greater number. The public, therefore, among a democratic people,' continued Tocqueville, 'has a singular power, which aristocratic nations cannot conceive; for it does not persuade others to its beliefs, but it imposes them and makes them permeate the thinking of everyone by a sort of enormous pressure of the mind of all upon individual intelligence.'[23]

The result would not be pretty. 'It may be foreseen,' Tocqueville concluded, 'that faith in public opinion will become for them a species of religion, and the majority its ministering prophet. … And I perceive how … democracy [could] extinguish that liberty of the mind to which a democratic social condition is favorable; so that, after having broken all the bondage once imposed on it by ranks or by men, the human mind would be closely fettered to the general will of the greatest number.'[24]

If the potential loss of political and intellectual freedom were not enough, Tocqueville also detected another fateful development that accompanied the rise of egalitarian democracy: the loss of civic virtue. It will be recalled from our earlier discussion of classical republicanism that traditional polities required a certain degree of intelligence and independence on the part of both leaders and followers, and a willingness to subsume individual interests to the good of the whole. Tocqueville found each of these attributes threatened by American realities.

In addition to widespread egalitarianism, Tocqueville found Americans to be dominated by bourgeois interests and sentiments, with a focus upon economic concerns, individual advancement and personal fulfillment. He found a culture of mediocrity, with 'a vast multitude of similar and equal men endlessly revolving around themselves in search of petty and vulgar pleasures with which to stuff their souls'.[25] The traditional constraints of civic virtue were a poor fit. In America, 'the people … find great difficulty in surmounting their inclinations'.[26]

In the odd brew of egalitarianism and bourgeois notions that characterized American society, Tocqueville also found a new phenomenon that appeared to be antithetical to traditional notions of civic virtue: the emergence of individualism. The chief culprit was, again, the pervasive equality to be found in American society. 'It must be acknowledged', he asserted, 'that equality, which brings great benefits into the world, nevertheless suggests to men … some very dangerous propensities. It tends to isolate them from one another, [and] to concentrate every man's attention upon himself….'[27] He elaborated: 'As social conditions become more equal, the number of persons increases who … have … acquired or retained sufficient education and fortune to satisfy their own wants'. As a result, 'they owe nothing to any man, they expect nothing from any man; they acquire the habit of always considering themselves as standing alone, and they are apt to imagine that their whole destiny is in their own hands'.[28]

Tocqueville was the first to describe and use the term 'individualism' to depict this new relation between man and society. 'Individualism', he said, 'is a novel expression to which a novel idea has given birth. Our fathers were only acquainted with *egoisme* (selfishness). Selfishness is a passionate and exaggerated love of self, which leads a man to connect everything with himself and to prefer himself to everything in the world. Individualism,' on the other hand, 'is a mature and calm feeling, which disposes each member of the community to sever himself from the mass of his fellows and to draw apart with his family and his friends, so that after he has thus formed a little circle of his own, he willingly leaves society at large to itself.'[29]

To one like Tocqueville who was steeped in traditional ways of civic virtue, this development posed a fundamental threat. 'Individualism', he said, 'saps the virtues of public life.'[30] Indeed, 'men who inhabit democratic countries ... can never, without an effort, tear themselves from their private affairs to engage in public business.... Not only are they naturally wanting in a taste for public business, but they frequently have no time to attend to it. Private life in democratic times is so busy, so excited, so full of wishes and of work, that hardly any energy or leisure remains to each individual for public life.'[31] Individualism and private interest thereby joined the lists of the challenges posed by democracy that would require his attention. Tocqueville would not shirk this duty. 'I am the last man to contend that these propensities are unconquerable,' he noted, 'since my chief object in writing this book has been to combat them.'[32]

There was also a perhaps even more ominous threat created by the American focus on individualism. We have seen already how 'men who inhabit democratic countries ... can never, without an effort, tear themselves from their private affairs to engage in public business'. This was bad enough from the standpoint of civic virtue, but Tocqueville also had the insight to recognize that it also led to a new and thoroughly modern form of despotism. According to Tocqueville, men's 'natural bias' toward their personal affairs 'leads them to abandon [public business] to the sole visible and permanent representative of the interests of the community; that is to say, to the state'.[33] This, in turn, led to a 'species of oppression by which democratic nations are menaced [that] is unlike anything that ever before existed in the world; our contemporaries will find no prototype of it in their memories'.[34]

The phenomenon was so novel that even Tocqueville struggled to articulate it. 'I seek in vain', he said, 'for an expression that will accurately convey the whole of the idea I have formed of it; the old words *despotism* and *tyranny* are inappropriate: the thing itself is new, and since I cannot name it, I must attempt to define it.'[35]

Tocqueville went on to describe it in this way: 'Above this race of men stands an immense and tutelary power, which takes upon itself alone to secure their gratifications and to watch over their fate. That power is absolute, minute, regular, provident, and mild.' That was the intriguing part. This new despotism was essentially benevolent. 'For their happiness,' he went on to observe, 'such a government willingly labors, but it chooses to be the sole agent and the only arbiter of that happiness; it provides for their security, foresees and supplies their necessities, facilitates their pleasures, manages their principal concerns, directs their industry, regulates the descent of property and subdivides their inheritances. What remains,' he asked, 'but to spare them all the care of thinking and all the trouble of living?'[36]

The impact upon the citizen was subtle yet profound. 'The will of man is not shattered, but softened, bent, and guided'. While 'men are seldom forced by it to act', nevertheless 'they are constantly constrained from acting. Such a power does not destroy, but it prevents existence; it does not tyrannize, but it compresses, enervates, extinguishes, and stupefies a people, till each nation is reduced to nothing better than a flock of timid and industrious animals, of which the government is the shepherd.'[37]

This brought Tocqueville to what was perhaps his most fundamental critique of democracy. It seemed that democracy produced leaders and followers who were ill suited to face the formidable catalogue of challenges Tocqueville had identified. The people, as a result of their quiescent acceptance of the operations of a paternalistic state, rarely met the requirements of democratic citizenship. 'By this system,' he noted, 'the people shake off their state of dependence just long enough to select their masters [via elections] and then relapse into it again. A great many persons at the present day are quite contented with this sort of compromise between administrative despotism and the sovereignty of the people; and they think they have done enough for the protection of individual freedom when they have surrendered it to the nation at large.' Unfortunately, the opposite was the case. Such limited political activity 'will not prevent them from gradually losing their faculties of thinking, feeling, and acting for themselves, and gradually falling below the level of humanity'. Once this occurs, 'no one will ever believe that a liberal, wise, and energetic government can spring from the suffrage of a subservient people'.[38]

This led Tocqueville to address one of the central issues of leadership in a democracy. Given the overwhelming influence of the people in a democracy, the question of their competence to govern was key. Tocqueville was not reassured. Even if the evils of bourgeois selfishness and individualism could be circumvented, there remained problems with popularly-based rule. Though Tocqueville was willing to 'admit that the mass of the citizens sincerely wish to promote the welfare of the country', the problem was 'it is always more or less difficult for them to discern the best means of attaining the end which they sincerely desire'.[39] In other words, in his view, 'it is impossible, after the most strenuous of exertions, to raise the intelligence of the people above a certain level.... It is therefore quite as difficult to imagine a state in which all the citizens are very well informed as a state in which they are all wealthy.' The conclusion was inevitable: 'I hold it to be sufficiently demonstrated', Tocqueville intoned, 'that universal suffrage is by no means a guarantee of the wisdom of popular choice. Whatever its advantages may be, this is not one of them.'[40]

If the people were not to be trusted to have sufficient wisdom to govern, the focus must shift to wise leaders. Unfortunately, Tocqueville found that democracy militated against this possibility as well. 'Many people in Europe,' he argued, 'are apt to believe without saying it, or say without believing it, that one of the great advantages of universal suffrage is that it entrusts the direction of affairs to men who are worthy of the public confidence. They admit that the people are unable to govern themselves, but they own that the people always wish the welfare of the state and instinctively designate those who are animated by the same good will and who are fit to wield supreme authority. I confess that the observations I made in America by no means coincide with those opinions.' Instead, reported Tocqueville, 'On my arrival in the United States, I was surprised to find so much distinguished talent among the citizens, and so little among the heads of government.'[41]

The reason for 'the constant fact that at the present day the ablest men in the United States are rarely placed at the head of affairs' was inherent in the system. As Tocqueville explained it, 'it must be acknowledged that such has been the result in proportion as democracy has exceeded all its former limits'.[42] He went on to analyze how American conditions were conducive to the selection of mediocre leaders.

One contributing factor was the great leveling nature of American egalitarianism. As Tocqueville put it, 'democracy not only lacks that soundness of judgment which is necessary to select men really deserving of their confidence, but [citizens of a democracy] often have not the desire or the inclination to [choose such qualified individuals]'. The reason was that 'democratic institutions awaken and foster a passion for equality which they can never entirely satisfy…. Whatever transcends their own limitations appears to be an obstacle to their desires, and there is no superiority, however legitimate it may be, which is not irksome in their sight.' As a result, 'the natural instincts of democracy induce people to reject distinguished citizens as their rulers'.[43]

The reluctance among democratic peoples to choose wise leaders was matched by a similar reluctance on the part of wise leaders to serve. 'In the United States,' observed Tocqueville, 'I am not sure that the people would choose men of superior abilities even if they wished to be elected; but it is certain that candidates of this description do not come forward.' This, in part, was again traceable to American social and economic realities. The American obsession with amassing personal fortunes was one aspect of the problem. In Tocqueville's view, 'The pursuit of wealth generally diverts men of great talents and strong passions from the pursuit of power…. The consequence is that in tranquil times public functions offer but few lures to ambition.' Consequently, 'it frequently happens that a man does not undertake to direct the fortunes of the state until he has shown himself incompetent to conduct his own. The vast number of very ordinary men who occupy public stations is quite as attributable to these causes as to the bad choice of democracy.'[44]

Another explanation for the lack of distinguished leaders struck at the heart of hopes for good leadership in a democracy. Another of the reasons 'that induces able men to retire from the political arena' was that in that arena 'it is so difficult to retain their independence, or to advance without becoming servile'.[45] The transcendant importance of this observation was that, in it, Tocqueville was suggesting that, in a democracy, the longstanding 'classical ideal' of the leader might no longer be operable. This, it will be recalled, called for wise, virtuous and independent leaders who could perceive the common good and act unhindered in its pursuit. According to Tocqueville, a far different relationship between leaders and the people had evolved in American democracy.

In short, as Tocqueville explained it, 'I attribute the small number of distinguished men in political life to the ever increasing despotism of the majority in the United States'. Because of it, 'Democratic republics extend the practice of currying favor with the many and introduce it into all classes at once'. Consequently, 'In the immense crowd which throngs the avenues of power in the United States, I found very few men who displayed that manly candor and masculine independence of opinion which distinguished the Americans in former times, and which constitutes the leading feature in distinguished characters wherever they may be found'.[46] In contrast, 'it often happens that mountebanks of all sorts are able to please the people, while their truest friends frequently fail to gain their confidence'.[47]

For all of these reasons, Tocqueville concluded that 'democracy, pushed to its furthest limits, is therefore prejudicial to the art of government'.[48] This was a striking criticism, and one with which he would grapple when he turned to the task of proposing solutions for the weaknesses that he observed in American democracy.

SOLUTIONS FOR THE PROBLEMS OF DEMOCRACY

As we turn to our consideration of Tocqueville's proposed remedies, a word of caution is in order. Tocqueville's *Democracy in America* is a sprawling narrative of his observations of American culture and politics. His own depiction, for example, of the problems of democracy is not nearly as linear as portrayed in the previous section. The same holds true for his proposed solutions to these difficulties. Tocqueville's discussions of the points made in this section are found almost willy-nilly throughout his two volumes; the ordering of the ensuing analysis is imposed from without. This also means that the solutions discussed below are not always precisely linked to a single antecedent problem. Tocqueville's focus upon various forms of political education, for example, addresses, at various levels, the problems of the tyranny of the majority, the pervasive influence of public opinion and his concern with individualism. Accordingly, this section will be organized according to Tocqueville's proposed solutions. Care will be taken, however, to make clear the links between the democratic ills identified earlier and their remedies discussed in this section.

It is important to note at the outset that, despite his many concerns about democratic functioning, Tocqueville was no enemy of democracy. To be sure, he took a measured view of the institution. 'When the opponents of democracy assert that a single man performs what he undertakes better than the government of all,' he allowed, 'it appears to me that they are right. The government of an individual is more consistent, more uniform, and more accurate in details than that of a multitude, and it selects with more discrimination the men whom it employs. If any deny this,' he concluded, 'they have never seen a democratic government....'[49]

But this is, perhaps, to take too narrow a view of the topic. Before judging democracy, Tocqueville argued, 'we must first understand what is wanted of society and its government'. He posed the alternatives himself: 'Do you wish to give a certain elevation to the human mind and teach it to regard the things of this world with generous feelings, to inspire men with a scorn of mere temporal advantages, to form and nourish strong convictions and keep alive the spirit of honorable devotedness...? If you believe such to be the principal object of society,' he said, 'avoid the government of democracy, for it would not lead you certainly to the goal.' On the other hand, 'if...you are of the opinion that the principal object of government is not to confer the greatest possible power and glory upon the body of the nation, but to ensure the greatest enjoyment and to avoid the most misery to each of the individuals who comprise it – if such be your desire, then equalize the conditions of men and establish democratic institutions.'[50] Tocqueville made no secret that he sometimes longed for a return to the aristocratic days of the past, but he was willing to acknowledge democracy's advantages. 'Democracy does not give people the most skillful government,' he admitted, 'but it produces what the ablest governments are frequently unable to create: namely, an all-pervading and restless activity, a superabundant force, and an energy which is inseparable from it and which may, however unfavorable circumstances may be, produce wonders. These,' he concluded, 'are the true advantages of democracy.'[51]

Tocqueville saw clearly the task before him. Reflecting upon the rise of equality and democracy that he saw so manifest in the United States, he recognized that 'the movement which impels [nations] is already so strong that it cannot be stopped'. Nevertheless, 'it is not yet so rapid that it cannot be guided. Their fate is still in their own hands, but very soon they may lose control.'[52] 'Thus', he conceded, 'the question is not how to reconstruct aristocratic society, but how to make liberty proceed out of that democratic state of society in which God has placed us.'[53] That being the case, said Tocqueville, 'let us endeavor to make the best of that which is allotted to us, and, by finding out both its good and evil tendencies, be able to foster the former and repress the latter to the utmost'.[54]

In conceptualizing his remedies for the ills of democracy, Tocqueville's overall approach was not all that different from that of Madison. That is to say, Tocqueville looked to, in his words, the erection of 'obstacle[s] which can retard [democracy's] course and give it time to moderate its own vehemence'.[55] Like Madison, Tocqueville sought to re-establish in a majoritarian society the influence of something akin to the classical ideal of the leader. His proposals were largely attempts to create individuals, institutions and beliefs that would bring wisdom and civic virtue to the workings of democracy. However, although he greatly admired Madison and his work, Tocqueville in many ways improved upon Madison. The great contributions of Tocqueville were, first, his willingness to engage democracy on its own terms (he did not, as Madison had, seek to circumvent it), and, second and perhaps more importantly, his more creative and expansive solutions. While Madison had concocted essentially institutional responses to the challenges of popular sovereignty, Tocqueville went beyond this and created what might be called 'cultural proxies' for the classical ideal. Moreover, it was in Tocqueville's creative use of the existing and naturally-occurring elements of democracy to restrain its own excesses that he displayed his genius. It is to those solutions that we now turn.

As indicated, Tocqueville did not ignore the more formal institutional remedies for democratic excesses. On the contrary, he approved of them, and had special praise for Madison's earlier efforts. In discussing such remedies, Tocqueville first made clear the essential challenge: 'The existence of democracies is threatened', he said, 'by two principal dangers: namely, the complete subjection of the legislature to the will of the electoral body, and the concentration of all the other powers of the government in the legislative branch.'[56] Looking back, he found that Madison and the other Founding Fathers had 'done all they could to render [those dangers] less formidable'.[57]

Specifically, Tocqueville held out the Constitution and its structures as worthy of the highest praise. He approved of the separation of powers as a brake on popular passions. If, he argued, in all governments, 'a legislative power could be so constituted as to represent the majority without being the slave of its passions, an executive so as to retain a proper share of authority, and a judiciary so as to remain independent of the other two powers, a government would be formed which would still be democratic while incurring scarcely any risk of tyranny'.[58]

We will return to the role of the judiciary in another context; here, the focus will be upon how Tocqueville believed the American Constitution structured the most popular branch to limit the tyranny of the majority and to help ensure the selection of wise leaders. He was particularly enamored of the Senate and its mode of election. Tocqueville saw long terms of office as a limit on popular passions. 'By granting to the senators the privilege of being chosen for several years,' he argued, '... the law takes care to preserve in the legislative body a nucleus of men already accustomed to public business, and capable of exercising a salutary influence....'[59]

Even more important was the indirect election of Senators provided for in the Constitution. Tocqueville contrasted the means of election to the House and Senate. 'How comes this strange contrast,' he asked, 'and why are the ablest citizens found in one assembly rather than the other? ... The only reason which appears to me adequately to account for it is that the House of Representatives is elected by the people directly, while the Senate is elected by elected bodies.... This transmission of the popular authority through an assembly of chosen men operates an important change in it by refining its discretion and improving its choice.' The result was the kind of leaders needed in a democracy. 'Men who are chosen in this manner accurately represent the majority of the nation which governs them,' he argued, 'but they represent only the elevated thoughts that are current in the community and the generous propensities that prompt its nobler actions rather than the petty passions that disturb or the vices that disgrace it.' Indeed, Tocqueville suggested that American democracy must extend this procedure. 'The time must come,' he said, 'when the American republics will be obliged more frequently to introduce the plan of election by an elected body into their system of representation or run the risk of perishing miserably among the shoals of democracy.'[60]

In sum, Tocqueville believed that the institutional safeguards thrown up by the Constitution were necessary everywhere democracy operated. As a result of such innovations, 'an attentive observer will soon notice that the business of the Union is incomparably better conducted than that of individual states. The conduct of the Federal government is far more fair and temperate than that of the states; it has more prudence and discretion, its projects are more durable and more skillfully combined, its measures are executed with more vigor and consistency.'[61]

Yet Tocqueville devoted little effort to elaborating detailed institutional solutions of the kind Madison had constructed. His focus was in a different direction. As the modern Tocqueville scholar Sheldon Wolin has phrased it, Tocqueville's contribution was 'the invention of a new battleground for the defense of freedom against majoritarian democracy, a shift from Madisonian constitutional devices to cultural formations, from strategies for preventing the coalescence of a majority to shaping or countering its beliefs and values'.[62] It is to such strategies that we now turn.

One far-reaching strategy addressed multiple concerns. According to Tocqueville, political education, broadly conceived, held the promise of moderating the tyranny of the majority and the force of public opinion, reinvigorating civic virtue, and resolving the problem of incompetence among the citizenry. And the most potent form of political education was political participation. We must 'use Democracy to moderate Democracy', Tocqueville wrote. 'It is the only path open to salvation to us.'[63]

Tocqueville went on to demonstrate the many benefits of political participation. His chief concern, it may be recalled, may well have been the lack of civic virtue in egalitarian democracy. Indeed, he had gone so far as to say that 'my chief object in writing this book has been to combat' the twin dangers of individualism and private interest.[64] Now, he put forward political participation as a remedy. 'I maintain', Tocqueville asserted, 'that the most powerful and perhaps the only means that we still possess of interesting men in the welfare of their country is to make them partakers in the government.'[65] 'It cannot be doubted', he continued, 'that in the United States the instruction of the people powerfully contributes to the support of the democratic republic.'[66] More specifically, 'When the members of a community are forced to attend to public affairs, they are necessarily drawn from the circle of their own interests and snatched at times from self-observation. As soon as a man begins to treat public affairs in public, he begins to perceive that he is not so independent of his fellow men as he had at first imagined, and that in order to obtain their support he must often lend them his cooperation.' Thus, democratic politics 'brings a multitude of citizens permanently together who would otherwise always have remained unknown to one another'. To this extent, 'Americans have combated by free institutions the tendency of equality to keep men asunder...',[67] and have created a commitment to public measures, even if they are at variance with individual interest (the very essence of 'civic virtue'). 'However irksome an enactment may be,' Tocqueville suggested, 'the citizen of the United States complies with it, not only because it is the work of the majority, but because it is his own, and he regards it as a contract to which he is himself a party.'[68]

Political participation also helped mitigate the tyranny of the majority, according to Tocqueville. This was accomplished through the emphasis upon individual rights, which, in turn, was honed by political participation. 'In America,' he observed, 'the lowest classes have conceived a very high notion of political rights, because they exercise those rights....' Indeed, Tocqueville maintained, 'I am persuaded that the only means which we possess at the present time of inculcating the idea of right and rendering it, as it were, palpable to the senses is to endow all with the peaceful exercise of certain rights'. This, in turn, moderated the tyranny of the majority. Citizens 'refrain from attacking the rights of others', he postulated, 'in order that their own may not be violated'.[69]

Participation also addressed the challenges posed by the creeping threat of paternalistic despotism that Tocqueville had warned against, as well as the evils of incompetent followers and unwise leaders in a democracy. He argued 'if education enables men at all times to defend their independence, this is most especially true in democratic times.'[70] When 'a nation which is ignorant as well as democratic an amazing difference cannot fail speedily to arise between the intellectual capacity of the ruler and that of each of his subjects. This completes the easy concentration of all power in his hands: the administrative function of the state is perpetually extended because the state alone is competent to administer the affairs of the country.'[71] All this changes, however, when the people take an active part in government. Although 'it is incontestable that the people frequently conduct public business rather badly; but it is impossible that the lower orders should take a part in public business without extending the circle of their ideas and quitting the old routine of their thoughts. The humblest individual who cooperates in the government of society acquires a degree of self-respect; as he possesses authority, he can command the services of minds more enlightened than his own.'[72] In sum, a democracy with a politically active citizenry enjoys committed citizens who choose wise leaders and who are more mindful of their rights and independence.

Tocqueville moved beyond generalization and provided a detailed example of how this form of political education worked in his study of the New England town. While Tocqueville has been criticized by some later scholars for offering up an uncritical paean to New England democracy when it was even then idiosyncratic and succumbing to the pressures of the times, such critics fail to realize that his purpose was to suggest how local government might be a part of the solution to the problems of democracy.

If political participation was a key ingredient in the recipe to cure the ills of democracy, the key to such participation was vigorous, participatory institutions at the local level. 'Municipal institutions', Tocqueville argued, 'constitute the strength of free nations.' They 'are to liberty what primary schools are to science; they bring it within the people's reach, they teach men how to use and how to enjoy it'.[73] 'I believe,' he continued, 'that provincial assemblies are useful to all nations, but nowhere do they appear to me to be more necessary than among a democratic people…. How,' he asked, 'can a populace unaccustomed to freedom in small concerns learn to use it temperately in great affairs? What resistance can be offered to tyranny in a country where each individual is weak and where the citizens are not united by any common interest? Those who dread the license of the mob and those who fear absolute power,' Tocqueville concluded, 'ought alike to desire the gradual development of provincial liberties.'[74]

Thus when Tocqueville turned to the application of his ideas about the political education of the people, he noted 'It is not without intention that I begin this subject with the township' of New England. It was in New England, 'a democracy more perfect than antiquity had dared to dream started in full size and panoply…. The new settlers did not derive their powers from the head of the empire …; they constituted themselves into a society …; continually exercised the rights of sovereignty; they named the magistrates and enacted the laws.'[75] In sum, 'the general principles which are the groundwork of modern constitutions … were all recognized and established by the laws of New England: the intervention of the people in public affairs, the free voting of taxes, the responsibility of the agents of power, personal liberty, and trial by jury were all positively established without discussion.'[76]

Again, the reason why such local governments proved so important was because they served as a prototype of how the evils of democracy could be harnessed, while its many advantages continued unabated. For example, vibrant local polities were useful in the battle against majority tyranny, since they 'form so many concealed breakwaters, which check or part the tide of popular determination'. The safety lay in the need for local administration of any law: 'If an oppressive law were passed, liberty would still be protected by the mode of executing the law'.[77] With strong local governments made up of citizens attuned to their liberties, the evils of tyranny would be minimized.

More important were the effects of local politics upon the nature of citizens. The New England towns were, for example, havens from individualism. In these towns, Tocqueville argued, 'the Americans have combated by free institutions the tendency of equality to keep men asunder, and they have subdued it'. When 'the local affairs of a district [are] conducted by the men who reside there, the same persons are always in contact, and they are, in a manner, forced to be acquainted and to adapt themselves to one another'.[78] These local political institutions 'remind every citizen, and in a thousand ways, that he lives in society. They every instant impress upon his mind the notion that it is the duty as well as the interest of men to make themselves useful to their fellow creatures.'[79]

The towns were likewise centers of civic virtue. Here, the local aspect of governing became all-important. 'It is difficult,' said Tocqueville, 'to draw a man out of his own circle to interest him in the destiny of the state, because he does not clearly understand what influence the destiny of the state can have upon his own lot. But,' Tocqueville continued, 'if it is proposed to make a road cross the end of his estate, he will see at a glance that there is a connection between this small public affair and his greatest private affairs, and he will discover, without its being shown to him, the close tie that unites private to general interest. Thus, … by entrusting to the citizens the administration of minor affairs,' it serves the purpose of 'interesting them in the public welfare and convincing them that they constantly stand in need of one another in order to provide for it.'[80] Thus, 'men attend to the interests of the public first by necessity, afterwards by choice; what was intentional becomes an instinct, and by dint of working for the good of one's fellow citizens, the habit and the taste for serving them are at length acquired'.[81]

Local polities such as the New England town thus created the ideal citizen for a democracy. Tocqueville painted a rosy picture of the consequences of such political bodies: 'The native of New England is attached to his township because it is independent and free: his cooperation in its affairs ensures his attachments to its interests; the well-being it affords him secures his affection; and its welfare is the aim of his ambition and of his future exertions. He takes a part of every occurrence in the place; he practices the art of government in the small sphere within his reach; ... he acquires a taste for order, comprehends its balance of powers, and collects clear practical notions on the nature of his duties and the extent of his rights.'[82] With citizens such as this, democracy did indeed stand a chance of operating for the good of all.

The New England experience also addressed another concern. Tocqueville was by nature and inclination an aristocrat, and he often appeared to regret the passing away of the type of aristocratic leadership represented by the classical ideal of the leader. He recognized that with the advent of equality and democracy, this particular form of leader no longer held sway. In the towns of New England, however, Tocqueville found the old deference to one's superiors remained. 'In New England', he noted, 'where ... society has acquired age and stability enough to enable it to form principles and hold fixed habits, the common people are accustomed to respect intellectual and moral superiority and to submit to it without complaint.'[83] Participation in local politics thus increased the possibility of good leaders in a democracy as well.

Tocqueville therefore strongly advocated the reinvigoration of local political entities. The requirements for their creation were relatively simple: they needed to be granted 'power and independence', for without those two essentials 'a town may contain good subjects, but it can have no active citizens'.[84] But with such active citizens, many of the problems of democracy Tocqueville had catalogued would become manageable.

It was not, however, only in vibrant local politics that remedies for the ills of democracy could be found. There was in America, Tocqueville discovered, a unique phenomenon, which he believed harbored the potential to constrain the excesses of democracy. Indeed, one of Tocqueville's great contributions was his recognition of the existence and contributions of what is often called 'civil society'. In America, 'instead of vesting in the government alone all the administrative powers ..., a portion of them may be entrusted to secondary public bodies temporarily composed of private citizens'.[85] These quasi-public bodies were supplemented by innumerable voluntary associations. As Tocqueville depicted it, 'When a private individual meditates an undertaking, however directly connected it may be with the welfare of society, he never thinks of soliciting the cooperation of government; but he publishes his plan, offers to execute it, courts the assistance of other individuals, and struggles mightily against all obstacles. Undoubtedly he is often less successful than the state may have been in his position;' Tocqueville acknowledged, 'but in the end the sum of these private undertakings far exceeds all that the government could have done.'[86] 'Americans of all ages, all conditions, and all dispositions', he concluded, 'constantly form associations.'[87] And, returning to his theme of political education, Tocqueville likened these political associations to 'large free schools where all citizens come to learn'.[88]

Again, Tocqueville was able to detail how such voluntary associations served to mollify the evils of democracy that he had previously identified. He found, for example, that 'the liberty of association has become a necessary guarantee against the tyranny of the majority.... In America,' Tocqueville explained, 'the citizens ... form ... minority associations in order, first, to show their numerical strength and so to diminish the moral power of the majority; and, secondly, to stimulate competition and thus to discover those arguments that are most fitted to act upon the majority....'[89]

Such associations also provided another of those 'breakwaters' against governmental despotism. Tocqueville had demonstrated earlier how individualistic, egalitarian democracy risked such an evil. 'The more enfeebled and incompetent the citizens become,' he observed, 'the more able and active the government ought to be rendered in order that society at large may execute what individuals can no longer accomplish.' Voluntary associations provided a potential remedy. 'Governments, therefore,' he argued strenuously, 'should not be the only active powers....' Instead, 'associations ought, in democratic nations, to stand in' the place of government.[90]

So, too, were voluntary associations useful to counter the evil of individualism. It was Tocqueville's observation that 'feelings and opinions are recruited, the heart is enlarged, and the human mind is developed only by the reciprocal influence of men upon one another. I have shown', he reminded his readers, 'that these influences are almost null in democratic countries; they must therefore be artificially created, and this can only be accomplished by associations.'[91]

Closely related to this were the lessons citizens learned about civic virtue; that is, the willingness to subsume individual desires to the good of the whole. According to Tocqueville, in voluntary associations men 'learn to surrender their own will to that of all the rest and to make their own exertions subordinate to the common impulse'.[92] Here, he saw in American practice a hopeful development. 'I have often admired', he wrote, 'the extreme skill with which the inhabitants of the United States succeed in proposing a common object for the exertions of a great many men and in inducing them voluntarily to pursue it.' Consequently, he found 'the most democratic country on the face of the earth is that in which men have, in our time, carried to the best perfection the art of pursuing in common the object of their common desires and have applied this new science to the greatest number of purposes.'[93]

Tocqueville was quite innovative when he turned to the consideration of how voluntary associations could remedy the democratic problem of incompetent leaders and ineffective followers. He began with one of his periodic eulogies to the aristocratic virtues of a lost age: 'Aristocratic countries abound in wealthy and influential persons who are competent to provide for themselves and who cannot be easily or secretly oppressed', he observed. Such independent leaders 'restrain a government within general habits of moderation and reserve'. Unfortunately, he acknowledged, 'I am well aware that democratic countries contain no such persons'. Here is where Tocqueville became creative. Although democracies did not supply such independent leaders 'naturally', nevertheless he believed 'something analogous to them may be created by artificial means. I firmly believe,' he continued, 'that an aristocracy cannot again be founded in the world, but I think that private citizens, by combining together, may constitute bodies of great wealth, influence and strength, corresponding to the persons of an aristocracy.' Thus, 'an association for political, commercial, or manufacturing purposes, or even for those of science or literature, is a powerful and enlightened member of the community....' In sum, private, voluntary associations held the potential of resurrecting the classical ideal of the leader. 'By this means,' Tocqueville concluded, 'many of the greatest political advantages of aristocracy would be obtained without its injustice or its dangers.'[94]

A similar argument applied to the citizens of a democracy. Aristocracies contain 'a small number of powerful and wealthy citizens' who 'can achieve great undertakings single-handed'. Thus, 'in aristocratic societies men do not need to combine in order to act'. Such was not true in a democracy. 'Among democratic nations, on the contrary, all the citizens are independent and feeble; they can do hardly anything by themselves.... They all, therefore, become powerless if they do not learn voluntarily to help one another.'[95]

The conclusion was clear: 'If [citizens] never acquired the habit of forming associations in ordinary life', democracy could not work.[96] To Tocqueville, 'the art of associating together must grow and improve in the same ratio in which the equality of conditions is increased'.[97] Accordingly, in the words of one scholar, 'Civil Society was ... the repository of Tocqueville's hopes for political vitalization'.[98]

Tocqueville's recognition of the role a revitalized political scene might play in the taming of democracy was insightful; his discovery of civil society innovative. Yet it was, perhaps, his attention to the impact of cultural norms and customs that set him apart. In a famous passage, he noted that 'the manners of the people may be considered as one of the great general causes to which the maintenance of a democratic republic in the United States is attributable. I here use the word *customs* ... [for] what might be termed *the habits of the heart*.'[99] These 'customs of the Americans of the United States are, then, the peculiar cause which renders that people the only one of the American nations that is able to support a democratic government'. Tocqueville was well aware of the role such customs played in his strategy to moderate the excesses of democracy. 'The Americans have shown', he pointed out, 'that it would be wrong to despair of regulating democracy by the aid of customs and laws.'[100] Thus Tocqueville came to place an enormous focus on what might be deemed the cultural elements of a functioning democracy. 'The importance of customs is a universal truth,' he concluded, 'to which study and experience constantly remind us. I find that it occupies the central position in my thoughts; all my ideas come back to it in the end.'[101]

Tocqueville devoted a large portion of his two volumes to a depiction of various aspects of American culture. The focus here will be upon those elements of his analysis that address his concern with the problems of an overweening democracy. In that analysis, Tocqueville created what might be deemed 'cultural proxies' for the classical ideal of the leader. That is, he looked to habits, customs and practices that served the purpose of restraining democracy's excesses and ensuring that it operated for the general good. Appropriately implemented cultural norms, or 'habits of the heart', could counteract excessive equality, restore civic virtue and serve as a neo-aristocratic brake upon the actions of leaders and the people. Perhaps most important, cultural norms, by their very nature, operated directly upon democratic citizens. They completed Tocqueville's extensive agenda for the political education of the people.

Turning to the agents of such cultural education, Tocqueville began with the role of law and legal institutions. To be sure, Tocqueville noted the distinction between law and custom, and he always acknowledged the primacy of the latter. But the distinction was less clear than might at first appear. It was at the point of nexus, that is, where 'the transmutation of laws and legal practices into [customs]' occurred, that Tocqueville found to be 'the key to American political culture'.[102]

Tocqueville was well aware of the institutional advantages the American judicial system provided in the effort to restrain the excesses of democracy. Of particular import was the role of judicial review. This restraint upon the more popular branch was an indispensable tool in the efforts to avoid majority tyranny. 'It will be found that an elective authority that is not subject to judicial power', he observed, ' will sooner or later elude all control....'[103] 'The strength of the courts of law has always been the greatest security that can be offered to personal independence,' Tocqueville noted, 'but this is especially the case in democratic ages. Private rights and interests are in constant danger if the judicial power does not grow more extensive and stronger to keep pace with the growing equality of conditions.'[104]

Even acknowledging the institutional role of judicial review, however, Tocqueville was even more interested in the cultural impact of the law and its institutions. The notion of law itself permeated American cultural understandings. 'In America,' he observed, '... it may be said that no one renders obedience to man, but to justice and law.'[105] This American devotion to law created a nobility in American aspirations equivalent to civic virtue. According to Tocqueville, 'men may be interested by the laws in the fate of their country. It depends upon the laws to awaken and direct the vague impulses of patriotism....' If such commitment to the greater good 'be connected with the thoughts, the passions, and the daily habits of life, it may be consolidated into a durable and rational sentiment'.[106] In this way the respect for the law transcended mere obedience and became the basis for virtuous citizenship.

The cultural imprint of the law extended far beyond an abstract respect for its provisions. Tocqueville found that Americans received a civic education in the actual operation of judicial institutions. The best example was the role of the jury. He perceived that 'trial by jury may be considered in two separate points of view: as a judicial, and as a political institution.... My present purpose is to consider the jury as a political institution.... The jury is, above all, a political institution,' he noted, 'and it must be regarded in this light to be duly appreciated.'[107]

To Tocqueville, the importance of the jury did not lay in its fact finding or in its verdict *per se*. Instead, 'Trial by jury ... appears to me an eminently republican element of the government'. By this he meant 'it places the real direction of society in the hands of the governed ... and not in that of the government'. Looking at it in this light, 'the jury system as it is understood in America appears to me to be as direct and as extreme a consequence of the sovereignty of the people as universal suffrage'.[108]

Jury service had the added advantage of serving as a tutorial for democratic citizens. One of its chief advantages was to infuse the wisdom of the judges – who for Tocqueville were representatives of the classical ideal of the leader – into the citizenry. As he put it, 'the jury ... serves to communicate the spirit of the judges to the minds of all the citizens, and this spirit, with the habits which attend it, is the soundest preparation for free institutions'. Tyranny of the majority was muted because jury duty 'imbues all classes with a respect for the judged and with the notion of right'. The jury also contributed to civic virtue. It 'teaches every man not to recoil before the responsibility of his own actions and impresses him with that manly confidence without which no political virtue can exist'. The jury also 'invests each citizen with a kind of magistracy; it makes them all feel the duties which they are bound to discharge towards society and the part which they take in government. By obliging men to turn their attention to other affairs than their own, it rubs off that private selfishness which is the rust of society.'[109]

The consequences were uniformly positive to a well-ordered democracy. As Tocqueville summed it up, 'the jury contributes powerfully to form the judgment and to increase the natural intelligence of a people; and this, in my opinion, is its greatest advantage'. Indeed, 'it may be regarded as a gratuitous public school, ever open, in which every juror learns his rights, enters into daily communication with the most learned and enlightened members of the upper classes, and becomes practically acquainted with the laws. I think', Tocqueville continued, 'the practical intelligence and political good sense of the Americans are mainly attributable to the long use that they have made of the jury.... I look upon it as one of the most efficacious means for the education of the people which society can employ.'[110]

If the law was one approach to inculcating the 'habits of the heart' conducive to a well operating democracy, other strategies included fostering patriotism and religion. According to Tocqueville, 'there is no true power among men except in the free union of their will; and patriotism and religion are the only two motives in the world that can long urge all the people towards the same end'.[111]

Patriotism, Tocqueville believed, was a powerful force that led men to look to the interests of the country as a whole rather than to individual interests, and thereby to practice civic virtue. Tocqueville delineated two forms of patriotism. The first was the 'instinctive, disinterested, and undefinable feeling which connects the affections of man with his birthplace'. This connection was essentially conservative in nature, and thus operated as a restraining influence upon sudden changes and passions of an emerging democracy. This form of patriotism lends itself to 'a taste for ancient customs and a reverence for traditions of the past'. Citizens who experience this sort of patriotism 'love their country ... and they are even pleased by living there in a state of obedience'.[112]

This sort of commitment to settled traditions obviously meshed well with Tocqueville's strategy of creating proxies for lost restraints on the activities of the people. Unfortunately for Tocqueville, however, this affection for institutions of the past was not a prominent characteristic of America's dynamic, materialistic and contemporary culture. Fortunately, he also found 'another species of attachment to country', one that 'is more rational', yet 'more fruitful and more lasting'. This form of patriotism sprang almost unbidden from the realities of American life, and exemplified a new and previously undetected link between perceived self-interest and the general good. We will turn to this 'self-interest rightly understood' in more detail momentarily. Here, suffice it to say that Tocqueville saw its operation in a form of patriotism that could only emerge in a well-organized democracy. This sort of patriotism 'springs from knowledge; it is nurtured by the laws; it grows by the exercise of civil rights; and, in the end, it is confounded with the personal interests of the citizen'. In its operation, 'a man comprehends the influence which the well-being of his country has upon his own; he is aware that the laws permit him to contribute to that prosperity, and he labors to promote it, first because it benefits him, and secondly because it is in part his own work'.[113] As a result, 'the citizen looks upon the fortune of the public as his own, and he labors for the good of the state, not merely from a sense of pride or duty, but from what I venture to term cupidity'.[114] Far from disparaging this somewhat alloyed public interest, Tocqueville found in it hope for a more deep-seated commitment to the common good.

Religion was even more central to Tocqueville's efforts to restrain democracy. Modern scholar Sheldon Wolin has best captured the role it played in shaping the cultural beliefs of Americans. According to Wolin, 'Tocqueville is less concerned with the solace furnished by religion than with its utility as a method, perhaps even the principal one, of social control'.[115] In other words, in the United States, 'religion was the single most important element in a web of restraints – legal, constitutional, moral, and geographical – on the powers of majorities.... [It] furnished the most effective restraint upon democratic passions and ambitions.'[116]

Tocqueville made it clear how religion served this important function. Essentially, religion counteracted the dominant cultural tendencies of American society. For example, while 'it must be acknowledged that equality, which brings great benefits into the world, nevertheless suggests to men ... some very dangerous propensities. It tends to isolate them from one another, to concentrate every man's attention upon himself; and it lays open the soul to an inordinate love of material gratification. The greatest advantage of religion', on the other hand, 'is to inspire diametrically contrary principles.'[117] 'Christianity ... teaches that men ought to benefit their fellow creatures for the love of God....'[118]

Society was similarly threatened by the evil of materialism. 'Materialism, among all nations, is a dangerous disease of the human mind,' Tocqueville noted, 'but it is especially to be dreaded among a democratic people because...this taste, if it becomes excessive, soon disposes men to believe that all is matter only; and materialism, in its turn, hurries them on with mad impatience to these same delights; such is the fatal circle within which democratic nations are driven round.' To the contrary, religion is a 'general, simple, and practical means of teaching men the doctrine of the immortality of the soul. This is the greatest benefit which a democratic people derives from its belief',[119] because it was 'the essential inhibitory ingredient in democratic self-restraint'.[120]

These influences upon American 'habits of the heart' made religion absolutely necessary. As Tocqueville put it, 'Although it is of great moment to man as an individual that his religion should be true, that is not the case for society. Society has nothing to fear or hope from another life; what is important for it is not that all citizens profess the true religion, but that they profess a religion.' Consequently, 'the lawgivers in democracies and all upright and educated men should tirelessly seek to elevate souls and to direct them toward heaven. It is urgent for all who are interested in the future of democratic societies to unite and, acting in concert, to make continual efforts to diffuse throughout society a taste for the infinite, an appreciation of greatness, and a love of spiritual pleasures.'[121] Only by so doing might the much more secular dream of good democracy be realized.

Tocqueville had isolated and identified a number of strategies that he believed would harness the restless spirit of egalitarian democracy and guide it in such a way that it operate in a manner akin to the classical republics he admired so much. That is to say, Tocqueville, in his many observations and recommendations, was seeking to create a polity that was based in a sovereign and equal people, yet would still have the advantages of civic virtue, wisdom and a commitment to the common good. His schemes were varied and creative, ranging from the institutional to the ideational. Yet, at bottom, the success of his many proposals rested – as they always do – on the nature and abilities of the individuals who were to implement them. Accordingly, he was confronted with the problem of leaders and followers in a democracy: the need for leaders with wisdom and a people committed to making the democracy work. Tocqueville, being the careful analyst that he was, did not shy away from this final challenge to leadership in a democracy. He addressed both in his usual insightful style.

In looking to the role of the people in the social relationship that we now call leadership, Tocqueville was inescapably called to consider the issue of virtue. In classical republicanism, a requirement of citizen and leader alike was a commitment to civic virtue, or the placing of the interests of the community above those of the individual. In the emerging egalitarian democracy of the nineteenth century, it was widely believed that such virtue was a thing of the past. Tocqueville himself, as we have seen, was well aware of the materialistic and individualistic ethos of modern democracy, the circumvention of which was the purpose of much of his writing. This makes all the more remarkable his ultimate finding that virtue, after a fashion, could still be found among the people of a modern democracy.

The virtue of modern democracy was not classical civic virtue, but a phenomenon Tocqueville called 'self-interest rightly understood'. He began by acknowledging that 'no power on earth can prevent the increasing equality of conditions from inclining ... every member of the community to be wrapped up in himself. It must therefore be expected', he reasoned, 'that personal interest will become more than ever the principal if not the sole spring of men's actions....' All this being said, however, 'it remains to be seen how each man will understand his personal interest'.[122] Here, Tocqueville came to one of his most penetrating insights. 'At the bottom of democratic institutions,' he observed, 'there is a hidden tendency which makes men promote the general prosperity in spite of their vices and errors ... in democracies men produce the good without having thought about it.'[123]

In the aristocratic world of the past, Tocqueville recalled, 'when the world was managed by a few rich and powerful individuals', the principles of the classical ideal of the leader was firmly in place. 'These persons', he noted, 'loved to entertain a lofty idea of the duties of man. They were fond of professing that it is praiseworthy to forget oneself and that good should be done without hope of reward....' Although Tocqueville expressed some doubt whether the reality matched the ideal, this perception was the dominant fiction, and aristocratic leaders 'were incessantly talking of the beauties of virtue'.[124]

In the contemporary American democracy, however, Tocqueville made an interesting discovery. The language of classical republicanism was no longer in currency. 'In the United States,' he observed, 'hardly anyone talks of the beauties of virtue.' Nonetheless, 'they maintain that virtue is useful and prove it every day'.[125] Looking back upon his observations, he reflected how 'I have already shown, in several parts of this work, by what means the inhabitants of the United States almost always manage to combine their own advantage with that of their fellow citizens; my present purpose is to point out the general rule that enables them to do so'.[126]

That 'general rule' had little to do with selflessness or traditional notions of virtue. 'The American moralists', Tocqueville maintained, 'do not profess that men ought to sacrifice themselves for their fellow creatures *because* it is noble to make such sacrifices....' To the contrary, the focus is upon the agent himself: 'They boldly aver that such sacrifices are as necessary to him who imposes them upon himself as him for whose sake they are made'. Therein lay the conundrum of virtue in a democracy: 'They therefore do not deny that every man may follow his own interest, but they endeavor to prove that it is the interest of every man to be virtuous'.[127]

The answer to this riddle was the conception of 'self-interest rightly understood'. According to this, Americans 'show ... how an enlightened regard for themselves constantly prompts them to assist one another and inclines them willingly to sacrifice a portion of their time and property to the welfare of the state'. The argument is that one's actions, and their consequences, must be viewed in the large perspective. Looking at one's interests in the longer view, it becomes clear that 'lasting happiness can be secured only by renouncing a thousand transient gratifications; and that a man must perpetually triumph over himself in order to secure his own advantage'.[128] Using the influence of religion as an example, Tocqueville suggested that Americans perceived how efforts made on behalf of others often led to a more beneficial result, in the long run, for those who made short-term sacrifices.

The result was something Tocqueville called 'enlightened selfishness'. He regarded 'the principle of self-interest rightly understood … [as] the best suited of all philosophical theories to the wants of men of our time, and … as their chief remaining security against themselves'.[129] In sum, Tocqueville thought he had discovered among the Americans a way of justifying popular sovereignty, even among an egalitarian and materialistic people.

If there was hope for a suitably 'virtuous' people, Tocqueville still faced the problem of securing wise leaders to lead them. Here, too, he did not disappoint. Again, he provided the sort of astute yet realistic analysis that was the hallmark of his entire work.

Tocqueville recognized that creating a cadre of leaders of the traditional sort – that is, leaders who conformed to the classical ideal – was a difficult task. 'In America,' he acknowledged, 'the aristocracy has always been feeble from its birth, and if at the present day it is not actually destroyed, it is at any rate so completely disabled that we can scarcely assign to it any degree of influence on the course of affairs.'[130] Indeed, 'all who attempt, in the ages upon which we are entering, to base freedom upon aristocratic privilege will fail…. At the present day, no ruler is skillful or strong enough … to preserve free institutions if he does not take equality for his first principle and his watchword.' Thus any attempt to create competent leaders must accept the new reality of equality: 'upon this depends the success of their holy enterprise'.[131]

From this premise, Tocqueville moved to a realistic assessment of the status of and possibility for the emergence of good leaders in American democracy. It will be recalled from his litany of problems of American democracy that one problem was that, in normal times, it was usually only the incompetent who emerged as leaders of the people. The problem was less acute in times of crisis: 'When serious dangers threaten the state,' he noted, 'the people frequently succeed in selecting the citizens who are most able to serve it…. At those dangerous times, genius no longer hesitates to come forward, and the people, alarmed by the perils of their situation, for a time forget their envious passions.'[132]

Even in more prosaic times, a regime grounded in popular sovereignty offered some safeguards against the incompetence and cupidity of its leaders. 'If, in a democratic state,' Tocqueville reasoned, 'the governors have less honesty and less capacity than elsewhere, the governed are more enlightened and more attentive to their interests.' This led to greater accountability. 'As the people in democracies are more constantly vigilant in their affairs and more jealous of their rights, they prevent their representatives from abandoning that general line of conduct which their own interest prescribes.' But there was a more fundamental safeguard as well. While 'it is no doubt of importance to the welfare of nations that they should be governed by men of talents and virtue; … it is perhaps still more important that the interests of these men not differ from the interests of the community at large'. That proved the ultimate protection. 'The men who are entrusted with the direction of public affairs in the United States are frequently inferior, in both capacity and morality, to those whom an aristocracy would raise to power', Tocqueville allowed. 'But their interest is identified and mingled with that of the majority of their fellow citizens. They may frequently be faithless and frequently mistaken, but they will never systematically adopt a line of conduct hostile to the majority, and they cannot give a dangerous or exclusionary tendency to the government.'[133]

This did not mean that the quest for more capable leaders should be abandoned. Tocqueville, in the words of one of his chroniclers, 'was engaged in a lifelong task of retrieving a receding aristocratic past in order to counteract the new forms of despotism.'[134] There was a need, Tocqueville was convinced, for an aristocratic influence of some sort, in the spirit of the classical ideal. 'Almost all the nations that have exercised a powerful influence upon the destinies of the world, ... from the Romans to the English, have been governed by aristocratic institutions.'[135] If a traditional aristocracy was no longer feasible in a democratic age, some proxy was necessary.

We have already seen some of Tocqueville's attempts to create proxies for aristocratic leadership. The role of voluntary associations is perhaps the best example. 'I am firmly convinced,' he said, 'that an aristocracy cannot be founded anew in the world; but I think that by associating ordinary citizens can constitute very rich bodies, very influential and very strong, in other words an aristocratic being. In this way,' he went on, 'one could gain many of the greatest political advantages of aristocracy without its injustices or dangers.'[136]

Another possibility, although one not fully developed by Tocqueville, was the potential role of political parties. Tocqueville distinguished between what he called 'great' and 'minor' political parties. 'The political parties that I style great,' he explained, 'are those which cling to principles rather than to consequences; to general and not to special cases; to ideas and not to men. These parties are usually distinguished by nobler features, more generous passions, more genuine convictions, and a more bold and open conduct than the others.... Minor parties, on the other hand, are generally deficient in political good faith. As they are not sustained or dignified by lofty purposes, they ostensibly display the selfishness of their character in their actions.'[137] Unfortunately, Tocqueville found that 'Great political parties ... are not to be met with in the United States at the present time.... The parties by which the Union is menaced do not rest upon principles, but upon material interests.'[138] Tocqueville essentially left his treatment of political parties at this descriptive level. However, given his later specifications for the type of leaders that democracy required, the role for 'great' political parties headed by individuals committed to the classical ideal could have been an enhanced portion of his portfolio of solutions.

Beyond mere proxies, there was still the possibility of a more traditional elite as well. For this, Tocqueville looked again to the pervasive influence of law in American society. He found two related groups in a position to exercise influence of the type traditionally associated with the aristocracy. The first was judges. The influence of judges in American society was a function of the unique institutional doctrine of judicial review. As a result, the American judge 'is invested with immense political power',[139] since 'scarcely any political question arises in the United States that is not resolved, sooner or later, into a judicial question'.[140] This political power was used, Tocqueville observed, in a manner consistent with wise leadership in a democracy. 'The courts of justice are the visible organs by which the legal profession is enabled to control the democracy.' An American judge 'cannot force the people to make laws, but at least he can oblige them not to disobey their own enactments, and not to be inconsistent with themselves'.[141] Thus, Tocqueville concluded, 'I am inclined to believe this practice of the American courts to be at once most favorable to liberty and public order'.[142]

Even more important – and more pervasive – was the role of lawyers. Tocqueville was quite strident in his championing of their influence. 'In visiting the Americas and studying their laws,' he wrote, 'we perceive that the authority they have entrusted to members of the legal profession, and the influence that these individuals exercise in government, are the most powerful existing security against the excesses of democracy.'[143] Indeed, 'the more that we reflect upon all that occurs in the United States, the more we shall be persuaded that the lawyers, as a body, form the most powerful, if not the only, counterpoise to the democratic element. In that country we easily perceive how the legal profession is qualified by its attributes, and even by its faults, to neutralize the vices inherent in popular government.'[144]

Tocqueville went on to elaborate upon those 'attributes' of lawyers that fitted them for leading a democracy. 'Men who have made a special study of the law', he explained, 'derive from this occupation certain habits of order, a taste for formalities, and a kind of instinctive regard for the regular connection of ideas, which naturally render them very hostile to the revolutionary spirit and unreflecting passions of the multitude.' Thus, 'some of the tastes and habits of the aristocracy may consequently be discovered in the class of lawyers. They participate in the same instinctive love of order and formalities; and they entertain the same repugnance to the actions of the multitude, and the same secret contempt of the government of the people.' In consequence, 'in a community in which lawyers are allowed to occupy without opposition that high station which naturally belongs to them, their general spirit will be eminently conservative and anti-democratic'.[145]

Fortunately, Tocqueville also found that 'the government of democracy is favorable to the political power of lawyers'. Lawyers constituted the only accepted aristocratic body in democratic society, he noted. 'The special information that lawyers derive from their studies ensures them a separate rank in society, and they constitute a sort of privileged body in the scale of intellect.... They are the only men of information and sagacity, beyond the sphere of the people, who can be the object of the popular choice.' In fact, 'the people in democratic states do not mistrust the members of the legal profession'. Because 'lawyers belong to the people by birth and interest, and to the aristocracy by habit and taste; they may be looked upon as the connecting link between the two great classes of society'. Therefore 'the profession of the law is the only aristocratic element that can be amalgamated without violence with the natural elements of democracy and be advantageously and permanently combined with them'.[146]

There was hope, then, for appropriate leaders in a democratic society. And, indeed, the reality was that, 'as the lawyers form the only enlightened class whom the people do not mistrust, they are naturally called upon to occupy most of the public stations. They fill the legislative assemblies and are at the head of the administration; they consequently exercise a powerful influence upon the formation of the law and upon its execution.'[147]

Once appropriate leaders were identified and in place, their duty was to act with the wisdom and virtue demanded by the classical ideal of the leader and, more specifically, to seek to implement the various stratagems that Tocqueville had identified.

For example, Tocqueville placed in the lap of leaders the obligation to create and maintain a vibrant civil society: 'It requires a great deal of intelligence, knowledge, and skill to organize and maintain in these conditions secondary powers and to create among independent but individually weak citizens free associations able to fight against tyranny without destroying order'.[148] Similarly, the cultural 'habits of the heart' were 'typically shaped by the Few: by priests, teachers ... writers, [and] editors.... These elites are the modern successors to aristocracy....'[149] It was, indeed, the role of 'enlightened leaders to bring about changes in the laws, ideas, habits and [customs]' that would lead to the kind of cultural beliefs that would sustain an effective democracy.[150]

More specifically with regard to the new social relation we call leadership, leaders had an obligation to help their followers to see the bigger picture; to go beyond immediate gratification to 'self-interest rightly understood'. 'Philosophers and rulers' must 'make [men] see that' their focus must be upon 'long term projects', rather than on satisfying 'a thousand mundane petty passions'.[151] More than this, however, it was the task of democratic leaders to get the people to see beyond themselves in a larger sense. They must lift the vision of the demos to its highest calling; that is, to an approach to democratic governing akin to what he detailed as consonant with the 'great' political parties. 'I think, then, that the leaders of modern society ... would have endeavors made to give [the people] a more enlarged idea of themselves and of their kind.'[152] 'The task of those in power is ... clearly marked out.... Governments must apply themselves to restore to men that love of the future with which religion and the state of society no longer inspire them.'[153]

Perhaps most important of all, leaders of a regime grounded in popular sovereignty must raise the level of the people themselves. 'It would seem as if the rulers of our time sought only to use men to make things great', Tocqueville observed. 'I wish they would try a little more to make great men.' For they must 'never forget that a nation cannot long remain strong when every man belonging to it is individually weak; and that no form or combination of social polity has yet been devised to make an energetic people out of a community of pusillanimous and enfeebled citizens'.[154] This was a tall order, but one that leaders of a democracy could not shirk.

Tocqueville summed up the leaders' tasks in his Introduction to his two volumes: 'The first of the duties that are at this time imposed upon those who direct our affairs is to educate democracy, to reawaken, if possible, its religious beliefs; to purify its morals; to mold its actions; to substitute knowledge of statecraft for its inexperience, and an awareness of its true interest for its blind instincts....'[155] With such leadership, democracy did indeed have a chance of success.

THE IMPLICIT LEADERSHIP THEORIES OF ALEXIS DE TOCQUEVILLE

Just as was the case with every other person struggling to come to grips with the new reality of popular sovereignty, Alexis de Tocqueville confronted the challenges of democracy with a constellation of often unstated premises and assumptions. Those 'implicit theories' guided the way he went about diagnosing the problems of democracy and, of course, shaped his proposed solutions. The protocol of questions that makes up our template of leadership helps to elucidate Tocqueville's key assumptions, and thereby facilitates our understanding of the underpinnings of the fiction he created to address the perceived challenges of democracy.

What is the Leadership Challenge?

As the preceding analysis makes plain, Tocqueville's carefully analytic tour of America identified a series of specific challenges brought about by the novel social and political realities of the United States of the 1830s. These challenges ranged from the tyranny of the majority, to the related hegemony of public opinion, to the loss of civic virtue and the rise of individualism. Taken in larger perspective, the problems Tocqueville identified stemmed from the emergence of large-scale, egalitarian democracy. Accepting the rise of democracy as a given, yet viewing its effects with alarm, Tocqueville's challenge could be viewed as the problem of somehow controlling democracy in such a way as to fulfill his expectations for a good society (a topic spelled out in more detail in his responses to subsequent queries of the template). Indeed, the perspective could be widened still further. Alexis de Tocqueville was among the first, and among the most astute, of the commentators to confront modernity. In his attempts to grapple with widespread political participation, egalitarianism and the effects of a highly commercialized and individualistic society, Tocqueville faced a world unknown to any of his predecessors. It was a formidable challenge indeed.

It was also a leadership challenge. If we view leadership as a new relation between the few and the many demanded by the realities of ultimate power residing in the many, the leadership element of Tocqueville's detailed study becomes clear. That is to say, as he sought to devise new ways that leaders and followers could seek to achieve societal objectives (our definition of leadership), Tocqueville was forced to consider the nature and characters of leaders and the people, and how they should relate. Furthermore, he had to contemplate how society's institutions, structures and processes could be reconfigured to facilitate his desired outcomes. This, as it turns out, amounts to the invention of a new fiction of leadership. It also, not coincidentally, parallels closely the substance evoked by the remaining questions of the leadership template.

What is the Perception of Human Nature?

The content of any desired outcome in terms of the relationship between leaders and the people is tied inextricably to assumptions concerning the nature of the human condition and human interactions. How one views man's proclivity for interaction with others, or one's conclusions regarding what inspires individuals to act, and any number of related assumptions, will largely determine how one will evaluate the success of existing arrangements and will form the foundation for any proposed reforms. Consequently, it is important to seek to identify Tocqueville's premises concerning the human condition, in order to evaluate more fully both his critique and his proposed solutions.

To his credit, Tocqueville refused to be simplistic in his articulation of the human condition. He combined a sharp eye for the realities humans faced in a modern democratic world with an idealistic yet unsentimental belief that these could be improved upon (according to his lights). This seeming dichotomy is best illustrated by turning to specific examples. In looking to man's relationship to man, Tocqueville was among the first to note one of the seeming desiderata of modernity: that individuals in society tended to interact with each other *qua* individuals, thus reversing millennia of assumptions concerning humans as essentially social beings who find fulfillment in communal settings. While perceiving this reality and acknowledging its pervasiveness, Tocqueville nonetheless refused to abandon the field to rampant individualism. Viewing such individualism as an unmitigated evil, he believed that, if not perfectible, men were at least capable of improvement. Such was the motivation for his elaborate schemes – from local political participation to the institutions of civil society – designed to enhance the individual's connection to the community. But

Tocqueville's approach was more sophisticated than merely an effort to tempt citizens to return to traditional values. As was the case in many of his applications, he accepted the new reality and sought to turn it in more productive directions. An example was his identification and efforts to foster 'self-interest rightly understood', an approach he also referred to as 'enlightened selfishness'. In this, Tocqueville sought to harness modern realities of human interaction with the ideals of an older commitment to a larger world.

In a similar vein, Tocqueville was among the first to perceive the political implications of another feature of modernity: the primacy of economic motivation for individual behavior. Capitalism had been a factor in Western life for centuries, and as recently as sixty years prior to the publication of Tocqueville's first volume, Adam Smith had explained this motivation in his *Wealth of Nations*. Yet it was Alexis de Tocqueville who contemplated what this might mean in a polity in which the will of the people was the driving force. He recognized that the inhabitants of the America of the 1830s often acted as *homo oeconomicus*, looking to individual economic consequences of any proposed public policy. Although he bemoaned the crass commercialism he saw in the United States, Tocqueville, again, was willing to adapt to the new reality. Rather than attempt to thwart something so deeply imbedded in the American psyche, he instead sought to guide it. This, too, was one of his motivations for stressing 'self-interest rightly understood', and, even more directly, his championing of the otherworldly values of religious belief.

Another aspect of human nature and interactions involved the issue of equality. As we will explore in more detail below in our discussion of the relations of leaders and the people, the extreme egalitarianism of the modern world of the early nineteenth century undercut long-held expectations about the relations between the common people and those who held political office. While lamenting the change in many respects, it was not Tocqueville's way to attempt (as Madison had done in an admittedly less democratic era) to resurrect past relations. Instead, Tocqueville sought a new leadership relation grounded in equality yet seeking to tap what tendencies remained that served to reinforce the values of the classic ideal of the leader. The details of that new relation will be spelled out presently.

The brief analysis above suggests that Tocqueville was astute in his perception of the emergence of a 'modern' individual: one who operated from novel premises about what it means to be human, and with new expectations concerning his relations with others and with those in positions of authority. Tocqueville would prove to be remarkably prescient in both his depiction of human behavior in modern democracies and, ultimately, in his proposals for adapting the polity to the new realities.

Are the People Capable of Governing?

Along with the new assumptions about human nature came the equally important matter of Tocqueville's stance regarding the ability of the people to govern themselves. Given his pragmatic acceptance of the reality (and inevitability) of democracy, his response to this issue could hardly be more important.

Again, Tocqueville demonstrated his ability to embrace nuanced shadings of interpretation. His opinion of the political capabilities of the people was essentially negative. Much of his fear of majority rule stemmed from his belief that citizens were not competent to handle the absolute power granted by pure democracy. They did not possess the requisite wisdom to discern their true needs. Moreover, they were damned at both ends of the political spectrum. On the one hand, their excessive individualism precluded civic virtue, and hence they tended toward selfish anarchy. On the other hand, that same single-minded focus upon individual interests often led them, through mere inattention, to an acceptance of a new form of benevolent tyranny. Perhaps worse still, Tocqueville believed that, in ordinary circumstances at any rate, the people did not even have the soundness of judgment to select good leaders (thus dashing Madison's hopes). It comes as little surprise, then, that we find Tocqueville intoning that 'Democracy, pushed to its furthest limits, is … prejudicial to the art of government'.[156]

Such concerns with the capability of the people to govern obviously fueled much of Tocqueville's extensive efforts to invent systems that moderated the risks of democratic government. At the same time, however, he was, again, also able to see the positive aspects of and potential for government by the people. In the first place, even though they were often unwise, Tocqueville felt that the people would never knowingly act against their own interests. This insight gave him hope that, in the long run, those interests would be 'rightly understood' to mean the support of the common good. Moreover, one of the premises of much of Tocqueville's agenda was that the abilities of the people could be honed. His lengthy encomiums of New England town meetings and jury service, for example, were dedicated to their role in creating individuals who were properly educated for the duties of citizenship.

Because Tocqueville saw democracy as the wave of the future – and, indeed, because he was attracted to its vast energy and creativity – he was not about to abandon it as impracticable. He turned his efforts instead to adapting and modifying it in such a way as to tap the promise of the people, while at the same time providing them with leaders of the type associated with the classical ideal or, failing that, creating surrogates that could serve the same function. It was this cautious, carefully circumscribed faith in the people that powered and shaped Tocqueville's reform agenda.

What is the Proper End or Purpose of Leadership?

In addressing this question, one can discern from Tocqueville's writings a multi-tiered response. At the first level, if you will, Tocqueville clearly articulated what he saw as the desired end of all political action. It was, in effect, a somewhat nostalgic embrace of the classic ideal. At many points in his analysis, Tocqueville waxed eloquent about the lost days of an aristocratic world in which wise leaders operated for the common good. Even though he acknowledged that the reality never quite matched this fiction, there can be no doubt that in Tocqueville's perfect world, the proper end of leadership was some consensual common good. At the second level of his analysis, however, Tocqueville acknowledged the *realpolitik* of democracy. That is to say, he saw in American democracy the reality that whatever the majority decided upon was sure to be the law of the land. And, because he held no great confidence in the civic virtue of the people, this result seemed destined to be the mere will of the majority, unalloyed by considerations of the common good or, indeed, the interests of any minority. Looking at the reality of modern democracy, then, Tocqueville found the 'end' or purpose of leadership to be whatever the majority decided upon. Finally, Tocqueville enunciated yet a third view of the ends of leadership, a view that was, in effect, a synthesis of his thesis of the classical ideal and the antithesis of democracy's *realpolitik*. This last version of the desired ends of political society was to become a part of Tocqueville's invented fiction of leadership. In it, he held out for a continued adherence to the notion that there existed some external, definable conceptualization of the good, and that this good was achievable in a democratic context. Where he departed from the classical ideal was in his willingness to abandon the traditional sole reliance upon virtuous leaders, and to contemplate novel and often unusual modes of determining and implementing the good.

What is the Epistemology of Leadership?

This issue cuts to the heart of the new relation between the few and the many that we are labeling leadership. It recalls the tension between the elitist and participationist approaches to democracy, discussed in the introductory chapter to this Part. In Tocqueville's contemplation of the topic, the strain was really between two desirable but potentially antagonistic themes: *participation* and *competence*.

It will be recalled that those who stress the merits of participation argue that all should be engaged in determining what is proper, and, in effect, that whatever is decided by a properly inclusive process is, by definition, correct. Those who are of the elitist mold counter that there are some individuals who know better what is best for society than others, and that the determination and implementation of policy should be entrusted to their hands. In articulating these two extreme ends of the spectrum, it should become clear that they advocate differing epistemic approaches, one grounding knowledge of the good on procedural inclusiveness, and one on the insights of competent elites.

Tocqueville, as we saw in our discussion of the previous query of the protocol, sought a synthesis of the two approaches in his new fiction of leadership. We need not repeat in detail Tocqueville's personal commitment to the elitist conceptions of the classical ideal. Nor is it necessary to revisit the reality he faced in America's raucous egalitarian democracy. In the America of the 1830s, suffice it to say, whatever the people decided *was* the proper result. Resisting this with all his aristocratic soul, Tocqueville devoted his two volumes to feeling out some acceptable synthesis that allowed the people to know and determine proper policy (participation) while under the guidance and/or restraint of individuals and institutions that emulated the virtues of the classical ideal (competence). Whether he succeeded or not is a matter of some conjecture, but in the attempt Tocqueville created one of the first versions of the new fiction we call leadership.

With such underlying premises laid bare, we can now turn to the portions of the leadership protocol that reveal the heart of the leadership relation.

What is the Role of the Leader?

When Tocqueville turned his attention toward the role leaders should play in a democratic polity, he engaged in his now-familiar dialectical analysis. There can be little doubt that the aristocratic Tocqueville harbored affection for those past days in which virtuous elites were permitted to seek, unfettered, the good of society as a whole. The actual workings of American democracy, however, posed fundamental challenges to this ideal. In the first place, he found American citizens so sensitive to claims of superiority by other members of society as to call into question the very idea of leaders of the traditional sort. To the extent that positions of authority were inescapable, he found that the system normally produced mediocre, unqualified leaders. It was this fundamental contradiction between his aspirations and democracy's reality that caused him to cast about for ways to superimpose the benefits of the classical ideal on to the base alloy of democracy.

Tocqueville's first challenge was to secure appropriate leaders or their substitutes. After considerable searching, he did have some success in this pursuit. There were, for instance, on occasion, leaders of the classical ideal in place. This happy occurrence came about when the New England town was working to its full potential, and at times in the neo-aristocratic South. Tocqueville saw much more potential, however, in the class of lawyers and judges that seemed to be the dominant force in political society. Here, he thought, was the replacement for the aristocracy of the past, and he pinned his hopes upon the possibility that their emergence might allow society to enjoy many of the benefits of the classical ideal.

Recognizing that more might be needed, Tocqueville trawled democratic society looking for existing institutions that might serve as surrogates for individual leaders committed to the long-term public good. It was in connection with this effort that he came to advocate the role of the voluntary associations of civil society, the creation of 'great' political parties, and the like.

We have also seen that Tocqueville was creative enough to look to non-traditional methods of advancing the long-term interests of society at the expense of short-term selfishness. These we have labeled 'cultural proxies', and include the 'habits of the heart', or societal customs that led people to have a longer-term vision, and indeed to raise the level of the people themselves. Commitment to law, patriotism and religious belief all served this function.

This detailing of Tocqueville's efforts to find appropriate leaders or their surrogates also helps to answer the question concerning the leader's proper role in this new democratic world. According to Tocqueville, leaders, ideally, would chart policy as in days of yore. Failing that, leaders and their proxies had the duty to inculcate appropriate values to the citizens of a democracy. Judges and juries, for instance, educated them about the rule of law and the need to decide matters according to standards beyond self-interest. Voluntary associations helped participants to understand the value of working together for group objectives. Religious commitment championed communal values and lifted one's vision to higher ends. Taken together, these 'habits of the heart' could raise citizens from narrow selfishness to 'self-interest rightly understood', which was perhaps as close to civic virtue as one could expect in a democratic society.

What is the Role of the People?

One of the realities of the democracy that Tocqueville studied was the omnipotence of the people. 'They are the cause and aim of all things;' he said, 'everything comes from them, and everything is absorbed in them.'[157] This seeming surrender of all power and authority to the citizenry constitutes, as we have seen, one of the fundamental challenges to the traditional leader. At the same time it creates the demand for the new fiction of leadership, which is devoted to setting forth the proper relationship between the few and the many when sovereignty resides in the many. Having assessed Tocqueville's conception of the appropriate role of the leaders, we can now look to his views on the appropriate role of the people in his new fiction.

His essential strategy was not to circumvent the people so much as to educate them and guide them in ways conducive to the making of wise policy. Much of Tocqueville's agenda was devoted to enhancing, in various ways, the political competencies of the people. Thus, his advocacy of local political participation, jury duty and voluntary associations all had the additional benefit of serving as schools for democratic citizenship. When it was possible, of course, Tocqueville gladly welcomed the guidance of wise and virtuous leaders, but he had resigned himself to a more indirect method of achieving the desired results.

In sum, Tocqueville was content (he had no other choice) to permit the people to be the driving force in the polity, but he extended himself to the utmost to harness the energies of the people in ways that befitted the public good.

How Should Leaders and the People Interact?

The reality that confronted Tocqueville as he assayed the relationship between leaders and the people was a revolutionary one. Throughout our chronological treatment of the relations between leader and follower since ancient times, we have been able to characterize the relationship as one of deference on the part of the people toward their leaders. It was this deference, indeed, that permitted something like the classical ideal to operate. Yet as the fiction of the people began to assert itself, we have also seen some chinks in the armor of deference. In the late seventeenth century, James Harrington created a fiction in which the elite deferred to the people as much as vice versa. And James Madison confronted a diminishing respect for traditional leaders as his career extended into the nineteenth century. It was, indeed, this decline in deference that historian Edmund S. Morgan claims generated the need for leadership. Yet it was Alexis de Tocqueville among our chosen commentators who first faced the full fury of egalitarian democracy and its implications for leader–follower relations. As we noted in the discussion of the role of the people, Tocqueville was quite cognizant of the revolutionary reversal implied by this development: now, rather than the many deferring to the superior wisdom and virtue of the few, it was expected that the few would serve as mere delegates of the many, obliged to fulfill their whims and desires.

Unfortunately for Tocqueville, he was not comfortable with this participationist version of the relations between leaders and the people. We know from our discussion of Tocqueville's views of the capabilities of the people to govern that he had no overwhelming respect for the wisdom or virtue of the many. Because of this, he admired the old deference to superior leaders and sought to replicate it where possible. Knowing this to be a frail reed upon which to support his efforts to secure wise policy, he also sought more innovative ways to modify the mindless, self-interested dominance of the many. He found relief, ironically enough, in the self-same self-interest. He had always maintained that the people would never knowingly do their own interests harm. It was this sense of self-preservation that Tocqueville relied upon when he advocated 'self-interest rightly understood.' One duty of good leaders and surrogates was to inject this notion into the mindset of the general populace. Once the people could be made to realize that acting in ways that preserved the good of the whole benefited each individual citizen in the long run, the way was also open to attempt to resurrect some of the old deferential relationships. That is to say, Tocqueville held out hope that democracy could be tamed, and it was through revised relations between leaders and the people that this might be achieved.

How is the Matter of Diversity and Minority Interests Addressed?

The related issues of diversity and minority rights did not receive primary attention until the emergence of two developments related to modernity. The first was the rise of egalitarian democracy and the accompanying decline of deference. Until the modern polity made its appearance on the scene, there was little sense that the actions of the leaders on behalf of society could be adverse to the interests of the whole. When such a perception did arise, such as in the case of the Stuarts in seventeenth-century England, the conclusion was that it was the oppressive leaders who were being revolutionary; they were transgressing the accepted norms (the norms themselves were fine). But once sovereignty truly gravitated to the people, the fiction of the ideal leader was exploded, and all actions by putative leaders came under increasing scrutiny. Now, for the first time (other than old-fashioned political oppression), the question arose as to whether elite actions were congruent with the interests of all.

Closely related to this was the second development: the recognition that there could be legitimate individual interests apart from, and even in conflict with, the interest of the majority. For millennia it had been a commonplace that the true interests of society were unitary, and that proper public policy was essentially a matter of discerning and addressing that interest. In the generation previous to Tocqueville, writers such as Adam Smith and James Madison (in his *Federalist Number 10*) had brought that traditional assumption into question. By Tocqueville's time, the longstanding premise had been reversed, and it was assumed that each citizen should pursue his or her own advantage.

This brings us to Tocqueville, who, typically, melded traditional inclinations with modern sensibilities. That is to say, Tocqueville remained attracted to the idea that there was a discernible external good in the public sphere, but he was also quite attuned to the reality of individual interests. To the outside observer, it was an uncomfortable marriage, but Tocqueville seemed unaware that he was straddling two divergent traditions (the liberal and the communitarian, addressed in the next two chapters, respectively). In any event, Tocqueville continued to call for leaders and institutions that looked to a public interest superior to self-centered activity, while at the same time demonstrating concern for individual interests. It is to the latter that this question of the leadership template focuses our attention.

With his railings against majority tyranny, Tocqueville staked out his concern for minority interests in democratic society. True to form, having identified the problem, he moved to suggest possible ways of protecting the minority in such a polity. One of his solutions was part-and-parcel with his advocacy of political education for citizens: he believed that local political participation and service on juries, and the like, would inculcate an appreciation of the rights of others. At a higher level of specificity, Tocqueville emulated Madison in his support for the specific legal protections of bills of rights, augmented by the actions of the judiciary. Then, too, Tocqueville sought ways in which those with interests inimical to that of the majority could bolster their position and give them a more effective voice, possibly even bringing the majority around to a new point of view. This was one of the chief benefits, Tocqueville believed, of voluntary associations.

Tocqueville's concern for minority interests in modern democracy represented a signal departure in the ongoing dialogue concerning this novel form of polity. A few years later John Stuart Mill would acknowledge Tocqueville's work as an inspiration for his classic work on the same topic, and the issue would thereafter become an unavoidable challenge for anyone contemplating the fiction of leadership in a democracy.

What Institutions and Processes Must be Designed to Accommodate the Premises and Assumptions about Leadership Articulated in the Response to the Leadership Template?

Much of the analysis of this chapter is devoted to cataloguing Tocqueville's responses to the leadership challenge as he perceived it. There is no need to replicate what has gone before, other than to indicate in broad outline the scope of his innovations. One attribute of his approach is worth noting, however. Tocqueville, when compared to earlier commentators, was quite forward-looking and modern in his response to democracy. It is of more than idle interest to note that while Madison called for 'a republican remedy for the diseases most incident to republican government',[158] Tocqueville instead argued that we must 'use Democracy to moderate Democracy'.[159] What this suggests is that while Madison confronted his challenges from the perspective of classical republicanism, Tocqueville accepted the actuality of modern democracy and sought remedies for its problems within that reality. This made Tocqueville, perhaps, the more relevant of our brace of early thinkers about leadership in a democracy.

Once he turned his attention to the problems of democracy, we have seen that Tocqueville was quite creative in his proposed responses. He embraced Madison's earlier institutional innovations – for example, his Constitutional separation of powers, bicameral legislature, indirect election of leaders and the like – but went far beyond those beginnings. He also advocated the resurrection of a vibrant local politics and the fostering of a robust civil society. Tocqueville also had the insight to reach beyond institutional solutions to advocate the cultivation of the 'habits of the heart' that were the cultural guideposts toward the wise operation of a modern democracy.

Tocqueville thus joins Madison as presenting a key early articulation of a blueprint for addressing the challenges of democracy. As such, he became the architect of a new fiction.

ALEXIS DE TOCQUEVILLE AND THE FICTION OF LEADERSHIP

We have defined the making of a fiction as the creation of an ideal set of values, institutions and processes designed to meet the demands of a current reality, and ultimately of sufficient suitability to the members of the populace to be accepted as correct, even if that fiction could never, in reality, become manifest in any pure sense. During the course of the historical analysis of this volume, we have put forward several 'fictions' as having reached the status of societal acceptability: the classical ideal of the leader, the divine right of kings, and the conception of the people as the constituting body of the state. With the emergence of the fiction of popular sovereignty, we also suggested that this created a demand for a new fiction that would guide, explain and justify the proper relations between the few and the many in a democratic world.

As Tocqueville said, 'a new science of politics is needed for a new world'.[160] With *Democracy in America*, he gave us all a substantial beginning toward that end. The next chapters will trace two more modern configurations of the appropriate relations in a democracy.

NOTES

1. Sheldon S. Wolin, *Tocqueville between Two Worlds: The Making of a Political and Theoretical Life* (Princeton: Princeton University Press, 2001), 3.
2. Ibid.
3. Alexis de Tocqueville, *Democracy in America* (1835, 1840), ed. Phillips Bradley, 2 vols (New York: Vintage Books, 1990), 1:7.
4. Ibid., 1:14.
5. Ibid., 1:7, 14.
6. Ibid., 1:53.
7. Ibid., 1:3.
8. Ibid.
9. Ibid., 1:53.
10. Ibid., 1:3.
11. Ibid., 1:54–55.
12. Ibid., 1:53, 58.
13. Ibid., 1:55.
14. Ibid., 1:173.
15. Ibid., 1:254.
16. Ibid., 1:155.
17. Ibid., 1:238.
18. Ibid., 1:259.
19. Ibid., 1:260.
20. Ibid., 2:290.
21. Ibid., 1:263.
22. Ibid., 2:10.
23. Ibid.
24. Ibid., 2:11.
25. Tocqueville, *Democracy in America*, quoted in Wolin, *Tocqueville between Two Worlds*, 342.
26. Tocqueville, *Democracy in America*, 1:230.
27. Ibid., 2:22.
28. Ibid., 2:99.
29. Ibid., 2:98.
30. Ibid.
31. Ibid., 2:293.
32. Ibid.
33. Ibid.
34. Ibid., 2:318.
35. Ibid.
36. Ibid.
37. Ibid., 2:319.
38. Ibid., 2:319, 321.
39. Ibid., 1:201.
40. Ibid., 1:200–202.
41. Ibid., 1:200.
42. Ibid.
43. Ibid., 1:201–202.
44. Ibid., 1:208.
45. Ibid., 1:202.
46. Ibid., 1:266–267.
47. Ibid., 1:201.
48. Ibid., 1:212.
49. Ibid., 1:251.
50. Ibid., 1:252–253.
51. Ibid., 1:252.
52. Ibid., 1:7.
53. Ibid., 2:322.
54. Ibid., 1:253.
55. Ibid., 1:260.
56. Ibid., 1:156.

57. Ibid.
58. Ibid., 1:261; *see also* 1:122, 1:154–156.
59. Ibid., 1:84; *see also* 1:154.
60. Ibid., 1:204–205.
61. Ibid., 1:156.
62. Wolin, *Tocqueville between Two Worlds*, 251–252 (see note 1).
63. Unpublished fragment, quoted in Wolin, *Tocqueville between Two Worlds*, 195.
64. Tocqueville, *Democracy in America*, 2:293.
65. Ibid., 1:243.
66. Ibid., 1:317.
67. Ibid., 2:103.
68. Ibid., 1:247–248.
69. Ibid., 1:245.
70. Ibid., 2:299.
71. Ibid., 2:300.
72. Ibid., 1:251.
73. Ibid., 1:61.
74. Ibid., 1:95.
75. Ibid., 1:35–37.
76. Ibid., 1:39.
77. Ibid., 1:272.
78. Ibid., 2:103.
79. Ibid., 2:105.
80. Ibid., 2:104.
81. Ibid., 2:105.
82. Ibid., 1:68.
83. Ibid., 1:203.
84. Ibid., 1:67.
85. Ibid., 2:223.
86. Ibid., 1:94.
87. Ibid., 2:106.
88. Tocqueville, *Democracy in America*, quoted in Wolin, *Tocqueville between Two Worlds*, 238 (see note 1).
89. Tocqueville, *Democracy in America*, 1:194, 196.
90. Ibid., 2:108–109.
91. Ibid.
92. Ibid., 2:116.
93. Ibid., 2:106–107.
94. Ibid., 2:324.
95. Ibid., 2:107.
96. Ibid.
97. Ibid., 2:110.
98. Wolin, *Tocqueville between Two Worlds*, 343.
99. Tocqueville, *Democracy in America*, 1:299.
100. Ibid., 1:325.
101. Tocqueville, *Democracy in America*, quoted in Wolin, *Tocqueville between Two Worlds*, 222; *see* Tocqueville, *Democracy in America*, 1:322.
102. Wolin, *Tocqueville between Two Worlds*, 223.
103. Tocqueville, *Democracy in America*, 1:74.
104. Ibid., 2:325.
105. Ibid., 1:94.
106. Ibid., 1:93.
107. Ibid., 1:280–282.
108. Ibid., 1:282–283.
109. Ibid., 1:284–285.
110. Ibid., 1:285.
111. Ibid., 1:93.
112. Ibid., 1:242–243.
113. Ibid., 1:242.
114. Ibid., 1:243.
115. Wolin, *Tocqueville between Two Worlds*, 324 (see note 1).
116. Ibid., 326, 224.

117. Tocqueville, *Democracy in America*, 2:22.
118. Ibid., 2:125.
119. Ibid., 2:145.
120. Wolin, *Tocqueville between Two Worlds*, 237.
121. Tocqueville, *Democracy in America*, quoted in Wolin, *Tocqueville between Two Worlds*, 325, 329.
122. Tocqueville, *Democracy in America*, 2:123–124.
123. Tocqueville, *Democracy in America*, quoted in Wolin, *Tocqueville between Two Worlds*, 280.
124. Tocqueville, *Democracy in America*, 2:121.
125. Ibid.
126. Ibid.
127. Ibid., 2:121–122.
128. Ibid., 2:125.
129. Ibid., 2:123.
130. Ibid., 1:52.
131. Ibid., 2:322.
132. Ibid., 1:202–203.
133. Ibid., 1:239–240.
134. Wolin, *Tocqueville between Two Worlds*, 9.
135. Tocqueville, *Democracy in America*, 1:236.
136. Ibid., 2:324.
137. Ibid., 1:175.
138. Ibid., 1:177.
139. Ibid., 1:100.
140. Ibid., 1:280.
141. Ibid., 1:278–279.
142. Ibid., 1:102.
143. Ibid., 1:272.
144. Ibid., 1:278.
145. Ibid., 1:273–274.
146. Ibid., 1:274–276.
147. Ibid., 1:279.
148. Tocqueville, *Democracy in America*, quoted in Wolin, *Tocqueville between Two Worlds*, 369 (see note 1).
149. Wolin, *Tocqueville between Two Worlds*, 378.
150. Ibid., 194.
151. Tocqueville, *Democracy in America*, quoted in Wolin, *Tocqueville between Two Worlds*, 336.
152. Tocqueville, *Democracy in America*, 2:248.
153. Ibid., 2:150–151.
154. Ibid., 2:329.
155. Ibid., 1:7.
156. Ibid., 1:251.
157. Ibid., 1:58.
158. James Madison, *Federalist Number 10*, in William T. Hutchinson, et al., eds, *The Papers of James Madison*, 17 vols. (Chicago: University of Chicago Press, 1962–77; Charlottesville: University Press of Virginia, 1977–), 10:267.
159. Tocqueville, unpublished fragment, quoted in Wolin, *Tocqueville between Two Worlds*, 195.
160. Tocqueville, *Democracy in America*, 1:7.

8. Inventing liberalism

In the previous two chapters, we have parsed the works of two of the most acute observers of the emerging phenomenon we call leadership. As we have seen, James Madison and Alexis de Tocqueville struggled mightily to concoct leadership solutions to the challenges posed by popular sovereignty, and in particular to its emergent form as mass democracy. It is not a coincidence that the productive portions of the careers of Madison and Tocqueville overlapped, if only slightly (in the 1830s). At about the same time – 1819 – another commentator was prescient enough to observe what may have been the most important development for the emergence of modern theory concerning leadership in a democracy. In that year, Benjamin Constant of Switzerland delivered an address that has since become a classic. Entitled *The Liberty of the Ancients Compared with That of the Moderns*, Constant was able to distinguish two fundamental philosophies, each of which would come to have important implications for modern thinking about leadership.[1] It is worth our while to begin this portion of our analysis by looking at the content of Constant's message:

'I wish to submit for your attention,' he began, 'a few distinctions, still rather new, between two kinds of liberty: these differences have thus far remained unnoticed, or at least insufficiently remarked. The first,' he continued, 'is the liberty the exercise of which was so dear to the ancient peoples; the second the one the enjoyment of which is especially precious to the modern nations.... The confusion of these two kinds of liberty,' he went on to assert, 'has been amongst us ... the cause of many an evil.'[2]

First, let us look at what Constant called 'the liberty of the ancients'. That form of liberty, Constant observed, 'consisted in an active and constant participation in collective power'. There was, he argued, 'the sharing of social power among the citizens.... This is what they called liberty', and 'the ancients were ready to make many a sacrifice to preserve their political rights and their share in the administration of the state.'[3]

Contrast this sense of communal political obligation with what Constant labeled 'the liberty of the moderns'. Looking around at his emerging modern world, Constant saw a much more individualistic conception of liberty. The moderns, he argued, are 'far more attached than the ancients to our individual independence.... The aim of the moderns is the enjoyment of security in private pleasures and they call liberty the guarantees accorded by institutions to these pleasures.' There was far less of a commitment to the political process. As Constant put it, modern 'freedom must consist of peaceful enjoyment and private independence.... The exercise of political rights ... offers us but a part of the pleasures that the ancients found in it....' In sum, he concluded, 'Individual liberty ... is the true modern liberty ...', and the role of the political system was solely to guarantee this individual liberty.[4]

Constant's perceptive distinctions serve us well as a point of departure for the next stage of our analysis. In this section of the text, it will be recalled, we are tracing the 'invention' of a new mode of social relations – a mode we call 'leadership' – which became a necessary response to the dialectic created by the emergence of notions of popular sovereignty alongside traditional notions of the ideal leader. Having reviewed the insights of two early commentators concerning the leadership challenges posed by the invention of a sovereign people (that is, those of Madison and Tocqueville), we now turn to two more systematic responses to this central challenge of the modern era.

These responses, which echo Constant's typology of ancient and modern conceptions of leadership, are best depicted by the modern scholar Charles Taylor. Taylor 'describes "two package solutions emerging out of the mists to the problem of sustaining a viable modern polity ..." which correspond roughly to the communitarian and liberal model[s]'.[5] This chapter and the next will explore two distinct constellations of ideas that we shall label, respectively, liberalism and communitarianism.

There arose, then, two central responses to the challenges posed by the emergence of popular sovereignty. In the language of this study, these responses can be viewed in terms of our now-familiar notion of 'fictions' – idealized constructs and systems created and utilized by those who accepted them as both intellectual and pragmatic solutions to the perceived challenges of a democratic era. These two fictions – liberalism and communitarianism – of course have deep roots in the past, yet at the same time have evolved into complex and sophisticated ideologies geared to modern needs.

It is important to note that these two modern leadership fictions are fundamentally at odds with one another. Constant recognized 'the opposed spirit of ancient and modern times'.[6] Modern political philosopher John Rawls adds, 'The course of democratic thought over the past two centuries or so makes plain that there is at present no agreement on the way the basic institutions of constitutional democracy should be arranged if they are to satisfy the fair terms of cooperation between citizens regarded as free and equal. This is shown,' he continues, 'in the deeply contested ideas about how the values of liberty and equality are best expressed....' Rawls ties this back directly to the distinction first articulated by Constant. 'We may think of this disagreement,' Rawls writes, 'as a conflict within the tradition of democratic thought itself, between the tradition associated with Locke, which gives greater weight to what Constant called "the liberties of the moderns," freedom of thought and conscience, certain basic rights of person and property, and the rule of law, and the tradition associated with Rousseau, which gives greater weight to what Constant called "the liberties of the ancients," the equal political liberties and values of public life.'[7]

These two approaches to the social relation we call leadership must be explored in some depth. They represent the most significant theoretical thinking about leadership at the present day. In the next two chapters, we will explore the nature of liberalism and communitarianism respectively, and relate our findings to the issue of leadership. To facilitate this, we will draw heavily upon the organizing function of the leadership template, although the questions contained therein may be rearranged to fit the logic of each commentator's argument, and, indeed, to fit the logic of the ideologies themselves. Use of the template will allow us to identify the contrasting underlying assumptions – the implicit theories – of these approaches, and to understand better, in Benjamin Barber's terms, the differing 'world views of individualism and communalism'.[8] Use of the template will also allow us to explore the leadership implications of each ideology. As we shall see, each approach poses certain difficulties for the operation of leadership in a democracy.

This chapter addresses the liberal solution to the challenges of democracy. We will look first to the works of two of the founding greats of modern liberalism, John Locke and

John Stuart Mill. We will then gain a sense of the current spectrum of liberal thought by exploring the ideas of modern commentators John Rawls and Robert Nozick. With this rich sampling of liberal thought in hand, we will be in a position to draw some conclusions about the nature of liberalism and its implications for leadership.

JOHN LOCKE

We can begin our examination of liberal thinking by looking to the works of one of liberalism's foundational figures, John Locke. Here, our chief focus will be upon a work entitled the *Second Treatise of Government*, which Locke subtitled as *An Essay Concerning the True Original, Extent, and End of Civil Government*.[9] Locke's work is familiar territory for most; here, through the mechanism of our leadership template, the objective is to distill from his work Locke's implicit theories concerning leadership in a democratic state. Accordingly, the analysis will pursue a series of questions patterned after our analytical template.

What is the (External) Leadership Challenge?

The initial query that has consistently guided our leadership analysis in this text is the following: What is the leadership challenge that generated the need to create (or 'invent') new ways of thinking about the relationship between the governed and their leaders? In our analysis of Locke – for reasons that should come clear shortly – the first question has been modified to address the 'external' leadership challenge facing Locke, by which we mean the surrounding societal and political circumstances that caused him to erect his system. Modern scholar Markate Daly provides us with a synopsis: 'The task of the early liberal philosophers [such as Locke] was to justify replacing the old monarchies with a democratic political order.... Locke [wrote] in the [era] of the English Revolution of 1688. Locke's purpose was to deny that monarchs have a divine right to rule and to establish that all political authority derives from the consent of the governed.'[10] In order to justify his ultimate response (which was to legitimate a liberal state controlled by the propertied classes), Locke first addressed with some care yet another fundamental question from the template of leadership.

What is the Perception of Human Nature?

Like Hobbes before him, Locke opened his analysis with a thoroughgoing exposition of what he calls a 'state of nature', which, for the sake of his argument at any rate, existed prior to the formation of society and civil government. As Locke scholar C.B. Macpherson indicates, however, 'Locke ... introduces the "natural" condition of mankind not as an historical condition existing before the emergence of civil society but as a logical abstraction from the essential nature of man'.[11] In Locke's own words, 'To understand political power right, and to derive from its original, we must consider, what state all men are naturally in'.[12]

Turning to this investigation of the nature of man in the state of nature, Locke's first emphasis was man's individual freedom. 'We must consider', he wrote, 'what state all men are naturally in, and that is a *state of perfect freedom* to order their actions, and dispose of their possessions and persons, as they think fit, within the bounds of the law of nature, without asking leave, or depending upon the will of any other man....' Indeed, he added, 'the *natural liberty* of man is to be free from any superior power on earth, and not to be under the will or legislative authority of man, but to have only the law of nature for his rule'. Moreover, said Locke, man's natural liberty is inviolable and non-negotiable. 'This freedom from absolute arbitrary power is so necessary to, and closely joined with a man's preservation,' he continued, 'that he cannot part with it, but by what he forfeits his preservation and life together....'[13]

In addition to men in their natural state having perfect freedom, it was, Locke found, 'a *state* also of *equality*, wherein all the power and jurisdiction is reciprocal, no one having more than another, there being nothing more evident, than that creatures of the same species and rank, promiscuously born to all the same advantages of nature, and the use of the same faculties, should also be equal one amongst another without subordination or subjection'.[14]

In addition to enjoying freedom and equality, man in his natural state was also rational. Indeed, according to Locke, 'the *freedom* then of man, and liberty according to his own will, is *grounded on* his having *reason*'.[15]

From the premises of individual freedom, equality and rationality, Locke derived a 'law of nature' that would prove to be the foundation for his theoretical edifice regarding the need for and purposes of government (and leadership). 'The *state of nature*', he said, 'has a law of nature to govern it, which obliges every one: and reason, which is that law, teaches all mankind, who will but consult it, that being all *equal* and *independent*, no one ought to harm another in his life, health, liberty, or possessions.'[16] Here , in conjunction with his original law of nature, we see Locke first propounding the centrality of the protection of his trilogy of life, liberty and property.

The issue of property, however, created some complications, and as a result, Locke's portrayal of the state of nature (and man's essential nature) was not so simple as it might first appear. As a defender of the propertied classes of England, Locke was faced with the challenge of justifying the accumulation of property and the inequalities that resulted. He began with a rather simple justification for the private ownership of property based upon one's individual labor. As Locke explained it, 'Though the earth, and all inferior creatures, be common to all men, yet every man has a *property* in his own *person*.... The *labour* of his body, and the *work* of his hands, we may say, are properly his. Whatsoever then he removes out of the state that nature hath provided ... he hath mixed his *labour* with and joined it to something that is his own, and thereby makes it his *property*.' This property then comes under the dominion of him who created it. Such ownership 'excludes the common right of other men: for this *labour* being the unquestionable property of the labourer, no man but he can have a right to what that is once joined to, at least where there is enough, and as good, left in common for others'.[17]

Locke thus had created a conception of private property from what had been held in common. In this natural state, however, the amount of property one man could own was limited by the necessity that he put it to good use – to possess only 'as much as any one can make use of to his advantage before it spoils ... whatever is beyond this, is more than his share, and belongs to others'.[18] Locke circumvented this natural roadblock to property accumulation by positing the eventual invention of money. This changed everything. As he explained it, 'the same *rule of propriety* ... that every man should have as much as he could make use of, would hold still in the world ... had not the *invention of money*, and the tacit agreement of men to put a value on it, introduced (by consent) larger possessions, and a right to them'. This served man's 'desire of having more than [he] needed ... [he] had *agreed, that a little piece of gold metal*, which would keep without wasting or decay, should be worth a ... whole heap of corn'.[19]

The invention of money allowed Locke to defend both the accumulation of property and the resulting inequality. It allowed the industrious to get ahead: 'as different degrees of industry were apt to give man possessions in different proportions,' Locke reasoned, 'so this *invention of money* gave them the opportunity to continue and enlarge them'.[20] A further consequence was that it legitimated inequality. Indeed, the very invention of money inferred this. 'Since gold and silver ... [have] ... value only from the consent of men ... it is plain, that men have agreed to a disproportionate and unequal *possession of the earth*, they having, by a tacit and voluntary consent, found out a way how a man can fairly possess more land than he himself can use the product of, by receiving in exchange for the overplus gold and silver, which may be hoarded up without injury to anyone.'[21]

Moreover, Locke thought that such individual accumulation and utilization of property was a great benefit to society. 'He who appropriates land to himself by his labours [or, Locke would argue, the labors of those under his guidance] does not lessen, but increase the common stock of mankind: for the provisions serving to support human life, produced by one acre of cultivated land, are .... ten times more than those which are yielded by an acre of land of an equal richness lying waste in common.'[22]

By way of this elaborate argument, Locke had put into place the last of his attributes of human nature that were destined to become the cornerstones of liberal thought. In addition to the fact that each individual is by nature free, equal and rational, Locke now had added man's innate love of property and its accumulation.

What is the (Internal) Leadership Challenge?

Locke's extensive exploration of the human condition by means of his state of nature laid the groundwork for his subsequent model for the relations between ruler and ruled. But there was yet one piece missing, a piece we will label the 'internal' leadership challenge. This challenge to Locke's desired ends has little to do with the surrounding political crisis of the late seventeenth century (the 'external' challenge); instead, it is a challenge that is internal to his theory. Specifically, Locke himself posed a challenge to his conception of life in his state of nature. And it was this second challenge that served as the catalyst for Locke's theory of governing, and a response that can be deemed to come under the rubric of 'leadership'.

In Locke's initial depiction of the state of nature, man's very rationality allowed him to self-police infringements on life, liberty and property. This early version he described as 'a state of peace and goodwill, mutual assistance, and preservation'.[23] But this rather idyllic state first portrayed by Locke was soon to be complicated. Later in his essay, Locke admitted that there is also a dark side to human nature that made the state of nature untenable. Although men could be rational, they could also be described as 'biased by their interests', 'partial to themselves', and motivated by 'passion and revenge'.[24] This, unfortunately, led to 'a state of enmity, malice, violence, and mutual destruction'.[25] In this state, men obviously behave badly. Rather than adhering to the rationality of the state of nature, 'the offender declares himself to live by another rule than that of reason and common equity ... and so he becomes dangerous to mankind ... [and] *would take away the freedom* that belongs to any'. Far from being a peaceful state of nature, this turn of events must 'be looked on as a *state of war*'.[26]

Locke's 'internal' leadership challenge, then, was how to construct relations among men that both preserved man's natural individual liberty and property while at the same time providing sufficient order to prevent unchecked liberty from undermining those same desired ends.

Locke's Proposed Solution

Locke's response to the seemingly inevitable state of war that occurs in the state of nature is justly famous. We will merely summarize it here, and devote most of our analytical efforts to the derivation of the implications for leadership through the application of the questions of the leadership template.

In summary form, as Locke puts it, in the state of nature '[man's] enjoyment of [liberty] is very uncertain, and constantly exposed to the invasion of others.... [T]he enjoyment of the property he has in this state is very unsafe, very insecure. This makes him willing to quit a condition which, however free, is full of fears and continual dangers: it is not without reason, that he seeks out, and is willing to join in the society with others ... for the mutual *preservation* of their lives, liberties, and estates, which I call by the general name, *property*.'[27] This constitutes the famous Lockean *social contract*. A key premise is that entry into this society is a voluntary act by each individual; man's very freedom in the state of nature requires that the move to civil society be voluntary and consensual: 'all men are naturally in [the state of nature] and remain so, till by their own consents they make themselves members of some politic society'.[28] Locke's reference to a 'politic society' is important. In addition to voluntarily coming together into a society, the constituents also agree to establish a government whose sole purpose it is to offer protection for those essential rights of life, liberty and property. '*Civil government*', he argued, 'is the proper remedy for the inconveniences of a state of nature.'[29]

The consequence of this momentous agreement to leave the state of nature and to form a political community was to create a new set of relationships, particularly among men and their rulers. 'Where-ever any number of men, in the state of nature, enter into society to make one people, one body politic, under one supreme government', says Locke, this action '*puts men* out of a state of nature *into* that of a *common-wealth*.'[30] The new social and political relations in Locke's commonwealth are at the heart of liberal notions of government and leadership. We can explore the nuances of Locke's thinking by returning to the guiding questions of the template of leadership.

What is the Proper End or Purpose of Leadership?

From the foregoing, the proper end or purpose of this new relationship among men and their government – a relationship that we deem a part of the leadership relation – becomes clear. As a result of the state of war that emerges in the state of nature, men come together in order to protect that which was endangered by the state of war. The general tenor of Locke's vision of the purpose of government (which for our purposes embraces the leadership relation as well) is shown by the epigraph he chose to place on the title page of his text: *Salus populi suprema lex esto*, which can be translated as 'the good of the people is the supreme law'.

Locke reinforced this essential message at several points in his text, each time making it clear that these expectations applied to those in charge of the state. In his most thoroughgoing exposition of this sentiment, he pointed out that *'political power* is that power which every man having in the state of nature, has given up into the hands of the society, and therein to the governors, whom the society hath set over itself, with this express or tacit trust, that it shall be employed for their good'.[31] At another point, he insisted that the power of government 'be directed at no other *end*, but the *peace, safety,* and *public good* of the people'.[32] And again: '*The first and fundamental natural law*, which is to govern the legislative itself, *is the preservation of the society* ... as far as will consist with the public good'.[33]

Having clearly staked out the general axiom, Locke went on to define with some precision what he meant by the public or common good. He simply returned to his now-familiar mantra: *'Political power'*, he said, 'can have no other *end* or *measure*, when in the hands of the magistrate, but to preserve the members of that society in their lives, liberties, and possessions.'[34] He placed a particular stress upon the protection of property. At more than one place in the text he stated that 'the great and *chief end*, therefore, of men's uniting into commonwealths, and putting themselves under government, *is the preservation of their property'*.[35] Indeed, at one point he specifically equated the common good with the protection of property. 'The power of society, or *legislative* constituted by them, can *never be supposed to extend further, than the common good*, but is obliged to secure every one's property by providing against those ... defects ... that made the state of nature so unsafe and uneasy.'[36] One modern scholar, C.B. Macpherson, has gone so far as to suggest that 'Locke's case for the limited constitutional state is largely designed to support his argument for an individual natural right to unlimited private property'. He went on to point out Locke's legacy in this regard: 'Defenders of the modern liberal state', Macpherson argues, 'see, or sense, that that right is at the heart of the state.'[37]

What is the Epistemology of Leadership?

One of the continuing queries in our analytical investigation of various theoretical formulations of the leadership relation involves how participants in that relation know what they are doing is 'right'; that is, how do they judge the propriety of actions? In some formulations, this matter takes a central place in the theoretical schema. Ironically, John Locke, known to have created one of Western civilization's foundational epistemological commentaries in his *Essay Concerning Human Understanding*, does not trouble himself overmuch with this question in the political realm. It is implied, however, that the epistemology of leadership is simply the reverse of that presented by the stated ends of leadership. That is to say, one judges the propriety of actions simply by looking at the extent to which they support or undermine the protection of life, liberty and property.

What Institutions and Processes are Needed?

Before turning to the next stage of the analysis, it may be useful to summarize Locke's argument thus far in leadership terms. In confronting the perceived challenges of his day created by the actions of the late Stuart kings, Locke had taken great care to justify his proposed response. He devoted a considerable amount of effort to the task of depicting (through his description of the state of nature) man's essential nature and his inherent rights. In language that would become crucial to liberal ideology, he depicted man as an independent entity who is by nature free, equal and rational. Moreover, humans – even in a state of nature – had developed, through the vehicle of the invention of money, the wherewithal to accumulate property. This, then, in Locke's emerging liberal ideology, was the reason men joined together into society, and indeed why society existed: to protect the individual's rights to life, liberty and property.

In Locke's schema, concomitant with the formation of society was the task of establishing the 'legislative', or government. As he put it, 'The great end of man's entering into society, being the enjoyment of their properties in peace and safety, and the great instrument and means of that being the law established in that society; *the first and fundamental positive law* of all commonwealths *is the establishing of the legislative power*, as the *first and fundamental natural law*, which is to govern even the legislative itself, *is the preservation of society*, and (as far as will consist with the public good) of every person in it'.[38] Locke next turned his attention, then, to the appropriate institutions, processes, and relationships among leaders and followers (that is, the people) to assure the intended ends of society (the preservation of life, liberty and property). In this section, we will explore what might be called the leadership structure of institutions Locke proposed. In subsequent sections, we will turn to a consideration of the respective roles of leaders and the people.

The first task of the sovereign people, then, once they had come together to form a society (a 'commonwealth'), was to establish a form of government to serve its intended purpose. Although Locke, in the context of late seventeenth-century England, was writing to justify a Parliamentary state, he took care in his theoretical statements to allow the people to choose any form of government. 'By *commonwealth*,' he said, 'I must be understood all along to mean, not a *democracy*, or any form of government, but *any independent community*.'[39] This could take any form, and indeed Locke echoed the classical typology of forms of government, familiar since the time of Aristotle. 'The majority having ... upon men's first uniting into society, the whole power of the community naturally in them, may employ all that power in making laws for the community.... [In that case], then the *form* of government is a perfect *democracy*....' However, the people could choose some other form. They could 'put the power of making laws into the hands of a few select men, and then it is an *oligarchy*; or else into the hands of one man, and then it is a *monarchy*.... Or, if desired, 'the community may make compounded and mixed forms of government, as they think good'.[40]

It is clear, however, that the ideal governmental form Locke had in mind was one modeled after the English Parliament, where the political power resided in a ruling legislature. 'In well-ordered commonwealths,' he wrote, 'where the good of the whole is to be considered, as it ought, the *legislative* power is put into the hands of divers persons, who duly assembled, have by themselves, or jointly with others, a power to make laws....'[41] Having placed sovereign power in the legislature, Locke also acknowledged the need for executive power, but such a power must be 'visibly subordinate and accountable to' the legislature.[42]

Beyond such general comments about the desired form of government, Locke remained relatively vague in terms of specifics. Nonetheless, he did enunciate two dominant principles that should guide all governmental undertakings, principles that have become central to all liberal states.

The first principle was that society should be governed according to the *rule of law*. According to Locke, 'absolute arbitrary power, or governing without settled *standing laws*, can neither of them consist with the ends of society and government'. Indeed, he stated in another place, *'Where-ever law ends, tyranny begins'*.[43] Consequently, a rule of law was necessary in a proper state, no matter what form it took. This notion of law, Locke believed, fulfilled, rather than restrained, liberty. As he put it, *'the end of law* is not to abolish or restrain, but *to preserve* and *enlarge freedom*; for in all the states of created beings capable of laws, *where there is no law, there is no freedom....* for law,' Locke elaborated, 'in its true notion, is not so much the limitation as *the direction of a free and intelligent agent* to his proper interest, and prescribes no farther than is for the general good of those under that law.'[44] For Locke, and for all subsequent liberals, government by laws and not by men was thus a necessity.

Locke's discussion of the rule of law highlights the second liberal essential: the fact that government is limited. Locke states that 'the *legislative* ... is *not*, nor can be absolutely *arbitrary* over the lives and fortunes of the people; for it being but the joint power of every member of society given up to that person or assembly, which is legislator'; therefore government 'can be no more than those had in a state of nature before they entered into society, and gave up to the community: for no body can transfer to another more power than he has himself ... and having in the state of nature no arbitrary power over life, liberty, or possession of another ... this is all he doth, or can give up to the commonwealth, and by it to the *legislative* power, so that the legislative cannot have more than this....'[45] 'Hence,' Locke concludes, 'it is a mistake to think, that the supreme or *legislative power* of any commonwealth can do what it will, and dispose of the estates of the subject *arbitrarily*, or to take any part of them at pleasure.'[46] With Locke and his liberal inheritors, then, comes the novel principle of a government of limited powers. It, too, has become a central tenet of liberal thinking.

Because those limitations on power were to be enforced by the only body superior to government – that is, the people – it behooves us now to look with some care at the respective roles of leaders and the people in Locke's liberal model.

What is the Role of the People?

Because John Locke is rightfully seen as one of the progenitors of popular sovereignty, his view of the respective roles of the people and their leaders is of particular importance to our ongoing study of various models of leadership in a democratic state. We will begin this part of our analysis of Locke by investigating his view of popular participation in the liberal state he advocates. The findings may be somewhat surprising to modern observers steeped in current mores of popular participation. Although he is fundamentally attached to the notion of the theoretical sovereignty of the people, that constituting body has little role to play in the day-to-day operations of the polity.

Perhaps the most dramatic of Locke's statements regarding the role of the people relates to the creation of the 'social contract' that serves as the foundations of society and government. The premise of this contract is that the people are indeed sovereign, and that this is their original act of sovereignty. The contract, acknowledged Locke, was most certainly an act of the people. 'The people', he noted, 'are … a society of rational creatures, entered into a community for their mutual good….' Once formed, their initial act was to 'set rulers over themselves, to guard, and promote that good'.[47] This 'constitution of the legislative', he affirmed, is 'the original and supreme act of the society [people]'.[48] It was thus an inescapable conclusion that all political '*power has its original only from compact and agreement, and the mutual consent of those who make up the community*'.[49]

Locke's mention of consent was not idle; because those coming to the contract were free individuals, they could enter into this new relationship only voluntarily. 'The *beginning of political society* depends upon the consent of the individuals, to join into, and make one society'; 'when any number of men have so *consented to make one community or government*, they are thereby presently incorporated, and make *one body politic*.'[50]

Once the body politic has been created, however, a new dynamic appears. Once the government is formed, political sovereignty, in effect, shifts to the elected leaders. The people thereafter are expected to be duly subservient to its actions – unless and until it oversteps its appointed bounds. Locke acknowledged that (in his case of England) 'the legislative consists of *representatives* chosen by the people'. Once in place, however, that body is sovereign, 'the *people … having … no power* to act as long as the government stands'.[51] The one, obvious, exception was on election day. On that day sovereignty was re-invested in the people. On that day the leaders were 'chosen … by the people, which afterward return into the ordinary state of subjects, and have no share in the legislative but upon a new choice….'[52] Once the new government is in place, again, 'the *legislative* is not only *the supreme power* of the commonwealth, but sacred and unalterable in the hands where the community have once placed it'.[53]

This brings us to one of Locke's important points regarding the limitations placed on the role of the people in his polity. He illustrated the point in the form of a question: '*May the commands of a prince be opposed? may* he be resisted as often as any one shall find himself aggrieved, and but imagine he has not right done him?' Locke's answer was in the negative. 'This will unhinge and overturn all politics,' he suggested, 'and instead of government and order, leave nothing but anarchy and confusion.'[54] This led to a peculiar sort of liberty in Locke's state. Man was free to do as he pleased, *so long as* it did not run afoul of the law. In Locke's liberal state, one had the liberty to be ruled by law, within the realm to which such law extended. '*Freedom of men under government*', Locke maintained, 'is, to have a standing rule to live by, common to every one of that society and made by the legislative power erected in it; a liberty to follow my own will in all things, where the rule prescribes not….' 'The *liberty of man*, in society', then, 'is to be under no other legislative power, but that established, by consent, in the commonwealth; nor under the dominion of any will, or restraint of law, but what that legislative shall enact, according to the trust put in it.'[55]

Locke summed it nicely in terms of a trade-off: 'For being now in a new state, wherein he is to enjoy many conveniences, from the labour, assistance, and society of others in the same community, as well as protection from its whole strength; he is to part also with as much of his natural liberty, in providing for himself, as the good, prosperity, and safety of the society shall require, which,' Locke concluded, 'is not only necessary, but just, since the other members of society do the like.'[56]

We have seen thus far that sovereignty resides in the people, and it is only through their actions that the state comes into being at all, via the social contract. Once the government – 'the legislative' – is in place, however, the role of the people changes. They continue to exercise their sovereignty on election days when they select their representatives, but thereafter, in the usual course of things, the people are expected to defer to the actions of the legislature and the prerogative of the executive. During the majority of the time, then, the people are to remain quiescent, and follow the rules of law established by the legislative.

However, just as the people are the constitutive force in the creation of the state, so too do they retain ultimate power to disband the state, albeit in limited circumstances. Locke described the dynamics well. He began with the general rule: 'In a constituted commonwealth ... there can be but *one supreme power*, which is the *legislative*, to which all the rest must be subordinate'. However, this was not without exception. 'Yet the legislative being only a fiduciary power to act for certain ends, there remains still *in the people a supreme power to remove or alter the legislative* when they find the *legislative* act contrary to the trust reposed in them.' This meant that, in actuality, 'the *community* perpetually *retains a supreme power* of saving themselves from the attempts and designs of any body, even of the legislators, whenever they shall be so foolish, or so wicked, as to lay and carry on designs against the liberties and properties of the subject'. Thus, 'the *community* may be said in this respect to be *always the supreme power*'. Locke was careful, however, to limit this ascendancy of the people to cases when the government had actually been dissolved due to its abuses. Popular supremacy cannot occur 'under any form of government, because this power of the people can never take place till the government be dissolved'.[57] Thereafter, however, the people returned to the sovereignty they had enjoyed at the time of the original social contract. 'In those and like cases, *when the government is dissolved*, the people are at liberty to provide for themselves, by erecting a new legislative, differing from the other, by the change of persons, forms, or both, as they shall find it most for their safety and good: for the *society* can never, by the fault of another, lose the native and original right it has to preserve itself....'[58]

We will return to the dynamics of the right of rebellion when we turn to a consideration of the template question about the appropriate relationship between leaders and the people in Locke's liberal polity. Suffice it to say for now that Locke posited a sovereignty in the people, who act as the constitutive body of the polity, and retain the right to abolish it as well. During the run of day-to-day activities, however – save for election day – Locke did not anticipate an active citizen presence. This conclusion raises another, related question that we have included in our template of leadership.

Are the People Capable of Governing?

Locke nowhere answers this question directly, although his view can be inferred from what has gone before. Certainly Locke created his entire liberal edifice upon his view of the individual as free, equal and rational, and there is no doubt that the government's authority came from the people (an innovation in his day that would undergird the rise of popular sovereignty). Moreover, the fact that governments are created and dissolved at the will of the people suggests that Locke believed the rational aspect of human nature fully capable of realizing, and acting on, the inherent natural rights of life, liberty and property. To further buttress his positive view of the people, he specifically rejected claims that the people might abuse the right of rebellion and easily revolt for small reasons.

To all these accolades, however, must be added a note of caution. Locke's work was created in the specific circumstances of the latter decades of the seventeenth century in England, and his ultimate purpose was to justify a dominant political role for the propertied classes in English society. This is the reason he went to such lengths to justify the right of the accumulation of property in his state of nature. Politically, he fully expected this group of elite to be the politically active portion of the populace, not the masses. As C.B. Macpherson has observed, 'Locke ... never intended [those without property] to be full members. He took for granted that the right to vote in elections to the legislature was to be confined to the propertied class.'[59] Further evidence of Locke's suspicions about popular competency arises internally within the text. Even (presumably) within the propertied classes who were to be active in Locke's state, he was careful to restrict popular activity, in the normal course of things, to voting on election day. All the day-to-day policy making was to be in the hands of elected representatives, presumably of superior capacities.

Locke thus becomes among the first in a long line of writers who champion 'popular sovereignty' without embracing popular participation, and/or adhering to continued rule by the elite (recall Edmund Morgan's depiction of the rise of popular sovereignty in England and America, and our extended treatment of the thought of American Founding Father James Madison). This will remain a central challenge of liberal – and indeed, all forms of – democracy.

Having traced the rather tentative role Locke envisioned for the people in his commonwealth (that is, the people were sovereign yet played little role in policy making), it is all the more important that we look to the expectations and constraints he placed upon those who were to serve in the role of leaders.

What is the Role of the Leader?

The dissonance of Locke's view of the people, where the ultimate sovereign in actuality plays a limited role in governance, is mirrored in his treatment of leaders (those in the 'legislative') who were seemingly circumscribed by his notions of limited government, but who in actuality had rather wide latitude for action. Given our concern with the leadership relation, it is worth our while to parse out Locke's thinking in this regard.

In looking to the expectations of the leader in Locke's schema, one finds an intriguing tension. On the one hand, Locke is quite careful to note that leaders, as part of government, are subject to the same limitations. As Locke put it, 'the power of the society, or *legislative*, constituted by them, *can never be supposed to extend farther, than the common good*, but is obliged to secure every one's property, by providing against those ... defects ... that made the state of nature so unsafe and uneasy'.[60] Locke took the time to spell out some of the specific expectations of those in leadership roles. 'Whoever has the legislative or supreme power of any commonwealth, is bound to govern by established *standing laws*, promulgated and known to the people, and not by extemporaneous decrees; by *indifferent* and upright *judges*, who are to decide controversies by those laws; and to employ the force of the community at home, *only in the execution of such laws....* And all of this to be directed to no other *end*,' Locke concluded, 'but the *peace, safety,* and *public good* of the people.'[61]

Locke's vehemence in articulating such limitations on those who promulgated and executed the laws gives – at first blush – the appearance of an emasculated government under his scheme. But this is an erroneous impression. So long as leaders did not overstep the bounds into arbitrary government, Locke allowed them rather vast leeway. A good example of this can be seen in what may be called the 'Lockean prerogative'.

The 'prerogative' is the power the executive has to act without specific legislative permission. As we have seen, in Locke's recommended polity the legislature held the reins of authority. That makes his treatment of the executive prerogative all the more impressive. Even in granting ascendancy to the legislature, Locke had acknowledged that there was an important executive function to perform as well. When the legislature was not in session, someone must, in Locke's words, 'make use of the prerogative for the public good ... and where else could this be so well placed as in his hands who was intrusted with the execution of the laws for the same end? ... it naturally fell into the hands of the executive'.[62] To accomplish this, the executive must be granted the prerogative, defined by Locke as 'being nothing but a power, in the hands of the prince, to provide for the public good'.[63] Or, in more detail, '*prerogative* can be nothing but the people's permitting their rulers to do several things, of their own free choice, where the letter of the law was silent, *and sometimes against the direct letter of the law* [emphasis supplied], for the public good, and their acquiescing in it when so done'.[64]

The prerogative thus was only limited, in practice, by the rather vague construct of the 'public good'. In framing it in these terms, Locke's grant of authority to the executive leader was rather staggering. At one point, Locke further defined the prerogative thus: 'This power to act according to the public good, *without the prescription of law, and some times even against it* [emphasis supplied], is that which is called *prerogative*'.[65] Moreover, Locke specifically restricted criticism of such a broad power in the hands of the executive. 'This power whilst employed for the benefit of the community, and suitably to the trust and ends of government, is *undoubted prerogative*, and never is questioned....' Thus the prerogative, when used within its limits, was exempt from popular scrutiny. Locke noted that the people 'are far from examining *prerogative*, whilst it is in any tolerable degree employed for the use it was meant, that is, for the good of the people, and not manifestly against it'.[66] And, indeed, 'a good prince, who is mindful of the trust put into his hands, and careful of the good of his people cannot have *too much prerogative*, that is, the power to do good....'[67]

We know – and Locke makes clear – that this power was not unlimited. Nevertheless, it is equally clear that Locke was content to place a considerable amount of discretionary power into the hands of his leaders – even to such lesser functionaries as those who did not make, but merely executed the laws. In sum, the role of the leader, too, was laced with ambiguity. In the next section, again turning to the template of leadership, we will seek to sort out Locke's complex equation of leaders and the people in his liberal state.

How Should Leaders and the People Interact?

We have now seen the somewhat paradoxical set of expectations that Locke posits for both the people and their leaders in his liberal state. The people are deemed to have absolute sovereignty, yet exercise little authority over those chosen to represent them in government. The leaders, on the other hand, are at all times subject to the sovereign power of the people, but in the actual course of events have a great deal of latitude in their actions. They are restricted only by the rather vague dictate to act in the people's interests. Other than indirectly through the ballot box, Locke provides only one instance in which the people dictate to their rulers: that is, in the people's right of rebellion. In this section, we will deduce Locke's expectations regarding the proper relationship between leaders and the people, then look to its limits, that is, the people's right to rebel. In the process, we can elucidate the boundaries of both leaders and the people.

One image that Locke evokes time and again is that leaders are granted a precious 'trust' that they must uphold and honor at all times. 'A good prince', Locke said, '... is mindful of the trust put into his hands....'[68] Likewise the 'legislative shall ... [act] according to the trust put in it'.[69] 'The legislative [has] ... only a fiduciary power to act for certain ends....'[70] Those ends are indeed the ends of leadership outlined previously. The powers granted to leaders must be utilized 'not as an arbitrary power ... but with this trust always to have it exercised only for the public weal', and leaders 'never have a right to destroy, enslave or designedly to impoverish the subjects'.[71]

Assuming the leaders honor this trust, the people are to remain subservient and quiescent. Although Locke nowhere uses the term, it is clear that what he expects is that the relationship between leaders and the people should be one of deference on the part of the people to their chosen leaders. Given both the limited activity allocated to the people in the normal course of events, and the wide powers granted the leaders when they act in good faith, no other interpretation is reasonably possible. Locke was thus able to graft his revolutionary doctrine of sovereignty in the people on to a quite conservative reading of leader–follower relations. His early version of liberalism, then, suggests that elite leadership and democracy are not necessarily antithetical.

It behooves us to explore briefly the limits of this deference, for the exception gives clarity to the rule. The exception, of course, is the people's standing right to rise up and overthrow any leader or government who betrays the trust granted them. In such a case, when the government or leaders 'go about to enslave or destroy' the people, although they 'have no appeal on earth', nevertheless they 'have a liberty to appeal to heaven', and 'they should rouze themselves, and endeavor to put the rule into such hands which may secure to them ends for which government was first erected' – that is, they have not only the right, but the duty to revolt and throw over the tyrannical leaders or government.[72]

What is striking, however, is how limited Locke envisioned this right of rebellion to be. 'Nor let one think', he allowed, 'this lays a perpetual foundation for disorder, for this operates not, till the inconveniency is so great, that the majority feel it and are weary of it, and find a necessity to have it amended.'[73] 'Such *revolutions happen*,' he asserted, 'not upon every little mismanagement in public affairs. *Great mistakes* in the ruling part, many wrong and inconvenient laws, and all the *slips* of human frailty, will be *born by the people* without mutiny or murmur.' It is only when 'a long train of abuses, prevarications, and artifices, all tending the same way, make the design visible to people', and they are 'persuaded in their consciences, that their laws, and with them their estates, liberties, and lives are in danger', that a rising is justified.[74]

With this limited right of revolution, Locke confirmed not only the central tenets of liberal thought regarding popular sovereignty, limited government, and the protection of individual rights, but also suggested that such a governing philosophy could operate comfortably within a regime having strong leaders with considerable latitude for action.

How is the Matter of Diversity and Minority Interests Addressed?

With the foregoing analysis, we have subjected Locke's liberal philosophy to a rigorous examination from the perspective of leadership – the new relationship among rulers and ruled that emerged as a result of the novel belief in the sovereignty of the people. The only query contained in our template of leadership left unaddressed – that is, the treatment of minorities and diversity, was left until last because it offers the perfect segue into the work of our second founder of liberalism, John Stuart Mill. This is because Locke, for his part, largely ignored this problem. He was, of course, fundamentally concerned with infringements on individual rights, but differences of opinion and views among the people were not his concern. Occupied as he was with legitimating resistance to a tyrannical king, he paid little attention to the potential problems experienced by those in the minority in a democratic state.

Locke's position was clear. 'When any number of men have so *consented to make one community or government*,' he said, 'they are thereby presently incorporated and make *one body politic*, wherein the *majority* have a right to act and conclude the rest.'[75] Indeed, Locke found it impossible to imagine how a polity could operate otherwise. The social contract formed a '*community* ... with a power to act as one body, which is only by the will and determination of the *majority*'. If this be not so, Locke reasoned, 'it is impossible it should act or continue [as] one body, *one community*'. Without majority rule, 'this *original compact*, whereby [an individual] incorporates into one society, would signify nothing'.[76]

The liberal concern with differences of opinion within society would await other commentators, concerned with other challenges. This brings us to the second of the twin towers of early liberalism.

JOHN STUART MILL

Standing alongside John Locke in the pantheon of early liberal thinkers is John Stuart Mill. While Locke was instrumental in setting forth the grounding principles of liberalism, Mill, writing in the middle of the nineteenth century, adapted those principles to the new demands of a democratic age. Confronting new challenges, and drawing upon a different justification (that is, utilitarianism), John Stuart Mill nonetheless was an equal contributor with Locke to the 'invention' of a coherent modern response to the emergence of a popular state. In 1859, nearly two centuries after Locke's seminal work, Mill wrote an essay entitled *On Liberty*. It stands next to Locke's *Second Treatise* as a foundational treatise of modern liberalism, and has been called 'the quintessential statement of liberal principles'.[77]

The initial portion of our treatment of Mill's thought, then, will involve the same kind of careful analytical treatment of *On Liberty* as we have just accorded Locke's *Second Treatise*. However, in our quest for the antecedents of the liberal version of the emerging leadership relation between rulers and the people, a consideration of *On Liberty* alone is insufficient. As brilliantly as it espouses the grounding principles of liberalism, it contains few details to guide its actual political application in the public sphere, to include its implications for the actions of leaders and the people, and the institutions and processes that are required. For this, we will turn to another of Mill's essential works, *Considerations on Representative Government*.[78] Between the two texts, we can glean Mill's contributions to the evolving liberal solution to emerging democracy. Again, the template of leadership will help us to structure our analysis. And, again, the ordering and wording of the questions of the template will be adapted to fit Mill's argument.

What is the Leadership Challenge?

From his vantage point in the mid-nineteenth century, Mill acknowledged the nature of the early leadership challenge that led Locke to midwife the emergence of liberalism in the late seventeenth century. 'The struggle between liberty and authority', he wrote, 'is the most conspicuous feature in … history. But in old times this contest was between subjects, or some classes of subjects, and the government. By liberty was meant protection against the tyranny of political rulers….'[79] However, as modern scholar Markate Daly notes, 'by the time Mill wrote in the middle of the nineteenth century, the basic political liberties at issue in the previous centuries had already been won'. Instead, Mill 'campaigns for liberty on a new front'.[80]

   That 'new front' was nothing less than the emergence of democracy. Writing in the mid-nineteenth century in Britain, Mill was deeply influenced by Tocqueville's recent work in America. As we know, Tocqueville, in the words of modern scholar Elizabeth Rapaport, 'described a society that was moving toward cultural homogeneity and conformity. In America, the tastes and prejudices of the mass public were a power to be reckoned with, potentially more inhospitable to deviants and innovators than crown, aristocracy, and established church had been.'[81] What concerned Mill, as it had Tocqueville, were the implications for liberty. 'The will of the people', he pointed out, '… means the will of the most numerous or the most active *part* of the people – the majority….' The problem was that 'the people … *may* desire to oppress a part of their number'. As a result, warned Mill, 'precautions are as much needed against this as against any other abuse of power'. Mill even borrowed Tocqueville's phrase when he concluded that '"the tyranny of the majority" is now generally included among the evils [against] which society requires to be on its guard'.[82]

   Like Tocqueville, however, Mill embraced democracy. Nevertheless, he sought a way to resolve this dilemma of a tyrannous majority, a dilemma that placed him squarely in the liberal camp: that is, in Rapaport's words, Mill sought a solution for the reality that '*democratic society does not automatically protect individual and minority liberty*'.[83] As Mill phrased it, 'The subject of this essay is … civil, or social liberty: the nature and limits of the power which can be legitimately exercised by society over the individual'. It was, Mill suggested, 'a question … [that] is likely soon to make itself recognized as the vital question of the future'.[84]

   It is important to recognize that Mill's concern for individual freedom went beyond Locke's merely political preoccupation. Mill acknowledged that 'like other tyrannies, the tyranny of the majority was at first … held in dread, chiefly as operating through the acts of public authorities'. However, 'reflecting persons perceived that when society is itself the tyrant – society collectively over the separate individuals who compose it – its means of tyrannizing are not restricted to the acts which it may do by the hands of its political functionaries'. Rather, 'society can and does execute its own mandates; and if it issues … mandates … in things with which it ought not to meddle, it practices a social tyranny more formidable than many kinds of political oppression…. Protection, therefore, against the tyranny of the magistrates,' Mill concluded, 'is not enough, there needs protection also against the tyranny of the prevailing opinion and feeling, against the tendency of society to impose, by other means than civil penalties, its own ideas and practices as rules of conduct on those who dissent from them….' Mill suggested that the answer to 'the practical question where to place the limit – how to make the fitting adjustment between individual independence and social control – is a subject on which nearly every thing remains to be done'.[85]

In consequence of this particular definition of the challenge confronting society, Mill crafted a response that has ever since been at the heart of the liberal rejoinder to the rise of democracy. His effort helped to further define the liberal perception of human nature, and the proper purposes and processes of government and leadership. In particular, Mill made a frontal assault on an issue that Locke had found inconsequential: the need for the protection of individual and minority interests in a majoritarian society. Mill's solution, as well as his justification for it, have become a part of the core of liberalism.

What is the Perception of Human Nature?

When John Locke set about justifying resistance to tyrannical governments, he devoted a good deal of effort to the construction of a fictional state of nature that depicted man's essential nature – a nature he portrayed as free, equal and rational, and devoted to the accumulation of property. Taking Locke's premises as a given, John Stuart Mill was much more focused. He stressed the glories of human individuality. 'There is no reason', he wrote, 'that all human existence should be constructed on some one or small amount of patterns. If a person possesses any tolerable amount of common sense and experience,' Mill allowed, 'his own mode of laying out his existence is the best, not because it is the best in itself, but because it is his own mode.' This was the key. 'Human beings are not like sheep,' he pointed out, 'and even sheep are not indistinguishably alike.'[86]

What is the Proper End or Purpose of Leadership?

Mill's perception that individuality defined the human condition made the segue to the appropriate ends or purposes of leadership easy. For Mill, man's laudable individuality gave rise to a metaphor of the human endeavor. 'Among the works of man which human life is rightly employed in perfecting and beautifying,' Mill asserted, 'the first in importance is surely man himself.... Human nature is not a machine to be built after a model, and set to do exactly the work prescribed for it, but a tree which requires to grow and develop itself on all sides, according to the tendency of the inward forces which make it a living thing.'[87]

This in turn, gave rise to the leadership obligation. It was the demand that each person be allowed to realize his or her (Mill was quite attentive to gender issues) possibilities, to achieve 'a Greek ideal of self-development'.[88] It followed from this that individuals must have the space to realize their own unique capabilities according to their own lights. 'It is the privilege and proper condition of a human being', Mill concluded, '... to use and interpret experience in his own way....'[89] A society structured to encourage this was Mill's ultimate purpose. 'It is only the cultivation of individuality which produces, or can produce, well-developed human beings', he maintained. 'For what more or better can be said of any condition of human affairs than that it bring human beings themselves nearer to the best they can be?'[90] For leaders and government, the path was clear. As Mill put it in the context of the larger society, 'It is not by wearing down into uniformity all that is individual in themselves, but by cultivating it and calling it forth, within the limits imposed by the rights and interests of others, that human beings become a noble and beautiful object of contemplation', he asserted. 'In proportion to the development of his individuality, each person becomes more valuable to himself, and is, therefore, capable of being more valuable to others.'[91] This explains Mill's choice of epigraph for his volume, from William von Humboldt's appropriately entitled *Spheres and Duties of Government*: 'The grand, leading principle, towards which every argument unfolded in these pages directly converges, is the absolute, essential importance of human development in its richest diversity'.[92]

How is the Matter of Diversity and Minority Interests Addressed?

The mention of 'diversity' in Humboldt's epigraph was more than coincidence. From Mill's choice of emphasis on individuality and human development – as opposed to Locke's concern with liberating the people as a whole from political oppression – it becomes clear that the leadership issue of most interest to Mill was the one Locke was concerned with least: the matter of diversity and minority interests. Rapaport has stated that 'John Stuart Mill was among the first to appreciate and explore the issues raised by the inevitable conflict between minority rights and majority rule. His essay *On Liberty* … remains the essential starting point for discussion of this vital and never fully resolved problem of democratic society.'[93]

Mill's rhetoric clearly suggests the importance of each of these issues to the version of liberalism that he was concocting. Regarding diversity, he wrote '… [T]here should be different opinions [and] … different experiments of living … free scope should be given to varieties of character, short of injury to others; and … the worth of different modes of life should be proved practically, when anyone thinks fit to try them.' In sum, 'diversity [is] not an evil, but a good'.[94] Similarly, Mill was keen to prevent the oppression of any minority by a majority. '… [T]he opinion of a … majority imposed … on the minority, on questions of self-regarding conduct is quite as likely to be wrong as right, for in these cases public opinion means, at the best, some people's opinion of what is good or bad for other people….'[95] In sum, it was Mill's considered view that 'to give any fair play to the nature of each [individual], it is essential that different persons should be allowed to lead different lives'.[96]

At the same time, Mill was not unaware of the legitimate demands of political – indeed, any – society. 'It would be a great misunderstanding of this doctrine to suppose', he warned, 'that it is one of selfish indifference, which pretends that human beings have no business with each other's conduct in life….'[97] He recognized that 'all that makes existence valuable to anyone depends on the enforcement of restraints upon the actions of other people. Some rules of conduct, therefore, must be imposed…. What these rules should be', he concluded, 'is the principal question in human affairs.'[98]

Mill's proposed resolution of the challenge of individual idiosyncrasy and minority interests is as justly famous as was Locke's answer to the problem of arbitrary tyrants. Mill sought to derive a universal principal to guide actions both governmental and personal. Indeed, he asserted that one of the problems had been the lack of such a standard: 'It seems to me,' he said, 'that in consequence of this absence of rule or principle, one side is at present as often wrong as the other; the interference of government is, with equal frequency, improperly invoked and improperly condemned.' Therefore, 'The object of this essay', he wrote in *On Liberty*, 'is to assert one very simple principle, as entitled to govern absolutely the dealings of society with the individual in the way of compulsion and control'.[99]

Mill then proceeded to state the principle: 'That principle', he said, 'is that the sole end for which mankind are warranted, individually and collectively, in interfering with the liberty of action of any of their number is self-protection'. To elaborate: 'The only purpose for which power can be rightfully exercised over any member of a civilized community against his will, is to prevent personal harm to others.... To justify that, the conduct from which it is desired to deter him must be calculated to produce evil to someone else.'[100] Mill eventually acknowledged that the rule was not quite as clear-cut as might first appear. There would be areas open to interpretation. 'As soon as any part of a person's conduct affects prejudicially the interests of others,' however, 'society has jurisdiction over it.' At that point, 'the question whether the general welfare will or will not be promoted by interfering with it becomes open to discussion'.[101] He went so far as to suggest a corollary to help guide the debate. 'When, by conduct of this sort, a person is led to violate a distinct and assignable obligation to any other person or persons, the case is taken out of the self-regarding class and becomes amenable to moral disapprobation....'[102] Mill devoted a great deal of the closing parts of his essay to the exploration of possible applications.

Interim Summary

In his classic essay *On Liberty*, then, John Stuart Mill achieved a revolutionary redefinition of the individual for whom the liberal state was created. Assuming that mankind remained the sort that deserved the protections of life and liberty championed by Locke (albeit for different reasons; see below), Mill went on to assert that each individual was a being of such inherent dignity and possibility that such individuality was also a right and privilege which had to be protected.

Consequently, Mill also created a state even more limited in some respects than the liberal edifice erected by Locke. Locke's state was limited by the illegitimacy of any interference with essential human rights. Mill's state prevented unwarranted impositions upon human thoughts, and, to a somewhat lesser extent, actions. Mill's liberal state was a citadel for the development of human potential.

Two other distinctions between Locke and Mill are worthy of note. Mill had a differing take on the basis of the state. He eschewed Locke's social contract as a necessary artifice. 'The society is not founded on a contract,' he proclaimed, 'and ... no good purpose is answered by inventing a contract in order to derive social obligations from it.' In so doing, Mill also, implicitly, undercut the social and political ties that accompanied Locke's contract, although Mill acknowledged that 'everyone who receives the protection of society owes a return for the benefit....'[103] The nature of political relations in Mill's liberal state is set out below.

Finally, it is useful to note one other important aspect of Mill's approach that distinguishes him from earlier writers such as Locke, as well as from several of the modern contributors to modern liberalism such as John Rawls. This is his 'utilitarianism'. Normally stated in the shorthand 'the greatest good for the greatest number', Mill's theory, in the words of modern scholar Michael Sandel, 'defends liberal principles in the name of maximizing the general welfare. The state should not impose on its citizens a preferred way of life, even for their own good, because doing so will reduce the sum of human happiness, at least in the long run. It is better that people choose for themselves, even if, on occasion, they get it wrong.'[104] As Mill himself put it, 'It is proper to state that I forego any advantage which could be derived to my argument from the idea of abstract right as a thing of independent utility.... I regard utility as the ultimate appeal on all ethical questions; but it must be utility in the largest sense, grounded on the permanent interests of man as a progressive being....'[105] Although his rationale differed, Mill came down squarely in the liberal camp with respect to the valuing of individual initiative and its fruits. However, as we shall see shortly, it was in part disagreement with Mill's utilitarianism that sparked Rawls to reinvigorate liberal thinking in the late twentieth century.

The Tensions of Democratic Leadership

Mill's essay *On Liberty* has become a landmark of liberal thinking, what with its focus upon the dignity of the individual and the limited role government should play in the lives of its citizens. Although the underlying values are clear, *On Liberty*, however, says very little about the pragmatic processes of leadership that also concern us. That is to say, it provides little guidance with respect to key questions from the template of leadership such as the appropriate role of leaders and the people, or the institutions and processes needed in a liberal democratic state. Fortunately, Mill did not ignore such essential issues. In other writings throughout his career he addressed them, most notably in one of his later works entitled *Considerations on Representative Government*. This work, when considered in conjunction with the earlier principles set forth in *On Liberty*, establishes a blueprint for a liberal state that has shaped thinking about leadership in a liberal state from that day to this.

According to Mill in *Representative Government*, the central challenge of leadership in a liberal state is to secure 'the advantage of government by the competent along with the advantage of government made responsible through participation by citizens'.[106] Modern scholar Dennis Thompson elaborates. 'Mill in effect invokes two principles. The first, which will be called the principle of participation, requires the participation of each citizen be as great as possible.... The second, which will be termed the principle of competence, stipulates that the influence of the more qualified citizens should be as great as possible....'[107] Mill thus identifies and seeks to address the dilemma made manifest by the emergence of the conception of sovereignty in the people, the dilemma that is at the heart of modern leadership: how does one honor popular participation while still seeking wise rulers? Mill faced the additional complication of seeking to do so in a way that honored the principles enunciated in *On Liberty*. To accomplish this, he would propose a system intended to bring out the best in both rulers and ruled, and indeed, so structured as to foster the kind of individual improvement so honored in *On Liberty*.

In practice, as we shall see, Mill provides no simple answers. According to Thompson, 'Mill does not intend to resolve fully the conflict between the principles of participation and competence, since a tension between the two principles is an essential feature of this theory of government. The theory defines the nature of that tension, sets limits to its resolution, and suggests practical ways in which resolution might be approximated.'[108] It is worthwhile, then, to examine Mill's argument more closely.

Are the People Capable of Governing?

It is important to note that the entirety of Mill's political theorizing is based upon his answer to this template question. Indeed, the question is central to the entire notion of leadership in a democracy. In previous chapters of this Part we have identified the continuing dilemma created by an ambivalent answer to this query. James Madison devoutly believed in popular sovereignty, but did not fully trust the people to govern wisely. As we have seen, he concocted a series of brilliant political innovations geared to retaining a competent elite in power, only to fail in his efforts. Alexis de Tocqueville, confronting the reality of mass democracy, embraced the juggernaut, but harbored deep reservations about the possibility that an unfettered majority could be trusted to govern well. Perforce, he largely abandoned Madison's backward-looking strategy of rule by an elite, but sought instead to craft other innovative solutions. John Stuart Mill considered Tocqueville his muse. He shared Tocqueville's concern with the masses (although he focused more narrowly upon their potentially negative impact upon personal liberty). Mill, however, was more optimistic concerning their perfectibility. That is to say, Mill had a deep faith in the possibilities of self-improvement. Therefore, in his democratic theory, he sought to ameliorate the evils of mass participation while creating a system that encouraged the people to become more capable of self-governing. Because of the importance of his premises in this regard, it is necessary to revisit briefly Mill's views about popular political abilities.

Many earlier proponents of popular sovereignty – to include Mill's father – had been more concerned with establishing universal suffrage than in its potential consequences.[109] Mill, writing as the full effect of complete democracy was beginning to be felt, took a different stance. Having read Tocqueville, 'Mill saw that his father had been wrong. The overthrow of traditional society and the development of popular institutions did not secure liberty.' Instead, 'it exposed liberty to potent dangers of a novel kind'.[110] Mill had identified the problem in *On Liberty*. He had rebutted the earlier undiluted praise for mass participation. 'In political and philosophical theories as well as in persons,' he noted, 'success discloses faults and infirmities which failure might have concealed from observation.' Such was the case with democracy. 'The notion that people have no need to limit their power over themselves might seem axiomatic, when popular government was only dreamed about…. In time, however, a democratic republic came to occupy a large portion of the earth's surface [referring to the United States] … and elective and responsible government became subject to … observations and criticisms [referring to Tocqueville].'[111] Mill offered his own reflections.

A part of the problem had to do with the capabilities of the people themselves. 'The general average of mankind', Mill opined, 'are not only moderate in intellect, but also moderate in inclinations.'[112] Indeed, when it comes to 'human understanding', Mill gave the dreary prediction that 'for any matter not self-evident there are ninety-nine persons totally incapable of judging of it for one who is capable, and the capacity of the hundredth person is only comparative….'[113] Thus Mill in *On Liberty* began with a pessimistic perception of the capability of the people to govern. 'In sober truth', he wrote, '… the general tendency of things throughout the world is to render mediocrity the ascendant power among mankind.' This most certainly applied to politics. In modern democracy, 'the only power deserving the name is the masses … that is to say, a collective mediocrity'.[114]

A part of Mill's solution in *On Liberty*, as we have seen, was his proposed enactment of a guiding principle designed to protect individuals from undue infringement by either the majority or its government. However, there was another, more positive, aspect of Mill's argument, which held the promise of redeeming humanity's weaknesses. Despite – or perhaps because of – his dour outlook regarding the masses, Mill was surprised to find that 'there is on the whole a preponderance among mankind of rational opinion and rational conduct'. Reflecting upon the seeming inconsistency, Mill found the answer in the redeeming power of human potential. 'It is owing to a quality of the human mind,' he allowed, 'the source of every thing respectable in man either as an intellectual or as a moral being, namely, that his errors are corrigible.' That is to say, 'he is capable of rectifying his mistakes by discipline and experience....'[115] This, then, is what gave Mill hope, and what helped to shape his political theory. It was the possibility that appropriate institutions and processes could 'raise ... even persons of the most ordinary intellect to something of the dignity of thinking beings'.[116] In other words, Mill harbored a redemptive hope for a democratic people, one he set out to realize through his proposals in his *Considerations on Representative Government*.

What is the Role of the People?

Mill's hopeful conclusion to the template query about the capability of the people to govern themselves informs his view of the role of the people in a democratic state. In order to realize the possibilities inherent in all citizens, they must first be encouraged to participate in the political process. In Mill's view, this expectation did not infringe upon one's individual liberty. Even in *On Liberty* he had acknowledged that 'the fact of living in society renders it indispensable that each should be found to observe a certain line of conduct toward the rest. This conduct consists ... in each person bearing his share ... of the labors and sacrifices incurred for ... society or its members....'[117] In fact, political duties were inherent in Mill's definition of democracy in *Representative Government*. Mill referred to '"sovereignty ... vested in the entire aggregate of the community," a voice for every citizen in the exercise of that sovereignty, and participation by every citizen in the "discharge of some public function"'.[118]

Mill found 'that any participation, even in the smallest public function, is useful'.[119] The advantage of political participation was, of course, the impact that it had upon the individual involved. In the first instance, such participation was likely to yield better decisions (the process by which that might occur will be the subject of our attention presently). Mill believed that 'active participants ... are ... more likely to have more sophisticated opinions, to be better informed about politics, and to be better able to perceive differences between parties and candidates than are less active citizens'.[120] Indeed, 'if circumstances allow the amount of public duty assigned him to be considerable, it makes him an educated man'.[121]

Equally important, political participation held out the hope of raising a citizen's sense of public obligation. Mill had shared Tocqueville's concern about the primacy of selfish interests in modern democracy. Political participation held out the promise to overcome this. As Mill saw it, 'It is not sufficiently considered how little there is in most men's ordinary life to give largeness ... to conceptions.... Giving him something to do for the public', he suggested, 'supplies [this].... He is called upon, when so engaged, to weigh interests not his own; to be guided, in case of conflicting claims, by another rule than his private partialities; to apply, at every turn, principles and maxims which have for their reason the existence of the common good.'[122] As a result, the citizen was more likely to 'consider the interest of the public, not his private advantage, and give his vote to the best of his judgment'.[123]

What is the Role of the Leader?

Despite his optimism about enhancing the political capabilities of the common man, Mill was well aware of the continued need for competent leaders in a liberal democracy. 'No government by a democracy', he said, '... ever did or could rise above mediocrity except in so far as the sovereign. Many have let themselves be guided ... by the counsels and influence of a more highly gifted and instructed *one* or *few*'. This was not mere 'hero-worship'; 'It does mean, however', Mill noted, 'that when the opinions of the masses of merely average men are everywhere become or becoming the dominant power, the counterpoise and corrective to that tendency would be the more and pronounced [role] ... of those who stand on the higher eminences of thought. It is in these circumstances most especially', Mill concluded, 'that exceptional individuals, instead of being deterred should be encouraged...'.[124]

There could be no question that some men possessed competence not characteristic of the common lot. Modern scholar Dennis Thompson has suggested that 'Mill's arguments implicitly employ two kinds of competence – instrumental and moral. Instrumental competence', he explained, 'is the ability to discover the best means to certain ends and the means to identify ends that satisfy individuals' interests as they perceive them'. On the other hand, 'moral competence is the ability to discern ends that are intrinsically superior for individuals and society. Morally competent leaders', Thompson continued, 'are able to recognize the general interest and resist the sinister interests that dwell not only in the government but also in the democratic majority'.[125]

As we shall see in our section on the leadership process, the task of these leaders was not to dictate from their higher eminence, but to work with the citizen, to 'supply reasons to his understanding, and stimulation to his feeling for the general interest'.[126] For his part, 'the honor and glory of the average man is that he is capable of following that initiative [of the leaders]; that he can respond internally to wise and noble things, and be led to them with his eyes open'.[127] For Mill, this was how the leadership process should unfold.

How Should Leaders and Followers Interact [I]: What is the Epistemology of Leadership?

Mill's treatment of the appropriate roles for leaders and the people in his democratic republic is incomplete without consideration of the important dynamic between them. As we have seen, the interaction was designed to achieve two essential purposes: to achieve wise policy outcomes and to encourage inherently selfish individuals to become more fitted as citizens. This aspect of Mill's analysis actually serves the ends of two of the template questions. In addition to exploring the dynamics of the interactions between leaders and the people, Mill also portrayed this process as the best way to come the closest to 'truth' in the policy-making process. Mill thus provides an important innovation in the pursuit of 'right' policy that continues to have important implications for modern, diverse democracies that have eschewed belief in *a priori* measures of the 'correctness' of policy outcomes.

In some ways, this interpretation of Mill's work cuts against the usual interpretation of him as following the guides of utilitarianism. There can be no question that Mill grounded the theoretical justification for his approach in its perceived superior utility. As we mentioned earlier, Mill's theory, in the words of modern scholar Michael Sandel, 'defends liberal principals in the name of maximizing the general welfare. The state should not impose on its citizens a preferred way of life, even for their own good, because doing so will reduce the sum of human happiness, at least in the long run. It is better that people choose for themselves, even if, on occasion, they get it wrong.'[128] As Mill himself put it, 'It is proper to state that I forego any advantage which could be derived to my argument from the idea of abstract right as a thing of independent utility…. I regard utility as the ultimate appeal on all ethical questions; but it must be utility in the largest sense, grounded on the permanent interests of man as a progressive being….'[129]

However – I argue here – this calculation was more relevant at the theoretical level than in the making of actual policy in a democracy that championed diverse viewpoints. In fact, Mill provides a rather elegant portrayal of how such a polity could achieve good policy outcomes. In it, he stressed the lack of any certainty of 'truth', and relied instead upon the dynamics of the policy-making process to come the closest to that elusive conception. In that process, the interactions between leaders and the people played a central role.

The premise of Mill's argument can be found in *On Liberty*, where he stressed the ultimate fallibility of man's judgment. At several points in that text, Mill stressed 'the fallibility of what is called the moral sense…. There is, in fact', he argued, 'no recognized principle by which the propriety or impropriety of government … [action] is customarily tested.'[130] He made a similar argument concerning ascertaining the 'truth' in open debate.

Given this, argued Mill, the remedy was to acknowledge human fallibility and attempt to overcome it through the full exchange of opinion and information. Mill took some care in *On Liberty* to elaborate his argument. 'Those who desire to suppress [another opinion], of course, deny its truth', he began. 'But they are not infallible. They have no authority to decide the question for all mankind and exclude every other person from the means of judging. To refuse a hearing to an opinion because they are sure that it is false,' Mill continued, 'is to assume that *their* certainty is the same thing as *absolute* certainty.' This returned to the root of the problem: 'All silencing of discussion,' he observed, 'is an assumption of infallibility'. The problem, however, went deeper still. 'The peculiar evil of silencing the expression of an opinion is that it is robbing the human race … those who dissent from the opinion, still more than those who hold it.' This was because 'if the opinion is right, they are deprived of exchanging error for truth; if wrong, what is almost as great a benefit, the clearer perception and livelier impression of truth produced by its collision with error'.[131] Even this did not exhaust the possibilities. 'There is a commoner case than either of these', he suggested. That occurred 'when the conflicting doctrines, instead of being one true and one false, share the truth between them, and the nonconforming opinion is needed to supply the remainder of the truth of which the received doctrine embodies only a part'.[132]

The solution was clear, and it was twofold. In *On Liberty*, Mill's call was for unfettered debate. 'It is the duty of governments, and individuals, to form the truest opinions they can; to form them carefully, and never impose them upon others unless they are quite sure of being right', he wrote. 'Complete liberty of contradicting and disproving our opinion is the very condition that justifies us in assuming its truth for the purposes of action; and on no other terms can a being with human faculties have any rational assurance of being right.'[133]

Mill's second method for deriving right policy in a democracy had more to do with the leadership relation, and comes from *Considerations on Representative Government*. It is here that the interchange between leaders and the people becomes critical. As Thompson notes, 'Mill recognizes that by itself this balance of competing factions will not consistently yield policies and laws that are in the general interest'. As a result, 'the political role of the instructed few becomes clear'.[134] The leadership relation between leaders and the people, in Mill's words, 'bring[s] ... inferior minds into contact with superior, a contact which in the ordinary course of life is altogether exceptional, and the want of which contributes more than anything else to keep the generality of mankind on one level of contented ignorance....' The importance of wise leaders is clear. 'A government which [does not show] ... any one else how to do anything', Mill elaborated, 'is like a school in which there is no schoolmaster, but only pupil-teachers who have never themselves been taught.'[135]

The dynamics of this interaction between leaders and the people is important, and holds implications for modern leadership activity. Again, modern scholar Dennis Thompson does a good job in ferreting out its nuances. 'Mill's description of this process, with its image of political teachers and pupils, sounds elitist, and to some degree it is', Thompson observed. 'But notice that, unlike many contemporary elitist theories of democracy, Mill does not justify the influence of the competent minority solely on the grounds of the superior ability to govern....' In Mill's scenario, 'the instructed few do not literally act like teachers in a classroom. They teach principally by example. Through deliberation in the representative assembly, electoral campaigns, and other public places, they demonstrate how to reason intelligently about the ends of politics.'[136] The objective is to inform their constituents of the nuances of the issue under consideration, so that the citizens can contribute more intelligently to the political process.

Under Mill's theory, the very process of debating public policy issues brings the polity closer to right action, while the interaction of leaders and followers also enhances the ability of the citizens to make informed contributions.

How Should Leaders and the People Interact [II]: The Nature of Representation

It is in the context of this dynamic between leaders and the people that we can also explore Mill's treatment of a theme that springs eternal in any polity dedicated to a representative form of government: what 'type' of representation is anticipated? Those even remotely familiar with political theory recognize that the two classic 'types' of representation are the 'trustee' type and the 'delegate' type. A representative who acts as a trustee was made famous by Edmund Burke, with his advocacy of a leader who best serves the interests of his constituents by applying his own best wisdom to the problem at hand, even if this at times contradicts the views of those constituents. A representative who is a delegate, on the other hand, is bound to follow the dictates and instructions of those he represents.

Mill's version is, again, nuanced. In his early writings, he appeared to come down foursquare in the 'trustee' camp. But, as Thompson points out, by the time he wrote *Considerations on Representative Government*, Mill 'expands the political role of ordinary citizens. Even though Mill still hopes that citizens will choose the wisest person to represent them, he now maintains that it is inevitable and even desirable that citizens' opinions about their own interests and about substantive political issues influence their choice of representatives.'[137] In fact, one of Mill's more sophisticated proposals (the Hare Plan) actually created representatives who specifically represented the interests of their constituents.[138] In so doing, Mill tried to create a system where leaders would have every incentive to be sensitive to constituent concerns. Although Mill did not pursue this to its logical extreme, this approach could be viewed as an early progenitor of what would become modern 'interest-group liberalism'.[139]

Perhaps the best way to conclude this overview of the relations between leaders and the people is to compare Mill to Locke. John Locke, it will be recalled, expected an attitude of deference on the part of the people toward their chosen leaders. Mill also created a deferential leadership relation, but it was a deference that recognized the dignity and the legitimacy of the people's views as well. Dennis Thompson, in his study of Mill, perhaps sums it up best: '... [C]itizens will ... defer to the competent, but it is a rather special kind of deference that Mill prescribes.... Even when Mill most strongly stresses rule by the elite, he insists that citizens defer to leaders only on rational grounds. It is men's reason that teaches them to respect the authority of still more cultivated minds....' As Mill himself said, 'Deference to mental superiority is not to go the length of ... abnegation of any personal opinion'. No longer may deference be construed as a 'blind submission of dunces to men of knowledge'; it becomes the 'intelligent deference of those who know much to those who know still more'.[140]

What Institutions and Processes are Needed?

Mill's frank acknowledgment of the central tensions that still challenge leadership in a democracy, that is, the dance between participation and competence, makes his proposed remedies of more than historical interest. Some of Mill's proposals have, of course, already found their way into the fabric of modern democratic institutions. Others, more radical, have not. In their spirit, if perhaps not in their specifics, modern reformers may find some inspiration.

If Mill was somewhat vague in his specific recommendations for the institutions and processes of democracy in *On Liberty*, he was much more forthcoming in *Considerations on Representative Government*. In that work, in which he had introduced the competing needs for participation and competency, he also devised a model of democracy that encouraged each.

Regarding participation, the first and most basic recommendation was for universal suffrage. As was the case for all of his theoretical proposals, his justification was that full participation would 'Further the general utility and thus make citizens better off'.[141] One of the significant implications of this justification emerged when the logic of it led Mill to support, in his later years, what modern commentators might call 'positive liberty'. In later works, Mill argued that government must compensate for any natural inequalities imposed upon citizens, and that an individual's effort and skill were often not sufficient to overcome poverty.[142] Such thinking is identical to that which underpins modern 'welfare liberals', who argue that one can only become an independent and fully functioning member of the political community if certain basic needs are met. Finally, because he saw voting as a public trust rather than an exercise of private interest, Mill proposed the return of *viva voce*, or public voting, to replace the secret ballot.[143]

To provide voters with the intellectual rigor, enlarged views and practical common sense necessary to participate successfully, Mill strongly supported various forms of public political education. These included civic education and, like Tocqueville, the encouragement of citizen involvement at local levels of government. As we have seen, a properly functioning leadership process, with intelligent and far-seeing leaders mentoring eager citizens, was the ideal.[144]

Turning to the issue of competence, Mill's challenge was also to create 'the political means by which the competent exercise influence in a democracy [in such a way that] ... that influence can in practice be combined with the demands of the principle of participation'.[145] One approach was to ensure that a competent elite had sufficient influence in the polity. One proposal Mill ventured was to abandon what today we would call the principle of 'one man, one vote', and instead allow individuals who were more competent (in Mill's scheme, the educated) to have more than one vote, although he took care to prevent the elite from outvoting the masses.[146] Mill also favored a complex electoral system called the Hare Plan. Under that system, rather than having a majoritarian system of single-member districts, voters indicated their preferences for multiple candidates, from any portion of the country, in rank order. In the rather complicated calculations of the results, 'excess' votes for the top candidate were reallocated to the next most popular candidate and so on, until a pool of representatives had been selected. The intended consequence was 'to strengthen the influence of the elite.... Distinguished persons, who might not win a majority in any local constituency, would be more likely to secure the required quota if they had the electorate of the whole nation to draw upon.... Moreover, the majority parties, faced with competition from these distinguished national candidates, would have a greater incentive to seek more competent persons to run under the party banner.'[147]

Mill also floated the possibility of various constitutional structures that could be instituted to enhance the influence of competence in the polity. Most obviously, he believed that the very presence of a representative body as the primary governing body (especially in conjunction with such innovations as the Hare Plan) would help guarantee that the competent would lead. Yet Mill went further still. In a structure reminiscent of Harrington's 'divide and choose' model, Mill proposed that a Legislative Commission should frame all laws and send them to the legislature. The legislature could then only 'pass, reject, or return a bill to the Commission for reconsideration'.[148] Mill was less enamored with the existing British bicameral system, but he did allow that a 'Chamber of Statesmen, composed of the most competent persons who have held important political office', could serve in an advisory role.[149]

In summary, John Stuart Mill is, in the words of one modern commentator, 'a valuable source for contemporary theorizing about democracy'.[150] He helped to establish the core values of modern liberalism. In terms of the new social and political relation we call leadership, he sought to guarantee not only a universal juridical right of the people to participate, but also to ensure real participation by 'leveling the playing field' of individual capability and competence. He also proposed numerous ways to ensure the necessary competence of leaders, and provide for their influence. Finally, he envisioned a form of 'rational deference' on the part of the people toward those leaders that embodied the best of both participation and competence.[151]

Although there could be other nominees to reside in the pantheon of the founders of modern liberalism, certainly John Locke and John Stuart Mill stand in the first rank. After Mill, it could be argued that it would not be until the latter decades of the twentieth century that a figure would have a similar sort of impact. That figure would be John Rawls.

JOHN RAWLS

Having set forth the foundational principles of the liberal response to the emergence of the sovereignty of the people, we now turn to a sampling of more recent attempts at adapting liberalism to our modern era. One name in particular stands out. As the scholar Jeremy Waldron has stated, 'Inevitably, because of our proximity, it is harder to identify canonical works of twentieth-century liberalism. There was a long period in the twentieth century in which liberal philosophers seemed to lose their taste (or their nerve) for grand theory on the scale of [Locke or Mill]....' However, Waldron said, 'That phase seems to have passed, and more confident versions of philosophical liberalism have re-emerged in the work of late-twentieth-century writers ... most importantly, John Rawls'.[152] Added Will Kymlicka: '[Rawls's] theory ... dominates the field, not in the sense of commanding agreement, for very few people agree with all of it, but in the sense that later theorists have defined themselves in opposition to Rawls.'[153]

Rawls is particularly important to our current study of liberal visions of the leadership relation in modern democracy. As another scholar, Markate Daly, has put it, 'John Rawls restructured liberal political theory to fit the world view of contemporary culture and institutions of American democracy'.[154] Rawls himself, in the introduction to his *Political Liberalism*, indicated that his work 'discusses, from the point of view of the political, the main moral and philosophical conceptions of a constitutional democratic regime: the conceptions of a free and equal citizen, [and] of the legitimate exercise of political power....'[155] Rawls, then, has much of importance to say to us. By engaging in our usual analytical treatment of his efforts, we can illuminate the leadership implications of this most important of modern versions of liberalism.

What is the Leadership Challenge?

Rawls, like the previous liberal theorists we have encountered, perceived a challenge – actually, a series of challenges – to existing ways of thinking about how members of society should respond to contemporary conditions. These challenges can be categorized under two heads: the theoretical and the practical.

The initial challenge that Rawls perceived was theoretical. He honored 'the historical origin of political liberalism ... [to include] controversies ... of crucial importance, such as those over limiting the powers of absolute monarchs by appropriate principles of con-stitutional design protecting basic rights and liberties.'[156] However, Rawls was concerned about the weaknesses inherent in the rationale used to justify such theories.

Rawls was particularly troubled by one trend in modern liberal theory. He noted that 'during much of the modern period of moral philosophy the predominant systematic view has been some form of utilitarianism'.[157] Utilitarianism had had its critics from its beginnings. According to Michael Sandel, 'The case against utilitarianism was made most powerfully by Immanuel Kant. He argued that empirical principles such as utility were unfit to serve as a basis for morality. A wholly instrumental defense of freedom and rights not only leaves rights vulnerable but fails to respect the inherent dignity of persons.'[158] Rawls added his opinion that 'these basic liberties could not be sacrificed or limited for the sake of an increase in general utility [which was theoretically possible under utilitarianism]'.[159]

More important, in the ensuing years since Mill, Rawls felt that 'critics failed to elaborate a workable and systematic moral conception that could oppose [utilitarianism]. The outcome was that we were often forced to choose between utilitarianism and rational intuitionism and were likely to settle for a variant of the principle of utility circumscribed and restricted by seemingly ad hoc intuitionist constraints.' According to Rawls, 'The aims of [his first work, *A Theory of Justice*] were to ... develop ... an alternative systematic account of justice that is superior to utilitarianism .... an alternative conception ... [to serve as] the most appropriate basis for the institutions of a democratic society'.[160] In sum, Rawls determined that what was needed was a better 'fiction' of liberalism, which he set out to produce in his path-breaking *A Theory of Justice*.

Rawls's *A Theory of Justice* [we will spell out its essential arguments presently] created nothing less than a sensation, as Rawls succeeded in reinvigorating liberal theory. It also spurred a raft of criticism. Upon reflection, Rawls agreed with one central challenge to his initial theoretical formulation. The problem, as Rawls saw it, was that his first attempt at creating a liberal theory contained the seeds of its own downfall. That is to say, in Rawls's words, 'the serious problem I have in mind concerns the unrealistic idea of a well-ordered society as it appears in *Theory*. An essential feature of a well-ordered society associated with justice as fairness [the term Rawls applied to the substance of his theory] is that all its citizens endorse this conception on the basis of what I now call a comprehensive philosophical doctrine.'[161] At another place, Rawls defined what he meant by a 'comprehensive philosophical doctrine'. A comprehensive doctrine was one that had one exclusive conception of 'the good'. As a set of examples, 'Plato and Aristotle, and the Christian tradition as represented by Augustine and Aquinas,' he said, 'fall on the side of the one reasonable and rational good. Such views hold that institutions are justifiable to the extent that they effectively promote that good. Indeed, beginning with Greek thought, the dominant tradition seems to have been that there is but one reasonable and rational conception of the good.... Classical utilitarianism,' Rawls noted, 'belongs to this dominant tradition.'[162] Returning to his own work in *A Theory of Justice*, he wrote: 'Now the serious problem is this. A modern democratic society is characterized by ... a pluralism of incompatible yet reasonable comprehensive doctrines. No one of these doctrines is affirmed by citizens generally.... The fact of a plurality of reasonable but incompatible comprehensive doctrines ... shows that, as used in *Theory*, the idea of a well-ordered society of justice as fairness is unrealistic....'[163]

Rawls's reformulated version of liberalism is found in his second major work, *Political Liberalism*. As Rawls puts it, 'By contrast [to *Theory*], ... *Political Liberalism* supposes that there are conflicting conceptions of the good, each compatible with the full rationality of human persons'. In consequence, in the place of a liberalism based upon a comprehensive doctrine, Rawls created what he called a 'political conception', or, more specifically, 'political liberalism'. To political liberalism, said Rawls, 'the question the dominant tradition has tried to answer has no answer: no comprehensive doctrine is appropriate as a political conception for a constitutional regime'.[164] 'Political liberalism,' he elaborated, 'is not a form of Enlightenment liberalism, that is, a comprehensive liberalism and often secular doctrine founded on reason and viewed as suitable for the modern age now that the religious authority of Christian ages is said to be no longer dominant.' Enlightenment liberalism, such as that proclaimed by Locke, was its own version of a comprehensive doctrine. Rawls's version of liberalism was something new: '*Political Liberalism*' Rawls continued, 'has no such aims. It takes for granted the fact of reasonable pluralism of comprehensive doctrines, where some of those doctrines are taken to be nonliberal and religious. The problem of *Political Liberalism* is to work out a political conception of political justice for a constitutional democratic regime that a plurality of reasonable doctrines, both religious and nonreligious, liberal and nonliberal, may freely endorse.... Emphatically it does not aim to replace comprehensive doctrines, religious or nonreligious, but intends to be equally distinct from both, and, it hopes, acceptable to both.'[165] 'Thus,' said Rawls, 'a main aim of *Political Liberalism* is to show that the idea of the well-ordered society in *Theory* may be reformulated so as to take account of the fact of reasonable pluralism. To do this it transforms the doctrine of justice as fairness as presented in *Theory* into a political conception of justice that applies to the basic structure of society.' Other than elaborating a new, political, justification for his doctrine of justice as fairness, 'otherwise [*Political Liberalism*] take[s] the structure and content of *Theory* to remain substantially the same'.[166]

Rawls's discussion of the theoretical challenge posed by the reliance upon comprehensive doctrines in previous theories of liberalism allows us to identify the accompanying pragmatic challenge. To get at this challenge and its resolution, we must explore two other issues posed by the template of leadership, namely, the challenge of diversity in a democratic polity and the end or purpose of leadership. Once we have introduced these central issues, we will provide a brief account of the theory Rawls devises in response, and then return to those template queries for a more analytical discussion.

How is the Matter of Diversity and Minority Interest Addressed [I]: the Challenge of Diversity

As we have seen from our discussion of the evolution of Rawls's theory, the underlying issue is quite a pragmatic one. Put simply, as Rawls himself posed it, the question is, 'how is it possible for there to exist over time a just and stable society of free and equal citizens, who remain profoundly divided by reasonable religious, philosophical, and moral doctrines?'[167] Put another way, in more political terms: 'Part of the problem is: What are the fair terms of social cooperation between citizens characterized as free and equal yet divided by profound doctrinal conflict? What is the structure and content of the requisite political conception, if, indeed, such a conception is even possible?' As Rawls stated it, 'The problem of *Political Liberalism* is to work out a conception of political justice for a constitutional democratic regime that the plurality of reasonable doctrines – always a feature of the culture of a free democratic regime – might endorse'.[168] Rawls's goal, then, was as noble as it was needed in modern democracy; that is, to create 'a new social possibility: the possibility of a reasonably harmonious and stable political society'.[169]

What is the Proper End or Purpose of Leadership [I]: a Political Conception of Liberalism

In sum, Rawls sought to adapt liberalism to the modern polity. To do so required creating a theory that remained true to the underlying liberal values honoring individual rights and opinions, yet which acknowledged the realities of modern society. Recall that in Rawls's modern polity, one could not assume that all members of society embraced traditional liberalism – 'given the fact of reasonable pluralism, this comprehensive view is not held by citizens generally, any more than a religious doctrine or some form of utilitarianism.'[170] Thus Rawls turned to a different approach to liberalism. Perforce, this was also a theory of leadership, if we recall that by democratic leadership we mean the new social and political relation among members of a society as they act together in the public sphere to accomplish public policy.

In effect, the new 'end' or purpose of Rawls's theory was to create the political conception of liberalism mentioned earlier. What Rawls meant by a strictly political conception requires, perhaps, some elaboration. Rawls begins by making an important distinction: 'Since there is no reasonable religious, philosophical, or moral doctrines affirmed by all citizens,' he wrote, 'the conception of justice affirmed in a well-ordered democratic society must be a conception limited to what I call "the domain of the political" and its values.'[171] The key construct in this statement by Rawls is 'the domain of the political'. Rawls envisioned a public, or political, arena into which all citizens could enter – no matter their personal comprehensive doctrines – and interact according to a shared set of premises and rules of engagement. While such premises and rules were certainly not value-free, Rawls believed they could be willingly embraced by all.

The content of this 'political conception', and how it is derived, will be the subject of our next section. Here, the key issue is that 'a political conception tries to elaborate a reasonable conception for this basic [political] structure alone and involves, so far as possible, no wider commitment to any other doctrine'. The important point is that 'it is normally desirable that the comprehensive philosophies and moral views we are wont to use in debating fundamental political issues should give way in public life'.[172] The end result, and indeed the desired end of Rawls's 'political liberalism', was that 'when citizens share a reasonable conception of justice, they have a basis on which public discussion of fundamental political questions can proceed and be reasonably decided....'[173]

Rawls's Proposed Solution

Rawls's chief task, then, was to create such a 'political conception' of liberalism that could be acceptable to all. We must 'specify the political domain and its conception of justice,' he said, 'in such a way that its institutions can gain the support of an overlapping consensus. In this case, citizens themselves within the exercise of their liberty of thought and conscience, and looking to their comprehensive doctrines, view the political conception as derived from, or congruent with, or at least not in conflict with their other values.'[174] In this section, we provide a brief overview of the processes and content of the conception Rawls puts forward – a conception he labels 'justice as fairness'.

The first stage of the process by which an acceptable political conception might be arrived at necessitated a new conceptualization of society itself. Rawls was not naïve. He recognized that, in his diverse society, there were likely to be fundamental conflicts. 'The public political culture', he acknowledged, 'may be of two minds at a very deep level [such as the] ... enduring controversy ... concerning the most appropriate understanding of liberty and equality.' In response, Rawls 'tries to ... [solve] this by using a fundamental organizing idea within which all ideas and principles can be systematically conceived and related. This organizing idea,' he said, 'is that of a society as a fair system of social cooperation between free and equal persons viewed as fully cooperating members of society over a complete life.'[175] This new conceptualization of society meant that the participating citizens must see each other as fellow sojourners in the quest for enduring political principles and processes, willing to cooperate as necessary.

Even assuming this basic assumption of societal commitment, however, the basic question remained: 'How are fair terms of cooperation to be determined? … these terms [should] be established by an undertaking among those persons themselves in view of what they regard as their reciprocal advantage'.[176] Thus Rawls called for a process he called 'political constructivism'. Under this concept, 'the principles of political justice are the result of a procedure of construction in which rational persons …, subject to reasonable conditions, adopt the principles to regulate the basic structure of society.'[177]

How this was to be accomplished constitutes one of Rawls's most famous innovations. He imagined a hypothetical scenario which he called the 'original position'. As he explained it, 'This idea is introduced in order to work out which traditional conceptions of justice … specifies the most appropriate principles for realizing liberty and equality once society is viewed as a fair system of cooperation between free and equal citizens'.[178]

The chief difficulty in deriving shared basic principles was the obvious one of disagreement based upon differing comprehensive doctrines, different statuses in society and the like. The challenge for Rawls was how to supersede such divisive and self-interested factors. 'The difficulty is this:' he said, 'we must find some point of view, removed from and not distorted by the particular features and circumstances of the all-encompassing background framework, from which a fair agreement between persons regarded as fair and equal can be reached.' Here, Rawls got creative. 'The original position, with the features I have called "the veil of ignorance," is this point of view….' He elaborated: 'To model this conviction in the original position, the parties are not allowed to know [their] social positions …, or [their] particular comprehensive doctrine …. The same idea is extended to information about people's race and ethnic group, sex and gender, and their various native endowments such as strength and intelligence…. We express these limits on information figuratively,' Rawls concluded, 'by saying the parties are behind a veil of ignorance.'[179]

Rawls confirmed the rationale underlying this fiction. 'We introduce an idea like that of the original position,' he explained, 'because there seems no better way to elaborate a political conception of justice for the basic structure from the fundamental idea of society as an ongoing and fair system of cooperation between citizens regarded as free and equal…. We must keep in mind that we are trying to show how to find principles specifying the basic rights and liberties and the forms of equality most appropriate to those cooperating, once they are regarded as citizens, as free and equal persons.'[180]

According to Rawls, 'the outcome of the original position yields … the appropriate principles of justice for free and equal citizens.'[181] Ultimately, as Will Kymlicka points out, 'Rawls argues that his principles are superior because they are the outcome of a hypothetical social contract. He claims that if the people in a certain kind of pre-social state had to decide which principles should govern their society, they would choose his principles.'[182]

And what are these principles? Rawls articulates 'the two principles that he believes any rational individual would choose as the foundation of social justice'.[183] The first principle, which is sometimes called the 'liberty principle', holds that '*Each person has an equal claim to a fully adequate scheme of basic rights and liberties, which scheme is compatible with the same scheme for all; and in this scheme the equal political liberties, and only these liberties, are to be guaranteed their fair value*'. The second principle, famously called the 'difference principle', states that '*Social and economic inequalities are to satisfy two conditions: first, they are to be attached to positions and offices open to all under conditions of fair equality of opportunity; and, second, they are to be to the greatest benefit of the least advantaged members of society'.*[184]

In sum, through the mechanism of the elaborate fiction of a 'social contract' entered into by individuals in the original position, Rawls puts forward the guiding principles of his political society. We can now use these principles to take a more substantive look at his response to the template queries introduced above; that is, the proper ends of leadership and the matter of diversity in a democratic society. Once these topics have received further consideration, we can turn to the implications of Rawls's liberal theory for the dynamics of the social and political relation we call leadership. Specifically, we can turn to the role the people should play in the polity Rawls has proposed.

What is the Proper End or Purpose of Leadership (II): Liberty

In our initial 'take' on the template question of the proper end or purpose of leadership, we suggested that Rawls was attempting to create a 'political' conception of the appropriate relations among members of the polity that honored – and avoided – their personal comprehensive doctrines. Having now outlined Rawls's solution to that conundrum – the approach he calls 'justice as fairness' that embodies the 'liberty principle' and the 'difference principle' – we are in a position to return to the template issues and to explore the content of each of these principles. Although there is considerable overlap, we will identify his first principle, the 'liberty principle', as his response to questions about the purpose of leadership, while the 'difference principle' can be viewed as his response to the inevitable diversity in status that occurs in modern democracies.

Unquestionably, Rawls's top priority was liberty, and, specifically, '[he] shows how self-interested individuals constructing their social order would choose principles of justice that establish the priority of individual liberty'.[185] Indeed, Rawls stated that 'political liberalism … must have the kind of content we associate with liberalism historically: for example, it must affirm certain basic rights and liberties, assign them a certain priority, and more'.[186] This is because the specification of such liberties is the foundation for the proper operation of his desired state. Guaranteeing their protection 'takes these guarantees off the political agenda and puts them beyond the calculus of social interests, thereby establishing clearly and firmly the rules of political contest'.[187]

Having these political liberties treated as sacrosanct, then, allows Rawls to avoid the essential difficulty of modern democracy. As Rawls framed it, 'A fundamental difficulty is that … under reasonable pluralism the religious good [for example; or any comprehensive doctrine] cannot be the common good for all citizens'. And precisely because no one's comprehensive doctrine can serve as the basis for a just resolution of policy differences, 'the political conception must employ, instead of that good, political conceptions such as liberty and equality together with a guarantee of sufficient all-purpose means [what he will call 'primary goods'] for citizens to make intelligent and effective use of their freedoms'.[188]

In sum, Rawls concluded that in his liberal polity, 'the definition of liberal conceptions is given by three conditions: first, a specification of certain rights, liberties, and opportunities (of a kind familiar from democratic regimes); second, a special priority for these freedoms; and third, measures assuring all citizens, whatever their social position, adequate all-purpose means to make intelligent and effective use of their liberties and opportunities.'[189]

Moreover, Rawls made an important statement about how these political rights must take primacy over all else, to include the comprehensive doctrines of individuals. He articulated this as a maxim stating that *the right is prior to the good*. He also at times referred to this as 'the priority of right'. 'This priority means', he said, 'that admissible ideas of the good must respect the limits of, and serve a role within, the political conception of justice.'[190] Modern political philosopher Michael Sandel perhaps explains the conception most succinctly. To Rawls (said Sandel), 'certain rights are so fundamental' that they cannot be overridden. 'The right is prior to the good ... in two senses. First, individual rights cannot be sacrificed for the sake of the general good; and second, the principles of justice that specify these rights cannot be premised on any particular vision of the good life.' Such rights, then, 'protect individuals from policies, even democratically enacted ones, that would impose a preferred conception of the good and so fail to respect people's freedom to choose their own conceptions'.[191]

John Rawls thus clearly falls within the traditional liberal paradigm that champions individual liberties from interference by governments or fellow members of society, albeit he came to this by a different route than had the others. Yet Rawls also went beyond the liberalism of many of his predecessors. Previous theorists had given lip service to both 'liberty' and 'equality', but while liberty received detailed consideration and treatment, the idea of equality tended to get short shrift. In general, equality was believed to be an inherent aspect of the human condition (for example, in the state of nature), and a rough equality of opportunity was generally assumed. John Rawls changed all that. He brought to modern liberal theory a new emphasis upon equality and, more important, he reinterpreted its meaning and operation for a modern society characterized by great variations in resources and status. This can best be seen through the operation of the second principle of Rawls's 'justice as fairness', particularly in the context of our next template question.

How is the Matter of Diversity and Minority Interests Addressed (II): Equality

We have seen how Rawls erected his entire philosophical system around what he called 'reasonable pluralism'. In that sense, he championed differences among members of society and sought their protection. But another form of difference or diversity troubled him greatly. This was the difference born (often literally) of distinctions in physical and mental capabilities, resources, social status and the like. Rawls' belief that these distinctions should not be the basis for differences in treatment was behind his invention of the 'veil of ignorance' in the 'original position'. The parties constructing rules of justice for such a society, not knowing where they might find themselves in the resulting society, were likely, Rawls thought, to create a society attentive to the circumstances of those worst off. Thus, it was 'rational to adopt a "maximin" strategy – that is, you *maximize* what you would get if you wound up in the *minimum*, or worst-off, position.... As a result, you select a scheme that maximizes the minimum share allocated under the scheme.'[192]

It is clear, then, that in addition to individual liberty, Rawls was also fundamentally concerned with issues of equality and inequality. Although he quite openly stated that his 'liberty principle' took priority over all else, he also acknowledged that 'guaranteed liberties taken alone are properly criticized as purely formal.... By themselves they are an impoverished form of liberalism, indeed not liberalism at all but libertarianism. The latter does not combine liberty and equality in the way liberalism does; it lacks the criteria of reciprocity and allows excessive social and economic inequalities as judged by that criterion.'[193] In short, Rawls was quite forthcoming in admitting that the principles of his justice as fairness 'express an egalitarian form of liberalism'. This included the familiar 'equality of opportunity', but also 'the so-called difference principle, which says that the social and economic inequalities attached to offices and positions are to be adjusted so that whatever the level of those inequalities, whether great or small, they are to the greatest benefit of the least advantaged members of society'.[194]

In analyzing this contribution to liberalism, one can discern differing levels of response to the challenge of this form of inequality in society. The most basic was the familiar equality of opportunity. As Rawls stated, 'citizens ... require for their advancement roughly the same ... basic rights, liberties, and opportunities ... as free and equal persons'.[195]

In addition to this rather traditional notion of equality of opportunity, Rawls went further still, and advocated what might be called 'positive liberty.' That is to say, there should be 'measures assuring to all citizens adequate all-purpose means to make effective use of their liberties and opportunities'.[196] Rawls thus promoted the notion that citizens should be provided with the things it takes for them to participate on an equal basis. These included 'certain fair equality ... in education and training ... a decent distribution of income and wealth ... [and] basic health care assured all citizens'.[197] The ultimate objective was that 'all citizens must be assured the all-purpose means necessary for them to take intelligent and effective advantage of their basic freedoms. In the absence of this condition,' Rawls noted, 'those with wealth and income tend to dominate those with less and increasingly to control political power in their own favor.'[198]

Rawls's classic case for 'positive liberty' implied even more radical stances (from the standpoint of traditional liberalism). In pursuit of the requirements of positive liberty, if other means failed, Rawls looked to 'society as employer of last resort through general or local government, or other social and economic policies'.[199] This suggests the notion of 'welfare liberalism'. Although Rawls himself never admitted this as his conclusion, Kymlicka is correct when he notes that his ideas have 'more radical implications than ... Rawls recognizes'.[200]

It was in Rawls's 'difference principle', however, that he took his most radical stance. In it, Rawls rejected notions of legitimate differences among individuals (even differences in intellect could be attributed to the luck of the draw). Accordingly, he sought to minimize the unfair distribution of resources. This was the inspiration for his famous 'difference principle'. As he said in *A Theory of Justice*, 'all social primary goods – liberty and opportunity, income and wealth, and the bases of self-respect – are to be distributed equally unless an unequal distribution of any or all of these goods is to the advantage of the least favored'.[201] The implications of Rawls's difference principle were revolutionary (albeit Marx had explored similar ground). Applied to the liberal tradition, no longer (according to Rawls) would Locke's unlimited accumulation of property and resulting inequalities be permitted. Inequalities *were* permitted, but only if in the creation of them the situation of the most disadvantaged in society was also improved. As we shall see when we look to the thinking of Robert Nozick, Rawls caused a divide here among modern liberals. Some continued to adhere to Lockean notions, while others embraced some form of the more activist approach of Rawls.

In sum, Rawls's form of liberalism took dead aim at the problems created by diversity in modern democratic society. Intellectual diversity, in the form of differing individual comprehensive doctrines, he vigorously defended, although he relegated their operation (for the most part) to the private sphere of human endeavor (in the public realm, the notions of public reason reigned). Diversity, then, was honored, but inequality was not.

In addition to his careful treatment of the principles of justice in a democratic society, Rawls took particular care in addressing such leadership issues as the role of the people and the nature of their interactions. It is to such matters that we now turn.

What is the Perception of Human Nature?

As noted in the introduction to Rawls, the announced focus of his work was to explore 'the main moral and philosophical conceptions of a constitutional democratic regime' (the topic we have been addressing in our treatment of justice as fairness). Also embodied in such a study, according to Rawls, are 'the conceptions of a free and equal citizen [and] of the legitimate exercise of political power'.[202] Rawls's *Political Liberalism* is all about conceiving of a political society in which individuals of differing characteristics and beliefs can create public policy by way of certain political processes. This way of looking at Rawls's work places it squarely within the parameters of leadership. It allows us to consider several interconnected issues concerning the capability and role of the people in a democratic regime.

One of these issues is raised by the template of leadership question about the presumptions concerning human nature. Rawls's assumptions are somewhat complex. They track the traditional liberal focus on the individual, yet at the same time acknowledge certain social aspects of the human condition.

There can be little doubt that Rawls, in his theory, 'regards the individual as of the ultimate importance'. This can be seen in the very way he structured his fictional 'original position'. As modern scholars Stephen Mulhall and Adam Swift observe, 'the way in which justice as fairness involves the idea of people agreeing to a contract certainly reflects this strand. Rawls's theory aims to take seriously the separateness of persons.'[203] Will Kymlicka adds, 'the idea of a state of nature [in Rawls is] not [intended] to work out the historical origins of society, or the historical obligations of governments and individuals, but to model the idea of the moral equality of individuals.... [His] idea of a state of nature does not, therefore, represent an anthropological claim about the pre-social existence of human beings, but a moral claim about the absence of natural subordination amongst human beings.'[204]

This belief in man's ultimate individuality is reinforced by Rawls's liberal acknowledgment of his agency. 'We ... think of citizens as free and equal persons', he pointed out, and 'presuppose that we are indeed individuals capable freely of forming, and changing, our own views about how we should live our lives'.[205] Yet at the same time, Rawls stressed the reality that human beings in society need to interact, and to some degree depend upon each other. Recall that his very definition of society was 'a fair system of social cooperation over time, from one generation to the next'.[206]

Rawls took great care to define the boundaries between the individual and other members of society. He confronted the issue directly: 'Let us begin by considering the objection that ... justice as fairness abandons the ideal of a political community and views society as so many distinct individuals ... cooperating solely to pursue their own personal, or associational, advantage without having any final ends in common.' In one sense, Rawls agreed with this comment. 'In reply,' he wrote, 'justice as fairness does indeed abandon the ideal of political community if …. we mean by community a society governed by a shared comprehensive religious, philosophical, or moral doctrine.'[207]

This did not mean, however, that Rawls's political society consisted of a collection of individual atoms randomly coming into contact with one another. His was a rather sophisticated depiction based, at least in part, upon his conception of the attributes of human nature. Rawls assumed that individuals were both *rational* and *reasonable*. The first attribute reflected man's individualistic nature, while the second acknowledged his capability also to move beyond pure self-interest. In his words, 'Rational autonomy … rests on persons' intellectual and moral powers. It is shown in their exercising their capacity to form, to revise, and to pursue a[n] [individual] conception of the good, and to deliberate in accordance with it.' On the other hand, 'Persons are reasonable in one basic aspect when, among equals, say, they are ready to propose principles and standards as fair terms of cooperation and to abide by them willingly, given the assurance that others will likewise do the same'. Thus, Rawls allowed, 'the reasonable is public in a way the rational is not'.[208] The dualistic nature of humans allowed them to engage in the 'fair system of social cooperation' without sacrificing each one's individual conceptions.

The fact that individuals would necessarily be interacting as a part of society also presupposed another key human trait. As Rawls puzzled it out, 'We must start', he said, 'with the assumption that a reasonably just political society is possible, and for it to be possible,' he reasoned, 'human beings must have a moral nature … that can understand, act on, and be sufficiently moved by a reasonable political conception of right and justice to support a society guided by its ideals and principles'.[209] More specifically, 'since persons can be full participants in a system of social cooperation, we ascribe to them two moral powers connected with the elements in the idea of social cooperation … namely, a capacity for a sense of justice and a capacity for a conception of the good.'[210]

In sum, John Rawls adds significantly to the portrayal of human nature as previously put forward by Locke and Mill (although, to be sure, he stands upon the shoulders of other greats, such as Immanuel Kant). In his liberal conception, man's core individualism remains, but is tempered by capacities that make it possible for him to interact productively in a society Rawls portrays as cooperative. Again, not all modern liberal philosophers go so far as Rawls, yet his is an important statement in the quest to adapt liberal thinking to modern realities.

What is the Role of the People?

Having deduced the essential attributes of the human condition from Rawls's work, we can turn more directly to the leadership issue of the role of the people in his projected polity. Rawls himself allowed that 'I shall focus on the idea of citizenship in a democratic regime and how it is connected with the ideas of political legitimacy and public reason'.[211]

Before we turn to the anticipated roles the people are to play in Rawls's democratic society, it is important to note that Rawls, like Locke and other 'social contract' theorists, posits certain 'pre-political' obligations on the part of citizens. Although it is hypothetical, the agreement upon basic principles in Rawls's original position is a product of a process he calls an 'overlapping consensus of reasonable comprehensive doctrines. In such a consensus,' Rawls explained, 'the reasonable doctrines endorse the political conception, each from its own point of view.'[212] The point is that Rawls assumes, as does Locke, that the justification for the political society stems from the consent of the people. This classic liberal democratic belief demonstrates the bedrock commitment to the people as the constitutive element of modern society.

Our focus here, however, will be the expectations Rawls places on citizens in the course of their participation in the political processes of the polity. First, it is necessary to recall once again his definition of a society. It is, he said, 'a fair system of cooperation over time, from one generation to the next'.[213] This has implications for the role of citizens. Rawls takes some time to spell out the expected role his citizens would play. 'A well-ordered society', he wrote, '… is not, then, a private society; for in the well-ordered society of justice as fairness citizens do have final ends in common. While it is true that they do not affirm the same comprehensive doctrine, they do affirm the same political conception of justice; … and this means', he continued, 'that they share one very basic political end, and one that has high priority: namely, the end of supporting just institutions and of giving one another justice accordingly…'.[214]

This, in turn, led to the central question that confronts every democracy: 'seeing political power as the power of citizens as a collective body, we ask: when [that is, under what conditions] must we, as free and equal citizens, be able to view ourselves as exercising that power if our exercise of it is to be justifiable to other citizens …?'[215]

The answer, in Rawls's view, was the concept of *public reason*. With it, Rawls spelled out what is expected of citizens. 'Now it is essential', he began, 'that a liberal political conception includes besides its principles of justice, guidelines of inquiry that specify ways of reasoning and criteria for the kinds of information relevant for political questions.' Such 'guidelines for public inquiry' were the 'values of public reason'.[216] Applying public reason, citizens 'should be ready to explain the basis of their actions to one another in terms each could reasonably expect the others might endorse as consistent with their freedom and equality'.[217] 'The point of the ideal of public reason is', Rawls elaborated, 'that citizens are to conduct their fundamental discussions … based on values that the others can reasonably be expected to endorse…. This means that each of us must have, and be ready to explain, a criterion of what principles and guidelines we think other citizens … may reasonably be expected to endorse along with us.'[218] 'Trying to meet this condition', Rawls assures us, 'is one of the tasks that this ideal democratic politics asks of us'. Thus, 'understanding how to conduct oneself as a democratic citizen', he concludes, 'includes understanding an ideal of public reason'.[219] 'Public reason', then, 'is characteristic of a democratic people: it is the reason of its citizens, of those sharing the status of equal citizenship'.[220]

Linked to the concept of public reason was the notion of *reciprocity*. Only if citizens are sincerely open to the possibility of acknowledging the reasoning of other citizens will public reason work. 'Only when we sincerely believe that the reasons we offer for our political action may reasonably be accepted by other citizens' is there a possibility of success.[221]

In addition to the core expectations of public reason and reciprocity, Rawls identified other public virtues that must be exhibited by citizens. 'The virtues of political cooperation that make a constitutional regime possible are, then', he said, 'very great virtues. I mean, for example, the virtues of tolerance and being ready to meet others halfway, the virtue of reasonableness, and the sense of fairness. When these virtues are widespread in society', he concluded, '… they constitute a very great public good, part of society's political capital'.[222]

One way to capture all this, according to Rawls, was through the concept of the 'duty of civility.' 'The ideal of citizenship,' he argued, 'imposes a moral, not legal duty – the duty of civility – to be able to explain to one another on those fundamental questions how the principles and policies they advocate and vote for can be supported by the political values of public reason. This duty also involves a willingness to listen to others and a fairmindedness in deciding when accommodations to their views should reasonably be made.' At another place, Rawls referred to the need for 'civic friendship'.[223]

What is the Epistemology of Leadership?

Rawls's call for public reason harbored another key insight related to leadership in a democracy. Somewhat akin to Mill, Rawls eschewed any claim to absolute truth in the public sphere; indeed, much of his energies were devoted to creating a political conception that could operate in the public arena, leaving individual claims of truth – that is, comprehensive doctrines – to the private realm of individual functioning. Again somewhat like Mill, Rawls looked to the give and take of the actual process of political interaction among citizens to achieve the 'best' policy outcome. In other words, the way to perceive the 'rightness' of one's actions – what we are calling the epistemology of leadership – was a function of the process itself, rather than a call to some comprehensive doctrine.

As Rawls saw it, there were two obstacles to the achievement of 'truth' in the public sphere. The first, pragmatic, obstacle was one that he called the *burdens of judgment*. Rawls recognized that 'many of our most important judgments are made under conditions where it is not to be expected that conscientious persons with full powers of reason, even after free discussion ... will all arrive at the same conclusion.' It was these conditions that Rawls called 'the burdens of judgment'.[224]

Rawls took the time to spell out these burdens of judgment at some length. They occurred when:

a. the evidence ... bearing on the case is conflicting and complex....
b. Even when we agree fully about the kinds of considerations that are relevant, we may disagree about their weight, and so arrive at different judgments
c. To some extent all our concepts ... are vague and subject to hard cases; this indeterminacy means that we must rely on judgment and interpretation
d. To some extent ... the way we assess evidence and weigh moral and political values is shaped by our total experience ... and our total experiences must always differ....
e. Often there are different kinds of normative considerations of different force on both sides of an issue and it is difficult to make an overall assessment....
f. ... [we are] forced to select among cherished values.[225]

Thus, even in the best of cases, when individuals of intelligence and good faith deliberated together, it was unlikely that they would always agree as to the 'right' policy outcome. Add to this, said Rawls, the unfortunate reality of 'prejudice and bias, self- and group interest, blindness and willfulness', and the challenge was clear.[226]

Given such burdens of judgment, which make even good-faith agreement on outcomes problematic, Rawls concluded that there could be only one reasonable response. 'Reasonable persons see that the burdens of judgment set limits on what can be reasonably justified to others', he acknowledged, 'and so they endorse some form of liberty of conscience and freedom of thought'.[227] Thus Rawls comes down alongside Mill in championing intellectual freedom.

Much more important than the pragmatic difficulties in coming to shared conclusions posed by the burdens of judgment was the reality of 'reasonable pluralism'. 'The diversity of reasonable comprehensive religious, philosophical, and moral doctrines found in modern democratic societies', Rawls observed, 'is not a mere historical condition that may soon pass away, it is a permanent feature of the public culture of democracy.' As a result, 'even after reasoned reflection, decent, intelligent people will come to different conceptions about the nature of the good life'.[228]

Again, the response was obvious to Rawls. 'Given the fact of reasonable pluralism,' he said, 'we should try to decide questions of justice and rights without affirming one conception of the good over others.'[229] The public response, then, must be neutrality among competing conceptions of the good. This 'impartiality [of political liberalism] is shown in various ways', Rawls noted. 'For one thing, political liberalism does not attack or criticize any reasonable view. As part of this, it does not criticize, much less reject, any particular theory of the truth of moral judgments.... Which moral judgments are true, all things considered, is not a matter for political liberalism', since 'it approaches all questions within its own limited point of view.'[230]

More broadly, Rawls looked to an approach to public policy formation that was again reminiscent of John Stuart Mill. Rawls advocated an approach he labeled 'political constructivism'. According to Rawls, 'the political constructivist regards a judgment as correct because it issues from the reasonable and rational procedure of construction when correctly formulated and correctly followed'. To elaborate, 'political constructivism ... does not ... use (or deny) the concept of truth.... Rather, within itself the political conception does without the concept of truth.' As Rawls saw it, 'political constructivism provides political liberalism with an appropriate conception of objectivity. Political constructivism ... says that ... the principles of political justice (content) may be represented as the outcome of a certain procedure of construction....'[231]

That procedure was nothing less than the demands of public reason and reciprocity that Rawls required of all citizens in his liberal polity. As a result, said Rawls, 'it is only by affirming a constructivist conception – one which is political and not metaphysical – that citizens generally can expect to find [outcomes] that all can accept'.[232]

Are the People Capable of Governing?

From the preceding, it should be clear that Rawls placed a great deal of reliance upon the people to take responsibility for the proper operation of the polity. 'Since our account of justice as fairness begins with the idea that society is to be conceived as a fair system of cooperation over time between generations,' he said, 'we adopt a conception of the person to go with this idea.' It was 'the concept of someone who can take part in, or who can play a role in, social life, and hence exercise and respect its various rights and duties. Thus we say that a person is someone who can be a citizen, that is, a normal and fully cooperating member of society over a complete life.'[233] More specifically, 'In order to fulfill their political role, citizens are viewed as having the intellectual and moral powers appropriate to that role, such as the capacity for a sense of political justice given by a liberal conception and a capacity to form, follow, and revise their individual decisions of the good, and capable also of the political virtues necessary for them to cooperate in maintaining a just political society.'[234]

What is the Role of the Leader?

If Rawls devoted a good deal of attention to the proper role and activities of the people in his liberal polity, the same cannot be said of the role of leaders. As a result, any conclusions are somewhat tentative, informed by hints in Rawls's writings and our general understanding of his liberal principles.

It is certainly reasonable to conclude that Rawls's political society would have leaders of some sort. As modern commentator Will Kymlicka has observed, 'Classical liberals were not anarchists ... who believe that governments are never acceptable. Anarchists believe that people can never come to have legitimate authority over others, and that people can never be legitimately compelled to obey authority.' 'These liberals were not anarchists', Kymlicka repeated; they believed 'having some people with the power to govern others is compatible with respecting moral equality because the rulers only hold this power in trust, to protect and promote the interests of the governed'.[235] Although Rawls was not a 'classical' liberal philosopher *per se*, he implied his acceptance of leaders when he wrote: 'This idea of equality recognizes that some persons have special traits and abilities that qualify them for offices of greater responsibility and their attendant rewards'.[236]

Despite this seeming acceptance of leaders, however, Rawls's discussion of 'public reason' provides an interesting insight that undercuts any idea of the kind of elite leadership articulated by Locke and Mill. Rawls observed that 'in aristocratic and autocratic regimes, when the good of society is considered, this is not done by the public, if it exists at all, but by rulers, whoever they may be'. However, 'Public reason is characteristic of a democratic people: it is the reason of citizens, of those sharing the status of equal citizenship'.[237]

The implication is clear: in the important business of determining what serves the public good, Rawls allocates the entire responsibility to the people. This may seem obvious on its face, until one recalls that Locke was content to allocate an enormous prerogative to the leader, and Mill stressed the key role of competence that the leader represents. Thus Rawls's work holds out the possibility of a new role for the leader in a democratic polity. Precisely what that role is Rawls does not make clear, but his work allows for some informed speculation.

We can say with a fair degree of certainty that Rawls's leader – and any government of which he or she might be a part – should maintain 'neutrality ... in terms of the aims of basic institutions and public policy with respect to comprehensive doctrines and their associated conception of the good'. That was because, 'when there is a plurality of reasonable doctrines, it is unreasonable, or worse to want to use the sanctions of state power to correct, or to punish, those who disagree with us'.[238]

Beyond the conception of neutrality as to particular conceptions of the good, Rawls remains silent as to his expected leader role and behavior. However, his discussion of public reason is, again, suggestive. If the decision of the people in matters pertaining to the public good is determinative, and if that determination is to be achieved through public reason and reciprocity, this suggests (as our discussion of epistemology made clear) that the focus of public action is upon the *process* and not any predetermined outcome. Although

Rawls nowhere states it, this, in turn, suggests that the Rawlsian leader should be an adept manager of the process, to ensure that the precepts of public reason play out appropriately. If so, this is quite a far cry from the substantive expertise both Locke and Mill expected their leaders to have. Because we are running so far ahead of any supportive evidence from Rawls that this speculation is true, we will leave this at the level of a hypothesis. We will, however, have reason to return to this vision of the role of the leader when we later turn to the future challenges to leadership in a diverse democratic society.

How Should Leaders and the People Interact?

In our discussion of the thinking of early liberal theorists, we have seen how their perception of the appropriate role for the leader led to certain expectations regarding the relationship between leaders and the people. Locke expected the people to exhibit deference toward their leaders, and Mill looked to what we labeled as 'rational deference'. If our speculations pertaining to Rawls's view of leaders are anywhere near correct, the accompanying relationship between leaders and the people would be similarly shifted. Replacing the traditional deference would be some other form of relationship, where the people respected their leaders not so much for their substantive knowledge but for their procedural expertise. Again, we will return to the implications of such a conception of leadership when we consider it more fully in our final chapter.

What Institutions and Processes are Needed?

Again, Rawls did not devote a great deal of time to setting forth the specific institutions needed to implement his conceptions. However, certain conclusions are warranted. First, he asserted that 'our exercise of political power is fully proper only when it is exercised in accordance with a constitution'.[239] Such a document would establish and protect the fundamental ideals and principles of the polity, as well as the basic liberties of the people. In addition, stated Rawls, 'it is fitting ... that the fair terms of social cooperation between citizens as free and equal should meet the requirements of full publicity'. This he called 'the publicity condition'; through it 'citizens are made aware of and educated to this conception'.[240]

Moreover, despite Rawls's protestations to the contrary, his insistence on including social and economic elements in his basic liberties, and the redistributive implications of his 'difference principle' all tend toward a modern welfare state, and thus place Rawls within the rather broad category of what might be called 'welfare liberals'. Although admittedly it goes beyond the specific recommendations of Rawls, it is useful – particularly in light of our upcoming discussion of Robert Nozick – to take this opportunity to introduce this form of liberalism. According to Kymlicka, 'the [Rawlsian] liberal favours a mixed economy and welfare state ... to achieve the best practical realization of the demands of equality itself'. Indeed, although Rawls himself does not go nearly so far, 'quite radical government policies might be required to eliminate those entrenched hierarchies – e.g., nationalizing wealth, affirmative action, worker self-ownership, ... public health, free university education, etc.'.[241] 'Some people argue [see Nozick, below]', Kymlicka admitted, 'that if liberals endorse these radical reforms, they have abandoned their liberalism.'

Kymlicka disagrees. This 'is misleading, for however far liberal principles take us from traditional liberal practices, they are still distinctively liberal principles'.[242]

Conclusion

The liberal philosophy of John Rawls fundamentally altered the debate concerning the proper response to modern democratic challenges. Rawls himself saw his work as merely the culmination of the liberal legacy we have been tracing in this chapter. 'Were justice as fairness' to be adopted, he wrote, 'it would complete and extend the movement of thought that began three centuries ago with the gradual acceptance of the principles of toleration and led to the nonconfessional state and equal liberty.... This extension is required', he argued, '... given the historical and social circumstances of a democratic society.'[243]

Certainly Rawls served as the prototype for an important new interpretation of liberalism generally, and the leadership relation in particular. However, his was not the only interpretation of liberalism for a modern state. For a counterpoint to Rawls, we must take a brief look at the work of Robert Nozick.

ROBERT NOZICK

If John Rawls has been credited with reinventing liberalism to meet the challenges of modern democracy, Robert Nozick is perhaps the best-known modern proponent of a countervailing approach. Rather than Rawls's stress upon equality and social cooperation, Nozick harked back to the 'classical liberalism' of John Locke (and Immanuel Kant) and fashioned a libertarian interpretation of the appropriate role for government and its leaders. Nozick's work allows us to perceive two realities of modern liberalism. First, the distinctions between Rawls and Nozick point up the great divide in modern liberalism, and help us to understand much about contemporary politics. More important for our purposes, Nozick's rather extreme position allows us to bring into focus an undercurrent of 'anti-leadership' that characterizes all of modern liberalism.

Because the purpose here is to illustrate the latter two points of bifurcated liberalism and the challenges modern liberalism poses for a rich understanding of the leadership relation, our approach here will not be to parse Nozick's thought in the detailed manner employed in our previous analysis of the chief contributors to the liberal tradition. Instead, we will provide only the briefest of summaries of Nozick's approach, and then use this as a starting point for the discussion of the larger issues.

Robert Nozick, somewhat akin to Rawls, was spurred to create his theory of liberalism as a result of weaknesses he perceived in existing liberal theory. Ironically, however, it was the work of Rawls and his ilk that caused Nozick the most distress. Nozick believed that much of modern liberal theory had gone too far in the direction of social and economic equality, to the extent that it violated Kant's maxim that individuals should only be ends in themselves, and never be used as means to other ends.[244]

One of the key areas in which distinctions can be drawn between Nozick and Rawls has to do with the underlying values that are stressed, and by implication, the resulting ends or purposes of government and leadership. Rawls, it will be recalled, gave liberty 'lexical priority', but also stressed 'equality or mutual advantage', and he elaborated a system whereby true social cooperation could be created and encouraged. Nozick, on the other hand, also mentioned both values of liberty and equality, but had another interpretation. For Nozick, liberty was 'a foundational moral premise', which could not be compromised (as welfare liberals were wont to do) with equality. While such a view placed Nozick solidly in the libertarian camp, he also used the rhetoric of equality, albeit differently than had Rawls. For Nozick, it was more of a Kantian equality: the right of 'self-ownership' – Kant had talked about individuals as 'ends unto themselves' – that Nozick used to justify his rejection of activist liberalism.[245]

The core of Nozick's theory is laid out in the first sentence of his book: 'Individuals have rights, and there are things no person or group may do to them (without violating their rights)'.[246] The core right, as we have seen, is that of 'self-ownership', which implied that no individual could be required to sacrifice his or her own interests for others. Indeed, Nozick took this to its logical conclusion, claiming that 'no one has the right to take [my resources] from me, even if it is to keep the disabled from starving'.[247]

Given this foundational assertion, Nozick elaborated a theory in which, as described by fellow scholar Jonathan Wolff, 'His conclusions fall into three parts: a defence of the minimal state; a theory of economic justice; and a utopian vision of society'.[248] Each of these strands of Nozick's thought parallel issues presented in the template of leadership.

Nozick's advocacy of a minimalist state is his response to the issue of the proper role of government and leaders. Having made his statement about rights quoted above in the first sentence of his book, in his second sentence Nozick contemplated the implications for leadership: 'So strong and far-reaching are these rights', he allowed, 'that they raise the question of what, if anything, the state and its officials may do'.[249] In response, he pointed out the evils wrought by an activist state. Nozick began with a Lockean portrayal of the acquisition of property through private effort. Thereafter, 'because people have a right to dispose of their holdings as they see fit,' he would argue, 'government interference is equivalent to forced labour – a violation ... of our basic moral rights'.[250]

Since such interference is unjustifiable, Nozick called for the 'nightwatchman' state of classic liberalism. Nozick stated that 'a minimal state limited to the narrow functions of protection against force, theft, fraud, enforcement of contracts, and so on, is justified; any more extensive state will violate persons' rights not to be forced to do certain things, and is unjustified'.[251] According to the logic of this, 'there is no public education, no public health care, transportation, roads, or parks. All of these involve the coercive taxation of some people against their will....'[252] In particular, Rawls's scheme could not be 'continuously realized without continuous interference with people's lives'.[253] The problem with Rawls was that 'people, left to their own devices, will engage in free exchanges that violate the difference principle'. Consequently, said Nozick, 'preserving the difference principle requires continually intervening in people's exchanges'.[254]

The extremely limited role of the government/leader in Nozick's scheme, and his emphasis on exchanges, is in part a reflection of his second theme of distributive justice. His theory was labeled the 'entitlement theory', and detailed the acquisition of property through one's individual efforts, and forbade its transfer unless that transfer was voluntary.[255] This, in turn, led to Nozick's reliance upon the market mechanism as the only appropriate vehicle of exchange. Nozick claimed that 'market exchanges involve the exercise of individuals' powers, and since individuals own their powers, they also own whatever comes from the exercise of those powers in the marketplace'.[256] Since the market is the vehicle through which man's moral nature is fulfilled, the protection of free market mechanisms – and the prohibition of redistributive policies of any sort by governments and leaders – was at the core of his theory.

Nozick also harbored what he believed was a utopian vision of society, one which 'is inspiring as well as right' – and one which calls up the template issue having to do with the proper role of the people. As Jonathan Wolff depicts it, in Nozick's scheme, within the confines of his basic protection of the individual's self-ownership, 'people may enter into whatever voluntary arrangements they wish. Thus Nozick argues that a group may set up any type of community they wish, provided they have the resources and do not coerce others to join them. Thus libertarianism is viewed,' according to Nozick, 'as a "framework for utopia" in which individuals can act out their own model of utopia, in company with like-minded others.'[257] Thus, although Nozick says little else about how the people would function in his polity, he nonetheless affirms the liberal principle that 'people have a right to the most extensive liberty compatible with a like liberty for all'.[258] The door is open, then, for the people to create a voluntary, consensual polity geared to serving their highest aspirations.

Nozick addresses a few other issues that we have identified as being crucial to an understanding of leadership in a democratic polity, albeit not overtly. One is the perception of human nature. More than Rawls, and more akin to the classical liberals, is Nozick's stress upon one's inviolate individuality. According to Nozick, the proper society treats individuals 'not as instruments or resources', but as 'persons having individual rights with the dignity this constitutes. Treating us with respect by respecting our rights', he continued, '[the proper society] allows us, individually or with whom we choose, to choose our life and realize our ends and our conceptions of ourselves, in so far as we can....'[259] With this, Nozick returns to the earlier liberal emphasis on atomistic individuals, and rejects the enforced cooperative gloss created by Rawls with his definition of a cooperating society.

With his praise of market mechanisms, Nozick also put forward a variant of the epistemology of leadership that has become a core belief among modern liberals of Nozick's stripe. It is a commonplace among all liberals that 'we promote people's interests by letting them choose for themselves what sort of life they want to lead'; indeed, 'to deny people this self-determination is to fail to treat them as equals'.[260] However, Nozick and others evince a particular way of knowing when policy decisions are the 'right' ones. It is simply to rely on an unfettered market. 'A just distribution is simply whatever distribution results from people's free exchanges' is one way to put it. Similarly, 'any distribution that arises by free transfers from a just situation is itself just'.[261] Thus Nozick and other modern 'libertarian liberals' equate capitalism to freedom and justice, and perforce, whatever the market determines is 'right.' Such a view avoids the potential evils and inefficiencies of such determinations being made through a political process.

Unfortunately for our study of leadership, this avoidance of the political give and take among the members of the polity obviates such central leadership questions as the nature of the interaction among leaders and the people, just as it ignores the challenge of minority interests. Still and all, the work of Robert Nozick, partly because he states his stance so boldly, permits us to discern a key fault line within modern liberalism and to consider its implications.

TWO LIBERALISMS

John Rawls and Robert Nozick, although both had important predecessors and both inhabit only a portion of the vast landscape that we call liberalism, nevertheless allow us to stake out a dichotomy that has shaped – and haunted – modern liberalism. For – if one will excuse the oversimplification – there have emerged not one but *two* liberalisms in the modern democratic polity. This has sparked, at a minimum, a confusion of nomenclature. The liberalism of John Rawls can be appropriately labeled *egalitarian liberalism* or *welfare liberalism*, and supports, in addition to the core liberal emphasis upon individual liberty, the idea of 'positive liberty', with its provision of certain social and economic rights to assure full participation. Provision of these rights often requires state intervention. In modern American political parlance, such individuals are simply called *liberals* and their beliefs *liberalism*. Ironically, it is those who profess beliefs along the lines of Nozick who can properly be called *classical liberals*, *libertarian liberals* or *laissez-faire liberals*. As we have seen, they defend the market economy and minimal government, and claim that redistributive policies violate people's rights. In the American political lexicon, such individuals are called *conservatives*. Thus a confusion arises. In American politics, those labeled 'conservatives' arguably have the best claim to the liberal tradition. However, to many of them the term 'liberal' is the dreaded 'L-word' of Rawlsian welfare liberalism. Meanwhile, 'Europeans are often disconcerted to hear "liberal" used ... as label for positions that they themselves would describe as left-wing or moderately socialist'.[262]

More important than mere nomenclature, however, is the realization that all American politics can be viewed as belonging to the liberal tradition. This will become all the more important when, in the next chapter, we trace an emerging alternative response to the challenges of leadership in a democracy. Before turning to that alternative, it is necessary to pull together the leadership implications of the long intellectual tradition we have been tracing.

CONCLUSION: THE LIBERAL FICTION IN LEADERSHIP TERMS

Now that we have explored in some depth the underpinnings of the philosophical approach that has become the dominant response to the emergence of popular sovereignty, it is useful to make some summary comments about the premises underlying the liberal outlook, and to consider their strengths and weaknesses for the fiction of leadership.

Although we have detailed various key contributions to the liberal fiction, it is helpful to begin this summary overview with the definition of liberalism provided by Jeremy Waldron in an entry to the *Routledge Encyclopedia of Philosophy*. According to Waldron, 'Liberal political philosophy explores the foundations of the principles most commonly associated with liberal politics: freedom, toleration, individual rights, constitutional democracy and the rule of law. Liberals hold that political organizations are justified by the contribution they make to the interests of individuals, interests which can be understood apart from the idea of society and politics. They reject both the view that cultures, communities and states are ends in themselves, and the view that social and political organizations should aim to transform or perfect human nature.' Waldron elaborated: 'People have purposes of their own to pursue,' he said, 'either economic or spiritual (or both). Since those purposes do not naturally harmonize with one another, a framework of rules may be necessary so that individuals know what they can count on for their own purposes and what they must concede to the purposes of others. The challenge for political philosophy [and leadership], then,' he concluded, 'is to design a social framework that provides this security and predictability, but represents at the same time a safe and reasonable compromise among the disparate demands of individuals.'[263]

In all liberal approaches there is general agreement of the 'priority of right', and governmental neutrality 'between competing conceptions of what is good in life or which way of life is morally justifiable'. In leadership terms, liberalism 'restrict[s] the scope of government to the status of referee: it must ensure each individual's freedom to form a conception of a good life and pursue it, provided that he or she does not infringe on the freedom of others to do likewise'.[264]

That being said, there are, as Rawls acknowledged, 'many variant liberalisms', and Waldron added that liberalism is not 'dogmatic formulae …,' nor is there a 'liberal catechism'. As we have seen from our surveys of Rawls and Nozick, 'liberals disagree about property, economic equality and the role of the state', as well as 'the connection between individual and social purposes'.[265] Given such diversity, hard-and-fast generalizations are difficult to come by. In the following paragraphs, we will attempt, however, to bring some clarity to the liberal world view, particularly as it relates to the focus of our attention, leadership. Again, the template of leadership can serve as our guide.

What is the Leadership Challenge?

We have taken pains to identify with care the specific challenges that each commentator perceived, and which spurred the creation of each theorist's particular version of a liberal response. However, it is fair to generalize to this extent: each liberal writer, in one form or another, addressed a challenge to liberty and individual autonomy and fulfillment. As we have seen, Locke responded to the tyranny of overreaching monarchs; Mill was concerned with the social and political tyranny of an overweening majority. Rawls, for his part, sought to create a polity that could sustain individual freedom in a society characterized by diversity and pluralism. Nozick's concern was that certain variants of modern liberalism intruded overmuch into personal freedom and property interests. Each, in his own way, sought to create a set of relations between the rulers and the ruled that would guarantee protection against the specific perceived threat to liberty. The various definitions of the challenge led inexorably to parallel conceptualizations of the purposes of the proposed leadership relation.

What is the Proper End or Purpose of Leadership?

When we turn to the question of the ends of leadership, the diversity of theories allow this generalization by Jeremy Waldron: 'Liberals hold that political organizations are justified by the contributions they make to the interests of *individuals* [emphasis added]'.[266] In general, all liberal theorists would say that the end purposes of leadership are individual liberty and equality, but they often disagree fundamentally over the meaning of those terms.

For example, there can be a call for 'negative liberty' or 'positive liberty'. 'Some define freedom in negative terms', Waldron explains. 'Freedom, they say, is what flourishes when these constraints are taken away, and [in the extreme libertarian form of liberalism] there is nothing apart from the removal of constraints that needs to be done politically in order for freedom to flourish.' On the other hand, 'Positive conceptions of liberty allow the state a much greater role than this: they may see freedom or autonomy as something to be achieved, rather than taken for granted, in the life of an unrestrained individual, something that requires educated individual capacities and favourable social conditions'.[267]

There is a similar generalized call for 'equality', but it tends to be more muted than the liberal call for liberty, and, again, there is disagreement over the meaning of this particular end of leadership. For instance, the egalitarianism of Rawls's difference principle contrasts sharply with Nozick's equality of basic worth (articulated in his conception of 'self-ownership'). And, of course, the resulting institutional and policy recommendations differ accordingly.

As Will Kymlicka points out, 'there is a "common good" present in liberal politics as well', but only in the minimalist sense that 'the policies of a liberal state aim at promoting the interests of the members of the community'. The stress of liberalism is upon the individual, and this individualism makes end goals less 'common', and more 'competing, but incompatible goods'. Nonetheless, liberals suggest various approaches to achieving something akin to the 'public interest', whether it be secured by commitment to some higher common values in the public realm (Rawls) or via market mechanisms (Nozick). In all cases, 'in a liberal society, the common good is a result of a process of combining preferences, all of which are counted equally'.[268]

What is the Perception of Human Nature?

The discussion of the liberal perception of the ends of leadership reveals the fundamental truism of the liberal conception of the human condition. C.B. Macpherson has stated that 'every political theory which sets out to justify or advocate a particular system of government, or a limited or unlimited degree of obligation of the citizen to the state, must rest on an explicit or implicit theory of human nature'.[269] For liberals, that conception of the human condition highlights its individualistic nature. Mulhall and Swift assert that 'it would be foolish to deny that liberalism regards the individual as of ultimate importance'.[270] More specifically, liberals stress, says Daly, 'the equal worth and dignity of each individual human being'. Michael Sandel describes a 'liberalism that conceives persons as free and independent selves, unencumbered by moral or civic ties they have not chosen'.[271] As portrayed by Daly, in the liberal conception 'each person has a unique identification defined by a subjective consciousness, forms and carries out projects that unfold in a personal history, [and] holds an inalienable right to pursue this life plan'.[272]

The sum total of these observations by commentators on the liberal philosophy is that liberalisms champions a view of human nature characterized by individual capabilities and a self-centered orientation. This is not to suggest, however, that all liberal thinkers agree as to the details. One strand of liberalism – represented in this chapter by Nozick – sees men as 'radically individualistic and solitary, ... hedonistic and prudential, and ... social only to the extent required by the quest for preservation and liberty in an adversarial world of scarcity'. Benjamin Barber has gone so far as to portray liberal man as *'homo economicus*

– the solitary seeker of material happiness and bodily security'.[273] John Rawls, on the other hand, represents those liberal thinkers who acknowledge both the necessity and benefit of some social cooperation, all the while retaining the traditional liberal emphasis upon the 'unencumbered self' – that is, 'unbound by prior moral ties, capable of choosing our ends for ourselves'.[274]

Given the liberal focus upon the individual, serious questions are raised when one turns to a consideration of a phenomenon like leadership, which implies leaders and the people interacting in the interests of society. We thus turn to several template questions that suggest how liberals have approached this conundrum.

Are the People Capable of Governing?
What is the Role of the People?

When we turn our attention to the actual workings of the relationship between leaders and the people, we must confront some difficulties that are posed for the very construct of leadership in a liberal democratic state. Some of these difficulties have to do with the place of the people in a liberal regime, and for this reason, in this summary we will consider the above two template questions together.

In the above paragraphs, we have identified the core concern of the liberal state as individual freedom. Perhaps surprisingly to some, this emphasis upon personal freedom is not necessarily linked to popular participation in government – as the concern about the tyranny of the majority demonstrates. Some liberals have gone so far as to question the need for popular participation at all. Isaiah Berlin, a 'leading defender of the liberal tradition' in the mid-twentieth century, acknowledged this. His stance is depicted by the communitarian critic of liberalism Michael Sandel. 'On the liberal conception', wrote Sandel, '… liberty is not internally but only incidentally related to self-government. Where liberty consists in the opportunity to pursue my own interests and ends, it may or may not coincide with democratic government.' Here Sandel quotes Berlin: 'Liberty in this sense is not incompatible with some kinds of autocracy, or at any rate with the absence of self-government', Berlin wrote. A democracy may violate individual rights that an enlightened despot could in principle respect. Thus, freedom is 'not logically connected with democracy or self-government…. There is no necessary connection between individual liberty and democratic rule.'[275] Modern liberal scholar Jeremy Waldron puts a point on this: 'Certainly, liberals do not regard participation in politics as an end itself', he wrote. 'They do not think that the most important virtues and activities are those oriented towards politics and the formal exercise of power over others.'[276]

This having been said, it is nonetheless true that each of the four liberal scholars detailed in this chapter (who represent the mainstream) worked from the premise of popular participation in government, and, indeed, some championed it. Berlin's caution and Waldron's insight simply highlight a tension that arises when liberal ideas co-exist cheek-by-jowl with participatory politics. We can now turn to the liberal handling of the template questions.

In the previous section, we quoted Macpherson to the effect that every political theorist must present an explicit or implicit theory of human nature. As a corollary, he added: 'The theorist must show, or assume, that the human beings who will have to submit to and operate the desired system do need it and are capable of running it'.[277] Our treatment of our chosen liberal theorists reveals, to some degree, an ambiguity among liberal theorists about the capabilities of the people to govern. John Locke never anticipated that anyone other than a propertied elite would be politically active, and even then placed the responsibility for governing, through his prerogative, in the leaders, rather than the people. John Stuart Mill, as we have seen, feared the tyranny of the majority. At the same time, he appeared to take a more optimistic view of the capabilities of the people. He was a proponent of universal participation, and perceived the civic educability of the people. For Mill, however, the people still had their limitations, which called forth his plea for the expertise of leaders. John Rawls had perhaps the most sanguine view of the capability of the people. His assumptions about their rationality and moral capabilities led him to propose a system that relied almost entirely upon popular activity. Nozick, on the other hand, wrote from that libertarian tradition apprehensive 'about the extent and intrusiveness of the power that a populist state is capable of exercising', and preferred not to rely upon popular wisdom, but rather looked to constraints upon the state.[278]

Thus far, we have seen a liberal tradition that acknowledges some underlying tension between popular participation and its core value of individual liberty, and which has demonstrated a mixed view of the wisdom of the people and their capability to govern themselves. Not surprisingly, these same ambiguities are reflected in the perception of the role the people should play in governing.

Again, it is the core values of liberalism that shape (and limit) the role of the people. Sandel (the critic of liberalism) describes this well. 'Conceived as unencumbered selves, [liberals] must respect the dignity of all persons, but beyond this, we owe only what we agree to owe.'[279] This explains the popularity of social contract imagery among liberals. According to Sheldon Wolin, 'Contract theory conceives of political society as the creation of individuals who freely consent to accept the authority and rules of political society on the basis of certain stipulated conditions…. The contractual element is needed, according to the theory, because, all persons being free and equal by nature and society being by nature in need of coercive power to protect rights [and] preserve peace … the freedom of individuals will have to be limited and regulated. Individuals will contract, therefore, to surrender some part of their rights in exchange for the protection of the law….'[280] Sandel reflects upon the implications of this. 'One striking consequence of this view,' he said, citing Rawls, 'is that "there is no political obligation, strictly speaking, for citizens generally." …. The average citizen', Sandel continued, 'is therefore without any special obligations to his or her fellow citizens, apart from the universal, natural duty not to commit injustice.'[281]

The scholars cited above (Sandel, Wolin) are critics of liberalism. Nevertheless, there is something to the fact that the liberal stress upon individual freedom sometimes rests uncomfortably next to any demand for political exertion on behalf of others. This results in uneven expectations of citizens. As Jeremy Waldron has observed, 'philosophical liberals are about equally divided on the question of whether voters in a democracy should orient their decisions to the common good or to their own interests (with the common good emerging as some sort of resultant from the political process)'.[282] From the perspectives of our four chosen commentators, we can see the variation, with a progression from Locke's passive and deferential citizens, through Mill, to Rawls's engaged citizens, but recall that even Rawls was hesitant to demand of citizens any political activity, and Nozick had little use for any citizen activity in government.

In sum, the point here is not that liberalism is antithetical to rule by the people. Indeed, it is being presented here as one response to the emergence of popular sovereignty, as it sought to protect individuals first from the state, and then from both the state and the tyranny of fellow citizens. The point is that liberalism's answer to the rise of the people has not always provided satisfactory answers to the issue of the proper role for the people in the new polity. In the next section, we will find a similar tension with respect to the leader. Taken together, this merely means that modern society faces a continuing challenge with respect to the new social and political relation we call leadership.

What is the Role of the Leader?

The commentators chosen as representative of liberal thinking for the purposes of this chapter provide us with the span of thinking among liberals with respect to the role of the leader. In our treatment of these commentators, one can detect a transition. The early writers such as Locke and Mill were more attuned to what we have put forward as leaders in the style of the classical ideal: individuals who have superior capabilities and intellect, who operate with the larger good in mind. By the time we encounter Rawls in a modern democratic setting, however, we have a different perception of the leader. For Rawls, it was somewhat difficult to discern a leader's role at all, but from careful analysis one could derive a new expectation for leader behavior: one who was committed to neutrality among various conceptions of the good, and who was process-oriented – that is, one who 'asserts the priority of fair procedures over particular ends'.[283]

If this were simply a matter of a 'newer' version replacing an older one, this would pose no undue problems. However, as our continuing discussion of the tension between 'participation' and 'competence' reveals, each version of leader behavior has its desirable aspects. Unfortunately, each also has its weaknesses. Those who advocate mere procedural leadership either must make the rather large and dangerous assumption that all individuals in the polity have the capability and the desire to act in ways that will serve all, or adopt the unproven position that the conflict among individual interests will automatically result in policies serving the interests of all. On the other hand, reliance upon traditional leaders of superior capability assumes that such leaders exist, and runs against a deep-seated modern aversion to elitism. Both approaches to leader behavior, then, leave something to be desired, and this template query remains relevant in our quest to create leadership for a democracy.

How Should Leaders and the People Interact?

Liberalism provides three nodal points at which the relations between the leaders and the people are articulated: the social contract, the idea of representation and the actual process of interaction between leaders and the people. We have seen the implications of the social contract: specifically, the limited government that results and the consensual nature of the relationship between leaders and the people (although recall that Mill dispensed with this fiction, and relied instead upon the claims individuals are entitled to make upon their government and society).

So, too, has representation been a central aspect of the relations between leaders and the people in a liberal state. As Benjamin Barber depicts it, 'Liberal democracy was ... an attempt to adapt pure democracy to the realities of governing large-scale nation states', in which 'representative democracy ... substituted ... as a form of government in which some of the people ... govern in all public matters'.[284] As we have seen, however, disputes arose concerning the nature of the relationship between representative and constituent – disputes that echoed the assumptions about the respective roles of leaders and the people. Some advocated a 'trustee' form of representation, in which elected representatives acted on their own best judgment in the interests of all, while others demanded that representatives be mere 'delegates', acting out the wishes of their constituents.

Finally, the liberal theorists also addressed the matter of the actual interaction between the leaders and the people. Locke restricted this, essentially, to the casting of votes on election day (and the unlikely event of revolution), and expected there to be deference on the part of the people to their leaders. Mill saw the interactions among leaders and the people as a mutually educative process, albeit the expertise of leaders was to be honored. He foresaw a kind of 'rational deference' to leaders. Rawls, for his part, appeared to regard leaders more as procedural experts, and suggested little in the way of deferential relations between leaders and the people (if anything, the deference now ran the other way, with leaders deferring to the activities of the people).

We see, then, that the liberal outlook admits of many possible models for relations between leaders and the people. One of the continuing challenges for leadership in our modern age is to delineate the appropriate relationship, backed, of course, by sufficient justifications. We will turn to such matters in the concluding Part of this book.

What is the Epistemology of Leadership?

All this relates to the topic we have called the 'epistemology of leadership', or, framed alternatively, 'How do we know what to do, or if what we are doing is right?' Our study thus far has suggested three rather broadly-conceived approaches taken by liberal thinkers to this central question.

Many theorists in the liberal pantheon look to what Rawls would call a 'comprehensive doctrine' of liberalism. Benjamin Barber asserts that 'liberal democratic theory ... depends on particular assumptions about the character of political knowledge.... The paramount assumption', he asserts, 'is Cartesian: that there exists a knowable independent ground ... from which concepts, values, standards and ends of political life can be derived by simple deduction.'[285] This might be the deontology of Kant or the utilitarianism of Mill.

Rawls, it will be recalled, objected to this in the context of what he called 'reasonable pluralism', and sought to escape its operation through his 'political conception' of liberalism, wherein comprehensive doctrines were to be set aside in the public arena, and all participants would agree to certain rules of engagement that ensured fair cooperation. This might be deemed a 'procedural' approach to achieving the 'best' policy in modern democracy.

Finally, Robert Nozick's work suggests what has become another dominant mode of achieving 'right policy'. He looks to market mechanisms. The assumption here is that there is no common good or public interest. Voters pursue their individual interests, and the operation of the free and unfettered market will guarantee a just outcome. One form of this is the 'pluralist model of democracy', which includes the 'interest group' theories of political scientist Robert Dahl and the like.[286]

Taken together, again we see that liberalism provides us with a rich vein of possibilities that can inform us in our ultimate task of deriving our own responses to the questions of the leadership template.

How is the Matter of Diversity and Minority Interests Addressed?

In this, we see even more than the usual span of liberal responses. Locke, concerned only with political oppression, satisfied himself with simple majoritarianism, ignoring the issue of diversity and minority interests. The remaining liberal commentators who have been the subject of our study here, however, took this matter quite seriously. Mill was intensely concerned with protecting the idiosyncratic thoughts and actions of all individuals, and Rawls erected an entire system around the premise of a diverse society. Nozick, for his part believed that 'collective coercion in matters political or economic [are] always ... illegitimate'.[287] In sum, one of the enduring glories of the liberal approach has been its consistent concern with this key issue. As we have seen, various theorists have come up with differing ways to address the matter. Taken together, the works of these liberal theorists provide a call for tolerance that one would be hard put to dispute.

What Institutions and Processes Must be Designed?

It is beyond the scope of this analysis to delve very deeply into the specific institutional and procedural modes of implementing the values and priorities of the liberal outlook. Suffice it to say that since liberalism has become paradigmatic in Western democracies, many of its manifestations have become commonplaces. One key area is the protection of rights, often through a constitutional guise such as a bill of rights. There are similar institutional protections against overweening power in the form of the separation of powers, federalism, and the like, as well as guarantees of participation via electoral regulations. Also, in general, the state has been viewed as a neutral framework within which individuals can pursue their own conceptions of the good. In terms of leadership processes, the liberal tradition has relied upon representative systems and proceduralist processes designed to guarantee a fair hearing to all.

Again, there are rather severe disagreements regarding some of the specifics, ranging the gamut from Nozick's *laissez-faire* state, dedicated to free market mechanisms, to Rawls's implied welfare state, with its redistribution of wealth and power.

Summation

Despite the amazing variety of specific applications, and some quite substantive disagreements, there is a discernible value set that is more-or-less common to all who carry the sobriquet of liberals in the philosophical sense. As Richard Dagger frames it (quoting Lance Banning), '*Liberalism* is a label most would use for a political philosophy that regards man as possessed of inherent individual rights and the state as existing to protect these rights, deriving its authority from consent.... Liberalism ... is comfortable with economic man, with the individual who is intent on maximizing private satisfactions and who needs no more in order to serve the general good.'[288]

However encapsulated, this constellation of ideas has become the dominant response to the emergence of popular sovereignty and modern society, and in many ways it has earned the respect and honor often heaped upon it. Unfortunately, this ideology, as a solution to the demands of the new relation between the few and the many that we are calling leadership, also has some flaws and weaknesses (a few of which are outlined above). Any acceptable proposal for a modified 'fiction' of leadership, such as the one we will present in the last Part of this book, will need to confront both the strengths and weaknesses of modern liberalism.

Before turning to this task, however, it is necessary to acknowledge that, despite its hegemony, liberalism is not the only unified body of assumptions and proposed responses to the challenges of modern society. There is another constellation of ideas, many antithetical to those of liberalism – an approach we will rather loosely call *communitarianism* – with equally deep roots in the western tradition, and which has emerged rather recently as a legitimate contender as an appropriate variant of the proper relations among leaders and the people in a democracy. It is to a consideration of this alternative fiction that we now turn.

NOTES

1. Benjamin Constant, 'The Liberty of the Ancients Compared with That of the Moderns', in Biancamaria Fontana, trans. and ed., *Political Writings of Benjamin Constant* (Cambridge: Cambridge University Press, 1988), 307–328.
2. Ibid., 309.
3. Ibid., 316–317.
4. Ibid., 317, 316, 323.
5. Quoted in Will Kymlicka, *Contemporary Political Philosophy: An Introduction* (Oxford: Clarenden Press, 1990), 225.
6. Constant, 'Ancients and Moderns', 319 (see note 1).
7. John Rawls, *Political Liberalism* (New York: Columbia University Press, 1996), 4–5.
8. Benjamin Barber, *Strong Democracy: Participatory Politics for a New Age* (Berkeley: University of California Press, 1984), 155.
9. John Locke, *Second Treatise of Government*, ed. C.B. Macpherson (Indianapolis: Hackett Publishing Company, 1690, 1980).
10. Markate Daly, ed., *Communitarianism: A New Public Ethics* (Belmont, CA: Wadsworth Publishing Company, 1994), xix.
11. C.B. Macpherson, 'Introduction' to John Locke, *Second Treatise of Government* (Indianapolis: Hackett Publishing Company, 1980), xiii.
12. Locke, *Second Treatise*, sec. 4.
13. Ibid., sections 4, 22, 23.
14. Ibid., sec. 4.
15. Ibid., sec. 63.
16. Ibid., sec. 6.
17. Ibid., sec. 27.
18. Ibid., sec. 31.
19. Ibid., sec. 36, 37.
20. Ibid., sec. 48.
21. Ibid., sec. 50.
22. Ibid., sec. 37.
23. Ibid., sec. 19.
24. Ibid., sec. 124, 125.
25. Ibid., sec. 19.
26. Ibid., sec. 8, 17.
27. Ibid., sec. 123.

28. Ibid., sec. 15.
29. Ibid., sec. 13.
30. Ibid., sec. 89.
31. Ibid., sec. 171.
32. Ibid., sec. 131.
33. Ibid., sec. 134.
34. Ibid., sec. 171.
35. Ibid., sec. 124, 85.
36. Ibid., sec. 131.
37. Macpherson, 'Introduction', vii–viii (see note 11).
38. Locke, *Second Treatise*, sec. 134 (see note 9).
39. Ibid., sec. 133.
40. Ibid., sec. 132.
41. Ibid., sec. 143.
42. Ibid., sec. 152, 144.
43. Ibid., sec. 137, 202.
44. Ibid., sec. 57.
45. Ibid., sec. 135.
46. Ibid., sec. 138.
47. Ibid., sec. 163.
48. Ibid., sec. 157.
49. Ibid., sec. 171.
50. Ibid., sec. 106, 95.
51. Ibid., sec. 157.
52. Ibid., sec. 154.
53. Ibid., sec. 134.
54. Ibid., sec. 203.
55. Ibid., sec. 22.
56. Ibid., sec. 130.
57. Ibid., sec. 149.
58. Ibid., sec. 220.
59. Macpherson, 'Introduction,' xix (see note 11).
60. Locke, *Second Treatise*, sec. 131 (see note 9).
61. Ibid.
62. Ibid., sec. 156.
63. Ibid., sec. 158.
64. Ibid., sec. 164.
65. Ibid., sec. 160.
66. Ibid., sec. 161.
67. Ibid., sec. 164.
68. Ibid.
69. Ibid., sec. 22.
70. Ibid., sec. 149.
71. Ibid., sec. 156, 135.
72. Ibid., sec. 168, 225.
73. Ibid., sec. 168.
74. Ibid., sec. 225, 209.
75. Ibid., sec. 95.
76. Ibid., sec. 96, 97.
77. John Stuart Mill, *On Liberty*, ed. with intro. by Elizabeth Rapaport (Indianapolis: Hackett Publishing Company, 1859/1978); Jeremy Waldron, 'Liberalism', in *Routledge Encyclopedia of Philosophy* (London: Routledge, 1998), 5:604.
78. John Stuart Mill, *Considerations on Representative Government* (London: John W. Parker and Son, 1859).
79. Mill, *On Liberty*, 1.
80. Markate Daly, *Communitarianism: A New Public Ethics* (Belmont, Calif.: Wadsworth Publishing Company, 1994), xx.
81. Elizabeth Rapaport, 'Introduction' to John Stuart Mill, *On Liberty* (Indianapolis: Hackett Publishing Co., Inc., 1859/1978), xiv.
82. Mill, *On Liberty*, 4 (see note 77).
83. Rapaport, 'Introduction', xiv.

84. Mill, *On Liberty*, 1.
85. Ibid., 4, 5.
86. Ibid., 64.
87. Ibid., 56–57.
88. Ibid., 59.
89. Ibid., 55–56.
90. Ibid., 61.
91. Ibid., 60.
92. Citing William von Humboldt, *Spheres and Duties of Government* (Bristol: Thoemmes Press, 1854/1996).
93. Rapaport, 'Introduction', vii (see note 81).
94. Mill, *On Liberty*, 54 (see note 77).
95. Ibid., 81.
96. Ibid., 61.
97. Ibid., 74.
98. Ibid., 5.
99. Ibid., 9.
100. Ibid.
101. Ibid., 73.
102. Ibid., 79.
103. Ibid., 73.
104. Michael J. Sandel, *Democracy's Discontent: America in Search of a Public Philosophy* (Cambridge: Harvard University Press, 1996), 8.
105. Mill, *On Liberty*, 10 (see note 77).
106. Mill, *Representative Government*, 116–117, quoted in Dennis Thompson, *John Stuart Mill and Representative Government* (Princeton: Princeton University Press, 1976), 10–11.
107. Thompson, *John Stuart Mill*, 3, 9–10.
108. Ibid., 91–92.
109. *See* Rapaport, 'Introduction', ix. (see note 81).
110. Ibid., xiv.
111. Mill, *On Liberty,* 3 (see note 77).
112. Ibid., 66.
113. Ibid., 19.
114. Ibid., 63.
115. Ibid., 19.
116. Ibid., 33.
117. Ibid, 73.
118. Mill, *Representative Government,* p. 53, quoted in Thompson, *John Stuart Mill*, 5 (see note 106).
119. Mill, *Representative Government*, p. 69, quoted in Thompson, *John Stuart Mill*, 13.
120. Thompson, *John Stuart Mill*, 39–40.
121. Mill, *Representative Government*, 68 (see note 78).
122. Ibid.
123. Mill, *Representative Government*, p. 201, quoted in Thompson, *John Stuart Mill*, 97.
124. Mill, *On Liberty*, 64 (see note 77).
125. Thompson, *John Stuart Mill*, 55.
126. Mill, *Representative Government*, 68, quoted in Thompson, *John Stuart Mill*, 38.
127. Mill, *On Liberty*, 63–64.
128. Michael J. Sandel, *Democracy's Discontent: America in Search of a Public Philosophy* (Cambridge: Harvard University Press, 1996), 8.
129. Mill, *On Liberty*, 10 (see note 77).
130. Ibid., 7–8.
131. Ibid., 16–17.
132. Ibid., 44.
133. Ibid., 18.
134. Thompson, *John Stuart Mill*, 70, 79 (see note 106).
135. Mill, *Representative Government*, 282, 294, quoted in Thompson, *John Stuart Mill*, 79–80.
136. Thompson, *John Stuart Mill*, 80–81.
137. Ibid., 21.
138. Ibid., 105.
139. Rapaport, 'Introduction', xx (see note 81).
140. Thompson, *John Stuart Mill*, 82–85; Mill, *Representative Government*, 234 (see note 78).
141. Thompson, *John Stuart Mill*, 96.

142. Ibid., 99.
143. Mill, *Representative Government*, 203–211; Thompson, *John Stuart Mill*, 98.
144. Thompson, *John Stuart Mill*, 46–47, 49, 126–127.
145. Ibid., 90.
146. Mill, *Representative Government*, 173–178; Thompson, *John Stuart Mill*, 99–100.
147. Thompson, *John Stuart Mill*, 104; Mill, *Representative Government*, 144–152.
148. Mill, *Representative Government*, 100–102, 318–319; Thompson, *John Stuart Mill*, 121–123.
149. Mill, *Representative Government*, 243; Thompson, *John Stuart Mill*, 94.
150. Thompson, *John Stuart Mill*, 175.
151. Ibid., 126.
152. Waldron, 'Liberalism', 5:599 (see note 77).
153. Kymlicka, *Contemporary Political Philosophy*, 52 (see note 5).
154. Daly, *Communitarianism*, 71 (see note 80).
155. John Rawls, *Political Liberalism* (New York: Columbia University Press, 1996), xli.
156. Ibid., xxvi.
157. Ibid., xvi.
158. Sandel, *Democracy's Discontent*, 9 (see note 128).
159. Thompson, *John Stuart Mill*, 97 (see note 106).
160. Rawls, *Political Liberalism*, xvii; *see generally* Rawls, *A Theory of Justice* (Cambridge: Belknap Press of Harvard University Press, 1971).
161. Rawls, *Political Liberalism*, xviii.
162. Ibid., 134–135.
163. Ibid., xviii–xix.
164. Ibid., 135.
165. Ibid., xl.
166. Ibid., xliii, xviii.
167. Ibid., 4.
168. Ibid., xxvii, xx.
169. Ibid., xxvii.
170. Ibid., xlii.
171. Ibid., 38.
172. Ibid., 13, 10.
173. Ibid., xxii–xxiii.
174. Ibid., 11.
175. Ibid., 9.
176. Ibid., 97.
177. Ibid., xxii.
178. Ibid., 22.
179. Ibid., 23–25.
180. Ibid., 26–27.
181. Ibid., 72.
182. Kymlicka, *Contemporary Political Philosophy*, 55 (see note 5).
183. Ibid., 71.
184. Rawls, *Political Liberalism*, 5–6 (see note 155).
185. Daly, *Communitarianism*, xxi (see note 80).
186. Rawls, *Political Liberalism*, 175.
187. Ibid., 161.
188. Ibid., xli.
189. Ibid., xlviii.
190. Ibid., 176.
191. Sandel, *Democracy's Discontent*, 10–11 (see note 128).
192. Kymlicka, *Contemporary Political Philosophy*, 65 (see note 5); *see* Rawls, *Theory of Justice*, 152–153 (see note 160).
193. Rawls, *Political Liberalism*, xli.
194. Ibid., 6.
195. Ibid., 180.
196. Ibid., 6.
197. Ibid., lviii–lvix.
198. Ibid.
199. Ibid.
200. Kymlicka, *Contemporary Political Philosophy*, 89.

201. Rawls, *Theory of Justice*, 303.
202. Rawls, *Political Liberalism*, xli.
203. Stephen Mulhall and Adam Swift, *Liberals and Communitarians* (Oxford: Blackwell Publishers, 1992), 14.
204. Kymlicka, *Contemporary Political Philosophy*, 60 (see note 5).
205. Rawls, *Political Liberalism*, 18–19 (see note 155); Mulhall and Swift, *Liberals and Communitarians*, 11.
206. Rawls, *Political Liberalism*, 15.
207. Ibid., 42, 201.
208. Ibid., 72, 49, 53.
209. Ibid., lxii.
210. Ibid., 19.
211. Ibid., xxxviii.
212. Ibid., 134.
213. Ibid., 15.
214. Ibid., 202.
215. Ibid., 137.
216. Ibid., 224.
217. Ibid., 218.
218. Ibid., 226.
219. Ibid., 218.
220. Ibid., 213.
221. Ibid., xlvi, li.
222. Ibid., 157.
223. Ibid., 217, li.
224. Ibid., 58.
225. Ibid., 55–57.
226. Ibid., 58.
227. Ibid., 61.
228. Ibid., 36, 18.
229. Ibid., 18–19.
230. Ibid., xxi–xxii.
231. Ibid., 96, 94, 128, 89–90.
232. Ibid., 98.
233. Ibid., 18.
234. Ibid., xlvi–xlvii.
235. Kymlicka, *Contemporary Political Philosophy,* 60–61 (see note 5).
236. Rawls, *Political Liberalism*, 80 (see note 155).
237. Ibid., 213.
238. Ibid., 192, 138.
239. Ibid., 137.
240. Ibid., 68, 71.
241. Ibid., 86.
242. Ibid., 90.
243. Ibid., 154.
244. Kymlicka, *Contemporary Political Philosophy*, 90, 106 (see note 5).
245. Ibid., 132, 103.
246. Robert Nozick, *Anarchy, State and Utopia* (New York: Basic Books, 1974), ix.
247. Kymlicka, *Contemporary Political Theory*, 104–105, 98.
248. Jonathan Wolff, 'Robert Nozick', in *Routledge Encyclopedia of Philosophy* (London: Routledge, 1998), 7:45.
249. Nozick, *Anarchy, State, and Utopia*, ix (see note 246).
250. Kymlicka, *Contemporary Political Theory*, 96 (see note 5).
251. Nozick, *Anarchy, State, and Utopia*, ix.
252. Kymlicka, *Contemporary Political Theory*, 97.
253. Ibid., 163.
254. Kymlicka, *Contemporary Political Philosophy*, 148.
255. Wolff, 'Robert Nozick', 7:45 (see note 248).
256. Kymlicka, *Contemporary Political Theory,* 107.
257. Wolff, 'Robert Nozick', 7:45–46.
258. Kymlicka, *Contemporary Political Theory*, 135.

259. Nozick, *Anarchy, State, and Utopia*, 334 (see note 246); Kymlicka, *Contemporary Political Philosophy*, 104 (see note 5).
260. Kymlicka, *Contemporary Political Theory*, 199.
261. Ibid., 96–97.
262. Waldron, 'Liberalism', 5:599 (see note 77).
263. Ibid., 5:598.
264. Daly, *Communitarianism*, xvi (see note 80).
265. Rawls, *Political Liberalism*, 6 (see note 155); Waldron, 'Liberalism', 5:599–600.
266. Waldron, 'Liberalism', 5:598.
267. Ibid., 5:600.
268. Kymlicka, *Contemporary Political Philosophy*, 206 (see note 5).
269. Macpherson, 'Introduction', x (see note 11).
270. Mulhall and Swift, *Liberals and Communitarians*, 14 (see note 203).
271. Daly, *Communitarianism*, p. xiv (see note 80); Sandel, *Democracy's Discontent*, 6 (see note 128).
272. Daly, *Communitarianism*, xiv.
273. Barber, *Strong Democracy*, 20, 213 (see note 8).
274. Sandel, *Democracy's Discontent*, 12.
275. Ibid., 26, citing Isaiah Berlin, 'Two Concepts of Liberty', in Berlin, *Four Essays on Liberty* (London: Oxford University Press, 1969), 129–130.
276. Waldron, 'Liberalism', 5:602 (see note 77).
277. Macpherson, 'Introduction', x (see note 11).
278. Waldron, 'Liberalism'. 5:599.
279. Sandel, *Democracy's Discontent*, 14 (see note 128).
280. Sheldon S. Wolin, 'Contract and Birthright', *Political Theory* 14 (May 1986): 180–181.
281. Sandel, *Democracy's Discontent*, 14, citing Rawls, *Theory of Justice*, 114 (see note 160).
282. Waldron, 'Liberalism', 5:602 (see note 77).
283. Sandel, *Democracy's Discontent*, 4.
284. Barber, *Strong Democracy*, xxii (see note 8).
285. Ibid., 46.
286. Ibid., 143–144.
287. Ibid., 252.
288. Richard Dagger, *Civic Virtues: Rights, Citizenship, and Republican Liberalism* (Oxford: Oxford University Press, 1997), 12, quoting Lance Banning, 'Jefferson Ideology Revisited: Liberal and Classical Ideas in the New American Republic', *William and Mary Quarterly* 43 (1986): 12.

9. Inventing communitarianism

The introduction to our previous chapter recalled the insight of Benjamin Constant, who in 1819 distinguished between the 'liberty of the ancients' and the 'liberty of the moderns'. 'The confusion of these two kinds of liberty', he had noted, 'has been amongst us ... the cause of many an evil.'[1] As we have seen, his 'liberty of the moderns' was closely akin to the values of what we have labeled classical liberalism, and our previous chapter was devoted to an exploration of the premises of classical and modern liberalism and their leadership implications. In this chapter we turn to the other half of Constant's dichotomy, the 'liberty of the ancients'. As opposed to the individualistic conception of liberty maintained by Constant's 'moderns', his 'liberty of the ancients ... consisted in an active and constant participation in collective power', with a conception of liberty that embraced not individual rights but communal obligations.[2] And, just as we treated liberalism in the previous chapter as the invention of a 'fiction' that depicted a new mode of social and political relation we can study in leadership terms, so too can we turn to an opposing constellation of ideas that we will label, for the sake of convenience, 'communitarianism'.

Like liberalism, communitarianism has roots in the past (Constant was harking back to the values of classical republicanism), but has taken on new life in recent decades as a complex and sophisticated ideology geared to modern needs. It represents the principal alternative to the dominant liberalism of the modern era. The first sections of this chapter will be devoted to a consideration of some of the classic early statements of communitarianism, by Aristotle, Hegel, and especially, Rousseau. Despite these deep roots, however, modern communitarian thought is a product of the revitalization of liberalism spearheaded by John Rawls. Indeed, as modern communitarian scholar Markate Daly has noted, modern 'communitarianism is a postliberal philosophy in the sense that it could only have developed within a liberal tradition of established democratic practices, in a liberal culture that had allowed community values to decline to the extent that a corrective seemed necessary'. Daly points out that 'communitarianism was proposed as just such a corrective', and purports to provide an alternative argument about 'the place of individual liberty, the structure of ethics, and the obligation of citizens'.[3] The bulk of this chapter will parse the literature of modern communitarian scholarship to identify its essential premises and, again, their implications for leadership in a democracy.

Our analysis is complicated by the fact that, as Allen Buchanan has observed, 'at present the communitarian critique of liberalism is more developed than is communitarianism as a systematic ethical or political philosophy'. As a result, 'For the most part, the positive content of communitarians' views must be inferred from their criticisms of liberalism'.[4] In these pages, then, rather than attempting to identify some 'iconic' modern statement – such as those provided by Rawls and Nozick for liberalism – we will draw upon numerous commentators, and again use the template of leadership to help us identify key assumptions and explore the leadership implications.

Prior to turning to our analysis proper, one definitional caveat must be entered. The ensuing analysis will conflate to some degree the overarching principles of the philosophical approach labeled *communitarianism* with one political variant, *republicanism*. These two traditions are in some ways distinct; where appropriate the differing sources for our conclusions will be pointed out.

Moving now to our analysis, our first task is to look to the historical roots of the community-based response to the challenges of modern leadership. For that, we focus (briefly) on the insights of Aristotle and G.W.F. Hegel, and then devote somewhat more attention to the work of Jean Jacques Rousseau.

ARISTOTLE

Although contemporary communitarians label their approach a modern phenomenon, most also acknowledge its deep roots in the past. Markate Daly, for example, asserts that 'communal relationships form the fabric of all human societies and community-centered philosophy goes back at least to ancient Greece'. Indeed, she says, 'the roots of a community-based philosophy are explored in ... Aristotle'.[5] We have encountered Aristotle before, chiefly in the context of the fiction of the classical ideal of the leader. We return to him now, to explore his fundamental assumptions about the nature of man, the importance of community and the role of the people.

When Aristotle turned his attention to the analysis of political forms and processes, he began by exploring human nature. 'We must certainly first obtain', he wrote, 'some general notion of the virtue of the citizen.' His response was that 'like the sailor, the citizen is a member of a community'.[6] Indeed, he maintained, 'it is only as participants in political association that we realize our nature and fulfill our highest ends.'[7] Thus, as a modern commentator puts it, Aristotle believed that 'humans are political by nature; that is, they live and find their fulfillment only in the polis'. This was not to preclude totally the possibility of individual aspiration and virtue, but, to Aristotle, individual 'freedom holds the place of an instrumental good', worthy to the extent that it fostered 'effective participation in government'.[8] In sum, man was, by nature, a creature of his community, and it was to his community that he owed his obligation and best action.

Aristotle reinforced this understanding with his explication of what was entailed in the 'good'. He first posed the question in his *Nicomachean Ethics*. There, he suggested the foundational issue: 'Let us ... state,' he began, 'in view of the fact that all knowledge and every pursuit aims at some good, what it is that we say political science aims at and what is the highest of all goods achievable by action.' The answer, Aristotle posited, was that it was 'happiness'. But this was not a sufficient response. 'To say that happiness is the chief good seems a platitude', he acknowledged. 'A clearer account of what it is is still desired.' Further insight might be gleaned, Aristotle reasoned, 'if we could first ascertain the function of man'. This function, it turned out, was to live 'a certain kind of life'. That kind of life, and indeed 'human good turns out to be activity ... in accordance with virtue'.[9]

Following Aristotle's reasoning, the 'good' was achieved by living a life of virtue. But this still begged the question of what he meant by the term 'virtue'. His answer came most dramatically in his work *Politics*. His focus there was upon the notion of man as a member of his polis, that is, as a citizen. 'We must certainly first obtain', he noted, 'some general notion of the virtue of the citizen'. That virtue derived from a 'common object'. To be more precise, 'the salvation of the community is the common business of them all'. Therefore, the 'virtue of the citizen' *qua* citizen was to be judged according to his commitment to the interests of the political community. 'What is to be just or right', Aristotle concluded, 'is to be interpreted … with reference to the advantage of the state, and the common good of the citizens.'[10] Thus we come to Aristotle's classic concept of 'civic virtue', in which individual interests and desires are to be subsumed to the interests of the community. This prioritization is what places him in the stream of communitarian sentiment.

Having envisioned a state grounded in such values, Aristotle went on to contemplate the leadership implications. In an earlier chapter we went over this ground in our exploration of the expectations for the leader; here, we traverse it again, from the broader perspective of the role that citizens must play. Given his communitarian leanings, it comes as no surprise that Aristotle defined 'a citizen [as] one who shares in governing and being governed'.[11] However, his perception of the leadership relation was quite nuanced.

It all had to do with his perception of the capability of the people to govern. Viewed individually, 'each individual is but an ordinary person', and hence could be little trusted to govern wisely. Here, however, Aristotle's view of the communal nature of politics redeemed the situation. 'For the many … when they meet together may very likely be better … if regarded not individually but collectively.' This was because 'each individual among the many has a share of virtue and prudence, and when they meet together, they become in a manner one man, who has many feet, and hands, and senses…. Hence,' he concluded, 'the many are better judges than a single man.'[12] This additive conception of human capability and virtue is logical only if one begins, as Aristotle does, from a premise of political activity as the subsuming of individual interest to the common good.

As we noted in that earlier chapter, this did not mean that there was no role for leaders. Although the people, taken collectively, were wise and virtuous enough, they remained unequal to the more complex and sophisticated tasks associated with governing. For such tasks 'good men' were needed, men 'who differ from any individual of the many'. From the ranks of those few good men should come 'the good *ruler*'. Such a ruler must be a 'good and wise man'; indeed 'he who would be a statesman must be a wise man'.[13]

The obvious challenge was to determine how to allocate political roles among the rulers and the ruled. Aristotle's answer was to distinguish between the greater and lesser offices of the state. As for the general run of the people, he opined, 'there is still a danger in allowing them to share the greatest offices of state, for their [individual] folly will lead them into error, and their dishonesty into crime'. Nonetheless, he maintained that 'when they meet together their perceptions are quite good enough, and combined with the better class they are useful to the state'. For Aristotle, the resolution of the dilemma was clear. As for the people, the wisest path was 'to assign them some deliberative and judicial functions', such as 'the power of electing to offices and of calling the magistrates to account'. On the other hand, 'Do not', he admonished, 'allow them to hold office singly'; the 'good men' mentioned previously should occupy 'the great offices of state'.[14]

Aristotle, with his careful elaboration of the communal aspects of man's nature and exposition of how men must act together in public life for the good of the whole, serves as a seminal statement of early communitarian principles. And, as Daly puts it, 'Aristotle's theory of a life of virtue and his conception of citizenship in an ancient Greek polis have inspired nearly everyone who has since written on democratic community'.[15]

G.W.F. HEGEL

Having suggested the classical roots of communitarianism, it would be remiss not to recognize also a more modern source of such thought. Foremost among these is the work of Georg Wilhelm Friedrich Hegel. G.W.F. Hegel's productive years spanned the first three decades of the nineteenth century. He was a product of his time, and wrote in response to a philosophical tradition that included such seminal liberal thinkers as Immanuel Kant and John Locke. It is difficult to do justice to Hegel in a few short paragraphs, and perhaps impossible to tap into his near impenetrable prose to illustrate his points usefully. Nevertheless, such an attempt is justified by the importance of his insights. Some have called Hegel 'the most important progenitor of modern communitarian philosophy', not only because of his influence upon Karl Marx, who framed his own dissent to liberal philosophy, but also due to the manner in which he framed the relation between the individual and the community. In the following brief paragraphs, the intent is to identify some of these contributions to the communitarian heritage.

Two insights stemming from Hegel's work are the social construction of self and the related harmony of interests between individuals and their community. He acknowledged that it is common for humans to believe, initially, at any rate, that 'they are for themselves only', and perceive themselves as a 'self-sufficient essence'. Accordingly, Hegel went on, this 'individuality ... may indeed believe that it acts only *for itself* or *for its own advantage*'. Little could be further from the truth. In reality, such an individual consciousness 'is better than it believes'. Inevitably, argues Hegel, each individual becomes conscious of others, who are seemingly equally partaking in this 'self-sufficient essence'. With this comes the first inkling of a connection to others: 'I behold the others as myself, and myself as them'. The individual thus becomes aware of his '*unity* with the other consciousness.... In the self-sufficiency of the *other* it can behold the complete *unity* with that other....' This leads to the ultimate communitarian insight: each member of the community finds that 'the *work* of the individual for his needs is just as much the satisfaction of the needs of others as it is of his own, and he achieves the satisfaction of his own needs only through the work of others'.[16]

From this line of reasoning came a third insight concerning how social values and practices are a product of group functioning and interaction. As scholar Kenneth Westphal explains Hegel's point, 'human beings are fundamentally social practitioners; there are no individuals or individual actions apart from social practices'. Societal ethics and practices emerge from interactions among its members. As Westphal puts it, 'There are no social practices apart from a group of people who engage in them'.[17] Hegel himself writes that as a result of such communal interaction 'consciousness raises itself to universality [and] it becomes *universal* reason'. Thus the interactions of the members of the community eventually generate a common ethical life. For Hegel, '*the realm of ethical life* unlocks itself in this concept'.[18] In sum, according to Hegel, social values are socially constructed, another key tenet of modern communitarian thinking.

Finally, Hegel suggests that individual liberty can only be realized within such a rational ethical community. As one scholar explained it, 'Hegel's political philosophy locates the preconditions of individual freedom in the proper functioning of this complex of social practices, objective norms, and rational self-conscious agents'. In the first instance, ethical notions are 'formed by the legal, political, and civil structures of their society and by the actions of individuals within these structures'. Thereafter, community members 'express their personal freedom by acting in accord with the social structure and adjusting it to meet their changing needs'.[19] In other words, for Hegel, individual liberty can only be realized as a part of ongoing social and political interaction with other community members, as they 'recognize and critically evaluate their own customs and change them'. Almost by definition, this can only be done through a process of mutual interaction with other rational members of the community. Thus Hegel conceives of liberty as exercised within the confines of the values, institutions and principles of action agreed to by community members. This, too, is a foundational premise of modern communitarianism.

If Hegel contributed many of the principles that underlie recent communitarian thinking, there is yet another early commentator who has exercised an even greater influence. It could be argued that the enigmatic and always-controversial Jean-Jacques Rousseau remains the intellectual inspiration for modern communitarian thought. Certainly his writings offer us an opportunity to explore the foundational premises of communitarian thought in more detail. It is to his work that we now turn.

JEAN-JACQUES ROUSSEAU

Jean-Jacques Rousseau has excited controversy and consternation from the moment he put pen to paper in the mid-eighteenth century. He has been claimed and disclaimed by liberals and communitarians alike, and the implications of his ideas have spurred no small amount of fear and loathing. Nonetheless, his ideas have made an enormous contribution to thinking about the relations among the people, the state and its leaders. And, although his reliance upon a 'social contract' borrows from a central mechanism of liberal thought, the actual content of his carefully-reasoned text is clearly communitarian in its essence. Moreover, the expanse and depth of his model permits us to parse it for its leadership implications. Accordingly, in the following pages we will dissect Rousseau's argument utilizing the leadership template as a means of identifying some of the key premises of this core communitarian text.

What is the Leadership Challenge?

Rousseau opened Chapter I of his work *On the Social Contract* with language that has become immortal: 'Man is born free, and everywhere he is in chains'.[20] His point, however, is not what it seems. Rousseau was not lamenting the fact that man had had a natural freedom that society had subsequently denied him; rather, he used this statement as a way of introducing his real concern, that is, how to structure a society that recognized legitimate authority while protecting freedom. 'I want to inquire', he wrote, 'whether there can be some legitimate and sure rule of administration in the civil order.'[21] Such language places Rousseau's quest squarely within the compass of leadership studies.

The task that Rousseau set for himself was by no means simple. In his words, he sought to 'find a form of association which defends and protects with all common forces the person and goods of each associate, and by means of which each one, while uniting with all, nevertheless obeys only himself and remains as free as before'.[22] A tall order, and Rousseau's solution would stir considerable controversy. Nonetheless, his model represents a thoroughgoing and credible communitarian response to the (leadership) challenge of creating a state that legitimates authority while protecting freedom.

Rousseau's Solution

Rousseau had stated the challenge; that is, designing a polity wherein one's life and property would be protected while preserving his liberty. 'This is the fundamental problem,' he said, 'for which the social contract provides the solution.'[23] This statement of the problem and its solution sounds remarkably Lockean, and is the chief justification for the liberals' tenuous claim to Rousseau. The reality was quite otherwise. A further explication of Rousseau's version of the social contract suggests why.

Rousseau imitated Locke's fiction of a state of nature, and even continued to echo his liberal predecessor in his rationale for the creation of a political society. He noted that 'men have reached the point where obstacles that are harmful to their maintenance in a state of nature gain the upper hand.... Such being the case,' Rousseau allowed, 'that original state cannot subsist any longer, and the human race would perish if it did not alter its mode of existence.'[24] This inspired a social contract among members of the society.

It is the nature of that contract that sets Rousseau apart. As he put it, the contract 'is reducible to the following terms. *Each of us places his person and all his power in common under the supreme direction of the general will; and as one we receive each member as an indivisible part of the whole.*' We will be exploring Rousseau's notion of the 'general will' presently; here, the focus should be on his emphasis upon 'each individual as an indivisible part of the whole'. Here he demonstrates his communitarian credentials. Indeed, Rousseau goes on to suggest 'these clauses [of the social contract], properly understood, are all reducible to a single one, namely the total alienation of each associate, together with all of his rights, to the entire community'.[25]

This surrender of rights to the community appears, at first blush, to breach his second condition of retaining individual freedom. And, indeed, Rousseau has been taken to task by some on precisely these grounds. We will explore the dilemma in more detail presently. However, Rousseau, for his part, did not admit of any such tension. 'First of all,' he reasoned, 'since each person gives himself whole and entire, the condition is equal for everyone; and since the condition is equal for everyone, no one has an interest in making it burdensome for the others.' Moreover, 'in giving himself to all, each person gives himself to no one. And since there is no associate over whom he does not acquire the same right that he would grant to others over himself,' Rousseau concluded, 'he gains the equivalent of everything he loses, along with the greater amount of force to preserve what he has.'[26]

Despite his rationalizations, Rousseau's social contract requires further study if we are to plumb its premises and its relationship to leadership. For that, we can turn to the remaining components of the leadership template.

What is the End or Purpose of Leadership?

Rousseau's articulation of the end or purpose of leadership, or, phrased alternatively, the end or purpose of those coming together into a political society via the social contract, is revealing of several attributes that characterize communitarian thinking.

The first of these is his embrace of a conception of the common good (as opposed to the liberal focus on individual goods). 'The first and most important consequence of the principles established above [referring to the social contract],' he said, 'is that only the general will can direct the force of the state according to the purpose for which it was instituted, which is the common good.' He took care to reject the liberal reliance upon competing individual interests. 'For if the opposition of private interests made necessary the establishment of societies,' he began, 'it is the accord of these same interests that made it possible. It is what these different interests have in common that forms the social bond, and, were there no point of agreement among all these interests, no society could exist.' His conclusion was unambiguous. 'For it is utterly on the basis of this common interest', he concluded, 'that society ought to be governed.'[27]

This led him to adopt a central tenet of classical republicanism: civic virtue. 'The better a state is constituted,' he wrote, 'the more public business takes precedence over private business in the minds of the citizens.'[28]

Rousseau was not content, however, merely to hark back to an age-old axiom. He was astute enough to recognize the primacy of individual interests in human affairs. Nonetheless, he argued that entering into his polity effected a transformation in its members, and in doing so Rousseau became perhaps the first to articulate a notion that has become dominant in modern leadership literature. The transformation Rousseau envisioned was in many ways a moral one. As he depicted it, 'this passage from the state of nature to the civil state produces quite a remarkable change in man, for it substitutes justice for instinct in his behavior and gives his actions a moral quality they previously lacked'. This 'moral quality' was clearly a turn from selfish interests to civic virtue. 'Only then,' he continued, 'when the voice of duty replaces physical impulse and right replaces appetite, does man, who had hitherto taken only himself into account, find himself forced to act upon other principles and to consult his reason before listening to his inclinations.'[29]

In addition to the salutary impact this had for the achievement of the common good, this move to civil society worked a transformation in the individual himself. 'Although in this state he deprives himself of several of the advantages belonging to him in the state of nature,' Rousseau admitted, 'he regains such great ones. His faculties are exercised and developed, his ideas are broadened, his feelings ennobled, his entire soul is elevated to such a height that … transformed him from a stupid, limited animal into an intelligent being and a man.'[30]

Thus, the process of joining the political community yielded a series of benefits to those who chose to enter. Again, Rousseau took care to spell out the advantages thus accruing. 'Let us summarize this entire balance sheet so that the credits and debits are easily compared', he suggested. 'What men lose through the social contract is his natural liberty and an unlimited right to everything that tempts him and that he can acquire.' On the other hand, 'what he gains is civil liberty and the proprietary ownership of all he possesses'. This 'civil liberty' was the sort of liberty constrained by the mutual obligations of society. Rousseau distinguished between 'natural liberty (which is limited solely by the force of the individual involved) and civil liberty (which is limited by the general will)'. This 'civil liberty' was made both possible and palatable by the final phase of the transformation. 'To the preceding acquisitions', Rousseau noted, 'could be added the acquisition in the civil state of moral liberty, which alone makes man truly the master of himself.' For to be driven by appetite alone is slavery, and obedience to the law one has prescribed for oneself is liberty.[31] With this rather startling transformation, then, achieved through entry into society, man is made capable of the type of common commitment necessary for a communal society.

In thus championing the civic responsibilities that enable members of society to achieve the common good, Rousseau also stressed the primacy of equality. He was quick to admit that 'the greatest good of all', which 'should be the purpose of every system of legislation … boils down to the two principal objects, *liberty* and *equality*'.[32] Yet despite his disquisition on natural, civil and moral liberty, Rousseau chose to focus on the value 'that should serve as a basis for every social system'. It was the commitment to equality, but even here, the move into society transformed its nature. 'Instead of destroying natural equality,' he pointed out, 'the fundamental compact, on the contrary, substitutes a moral and legitimate equality to whatever physical inequality nature may have been able to impose upon men, and that, however unequal in force and intelligence they may be, men all become equal by convention and by right.'[33] In Rousseau's political community, then, the stress was on political equality. This, of course, is not at odds with liberal conceptions, yet the seeming primacy of equality over liberty is a communitarian attribute.

If the ends of leadership in Rousseau's scheme partook of a commitment to a communal approach, his depiction of the processes for determining right or true policy reinforced this tendency.

What is the Epistemology of Leadership?

The 'epistemology of leadership', it will be recalled, is the term we have given to the manner in which the members of a polity 'know' when a policy is right and correct. In the liberal mode of politics, we have seen a reliance upon freely competing private interests that, assuming the 'market' is fair, results in a policy that is, almost by definition, fair and appropriate. In Rousseau's political community, however, the determination of 'right' policy is quite different. Rousseau builds upon the citizens' transformation to a life of civic virtue (depicted above) to create a unique approach to determining correct policy.

That approach is his famous conception of the *general will*. As Markate Daly describes it, 'the general will is formed through the collective deliberations of a community's citizens. The interests they seek are not their private interests, but rather the good of the whole community….' As a result, 'the general will is the collective embodiment of the moral will of the people'.[34] This comes about only when, in Rousseau's polity, the citizens have left behind their private interests. In such a case, as Rousseau put it, 'since the citizens have but one interest, the people had but one will'.[35]

Of course, the mechanics of this determination of the general will were not always easy. As Rousseau acknowledged, 'there is often a great deal of difference between the will of all and the general will. The latter considers only the general interest, whereas the former considers private interest and is merely the sum of private wills.'[36] However, if the citizens abide by their new commitment to the good of all (the common good), the determination of appropriate policy can safely be entrusted to a majority vote. Although there will be honest differences of opinion, 'the general will would always result from the large number of small differences' because 'the pluses and minuses … cancel each other out, and what remains as the sum of these differences is the general will'. Thus, if the premise of commitment to the common good can be maintained, 'the deliberation would always be good.'[37]

One important implication of Rousseau's approach to determining right policy marks a departure from some of the assumptions of earlier republican theory. In the words of a modern scholar, under Rousseau's approach to the general will, 'citizens do not identify a pre-existing public interest, but instead define that interest in the process of choice'.[38] This constructivist conception of the public interest and common good would become a mainstay of much modern communitarian thought.

What is the Role of the People?

Discussion of the general will inevitably leads to a further consideration of the role of the people in Rousseau's polity. A number of modern scholars have reflected upon Rousseau's expectations of the citizenry. Richard Dagger notes that 'for Rousseau ..., citizenship was not simply a matter of legal status that carried with it various privileges and immunities'. Instead, 'citizenship was a way of life that required commitment to the common good and active participation in public affairs'.[39] Peter Gay depicts how Rousseau's community would 'govern itself, calmly, wisely, and generously'. In this endeavor, said Gay, 'the key element in the citizen's activity is his participation in decision-making'. And, as a 'sound citizen, he will cast his vote by listening not to his own selfish interests, but to his perception of the public weal'.[40]

Thus, according to Rousseau's model 'equality among citizens and their direct participation in self-government are necessary features'. And as the modern scholar Markate Daly points out, 'many contemporary communitarians have used Rousseau's defense of participatory democracy and his portrait of public spirited citizens as support for their own theories'.[41]

Are the People Capable of Governing?

For a commentator that placed so much reliance upon the civic virtue of the people for the success of his polity, Rousseau was remarkably ambiguous about the capability of the people to govern themselves. Certainly his championing of the moral transformation that accompanied entry into the body politic, and his reliance upon the possibility of a general will unalloyed by individual interests, suggests that, at base, he placed his reliance upon a citizenry capable of meeting the demands placed upon it.

Nevertheless, Rousseau was not naïve in his belief in citizen capability. Echoing Machiavelli in the *Discourses*, he believed that, particularly at the outset of a political community, its members may not manifest the necessary vision and skills. This reality led Rousseau to contemplate, like Machiavelli, a role for a strong leader, at least in the formative stages of political society. This can best, then, be explored under the next heading.

What is the Role of the Leader?

Like Machiavelli before him, Rousseau appeared to distinguish between the challenges facing a political society at its inception, and those once the polity was functioning normally. As a consequence, the anticipated role for leaders was dramatically different in the two instances. Here, Rousseau cited Montesquieu (who in turn relied upon Machiavelli). As Rousseau put it, 'at the birth of societies, says Montesquieu, it is the leaders of republics who bring about the institution, and thereafter, it is the institution that forms the leaders of the republic'.[42] Although there remains some ambiguity in his presentation, Rousseau apparently believed that the dramatically differing contexts of early versus established republics would lend consistency to his dichotomous view of the role of the leader. Nonetheless, his analysis points up some problematic areas for conceptions of the leader in communitarian societies. Let us pursue these by tracing his argument.

Rousseau began with cautionary language about the capabilities of the people to govern themselves. 'How will a blind multitude,' he began, 'which often does not know what it wants (since it rarely knows what is good for it) carry out on its own an enterprise as great and as difficult as a system of legislation? By itself, the populace always wants good, but by itself it does not often see it. The general will is always right,' he said ambiguously, 'but the judgment that guides it is not always enlightened.'[43]

This led Rousseau to call for a leader for the people. 'Everyone is equally in need of guides', he said, in particular the mass of the people. 'It must be made to see objects as they are, and sometimes as they ought to appear to it. The good path it seeks must be pointed out to it.' In addition to guidance toward specific policy goals, 'it must be made safe from the seduction of private wills'. Moreover, the general public must be made to extend its vision beyond immediate rewards. 'It must weigh present, tangible advantages against the danger of distant, hidden evils.' If the public is guided thus, 'public enlightenment results in the union of the understanding and the will in the social body; hence the full cooperation of the parts, and, finally, the greatest force of the whole'.[44]

Although the language quoted, on its face, would seem to apply to any gathering of the people at any time, Rousseau was thinking only of the populace before they had been re-formed by entry into a commonwealth. This is made clear by the fact that his remedy for the deficiencies in public reason listed above was the introduction of his concept of a particular kind of leader. In Rousseau's words, 'there arises the necessity of having a legislator'.[45] The term *legislator* was fraught with meaning. From time immemorial in republican political philosophy, to include the works of Machiavelli, Harrington and Montesquieu, there was a theoretical conceit that the desired polity could never spring forth in full flower on its own. This could only come at the hands of a single man – a man often endowed with extraordinary, non-republican powers – who, once the republic was created, stepped aside, to be replaced by more republican leaders. This was the meaning behind the language quoted earlier, when Rousseau cited Montesquieu: 'At the birth of societies, says Montesquieu, it is the leaders of republics who bring about the institution, and thereafter it is the institution that forms the leaders of the republic'.[46]

Our initial focus of attention, then, must be on that first extraordinary leader called the legislator. Although he was expected to disappear from the scene once the republic was operational, it is nevertheless instructive to students of democratic leadership to understand the type of leader needed when the public fails to meet expectations of sagacity and wisdom. Rousseau made it clear that his legislator was *sui generis*. 'The legislator is in every respect an extraordinary man in the state', he wrote. 'If he ought to be so by his genius, he is no less so by his office, which is neither magistracy nor sovereignty.' He made clear the limits of the legislator's function: 'this office, which constitutes the republic, does not enter into its constitution. It is a particular and superior function having nothing in common with the dominion over men.'[47]

Rousseau's 'legislator' was thus something of a midwife, assisting – even forcing – the birthing process of the new polity. Perhaps more important, the legislator also acted in a transforming capacity with respect to the people. As Richard Dagger points out, 'the legislator should feel capable of transforming human nature because such a transformation is necessary to replace the *natural* life of men with the *moral* life of the citizen'. Thus, Rousseau did not assume that citizens would necessarily automatically be transformed into moral beings committed to the common good merely by entry into the social contract. 'The legislator's task, in a sense, is to complete the passage from the state of nature to the civil state that Rousseau describes in … the *Social Contract*.'[48] Or, as Rousseau himself puts it, the legislator 'should feel that he is capable of changing human nature, so to speak; of transforming each individual, who by himself is a perfect and solitary whole, into a part of a larger whole'.[49] Thus it was the legislator's responsibility, among other things, to marshal the transformation from individual selfishness to civic virtue.

Once the social contract had been consummated and the body politic duly transformed, Rousseau perceived quite a different role for the leader. Once the body politic is in place via the social contract, there is no need to have a leader who guides it in the proper direction. 'For since the sovereign [that is, the body politic] is formed from the private individuals who make it up, it neither has nor could have an interest contrary to theirs. Hence, the sovereign power has no need to offer a trustee to its subjects, as it is impossible to harm all of its members.' In other words, 'the sovereign, by the mere fact that it exists is always all that it should be'.[50]

This was not to say that there should be no individuals in leadership positions. Rousseau acknowledged that 'the public force must have an agent of its own that unifies it and gets it working in accordance with the directions of the general will'. The key term in that statement, however is *agent*. The role of the leader in the well-constituted state was merely to serve the general will as evinced by the body politic. Leaders were to facilitate 'mutual communication, and charges with the execution of the laws and the preservation of liberty, both civil and political'. 'This', concluded Rousseau. 'is the reason for having government in the state.'[51]

Rousseau took great care to distinguish this act of agency from more assertive forms of leading. Although such leaders 'are called magistrates or *kings*', he noted, such labels are 'often badly confused with the sovereign, of which [they are] merely the minister'. Instead, 'the dominant will of the prince is not and should not be anything other than the general will or the law. His force is merely the public force concentrated in him.' Indeed, 'as soon as he wants to derive from himself some absolute and independent act, the bond that links everything together begins to come loose'. In fact, 'if it should finally happen that the prince had a private will more active than that of the sovereign and that he had made some use of the public force that is available to him in order to obey this private will', Rousseau concluded, '… at that moment the social union would vanish and the body politic would be dissolved'.[52] Rousseau entered one caveat to his rule that a leader could never act unilaterally, but it was an exception fully in line with his underlying principle. 'This is not to say that the commands of leaders could not pass for manifestations of the general will,' he allowed, 'so long as the sovereign, who is free to oppose them, does not do so. In such a case, the consent of the people ought to be presumed on the basis of universal silence.'[53]

With his careful delineation of the need for a strong leader when the people do not meet the requirements of the civil polity, and the contrasting requirement of only a facilitator and administrator when the polity is operating properly, Rousseau inadvertently revealed a tension inherent in the leading of his political community. His (and the communitarians') advocacy of 'caretaker' leaders holds only insofar as the premise of public virtue holds. If that assumption proves wanting, the role of the leader, and indeed the entire system, becomes problematic. This tension remains a challenge to modern communitarian thought.

Rousseau's discussion of the links between the body politic and the leader inevitably bring to the fore several issues relating to the relationship among the people and their leaders.

How Should Leaders and the People Interact?

As we have seen, the best metaphor for the appropriate relationship between the people and their leaders in Rousseau's model is that of principal and agent, where the principal is the body politic and the agent's role is filled by the leader. Underpinning this depiction is an assumption about the relationship of the people to their leaders that stands in marked contrast to the liberal position staked out by Locke. The distinction can best be demonstrated by revisiting the opposing views of the underlying political contract.

Rousseau noted the differences with some clarity. 'Some people [such as Locke]', he said, 'have claimed that this act of establishment [of the government] was a contract between the populace and the leaders it gives itself.' Not only were the parties to Locke's contract the leaders and the people, but the ensuing relationship was also characterized as an unequal one. In the liberal version, what was created was 'a contract by which are stipulated between the two parties the conditions under which the one obliges itself to command and the other to obey'.[54]

Rousseau rejected both notions. First, he denied that the parties to the contract were the people and their leaders. Rather, the only parties to the social contract were the people themselves. 'It is', argued Rousseau, 'not a convention [that is, agreement] between a superior and an inferior, but a convention of the body with each of its members.' Second, Locke's vision of a relationship between superior and inferior was misguided. According to Rousseau, 'the act that institutes government is not a contract but a law', created by the body politic, and as a result, 'the trustees of the executive power are not the masters of the populace but its officers'.[55] And again: 'those who claim that the act by which a people submits itself to leaders is not a contract are quite correct. It is absolutely nothing but a commission, an employment in which the leaders, as simple officials of the sovereign, exercise in its own name the power with which it has entrusted them.'[56] Rousseau's underlying premises concerning the relationship between the people and their leader thus marks an important distinction between his model of leadership and that of John Locke.

An equally dramatic departure from previous liberal theory can be found in Rousseau's view on representation. Rousseau rejected any form of representation in his polity. As we have seen, the premises underlying such liberal commentators as Locke and Mill allowed – even encouraged – the emergence of representation and representative institutions to guide the political community. Rousseau would have none of this. 'Sovereignty [which resided in the body politic] cannot be represented for the same reason it cannot be alienated', he reasoned. 'It consists essentially of the general will, and the will does not allow of being represented.' Indeed, 'the moment a people gives itself representatives, it is no longer free;

it no longer exists'.[57] Rousseau stakes out what is perhaps an extreme position, but his refusal to allow any but the actual members of the political community to make policy determinations suggests an inherent tension between the communitarian ideal and the notion of political leadership. At best, it appears to admit of only the 'leader as facilitator', and rejects any substantive contributions by leaders.

If Rousseau's (and by implication, the communitarians') version of the leader–follower relation was somewhat unique, his conception of *liberty* was jarringly at odds with traditional liberal notions. By playing out the implications of Rousseau's model in this realm, we can gain real insight into another enigma of modern communitarianism. This can best be achieved by addressing the next template issue.

How is the Matter of Diversity and Minority Interests Addressed?

Rousseau's communitarian premise was that not only was the body politic sovereign, but that its collective intent – the 'general will' – was unitary. The consequences were profound for those who dissented from the majority view (which, it will be recalled, was the decision rule for determining the general will). All this led to one of the striking paradoxes of his model: in Rousseau's classic statement, members of the polity could be 'forced to be free'.[58]

The difficulties arose when there was a lack of unanimity concerning what manifested the general will. It was inevitable, Rousseau knew, that not everyone would necessarily agree as to what constituted the appropriate policy outcome. Inescapably, then, there would be some in the minority who were outvoted when it came time to determine the general will. This appeared, at first blush, to undercut his declared objective of constructing a polity 'by means of which each one, while uniting with all, nevertheless obeys only himself and remains as free as before'.[59] According to Rousseau, however, this contradiction was more apparent than real.

Rousseau did not duck the issue; indeed, he confronted the challenge directly. He began by acknowledging that 'the vote of the majority always obligates all the others. But,' he continued, 'it is asked how a man can be both free and forced to conform to wills not his own.' In other words, 'how can the opponents be both free and be placed in subjection to laws to which they have not consented?' For Rousseau, a proper understanding of the nature of the political community resolved the conundrum. 'I answer', he said, 'that the question is not put properly. The citizen consents to all the laws, even to those that pass in spite of his opposition, and even those that punish him when he dares to violate any of them.' This was because 'the constant will of all members of the state is the general will; through it they are citizens and free'. This being the case, 'when a law is proposed in the people's assembly, what is asked of them is not precisely whether they approve or reject, but whether or not it conforms to the general will that is theirs'. Thus, 'each man, in giving his vote, states his opinion on this matter, and the declaration of the general will is drawn from the counting of the votes'. This resolves the apparent contradiction. 'When, therefore, the opinion contrary to mine prevails, this proves merely that I was in error, and what I took to be the general will was not so.' Indeed, 'if my previous opinion had prevailed,' Rousseau reasoned, 'I would have done something other than what I had wanted [which was to establish the general will]. In that case', he continued, 'I would not have been free', and so by the enforced compliance to the general will, the citizen is 'forced to be free'.[60]

This rather startling turn of logic holds only if certain key assumptions are made about the nature of community membership. As Rousseau put it, 'in order for the social compact to avoid being an empty formula, it tacitly entails [a] commitment', he argued. This commitment 'is not a convention between a superior and an inferior, but a convention of the body with each of its members'. Accordingly, 'so long as the subjects are subordinated only to such convention, they obey no one but their own free will'.[61] In this, we see the classic articulation of the communitarian ideal of freedom. Rather than the liberal championing of individualistic liberty, communitarians become free *through* their participation in the community, even if, at times, this requires that their individual desires are overridden.

This also has obvious implications for ideas of diversity and minority interests. There is no room for either in Rousseau's polity, and communitarian philosophy has labored ever since to alleviate the tension between the commitment to community interests and the countervailing ideal of individual liberty.

What Institutions and Processes are Needed?

Given the rather unique expectations of his model, Rousseau admitted that, for it to operate properly, his polity must have certain characteristics. Foremost among these was his belief that his community should be small, homogeneous and relatively equal.

The need for a small community was mandated by the requirement for direct participation. 'With regard to the best constitution of a state,' Rousseau said, 'there are limits to the size it can have, so as not to be too large to be capable of being well governed.... All things considered,' he added, 'I do not see that it is possible henceforth for the sovereign to preserve among us the exercise of its rights, unless the city is very small.'[62]

Likewise, Rousseau's notion of a unitary general will was premised on the existence of a homogeneous population. He admitted that 'the same laws cannot be suitable to so many diverse provinces which have different customs, live in contrasting climates, and which are incapable of enduring the same form of government'.[63] By implication, there would be similar difficulties confronted by a body politic characterized by internal differences.

Finally, Rousseau's small and homogeneous state must also have a rough equality of resources distributed among its inhabitants. 'Do you want to give consistency to the State?' he asked. If so, then, 'bring the extremes as close together as possible. Tolerate neither rich men nor beggars. These two estates, which are naturally inseparable, are equally fatal to the common good.' This did 'not mean ... that degrees of power and wealth are to be absolutely the same', but the distribution of wealth and power must be sufficiently equal to prevent abuses from those on either end of the spectrum.[64]

What Rousseau was calling for, then, was an Aristotelean community – his more immediate ideal was undoubtedly Geneva – in which his particular version of popular government could succeed. In so limiting his state, Rousseau has posed a continuing challenge to modern communitarian theorists, as they have tried to adapt the core of communitarian ideology to more modern and diverse situations.

Having parsed Rousseau's work to elucidate his conception of leadership, the foregoing analysis can be used as an inductive route to uncover his basic assumption about the nature of the human condition, an assumption upon which all subsequent communitarian arguments would likewise rest.

What is the Perception of Human Nature?

Rousseau's perception of the nature of man was nuanced, one reason that he has been claimed by liberals as well as communitarians. In his 'state of nature', each person was indeed an individual, and 'no man has a natural authority over his fellow man'.[65] This echoed Locke, and, like Locke, Rousseau's natural man quickly discovered the disadvantages of living unprotected in a state in which unbridled force often predominated.

Where Rousseau departed from Locke and his liberal brethren was in the nature of the ties among individuals resulting from the ensuing social contract. While Locke considered the signatories as remaining as individual entities who had entered into a rational pact designed to protect each one's self-interest, Rousseau, as we have seen, viewed the entry into the social contract as effecting a transformation of the individual into a part of a collective whole. 'At once', Rousseau pointed out, 'in place of the individual person of each contracting party, the act of association produces a moral and collective body ... which receives from this same act of unity, its common *self*, its life, and its will.'[66] The consequences were significant.

Among the foremost of these consequences was the fact that one's individual rights and property became subordinate to the community. Once it is in existence, 'the social order ... serves as the foundation for all other rights'.[67] And, although Rousseau argued that in practicality one's property would be more safe under the social contract than it had been in the state of nature, nonetheless 'each private individual's right to his very own store is always subordinate to the community's right to all'.[68]

Such sacrifice of individual liberty and property rights, which would make liberals shudder, nevertheless, in the view of a communitarian like Rousseau, was compensated for by the many advantages attaching to community membership. 'As soon as this multitude is thus united in a body,' he pointed out, 'one cannot harm one of the members without attacking the whole body.'[69] In a similar fashion, the constituents of the body politic received innumerable benefits from their membership in the community, ranging from the pragmatic betterment of their condition to the individual moral transformation linked to their commitment to the community.

Indeed, Jean-Jacques Rousseau, for all his perverse and controversial stances, can be viewed as a visionary who attempted to create a solution for the insecurities of his world by turning to a novel form of political relationship. Modern scholar Richard Dagger has written: 'I argue that Rousseau's attempt to formulate the general will is an attempt to provide the foundation for a body politic as a cooperative venture in which all citizens are treated fairly'.[70] This was a worthy goal, and Rousseau has earned his designation as one of the key figures in the transformation of classical republicanism into modern communitarianism. The modern communitarians have been left with the task of creating a working, communally-based polity that also successfully adapts to a complex and diverse modern society. They have been engaged, in a sense, in the 'inventing' of an alternative to liberalism that serves as a competing model for leadership in our postmodern age. It is to their contributions that we now turn.

MODERN COMMUNITARIAN THOUGHT

We have traced, in brief, the thinking of some of the foundational figures in communitarian thought. We have seen that, in response to the need for the coming together of members of a society to address societal challenges and goals (a process that we have studied under the rubric of 'leadership'), these commentators have 'given a central place to the ideal of community and ... have analyzed human life and action in terms of the social relationships among members of the community'.[71] This long tradition of thinking about the human condition and human endeavors in communal terms has been given new life in recent years, primarily by those uncomfortable with the liberal response to the challenge of leading in regimes characterized by popular sovereignty.

Perhaps the most famous of these modern-day communitarians is the sociologist Amitai Etzioni. Etzioni resisted the centrifugal individualism that he detected in much of modern liberalism. In his *The Spirit of Community: Rights, Responsibilities, and the Communitarian Agenda*, he argued that 'the pendulum has swung too far toward the radical individualist pole and it is time to hurry its return'.[72] Looking back to some of the same texts we have summarized here, he noted that 'the ancient Greeks understood ... well... [that] a person who is completely private is lost to civic life'.[73] Instead Etzioni called for 'a new social, philosophical, and political map' that champions 'a return to the language of social virtues, interests, and, above all, social responsibilities [that] will reduce contentiousness and enhance social cooperation'.[74]

Yet in making this call for a return to communal values, Etzioni was not prepared to erase three centuries of liberal advances. Indeed, he acknowledged the conundrum of modern communitarianism: few wish to reverse the gains in individual liberty and human dignity that are the fruits of liberal thinking. As Etzioni put it, 'We do *not* seek to push it to its opposite extreme, of encouraging a community that suppresses individuality. We aim for a judicious mix of self-interest, self-expression, and commitment to the commons – of rights and responsibilities, of I and we.'[75] In sum, Etzioni explained in another place, 'Contemporary communitarian thinking ... is a balancing act, a reaction to excessive individualism' without abjuring individualism in its entirety.[76]

Make no mistake, however: the modern communitarian argument holds that 'free individuals require a community'. The communitarian insight is that individuals are not truly so. Rather, as Etzioni put it, 'We gain our initial moral commitments as members of a community into which we are born. Later, as we mature, we hone our individualized versions out of social values that have been transmitted to us.' As a consequence, 'as a rule, ... these [individual values] are variations on community-formed themes'.[77] Thus, modern individuals are much more linked to community than liberals would have us believe.

Moreover, there is a moral aspect to the communitarian argument. Acknowledging community, Etzioni's argument goes, will allow us to recapture the moral high ground of shared obligations in the pursuit of mutual goals. 'As we restore the moral voice of communities (and the web of social bonds, the Communitarian nexus, that enables us to speak as a community),' he wrote, 'we ... will also be more able to encourage one another to live up to our social responsibilities.' This is central, 'for at the heart of the Communitarian understanding of social justice is the idea of reciprocity: each member of the community owes something to all the rest, and the community owes something to each of its members'. In our modern society, then, 'justice requires responsible individuals in a responsive community'.[78]

In a later work, Etzioni summarized the place of modern communitarianism in the ongoing evolution of social and political thought. 'Communitarian tracks and traces ... can be found throughout the ages', he began. 'However, it was only in the 1990s that Communitarian thinking became a widely known public philosophy, a social force. This was achieved', Etzioni posited, 'by expanding the [traditional republican] thesis to include not only the emphasis on the common good and social bonds but also the notion of balance between the communal and the personal, between individual rights and social responsibilities, and the notion of pluralism bounded by a core of shared values.'[79] He concluded that 'the success of the democratic experiment ... depends ... on building shared values, habits, and practices that assume respect for one another's rights and regular fulfillment of personal, civic, and collective responsibilities.'[80]

Although Etzioni sought to portray communitarianism in a coherent fashion, the truth is that much of this recent current of communitarian writing has been generated by the renaissance in liberalism sparked by the work of John Rawls. As such, much of recent communitarian writing is reactive, and does not always put forward an organized set of proposals upon which to construct a polity in accordance with its principles. Nevertheless, communitarian scholar Markate Daly has suggested that there is a consistent ideology underlying this diverse set of writings, an ideology that 'embraces a metaphysics of the person, an ethics, a concept of community, and a political philosophy'.[81] As such, modern communitarian writers are in the process of 'inventing' an alternative response to the challenges of leading in a democracy.

Because there is no single, iconic portrayal of modern communitarian thought, but rather a plethora of important contributions and contributors, the ensuing analysis of the essence of the communitarian 'fiction' will draw from a number of commentators. To bring coherence to our analysis, and to facilitate a comparison of the contrasting premises communitarian thought brings to leadership issues, the analysis will again adhere to the issues put forward by our template of leadership.

What is the Leadership Challenge?

Proper comprehension of modern communitarian thought requires an understanding of the communitarians' perception of the challenge facing contemporary society and politics. That challenge is nothing less than the current dominance of liberal ways of thinking. It is this focus upon the weaknesses of a competing philosophy that makes so much of modern communitarian writing to appear to be so 'reactive'. Rather than limning out an elegant and comprehensive competing ideology based upon communitarian principles, many writers devote their efforts to excoriating the dominant liberal paradigm. Nonetheless – that being said – recent communitarian writers, when taken as a whole, have etched the beginnings of an approach to contemporary politics and society – and to leadership – that harbors promise for our postmodern world. Let us begin, however, with their perception of the current challenge.

One of the most articulate critics of the liberal paradigm has been Charles Taylor. Taylor's work over the last decades of the twentieth century has indicated that in liberalism we have experienced too much of a good thing. Embodied more formally in his concept of 'hypertrophy', Taylor expressed the fear that 'the very things which define our break with earlier "traditional" societies – our affirmation of freedom, equality, radical new beginnings, control over nature, democratic self-rule – will somehow be carried beyond feasible limits and will undo us'.[82]

For example, Taylor found liberal individualism to be ultimately destructive. 'Our modern idea of the free, self-defining subject', he pointed out, 'is of an agent who finds his ... purposes in himself.' While this has a superficial allure, Taylor maintained that 'the ideally free agent faces total emptiness'. Instead, 'The ultimate viability of all horizons rested on the sense of being embedded in [some community] order'. As a result, 'Modern freedom undermines itself by destroying meaning'.[83]

So, too, was the case of liberal equality and democracy. According to Taylor, 'the insistence on political equality and mass participation ... puts impossible demands on modern societies and leads to their downfall'. Simply put, 'Modern democratic states were becoming "ungovernable"'.[84]

Related to this was the fact that liberal democratic principles had undercut the very incentives that led people to come together into a political community in the first place. According to Taylor, 'the neutral [liberal] state undermines the shared sense of the common good which is required for citizens to accept the sacrifices demanded by the ... state'. In Taylor's view, there is a 'common form of life' which surpasses bare individualism. This attachment to community and the common good 'is seen as a supremely important good, so that its continuance and flourishing matters to the citizens for its own sake'. In the modern liberal state 'this sense of the common good has been undermined, because ... we now have a political culture of state neutrality in which people are free to choose their goals independently' of the common good and communal priorities are trumped by individual rights.[85] Taylor's conclusion was that the modern liberal assumptions 'deny community ... [and] are exploitative', and that citizens are less and less willing to make sacrifices for such an unrewarding polity.[86]

As a consequence of all this, Taylor suggested that liberal democracies are undergoing a 'legitimation crisis'. 'The modern exaltation of individual freedom', he argued, 'ends up eroding the loyalties and allegiances of the wider community which any society needs to survive.... In sum, ... we have been led ... to lose confidence in our definitions of the good life ... [and] to feel alienated from and even cynical about our governmental institutions.'[87]

Communitarian philosopher Michael Sandel built upon Taylor's insights. 'The liberal vision of freedom', he argued, 'lacks the civic resources to sustain self government.... The public philosophy by which we live cannot secure the liberty it promises, because it cannot inspire the sense of community and civic engagement that liberty requires.'[88]

Likewise, political scientist Benjamin Barber agreed that 'an excess of liberalism has undone democratic institutions: for what little democracy we have had in the West has been repeatedly compromised by the liberal institutions with which it has been undergirded and the liberal philosophy from which its theory and practice has been derived'. Like Taylor and Sandel, Barber attributed the problem to liberalism's denial of community. Liberal democracy, he argued, 'yields neither the pleasures of participation nor the fellowship of civic association, neither the autonomy and self-governance of continuous political activity nor the enlarging mutuality of shared public goods'. In sum, liberalism, according to Barber, is 'oblivious to that essential human interdependency that underlies all political life'. As a result, 'liberalism serves democracy badly if at all'.[89]

Perhaps even worse, many communitarian observers of the contemporary scene argue that not only is the liberal paradigm making for unfulfilling lives and unresponsive political institutions, but it is also responsible for moral decay. Alasdair MacIntyre phrased this argument most directly. MacIntyre argued that in our liberal world our entire moral vocabulary of rights and the common good, is in such grave disorder that 'we have – very largely, if not entirely – lost our comprehension, both theoretical and practical, of morality'.[90] Benjamin Barber provided some substantive elaboration: under liberalism can be found 'individuals defined by their privacy and their property yet unable to determine who they are, emancipated by rights and freedoms but unable to act as morally autonomous agents'.[91] Sociologist Robert Nisbet concurred. 'The problem before us is in one sense moral', he said. 'It is moral in that it is closely connected with the values and ends....' In the case of liberalism, what has been abandoned are those values and ends that 'have traditionally guided and united men but that have in so many instances become remote and inaccessible'. Consequently, 'our age has come to seem a period of moral and spiritual chaos, of certainties abandoned, of creeds outworn, and of values devalued'.[92]

These perceived weaknesses of liberalism have caused many in modern society to pursue what Nisbet has called 'the quest for community'. As both Nisbet, and more recently, political scientist Robert Putnam, have found, 'the real problem is not ... the loss of old [community] contexts but rather the failure of our present democratic and industrial scene to create new contexts of association and moral cohesion'.[93]

More important for our task of tracing the rise of a new conception of the leadership relation, this perceived need for community also created the challenge of devising a coherent intellectual justification for whatever is to replace the liberal paradigm. As commentator Markate Daly phrased it, 'By now, the defects of liberalism are available for all to assess. But a communitarian political philosophy has yet to be tried or even well formulated.'[94] Charles Taylor put it more simply: 'We [need to] turn to other models'.[95]

This, then, was the ultimate leadership challenge facing the communitarians. They had to invent nothing less than a new political philosophy dedicated to resurrecting the role of community and of communal relations among members of the polity. At the same time, no one seriously contemplated abandoning entirely the salutary contributions of liberalism. Daly pointed out that 'the question for communitarian philosophy is, Can a philosophy whose aim is to strengthen the community that supports its members' fulfillment also conserve and deepen personal liberty? Can communitarian philosophy also legitimate democratic institutions as it cultivates a richer and fuller moral life?'[96] And Taylor added: 'Our agenda will then no longer be defined as limiting or slowing down the progress of modern values, but rather as finding a way to rescue them in their integrity, as against the distortions and perversions that have developed in modern history'.[97] In sum, as Daly put it, 'the modern communitarian proposal' must be wedded to 'the traditional liberal values of freedom and equality'. The result will be 'the ideal of a democratic community'.[98]

To understand and evaluate the nature of the communitarians' accomplishment, we must begin by looking closely at their underlying premises.

What is the Perception of Human Nature?

The modern communitarian conception of the essential attributes of the human condition has been developed, predictably enough, as a counterpoint to the perceived radical individualism of liberal thought. As Michael Sandel has written, 'the liberal conception of the person is too thin to account for the full range of moral and political obligations we commonly recognize'. Such a notion is 'too weak to support the ... communal obligations expected of citizens'.[99] The most cogent critiques of the liberal approach, however, were penned by Charles Taylor and Benjamin Barber.

We have encountered Taylor's work before, in our discussion of the challenge posed by liberalism. Taylor took to task 'our widespread conception of ourselves as autonomous individuals, choosing our own values and modes of life'. The liberal notion of the individual, he noted, had its roots in the theories of Locke and others. In Locke's approach, 'the free subject becomes someone who follows an internal purpose and who owes no a priori allegiance to a pre-existing order but gives it only to structures that were created by his/her own consent'. As a consequence, 'we find atomist conceptions of freedom developing where persons are seen to enjoy "natural liberty" in a state of nature'.[100]

Yet such a portrayal of the person, argued Taylor, ignored both ancient conceptions and modern realities. As he put it, 'some of our self-attributions would be shocking or even incomprehensible to our ancestors'. Instead, 'the ancient conceptions ... of the citizen ... were essentially defined as a certain relation to the whole'. Nor is the modern citizen any less imbedded in his/her surrounding world. 'The modern subject', he posited, '... is far from being an independent, atomic agent.... On the contrary, an individual is sustained, on one hand, by the culture which elaborates ... his or her self-understanding and, on the other, by the society.... All of this underpins one's identity as a free individual', Taylor pointed out, and, if truth be known, liberalism's atomistic individual 'could not long survive a state of nature', let alone operate successfully in our contemporary world.[101]

Benjamin Barber was even more direct in his assault upon liberal notions of the self. 'There is no better way to elucidate the difference between [communitarian] democracy and liberal democracy', he pointed out, 'than by comparing how they portray human nature.' Like Taylor, Barber acknowledged the historical legacy of liberalism's battle against tyranny. For Barber, however, 'historical irony has left its mark here'. The irony was this: 'the defense of the individual against old tyrannies of hierarchy, tradition, ... and absolute political power has been sustained by a theory of the radically isolated individual defined by absolute rights and liberties. Yet this theory, as put into practice in the world of actual social relationships,' he argued, 'has eroded the nourishing as well as the tyrannical connections and has left individuals cut off not only from the abuses of power but from one another.' In sum, according to Barber, 'what the liberal theory of human nature does, in short, is to define man in ways that deprive him of the potential strength of mutuality, cooperation, and common being'.[102]

If Taylor and Barber provide perhaps the clearest critique of liberal notions of the self, it is other communitarian commentators who invent an alternative conception of the human condition. Two of the most influential have been Michael Sandel and Alasdair MacIntyre.

Much of Michael Sandel's work has been inspired by the publication of John Rawls's *A Theory of Justice*. In his 1982 work, *Liberalism and the Limits of Justice*, Sandel provided a thoroughgoing critique of Rawls's position.[103] Here, we can focus upon two of Rawls's contentions with which Sandel took issue. The first was that 'subjects are mutually independent from each other'.[104] Sandel rejected this notion categorically. Instead, 'the relevant description of the self may embrace more than a single, individual human being, as when we attribute responsibility or affirm an obligation to a family or community or class or nation'.[105] Indeed, 'members of a society ... conceive their identity ... as defined to some extent by the community of which they are a part. For them, community describes not just what they *have* as fellow citizens, but also what they *are*, not a relationship they choose ... but an attachment they discover, not merely an attribute but a constituent of their identity.'[106]

Closely related to this was Rawls's claim that 'the self is prior to whatever values that self might have', or, worded another way, 'the self is prior to its ends'. According to Rawls, then, the individual self exists *a priori*, and any decisions about one's ends or values are the product of rational choice. Sandel points out, however, that this 'notion of the self, ... taken alone, does not complete the picture'.[107] Liberals such as Rawls portray 'a picture of the self given prior to its ends', Sandel acknowledged. 'But how plausible is this self-conception? Despite its powerful appeal, the image of the unencumbered self is flawed', wrote Sandel. 'It cannot make sense of our moral experience, because it cannot account for certain moral and political obligations that we commonly recognize, even prize.' Instead, we should 'think of ourselves as encumbered selves, already claimed by certain ... commitments'.[108] In sum, contrary to the independent self posited by Rawls, 'our selves are at least partly constituted by the ends we do not choose, but rather discover by virtue of our being imbedded in some shared social context'.[109]

This point is made even more dramatically by Alasdair MacIntyre. MacIntyre joined Sandel in rejecting the assumptions of liberal individualism, and, indeed, provided a striking counterpoint to the individualist conception of human nature provided by the liberals. Contrary to the liberal idea of the self as prior, MacIntyre maintained 'there is no way of *founding* my identity – or lack of it – on the psychological continuity or discontinuity of the self'.[110] Instead, 'I am never able to seek for the good or exercise the virtues only *qua* individual.... We all approach our own circumstances as bearers of a particular social identity. I am someone's son or daughter, someone else's cousin or uncle; I am a citizen of this or that city, a member of this or that guild or profession; I belong to this clan, that tribe, this nation. Hence what is good for me has to be the good for one who inhabits these roles.' The consequences yield a quite different person from that envisioned by the liberal paradigm. To MacIntyre, 'I inherit from the past of my family, my city, my tribe, my nation, a variety of debts, inheritances, rightful expectations and obligations'. Rather than being unencumbered as the liberals would have it, 'these constitute the given of my life, my moral starting point'.[111]

MacIntyre reinforced his point by introducing what he labeled 'the narrative view of self'.[112] As he explained it, 'man is in his actions and practice, as well as in his fictions, essentially a story-telling animal'. Furthermore, 'the story of my life is always embedded in the story of those communities from which I derive my identity. I am born with a past; and to try to cut myself off from that past ... is to deform my present relationship.' Indeed, 'the narrative of any one life is part of an interlocking set of narratives'. The bottom line was clear: 'It does follow of course,' MacIntyre continued, 'that all attempts to elucidate the notion of personal identity independently of and in isolation from the notions of narrative, intelligibility and accountability are bound to fail ... For the story of my life is always embedded in the story of those communities from which I derive my identity.'[113]

Other communitarian writers echoed Sandel's and MacIntyre's notion of human nature as 'embedded' in a societal and historical context. Sheldon Wolin, for example, summoned up the metaphor of 'birthright' to depict man's connections to his community. 'In ancient times', he explained, 'a birthright usually fell to the eldest son. He succeeded his father and received the major portion of his father's legacy.' The significance was that 'a birthright was thus an inherited identity and implicitly an inherited obligation to use it, take care of it, pass it on, and improve it'. This notion of an individual birthright can also be expanded, Wolin argued: there is also such a thing as 'a collective identity bound up with a people and extending over time'.[114]

Wolin's conception of birthright held implications for conceptions of the person. As Wolin put it, 'It is a way of "conceiving" the person.... Birthright language conceives the person as preformed [in direct opposition to the liberal conception], as an incorporation of elements of family, culture, and community. It asserts', he suggested, 'that we come into the world preceded by an inheritance.'[115] As a consequence, Wolin concluded, 'we can never renounce our past without rendering the idea of a political community incoherent'.[116]

If Wolin reinforced MacIntyre's historical perspective, Benjamin Barber came closer to Sandel's social constructivist approach to the human condition. Barber explicitly rejected the liberal view of the self. 'The liberal portrait of human nature', he pointed out, 'construes the human essence as radically individual and solitary, ... as social only to the extent required by the quest for preservation and liberty....' In the liberal world, 'people enter ... into social relations only in order to exploit them for their own individual ends'.[117] Instead, Barber took a constructivist approach. Citing Marx, Barber argued that 'the essence of man ... is the ensemble of social relationships'. Thus, said Barber, 'human nature [is] socially determined', a process through which 'the social construction of man ... [is] an ongoing interaction by which world and man together shape each other'. Human identity, then, is created '*within* the families, tribes, nations, and communities into which we are born'.[118]

This communitarian conception of the individual as social and embedded in societal and historical contexts had implications for the public political relationships of which leadership is a part. As Markate Daly put it, 'Communitarians argue that not only is the communitarian conception of the person a more accurate description of human life, but if it were the cultural ideal informing our policies and institutions, community bonds would be strengthened and the character of its members reinforced'. If communitarian ideals were acknowledged and pursued, it 'would lead not only to greater personal satisfaction but also to a superior public ethics and a more effective democracy.'[119] The specific connections of communitarian thought to the leadership relation are spelled out below.

What is the End or Purpose of Leadership?

When one turns to the foundational issue of the ultimate purposes of the leadership relation, most modern communitarian writing is, again, phrased in response to liberal premises. Allen Buchanan pointed out that 'liberal ontology asserts that only individuals exist and all putative properties of groups can be reduced to properties of individuals'. This perspective, in turn, determines the appropriate ends of leadership in a liberal state. 'Liberal motivational theory', Buchanan continued, 'assumes that individuals are motivated solely by preferences for private goods, and that they desire participation in groups only as a means to achieving such goods.'[120]

In contrast to this liberal preoccupation with the achievement of private ends, modern communitarians resurrect the ancient republican notion of the common good. As one commentator put it, communitarians agree 'that a common social life exists prior to the formation of individuals and that notions of the right and justice [for our purposes here, we can equate these to the ends of leadership] have to be conceptualized so that they are consistent with a society's common good'. This focus on a truly common good marks a central fault line dividing liberals from communitarians. Indeed, 'The specification of the concept of a common good in this sense is central to debates between liberals and communitarians'.[121] It behooves us, then, to explore this notion further.

Several communitarian writers have addressed the nature of the common good. For our purposes, brief mention of two in particular help us to understand communitarian thinking. The first is William Sullivan, who grounded his interpretation in the traditions of civic republicanism, and thereby acknowledged its deep roots in Western intellectual history. Sullivan began by articulating the liberal conception of the common good (when, indeed, the liberals admitted of the possibility at all). 'But what should the common good be?' he asked. 'As a liberal would see it, … political, even social vitality and progress are measured according to economic criteria. The public good, seen that way,' he reasoned, 'becomes the utilitarian sum of individual satisfactions. A common interest can be presumed to lie only in ensuring advantageous conditions of general exchange.' From such a vantage point, 'the civic [republican] language of the common good sounds to the liberal somehow darkly mystical or at least unnecessarily grandiose'.[122]

Sullivan sought to rescue liberal misconceptions about the common good by portraying it not as an entity to be bargained over, but instead something greater. 'The common good,' he argued, 'with its long history in the civic tradition, is part of a language that articulates a way of living … a way of life which is meaningful in its own terms.'[123] For Sullivan, then, the common good is merely the necessary (even unavoidable) concomitant of a healthy civic life, and emerged as a result of the interactions of citizens when guided by the Aristotelian ideal of civic virtue.

Benjamin Barber built upon this conceptualization of the common good to articulate a modern version of the construct. While some in the past seemed to depict the common good as some knowable entity awaiting discovery, Barber harked back to Rousseau (and Hegel) and suggested that the content of the common good was socially constructed. As Barber phrased it, 'Liberal democrats … render the critical democratic question as "What will we choose?"' On the other hand, communitarian democrats pose 'the alternative question, "How do we will?"' As Barber explained it, 'In treating decision-making as an activity of the will, [communitarians] honor the tradition of Rousseau … for whom the aim was not to choose common ends or to discover common interests but to will a common world by generating a common will'.[124]

This recent focus upon the participatory process as a part of the end itself brings us to the template question of the 'epistemology' of leadership in a communitarian polity.

What is the Epistemology of Leadership?

Recall once again that what we have been calling the 'epistemology' of leadership is merely the grounds upon which leaders and the people determine what is 'right' policy. In modern communitarian writing, again, the answer has emerged in response to liberal assumptions, most specifically those articulated by John Rawls. In brief summary, right policy in a liberal polity is a result of (a) individual choices based upon personal interest, with (b) the differences among individuals mediated by some appropriate market-like mechanism. The only restriction on process and outcome is that such determinations (c) must adhere to certain modal values (such as fairness in interaction) and further such end values as liberty, justice, equality and happiness. Communitarians, while accepting such liberal outcomes, nonetheless put forward a very different model for the determination of right policy.

First, in contrast to the individualistic bias of the liberals, communitarians stress the 'embeddedness' of those considering any political action. This can perhaps best be understood by looking at Rawls's formulation, and the communitarian response to it. According to Rawls, 'the self is prior to the ends that are affirmed by it'.[125] By that Rawls meant that individuals behave as unfettered actors who choose desired outcomes independently. Michael Sandel notes that this is, among other things 'an epistemological claim ... about the forms of self-knowledge of which we are capable'.[126] Communitarians, for their part, deny that individuals can make determinations in so atomistic a fashion.

Sandel points out that 'in contrast to Rawls notion [of] "the self [as] prior to [its] ends," it is possible that the opposite is the case, that is, that ends [that is, values and goals] predate the self. This', he noted, 'creates an entirely new perspective.'[127] Sandel buttressed this with two arguments. His first point is a logical one. In assessing 'Rawls's contention that each person chooses what values to adopt and what fundamental aims to accept', he poses the question: 'what could be the basis for these choices, if a person has no prior conception of the good?'[128] His second point puts forward the communitarian response: 'ethical reasoning [and concomitant choices regarding values and goals] must proceed within the context of a community's traditions and cultural understandings'.[129]

Other communitarians expand upon this notion. Charles Taylor noted that rather than the liberal 'rational self-determination', all individual actions 'must be situated'. Indeed, one 'cannot specify any content to our action outside of a situation which sets goals for us, which thus imparts a shape to rationality and provides an inspiration for creativity'.[130]

But it is Alasdair MacIntyre who best captures the communitarian concept of 'embeddedness', and what that means for determining appropriate choices. 'For I am never able to seek for the good or exercise the virtues only *qua* individual,' he wrote. 'It is not just that different individuals live in different social circumstances; it is also that we all approach our own circumstances as bearers of a particular social identity. I am someone's son or daughter, someone else's cousin or uncle; I am a citizen of this or that city, a member of this or that guild or profession; I belong to this clan, that tribe, this nation.' What this means in terms of determining what is 'right' policy is clear: 'The self has to find its moral identity in and through its membership in communities such as those of the family, the neighbourhood, the city and the tribe'. Consequently, 'The individual's search for his or her good is generally and characteristically conducted within a context defined by those traditions of which the individual's life is a part'.[131]

If the communitarians reject the individualism that is central to the liberal view of knowing what is best, so too do they renounce the notion that market-type interactions are the correct method for a society to determine right policy, or, indeed, that any approach based upon the assumption of individualistic preferences is sufficient. As Michael Sandel put it, 'republicanism [communitarianism] thus affirms a politics of the common good. But the common good it affirms does not correspond to the utilitarian notion of aggregating individual preferences.'[132] And William Sullivan added: 'The liberal penchant for modeling political questions on economic choices in a marketplace shows its most dangerous and morally irresponsible side. Against the liberal claim that free institutions ... can be sustained merely by concentration upon an expanding market system, civic republican insight and historical experience strongly suggest that such a course is folly, because it rests on a misconception of politics and, finally, on too narrow an understanding of the reality of social life.'[133]

Drawing upon this insight, many communitarians propose another method for determining right policy: civic dialogue. Sullivan continued: 'Because these political decisions so affect the kinds of life that will prevail, public debate is critical for developing a shared understanding of the consequences of policy choices, of hidden costs and benefits to the whole community'.[134] It is in the works of Benjamin Barber and Jürgen Habermas, that we see developed this version of communitarian epistemology to its highest form.

In his own words, Barber argues for 'an epistemology of process', or, in another place, 'conceiving politics *as* epistemology'.[135] In other words, citizens decide for themselves what is 'right', based upon ongoing dialogue. In his system democracy 'relies on participation in an evolving problem-solving community that creates public ends where there were none before by means of its own activity.... In such commons,' he suggested, 'public ends are neither extrapolated from absolutes nor "discovered" in a preexisting "hidden consensus." They are literally forged through the act of public participation, created through common deliberation and common action and the effect that deliberation and action have on interests, which change shape and direction when subjected to these particular processes.'[136] In sum, 'the rightness of public acts depends then neither on a prepolitical notion of abstract right nor on a simple conception of popular will or popular consent. For what is crucial is not consent pure and simple but the active consent of participating citizens who have imaginatively reconstructed their own values as public norms through the process of identifying and empathizing with the values of others.'[137]

Habermas explores this epistemic approach in more depth. As portrayed by one recent scholar, Habermas creates 'a rather elaborate and somewhat obtuse model of dialogue-based normative accounting' that he calls 'inter-subjective discourse (as opposed to personal reflection)'. As Habermas himself puts it, 'Ultimately, there is only one criterion by which beliefs can be judged valid, and that is that they are based on agreement reached by argumentation'. He goes into considerable detail concerning the rules and parameters of such discourse, but for our purposes the important point is that his approach 'points to a *procedural* rather than a *substantive* normative criterion. It is presumed that if a group follows such a procedure, it will not come up with what could be claimed as "wrong" values'.[138]

Barber and Habermas also conjure up the third epistemological distinction between communitarians and liberals. As Stephen Mulhall and Adam Swift have suggested, liberalism appears to adhere to a certain 'universalism' of values, and 'claims that its conclusions apply universally and cross-culturally'.[139] The best example, perhaps, is John Rawls. Michael Walzer depicted Rawls's stance as claiming 'there is one, and only one, distributive system that philosophy can rightly encompass'. In Rawls's case, this is 'the one that ideally rational men and women would choose if they were forced to choose impartially, knowing nothing of their own situation, barred from making particularist claims, confronting an abstract set of goods'. Walzer rejects that claim. 'It is surely doubtful', he responded, 'that these same men and women, if they were transformed into ordinary people, with a firm sense of their own identity, with their own goods in their hands, caught up in everyday troubles, would reiterate their hypothetical choice or even recognize it as their own.'[140] That is to say, in Markate Daly's words, many communitarians believe that 'universalistic morality is arrogant, or at least undemocratic in that it supposes that an intellectually satisfying set of principles or ideals is a higher standard than the customs and practices developed by many intelligent people in the conduct of their daily lives'. Instead, the communitarian approach is 'highly particularistic. It arises out of the particular interactions of real people who form and are formed by the historical tradition in which they live'.[141]

This aspect of communitarian thinking we will explore in more depth when we turn to the challenges of diversity and minority interests. For now, suffice it to say that communitarians, in response to liberal claims, have staked out their own version of the epistemology of leadership, a version that demands a quite different sort of leadership relation. This brings us to a more focused consideration of the workings of leadership in a communitarian polity.

What is the Role of the People?

As usual, modern communitarians tend to begin their discussion of the proper role of the people in a democratic polity by first rejecting the liberal approach. In our previous chapter, we traced out how John Rawls proposed a polity grounded upon universal rules of justice, within which individuals acted according to their respective comprehensive doctrines. This created some difficulties when it came time for the individuals to act in concert in the public sphere, but Rawls glossed over this his commitment to the notions of public reason and reciprocity.

Modern communitarians reject this schema. In terms of citizen activity, they view liberal thinking as imposing, in Benjamin Barber's term, 'skepticist minimalism'. That is to say, because one cannot know any absolute or unitary truth, one cannot impose one's own ideas on others. 'Afraid of overstepping the prudent boundaries set by skeptical reason,' Barber elaborated, 'the liberal is politically paralyzed. Because he is uncertain of his beliefs, he hesitates to act.' Instead, 'he willy-nilly permits market forces, which are neither public nor just, to ride roughshod over fellow citizens'.[142] And, according to Michael Sandel, this is overseen by a liberal polity that is nothing more than a 'procedural republic', in which the objective is to adhere to 'principles of justice that treat persons fairly as they pursue their various interests and ends'.[143]

Communitarians, with their classical republican roots, reject the procedural state with its minimalist citizens. As Sandel put it, the republican (communitarian) 'begins by asking how citizens can be capable of self-government, and seeks the political forms and social conditions that promote its meaningful exercise'. While liberals view individual liberty as something in tension with government and imply that participation with others is a kind of necessary evil, the communitarians embrace a different view of liberty. But to Sandel, 'we are free only insofar as we exercise our capacity to deliberate about the common good, and participate in the public life of a free city or republic'. Thus, to Sandel, 'I am free insofar as I am a member of a political community that controls its own fate, and a participant in the decisions that govern its affairs'.[144]

These communitarian beliefs have important implications for the expected role of the people in such a polity. As Markate Daly summarizes it, 'The common threads among all the [communitarian] writings are that citizens of a democratic community rise above their own self-interest in public matters to seek the common good, that they join together with others to form public policy, and that they act to bring this vision to fruition. In brief, citizenship is *virtuous* and *participatory* [emphasis added]'.[145]

There are, then, two aspects of communitarian expectations of the people in a democratic polity. The first has to do with the duty to participate. John Dewey, a communitarian writer from early in the twentieth century, was one of the most articulate proponents of the requirement for citizen participation in government. He defined community in terms of 'an association of free and equal citizens who join together to form a common vision of their communal life and participate in the activities necessary to achieve this common good'.[146] Indeed, for Dewey, 'the essence of community life, and democracy itself, is the joint activity of free and equal citizens who form the values and set the policies of the groups to which they belong'.[147] Modern scholar Benjamin Barber echoed this sentiment. 'To be a citizen,' he argued, '*is* to participate in a certain conscious fashion that presumes awareness of and engagement in activity with others…. Indeed, from the perspective of strong democracy, the two terms *participation* and *community* are aspects of one single mode of social being: citizenship.'[148]

Mere participation is not enough, however. Communitarians also require a different *kind* of citizen than is expected in the liberal state. 'Republican freedom', wrote Sandel, 'requires a certain form of public life, which depends in turn on the cultivation of *civic virtue* [emphasis added]'.[149] In calling for 'civic virtue', as Sandel implied, communitarians hark back to a republican tradition that can be traced at least as far back as Aristotle. The term itself, in Richard Dagger's capsulization, means 'the disposition to further public over private good in action and deliberation'.[150]

Such selfless virtue is diametrically opposed to the image of citizens in the liberal tradition, in which 'citizens voluntarily form a society for their own prosperity'.[151] Rather than a political community based upon a rational contract between individuals, as the liberals claim, with its limited and delineated responsibilities grounded in self-interest, there is instead what William Sullivan has called 'the classical notion of citizenship'. For Sullivan, 'citizenship has traditionally been conceived of as a way of life that … is essentially a collective experience. Indeed,' said Sullivan, 'the notion of *citizen* is unintelligible apart from that of *commonwealth*, and those terms derive their sense from the idea that we are by nature political beings…. Thus,' Sullivan concluded, 'mutual interdependency is the foundational notion of citizenship.'[152]

There is yet another aspect to most communitarian conceptions of citizenship. Like Rousseau's depiction of the transition from natural liberty to civil liberty to moral liberty, modern communitarian citizenship transforms the members of the polity. For Sullivan, citizenship is 'a way of life that changes the person entering it'.[153] Barber added, 'in strong democratic community [his term for the communitarian model] … individual[s] [are] transformed … their vision of their own freedom and interest has been enlarged to include others'. Indeed, 'Involvement in the community is the means by which citizens transform their private interests into a conception of the common good'.[154] It is such a Rousseauian transformation that makes the communitarian model possible in the modern era, and it lies at the heart of communitarian hopes at the present day.

Are the People Capable of Governing?

The responses to the previous template questions suggest that the communitarian model of the leadership relation makes heavy demands upon its members. Michael Sandel wrote that 'to deliberate well about the common good requires more than the [liberal] capacity to choose one's ends and to respect others' rights to do the same. It requires a knowledge of public affairs and also a sense of belonging, a concern for the whole, a moral bond with the community whose fate is at stake. To share in self-rule, therefore,' Sandel concluded, 'requires that citizens possess, or come to acquire, certain qualities of character, or civic virtues.'[155] Communitarians tend to argue that the people do have some of these capabilities, but acknowledge some doubt as to others.

To be more specific, almost by definition, they also make some assumptions about the inherent capabilities of the people that bode well for the type of polity that they desire. They assume, for example, that members of the polity do have the requisite commitment to the community. Drawing upon the republican tradition, William Sullivan proclaimed that 'civic life is possible because human nature is naturally disposed to find its fulfillment in what is called a life of virtue'. Drawing upon the Aristotelian tradition, he elaborated: 'Since humans are by nature social beings,' Sullivan posited, 'living well requires a shared life.... To participate in such a shared life is to show concern and reciprocity to one's fellows....'[156] Moreover, as Will Kymlicka has summarized their position, communitarians argue that 'the self is "embedded," or "situated" in existing social practices.... Our social roles and relationships must be taken as given for purposes of personal deliberation.'[157]

On the other hand, others acknowledge that one must not be sanguine about such matters in the modern world. John Dewey – writing early in the twentieth century, and his insight is certainly more relevant today – noted 'the disintegration of family life and the shifting composition of local communities'.[158] Hence, said Dewey, 'the prime difficulty ... is that of discovering the means by which a scattered, mobile ... public may so recognize itself as to define and express its interests'.[159] In a similar vein, Robert Nisbet noted 'the growing realization that the traditional primary relationships of men have become functionally irrelevant to our State and economy and meaningless to the moral aspirations of individuals'.[160]

Moreover, one of the qualifications Sandel sets out above, namely, that citizens in a communitarian polity must have a 'knowledge of public affairs', may not be inherent in the populace. Dewey expressed his concern that 'America is lacking the concerned, well-informed public needed for the formation of effective public opinion'.[161] He questioned whether an individual is 'competent to frame policies, to judge their results; competent to know in all situations demanding political action what is for his own good ... and the will to effect it against contrary forces'. In sum, wrote Dewey, 'The prime condition of a democratically organized public is a kind of knowledge and insight which does not yet exist'.[162] Such concerns remain among some more recent commentators. Benjamin Barber, one of the foremost proponents of citizen action, acknowledged that such concerns are genuine. Nonetheless, in the long republican tradition of Aristotle and, specifically, Machiavelli, Barber concluded that 'the multitude will on the whole be as wise or even wiser than princes'.[163]

Barber's reference to Machiavelli's discussion of leaders and the people serves as an appropriate segue to a matter of some complexity for communitarian thinkers: the role of the leader.

What is the Role of the Leader?

It may be recalled that in our previous chapter we found that those of the liberal persuasion had an ambiguous view of leaders. On the one hand, Locke granted them extensive prerogative powers (so long as they did not infringe upon fundamental liberties), and Mill championed a system of representation and sought to incorporate 'competence' into the ruling of the state. On the other hand, the liberal emphasis upon individual rights and negative liberty also engendered considerable suspicion of exercising power over others. In modern liberal thought, this can be seen in Rawls's call for state neutrality, and perhaps reaches its greatest extent in the libertarianism of Nozick.

Modern communitarian thought has likewise experienced some difficulty in reconciling the role of the leader with its fundamental premises. As we saw in earlier chapters, the classical republicanism that forms the intellectual progenitor of modern communitarianism had no particular difficulty with calling for a leader who fit what we have called 'the classical ideal' of the leader. Despite their encomia pertaining to the wisdom of the people when considered as a whole, both Aristotle and Machiavelli made a place for leaders of merit. Even modern republicans like William Sullivan have allowed that 'statesmanship must, then, by its very nature remain a prudential art'.[164] With the erosion of elitist assumptions, however, most modern communitarians have had some difficulty with the role of leaders – indeed, when they address the issue at all.

Political scientist Benjamin Barber is perhaps the most forthcoming communitarian writer with respect to the dilemma. Barber is, at base, deeply suspicious of leaders and leadership. 'It is only in systems where self-government and vigorous individual participation are central,' he wrote, 'that leadership takes on a problematic character. On its face,' he continued, 'leadership is opposed to participatory self-government; it acts in place of or to some degree encroaches on the autonomy of individual actors.... As a consequence,' Barber concluded, 'one might wish to say that in the ideal participatory system leadership vanishes totally. Complete self-government by an active citizenry would leave no room for leaders or followers.'[165]

Nonetheless, Barber recognized a further reality. 'Yet for all of this,' he admitted, 'actual participatory systems ... are clearly burdened with the need for leadership.' He mentioned several types. Echoing in some way 'the Legislator' found in the republican theories of Machiavelli, Harrington and Rousseau, Barber acknowledged 'the need for *transitional leadership* ... to guide people toward greater self-government'. Moreover, he recognized 'the inescapability of *natural leadership*', which is the inevitable result of differential capabilities, 'even in the most egalitarian communities'.[166]

More important for our consideration of the role of leaders in communitarian polities – and despite his earlier theoretical concerns – Barber saw a role for leaders in a well-functioning political community. Leaders, he believed, could play two central roles. The most important of these is what Barber calls *facilitating leadership*. For Barber, this is a limited role. 'The facilitator', he suggested, 'is responsible to a process rather than to specific outcomes', and 'to the integrity of the community rather than to the needs of particular individuals.'[167] The chief role for the communitarian leader, then, was to manage the process in the interests of the community and the common good.

Barber also allowed for a leader role that had the appearance of having a more substantive contribution. He called it *'moral leadership'*, which he said 'promotes social cohesion and community and celebrates the freedom and individual dignity on which democracy depends'. Yet this leader, again, is, for Barber, more oriented to creating the appropriate facilitating conditions for a communitarian polity. He called for a 'moral leader who incarnates the spirit of the community, and who therefore encourages a mutualist and cooperative approach'. The principal objective of such a leader was 'to create a community in which men lead themselves, in which they can be moved only by the common will in which they participate'.[168]

In sum, communitarians such as Barber acknowledge, however grudgingly, the need for leaders, but do not grant them latitude to direct the people in matters of substance. This, implicitly, also suggests the communitarian response to the next template question.

How Should Leaders and the People Interact?

The focus, for communitarians, of the nexus between leaders and followers, is a focus on the *process* of their interaction. As Barber put it, communitarians 'honor the tradition of Rousseau', and turn their attention to the challenge of 'generating a common will'.[169] The leadership process, then, in the words of Will Kymlicka, stresses 'the essentially political activities of discussion, criticism, example, and emulation ... in which men offer and test ideas against one another'.[170]

The communitarian ideal of leader–follower interaction differs from the liberal standard. Benjamin Barber, one of its stronger critics, described 'modern liberal democracies'. 'In our current system,' he said, 'citizens, who are often guided by their own self-interest, elect representatives by majority vote, and those representatives form public policy....'[171]

This might appear unobjectionable to most modern observers at first blush, but Barber went on to detail the communitarian objections to such an approach. Liberal, representative modes of democracy, he wrote, 'make politics an activity of specialists'. Moreover, 'The representative principle steals from individuals the ultimate responsibility for their values, beliefs, and actions'. Indeed, concluded Barber, 'An ostensibly free citizenry that leaves this ... to elites, thinking that it makes a sufficient display of its freedom by deliberating and voting on issues already formulated in concepts and terms over which it has exercised no control, has in fact already given away the greater part of its sovereignty'.[172]

According to Barber, communitarian democracy does not 'lend ... itself' to 'delegation'. Rather, what is needed is 'politics in the participatory mode: literally, it is self-government by citizens rather than representative government in the name of citizens. Active citizens govern themselves directly here.'[173]

Such an approach to leadership requires, of course, 'institutions designed to facilitate ongoing civic participation in agenda-setting, deliberation, legislation, and policy implementation'.[174] Such topics will occupy our discussion of the final question of the template of leadership. Before turning to institutional implications, however, there remains one other template issue; one that poses more difficulty for communitarians than it does for liberals.

How is the Matter of Diversity and Minority Interests Addressed?

Although all democratic states must confront issues of diversity and the treatment of minority interests, the challenges posed thereby are particularly acute in a polity dedicated to communitarian ideals. William Sullivan, a leading proponent of a modern version of civic republicanism, himself acknowledged 'the dangers of misguided, fanatical, and irresponsible civic involvement', and Russell Hanson noted that 'democratic republicanism [can lead] ... straight to majoritarianism'.[175]

The issue is complex, however, and in some spheres, communitarians actually stake a claim to superiority. Perhaps the best example has to do with liberal assumptions of ethical universalism. That is to say, as liberal writer Amy Gutmann phrased it, liberalism assumes that 'the claims of justice are absolute and universal'.[176] Communitarians tend to reject such universalistic assumptions, and assert that their localistic approach is better suited to a diverse world. Stephen Mulhall and Adam Swift noted that 'a significant strand of communitarian thinking has been directed at liberalism's alleged failure to attend to cultural peculiarity, to ways in which different cultures embody different values and different social forms and institutions'.[177] Because communitarians look to particular communities, each with its own 'traditions and practices that should be regarded as the locus of moral values', they can claim to be more sensitive to localistic patterns.[178]

By the same token, in both ethical and political affairs, communitarianism, with its focus on achieving a unitary, 'common' outcome, risks the exclusion of deviant outlooks. One of the more creative efforts to escape such an outcome was Michael Walzer's conception of 'spheres of justice'.[179] In his work, Walzer proposed 'a model of justice based upon the shared understandings of a particular community'.[180] In this, he was well within the communitarian mainstream, but he took his conceptions a step further, and emphasized that even *within* communities there should be 'an appreciation of cultural peculiarity'.[181]

The way to guarantee justice in a pluralistic society, Walzer asserted, was to think of it as consisting of a number of different and autonomous 'spheres'. These could be 'business, family, religion, neighborhood, ethnic group'. Each sphere would have its own sense of the 'good', and accordingly its own 'standard of justice'. Because the determinations of any one sphere had no claim to legitimacy in any other sphere, Walzer called this approach 'complex equality'.[182] In Walzer's words, with his approach 'there is room … for cultural diversity and political choice'. This is because 'the principles of justice are themselves pluralistic in form; … different social goods ought to be distributed for different reasons, in accordance with different procedures, by different agents', the manner in which this plays out to be determined by the reality of 'cultural particularism'.[183] In sum, for Walzer, this approach 'rules out the possibility of domination and guarantees justice in a pluralistic society'.[184]

Although Walzer's approach is undoubtedly the most well known, his was not the only attempt by a communitarian to avoid the charge of the oppression of minorities. Others harked back to the transformative aspect of a communitarian polity as a safeguard. Such commentators echoed Rousseau's assertion that men, once they entered into his particular version of the 'social contract', progressed from individual liberty to civil liberty to moral liberty, in which the needs of the community became paramount. So, a modern writer like Benjamin Barber could claim that the problem of minority interests could be addressed, in part, by 'a politics of mutualism that can overcome private interests'.[185]

Of course, Barber was not totally sanguine about the concerns for minority interests. He also called for 'safeguards for individuals, for minorities, and the rights that majorities governing in the name of a community may often abuse'.[186] This leads us, in turn, back to a consideration of the institutional implications of creating a polity dedicated to communitarian principles.

What Institutions and Processes are Needed?

Many communitarians, as a part of their discussion of the ideal of a communitarian polity, have sought to identify, in Sandel's words, 'the political forms and social conditions that promote it'.[187] In particular, they have looked to 'institutions designed to facilitate ongoing civic participation'.[188] Such proposals can be broken down into several strategies.

In most communitarian models, there were attempts to create institutions and processes where there can be, in the words of Jane Mansbridge, 'face-to-face interactions'.[189] This required, in most models, politics on a small scale. As Sheldon Wolin put it, there is a need for 'a political life that would be decentered rather than centralized'. For Wolin, 'democracy means diffusion of power rather than centering it'. In turn, 'power can only be diffused if problems are defined in smaller terms'.[190] This meant in the Mansbridge model, that 'decisions in ... government' should be 'decentralized to the level of ... neighborhood assemblies'.[191]

Even in the larger sphere of national politics, those seeking to redress the impersonal structures of liberal democracy have made creative suggestions. Robert Nisbet, for example, was an early advocate of what have come to be called 'mediating institutions'. As early as the 1950s Nisbet bemoaned 'the great formal associations in modern life – industrial corporations, governmental agencies, large-scale labor and charitable organizations', and argued 'it is plain that not many of these answer adequately the contemporary quest for community'. The answer, Nisbet maintained, was the rebuilding of more intimate social structures. He called for 'groups and associations lying intermediate to the individual and the larger ... society'.[192] In more recent times, Robert Putnam has similarly called for a resurrection of voluntary civic associations that help 'make democracy work'.[193]

Within such smaller political spheres, the democratic process that is to be pursued is familiar from our previous discussion. Benjamin Barber, perhaps the commentator most focused upon such processes, called for a 'participatory politics deal[ing] with public disputes and conflicts of interest by subjecting them to a never-ending process of deliberation, decision, and action'.[194]

Other commentators sought to identify the facilitating conditions necessary for such a democratic process. John Dewey focused upon the need for information and its widespread communication. 'Genuinely public policy cannot be generated', he argued, 'unless it be informed by knowledge'. Such knowledge was made useful, however, only by 'perfecting ... the means and ways of communication'.[195]

Subsumed within the perceived need for knowledge and its communication is a key communitarian premise: the requirement for civic education. Various communitarian writers stressed different valued outcomes of such civic education. John Dewey believed it helped to form the community itself. 'The young', he wrote, 'have to be brought within the traditions, outlook and interests which characterize a community by means of education.'[196] Modern republican William Sullivan saw the purpose of civic education as training individuals 'in the civic virtues', or, as Benjamin Barber put it, 'educat[ing] individuals how to think publicly as citizens'.[197] Barber elaborated: 'Strong democracy is a distinctively modern form of participatory democracy. It rests on the idea of self-governing citizens who are united less by homogeneous interests than by civic education and who are made capable of common purpose and mutual action by virtue of their civic attitudes and participatory institutions than by their altruism or their good nature.'[198]

Good intentions, in terms of possessing civic virtue, however, were not sufficient for more pragmatic communitarians. They also looked to a *realpolitik* of, in Walzer's term, a 'relative equality of power'.[199] Traditional republicanism had not required that the relative power of the one, the few and the many be equalized, but, with the decline of deference toward elites, communitarians increasingly called for a rough equality of the distribution of wealth and power. Rousseau had done so in his *On the Social Contract*, and modern commentators such as Jane Mansbridge have noted the links between 'economic equality ... [and] ... a comparable degree of political equality'.[200]

Finally, most modern communitarians also agree with Benjamin Barber that they are looking to reform liberal democracy without risking liberalism's rightful concerns with the protections of individual rights. Accordingly, they embrace a continuation of constitutional protections for individuals and minorities.[201]

Taken together, such institutional proposals by communitarian writers are designed to help implement an alternative version to the dominant liberal strand of democracy. They stress communitarianism's 'importance for the future of our country'. Indeed, says one, 'If democracy is to survive, we have no other option' than to look to such reforms.[202]

These contemporary calls for the reform of the leadership relation provide an appropriate segue into the final segment of this book.

NOTES

1. Benjamin Constant, 'The Liberty of the Ancients Compared with That of the Moderns', in *Political Writings*, trans. and ed. Biancamaria Fontana (Cambridge: Cambridge University Press, 1988), 309.
2. Ibid., 316.
3. Markate Daly, ed., *Communitarianism: A New Public Ethics* (Belmont, Calif.: Wadsworth Publishing Co., 1994), x, xiii, ix.
4. Allen Buchanan, 'Community and Communitarianism', in *Routledge Encyclopedia of Philosophy* (London: Routledge, 1998), 2:465.
5. Daly, *Communitarianism*, xiii, xx.
6. Aristotle, *Aristotle's Politics*, trans. Benjamin Jowett (New York: Random House, 1943), III.4.1276b17–21, p. 130.
7. Michael J. Sandel, *Democracy's Discontent: America in Search of a Public Philosophy* (Cambridge: Belknap Press of Harvard University Press, 1996), 7.
8. Daly, *Communitarianism*, xx, 22 (see note 3).
9. Aristotle, *Nicomachean Ethics*, trans. W.D. Ross, in *The Works of Aristotle*, vol. 2 (Chicago: William Benton, 1952), I.4.1095a14, p. 340; I.7.1097b22–25, p. 343; I.7.1098a13–16, p. 343.
10. Aristotle, *Aristotle's Politics*, trans. Benjamin Jowett, III.4.1276b19–20, p. 130; III.4.1276b29–30, p. 131; III.13.1283b40–44, p. 153.
11. Ibid., III.13.1283b44–45, p. 153.
12. Ibid., III.11.1281b1–8, pp. 145–146.
13. Ibid., III.11.1281b11, p. 146; III.4.1277a16–17, p. 132.
14. Ibid., III.11.1281b26–34, pp. 146–147.
15. Daly, *Communitarianism*, xx (see note 3).
16. G.W.F. Hegel, excerpts from *The Phenomenology of Spirit*, trans. Kenneth R. Westphal, in Markate Daly, ed., *Communitarianism: A New Public Ethics* (Belmont, CA: Wadsworth Publishing Company, 1994), 37–39.
17. Kenneth R. Westphal, annotation to G.W.F. Hegel, *The Phenomenology of Spirit*, in Markate Daly, ed., *Communitarianism: A New Public Ethics* (Belmont, CA: Wadsworth Publishing Company, 1994), 40.
18. Hegel, *Phenomenology of Spirit*, 37.
19. Daly, *Communitarianism*, 36.
20. Jean-Jacques Rousseau, *On the Social Contract*, trans. and ed. by Donald A. Cress (Indianapolis: Hackett Publishing Company, 1762/1987), 17.
21. Ibid.
22. Ibid., 24.
23. Ibid.
24. Ibid., 23.
25. Ibid., 24.
26. Ibid.

27. Ibid., 29.
28. Ibid., 74.
29. Ibid., 26–27.
30. Ibid., 27.
31. Ibid.
32. Ibid., 46.
33. Ibid., 29.
34. Daly, *Communitarianism*, 28 (see note 3).
35. Rousseau, *On the Social Contract*, 81 (see note 20).
36. Ibid., 31.
37. Ibid., 31–32.
38. Albert Weale, 'Public Interest', in *Routledge Encyclopedia of Philosophy* (London: Routledge, 1998), 7:832.
39. Richard Dagger, *Civic Virtues: Rights, Citizenship, and Republican Liberalism* (Oxford: Oxford University Press, 1997), 99.
40. Peter Gay, 'Introduction' to Jean-Jacques Rousseau, *On the Social Contract* (Indianapolis: Hackett Publishing Company, 1987), 9.
41. Daly, *Communitarianism*, 28 (see note 3).
42. Rousseau, *On the Social Contract*, 39 (see note 20).
43. Ibid., 38.
44. Ibid.
45. Ibid.
46. Ibid., 39.
47. Ibid.
48. Dagger, *Civic Virtues*, 95 (see note 39).
49. Rousseau, *On the Social Contract*, 39 (see note 20).
50. Ibid., 26.
51. Ibid., 49.
52. Ibid., 52.
53. Ibid., 30.
54. Ibid., 76.
55. Ibid., 34, 78.
56. Ibid., 49–50.
57. Ibid., 74–75.
58. Ibid., 26.
59. Ibid., 24.
60. Ibid., 82, 24.
61. Ibid., 34.
62. Ibid., 43, 75.
63. Ibid., 43.
64. Ibid., 46.
65. Ibid., 20.
66. Ibid., 24.
67. Ibid., 17.
68. Ibid., 29.
69. Ibid., 26.
70. Dagger, *Civic Virtues*, 84 (see note 39).
71. Daly, *Communitarianism*, ix (see note 3).
72. Amitai Etzioni, *The Spirit of Community: Rights, Responsibilities, and the Communitarian Agenda* (New York: Crown Publishers, 1993), 26.
73. Ibid., 259.
74. Ibid., 15, 7.
75. Ibid., 26.
76. Amitai Etzioni, *The New Golden Rule: Community and Morality in a Democratic Society* (New York: Basic Books, 1996), 39.
77. Etzioni, *The Spirit of Community*. 15, 30–31.
78. Ibid., 10, 263.
79. Etzioni, *The New Golden Rule*, 40.
80. Etzioni, *The Spirit of Community*, 255.
81. Daly, *Communitarianism*, xiv (see note 3).

82. Charles Taylor, 'Alternative Futures: Legitimacy, Identity and Alienation in Late Twentieth Century Canada', in Alan Cairns and Cynthia Williams, eds, *Constitutionalism, Citizenship and Society in Canada* (Toronto: University of Toronto Press, 1985), 183.
83. Ibid., 184.
84. Ibid.
85. Will Kymlicka, *Contemporary Political Philosophy: An Introduction* (Oxford: Clarendon Press, 1990), 224–225.
86. Taylor, 'Alternative Futures', 195.
87. Ibid., 188, 184, 203.
88. Sandel, *Democracy's Discontent*, 6 (see note 7).
89. Benjamin Barber, *Strong Democracy: Participatory Politics for a New Age* (Berkeley: University of California Press, 1984), xix, 24, xxii.
90. Alasdair MacIntyre, *After Virtue: A Study in Moral Theory* (Notre Dame: University of Notre Dame Press, 1981), 2.
91. Barber, *Strong Democracy*, 97–98.
92. Robert A. Nisbet, *The Quest for Community* (New York: Oxford University Press, 1953), 46.
93. Ibid., 73. *See also* Robert D. Putnam, *Bowling Alone: The Collapse and Revival of American Community* (New York: Simon & Schuster, 2000).
94. Daly, *Communitarianism*, xiv (see note 3).
95. Taylor, 'Alternative Futures', 205 (see note 82).
96. Daly, *Communitarianism*, xvii.
97. Taylor, 'Alternative Futures', 186.
98. Daly, *Communitarianism*, x.
99. Sandel, *Democracy's Discontent*, 16 (see note 7).
100. Taylor, 'Alternative Futures', 188–190.
101. Ibid., 189, 190, 194.
102. Barber, *Strong Democracy*, 213, 101, 75 (see note 89).
103. Michael J. Sandel, *Liberalism and the Limits of Justice*, 2nd ed. (Cambridge: Cambridge University Press, 1998).
104. Daly, *Communitarianism*, 79 (see note 3).
105. Sandel, *Liberalism and the Limits of Justice*, 63.
106. Ibid., 150.
107. Ibid., 55.
108. Sandel, *Democracy's Discontent*, 13–14 (see note 7).
109. Sandel, *Liberalism and the Limits of Justice*, 152–154.
110. MacIntyre, *After Virtue*, 202 (see note 90).
111. Ibid., 204–205.
112. Ibid., 205.
113. Ibid., 201, 205, 203.
114. Sheldon S. Wolin, 'Contract and Birthright', *Political Theory* 14 (1986): 179.
115. Ibid., 180.
116. Ibid., 188.
117. Barber, *Strong Democracy*, 213–214 (see note 89).
118. Ibid., 91, 214.
119. Daly, *Communitarianism*, xiv (see note 3).
120. Buchanan, 'Community and Communitarianism', 2:466 (see note 4).
121. Weale, 'Public Interest', 7:833 (see note 38).
122. William M. Sullivan, *Reconstructing Public Philosophy* (Berkeley: University of California Press, 1982), 161.
123. Ibid., 161–162.
124. Barber, *Strong Democracy*, 200 (see note 89).
125. John Rawls, *A Theory of Justice* (Cambridge, Mass.: Harvard University Press, 1971), 560.
126. Sandel, *Liberalism and the Limits of Justice*, 54 (see note 103).
127. Ibid., at Daly, *Communitarianism*, 82.
128. Daly, *Communitarianism*, 79 (see note 3).
129. Buchanan, 'Community and Communitarianism', 2:465 (see note 4).
130. Quoted in Kymlicka, *Contemporary Political Philosophy*, 208 (see note 85).
131. MacIntyre, *After Virtue*, 204–207 (see note 90).
132. Sandel, *Democracy's Discontent*, 25 (see note 7).
133. Sullivan, *Reconstructing Public Philosophy*, 166 (see note 122).
134. Ibid.

135. Barber, *Strong Democracy*, 65, 166 (see note 89).
136. Ibid., 152.
137. Ibid., 137.
138. Jürgen Habermas, *Moral Consciousness and Communicative Action* (Cambridge, Mass.: MIT Press, 1990), 14; Etzione, *The New Golden Rule*, 228 (see note 76).
139. Stephen Mulhall and Adam Swift, *Liberals and Communitarians* (Oxford: Blackwell Publishers, 1992), 19.
140. Michael Walzer, *Spheres of Justice: A Defense of Pluralism and Equality* (New York: Basic Books, Inc., 1983), 5.
141. Daly, *Communitarianism*, xviii, xxiv (see note 3).
142. Barber, *Strong Democracy*, 106 (see note 89).
143. Sandel, *Democracy's Discontent*, 27 (see note 7).
144. Ibid., 27, 25–26.
145. Daly, *Communitarianism*, xxiii.
146. Ibid., xxii.
147. Ibid., 154.
148. Barber, *Strong Democracy*, 155.
149. Sandel, *Democracy's Discontent*, 26.
150. Richard Dagger, *Civic Virtues: Rights, Citizenship, and Republican Liberalism* (Oxford: Oxford University Press, 1997), 14.
151. Daly, *Communitarianism*, 181 (see note 3).
152. Sullivan, *Reconstructing Public Philosophy*, 157–158 (see note 122).
153. Ibid., 157.
154. Barber, *Strong Democracy*, 232; and Daly, *Communitarianism*, 213.
155. Sandel, *Democracy's Discontent*, 5–6 (see note 7).
156. Sullivan, *Reconstructing Public Philosophy*, 163.
157. Kymlicka, *Contemporary Political Philosophy*, 207 (see note 85).
158. Daly, *Communitarianism*, 154 (see note 3).
159. John Dewey, *The Public and Its Problems* (New York: Henry Holt and Company, 1927), 146.
160. Nisbet, *The Quest for Community*, 49 (see note 92).
161. Daly, *Communitarianism*, 154.
162. Dewey, *The Public and Its Problems*, 158, 166.
163. Barber, *Strong Democracy*, 151 (see note 89).
164. Sullivan, *Reconstructing Public Philosophy*, 171 (see note 122).
165. Barber, *Strong Democracy*, 238.
166. Ibid.
167. Ibid., 238, 240.
168. Ibid., 238, 241, 242.
169. Ibid., 200.
170. Kymlicka, *Contemporary Political Philosophy*, 220 (see note 85).
171. Daly, *Communitarianism*, 213 (see note 3).
172. Barber, *Strong Democracy*, 152,145, 196 (see note 89).
173. Ibid., 198, 151.
174. Ibid., 151.
175. Sullivan, *Reconstructing Public Philosophy*, 158 (see note 122); Russell L. Hanson, 'Republicanism', in *Routledge Encyclopedia of Philosophy* (London: Routledge, 1998), 8:281.
176. Amy Gutmann, 'Communitarian Critics of Liberalism', *Philosophy and Public Affairs* 14 (Summer 1985): 310.
177. Mulhall and Swift, *Liberals and Communitarians*, 19 (see note 139).
178. Ibid., 20.
179. Walzer, *Spheres of Justice* (see note 140).
180. Daly, *Communitarianism*, 101 (see note 3).
181. Mulhall and Swift, *Liberals and Communitarians*, 19.
182. Daly, *Communitarianism*, xxi.
183. Walzer, *Spheres of Justice*, 5–6.
184. Daly, *Communitarianism*, 101.
185. Barber, *Strong Democracy*, 198 (see note 89).
186. Ibid., 262.
187. Sandel, *Democracy's Discontent*, 27 (see note 7).
188. Barber, *Strong Democracy*, 151.
189. Jane J. Mansbridge, *Beyond Adversary Democracy* (Chicago: University of Chicago Press, 1983), 28.

190. Wolin, 'Contract and Birthright', 193, 192 (see note 114).
191. Mansbridge, *Beyond Adversary Democracy*, 34.
192. Nisbet, *The Quest for Community*, 71–72, 70.
193. Putnam, *Bowling Alone* (see note 93); Robert D. Putnam, et al., *Making Democracy Work: Civic Traditions in Modern Italy* (Princeton: Princeton University Press, 1993).
194. Barber, *Strong Democracy*, 151 (see note 89).
195. Dewey, *The Public and Its Problems*, 178–179, 155 (see note 159).
196. Ibid., 154.
197. Daly, *Communitarianism*, 190 (see note 3); Barber, *Strong Democracy*, 152.
198. Barber, *Strong Democracy*, 117.
199. Daly, *Communitarianism*, 101.
200. Mansbridge, *Beyond Adversary Democracy*, 10 (see note 189).
201. Barber, *Strong Democracy*, 262.
202. Daly, *Communitarianism*, ix; Sullivan, *Reconstructing Public Philosophy*, 167 (see note 122).

PART IV

Reinventing Leadership

10.   A new fiction of leadership

As the preceding chapters have demonstrated, the challenge of designing new institutions and processes to accommodate the novel assumptions and realities of a democratic world has occupied the attention of theorists and practitioners for centuries. In particular, most of this volume has been devoted to a parsing of the various responses of a long and rich lineage of individuals and societies to the challenges posed by leadership in popular regimes.

These attempts were nothing less than efforts at inventing a new fiction. A 'fiction', it will be recalled, as used in this text, is an idealized construct or system created and utilized as both an intellectual and pragmatic solution to a perceived societal challenge. In this case, a new social and political relation we have labeled 'leadership' was needed to respond to the tensions created by the need to describe (and enact) the appropriate relationship between rulers and ruled in regimes committed to ultimate power in the people. In addition to, in Edmund S. Morgan's words, 'a new way of determining who should stand among the few to govern the many',[1] there was a need to specify the parameters of the relationship between the two groups as they sought to achieve societal goals. Those parameters, in turn, were grounded in specific values and assumptions that we have attempted to elucidate through the use of the 'template of leadership'. Taken together, this constellation of values, institutions, processes and relationships make up what we have called leadership.

In the course of our analysis, the varied efforts by many influential commentators to create a workable fiction of leadership have yielded a catalogue of potential solutions to contemporary leadership challenges. Unfortunately, no unified or coherent approach toward leadership in a modern democracy has been forthcoming. This should not be surprising. One of the purposes of applying our leadership template to each of the proposed solutions has been to suggest the tentative, complex – and conflicting – responses that are possible once the sovereignty of the people is assumed. When the sovereignty of the people is accepted as appropriate and right, as democracy most certainly does, the very complexity of the challenges posed allows for more flexibility in responding. In this sense our long foray into the historical antecedents of modern leadership has armed us properly for our own challenge: the construction – invention – of a more coherent and useful model (fiction) of the leadership relation, suited to contemporary democratic functioning.

The final task of this volume, then, is to create a normative theory of leadership in a democracy. To paraphrase the task John Rawls set out for himself when he endeavoured to create the basis for a just society, we must 'develop … [a] systematic account' of the leadership relation, to serve as 'the most appropriate basis for the institutions of a democratic society'.[2] In sum, what is needed is a better 'fiction' of leadership; as leadership scholar Kenneth Ruscio has put it, 'we need to identify and elaborate upon the crucial elements of a normative theory of leadership that supports a democracy' of the sort we aspire to.[3] In the words of the estimable Alexis de Tocqueville, 'a new science of politics is needed for a new world'.[4]

In so doing, it will be incumbent upon me (notice the turn to the first-person singular) to make explicit the otherwise implicit assumptions that guide my arguments – what I have called my 'implicit theories'. In keeping with the remainder of the volume, this will be accomplished by means of the protocol of questions that comprise the template of leadership.

The significance of this careful attention to my implicit theories of leadership should perhaps be expanded upon. Ruscio notes 'the importance of revealing the assumptions we use to construct our preferred models of leadership'.[5] The reason is to permit and encourage informed debate and disagreement. Once we recognize that our debates about democracy and leadership are grounded in certain fundamental assumptions, we create the possibility that we might be able to move beyond polemics and move toward a constructive resolution of our problems. Only after our foundational beliefs are brought into the open can we hope to have truly productive debates about their implications.

This, then, to borrow from leadership scholar Ronald Heifetz, 'is an argument about the strategies of leadership most suitable to a democratic society', a fiction designed to 'inspire … commitment' from those most interested in successful leadership in a democracy – its participants.[6]

The analysis now turns to the questions that comprise the template of leadership. For each, reference will be made to relevant lessons from our historical analysis. I will append my own resolution of each issue, drawing upon both historical and contemporary commentators to buttress my position. Where appropriate, I will suggest methods by which my recommended approach might be implemented.

WHAT IS THE LEADERSHIP CHALLENGE?

If my objective – my overall challenge – is to create a new fiction (idealized model) of the leadership relation, there are several tensions inherent in leadership in a modern democracy that must be addressed (it is too bold to say such tensions can be resolved, nor is this desirable in all cases). That is to say, if my version of the fiction of leadership is to achieve hegemony, or even widespread acceptance, it must address productively the chief dilemmas posed by the emergence of the people as the constitutive power in the regime.

In this volume, we have encountered many commentaries. Although each contributor to the discourse on leadership in a democracy brings a unique constellation of assumptions and premises to the debate, it is also possible to identify several common issues that each has addressed. Indeed, there are certain issues that are so central to a fiction of leadership in a democracy that every attempt to construct a working model of the relation between leaders and followers as they seek mutual objectives must confront and resolve them. I provide a brief introduction to the key dilemmas of leadership in a democracy below.

Participation versus Competence

The new social and political relation we call leadership came about when the emergence of the people as the constitutive element of the polity required a rethinking of the relationship between leaders and their new sovereigns. Predictably, a tension arose between traditional ways of viewing the leader – the classical ideal – and the new fiction that the people are sovereign. One of the great challenges facing those who attempted to frame a new leadership relation consisted of the dilemma posed by the effort to honor a commitment to the sovereignty of the people while at the same time securing the advantages of the classical ideal, in which the pursuit of the public interest is carefully guided by wise and disinterested leaders.

One way to characterize the dilemma inherent in this challenge is to depict it in terms of *elitist* versus *participationist* approaches to leadership. In its most normative form, elitism calls for deference to leaders with supposedly higher levels of knowledge and ability to govern society. This is best represented in those writers linked to the classical ideal. The other horn of the elitist–participationist dilemma is the participationist viewpoint. Participationism, despite existing in several forms, is simply a stance in favor of giving decision-making power to the people. As such, it has become almost a truism (in theory, if not in practice) in the modern democratic polity.

As we have seen, several historical commentators have attempted to conjure up some synthesis for this dialectic. Aristotle, Machiavelli and Harrington each were aware of the tension. Madison, Tocqueville and Mill all made concerted efforts to resolve it. Indeed, into modern times, this dichotomy has proven to be a fault line among theories of democratic leadership. The dilemma for those seeking to construct a workable conception of leadership is that both approaches have their virtues and their flaws. The elitist view has ever had its attractions. It is difficult not to be lured by the siren call of great and virtuous leaders looking out for our good. Moreover, an argument can be made for the claim that some individuals *are* more capable than others, and so have claims to positions of influence. On the other hand, it takes no imagination to realize the down side of relying upon other individuals purportedly acting on our behalf. More important, the very commitment to democratic, participatory government argues against undue reliance upon the guidance of superiors.

In terms of the fiction of leadership to be posited here, I think the comment by J.S. Mill scholar Dennis Thompson is prescient: 'Mill', he wrote, 'does not intend to resolve fully the conflict between the principles of participation and competence, since a tension between the two principles is an essential feature of [his] theory of government. The theory defines the nature of that tension, sets limits to its resolution, and suggests practical ways in which the resolution might be approximated.'[7] Mill's acceptance of the tension is given further elaboration by modern leadership scholar Matthew Trachman. 'Elitist and participationist views might seem to be diametrically opposed, one suggesting that democracy threatens leadership, and the other that leadership threatens democracy', he acknowledges. But what strikes Trachman is 'what they share in common.... Rather than emphasizing the social logic of threat,' he concludes, 'I would emphasize that the discourse of leadership and modern democracy are *mutually constitutive*.'[8] That is, participation and competence are inextricably linked.

In sum, clearly, a successful fiction of leadership will have to negotiate this tension. Pure, unalloyed democracy appears neither feasible nor even desirable. Yet the reality of popular sovereignty (at least in its modern configuration) forbids swinging too far in the direction of elite rule. The reality is that there must be both leaders and the people operating in tandem in our democracy. The challenge of leadership is that we need to balance the power and abilities of a competent elite with the will of the people.

The Common Good

The second dilemma or challenge that any fiction of leadership must confront relates to the end or purpose of leadership, which calls up questions concerning the existence of the common good, its nature and the mode of achieving it. It will be recalled from our historical overview that the notion of the common good was not problematic during the vast majority of the time period covered. Under classical republicanism, the existence of a common good was simply assumed (and we could rely upon our leaders to discern it and act upon it). It was not until classical liberalism made its appearance in the seventeenth and eighteenth centuries, with its emphasis upon individual rights and its fear of coercion, that the idea of the common good came into question. This dichotomy has continued to the modern day, in the form of the distinction between the modern liberal and communitarian approaches. At one extreme, the concept was conceived of, at most, as the collection of all individual interests. At the other, there remained a commitment to a monolithic good that could provide guidance and sustenance for the community.

Linked with the question of the existence and nature of the common good has been a debate over how one might perceive or derive it. Those who invoke such a good rely upon various modes of determining it. Either leaders perceive it, or followers do (for example, the 'General Will'), or it is derived through participant interaction. Others, less enamored of the notion, are content to rely upon the outcome of 'market forces' to determine what is 'good', or to measure policy ends according to an arbitrary external standard such as the protection of personal property.

It should be obvious from the preceding that anyone proposing a new model of leadership will need to come down on one side or the other, and provide his or her justifications. At the least, there must be, in the words of Kenneth Ruscio, a proposal for 'reasonable and just collective action through political engagement'.[9] That, after all, is the essence of the leadership relation.

The Individual and the Community

Related in many ways to the discussion of the common good is a broader issue of the individual and community. To quote Ruscio again, 'a central, if not *the* central theme of Western politics [and, as we have seen, Western political thought] is reconciling individual pursuits with the collective purpose of a community'. And, as Ruscio further notes, 'it manifests itself in a seemingly endless number of variations: the tension between private and public interest; the yearning for communal bonds in a culture that values individuality; the debate over whether human nature is inherently selfish or sociable' and the like.[10]

Our study of the Western political tradition reflects the importance of this tension. We framed the split in terms of Benjamin Constant's 'liberty of the ancients' and 'liberty of the moderns'. Those stressing the modern emphasis on individuality included Locke, Mill, Rawls (to a large extent) and Nozick. Those harking back to 'ancient' views were Aristotle, Hegel, Rousseau, MacIntyre, Sandel and others. Again, both sides present powerful arguments. Communitarian Michael Sandel acknowledges the concerns of the individualists. 'From the liberal standpoint, the republican emphasis … leaves individual rights vulnerable to the tyranny of the majority. Moreover, … republican claims … may open the way to coercion and oppression.'[11] On the other hand, as Richard Dagger explains it, the liberal approach may be 'too one-sided and individualistic'. It 'encourages us to think of ourselves as apart from and threatened by ... society .... We fail to realize how we depend upon communities that not only give meaning to our lives but also largely constitute our identities.'[12]

Fortunately, the more astute commentators recognize the possibility of a middle ground. Communitarian Markate Daly points out that 'this debate is not a conflict between the values of liberty and community. None of the great philosophers disparaged either.... Nor are the extreme positions – self-seeking individualism and unreflective collectivism – under consideration.' Instead, 'the debate focuses on the theoretical and social consequences of stressing either liberty or community as the primary value in society.... The debate now turns on the question of whether circumstances still justify stressing the ideal of personal liberty, or whether the problems facing our society are sufficiently different to justify forming a new philosophy stressing a different ideal, that of community.'[13] The liberal Amy Gutmann agrees that 'we may be able to discover ways in which local communities *and* democracy can be vitalized without violating individual rights'. The bottom line, says Gutmann – and this is particularly relevant for our current endeavor of creating a fiction of leadership – is that 'we would be better off, by both Aristotelian and liberal democratic standards, if we tried to shape it according to our present moral understandings'.[14] That will be my objective here.

Diversity and Minority Interests

A (relatively) modern offshoot of the tension between the individual and community is the treatment of those in the minority and, particularly, the handling of the modern reality of diversity. Again, we have already traced the responses of several commentators. James Madison and John Stuart Mill concerned themselves with the protection of minority interests. Tocqueville devoted the better part of two volumes to the topic. This issue is the foundation for the liberal stress upon individual rights. A more complex subject is the modern development of highly diverse societies, which obviate previous assumptions of homogeneity. Modern liberals such as John Rawls (and communitarians such as Michael Walzer) have attempted to address this issue as well.

It is Rawls who frames the issue best: 'How is it possible', he asks, 'for there to exist over time a just and stable society of free and equal citizens, who remain profoundly divided by reasonable religious, philosophical, and moral doctrines?'[15] Having framed the issue perfectly, most would agree that Rawls and others have only imperfectly responded to this challenge of leadership in a democracy. One cannot expect a final resolution to this issue that has occupied the attention of the greatest minds of our heritage, but no model of leadership in a democracy can duck it.

Toward a New Fiction of Leadership

Having identified what I believe to be the central dilemmas that must be addressed in the process of creating a workable fiction of leadership for modern democracy, I now turn to the remaining issues posed by the template of leadership. From the answers will come a normative theory of leadership designed to address those challenges and geared to our modern realities.

WHAT IS THE END OR PURPOSE OF LEADERSHIP?

I have often referred to leadership as a 'social or political relation'. That is accurate, and it places the emphasis squarely where it belongs: on the relationship between leaders and the people. Before turning to these central elements of the leadership relation, however, it is important to establish the context that frames – and indeed shapes – that relationship. That is, we must explore the *purpose* for which leaders and the people relate – the 'end' of leadership, and something about how it is achieved.

The Common Good: a Reprise

Our discussion of the ends of leadership must begin with a reprise of the debate summarized in the previous section concerning the common good. Prior to the modern era, the answer to the question of the proper end of leadership could be succinctly answered by reference to the 'common good'. Moreover, prior to the emergence of the notion of the sovereignty of the people, there was little concern over what that term entailed or how it was to be discerned and implemented. Both the discerning and the implementing were the task of the wise and virtuous leader, who, by definition, was responsible for securing the common good of all. Even Rousseau, who wrote in support of popular sovereignty and who had moved beyond a simple reliance upon a virtuous leader, was in accord as to the essential end of leadership. 'It is utterly on the basis of the common interest', he concluded, 'that society ought to be governed.'[16] Modern communitarians have carried this concept forward, and make the common good central to their claims to the good life.

The conception of the 'common good' thus retains its currency and continues to influence thinking about leadership to this day. However, with the emergence of the people as a sovereign entity, and particularly with the appearance of liberal thought, came important shifts in the rationale and purpose of leadership. Liberalism, with its focus on individualism, in important ways brought into question the very conception of a common good. At the very least, the new focus upon private interests turned the notion of the common good upside down. Traditional republican thinking had viewed the common good as something wholly distinct from – and in most cases antagonistic to – private interests. Now, as historian Gordon Wood puts it, 'the pursuit of private interests was the real source of the public good'. Given these radically different priorities, the purpose of leadership shifted as well. Rather than seeking a unitary common good, the purpose of leadership was to facilitate 'the pursuit of private interests rather than the public good'.[17] In many (but not all) modern liberal conceptions, the public good has become nothing more than the utilitarian sum of individual satisfactions.

A Shift to Values

The debate over the existence and nature of the common good has become a staple of our political discourse. However, I propose that we turn to more productive ways to think about the ends of leadership. An important first step is provided by leadership scholar James MacGregor Burns. For Burns, 'leadership is … a moral undertaking, a response to the human wants expressed in public values'.[18] Burns's emphasis on values opens up whole new vistas in our thinking about leadership. More precisely, it is entirely possible to think about leadership and its ends in terms of human values.

Fellow leadership scholar Ronald Heifetz suggests how this might work. Heifetz envisions leadership as 'developing the organizational and cultural capacity to meet problems successfully according to our values and purposes. And when there are conflicts over values and purposes, which happen frequently, the clarification and integration of competing values itself becomes' the task of leadership, which he calls 'adaptive work'. More specifically, Heifetz maintains that 'adaptive work [leadership] consists of efforts to close the gap between reality and a host of values'. Thus, for Heifetz, 'tackling the tough problems – problems that often require an evolution of values – is the end of leadership; getting that work done is its essence'.[19]

If values are an appropriate way to frame the workings of leadership, it remains to discuss such values with some specificity, and to speculate regarding how they might shape the ends of leadership. As Heifetz himself acknowledges, 'clearly, we have a host of quite precious values – liberty, equality, human welfare, justice, and community – for which we take risks, and a concept of adaptation [leadership] applied to human organizations and societies must account for these squarely'.[20] Indeed, it might be said that we have hierarchies of values that guide our actions. The distinctions here are often subtle and rarely clearly articulated, yet they exert a substantial influence upon one's perception of the ends and obligations of the leadership relation. Modern democracies are founded upon such iconic declarations of 'life, liberty, and the pursuit of happiness', or 'liberty, equality, fraternity', but such widely accepted enunciations mask substantive differences in interpretation and priority. Some, for example, stress the 'negative' liberty of the absence of governmental interference in one's private affairs, while others champion the 'positive' liberty that comes from having sufficient economic and political resources. Equality can mean the equality of opportunity or the equality of condition. Another widely accepted value, justice, can take on quite different meanings. Other values are overtly antagonistic. Equality and fraternity, for instance, can be at odds with conceptions of liberty. Such distinctions can be elaborated almost without end.

In keeping with the ultimate model or fiction of leadership that I will endorse, I do not here espouse or lay claim to a particular ranking of values. That is for the people to decide. The important thing is that the relevant values must be identified and articulated as we move forward toward the accomplishment of our goals. This is conducive to a more informed evaluation of the proposed leadership solution, which then becomes the end of leadership. It is critical to our understanding of leadership, however, to recognize that there will rarely be consensus regarding the ranking of values. As Heifetz acknowledges, 'competing values are often at stake'.[21]

Conflicts are to be expected; however, if my fiction of leadership is to be successful, their resolution must involve more than the preponderance of power. To the extent that I take a normative stance on an issue that I view as essentially to be resolved by the people, it is to recommend that the resolution be more inclusive than delimiting (later I will articulate several strategies that will increase the likelihood of such an outcome). That is to say, in today's diverse society, it becomes necessary to expand upon the guiding core values underpinning democratic government. The classic natural rights of man are life, liberty, property and the pursuit of happiness (combining the ideas of Locke, Jefferson and, more recently, Burns). Such values are classically individualistic. However, other values such as justice (Rawls), equality (Rousseau), fraternity (Taylor) and mutual activity (Tocqueville) are more social in nature, and also need to be included in the principles that shape our democracy. Thus we need to value both what is good for the individual, and what is good for society as a whole.[22]

All this brings us back to the inevitability of conflict among values, and the individuals espousing them. In the next segment on the epistemology of leadership I will begin to suggest a productive approach to this challenge, which will eventually bring us to the heart of the leadership relation itself. Before moving in that direction, however, I wish to posit another insight concerning the purpose of leadership, an insight linked to our new focus on values yet one which represents a shift of perspective of rather seismic proportions.

A Tradition Inverted: the People's Needs

The shift to discussing the ends of leadership in terms of values rather than outcomes has helped us to escape from the conundrum of the liberal–communitarian debate over the common good. That being said, it is my claim that values merely shape the debate over leadership ends, as they explain and justify our priorities. There is something more basic that we have yet to uncover. Recall what James MacGregor Burns wrote in a passage quoted earlier: 'leadership is … a moral undertaking, *a response to the human wants* expressed in public values [emphasis supplied]. In another place Burns added: 'More than anything else, wants and needs motivate leaders and followers to struggle for social change. They are the powerhouses of leadership.'[23] This, then, leads us to the real genesis of leadership.

This observation is arguably valid for all legitimate regimes, but it is assuredly true for democracies. Burns's emphasis on people's wants and needs as the generative force on leadership is reinforced by the priorities of popular sovereignty. The truly revolutionary aspect of viewing leadership through the lens of popular sovereignty – literally, 'power in the people' – is the fact that it turns traditional thinking about the ends of leadership upside down. Instead of a teleological process geared toward achieving some desired end (such as an abstract common good or the result of applying some independent standard), the purpose of leadership is rooted in identifying and addressing the pre-existing needs of the people. Thus, leadership is not driven by ends, but by initiating needs. These needs, in turn, are evaluated according to the values society has settled on as important (indeed, it is an iterative process, as needs generate new value claims while existing values winnow out mere 'wants' from 'needs' – I distinguish the two).

The result of this way of thinking is, I think, a more productive – and more realistic – assessment of the ends and purposes of leadership. It will bring us, eventually, to a deeper understanding of the interactions between leaders and the people. Before leaving this topic of the ends of leadership, however, it is worthwhile to add one further observation that, somewhat ironically, brings us full circle back to our seemingly rejected notion of the common good.

A Public Interest, not a Common Good

Having made the argument that the ends of leadership have their genesis in the initiating needs of the people is not to say that there are no important outcomes as well. As a result of the process I will depict in the next section on the epistemology of leadership – and elaborate in my subsequent analysis of leaders and the people – the interactions of the people and their leaders, in the process of identifying and addressing their needs, generate certain outcomes. It is my argument that this outcome is more than the sum of its parts. That is to say, it is not merely the accumulated sum of private interests. The very process of engaging with one another yields something more. This echoes the perspective of Montesquieu. Recent commentator Kenneth Ruscio summarizes him well: 'Montesquieu's claim ... is ... that the public good is not merely some derivative of everyone's private interests. The whole is greater than the sum of its parts.'[24] As modern leadership scholar James MacGregor Burns puts it, the result of such interactions is a 'broadening [of] individual aspirations'.[25] The outcome is something that might be labeled a 'public interest' that is distinct from the calculus of the private claims that incited the need for leadership.

In sum, I argue that there is indeed a 'public interest' that is at the heart of leadership. I decline to use the term 'common good', partly because of the baggage it carries, and partly because the term implies a more reified outcome than I have in mind. By its very nature, this public interest is dynamic and ever subject to reassessment and review. It is unlike traditional notions of the common good.

At this point in my argument, I must acknowledge a weakness in my reasoning, and plead for the reader's suspension of judgment until I have had the opportunity to buttress my claims. I must admit that my conclusion that there is a 'public interest' (if not a common good) above and beyond the sum of private interests requires a bit of a leap of faith. That is to say, I can adduce no scientific, or social scientific evidence to justify this conclusion. My seemingly optimistic stance is not, however, the product of some fuzzy-cheeked naïvety. I strongly suspect that my penchant for hard-headed realism will become evident soon enough as my argument unfolds. At this point, I will only say that my belief in a public interest is part-and-parcel of my later claims about the transformation of individuals into citizens. For now, the reader can be comforted by the fact that I am not alone in my stance. Somewhat predictably, the communitarian Benjamin Barber maintains that in democratic discourse private interests will be transformed into public goods. Perhaps more impressively, the liberal Kenneth Ruscio insists that 'there is indeed a common good that transcends individual interests'.[26]

WHAT IS THE EPISTEMOLOGY OF LEADERSHIP?

Once it has determined the essential purpose or end of leadership, an effective model of leadership must establish the criteria or processes by which the polity can discern 'right policy' that accords with the desired purpose. This aspect of the leadership fiction I have labeled the 'epistemology of leadership'. Put another way, it is the question of the standard by which one judges the propriety or success of actions.

The Traditional Approaches

In the long tradition of the classical ideal, the epistemology of leadership posed no particular problem. In regimes where such leaders held sway, it was assumed that the wise and virtuous leader – in republics in association with an equally virtuous body of citizens – comprehended the common good and the means to achieve it. As Aristotle would have it, policy was to be evaluated 'with reference to the advantage of the state, and the common good of the citizens'.[27]

This approach was not without its problems, even in the earliest of times. Recall that as early as Plato, those looking to leaders of the classical ideal acknowledged the need for proxies. We have seen how Plato himself rather belatedly and reluctantly came around to advocating a rule of law in the apparent absence of virtuous leaders. Aristotle came to a similar conclusion regarding the need for law, albeit for different reasons. Aristotle was never so confident in the godly nature of his rulers, nor was he as suspicious of the virtue of the people. Nonetheless, he came to view the rule of law as a safeguard for the accomplishment of the desired ends of justice and the common good (especially in regimes where the many were dominant). Likewise Machiavelli (in the *Discourses*) championed the rule of law, and this tactic to keep leaders and the people from discretionary action has become a commonplace in the Western tradition.

Neither reliance upon virtuous leaders nor upon the rule of law is, however, a satisfactory answer to the requirements of the epistemology of leadership. Those relying upon the classical ideal of the leader to discern the common good confront the twin weaknesses of few leaders that fit the bill and the problematic notion of a truly common good in a diverse society. It is also difficult to conceive of the common good as an external, pre-existing conception by which to measure actions. The rule of law, which was conceived as a response to both of these problems (that is, the problem of imperfect leaders and the need to articulate the common good), is not a satisfactory answer to the epistemological challenges of leadership. First, as James Harrington and James Madison acknowledged, laws are made by men, and thus can hardly be conceived to be some independent standard by which to gauge men's actions. Second, with the partial exception of the constitutionalism advocated by Henry Vane and the American Founding Fathers, looking to the rule of law as the measure of proper policy is tautological, since in a democracy most policy outcomes take the form of law. In sum, the 'ancients', in Constant's phrase, have not devised a useful model for the epistemology of leadership in a modern democracy.

For that matter, neither have, in Constant's terms again, the 'moderns'. With the rise of liberal individualism, the conception of an overarching common good went into eclipse. In a comment attributed to Thomas Jefferson, now 'the public good is best promoted by the exertion of each individual seeking his own good in his own way'.[28] Several variants of the measure of 'right policy' emerged under liberal conceptions of the epistemology of leadership. One primary mechanism of determining right policy was simply the operation of the market. Using market imagery first articulated by Bernard de Mandeville and Adam Smith, many liberals perceive appropriate policy as the outgrowth of general exchange. One version of this matured into the theory of modern interest-group pluralism of contemporary political scientists Robert Dahl and David B. Truman.[29] Others looked to some 'independent ground' to derive appropriate policy, such as Mill's utilitarian approach or the natural rights of Locke. We have seen Robert Nozick erect an entire liberal theory upon Lockean foundations.

Despite their rise to predominance in modern conceptions of democracy, the various approaches to the epistemology of leadership under the liberal rubric suffer their own inconveniences. They evoke no sense of engagement with fellow members of the polity, and thus seem ill-equipped to serve a modern democratic system dedicated to government, in Lincoln's words, 'of the people, by the people, and for the people'. In a similar vein, for those (like me) who preserve a conception of the public interest, the liberal conception of the mere sum of individual interests as the mode of determining right policy seems rather barren.

Neither of the traditional approaches to the determination of right policy, then, appears satisfactory to the demands of a diverse modern democracy. Neither taps into my own announced 'end or purpose of leadership', which involves drawing upon the perceived needs of the people. Nor do they faithfully acknowledge the reality of popular sovereignty, which is indeed a regime grounded in the power of the people. My proposed solution will tap into a third historical tradition, a tradition that has been expanded and elaborated in the modern era.

A Constructivist Approach

The emergence of the fiction of the people as the constituent power of the polity created significant new complexities for the epistemology of leadership that have yet to be fully resolved. Ardent participationists are satisfied with a majoritarian approach, suitably modified by protections for minority rights. Others continue to maintain that participation must still be leavened with competence. Ultimately, the fiction of leadership invented here will take the latter approach. But before the nuances of that proposal can be put forward, it is necessary first to construct an epistemology of leadership that draws its core strength from the interactions of the people themselves, even if those interactions need to be tempered by a new leadership relation.

To understand the historical dimensions of the issue of epistemology in a regime dedicated to the sovereignty of the people, we can begin with the work of Rousseau in the eighteenth century. Recall that Rousseau argued that true freedom could best be attained by men joining together into society, a process that transformed individuals from a commitment to selfish interests to an appreciation of the needs of the community. That community, then, would determine right policy according to the 'General Will', a complex concept to be sure, but in essence one designed to capture and reflect the common interests of the citizenry. All that is needed, for Rousseau, is the requisite commitment to that common interest. If the commitment to the common good can be maintained, 'the deliberation would always be good'.[30]

For our epistemological purposes, the important point is one made by a modern scholar, who writes that under Rousseau's approach to the General Will, 'citizens do not identify a pre-existing public interest, but instead define that interest in the process of choice'.[31] This is an early instance of a conception of the people 'constructing' a definition of the common good in the process of their deliberations. The notion was not without difficulties however. One was in the form of determining the General Will. This, according to Rousseau, was by majority vote. At first blush, this was simple majoritarianism, but Rousseau was more sophisticated than that. For one thing, the General Will was for him more than the majority of individual interests. It was something 'realized and desired by all'. This conception led to one of Rousseau's otherwise most puzzling statements: those who were outvoted were merely mistaken as to the content of the General Will, and in their subordination to the majority they were 'forced to be free'.

From a modern perspective, the weaknesses of Rousseau's approach are his unitary conception of the General Will and the related fact that those who disagree with it are 'forced to be free'. Nevertheless, Rousseau is an important figure. He shifted the focus of the epistemology of leadership to the people, and he suggested an approach wherein the people created or 'constructed' their own interpretation of right policy. Likewise, he (unknowingly) revealed to us the most troubling aspects of that shift to an epistemology based upon the people, in the drastic implications of his vision of the General Will.

Rousseau, of course, was a theorist. Yet historian Gordon S. Wood suggests that within a century – that is, by the time of Tocqueville – something akin to the General Will had become a reality, and the epistemological issues of popular determination of public policy became much more than theoretical. By the nineteenth century, wrote Wood, 'the result of all these assaults on elite opinion and celebrations of common ordinary judgment was a dispersion of authority and ultimately a diffusion of truth itself to a degree never before seen. With every ordinary person being told his ideas and tastes were as good, if not better, than those [of the elite] …, it is not surprising that truth and knowledge became elusive and difficult to pin down. Knowledge and truth … now indeed had to become more fluid and changeable, more timely and current….' As a result of this new frame, says Wood, 'Americans experienced an epistemological crisis as severe as any in their history'.[32]

The early nineteenth century response to this epistemological crisis was to embrace the will of the majority, but without the nuances appended by Rousseau. As Wood put it, the American people eventually devised 'a criteria for determining who was right and who was wrong, and it was the opinion of the whole people…. Truth was actually the creation of many voices … no one of which was more important than the other.' As a result, Americans had created 'something like a general will'.[33]

Even more than had been the case with the theoretician Rousseau, the actual turn to the people as the source of epistemological truth raised the twin specters of the tyranny of the majority and the championing of participation over competence. I will need to attempt to resolve both in order to create a credible theory of leadership, but first I wish to build upon these historical foundations. That is, I wish to put forward a justification for an epistemology grounded in the people based upon my previous conclusions that the end of leadership is to fashion from the needs of the people something that might legitimately be called the public interest.

My commitment to the underlying principle of popular sovereignty is absolute, in the sense that I endorse the claim that the people are the constituting force of the polity. This is also reflected in my argument that the ends of leadership must be based in its beginnings; that is, in the needs of the people. All of this is well and good, but it does not move us very far along the path to a defensible epistemology of leadership in a democratic state. That is to say, I need to address by what standard 'right policy' can be assessed and determined. Such an epistemology is possible, however. In order to create it, I need to address both its processes and its standards.

With respect to the appropriate epistemological process, its origins can be found in the works of those writers who might be said to take a 'constructivist' approach to the epistemology of leadership. I have already noted that Rousseau hinted at this approach when his majority defined the public interest in the process of choice. Two nineteenth-century commentators address this approach more specifically. Hegel introduced the notion of constructivism in a general sense. For him, social values and practices are a product of group functioning, and emerge from interactions among its members. In sum, social values are socially constructed.

John Stuart Mill applied this constructivist approach to the leadership relation. As he explored the interactions between leaders and the people, Mill portrayed this process as the best way to come the closest to 'truth' in the policy-making process. Actually, Mill stressed the lack of any certainty about 'truth', and relied instead upon the dynamics of the interactions between leaders and the people to approximate most closely this elusive concept.

This constructivist approach has been carried forward in modern times by theorists of both the liberal and communitarian traditions, albeit in differing forms. Both, in their own way, look to citizens to construct their own answers to civic questions. On the liberal side of the equation is John Rawls. Somewhat akin to Mill, Rawls eschewed any claim to absolute truth in the public sphere; indeed, much of his energies were devoted to creating a political conception that could operate in the public arena, leaving claims of truth to the private realm of individual functioning. Again somewhat like Mill, Rawls looked to the give and take of the actual process of political interaction to achieve the 'best' policy outcome. All this was to take place within the confines of agreed principles of justice – what Rawls called 'justice as fairness' – but within those rather minimalist restrictions, citizens of the polity should engage in what he called 'political constructivism'. According to Rawls, 'the political constructivist regards a judgment as correct because it issues from the reasonable and rational procedure of construction'. To Rawls, 'political constructivism ... does not ... use (or deny) the concept of truth.... Rather, within itself the political conception does without the concept of truth.' For matters in the political realm, 'political constructivism provides political liberalism with an appropriate conception of objectivity'.[34]

Interestingly, many communitarians endorse a similar type of approach to the determination of right policy. While they reject what they perceive to be the over-restrictive universalism of Rawls's conceptions of justice as expressed in his 'justice as fairness', and challenge his notion that 'the right is prior to the good', nonetheless they also endorse a form of constructivism. Many communitarians propose a similar method for determining right policy: civic dialogue. William Sullivan argues that because 'political decisions so affect the kinds of life that will prevail, public debate is critical for developing a shared understanding of the consequences of policy choices, of hidden costs and benefits to the whole community'.[35] Benjamin Barber directly addresses the epistemological aspect. He argues for an 'epistemology of process', or, in another place, 'conceiving politics *as* epistemology'.[36] Habermas explicated such an approach at great length.

In sum, the first piece of my claim about the epistemology of leadership is about the process required to understand and derive right policy. The upshot of the preceding discussion is that our understanding of what outcomes are deemed to be good and wise emerges as part and parcel of the process of discussion and deliberation among citizens. This understanding cannot be handed down by a leader after the fashion of the classical ideal, nor are there appropriate and sufficient 'independent grounds' by which to measure the quality of an outcome. As Barber suggests, we cannot know the specifics of what is right for our society until we work through the process of deliberation that leads us to our conclusion. Moreover, because it is quite obvious that there will be potentially conflicting ideas as the process unfolds, there must be some balancing of individual and collective values, of our claims to individual rights and our recognition of our societal obligations. The reality of it is that neither natural rights nor societal values are absolute, and therefore a process is needed to reconcile tensions.

The specifics of that process we will explore when we turn to the specifics of the fiction we call leadership. To preview, however, a part of the answer will be structural. Our focus moves away from the contents of the outcomes of societal debates and instead focuses on the process of the debate itself. What is required is to ensure that stakeholders have the opportunity to participate on something near an equal basis, and that the debate itself allows all views to get a fair hearing. If such procedural safeguards operate correctly, the outcome, almost by definition, is acceptable, and, because all have participated in its formulation, it could even be considered as in the public interest. In addition to the necessary structural protections, there are also – or so I will claim – important roles that must be played by the people and their leaders. The details of these must await my treatment of the heart of the leadership relation. Taken together, however, these comprise the elements of an epistemology of leadership that is distinct from historical traditions, and attuned to the needs of modern democracy.

The Public Interest Redux

This approach to the epistemology of leadership that I am espousing harks back, as do all epistemologies, to initial premises. It will be recalled that in the previous section I had marshaled my support behind an approach to leadership that centered on the people coming together to determine what is in the public interest. My take on the epistemology of leadership is merely an extension of that.

However, there is also a 'twist'. I also make a seemingly tautological claim: at the same time that the public interest is the *product* of the epistemological process depicted above, I also assert that a conception of the public interest also *guides* the policy-making (and leadership) process. How can this be? Here, I distinguish between policy outcomes and guides or standards to measure the propriety of potential outcomes. As one modern scholar has put it, 'The concept of the public interest can be used in a wide variety of ways, and this has led many to say that it is devoid of meaning. However, the concept enables us to evaluate the tendency of policies and institutions to promote the interests of the members of a society.'[37] It is this that I would like to explore further.

The resolution of the riddle of the public interest as both evaluative standard and desired outcome lies in an issue I have repeatedly returned to in the course of creating my fiction: the distinction between individual and citizen. To the extent that individuals become citizens, they adopt the broader perspectives predicted by Rousseau when individuals are transformed by entry into the social contract. And, while I do not subscribe to Rousseau's seemingly automatic transformation (albeit with the help of his 'Legislator'), I maintain that it is possible that individuals can acquire something akin to the traditional conception of civic virtue, and thereby desire outcomes that benefit the community in addition to their more purely selfish motives. Similarly, although again the authors appear too cavalier in their assumptions about the ease of achieving this result, I believe Sidney Verba and colleagues may have it right when they say 'In fuller participatory democracy, political activity becomes a mechanism whereby citizens engage in enlightened discourse, come to understand the views of others, and become sensitized to the needs of the community and nation. Thus educated, they transcend their own interests to seek the public good.'[38] Or, as the more pragmatic Kenneth Ruscio puts it, 'Deliberation aspires to more than simply the pursuit of private interests. It rises above a mere contest for position and power....

Public interest [is] discoverable by means other than each individual simply pressing his or her own preference without concern for others.' Indeed, continues Ruscio, 'That "true interest" of the people [can] only be discovered through reason and deliberation.'[39]

How this transformation from individual to citizen might come about will be the subject of ensuing sections. To the extent the transformation occurs, however, participants in the leadership process evaluate challenges and needs and the means of redress in terms of what can only be thought of as the public interest. At the same time, *because* this is the standard of evaluation, the resulting policy will likely embody the public interest as well. The public interest, then, is not, in my conception, so much an independent ground for evaluating policy as it is a way of thinking, a cognitive frame that helps to ensure appropriate outcomes for a polity, which then become manifestations of the public interest as well.

Leadership Redux

It may appear from the preceding that the simple act of the gathering together of individuals will ultimately lead to the public interest being enacted, but such is not the case. Achieving the desired outcome demands a certain level of competence in the people, an expectation that might be optimistic (more on this presently). To the extent that the people fall short, it remains for those with more competence – leaders – to inform and guide the deliberations. The matter cuts to the heart of the new relation between the few and the many that we are labeling leadership. It recalls the tension between participation and competence. My task, ultimately, will be to achieve a synthesis of the two that is satisfactory to our democratic sensibilities. Before we get to the heart of the matter, however, it is appropriate here to address another template issue, because it is so linked to our concern with democratic epistemology: the role of diverse interests.

HOW IS THE MATTER OF DIVERSITY AND MINORITY INTERESTS ADDRESSED?

The template issue of the handling of diversity and minority interests could be placed almost anywhere within the logic of the fiction I am creating, so pervasive is its importance. I have chosen, rather arbitrarily, to place it here, because it fits so nicely with our consideration of the epistemology of leadership. As will become evident, however, the inclusion of diverse interests is central to all aspects of a successful leadership relation.

Encouraging Diverse Interests

Somewhat surprisingly to modern sensibilities, concerns with diversity and/or minority interests are relatively recent. The related issues of diversity and minority rights did not receive primary attention until the emergence of two developments related to modernity. The first was the rise of egalitarian democracy. With democratic majorities holding sway, issues of minority interests inevitably arose.

The second issue was related, albeit perhaps more subtle. It was the recognition that there could be legitimate individual interests apart from, and even in conflict with, the interests of the majority. The idea that members of society might not be homogeneous, but rather are characterized by diversity and difference, was a surprisingly late addition to the political consciousness of democratic polities. For millennia it had been a commonplace that the true interests of society were unitary, and that proper public policy was essentially a matter of discerning and addressing that interest. To the extent that the polity still remained dedicated to a monolithic common good that fairly represented the needs of a homogeneous society, issues of diversity and minority interests were moot. In modern times, however, that longstanding premise has been reversed, and it is assumed that each citizen has individual interests that should be pursued. Moreover, today, any unitary notion of the common good appears to be, in the words of political scientist Richard Dagger, 'at odds with cultural pluralism'. Indeed, 'the ideal itself is objectionable'; it 'threatens to ignore the deep differences among groups of people and to impose an artificial homogeneity on them'.[40]

In a modern democracy, then, these matters cannot be ignored. In the modern literature, the issue of diversity is often portrayed as a challenge to be addressed. John Rawls provides perhaps the classic formulation. 'How is it possible', he asks, 'for there to exist over time a just and stable society of free and equal citizens, who remain profoundly divided by reasonable religious, philosophical, and moral doctrines?'[41] Rawls's question is precisely on point and, indeed, his response will be central to my treatment of the issue. Nevertheless, I wish to begin the discussion by striking a different note, a more positive one. Diversity, especially when one thinks of it in connection with the epistemology of leadership, is a thing greatly to be desired. Leadership scholar Ronald Heifetz perhaps articulates this best.

As we have seen (and shall see in more detail later), Heifetz conceives of leadership as 'adaptive work'. A part of adaptive work, he says, 'consists of the learning required to address conflicts in the values people hold, or to diminish the gap between the values people stand for and the reality they face'. This 'ability to adapt requires the productive interaction of different values'. For Heifetz, 'the implication is important: *the inclusion of competing value perspectives may be essential to adaptive success* [emphasis in the original]'. 'Without conflicting frames of reference,' he continues, 'the social system scrutinizes only limited features of its problematic environment.' Speaking epistemologically, 'the mix of values in a society provides multiple vantage points from which to view reality. Conflict and heterogeneity are resources for social learning. Although people may not come to share another's values, they may learn vital information that would ordinarily be lost to view without engaging the perspectives of those who challenge them.'[42]

In Heifetz's view, then, diversity is not only a reality to be adapted to; it is the linchpin of an effective leadership process. As such, the first task of leadership is to design processes and institutions that incorporate in meaningful ways the variety of views on topics for which (in our new epistemological reality) there are no fixed answers. In terms of the necessary processes, both Rawls and Heifetz will become central players in the fiction I am creating. However, I will postpone a more thorough consideration of their thinking until we come to the discussion of the roles of the people and their leaders, respectively. A discussion of the institutions necessary to ensure that all voices and stakeholders are heard is appropriate here, however, since it overlaps with the need to protect minority interests in a majoritarian society. My fiction of leadership, if it is to be effective, must address this.

Protecting Minority Interests

With the rise of democracy, concerns about minority rights came to the fore. The very definition of majority rule posed difficulties for minorities. As Madison had written, 'True it is that no other rule exists by which any question which may divide a Society, can be ultimately determined, but the will of the majority, but it is also true that majority may trespass on the rights of the minority'.[43] In response, thoughtful commentators, to include Madison and many others analyzed in this book, proposed solutions. Those that appear to be the most useful are highlighted below.

One attempt at protecting the voices of those in the minority was not institutional so much as it was attitudinal. It is embodied best in the liberal philosophy of John Stuart Mill. In his paean to individual liberty, he had written: 'The object of this essay is to assert one very simple principle, as entitled to govern absolutely the dealings of society with the individual in the way of compulsion and control'. His now-famous dictum was that 'The only purpose for which power can be rightfully exercised over any member of a civilized community against his will, is to prevent personal harm to others'.[44] A stronger statement on behalf of the individual voice is difficult to conceive.

A more pragmatic approach was to act to protect specific rights of individuals and minorities through institutional means. This approach has enjoyed a history dating back to the English battles with the Stuart kings in the seventeenth century. From the Petition of Right to the Declaration of Rights in England, to the American state bills of rights to Madison's federal Bill of Rights, the protection of certain basic liberties for those in the minority has emerged as a central element of our constitutionalism. It remains a bulwark protecting minority interests.

Closely related to the principle of enunciated rights is the practice of judicial review, a concept endorsed in *The Federalist Papers*, famously enunciated by John Marshall, and applauded by Tocqueville as one of the more effective antidotes for majority tyranny. Although 'non-democratic' in its own way, judicial review, in the words of modern political scientist Benjamin Barber, 'protects civil rights with a wariness that the people often lack'.[45]

Another element of our constitutionalism that is designed to prevent overbearing majorities lies in institutional design. Madison, in *Federalist No. 10*, had argued for a large republic to prevent the formation of 'majority factions'. Madison also drew upon his predecessor Montesquieu to create 'checks and balances activated by the design of the institutions', with each branch of government serving as a carefully weighted counterpoise to the actions of the others, all with the avowed purpose 'to guard against the abuse of power'.[46]

It is beyond the scope of this section to delve deeply into this important topic, but we can draw upon the work of Philippe Schmitter and Terry Lynn Karl for some other institutional possibilities that extend beyond individual liberties and into the realm of protecting the voice of minority groups. 'What happens', they ask, 'when a properly assembled majority ... regularly makes decisions that harm some minority (especially a threatened cultural or ethnic group? In these circumstances,' Schmitter and Karl suggest, 'successful democracies tend to qualify the central principle of majority rule in order to protect minority rights'. One approach is to require that 'concurrent majorities' of the principal interest groups must agree on major policy issues (recall John C. Calhoun and his proposal to protect the antebellum South from the dominant North). Another approach is to construct 'grand coalition governments that incorporate all parties', or to 'negotiate pacts between major social groups'.[47]

Finally, say Schmitter and Karl, 'the most common and effective way of protecting minorities ... lies in the everyday operation of interest associations and social movements.... In contemporary political discourse, this ... activity goes under the rubric of "civil society"'.[48] This is not the first time we have come across this argument. Recall Tocqueville had perceived that voluntary associations serve to mollify the evils of democracy. He found, for example, that 'the liberty of association has become a necessary guarantee against the tyranny of the majority.... In America, the citizens ... form ... minority associations in order, first, to show their numerical strength and to demolish the moral power of the majority; and secondly, to stimulate competition and thus to discover those arguments that are most fitted to act upon the majority....'[49]

In sum, a necessary bulwark against the oppression of minorities must be the institutional/ constitutional protection of rights and interests. We now turn to the heart of the matter: the actual interplay of the few and the many – the people and their leaders – as they go about accomplishing their mutual objectives. In order to begin this analysis properly, I must take some care to uncover my assumptions about the constituting force of the polity: the people. The next three template questions explore their nature and their expected role in the fiction of leadership that I am inventing.

WHAT IS THE PERCEPTION OF HUMAN NATURE?

This first of the triumvirate of leadership template questions devoted to the people is the most fundamental. As fellow theoretician Kenneth Ruscio allows, 'Constructing theories of leadership without a realistic appraisal of human nature ... is to create an untenable portrayal of the responsibilities of leaders [and the people]'.[50] Thus, as I go about framing my own fiction of leadership, I must take care to reveal my own 'implicit theories' on the matter.

Social or Asocial

We have devoted considerable attention in this volume to one of the great ideological divides in the history of leadership in a democracy, namely, the liberal–individualistic approach, which begins with the assumption that humans are at base solitary beings seeking out their own interests, versus the republican–communitarian approach, which assumes that humans are by nature political and social, in the sense that they exist and reach their full potential only in concert with fellow human beings. This disagreement has important stakes for our conceptions of leadership, and deserves fuller discussion.

Throughout much of Western history, the communal nature of humankind went unchallenged. Benjamin Constant had called this 'the liberty of the ancients, which consisted in an active and constant participation in collective power'.[51] Constant had a wealth of material to draw upon when he made this claim. Despite the plethora of historical commentators favoring humankind's cooperative and social nature, however, the interpretation that seems to hold sway in our contemporary world is the individualist claim. Constant had called this 'the liberty of the moderns'. The moderns, he argued, are 'far more attached than the ancients to our individual independence.... The aim of the moderns is the enjoyment of security in private pleasures.'[52] This focus upon the individualistic nature of human nature does not have the lengthy historic legacy of its communal counterpart, but it has a strong intellectual heritage nonetheless.

The theorizing about this fundamental attribute of human nature has thus been dichotomous, engendering considerable controversy. However, it is my claim that what has been created has been a false dichotomy, or at least a false perception of the incompatibility of the two approaches.

Bridging the Gap: the 'Unsocial Sociability' of Humankind

Some commentators have suggested that we need not be condemned to assert one position with respect to human nature at the expense of the other. Political scientist Richard Dagger has argued 'we are not forced to choose between a thoroughly instrumental vision in which everyone's sole concern is "What's in it for me?" and a thoroughly constitutive version within which everyone's constant preoccupation is "doing what is best for the group." There is a middle ground between these two visions, and it is likely to provide a more solid foundation' for such things as (for us) the leadership relation.[53]

Upon closer inspection, even the most individualistic interpretations of human nature leave room for behavior that acknowledges the interests of others. Tocqueville, it may be recalled, linked his acknowledgment of individualism with the concept of 'self-interest rightly understood'. Under that conception, he believed it was possible, if only individuals could be made to see the larger picture and perceive long-term implications, that they might willingly forego immediate individual advantage in the interest of policies that benefited the community. Such commitment to the community would not be the result of sacrifice or altruism, but of an educated calculation that it is important, ultimately, to one's self-interest to preserve the community that provides one's sustenance. This ancient debate can be illuminated by the findings of modern social science.

In our contemporary era, an assumption of humankind's individualistic approach toward the world underpins modern social scientific rational choice theory and game theory. As Kenneth Ruscio points out, the modern view of human nature in 'its current manifestation is the attempt to explain most human behavior in terms of the single-minded pursuit of self-interest'. According to this approach, 'humans are rational decision-makers ... [and] life is a series of choices', based on 'the highest [personal] payoff or the maximum utility'. Such individualistic choices, in turn, form the basis for 'collective action' in the polity, which amounts merely to 'aggregating the multitudes of individual rational choices'.[54] Other social scientists explore this individualistic calculus through the use of game theory. The most famous of these exercises is the 'Prisoner's Dilemma', in which individuals with incomplete information and selfish motives end up choosing suboptimal strategies in which 'the outcome will be less desirable to all than the outcome that follows from everyone's choosing to cooperate'.[55] The consequences of such individualistic behavior in the public realm are depicted in Garrett Hardin's classic piece, 'The Tragedy of the Commons'.[56]

It is in the sphere of game theory, however, where the intersection of individual interest and concern for other's outcomes takes an interesting turn. This is portrayed well by Dagger. As we have seen, the classic scenario called the Prisoner's Dilemma leads participants to choose individualistic ends to the detriment of all. But in certain situations – situations much like the reality of democratic polities – the individualistic Prisoner's Dilemma turns into something more cooperative. When the conditions of the 'game' called the Prisoner's

Dilemma are played out in circumstances in which the participants know that they will be engaging in multiple interactions over time, the outcome is quite different. 'In the single-shot dilemma,' explains Dagger, 'the rational course for each player, acting independently, is to [choose individualistic and suboptimal outcomes]. In the iterated dilemma, however, … rational actors will gradually come to cooperate with one another to produce the collectively desirable outcome *if* certain conditions are met…. When these circumstances prevail,' he concludes, 'people will find cooperation in a collective effort rational….'[57]

It becomes rather important for our fiction of leadership, then, to look further at the 'certain conditions' that appear to cause even individualists to perceive it as in their best interests to cooperate with others. According to Dagger, the conditions which spark such behavior are 'prolonged interaction and interdependency, a sense of common condition, and bonds that grow with familiarity'. Such facilitating conditions are certainly within the reach of a well-functioning democratic polity, and raise hopes for my project of 'inventing' a leadership relation that will operate on the basis of the public interest. To accomplish this, one of the strategies must certainly be to create the structural conditions conducive to such interactions. Dagger identifies five factors that foster the necessary conditions: (1) small communities of interaction; (2) a sense of stability; (3) fairness in interactions; (4) open communications; and (5) extensive participation.[58] As the specifics of my proposed fiction of leadership unfold, such structural features will have an important place.

In addition to the structural aspects that foster an enhanced concern for the outcomes of others, these experiments in game theory also suggest something subtle and important that occurs as the 'players' adapt to the new conditions: there is a concomitant shift in the psychology of interaction, which in turn yields new assumptions about human interaction. As the new facilitating conditions are incorporated, the nature of the game shifts from that of the Prisoner's Dilemma to something called the 'Assurance Game'. Dagger again summarizes the psychological implications. 'In the Prisoner's Dilemma', he begins, '… the assumption is that the parties involved are rational and narrowly self-interested.' But as the Assurance Game emerges, there is a transformation. 'In the Assurance Game, the assumption is that the parties are rational and conditionally altruistic.' This new approach of 'conditional altruism' deserves a closer look. According to Dagger, in the new game 'their altruism is qualified or conditional because they are not willing to cooperate when they believe that others will take advantage of their cooperation'. That is to say, 'if they are to act cooperatively … they must have … assurances … that others will indeed cooperate'. If these assurances are not forthcoming, 'the Assurance Game degenerates into the Prisoner's Dilemma'.[59]

All this suggests that, in addition to structural concerns, we must also pay close attention to processes. In light of the findings of game theory, the Rawlsian concepts of public reason and reciprocity take on even more significance. In sum, these findings of the social sciences are promising. As Dagger concludes, 'there is no reason to reject the possibility that conditional altruism may be cultivated…. If it is possible to establish this basis, furthermore, it is also possible to convert the political order into an assurance game.'[60] It is such a transformation that fuels my own fiction of leadership.

Having made the case that even the individualistic conceptions of human nature allow for activity of mutual advantage, I now make the further argument that the essence of the human condition is not individualistic; not purely, anyhow. Within the human breast their resides an amalgam of motives, both individualistic and communal. And although I am realistic (or cynical) enough to believe that the individual parts tend to predominate, the very presence of the opposing motivation to engage with others in the community opens up other possibilities when considering the leadership relation.

Several commentators have suggested the existence of the dual inclinations toward the individual and the cooperative. Immanuel Kant spoke of the 'unsocial sociability' of humans; that is, 'their hard-wired nature that compels them to express their individuality even as they seek the companionship of fellow citizens'.[61] James Madison, as we have seen, was among the most penetrating of observers of human nature in this regard. He was a realist and pragmatist, and readily acknowledged that humans often evinced a self-interested narrowness of purpose. Yet, under the proper conditions (and the proper leaders), he found them also capable of high aspirations and the ability to look beyond themselves. It was upon that delicate balance that he fashioned his own leadership fiction.

In our modern era, the most penetrating observer of this dualistic aspect of human nature may have been the philosopher John Rawls. Rawls's assumptions are somewhat complex. They track the traditional liberal focus on the individual, yet at the same time acknowledge certain social aspects of the human condition. There can be little doubt that Rawls regards the individual as of the highest importance: he had proclaimed that 'the self is prior to the good'. Yet at the same time, Rawls stressed the reality that human beings in society need to interact, and to some degree depend upon each other. Recall that his very definition of society was 'a fair system of social cooperation over time'.[62] Rawls took great care to define the dualism he found in human nature. He assumed that individuals were both *rational* and *reasonable*. The 'rational' aspect looked out for one's individual interests, while the 'reasonable' allowed the individual to cooperate with others in ways remarkably akin to those depicted in the Assurance Game: 'persons are reasonable', he said, when 'they are ready to propose principles and standards as fair terms of cooperation and to abide by them willingly, given the assurance that others will likewise do the same'. In sum, for Rawls, 'the reasonable is public in a way the rational is not'.[63] Both aspects of human nature are necessary if a polity is to be successful.

Taking all the foregoing into account, my claim is that human nature partakes of both the individualistic and the communal. I am pragmatic enough to agree with Kenneth Ruscio's portrayal of the modern liberal perception of 'a belief in a flawed human nature – a social nature to be sure, but also one that is hard-wired to calculate self-interest before the good of the whole'.[64] Yet I also claim that this tendency toward self-interest can be overcome (or at least moderated) both by structuring situations so as to highlight the self-interest involved in cooperative action, and by tapping the instincts toward communal endeavor that reside in all of us. Because of my claim that proper democratic functioning requires some commitment to cooperation, both of these objectives will be, at least in part, a function of leadership.

The Perfectibility of Humankind

One of the assumptions implicit in my emerging claims for the transformation from individual to citizen as the basis for a successful leadership relation in a democratic polity is the belief that such a transformation is possible. This raises, in turn, another fundamental question about the human condition: are humans perfectible – that is, can human behavior be changed and, hopefully, improved? This is another classic debate, but from at least the time of Locke's *tabula rasa* there has been an assumption that the beliefs, attitudes and behavior of humans can be shaped in desired ways. In the present context, the assumption is that humans can be made more 'virtuous' in the sense that they can become more other-regarding. That, indeed, was the assumption underlying most of Tocqueville's proposed reforms, and many like his over the years. And Rawls explicitly posited that 'human beings have a moral nature', a 'capacity for a sense of justice and a capacity for a conception of the good'.[65] Both augured for an ability to move beyond selfish interests toward larger concerns. My conclusion is, then, that it is possible, albeit perhaps difficult, to address perceived concerns and seek to make my desired fiction of leadership more achievable. This perception forms an appropriate segue into the next, closely related, topic.

ARE THE PEOPLE CAPABLE OF GOVERNING?

Given the fact that this study assumes popular sovereignty in its democratic mode, the answer to this question would appear to be obvious. James Madison had acknowledged that all efforts to create a polity in a regime of popular sovereignty depended 'on the capacity of mankind for self-government'.[66] Indeed, this template question is so central to the operation of a democracy that a response in the negative would seem to be dispositive of all further discussion. Yet it is not so simple as all that, and my analysis and conclusions regarding this matter will both reflect its complexity as well as draw us deeply into the folds of leadership itself.

In point of fact, the matter of the capacity of the people to govern themselves has long been one of controversy. During the course of the analysis in this volume, we have uncovered essentially two stances on this matter. The first, implicit in the centuries-old tradition of the classical ideal of the leader, holds that the people as a whole cannot be trusted – not fully, at any rate – to govern themselves wisely, and therefore need the guidance of wiser and more virtuous leaders. This, of course, tracks closely the elitist school of leadership, as well as the trustee form of representation. The opposite stance is the implicit theory underlying the participationist approach to leadership and the delegate form of representation. This side of the argument maintains that the people themselves are capable of governing, and, indeed, are best positioned to know the common good.

The emergence of the construct of the people did not resolve the issue. Recall that in its earliest manifestations, the fiction of the people was merely a prop to support one faction of elite leaders in their arguments with another. It was not until the nineteenth century that anything approaching real popular sovereignty appeared on the scene. After that, the notion of the capability of the people to govern became a commonplace – *as a fiction*. This fiction has become so dominant that in today's democracy one would be hard pressed to find anyone challenging the capability of the people to govern. At best it would be 'politically incorrect' to issue such a challenge, and at worst it might be considered positively subversive. In the following argument I intend to pick up that gauntlet, and argue, in effect, that 'the emperor has no clothes'. That is, I will maintain that the capability of the people to govern themselves is an assumption made too cavalierly, and instead requires more intense scrutiny.

A Basic Incompetence

In maintaining such an iconoclastic position, it is important to support my assertions. In keeping with the approach of this concluding chapter, I will place my arguments within the rich stream of historical insight that we have been tracing, a stream that is so important to full understanding, yet has been so neglected by most modern commentators. And, again in keeping with my approach in devising this new fiction of leadership, I will buttress the historical argument with contemporary observers and my own rationale.

I must first acknowledge that the modern presumption of the capabilities of the people is not without support in the historical record. Indeed, that stance has its own proud heritage. Even prior to the acceptance of popular sovereignty, there were those who believed in the people. Aristotle, although he did not go so far as to trust all the people with all the power, and, as we have seen, held out a place for wise leaders, nevertheless thought that the people, when taken together, harbored the seeds of competent government. 'For the many,' he noted, '… when they meet together may very likely be better … if regarded not individually but collectively.'[67] Similarly, Machiavelli built upon Aristotle. Although he was willing to accept that the people could be mistaken and sometimes evil, he also perceived the potentialities of the people, and went so far as to say that 'the voice of the people is likened to that of God'.[68]

Once the fiction of 'the people' came to be accepted, and particularly after it assumed its modern democratic guise, belief in the capability of the people was a logical extension of contemporary developments. With the rise of egalitarianism and individualism, and the accompanying eclipse of notions of deference to leaders and the undermining of civic virtue, together with the disintegration of notions of a unitary common good, there was little to hinder the emergence of a belief that all could take an equal share in governing society. The result was an almost unthinking belief in the capacity of the people to rule themselves. Modern commentator Brian O'Connell, for instance, enthuses that 'we became all the more committed to this kind of participatory society. Along the way we constantly renewed our faith in the basic intelligence and ability of the people. We have never found a better substitute for safeguarding freedom than placing responsibility in the hands of the people and expecting them to fulfill it.'[69]

Such paeans to the abilities of the people, however, run against a strong and deep counter-current in the intellectual history of leadership that warns that such confidence may be misplaced, perhaps dangerously so. Thoughtful commentators over the centuries have compiled a damning litany of charges against the people's abilities. Plato excoriated the people, and considered them totally unfit to govern. Thomas Hobbes believed that leaving the people to their own devices would result in 'a war of all against all', and a world in which life would be 'solitary, poor, nasty, brutish, and short'.

Likewise, several commentators who supported the emergence of popular sovereignty nonetheless harbored reservations about the capabilities of the people. Locke and Rousseau had their reservations about popular competence, and even John Stuart Mill sought to overcome what he perceived to be a lack of political acumen on the part of the people. Once true democracy became the reality of the day, observers like Tocqueville expressed serious reservations about the ability of the people to govern well. Indeed, Tocqueville made a baleful proposition: 'Democracy, pushed to its furthest limits', he said, 'is … prejudicial to the art of government'.[70]

Nor is it merely historical personages who take the people to task. Although the paradigm of modern democracy almost precludes dissenting voices, elite theorists Thomas Dye and Harmon Zeigler point out the more nefarious side of popular rule. 'Despite superficial commitment to the symbols of democracy,' they argue, 'the masses have surprisingly weak commitments to the principles of individual liberty, toleration of diversity, and freedom of expression when required to apply these principles to despised or obnoxious groups or individuals.' They provide 'recent examples' such as 'racial hatred, anti-intellectualism, class antagonisms, [and] anti-Semitism'.[71]

I have taken some care to lay out the historical indictment of the people as a reliable foundation for democratic government. In my view, despite obvious advances in education, communication and the like, there is little modern evidence to refute the concerns long associated with rule by the people. Dye and Zeigler are particularly helpful in this regard, as they point out the continued evidence of popular prejudice. I will go them one better. I believe an argument can be made that in addition to prejudice, the people continue to exhibit either a lack of intelligence or an overweening commitment to their own selfish interests, or both. At the risk of appearing topical in a volume intended to have a more long-term impact, I can cite the early twenty-first century American penchant for blindly favoring tax reductions no matter what the cost to necessary services, or the sad tale of many of the popular ballot initiatives in California.

To conclude, despite the unquestioned – and I believe cavalier – modern assumptions about popular capabilities in modern democracy, I believe, at the very least, there is reason for concern. This is not to denigrate the people totally (I have already expressed my commitment to placing government in their hands), but only to fix with a cold, clear gaze the problematic nature of our quest for a workable democracy. Much of the remainder of my analysis will be devoted, in various ways and in a variety of venues, to suggesting ways in which the leadership relation can be structured and utilized to either remedy my concerns with the people or to counteract their effects.

The Possibility of Redemption

Despite all the pessimism, there is another strong theme in the literature: the possibility of redemption. Many of the same theorists who expressed such skepticism about the capability of the people to govern married that skepticism with a belief that it is possible to reform and educate the people, and to create structures that maximize the possibility that this weakness in democratic functioning could be turned into a strength.

Madison had paired his skepticism of popular capabilities with a parallel belief in a certain degree of popular wisdom and virtue. And, as democracy began to take hold in the nineteenth century, two other skeptics of popular capability – Tocqueville and Mill – also voiced support for such a resurrection of popular political abilities. Tocqueville was deeply devoted to the transformation of the masses into responsible citizens. For Mill, it was the possibility that appropriate institutions and processes could 'raise … even persons of the most ordinary intellect to something of the dignity of thinking beings'. In other words, Mill harbored a redemptive hope for a democratic people.[72]

Modern scholars such as James MacGregor Burns also express a commitment to such an uplifting of the people. In terms of what this means in terms of specifics, proposals for reform generally fall under two rather broad rubrics: (1) the enhancement of the education and skill of the people; and (2) a transformation from individual to citizen.

The Tools of Redemption

If there is a chance that individuals can be educated and transformed into citizens, it is important to contemplate how to go about doing so. Our historical analysis, when coupled with the insights of recent scholarship from various disciplines, offer us a rich palette with which to paint a portrait of reformation. As we move forward, we should keep in mind the insights already uncovered, such as the litany of circumstances that game theorists suggest make it most likely that selfish individualism will be transformed into conditional altruism. Whatever the specifics, all proposals below have similar objectives: to tap that wellspring of cooperativeness with others that resides within us all, and to enhance the skills and conditions that make such cooperation possible.

The concept that best captures the intent of this endeavor is to engender a transformation *from individual to citizen*. As Richard Dagger puts it, 'the size, diversity and complexity of the modern state make it difficult for us to see ourselves as members of a body politic that is also a cooperative enterprise. If we cannot see ourselves as citizens, we cannot act as citizens.' For my leadership fiction to work, then, 'it must be possible to overcome these difficulties by finding a way to foster citizenship'. This means that individuals must internalize an approach somewhat akin to civic virtue, whether it be 'self-interest rightly understood', or the result of tapping the more communal aspects of the human character. Either way, the objective is to create a citizen who 'will bear his or her share of the civic burdens when others are bearing theirs'.[73] The following proposals promote such things as education, participation and mutual respect as strategies for shaping the individual into a potentially virtuous being.

A more level playing field

One underlying assumption is that participation in political processes *per se* is an important opportunity for individuals to become more cognizant of the needs of others, and of the advantages of mutual endeavor. As John Stuart Mill (and Tocqueville) pointed out, such active participation 'promises to widen individuals' horizons and deepen their sense of how their lives are involved with others'.[74] We will explore the dynamics of this in more detail in a moment, but first it is important to address a necessary condition precedent to this result: the meaningful opportunity to participate on something like an equal basis. It has long been the argument of many theorists that an individual will have an incentive to participate in the political process when two threshold requirements are met. First, the individual must have sufficient resources (broadly defined) to allow him or her the 'luxury' of participating politically. This notion is often linked to the concept of 'positive liberty'. Second, if individuals are going to engage in political discourse, they must have enough power actually to have a meaningful impact. These related but distinct objectives I lump together under the rubric of 'leveling the playing field'.

The argument for positive liberty troubles some, not so much because of the desired end of political participation, but because it implies unacceptable means that smack of a welfare state. Those who are troubled by positive liberty will undoubtedly be livid at my parallel suggestion that some equalization of power is necessary, which suggests an equalization of resources, which suggests the possibility of a redistribution of resources. I will not delve into specific modes of implementation here, but content myself with a justification for my conclusion.

The essential rationale for a proposal that advocates narrowing the resource gap between members of the polity is voiced quite succinctly by Rawls. 'Those with wealth and income', he says, 'tend to dominate those with less and increasingly to control political power in their own favor.'[75] James Harrington had put a more positive spin on this in the seventeenth century. 'Equality of estates causeth equality of power,' he had argued, 'and equality of power is the liberty not only of the commonwealth, but of every man.'[76] Rousseau, another proponent of such a policy, had indicated that this equalization need not be absolute, but only relative. It is only necessary that 'the distribution of wealth and power ... be sufficiently equal to prevent abuses from either end of the spectrum'.[77]

The reason this equalization of resources is important is the impact it has on individual attitudes toward the political process. As Dagger says, 'if there is reason to believe that [there is] ... an inequality of power or influence that gives some people's interests greater weight than others, then those with less influence may see themselves as locked in an exploitative relationship rather than a reciprocal one. ... When that happens, cooperation will collapse.'[78] Without cooperation, this fiction or model of leadership fails.

Local political participation

Recall that in game theory one of the factors found to cause a shift from the self-interested Prisoner's Dilemma to the more other-embracing Assurance Game was the extensive participation by all the players. This echoes the insights of many others, who see political participation as a means to shift focus from the self to the needs of others.

Tocqueville presents perhaps the classic argument. According to Tocqueville, political education, broadly conceived, held the promise of reinvigorating civic virtue and resolving the incompetence among the citizenry. A consequence of his many proposals was that individuals 'have created a commitment to public measures even if they are at variance with individual interests' – which is, of course, the very definition of civic virtue.[79] Likewise, John Stuart Mill believed that in order to realize the possibilities inherent in all citizens, they must be encouraged to participate in the political process. As a result, the individual was more likely to 'consider the interest of the public, not his private advantage, to give his vote to the best of his judgment'. Moreover, that judgment would be enhanced, because such participation was likely to yield better decisions. Indeed, 'if circumstances allow the amount of public duty assigned to him to be considerable, it makes him an educated man'.[80]

Richard Dagger is among the modern commentators who endorse the positive impact of political participation upon individuals. 'Through political activity ... the citizens of [the] polity ... exercise and continue to develop [their] capacity....' Moreover, they 'develop ... the conviction that the well-being of the individual is closely tied to the well-being of the polity as a whole'.[81] In sum, in the words of Sidney Verba and colleagues, 'In ... participatory democracy, political activity becomes a mechanism whereby citizens engage in enlightened discourse, come to understand the views of others, and become sensitized to the needs of community and nation. Thus educated, they transcend their own interests to seek the public good.'[82]

If political participation is so valuable, it behooves any democracy to maximize opportunities to engage in it. Tocqueville had championed the reinvigoration of local government; political philosopher Amy Gutmann went so far as to suggest 'creating new political institutions rather than increasing the power of existing institutions or reviving old ones'.[83] Along these lines Benjamin Barber has suggested the invention of neighborhood assemblies, and political scientist James A. Morone has provided a model of local participation in federal initiatives with his description of the Community Action Agencies of the 1960s War on Poverty.[84] Again, the purpose here is not to present detailed implementation strategies, but to suggest potential avenues leading toward the achievement of the desired objectives.

Strengthening civil society

My next recommendation is one that has become a commonplace in recent years, particularly among communitarians. It is the reinvigoration of what is called 'civil society'. Although there is some disagreement as to the meaning of the term, Jean L. Cohen captures it well enough in saying it is 'a sphere of human activity and a set of institutions outside state or government. It embraces families, churches, voluntary associations and social movements.'[85] More important than its precise definition is the function the institutions of civil society can perform in our quest to transform individuals into engaged citizens. We find that civil society serves many of the same purposes as political participation. Tocqueville, a great champion of civil society, notes that in 'voluntary associations' men 'learn to surrender their own will to that of the rest and to make their own exertions subordinate to the common impulse'.[86] Indeed, Tocqueville points out that the activity of civil society 'generates reciprocity that spills over into the political arena'.'[87]

The great proponent of civil society in the modern era is political scientist Robert Putnam. The institutions of civil society, he argues generate 'social capital', which in turn leads to civic virtue. According to Putnam, 'voluntary associations and the social networks of civil society ... contribute to democracy in two different ways: They have "external" effects on the larger polity, and they have "internal effects" on participants themselves. Externally, voluntary associations ... allow individuals to express their interests and demands on government.... Internally, associations and less formal networks of civic engagement instill in their members habits of cooperation and public-spiritedness, as well as the practical skills necessary to partake in public life....' Indeed, voluntary associations are places where social and civic skills are learned – 'schools for democracy'.[88]

Civic education

Putnam's reference to the institutions of civil society as 'schools for democracy' provides the perfect segue to my next proposed strategy for stimulating a commitment to the tasks and burdens of self-government. It is the need for civic education of the citizens of a democracy.

James Madison had advocated such measures, Tocqueville had advocated strongly for such a civic education (in addition to that received by service on juries and the like), and John Stuart Mill had as well. In the modern era, it has been the communitarians, with their emphasis upon citizen participation, who have advocated most strongly for civic education. Early in the last century John Dewey had expressed his concern that 'America is lacking the concerned, well-informed public needed for the formation of effective public opinion', and more recently Michael Sandel agreed that 'citizens must have knowledge of public affairs'.[89]

Civic education, however, means more than being current regarding important issues. What I am recommending here includes an attempt at the reorienting of values toward democratic cooperation, as well as a nuts-and-bolts, skills-based program. Benjamin Barber has been at the forefront of this initiative. According to Barber, 'without civic education, democratic choice is little more than the expression and aggregation of private prejudices.... Citizens are certainly not born,' he says, 'but made as a consequence of civic education and political engagement in a free polity.' Barber even gets into specifics. In his 'schools', 'individuals would undergo a rigorous training period ... in civic education, including parliamentary and electoral skills, community structure and organization, some elementary social science, and perhaps American history'.[90] Another model might be that famed training ground for civil rights activists in the 1960s, the Highlander Research and Education Center. However they are eventually structured, the proposal here is for the institution of 'Democracy Schools' required of all citizens, framed with the intention to furnish individuals with the tools to become effective citizens.

Cultivating civic virtues

Closely related to the issue of civic education is the cultivation of civic virtues. It is important here to distinguish between *civic virtue*, a term used throughout this volume, and *civic virtues*. In its singular form, I mean it in the traditional sense of subsuming individual interests to the good of the whole. In the plural, the term means the character traits necessary for the type of productive interaction demanded by democracy – and by this fiction of leadership.

As usual, Tocqueville is the first source we turn to when contemplating strategies for converting individuals into citizens. He was certainly well aware of the impact of civic virtues. He observed that 'the manners of the people may be considered as one of the great causes ... [of the] maintenance of a democratic republic.... Customs and practices serve ... the purpose of restraining democracy's excesses and ensuring that it operate[s] for the general good.'[91]

There have been various formulations of the necessary virtues. John Rawls provides perhaps the most influential litany. In addition to his core expectations of public reason and reciprocity (concepts to be addressed in the next section), Rawls identified other public virtues that must be exhibited by citizens, to include 'the virtues of tolerance and being ready to meet others halfway, the virtue of reasonableness, and the sense of fairness. When these virtues are widespread in society,' he concludes, 'they constitute a very great public good, part of society's political capital.'[92] One way to capture the essence of the virtues, according to Rawls, is through the concept of the 'duty of civility'. According to Rawls, 'the ideal of citizenship imposes a moral, not legal duty – the duty of civility .... This duty ... involves a willingness to listen to others and a fairmindedness in deciding when accommodations to their views should reasonably be made.'[93] Another version is that by Richard Dagger. In his book by that name, he lists six 'civic virtues'. For Dagger, a 'citizen is someone who respects individual rights, values autonomy, tolerates different opinions and beliefs, plays fair, cherishes civic memory, and takes an active part in the life of the community'.[94]

Such civic virtues must be cultivated if we are to have any chance of escaping the dark picture I earlier portrayed of the competence of the people to govern. Without them, we go our separate, individualistic, selfish ways. With them, we do not surrender our autonomy, but we do open ourselves to the needs of others, and make possible the type of interactions necessary for this model of leadership to work.

Of Pessimism and Optimism

In this discussion of the capability of the people to govern, I have been somewhat Janus-faced. I have portrayed the people as essentially self-centered and of limited horizons, yet I have also devoted considerable effort to the task of articulating a plan of redemption. In more than one place, I have mentioned a 'transformation' of the people. This transformation is somewhat parallel to that predicted by Rousseau when individuals enter the social contract. The transformation Rousseau envisioned was in many ways a moral one. As he depicted it, 'this passage from the state of nature to the civil state produces quite a remarkable change in man, for it substitutes justice for instinct in his behavior and gives his actions a moral quality they previously lacked'. This 'moral quality' was clearly a turn from selfish interests to civic virtue. 'Only then,' he continued, 'when the voice of duty replaces physical impulse and right replaces appetite, does man, who had hitherto taken only himself into account, find himself forced to act upon other principles and to consult his reason before listening to his inclinations.'[95]

Make no mistake, however: in advocating procedures for transforming individuals to citizens I have not abandoned my earlier skepticism. At best, it will be a hard slog to effect the conversion. I am not a Pollyanna concerning the likelihood of total success. This does not mean, however, that my proposed fiction of leadership is untenable. I will also propose an elaborate backup and support system, if you will, in the form of the role of leaders. Taken together, the people, transformed to some extent by the structures, programs and processes recommended above, together with the guidance and support of competent and virtuous leaders, can create an effective democracy. More to the point, it is possible to create a leadership relation that acknowledges hard realities yet provides a reasonable prospect of achieving the public interest.

Our discussion thus far has brought us at last to a discussion of the activities of the principals: the people and their leaders. Because this fiction of leadership is grounded in the assumption that the people constitute the polity and are most responsible for its workings, it makes sense to begin with them.

WHAT IS THE ROLE OF THE PEOPLE?

The essential challenge to which this entire volume has been addressed is that of leadership in a regime of popular sovereignty, and in particular, in a democracy. When contemplating the role of the people in such regimes, our analysis has shown how it has evolved. In the early days – from Locke through the American founding – the people, while technically sovereign, were not expected to be particularly active. It was not until the American founding that the real implications of popular sovereignty became clear. As the historian R.R. Palmer said, 'the idea of the people as the constitutive power of government was distinctively American. The idea reached its purest expression in the Preamble to the Constitution, in the revolutionary phrase, "We, the People"'.[96] Despite these important conceptual beginnings, it was really the onset – the onslaught – of democracy that had the greatest impact upon the people's role. As Tocqueville noted in the nineteenth century, 'The democratic principle ... has gained so much strength ... as to have become not only predominant, but all-powerful.... The people reign in the American political world as the Deity does in the universe. They are the cause and aim of all things; every thing comes from them, and every thing is absorbed in them.'[97]

With this new power came new responsibilities and, for the first time, really, since the era of the classical republics, the role of the citizen became a salient issue. Certainly it could be argued that the most momentous change in the leadership relation had to do with the role of ordinary citizens in government. The consequences of the democratic revolution were not only that ordinary men took part in ruling society – an outcome radical enough in its own right – but also that ordinary men had the responsibility to enact wise social policy. This brings us full circle to the challenge of leadership. The next step, then, is to explore ways in which this democratic discourse can best be structured and facilitated. The answer to this question will occupy our attention for the remainder of this chapter, as we look to the roles of both the people and their leaders.

The Public Reason of John Rawls

In inventing this fiction of leadership, I have found some aspects of the work of John Rawls to be persuasive, and in particular, I like the political process he outlines in his concept of 'public reason'. In using Rawls as my foundation for the proper role of the people, I am not necessarily siding with the 'liberals' as opposed to the communitarians. Indeed, in keeping with my penchant for being an equal-opportunity offender, I have no doubt that I disappointed liberals with my citations to communitarians in seeking a transformation from individuals to citizens committed to the public interest. Moreover, I would argue that in this case, at least, the distinctions are more apparent than real. Certainly Rawls is no communitarian, in any generally-understood sense of the term. Indeed it is the perceived wrongheadedness of Rawls against which modern communitarians have inveighed. In that sense, modern communitarian thinking might be seen as the 'anti-Rawls'. On the other hand, once one moves beyond the disparate premises held by the communitarians and Rawls, it is possible to perceive Rawls's portrayal of the democratic process itself – his 'public reason' – as something to be admired. That is to say, it is not necessary to accept Rawls's premise of 'justice as fairness' – for example, to accept his 'liberty principle' and his 'difference principle' as universal – in order to endorse a public discourse grounded in the civic virtues mentioned earlier. Likewise a communitarian like Michael Sandel can reject Rawls's claim that individuals can and should 'bracket' their 'comprehensive doctrines' (their deepest beliefs and values) when they enter public discourse, yet still accept the 'rules of engagement' that Rawls's public reason offers. The discussion of the activities of the people in a democratic regime that follows, then, is one based more upon process than ideology.

Given the ends of leadership I have enunciated, and the process necessary for perceiving and achieving them, it is clear that disagreement will exist over ends and means within any reasonably diverse democratic polity. It was this challenge that had inspired Rawls to write *Political Liberalism*. The answer, in Rawls's view, is the concept of public reason. In it, according to one observer, 'Rawls weaves together a set of ideas and concepts that serve as ground rules for political discourse in a pluralistic society where people differ profoundly in their beliefs and principles. Public reason,' then, '... is the way we should disagree on fundamental political questions, given that disagreement is inevitable and permanent in societies of free and equal citizens....' In such problematic circumstances, 'the decision must be arrived at legitimately'. That is to say, the process by which the decision is made must be such that all participants can accept the outcome. 'One criterion for legitimacy is whether the reasons for the action were publicly explained and understood by those affected, even if some remain opposed.'[98] Public reason, then, outlines the manner in which citizens should interact in our polity.

Turning to Rawls himself, he calls for a conception of public reason that is devoted to the public good. As to what public reason actually entails, Rawls points out that 'the ideal of citizenship imposes a moral, not a legal duty – the duty of civility – to be able to explain to one another on ... fundamental questions how the principles and policies they advocate and vote for can be supported by the political values of public reason. This duty also involves a willingness to listen to others and a fairmindedness in deciding when accommodations to their views should reasonably be made.' Specifically, citizens 'should be ready to explain the basis for their actions in terms each could reasonably expect the others might endorse as consistent with their freedom and equality'. In sum, says Rawls, 'Trying to meet this condition is one of the tasks that the ideal of democratic politics asks of us. Understanding how to conduct oneself as a democratic citizen includes understanding an ideal of public reason.'[99]

Thus the citizen must approach the discourse dedicated to achieving public ends from differing interests with a particular mindset, which can be evidenced by the practice of the 'civic virtues' mentioned in the previous section: 'civility, tolerance, reasonableness, a sense of fairness, mutual trust', and a commitment to reciprocity.[100] Armed with these, the chances of this model of leadership working become high indeed. As Ruscio notes, 'public reason ... is also an aspiration, for it seeks to elevate public discourse'. And, indeed, 'the stakes are high'. If our form of democracy is to work well, 'public reason becomes one of the fundamental obligations of citizens, a defining characteristic of citizenship itself'.[101]

In sum, citizens *should* act in this way, and if my fiction of leadership becomes paradigmatic, it will be increasingly easy to assume that they *will* act this way. However, as discussed in the previous section, we are dealing with flawed raw materials in the form of individuals who can be selfish, narrow-minded and intolerant. For this and other reasons, there remains in our polity a substantial need for leaders. In the discussion of the next two template questions, we have the opportunity to explore the complexities of leaders in regimes where the constituent power resides in the people.

WHAT IS THE ROLE OF THE LEADER?

In turning to the role of the leader in our fiction of leadership, we reach at last what is perhaps the most perplexing challenge of the modern democratic era. In the ensuing analysis, I will suggest the nature of the problem, and then argue the case for a continued need for the 'competence' of leaders to balance our commitment to the participation of the people. However, in view of our democratic realities, that 'competence' must be reconceptualized: we can no longer rely upon the simplistic notions of the classical ideal. In its place there must be a new role for leaders – demanding no less in the way of competence, but nevertheless requiring considerable revision of our traditional image of the leader and his or her role. Finally, I will propose two specific protocols for leader behavior: one designed to meet the substantive and epistemological needs of modern democracy, and the other fashioned to realize the ultimate objective of effecting the transformation of the constituents of the polity from self-centered individualists to citizens dedicated to the public interest.

The Problem of Leaders in a Democracy

Kenneth Ruscio has written: 'The theory of democracy does not treat leaders kindly. Suspicion of rulers, concern over their propensity to abuse power in their own self-interest, the need to hold them accountable, and the belief that legitimate power is lodged originally in the people and granted only in severe contingencies, all are fixed stars in the democratic galaxy. In many respects,' adds Ruscio, 'democracy came about as the remedy to the problems of [leaders]....' Indeed, 'fear of leadership is a basic justification for democratic forms of government'.[102] As a result, the role of the leader in modern democracies has been a topic of considerable controversy. Thinking back to our framing of the topic, one can easily imagine the contrasting role for the leader in an elitist as compared to a participationist approach to leadership. Similarly, a 'trustee' type of representative will carry different expectations from a 'delegate' type.

Carrying this line of thinking into the controversies of the modern era, recent conceptualizations of the operations of a democratic state evince considerable ambiguity about the role of leaders. In our sampling of liberal thinking, we have seen a range of positions on this issue which appear to mark a transition. The early writers such as Locke and Mill, while stressing rights and individualism, were still comfortable with what we had put forward as leaders in the style of the classical ideal. More modern liberals have had more difficulties with the concept of the leader. Some purists (recall Nozick) are much more concerned with the protection of rights than with notions of a leader. John Rawls is more in the mainstream, but even here, upon initial reading it is somewhat difficult to discern a leader's role at all in his work. With closer scrutiny one can derive a role for the leader, but it embraces a new expectation for leader behavior. Under Rawls, a leader must be committed to neutrality among various conceptions of the good, one who takes a process-oriented approach and who 'asserts the priority of fair procedures over particular ends'.[103]

In a similar vein, modern communitarians have had some difficulty with the role of leaders – indeed, when they address the issue at all. Many communitarians seemingly reject the very idea of a leader as elitist. Benjamin Barber is perhaps the most forthcoming on this count. Barber is, at base, deeply suspicious of leaders and leadership. 'In systems where self-government and vigorous individual participation are central,' he writes, '... leadership takes on a problematic character. On its face,' he continues, 'leadership is opposed to participatory self government; it acts in place of or to some degree encroaches on the autonomy of individual actors.... As a consequence,' Barber concludes, 'one might wish to say that in the ideal participatory system leadership vanishes totally. Complete self-government by an active citizenry would leave no room for leaders or followers.'[104]

These various perspectives on the role of the leader reveal the tensions inherent in the very concept of a leader in modern democracy. However, as our continuing discussion of the tension between 'participation' and 'competence' has shown, various versions of leader behavior have their desirable aspects. Unfortunately, each also has its weaknesses. Reliance upon traditional leaders of superior capability assumes that such leaders exist, and runs against a deep-seated modern aversion to elitism. Those who advocate mere process-oriented leaders must either make the large and dangerous assumption that all individuals in the polity have the capability and the desire to act in ways that serve all, or adopt the unproven position that the conflict among individual interests will automatically result in policies serving the interests of all.

All this complexity calls for a thoughtful and grounded consideration of the role of leaders in a democracy. As Ruscio says, 'If we want vibrant, dynamic, and progressive democracies, we need to be very clear about how we expect leaders to perform, the demands we can appropriately place on them, and their responsibilities to the polity and the citizens'.[105] And, as historian Gordon S. Wood points out, 'the emergence of democracy [requires] political leaders different from any that [have] ever existed anywhere in the history of the world'.[106] Thus 'democratic leadership' – Ruscio again – 'requires something [unique]. Especially if … public reason and careful deliberation, political trust, and the possibility of the [public interest] are central features of a vigorous, healthy, and vibrant democracy.'[107]

I now turn to my own proposed resolution of the problem of the leader in a democracy by suggesting what is needed, and how it can be provided.

An Infusion of Competence

In an earlier section, I questioned any unthinking reliance upon the capability of the people to govern themselves wisely. At the same time, I have steadily maintained a commitment to a democratic process based upon citizen discourse. The conjunction of these two claims sets up an obvious dilemma. Part of the tension, as we have seen, can be lessened by efforts to develop better citizens. But, while promising, this is not a development that we can count on sufficiently to resolve the problem. Something more is needed, and it is my assertion that what is needed is intervention by those who are prepared to shore up and, if necessary, take an active role in shaping and facilitating the discourse among citizens. What is needed are leaders, leaders who infuse competence into the workings of democracy. This is likely to be a debated claim, so I will begin by exploring my notion of the necessary competencies of a democratic leader.

As we begin our discussion of competence, it is useful to recall Rousseau's caution about the competence of the people and his remedy. Rousseau had captured the essential argument regarding the need for competence in the leadership relation: the people, though well-meaning, can be too self-interested, and not sufficiently cognizant (or interested in) subtleties and long-term implications. The traditional solution down through the ages was, as we have seen, the reliance upon a leader who embodied the classical ideal – one who used his (it was normally a male) wisdom and virtue, or commitment to the common good, to sort out the complexities and to derive policy that was in the true best interests of the people.[108] John Stuart Mill perhaps put it best: 'No government by a democracy,' he wrote, '… ever did or could rise above mediocrity except in so far as the sovereign Many have let themselves be guided … by the counsels and influence of a more highly gifted and instructed *one* or *few*…. When the opinions of the masses of merely average men are everywhere become or becoming the dominant power,' he continued, 'the counterpoise or corrective to that tendency would be the more and pronounced [role] … of those who stand on the higher eminences of thought. It is in these cases most especially,' Mill conceded, 'that exceptional individuals, instead of being deterred should be encouraged.'[109]

As the reality of democracy unfolded, one problem that arose was the fact that, just as there appeared to be a scarcity of qualified citizens, so too was there a paucity of leaders who met the classical ideal. More fundamentally, however, it is my claim that the traditional definition of 'competence' in a leader was inappropriate to a democratic world. From the analysis put forth in this volume, we know well the competence expected of a traditional leader. James Madison captured it perfectly in *Federalist No. 57*: 'The aim of every political constitution is, or ought to be, to obtain for rulers men who possess most wisdom to discern and most virtue to pursue the common good of society'.[110] But given the assumptions of democracy, the traditional expectations of the leader became unrealistic. As I tried to make clear in my earlier arguments, there is probably no independent, external common good to 'discern,' and even if there were, it is unlikely that some elite leader would be perceived as having sufficient 'virtue to pursue' it. In sum, we simply today do not accept the premises of the classical ideal.

Yet this does not mean that some new, reconceptualized leader could not provide real value and service to the polity, without doing undue violence to the underlying premises of democracy. That is to say, it is not inconceivable that a modern democratic polity might have – even require – both strong and competent leaders. The difference from the classical ideal must be in the nature of the competence. Such leaders must supply strength in areas in which the people are weak, without eclipsing the ultimate power of the people to debate and decide. This is a delicate balance, and one that will be the focus of our attention for most of the remaining analysis. It is possible here, however, at least to suggest the competencies of this new democratic leader. They are to awaken, to educate, to suggest future direction, to guide and to transform.

To awaken

One fruitful function a leader must perform is to keep the people from becoming complacent, and to alert them to leadership challenges that may not be readily discernible in the regular course of things. Thus, to quote James MacGregor Burns, the leader can 'critique … the gap between wants and values and actualities',[111] or, in the language of Ronald Heifetz, identify 'the gap between the values people stand for and the reality they face'.[112] In saying this, I am not making the argument that the leader *resolve* this conflict or bridge this gap; that is the task for the people. However, by bringing such discrepancies to the people's attention – indeed, at times *forcing* the people to take such notice – the leader performs the estimable function of what Benjamin Barber calls 'challenging the paradigmatic present'.[113] In doing so, the leader, although creating some immediate discomfiture, nonetheless ensures the long-term health of the polity.

To educate

Another leader role that enhances but does not usurp the role of the people is the ability to educate them concerning matters relevant to their discourse. A couple of examples should suffice. For example, leaders have an obligation to help the people see the bigger picture. As Tocqueville put it, the people need to 'go beyond immediate gratification', and their focus must be upon the 'long term'. More than this, however, it is the task of democratic leaders to help the people see beyond themselves in a larger sense. They must lift the vision of the demos to its higher calling of the public interest.[114]

A democratic leader can also educate the populace by helping them to define their realities – and their values. Recall that one definition of a leadership challenge – by both Burns and Heifetz – is the existence of a gap between values and reality. Again, in this example the leader does not do the work of the people, but instead helps them to perceive the issues and to work through them on their own. This is no small matter. In effect the leader is helping the populace to 'frame those issues', and in so doing to 'determine the direction of public debate'.[115] We again face that delicate balance in which the leader must intervene in the democratic discourse to ensure its quality while not intruding overmuch into the proper sphere of the people. It is the dance of leadership in a democracy, and one that must be constantly attended to.

To suggest future direction

Another intervention which involves the competence of the leader – and another instance of the 'dance of leadership in a democracy' – is the role the leader can play in suggesting future directions and potential solutions. Again, this reveals the assumption that some individuals *do* see farther than others in terms of future implications, *do* have the capability to perceive connections in the midst of complexity, and *do* have the spark of creativity needed to craft innovative solutions. The key point is that these leaders may have 'a potent vision of what is and what might be',[116] but cannot impose their insights and solutions upon the people, but only fold them into the mix in the most persuasive way possible. Ultimately the people will make the determination, and then be accountable for the results.

To guide

The competence of the leader is also needed as the public discourse moves forward. This competence is both substantive (evoking the 'dance' again) and procedural. On the substantive side of the ledger, Ruscio notes how leaders 'are obligated' to 'transcend' the 'vices' of the people, and to 'control and guide the irrational while promoting the rational'.[117] That is, it is imperative that leaders provide both insights and guidance as the debate moves along. Again, this is not intended to promote leader tyranny (indeed, if we have structured the system according to my earlier recommendations with the equalization of resources and power, this is unlikely in any event), but to leaven participation with competence.

On the process side, I will shortly explore a model of leadership inspired by Ronald Heifetz that suggests the many varied and important ways that a leader can ensure that the actual discourse of democracy is substantive and effective. In Heifetz's own words, his approach 'departs from Plato's perspective [the classical ideal] in a fundamental way'. In Heifetz's model, a leader's 'actions are nothing if not expert, but they are expert in the management of processes by which the people with the problem achieve the resolution'. This involves 'the orchestration of conflict' and bringing 'these conflicting voices into some sort of harmony'.[118] In both substance and process, then, the leader brings competence to the table in important ways.

To transform

As I will detail below, I believe that it is possible for the leader to create a leadership process in which the actions of the leader can have a direct impact upon the capabilities of the people, in such a way that the desired transformation from individual to citizen is accelerated. This, too, requires a certain competence on the part of the leader, and I believe it is a competence necessary in every good democratic leader.

In sum, it is important to note that leaders under my fiction of leadership bring their own version of competence to the table, but it is not the all-knowing competence of the classical ideal, nor are the people expected to defer unthinkingly to the leaders' ideas. Instead, the competence of the leader intersects with the autonomy (participation) of the people in such a way that both principles are served. How this might play out is the topic of the next segments.

The Facilitative Leader

In the following subsections I present two protocols for leader behavior in a modern democracy. Both are a function of the demands I have placed on the leader role in the course of devising this fiction of the leadership process. The first protocol is one I call the 'facilitative leader'. The necessity for the facilitative leader arises from the fact that I have placed the responsibility for determining the polity's needs and the appropriate responses to those needs squarely upon the backs of the people. The constructivist process that I have outlined is guaranteed to be messy and conflict-ridden, given the reality of diversity and the flawed human characters I have portrayed. Although there have been efforts in this fiction to ameliorate this by refitting the leadership structure, improving the capabilities of the people and specifying a process based on public reason, there is no reason to expect neat and tidy results. There is a need for leaders: strong leaders who combine procedural expertise with the kind of competence defined in the previous section. In the end, as Kenneth Ruscio has written, there is a need for leaders who 'possess a set of qualities and talents that allow them to participate in and manage a process that extracts from the citizens their "true interests"'.[119] This brings us to a fuller consideration of the concept of the facilitative leader.

If the decision of the people in matters pertaining to the public interest is determinative, and if that determination is to be achieved through public reason and reciprocity, this suggests (as my discussion of epistemology made clear) that the focus of public action is upon the *process*, not any predetermined outcome. This, in turn, suggests that the leader should be an adept manager of the process, to ensure that the precepts of public reason play out properly. At the same time, as my discussion of the new typology of leader competence also made clear, the leader is also more than merely a process manager. There are many areas in which the leader can 'infuse competence' into the process through the communication of her or his vision, ideas concerning possible resolutions to the challenge and the like. A model of leadership behavior that I believe to be useful and important is the one put forward by Ronald Heifetz. He too, argues for a strong leader role, albeit my claims for the importance of leader competence may make him somewhat uncomfortable. Nevertheless, I think his approach fits my fiction nicely.

The essence of Heifetz's approach is something he calls 'leadership as adaptive work'. To understand adaptive work, it is necessary to understand first the nature of an 'adaptive challenge' to society. According to Heifetz, such a challenge 'consists of a gap between the shared values people hold and the reality of their lives, or a conflict among people in a community over values or strategy'. It is a challenge, then, that goes to the heart of the polity's functioning. In response to such a challenge, adaptive work is 'the hard work of clarifying [society's] competing values and purposes, and of facing the painful trade-offs and adjustments required to narrow the gap between current conditions and purposes'. Leadership in such situations then, amounts to 'mobilizing people to tackle tough problems'.[120]

Heifetz takes great care to specify the tasks of a leader in this process of adaptive work. As we will see, although he explicitly grounds his process in the actions of the people, he nonetheless anticipates that leaders will play an instrumental role. In the paragraphs below I will describe the leader's expected role in adaptive work. In addition, I will graft on to Heifetz's portrayal of leadership responsibilities my own assessment of how the leader competencies I have depicted – that is, the ability to awaken the people, to educate them, to suggest future directions, to guide the process both in terms of substance and procedure, and to transform the participants – can play out in the process of adaptive work. Here are Heifetz's 'five strategic principles of leadership':[121]

1. *Identify the adaptive challenge.* According to Heifetz, this means identifying 'the gap between aspirations and reality'. In doing so, the leader must 'diagnose the situation in light of the values at stake, and unbundle the issues that come with it'. In the process, it is also the responsibility of the leader to frame the matter in such a way that the people can tackle it. S/he must 'produce questions about problem definitions and solutions'.[122] Thus, while it is clear that the objective is ultimately to turn the definition and resolution of the issue over to the people, Heifetz's initial strategy also invites the sort of leader competence I have been advocating. Clearly, this calls upon the leader to 'awaken' the people, to 'educate' them, and, I would argue, there is also a significant amount of substantive guidance involved in both identifying the challenge and in framing questions for how to go about addressing it. Indeed, Heifetz hints at this. He points out that his approach does not 'forsake the image of leadership as a visionary activity'. To the contrary, he says, 'it places emphasis on the act of giving clarity and articulating a community's guiding values'. Likewise, he anticipates that the leader will 'produce socially useful outcomes by setting goals that meet the needs of both the leader and followers'.[123]

2. *Keep the level of distress within a tolerable range.* Under this strategy, Heifetz likens the leader's role to operating a pressure cooker. It is important, on the one hand, to keep the pressure on the people to engage the tough issues. On the other hand, it is also the leader's responsibility not to give the people more than they can handle, and not to allow the pressure on them to rise to an extent that they cannot function. This takes an insightful leader who 'pace[s] the rate of challenge' in 'an effort to prepare people to undertake a hard task at a rate they can stand'.[124] It also assumes that the leader has the insight and competence to understand the frailties of the people, and it gives the leader considerable latitude with respect to the agenda for popular discourse.

3. *Focus attention upon ripening issues and not on stress-reducing distractions.* This goes hand in hand with the previous leader strategy. Here, the leader must 'identify which issues can currently engage attention'. One aspect of this is to 'keep attention focused on relevant issues'. It is tempting for the people to duck the hard work of adaptive leadership. Heifetz calls these avoidance strategies 'work avoidance', which includes 'mechanisms like denial, scapegoating, externalizing the enemy, pretending the problem is technical [and thus relying upon a leader for simplistic answers], or attacking individuals rather

than issues'. Whenever a leader perceives any work avoidance going on s/he must force the people back on task. Again, Heifetz's description reveals how important – and how substantive – a leader's role might be. Any leader who keeps people on task against their inclinations is no shrinking violet. Moreover, the duty to identify relevant issues has many substantive implications. As Heifetz himself says, this task of the leader amounts to 'directing attention' to certain issues. To Heifetz, 'attention is the heart of leadership', and 'getting people to pay attention to tough issues rather than diversions is at the heart of strategy'.[125] Again, elements of my argument for the infusion of leader competence seem to be in play.

4. *Give the work back to the people, but at a rate they can stand.* This strategy embodies Heifetz's basic premise that it is the province of the people to resolve their own challenges. At the same time, he, as usual, allows room for leader discretion in monitoring the process. Thus the leader should 'devise a strategy that shift[s] responsibility for the problem to the primary stakeholders'. This could easily tap the leader's substantive competence as well. Heifetz notes that the leader 'may be able to help or push the society to do the hard work of clarifying its competing values and purposes, of facing the painful trade-offs and adjustments required to narrow the gap between current conditions and purposes'.[126] In doing so, it is difficult to imagine – or even desire – that the leader should abjure the insights that his or her larger vision and appreciation of complexity might bring.

5. *Protect voices of leadership without authority.* This task of the leader has two elements. The first is to assure that all relevant stakeholders are 'at the table' – that is, engaged in the discourse. The second is to assure that all voices are heard once the discourse gets underway. The leader must 'give cover to those who raise hard questions and generate distress – people who point to the internal contradictions of the society. These individuals often will have latitude to provoke rethinking that authorities do not have.'[127] This is somewhat of a radical notion. Heifetz is asking the leader to bring into the discussion all who have a stake in it, even if they are troubling and seemingly subversive elements from outside the mainstream. This is an intent not unlike my recommendation for a redistribution of wealth and power.

Taken together, Heifetz's 'strategies' for leaders in a democratic polity constitute a useful depiction of the necessary activities of my 'facilitative leader'. These strategies allow the people to assume their appropriate place as the chief carriers of the discourse, but they also provide ample space for the competency of the leader to help frame the discourse and guide its progress. Ronald Heifetz thus helps to articulate one aspect of the leader's role in this fiction of leadership. But there is one more, as well.

The Transformative Leader

Just as the proposal for a facilitative leader grew out of the logic of the theory of leadership I have been creating, so too does the second aspect of the leader role, what I call the 'transformative leader'. One of the themes weaving itself throughout the fabric of the fiction is that for democracy to work well, the people need to be committed to it and its processes. As I have suggested, this is not necessarily their natural inclination, although I believe individuals harbor some natural cooperative sentiments. It has been my argument that such sentiments must be nurtured, and/or the individual's own self-interest must be 'rightly understood' in such a way that each sees it as in his or her interest to become productive participants in the democratic discourse. This brings us to the transformative leader.

As we move into this discussion, I wish to make a preliminary point about my use of the term 'transformative' leader. This term is chosen in order to distinguish what has gone before. The term 'transformational' leadership was coined by James MacGregor Burns in 1978 to depict a certain type of leadership that affected both leaders and followers as they set about creating major social change. In subsequent years the term has been hijacked by social scientists in today's leadership literature, so Burns has recently (2003) taken to calling his form of leadership 'transforming' leadership. The work of Burns is in many ways an inspiration for my own approach, but my claims are much more limited, and therefore, I believe, less problematic. Because my claimed transformation is limited to that from individual to citizen, I try to distance myself from the larger claims of Burns by calling my leader a 'transformative' leader.

Let us turn, then, to a discussion of transformation and my version of it. The kind of transformation I am talking about first came into the modern lexicon by way of Rousseau. He articulated two transformations: one social, the other individual. Both were linked to his 'social contract'. The social transformation was from a collection of individuals to a body politic. 'At once,' he pointed out, 'in place of the individual person of each contracting party, the act of association produces a moral and collective body ... which receives from this same act of unity, its common *self*, its life, and its will [emphasis in the original]'.[128] There was, according to Rousseau, an individual transformation as well: 'This passage from the state of nature to the civil state produces a remarkable change in man, for it substitutes justice for instinct in his behavior and gives his actions a moral quality they previously lacked. Only then, when the voice of duty replaces physical impulse and right replaces appetite, does man, who had hitherto taken only himself into account, find himself forced to act upon other principles and to consult his reason before listening to his inclinations.'[129] There could hardly be a better depiction of what I perceive as the distinction between individual and citizen.

The other principal source for the concept of transformation is James MacGregor Burns. He depicted transformational leadership in his classic 1978 book as what 'occurs where one or more persons *engage* with others in such a way that leaders and followers raise one another to higher levels of motivation and morality [emphasis in original]'. When he spoke of higher levels of 'motivation', he did not mean the traditional incentive to work harder, but the movement up Maslow's motivational hierarchy toward 'self-actualization'. And, according to Burns, 'the relationship becomes *moral* in that it raises the level of human conduct and ethical aspiration of both leader and led, and has a transforming effect on both [emphasis in the original]'. Neither of these elements of transformation are a part of my conception. While I am not denying the possibility that they exist, they are not necessary to the success of my fiction, and by excluding them from my model I also avoid, to an extent, some of the concerns raised about Burns's approach as articulating a set of overweening values that may not be acceptable to all. On the other hand, one derivative claim that Burns makes about his approach is much more useful. He also mentions 'followers who ... feel "elevated" by [the leadership process] and often more active themselves'.[130] *This* is more akin to my transformative notions.

When Burns returned to the topic of what he now calls transforming leadership in 2003, he provided some further insights into the leader–follower relationship. For Burns, the transforming leader has an important but limited role. As he put it, 'instead of exercising power over people, transforming leaders champion and inspire followers.... Leaders encourage followers to rise above narrow interests and work together for transcending goals.' This echoes my own approach, albeit my 'transcending goal' is a public interest determined by constructivist means, and Burns has a more limited vision of the role of the leader. For Burns, 'leaders take the initiative in mobilizing people for participation in the processes of change, encouraging a sense of collective identity and collective efficacy, which in turn brings stronger feelings of self-worth and self-efficacy', yet he does not admit to a role for leader competency as I have advocated. Burns does, however, have insights into what I have labeled the 'dance of democratic leadership', as leaders and followers negotiate roles and primacy. 'As leaders encourage followers to rise above narrow interests and work together for transcending goals,' he acknowledges, 'leaders can come into conflict with followers.' Burns does not bemoan this, but welcomes it. Increased follower activity 'is what makes transforming leadership participatory and democratic'.[131] I tend to agree.

The work of James MacGregor Burns, while not perfectly analogous, nicely complements Rousseau. Rousseau, it will be recalled, described almost perfectly the transition from individual to citizen, but did not sufficiently depict the process by which his transformation occurred. Burns, although his claimed transformation is more grandiose than I am prepared to accept, nevertheless does suggest that the transformation is a part of the dynamic between leader and the people. With these theorists as background, let us look more closely at the transformative leader in my own fiction.

There can be no question that the transformative leader places a central role in my fiction. Although my leadership model is based upon the premise of popular sovereignty and depends upon public discourse on public issues, I nevertheless have assigned important responsibilities to the leader. In one sense, despite the fact that it is the people who ultimately determine the substantive result, in another sense the achievement of the public interest is the responsibility of the leader. That is to say, only when competent leaders ask the correct questions and properly facilitate the political process are private concerns converted into public interest. In addition to the appropriate epistemological result of an acceptable policy outcome, there is what is in some ways a more important consequence: the possibility of transforming individuals into citizens. It is that latter, transformative, aspect of leadership that deserves more attention here.

There is a distinguished history of commentators who have called for leaders to inspire the necessary transformation in the people. We can begin by returning to Rousseau. Although he was somewhat vague as to the dynamics of his transformation from individual to citizen, he acknowledged that this was one of the few times when the actions of a leader – he called him the 'legislator' – were important (in the normal course of events, the body politic deliberated without the interference of a leader). During the early history of a polity, when the transformation from individual to citizen must take place, a leader was indispensable. Rousseau did not assume that individuals would automatically be transformed into moral beings committed to the common good merely by entry into the social contract. As commentator Richard Dagger explains it, 'The legislator's task, in a sense, is to complete the passage from the state of nature to the civil state'.[132] Or, as Rousseau himself put it, the legislator 'should feel like he is capable of changing human nature, so to speak; of transforming each individual, who by himself is a perfect and solitary whole, into a part of a larger whole'.[133] Thus it was the legislator's responsibility, among other things, to marshal the transformation from individual selfishness to civic virtue.

Similarly, Alexis de Tocqueville noted that leaders in a regime of popular sovereignty must raise the level of the people themselves. 'It would seem', he wrote, 'as if the rulers of our time sought only to use men to make things great. I wish they would try a little more to make great men.' For they must 'never forget that a nation cannot long remain strong when every man belonging to it is individually weak; and that no form or combination of social polity has yet been devised to make an energetic people out of a community of pusillanimous and enfeebled citizens'.[134]

John Stuart Mill also called upon leaders to be transformative. He took some care to portray how leaders could effect a more capable populace. In Mill's scenario, 'the instructed few [that is, the leaders] ... teach principally by example: Through deliberation in the representative assembly, electoral campaigns, and other public places they demonstrate how to reason intelligently about the ends of politics'.[135] Under Mill's theory, the very process of debating public policy issues better prepared the citizens for governing, and, of course, participation in the process itself had a similar effect.

Turning to the modern era, it is of significance to note that our champion for the facilitative leader – Ronald Heifetz – also makes several statements in support of what I have labeled the transformative leader. 'Making progress on these [adaptive] problems,' he writes, 'demands not just someone who provides answers from on high but changes in our attitudes, behaviors, and values. To meet challenges such as these [that is, adaptive challenges], we need a different idea of leadership and a new social contract that promote our adaptive capacities, rather than inappropriate expectations of authority [leaders]. We need,' he concluded, 'to reconceive and revitalize our civic life and the means of citizenship.' Heifetz views this transformation of the people in terms of social learning. According to Heifetz, 'Adaptive work requires ... mobilizing people to learn new ways'. Indeed, the very essence of adaptive work 'calls for leadership that induces learning'. This, in turn, is the obligation of the leader. A leader 'can induce learning by asking hard questions and by recasting people's expectations to develop their response ability'. As a result of the leader's actions, 'people discover, invent, and take responsibility'. The transformation is complete.[136]

The question, logically enough, becomes *how* to achieve this desired transformation. I believe it is possible to realize this type of transformation from individual to citizen through the effective implementation of my first type of leader behavior, that is, through the actions of the facilitative leader. That is to say, although the leader certainly should be conscious of his/her transformative impact, and foster the transformation whenever possible, in reality this transformative result is derivative of a properly working leadership process. To explain: if this fiction of leadership is structured properly, and if the leader plays well the role of facilitative leader by shepherding the public along the path of democratic discourse, using the strategies outlined earlier (identifying the adaptive challenge, focusing attention, giving the work back to the people and so on), the desired transformation from individual to citizen will be a natural byproduct of this process. Thus, you will see here no catalogue of 'strategies' for the transformative leader; the transformation is a natural by-product of the leader performing her or his other duties well. The conscientious action of the leader in engaging the people in the real work of the leadership process will have the effect of transforming them from individuals into citizens. Thus, like the public interest discussed earlier, the desired effect is both a constituent part and desired outcome of the process. But the role of the leader is crucial: without the leader, there is no transformation.

The distinction between the facilitative leader and the transformative leader is not one of substance so much as of cognitive approach. As the facilitative leader goes about his or her 'dance' of participation versus competence, the most important outcome s/he must have in mind must be the objective of transforming individuals into citizens. Although it is trite, the old chestnut about 'giving a man a fish versus teaching him to fish' is pertinent here. That is, once this transformation is complete, and we have a body politic of citizens and not merely individuals, the leadership process in a democracy has a better than fair chance of securing the public interest. Thus, although the underlying transformation is derivative of the process itself, it is critical that the leader be conscious – and conscientious – about this fundamental objective. To sum up: if it is the purpose of leaders to ask the right questions and facilitate the process of public discourse toward achieving the public interest, it is also the responsibility of the leader, using the process itself, to transform individual interests into public ones, and individuals themselves into citizens.

A Summing Up

In this section on the role of the leader, I have attempted to draw together several important themes from this emerging theory or fiction of leadership. I have posited that it becomes the role of leaders to guide the process of politics (leadership) in the pursuit of what passes for epistemological 'truth' in the polity. The role of leaders and the epistemological foundation of this fiction are interrelated. As much as we might like to be led by a leader after the fashion of the classical ideal who 'knows' truth and the common good and can educate about its elements and how to achieve them, we clearly have no such leaders. With our reliance upon the populace ultimately to identify and respond to the challenges facing the polity, leaders take on a different role. I continue to claim that there are individuals who have more substantive competence than others – who see things more clearly, who can make sense of complexity, who can imagine workable alternatives. It is important that the polity tap these resources of competence, but not at the expense of the underlying sovereignty of the people. I have labeled the resolution of this tension the 'dance of democratic leadership'. Even more important, the leaders in this model must have the capability to facilitate Heifetz's process of adaptive work. In so doing, the real goal of democratic leadership is achieved: individuals are transformed into citizens, and the discourse among citizens yields policies in the public interest.

HOW SHOULD LEADERS AND THE PEOPLE INTERACT?

The interaction of leaders and the people is the essence of this new social and political relation we call leadership. As such, it partakes of the responses to each of the preceding queries of the template of leadership. This question, it will be recalled, ferrets out the dynamics of the expected relationships of leaders and the people. As such, it reveals much about the complexities posed by the seemingly simple assertion of popular sovereignty. Leadership, as historian Edmund S. Morgan has told us, is 'a new mode of social relations and a new way of determining who should stand up among the few to govern the many'.[137] And, indeed, what form the leadership relation takes – that is, the nature of the relations between leaders and the people, who have sovereign power – remains the central challenge of leadership in a democracy.

One way to frame the issue is through the concept of representation. In the large and complex modern democratic state, unless one takes an extreme participationist stance, some form of representation is inevitable. As political scientists Schmitter and Karl point out, 'the central question, therefore, is not whether or not there will be a political elite ..., but how these representatives are chosen and then held accountable for their actions'.[138] Accordingly, representation has been a central aspect of the relations between leaders and the people in a modern state. As we have seen, however, disputes arose concerning the nature of the relationship between representative and constituent – disputes that echoed the assumptions about the respective roles of leaders and the people. Some advocated a 'trustee' form of representation, in which elected leaders acted on their own best judgment in the interests of all (a version of the classical ideal), while others demanded that representatives be mere 'delegates', acting out the wishes of their constituents.

Another related aspect of this new social and political relation called leadership is the nature of the interaction itself; the dynamic interchange between leaders and the people as they interact in the face of challenges to desired ends. This we can call the leadership *process*, and it embodies all the issues and dilemmas we have devoted so much time to parse out in the course of this volume.

One theme that has captured the dynamics of both representation and the nature of the relationship between leaders and the people over the years has been the concept of deference.

A Short History of Deference

The classical ideal of the leader's approach to leader–follower relations introduced the conception of *deference*. It was expected that those who were in the inferior position – that is, the people – would willingly accept that status because they recognized the superior capabilities of their leaders.

The initial move to conceptions of popular sovereignty did not change this underlying dynamic. Edmund S. Morgan provided us with a narration of the rise of Parliament in England. This rise in status of a representative body was, in some respects, less one of popular sovereignty than a move from a Platonic fiction (the divine right of kings) to one more in line with the classical republican fiction, in which there was some participation by propertied citizens, but the burdens of leading remained with a propertied elite.

The best example of this new relationship between leaders and the people remains that of John Locke. Locke, although fundamentally attached to the theoretical sovereignty of the people – embodied in his social contract – nonetheless allowed them little role to play in the day-to-day operations of the polity. Once the political community was formed, the initial act of the people was to 'set rulers over themselves, to guard and promote [the common good]'.[139] Once the government (the 'legislative') was in place, the role of the people changed. Although they continued to exercise their sovereignty on election days, in the usual course of things the people were expected to defer to the actions of the legislative and the prerogative of the executive. During the majority of the time, then, the people were expected to remain quiescent, and follow the rules of law propounded by the legislative. In sum, in all but the most extraordinary of circumstances, it was expected that the relationship between leaders and the people should be one of deference on the part of the people to their chosen leaders.

In terms of our construct of representation, implicit in this mode of representation is the concept of the representative as a trustee for his (it would not be her) constituents. Dye and Zeigler point out that such an approach 'envisioned decision-making by representatives of the people, rather than direct decision-making by the people themselves'.[140]

That would change, as the logic of popular sovereignty played itself out, and the concept of deference to leaders came under increasing pressure. Although James Madison belatedly came to recognize it, it was Alexis de Tocqueville who first confronted the implications that democracy held for relations between leaders and the people. The reality that confronted Tocqueville as he assayed this relationship was in many ways a revolutionary one. Since ancient times, it had been possible to characterize the attitude of the people toward their leaders as one of deference. It was this deference, indeed, that permitted something like the classical ideal to operate. Yet, as the fiction of popular sovereignty began to assert itself, this began to change. By Tocqueville's time, the egalitarianism of America's democracy had undercut the traditional notion of deference to leaders. As he put it, 'The nearer the people are drawn to the common level of an equal and similar condition, the less prone does each man become to place implicit faith in a certain man or class of men'.[141]

This, in turn, led to a new relationship between leaders and the people. Now, rather than the many deferring to the superior wisdom and virtue of the few, it was expected that the few would serve as mere delegates for the many, obligated to fulfill their whims and desires. In sum, the new ideology of the common man and the stress upon private interests generated a new set of expectations regarding the proper linkages between leaders and the people. It seemed that all the governing assumptions that had guided society had been turned upside down. The traditional deference paid to leaders disappeared. In such a wildly egalitarian culture, elite leaders were not only unnecessary; to some, they were undesirable. The new commitment to the common man left a lingering resentment of elite leadership.

This development brings us back to notions of representation. As we have seen in our review of Locke, in seventeenth-century England, the members of Parliament saw themselves as trustees for the interests of the people. Under the stresses of democratization, this morphed into the 'delegate' version of representation. There were no longer strong claims that the delegates were markedly superior to their constituents. If anything, since sovereignty was acknowledged to be in the people, a new possibility arose: the people could actually be *superior* to their leaders. What this meant in terms of the relations between leaders and the people was a total reversal of traditional assumptions and practices. Under the traditional, trustee-type of relation, the relationship was characterized by deference on the part of the people toward their superior leaders. But when the representatives became mere delegates of their constituents, a quite different relationship ensued.

Despite the almost paradigmatic shift in the perception of the relationship between leaders and the people, it was not quite that simple. What has complicated things is the fact that neither extreme has gained unchallenged ascendancy, and democratic political thought ever since has been a mishmash of one version or the other, or, more commonly some mixture of the two. We have traced in this volume several of these variations in the treatment of the appropriate relationship between leaders and followers. In the new fiction of leadership I am positing, I draw upon the more insightful of these historical approaches to devise a new approach to the relationship between leaders and the people, one better suited to modern democratic realities, yet also encompassing my call for a partial return to a reliance upon leader competence in the leadership relation.

A New Model of Deference

As I confront the issue of the proper relationship between leaders and the people in a modern democracy, I begin with two essentials: the need for leaders with wisdom and a people committed to making democracy work. My previous discussion has, I trust, sufficiently justified the need for both. The challenge, of course, is how to integrate leader competence with the participation – and ultimate sovereignty – of the people into a pragmatic, workable relationship best fitted to our modern democratic realities.

Ultimately, the relationship can be thought of in terms of our ongoing discussion of representation. Representation is the point of nexus between leaders and the people. The dialectical debate between competence and participation has the potential to yield a synthesis through the character of representation adopted as a part of the leadership fiction. Representation, then, links together competent leaders with the will of the people; it is one method of bridging two disparate ideological streams. The synthesis I have in mind can be summed up neatly in the concept of 'mutual deference', although it will take me some time to explicate it adequately.

A historical perspective

It is useful to begin by tapping the rich vein of historical commentary that has proven to be so useful throughout this volume. Various commentators have long attempted to portion out the responsibilities of leaders and the people. Aristotle, for example, distinguished between their relative merits. As for the general run of the people, he argued, 'there is still a danger in allowing them to share the greatest offices of state, for their [individual] folly will lead them into error, and their dishonesty to crime'. Nevertheless, he maintained that 'when they get together their perceptions are good enough, and combined with the better class they are useful to the state'. For Aristotle, the resolution was clear. As for the people, the wisest path was 'to assign them some deliberative and judicial functions', such as 'the power of electing officers, and of calling magistrates to account ... [and of] discuss[ing] policy'. This, however, came with a caveat: 'Do not', he admonished, 'allow them to hold office singly.' Any policy initiative of the people, moreover, was subject to veto by the leaders.[142] Thus, Aristotle was among the first to imply that both leaders and the people had a role to play. While competent leaders should be deferred to in their direction of the state, at the same time, the people, whose wisdom could be found in the collective, were the appropriate body to restrain excesses by the leaders, and their insights were useful in policy making. In this lay the seeds of a mutual deference.

James Harrington, writing in seventeenth-century England, moved us closer to the conception of mutual deference with his brilliant institutional arrangements. The task Harrington set for himself was similar to our own: he was concerned with interweaving the aristocratic element with that of the people without incurring unacceptable rule by a corrupt elite or the unwisdom of an unchecked democracy. In a larger sense, he was tackling the proper relations between leaders and the people.

His solution was an innovative political mechanism that ensured leaders who emulated the classical ideal while at the same time capturing the benefits of popular participation. To accomplish this, Harrington, like Aristotle, had to consider the differing capacities of the participants in his commonwealth. He perceived a natural aristocracy (a meritocracy) who had the wisdom and virtue to debate and discuss matters of public policy. The people, on the other hand, while not possessing the wisdom of the meritocracy, nevertheless, when presented with the ideas of the leaders, could best judge the merit of such proposals because the people had the best sense of the public interest.

Harrington thus advocated a senate made up of representatives of the meritocracy (in traditional classical republican fashion, wealth was a proxy for wisdom and virtue). This group of wise leaders would debate and propose policy initiatives. However, the senate could not enact policy. Another body, the assembly (recall Harrington substituted outlandish names for all of these institutions), was needed for this. The assembly included representatives of both elites and common people, but the commoners predominated by a four to three ratio. This body could not debate at all, but simply voted senate proposals up or down, thus serving its function of judging proposals against the assembly's sense of what was in the public interest.

Most important for our purposes, this elaborate institutional mechanism amounted to a new system of leading, with new expectations of both leaders and the people. Harrington articulated a sophisticated relationship between the people and their leaders. It was one marked by an intriguing mix of deference and mutual respect. On the one hand, he demanded that the many yield to the wisdom of the superior few in policy formation. In that manner, the principle of deference made its appearance. Yet the notion of deference is inadequate to depict fully the relationship between leaders and the people. As Harrington scholar J.G.A. Pocock put it, 'If the Many choose the Few by showing them deference, there is a real sense in which the Few must defer to the Many. Only on those principles will equality, authority, and virtue be simultaneously guaranteed.'[143] In other words, only the two, working together in mutual respect, could achieve wise policy in the public interest.

Harrington's model comprises a creative attempt at tapping the wisdom of the competent as well as the common sense of the people. He is also innovative in the way he embraced both versions of representation in the same polity. His senators served as trustees for the people, while the members of the assembly assumed more of a delegate function. This marriage of the differing functions of representation likewise marks James Harrington as a useful source in my attempt to establish a similar synthesis.

John Stuart Mill had yet another 'take' on the relationship between leaders and the people in a democracy. His challenge remained essentially the same as that of Harrington (it is our challenge as well): to create 'the political means by which the competent exercise influence in a democracy [in such a way that] ... that influence can in practice be combined with the demands of the principle of participation'.[144] In addition to facing the identical challenge with regard to the relationship of the leaders and the people, Mill also had precisely the same ends in mind: to achieve wise policy, and to encourage inherently selfish individuals to become more fitted as citizens.

In seeking these ends through the interactions of leaders and the people, Mill did not follow Harrington's institutional solution so much as look to an intellectual nexus. In Mill's conception, the leadership relation 'bring[s] ... inferior minds into contact with superior'. Here, the importance of leaders is clear. 'A government which [does not show] ... any one else how to do anything', he elaborated, 'is like a school in which there is no schoolmaster, but only pupil-teachers who have never themselves been taught.'[145] The people, on the other hand, were the pupils. 'The honor and glory of the average man', Mill stated, 'is that he is capable of following the initiative [of leaders]; that he can respond internally to wise and noble things, and be led to them with his eyes open.'[146]

This didactic conception yields a different version of the relations between leaders and the people. As Mill scholar Dennis Thompson points out, 'unlike many contemporary elitist theories of democracy, Mill does not justify the influence of the competent minority solely on the grounds of the superior ability to govern'.[147] Instead, they teach by example, with an eye toward enhancing the capabilities of their constituents. The objective is to inform the people of the nuances of the issue under consideration, so that citizens can contribute intelligently to the political process.

Likewise, the Mill approach suggests a different form of deference. We do not see the mutual deference institutionalized by Harrington, but Mill does provide us with an enhanced conception of the type of deference the people should show to their leaders in a democracy. It is a limited and conditional deference that recognizes the dignity and legitimacy of the people and their views. As Thompson says, 'citizens will ... defer to the competent, but it is a rather special kind of deference that Mill prescribes .... Even when Mill most strongly stresses rule by the elite, he insists that citizens defer to leaders only on rational grounds.' Or, as Mill put it, no longer may deference be construed as a 'blind submission of dunces to men of knowledge'; instead, it becomes the 'intelligent deference of those who know much to those who know still more'.[148] In other words, traditional deference was slaked by the people's rational judgment. In a sense, then, Mill *did* advocate a form of mutual deference: the people to the wisdom of the leaders, and the leaders to the dignity and inherent good sense of the people.

With such precedents concerning the appropriate deferential relationships in mind, we can turn to a consideration of the nature of the relations between leaders and the people in my own proposed fiction or model of leadership. I have labeled my approach 'mutual deference', and we have now seen that it has significant historical roots. Turning to my own notions, it may be helpful to look at this deference from the perspective of each side, and then to suggest how these conceptions can be integrated.

Leaders defer to the people
The 'default' position in modern democratic thinking is that leaders should defer to the wishes of the people. Certainly this is not an unreasonable stance given the modern constellation of beliefs in popular sovereignty, egalitarianism and commitment to individual liberty. In my approach to the ideal leadership relation, I accept and endorse this fundamental commitment to the priority accorded to the role and wishes of the citizens. Throughout my development of this 'fiction' of leadership I have attempted to place citizen action at the forefront of every aspect of the leadership process. Yet because I also claim an important role for competent leaders, it is not possible for me to leave my analysis at the level of leadership 'of the people, by the people, and for the people'. The reinvention of deference to the leader will be the substance of my next subsection. But even when considering the more accepted deference to the people, my call for substantive participation by both leaders and the people requires me to reconsider the deference to the people as well.

To be specific: my claim that there are times when the people should defer to their leaders grants those leaders a scope of action not often found in modern democratic theory. This new latitude on the part of leaders requires me to establish a standard beyond which a leader cannot go without violating the fundamental deference to the people that popular sovereignty and democracy requires. So it is that I turn now to an attempt to establish some parameters – 'rules of the game', if you will – that sketch the requirements for leader deference to the people. These requirements are intended as limitations on leaders: any leaders transgressing these expectations in any material way must be brought to account. In concept it is not unlike the 'long train of abuses' identified by Locke as the limit beyond which the leaders no longer deserved popular support. Unlike Locke, however, whose broad prerogative and limited exceptions to leader behavior carved out a large space for leader autonomy (limited only by a vague conception of the common good), in my fiction the standard applied to leaders is more thoroughgoing, more intrusive into leader activity, and better situated to preserve real autonomy on the part of the people. In creating such a standard, I place limits on leader behavior, and ensure the proper amount of deference to the people.

The most promising avenue for establishing such guidelines for the leader stems from an intriguing analysis recently put forward by scholar Norman Bowie, entitled *A Kantian Theory of Leadership*.[149] Bowie begins by admitting that the application of the thinking of Immanuel Kant to the concept of leadership might at first blush appear to be 'an oxymoron. After all,' he elaborates, 'it is a conceptual truth that [in leadership] a leader must have followers.' This is further complicated by the fact that 'people tend to think that a follower is of lesser rank than the leader', and 'for many, the term "leader" has hierarchical and even elitist connotations'.[150] All such conceptualizations seem to refute a Kantian approach.

In reply to such arguments, Bowie acknowledges that 'Kant's moral philosophy is basically egalitarian'. In it, 'persons are ... entitled to be treated with dignity and respect. That is why Kant argues that one cannot use another as a means merely.' It is also the basis for his 'categorical imperative': that 'action must be based on a maxim that can be universally endorsed'.[151]

Yet Bowie perceives the possibility that Kantian thinking can be applied to the leadership relation. 'First,' he argues, 'it should be pointed out that leaders need not violate the respect for persons formulation of the categorical imperative. Leaders need not use followers as means to their own ends.' 'Consequently,' says Bowie, 'a Kantian theory of leadership will insist on more participation on the part of followers and will be more protective of dissenting voices.' When thinking about the process of leadership, he points out that 'the Kantian leader is not so naïve as to believe that there will be unanimity regarding all decisions ... but the rules that govern decision-making should be rules that everyone living under them has had a hand in making and can endorse'.[152]

Bowie isolates one of Kant's formulations as being particularly relevant to our analysis of leadership. It is called the 'kingdom of ends'. In such a kingdom, according to Kant, 'one should act as if one were a member of an ideal kingdom of ends in which one was subject and sovereign at the same time'. Imagining oneself in such a position as both sovereign and subject is likely to ensure outcomes acceptable to all. (Recall Rawls took a similar tack with his 'original position' and 'veil of ignorance'.) For Bowie, 'the kingdom of ends formulation of the categorical imperative is the key to a positive theory of leadership'.[153]

Such a formulation 'acts as a significant restraint on [the leader] as [his or her role] is traditionally understood. Many people think of the leader as ... the person who makes decisions. A Kantian', Bowie posits, 'does not accept this view. To be consistent with the kingdom of ends formulation ..., a Kantian leader, contrary to the popular stereotype, is not one to whom you look for a decision. The Kantian leader empowers others in the [polity] to take responsibility for a decision.' That is to say, 'the leader is a decision proposer rather than a decision imposer.... The Kantian leader assists in the resolution of disagreement, but he or she does not make the decision herself. To do so would violate the autonomy of the other members of the [polity].' Indeed, Bowie goes so far as to establish 'principles' to 'guide a leader'. Among them is the assertion that 'the leader should consider the interests of all affected stakeholders in any decision'. Moreover, 'the leader should have those affected by ... the [outcome] participate in the determination of those rules and policies before they are implemented'. And, finally, 'every leader must in cooperation with others in [the polity] establish procedures to ensure that relations among stakeholders are governed by rules of justice'.[154]

If this sounds a great deal like the 'public reason' of Rawls and the 'adaptive work' of Heifetz, this is no coincidence. Both are clearly within the parameters of the Kantian approach, and this reflects my effort to construct a fiction of leadership consistent with its underlying principles. In terms of our current focus upon leader deference to the people, the consequence of the application of Kantian limits on leader behavior suggests that any act in contravention of these expectations breaches the deference required toward the people. On the other hand, this conceptualization also leaves room for an area of discretion for competent leaders. This brings us to the second thread of my conception of 'mutual deference'.

The people defer to their leaders
If the 'default position' for relations between leaders and the people is – and properly so – the deference of leaders to the will of the people, it takes somewhat more elaboration to justify the opposite claim: that the people also should defer to their leaders in certain instances.

Ronald Heifetz makes this point in his discussion of 'appropriate dependencies' in a democratic regime. According to Heifetz, '"appropriate dependencies" ... arise every day. Whenever we develop ... a political community, we establish a system of authorizations by which various persons or groups coordinate their efforts and take on specialized roles and functions. We construct a network of appropriate dependencies based on a realistic appraisal of what we and others can provide.' Heifetz hastens to assure us of the positive impact such dependencies can have on the leadership relation. 'To the extent that dependence ... functions realistically to meet a set of agreed upon goals, dependency seems quite appropriate ... within the context [of having] mutual interests and suitable skills to meet those interests.'[155] What those 'suitable skills' might be I have set forth in my section on the 'role of the leader': because some individuals do have more 'competence' than others – meaning clearer vision, a greater ability to deal with complexity, more creativity, better 'people skills' – it is both logical and necessary to tap such expertise in appropriate ways. When such competent individuals are permitted to draw upon their capabilities to shape and facilitate public discourse, their followers (that is, the people) are perforce deferring to their expertise.

The essential point is that this notion of deference to leaders does not have to be a nefarious development, robbing citizens of their autonomy. The Kantian restrictions on leaders in my proposed fiction are designed to forestall this. At the same time, there is a need for a more in-depth consideration of the nature of this deference toward leaders that is being asked of citizens. This deference should not be absolute; to expect as much would be to undercut the basis of the fiction, which is the sovereignty of the people. Instead, this deference must be limited; hemmed in by reasonable expectations of leader behavior, and ultimately, by institutional protections against abuse.

When considering the parameters of the people's deference to their leaders, we need to proceed with care. As Kenneth Ruscio has observed, 'arguing for "restraint" [of the people, as deference does] is not a comfortable posture for those with liberal instincts'.[156] Nevertheless, it is Ruscio who gives us the most sophisticated guide for the people's relationship to their leaders. It is embodied in his treatment of 'trust' in the political context.

Ruscio frames the issue well. 'In the modern ... state,' he says, 'the story of trust is the decision when and under what conditions we grant discretion to others [in this case, to our leaders]. With only slight exaggeration,' Ruscio continues, 'we might even claim that *the* dilemma of modern ... leadership as it confronts the demands of democracy is establishing equilibrium between accountability and discretion, between setting limits on leaders' actions while allowing them the flexibility to act.' This dilemma must be resolved if the leadership process is to function properly. As Ruscio puts it, 'understanding trust in leaders goes to the heart of the everyday formation and implementation of public policy', which is what leadership is all about.[157]

The actual dynamic of trust is central. The philosopher Robert C. Solomon provides some insight into this. 'Trust', he argues, '... is a relationship between a leader and his or her followers ... [a]nd relationships by their nature involve much more than a calculation of probabilities and outcomes'. Instead, 'trust is ... necessarily a reciprocal relation'. It is important to note that trust is a two-way street. 'Whereas leaders may be said to earn the trust of their followers,' says Solomon, 'it is the followers who have the capacity to give trust. Trust thus becomes a part of the dynamics of the relationship between those who would be leaders and their followers.'[158]

Ruscio here picks up the thread again. The goal, he suggests, is to develop sufficient trust so as to allow leaders the opportunity to contribute the benefit of their competence, without risking overmuch unacceptable leader behavior. Ruscio argues for the development of a 'zone of discretion'. According to him, 'a high level of trust does not eliminate the need for accountability, but it [does] ... provid[e] ... discretion for leaders and a greater willingness to delegate [responsibility to leaders]'. Drawing upon the insights of management theorist Chester I. Bernard, Ruscio posits 'a zone of discretion, the size of which depends upon the level of trust among citizens, their elected representatives, and administrators'. Thus, 'trust expands the zone, and mistrust causes it to contract'. This variability in the zone of discretion reinforces the important maxim that 'political trust is always conditional', and hence the importance of paying close attention to how trust is nurtured, and, on the other hand, how the people can be protected from its abuse.[159]

As Ronald Heifetz says, 'to build trust, we need to know what generates it'.[160] Ruscio provides us with some answers. First, what is needed are trustworthy leaders. One 'factor that determines the boundaries of discretion is the nature of the leaders themselves, their wisdom, and integrity.... Trust rests on the perception that leaders are pursuing a public good rather than their own self-interest.'[161]

Ruscio is thus calling for leaders who conform to the classical ideal. Unfortunately, he does not indicate where such leaders can be found. If the electoral system worked perfectly, we could count on such leaders being chosen by the voters. Unfortunately, I perceive that the same foibles of the people that impede their policy making also make unreliable their choice of appropriate leaders. Although I am venturing into seriously politically incorrect territory here, I would argue that we should consider returning to a practice long ago abandoned as being insufficiently democratic. Recall that in the classical republican tradition, wisdom and virtue were believed to reside in those who owned property (especially of the 'real' variety). We no longer accept this facile equation, but there was another traditional method of assuring appropriate leaders: through indirect election. Madison had championed this approach, but it is Tocqueville who was its most articulate defender. According to Tocqueville, the 'transmission of the popular authority through an assembly of chosen men operates an important change in it by refining its discretion and improving its choice'. Tocqueville argued that 'men who are chosen in this manner accurately represent the majority of the nation which governs them'; however, such indirectly-elected leaders 'represent only the elevated thoughts that are current in the community and the generous propensities that prompt its nobler actions rather than the petty passions that disturb or the vices that disgrace it'.[162]

Although not so sanguine about the virtuous results of indirect elections as Madison and Tocqueville, I still maintain that it holds the real possibility of securing leaders committed to the larger interests of society, and it is one of the few strategies that remains, arguably, within the scope of modern conceptions of popular sovereignty. In making this claim, I acknowledge that I am swimming upstream in the current of modern democracy. But, again, I agree with Tocqueville when he wrote: 'The time must come when the American republics will be obliged more frequently to introduce the plan of election by an elected body [that is, indirect election] into their system of representation or run the risk of perishing miserably among the shoals of democracy'.[163] I believe that time is upon us. The popular election of judges threatens an independent (and competent) judiciary and the Seventeenth Amendment (providing for the direct election of Senators, by now a progressive and democratic truism) has had, in my view, unfortunate consequences as well. Although difficult, this reform may be our best opportunity to create institutional assurance of good leader selection.

In addition to leaders with wisdom and virtue, a second factor that yields an increase in trust in leaders is the perception of a congruence of interest between leaders and the people. Heifetz argues that 'maintaining ... [the] trust' of the people is dependent upon 'meeting their expectations', and Ruscio adds that 'we trust those who seem to acknowledge the legitimacy of our interests'. In the political context, Ruscio is referring not to the championing of individual interests, but on the leaders' 'ability to respond and work towards our collective purpose'.[164] Thus leaders *earn* trust by demonstrating that their competence is used in the service of the people.

On the one hand, then, the objective is to widen the 'zone of leader discretion' by building trust, thereby allowing for leader competence to operate through a form of deference on the part of the people. Yet in keeping with my fundamental commitment to a constructivist approach to policy making grounded in the people, that zone of leader discretion cannot be overlarge. One limit to leader abuse of discretion lies in the Kantian parameters placed on leader behavior, as discussed in the previous subsection. But there is need for more pragmatic institutional restrictions on leaders as well. As Ruscio phrases it, 'trust [in leaders] is bounded and conditional, the risk moderated by a kind of institutional insurance policy that acts as an additional "motive to good behavior"'.[165] Such institutional protections are the familiar ones advanced by Montesquieu, Madison and others: a bill of rights, separation of powers, a federal system, judicial review and the like.

Having now articulated the two strands of deference which together comprise my conception of mutual deference, we can now turn to a more holistic view.

A New Social Contract

Through our discussion of the mutual deference that must exist between leaders and the people, we can move to an analysis that confirms the respective duties and obligations of those engaged in the leadership process. I will argue that the dynamics of the system of mutual deference create a unique relationship between leaders and the people, and from that relationship we can discern an implicit social contract that structures expectations of behavior. That social contract, where each party (leaders and the people) come to expect certain contributions from the other, is, in turn (to complete the circle), the root of that deference that allows both leaders and the people to occupy and perform their appointed roles. The upshot of these sophisticated renderings of leader–people relations can ultimately be seen in the acceptance of an approach to representation that becomes a hybrid of the trustee and delegate traditions.

To expound briefly upon the synopsis of the preceding paragraph, we have seen in the course of discussing this proposal for the adoption of an ideal fiction of leadership that in it the relationship between leaders and the people is complex. Absolute deference to either leaders or the people is neither the correct answer to the challenges of leadership nor the best way to identify and resolve the issues that confront the polity. Instead, what is needed is a creative and complex interaction – I have sometimes used the metaphor of a 'dance' – in which the people are the constituting force and vector toward change, while at the same time having their energies shaped and guided by competent leaders, who operate within a zone of discretion created by trust. The resulting discourse, characterized by the attributes of public reason and adaptive work, yields appropriate democratic outcomes.

By looking beneath the surface of these interactions, we can discern an underlying set of expectations – a social contract, if you will – that serves as the basis for the respective activities of leaders and the people. As Ronald Heifetz has noted, 'implicit in people's notions of leadership are images of a social contract'.[166] The social contract that underpins this fiction has, as all contracts do, explicit expectations placed upon the respective parties. From leaders we expect *competence* (I have articulated this to mean vision, the ability to deal with complexity, creativity and such 'people skills' as facilitation and conflict resolution). That competence, however, should be employed in advancing a form of leadership I have identified as 'adaptive work', in which leaders give work back to the people as they are able to handle such work, all the while transforming them into capable citizens better able to move forward on their own. Expectations are also placed upon the people. First, there is the expectation of *commitment*. By this I mean a commitment to the polity that rises above mere self-interest. I have devoted considerable attention to how the needed transformation from individual to citizen might be effected. Also expected of citizens is *activity*. This means real participation in the public discourse, along the lines specified by the requirements of public reason. At the same time, the people must recognize that there is such a thing as leader competence, and the consequent need for them to observe appropriate deference.

There remains one last piece of the puzzle to put into place. When politics are on the local level, we can utilize the pure form of 'adaptive work', in which all the interested parties are actively involved in the actual discourse. The realities of size, if nothing else, however, require that most public policy making be carried out by representatives of the people. The requirements of public reason and adaptive work continue to apply to the interactions of these representatives, of course, but the fact of representation requires us also to consider the proper relationship between representatives and their constituents. It is here that we come to grips one final time with the tension between competence and participation.

Representation, as it turns out, provides a decent construct by which to resolve the dialectical debate between competence and participation. Representation looks to both parties of the social contract, and serves as a nexus that ties competent leaders to the will of the people. The challenge is to so characterize the representative relation as to capture the benefits of both competence and participation. Kenneth Ruscio provides us with a nice beginning with his depiction of Montesquieu's approach, in which he 'refine[d] the function of representation. Representatives would be accountable to the people and responsive to their wishes but not in every detail. Their [the representative's] great advantage ... is that they can deliberate about public affairs and instruct each other in the orderly forum of the legislature.'[167] The people's strength, on the other hand, derives from their constituting role in the polity.

Each of these aspects can be addressed by devising a form of representation that combines the trustee and delegate theories of representation. While representatives must use their own judgment, expertise and ability to make decisions reflective of the best interests of society in general (the trustee approach), they must also actively attempt to solicit the opinions of their constituents, when the situation warrants doing so (the delegate approach). This gets us back to mutual deference. We must entrust a certain level of decision-making authority to the hands of our elected representatives, yet, at the same time, we must also expect that they will provide the opportunity for their constituents to input toward the decisions that must be made. Therefore, through the leadership process contained within politics itself, participationists are satisfied with their ability to influence the decision making of their representatives, while those committed to competence are satisfied with the corresponding latitude granted representatives to use their abilities to produce final outcomes that meet the ultimate epistemological test, the public interest.[168]

WHAT INSTITUTIONS AND PROCESSES ARE NEEDED?

This is a critical question that has occupied a place in our template of leadership because it is imperative to support one's theoretical musings with specific recommendations for the implementation of one's ideas. In this chapter, I have attempted to introduce needed institutions and processes at appropriate places in the discussion, and there is no need to address this issue further in this place.

LET THE GAMES BEGIN

In this chapter I have endeavored to build upon our earlier thoroughgoing analysis of the intellectual history of leadership by creating my own proposed ideal model of leadership, the type of model that throughout this work I have labeled a 'fiction'. It is my claim that, were modern democratic societies to embrace my version of the leadership relation (after accommodation to idiosyncratic cultural factors and the like), the polity stands the greatest chance of realizing the possibilities of democracy.

In my proposed new fiction of leadership I have attempted to address and to begin to resolve the essential leadership challenges of modern democracy: participation versus competence; the problem of the common good; the tension between the individual and the community; the championing of diversity and the protection of minority interests. Such a fiction stands on the shoulders of giants: it would not be possible to frame it adequately without the understanding provided by the historical commentators detailed in this volume. At the same time, it draws upon the insights of modern scholars who have added the insights of the social sciences and contemporary analyses of the leadership relation.

Of course, I am not so naïve as to believe that my proposal will meet universal acclamation. Indeed, there is surely fodder enough here to enrage those on both the left and right of the political spectrum. That is to the good. The measure of the benefit of this modest beginning will consist in the extent to which it sparks debate over these critically important issues. But it must be informed debate, and not just impassioned polemics. That is why I have taken such care to uncover the assumptions and premises – the 'implicit theories' – of my work and that of others. Only by acknowledging underlying assumptions, and then constructing arguments grounded in those assumptions, can we hope to have the sort of discourse over leadership in a democracy that is so sorely needed. As I indicated in the preface, I believe we are at a historical crossroads, one potentially as important as that of the American founding. We must define our own fiction of leadership in a democracy, or risk floundering through a dangerous future.

Let the games begin.

NOTES

1. Edmund S. Morgan, *Inventing the People: The Rise of Popular Sovereignty in England and America* (New York: W.W. Norton & Company, 1988), 306.
2. John Rawls, *Political Liberalism* (New York: Columbia University Press, 1996), xvii.
3. Kenneth P. Ruscio, *The Leadership Dilemma in Modern Democracy* (Cheltenham, UK: Edward Elgar Publishing, Ltd., 2004), 6.
4. Alexis de Tocqueville, *Democracy in America* (1835, 1840), ed. Phillips Bradley, 2 vols. (New York: Vintage Books, 1990), 1:14.
5. Ruscio, *The Leadership Dilemma*, xiii.
6. Ronald A. Heifetz, *Leadership Without Easy Answers* (Cambridge, Mass.: Belknap/Harvard University Press, 1994), 8.
7. Dennis Thompson, *John Stuart Mill and Representative Government* (Princeton: Princeton University Press, 1976), 91–92.
8. Matthew Trachman, 'Historicizing Leadership/Democratizing Leadership Studies,' paper delivered at the annual meeting of the International Leadership Association, Toronto, Canada, 7 November 2000, 7.
9. Ruscio, *The Leadership Dilemma*, 12 (see note 3).

10. Ibid., 62.
11. Michael J. Sandel, *Democracy's Discontent: America in Search of a Public Philosophy* (Cambridge, Mass.: Harvard University Press, 1996), 27.
12. Richard Dagger, *Civic Virtues: Rights, Citizenship, and Republican Liberalism* (Oxford: Oxford University Press, 1997), 3–4.
13. Markate Daly, ed., *Communitarianism: A New Public Ethics* (Belmont, Calif.: Wadsworth Publishing Company, 1994), xix.
14. Amy Gutmann, 'Communitarian Critics of Liberalism', *Philosophy and Public Affairs* 14 (summer 1985): 321, 322.
15. Rawls, *Political Liberalism*, 4 (see note 2).
16. Jean-Jacques Rousseau, *On the Social Contract*, trans. and ed. by Donald A. Cress (Indianapolis: Hackett Publishing Company, 1762/1987), 29.
17. Gordon S. Wood, *The Radicalism of the American Revolution* (New York: Alfred A. Knopf, 1992), 293–294.
18. James MacGregor Burns, *Transforming Leadership: A New Pursuit of Happiness* (New York: Atlantic Monthly Press, 2003), 2.
19. Heifetz, *Leadership Without Easy Answers*, 3, 31, 26 (see note 6).
20. Ibid., 27.
21. Ibid., 86.
22. I am indebted to Evan Baum for many of the insights of this section. *See generally* Baum, unpublished essay, University of Richmond, 2001.
23. Burns, *Transforming Leadership*, 2, 144.
24. Ruscio, *The Leadership Dilemma*, 76 (see note 3).
25. Burns, *Transforming Leadership*, 147.
26. Ruscio, *The Leadership Dilemma*, xii.
27. Aristotle, *Aristotle's Politics,* trans. Benjamin Jowett (New York: Random House, 1943), III.13.1283b43–44, 153.
28. Thomas Jefferson, quoted in Wood, *The Radicalism of the American Revolution*, 296 (see note 17).
29. Robert A. Dahl, *Dilemmas of Pluralist Democracy: Autonomy and Control* (New Haven: Yale University Press, 1982); Dahl, *A Preface to Democratic Theory* (Chicago: University of Chicago Press, 1956); David B. Truman, *The Governmental Process* (New York: Alfred A. Knopf, 1957).
30. Rousseau, *On the Social Contract*, 31–32 (see note 16).
31. Albert Weale, 'Public Interest', in *Routledge Encyclopedia of Philosophy* (London: Routledge, 1998), 7: 832.
32. Wood, *The Radicalism of the American Revolution*, 361–364 (see note 17).
33. Ibid, 359–364.
34. Rawls, *Political Liberalism*, 96, 94, 128, 89–90 (see note 2).
35. William M. Sullivan, *Reconstructing Public Philosophy* (Berkeley: University of California Press, 1982), 166.
36. Benjamin Barber, *Strong Democracy: Participatory Politics for a New Age* (Berkeley: University of California Press, 1984), 65, 166.
37. Weale, 'Public Interest', 7: 832.
38. Sidney Verba, Kay Lehman Schlozman and Henry E. Brady, *Voice and Equality: Civic Volunteerism in American Politics* (Cambridge, Mass.: Harvard University Press, 1995), 35.
39. Ruscio, *The Leadership Dilemma*, 27, 65, 28 (see note 3).
40. Dagger, *Civic Virtues*, 175 (see note 12).
41. Rawls, *Political Liberalism*, 4 (see note 2).
42. Heifetz, *Leadership Without Easy Answers*, 22–23, 33–35 (see note 6).
43. James Madison, 'Vices of the Political System of the United States', in *The Papers of James Madison*, William T. Hutchinson et al., eds (Charlottesville: University Press of Virginia, 1977–), 9:354.
44. John Stuart Mill, *On Liberty*, ed. with intro. by Elizabeth Rapaport (Indianapolis: Hackett Publishing Company, 1859/1978), 9, 7.
45. Barber, *Strong Democracy*, 308 (see note 36).
46. Ruscio, *The Leadership Dilemma*, 82–83 (see note 3).
47. Philippe C. Schmitter and Terry Lynn Karl, 'What Democracy Is ... and Is Not', *Journal of Democracy* 2 (1991): 79.
48. Ibid.
49. Tocqueville, *Democracy in America*, 1: 194, 196 (see note 4).
50. Ruscio, *The Leadership Dilemma*, 8.

51. Benjamin Constant, 'The Liberty of the Ancients Compared with that of the Moderns', *Political Writings of Benjamin Constant*, trans. and ed. by Biancamaria Fontana (Cambridge: Cambridge University Press, 1988), 316.
52. Constant, 'The Liberty of the Ancients', 317.
53. Dagger, *Civic Virtues*, 58 (see note 12).
54. Ruscio, *The Leadership Dilemma*, 41 (see note 3).
55. Dagger, *Civic Virtues*, 109.
56. Garrett Hardin, 'The Tragedy of the Commons', *Science* 162 (13 December 1968): 1243–1248.
57. Dagger, *Civic Virtues*, 111.
58. Ibid., 113.
59. Ibid., 112.
60. Ibid., 112–113.
61. Immanuel Kant, "Idea for a Universal History from a Cosmopolitan Point of View', in Ernst Behler, ed., *Philosophical Writings* (New York: Continuum, 1986), 252, cited in Ruscio, *The Leadership Dilemma*, 62.
62. Rawls, *Political Liberalism*, 15 (see note 2).
63. Ibid., 72, 49, 53.
64. Ruscio, *The Leadership Dilemma*, 32–33 (see note 3).
65. Rawls, *Political Liberalism*, lxii, 19.
66. James Madison, 'Federalist No. 39', in *The Federalist*, Bicentennial edition, by Alexander Hamilton, John Jay and James Madison (Washington, DC: Robert B. Luce, 1976), 243.
67. Aristotle, *Politics*, III.11.1281b1–2, pp. 145–146 (see note 27).
68. Niccolo Machiavelli, *Discourses on Livy*, trans. Harvey C. Mansfield and Nathan Tarcov (Chicago: University of Chicago Press, 1996), I. 58.
69. Brian O'Connell, *Civil Society: The Underpinnings of American Democracy* (Hanover, NH: University Press of New England, 1999), 29.
70. Tocqueville, *Democracy in America*, 1:200–202, 251 (see note 4).
71. Thomas R. Dye and Harmon Zeigler, *The Irony of Democracy: An Uncommon Introduction to American Politics*, 9th edn. (Belmont, CA: Wadsworth Publishing Company, 1993), 18.
72. Mill, *On Liberty*, 19, 33 (see note 44).
73. Dagger, *Civic Virtues*, 98, 195 (see note 12).
74. Ibid., 103.
75. Rawls, *Political Liberalism*, lviii–lvix (see note 2).
76. James Harrington, *The Commonwealth of Oceana*, in Harrington, *The Political Works of James Harrington*, ed. J.G.A. Pocock (Cambridge: Cambridge University Press, 1977), 170, 199.
77. Rousseau, *On the Social Contract*, 46 (see note 16).
78. Dagger, *Civic Virtues*, 114–115.
79. Tocqueville, *Democracy in America*, 1: 243, 247–248; 2: 103 (see note 4).
80. John Stuart Mill, *Considerations on Representative Government* (London: John W. Parker and Son, 1859), 68, 201.
81. Dagger, *Civic Virtues*, 191 (see note 12).
82. Verba, et al., *Voice and Equality*, 528–529 (see note 38).
83. Amy Gutmann, 'Communitarian Critics of Liberalism', *Philosophy and Public Affairs* 14 (Summer 1985): 321.
84. James A. Morone, *The Democratic Wish: Popular Participation and the Limits of American Government*, rev. ed. (New Haven: Yale University Press, 1998), 246–247.
85. Jean L. Cohen, 'Civil Society', in *Routledge Encyclopedia of Philosophy* (London: Routledge, 1998), 2:369.
86. Tocqueville, *Democracy in America*, 2: 116 (see note 4).
87. Ibid., quoted in Dagger, *Civic Virtues*, 116.
88. Robert Putnam, *Bowling Alone: The Collapse and Revival of American Community* (New York: Simon & Schuster, 2000), 338.
89. Daly, *Communitarianism*, 154, 159–160 (see note 13).
90. Barber, *Strong Democracy*, xvii, 278, 300 (see note 36).
91. Tocqueville, *Democracy in America*, 1: 299, 325.
92. Rawls, *Political Liberalism*, 157 (see note 2).
93. Ibid., 217, li.
94. Dagger, *Civic Virtues*, 195–196 (see note 12).
95. Rousseau, *On the Social Contract*, 26–27 (see note 16).
96. R.R. Palmer, quoted in John W. Gardner, 'Foreword: The American Experiment', in O'Connell, *Civil Society*, xi (see note 69).

97. Tocqueville, *Democracy in America*, 1: 53, 58.
98. Ruscio, *The Leadership Dilemma*, 22–23 (see note 3).
99. Rawls, *Political Liberalism,* 213, 217–218.
100. Ruscio, *The Leadership Dilemma*, 109; Rawls, *Political Liberalism*, 157.
101. Ruscio, *The Leadership Dilemma*, 27, 23.
102. Ibid., ix.
103. Sandel, *Democracy's Discontent*, 4 (see note 11).
104. Barber, *Strong Democracy*, 238 (see note 36).
105. Ruscio, *The Leadership Dilemma*, ix (see note 3).
106. Wood, *The Radicalism of the American Revolution*, 232 (see note 17).
107. Ruscio, *The Leadership Dilemma*, 5.
108. Rousseau, *The Social Contract*, 38 (see note 16).
109. Mill, *On Liberty*, 64 (see note 44).
110. James Madison, 'Federalist No. 57', in *Papers of James Madison*, 10: 521 (see note 43).
111. Burns, *Transforming Leadership*, 167 (see note 18).
112. Heifetz, *Leadership Without Easy Answers*, 22 (see note 6).
113. Barber, *Strong Democracy*, 194 (see note 36).
114. Tocqueville, quoted in Sheldon S. Wolin, *Tocqueville between Two Worlds: The Making of a Political and Theoretical Life* (Princeton: Princeton University Press, 2001), 336; Tocqueville, *Democracy in America*, 2:248 (see note 4).
115. Heifetz, *Leadership Without Easy Answers*, 116.
116. Burns, *Transforming Leadership*, 223.
117. Ruscio, *The Leadership Dilemma*, 23–24.
118. Heifetz, *Leadership Without Easy Answers*, 85, 117–119.
119. Ruscio, *The Leadership Dilemma*, 21 (see note 3).
120. Heifetz, *Leadership Without Easy Answers*, 15, 254, 25.
121. Ibid., 128.
122. Ibid., 128, 99, 127.
123. Ibid., 23, 20.
124. Ibid, 128, 99, 39–40.
125. Ibid., 128, 100, 113.
126. Ibid., 128, 100, 25.
127. Ibid., 128, 22.
128. Rousseau, *On the Social Contract*, 24 (see note 16).
129. Ibid., 26–27.
130. James MacGregor Burns, *Leadership* (New York: Harper and Row, 1978), 19–20.
131. Burns, *Transforming Leadership*, 25–26 (see note 18).
132. Dagger, *Civic Virtues*, 95 (see note 12).
133. Rousseau, *On the Social Contract*, 39.
134. Tocqueville, *Democracy in America*, 2: 329 (see note 4).
135. Thompson, *John Stuart Mill and Representative Government*, 80–81 (see note 7).
136. Heifetz, *Leadership Without Easy Answers*, 2, 22, 75, 84, 244–245 (see note 6).
137. Morgan, *Inventing the People*, 306 (see note 1).
138. Schmitter and Karl, 'What Democracy Is ... and Is Not,' 80 (see note 47).
139. Locke, *Second Treatise of Government*, ed. C.B. Macpherson (Indianapolis: Hackett Publishing Company, 1690, 1980) sec. 163.
140. Dye and Zeigler, *The Irony of Democracy*, 7 (see note 71).
141. Tocqueville, *Democracy in America*, 2: 10 (see note 4).
142. Aristotle, *Politics*, III.11.1281b26–28, 1281b32–35, pp. 146–147 (see note 27).
143. J. G. A. Pocock, 'Introduction to James Harrington', in *The Political Works of James Harrington* (Cambridge: Cambridge University Press, 1977), 107.
144. Thompson, *John Stuart Mill and Representative Government*, 90 (see note 7).
145. Ibid., 70, 79; Mill, *Representative Government*, 282, 294, quoted in Thompson, *John Stuart Mill and Representative Government*, 79–80.
146. Thompson, *John Stuart Mill and Representative Government*, 80–81.
147. Ibid.
148. Ibid., 82–85; Mill, *Representative Government*, 234 (see note 80).
149. Norman Bowie, 'A Kantian Theory of Leadership', *The Leadership and Organization Development Journal* 21 (2000): 185–193.
150. Ibid., 185.
151. Ibid., 185–186.

152. Ibid., 185, 188.
153. Ibid., 189.
154. Ibid., 190–191.
155. Heifetz, *Leadership Without Easy Answers*, 70–71 (see note 6).
156. Ruscio, *The Leadership Dilemma*, 24 (see note 3).
157. Ibid., 32.
158. Robert C. Solomon, 'Ethical Leadership, Emotions, and Trust: Beyond "Charisma"', in Joanne B. Ciulla, ed., *Ethics, the Heart of Leadership* (Westport, Conn.: Praeger Publishers, 1998), 88, 99, 100, 102.
159. Ruscio, *The Leadership Dilemma*, 35, 40.
160. Heifetz, *Leadership Without Easy Answers*, 107.
161. Ruscio, *The Leadership Dilemma*, 28, 40.
162. Tocqueville, *Democracy in America*, 1:205 (see note 4).
163. Ibid.
164. Heifetz, *Leadership Without Easy Answers*, 83 (see note 6); Ruscio, *The Leadership Dilemma*, 42, 57 (see note 3).
165. Ruscio, *The Leadership Dilemma*, 41.
166. Heifetz, *Leadership Without Easy Answers*, 14.
167. Ruscio, *The Leadership Dilemma*, 79.
168. As has been the case at a number of points in the preceding analysis, I have benefited by the clarity of exposition of these issues found in Evan Baum, unpublished essay (University of Richmond, 2001).

Index

Adams, John 107, 142
adaptive work 341, 350, 370, 383, 386–7
agrarian law 73, 78, 79–80, 85
Agreement of the People 100
Alien and Sedition Acts 182–3
altruism, conditional 354–5, 359
Anti-Federalists 160–61, 166–7
Aquinas, Thomas
    Aristotle, links to 30, 32, 41, 46
    democracy, view of 32–3
    introduction to 29–30
    leader, view of 33–6
    leaders and followers 34–5
    leadership, purpose or end of 31, 34–5
    people, role of 35–6
    Rawls, John and 265
Arendt, Hannah 133, 147, 161
Aristotle
    Aquinas, Thomas, links to 30, 32, 41, 46
    community, role of 297–8
    democracy, view of 48–9, 50–51, 56
    institutions needed 49, 53–5
    introduction to 46–7, 296–7
    law, rule of 56
    leader, role of 51–7, 298, 379
    leaders and people, interaction between
        47–8, 52–4, 298
    leadership, purpose or end of 48, 55–6, 297
    Locke, John, link to 244
    man, nature of 47, 297–8
    people
        capability of governing 298
        role of 49–57, 297–8
    Plato, link to 47–8, 55–6
    Rawls, John, and 265
Assurance Game 354–5, 360

Bailyn, Bernard 70
Banning, Lance 289
Barber, Benjamin
    communitarian vs. liberal 238
    constructivism 317–18, 320, 327
    education, role of 327, 362
    epistemology of leadership 288, 317–18, 320,
        347
    human nature 284–5, 315, 317

inertial frames 4
leaders, role of 324–5, 366
leadership, epistemology of 288, 317–18,
    320, 347
liberalism critiqued 313, 315, 317
minority interests 326
morality, role of 314
participation 317–18, 320, 322
public goods 343
representation 287–8, 325
Berlin, Isaiah 285
Bernard, Chester I. 384
Bill of Rights 351
Blythe, James M. 47
Bowie, Norman 382–3
Buchanan, Allen 296, 317
Burke, Edmund 107, 141–2, 261
Burns, James MacGregor 134, 340, 342–3, 358,
    368, 373–6

Calhoun, John C. 351
challenge, what is the leadership
    Aquinas and 30, 37
    communitarianism and 296, 310, 312–14
    democracy, of 162–3
    Harrington, James and 69–71
    leadership, applied to fiction of 135–7
    liberalism and 283
    Locke and 239, 241–2
    Machiavelli and 57–8
    Madison and 171, 173–5, 178–9, 183–6, 193,
        197
    Mill and 252–3, 256
    Plato and Aquinas compared 37
    popular sovereignty, implied in 119
    Rawls, John and 264–6
    republicans, classical and 82
    Rousseau and 300–301, 304–5
    solution, proposed 37
    template question, explanation of 5
    Tocqueville and 203–8, 210–11, 225–6
    Wren, J. Thomas and 335–9, 377
Charles I 96–100, 102
Charles II 102–3
citizen *see* people, the; role of the people; Wren
    model of leadership